JOHN RUSKIN: THE EARLY YEARS

JOHN RUSKIN

THE EARLY YEARS
1819–1859

TIM HILTON

YALE UNIVERSITY PRESS
NEW HAVEN AND LONDON

TO
JEANNE CLEGG

Frontispiece. *The Author of 'Modern Painters'*, reproduced from the photogravure of the water-colour drawing by George Richmond, R.A., 1843 (Library Edition, Volume III)

Filmset by Clavier Phototypesetting, Southend-on-Sea, Essex
Printed in Great Britain by the Bath Press, Bath

Library of Congress catalog card number 85–50177
ISBN 0–300–03298–6 (hbk.)
ISBN 0–300–08265–7 (pbk.)

A catalogue record for this book is available from the British Library

2 4 6 8 10 9 7 5 3 1

CONTENTS

LIST OF PLATES

FOREWORD

Of great English writers, there is none so prolific as Ruskin: nor, for those who love to study him, is there any writer so valued for every sentence, every touch of the pen — right down to that individual, flickering, hurrying punctuation that, as one reads his manuscripts, seems to drive his thoughts from one page to the next. His literary production was enormous, yet nothing is redundant. In a writing career of fifty-nine years, he published some 250 titles, to which we must add his lectures, contributions to periodicals, more than thirty volumes of diary, around forty volumes of published correspondence, and dozens of thousands of letters which remain unpublished, and will not see print for many a year yet. It is not easy to come to a moderately informed view of Ruskin, and not only because of his fecundity. There are no useful modern editions of his famous early works, *Modern Painters* (1843-60) and *The Stones of Venice* (1851-3). *Unto this Last* (1860) has been given an importance it does not really possess. *Fors Clavigera* (1871-84), Ruskin's best and most extensive work, was ignored in his lifetime and has scarcely been studied from that day to this. *Præterita* (1885-9), his autobiography, is an extended rumination on his childhood rather than a statement of Ruskin's purposes in adult life; and of his mature works, what does this century really know of those gnomically-entitled volumes, so often seen in second-hand bookshops, never reprinted, *The Harbours of England*, *The Two Paths*, *Munera Pulveris*, *Time and Tide by Weare and Tyne*, *The Ethics of the Dust*, *The Queen of the Air*, *Mornings in Florence*, *St Mark's Rest*, *Love's Meinie* and *The Storm-Cloud of the Nineteenth Century*?

Ruskin's books, even *The Elements of Perspective*, are without exception personal. They were formed by the events of his life, his reading, his friendships and loves, dreams, travels and memories. No doubt this is so of many imaginative writers: but Ruskin believed his life's work to be factual and analytical. This is the first problem of understanding Ruskin's writing, and one reason for a biography. A knowledge of his life, rewarding in itself, is also the best way to approach his books. They are neither straightforward nor self-explanatory, and they have an especial unlikeness to anyone else's writing. Few of them are in an obvious sense works of literature. They rarely conform to the classic *genres* of writing. Moreover, from some point in the 1850s it is

impossible to prefer Ruskin's 'major' to his 'minor' works, and
unfinished or unfinishable books may be more rewarding than his
more crafted productions. In later years he tried to give his readers all
he thought they should know about him in order to understand his
writings. But his audience, such as it was, then became further confused and sometimes alienated. This was the fate of *Fors Clavigera,*
which the present biographer believes to be Ruskin's masterpiece. *Fors*
was the monthly letter written (nominally) to instruct and inspire a
class that certainly did not read it, 'the workmen and labourers of
Great Britain'. Its six hundred thousand words, a commentary on
Ruskin's thoughts and experiences between 1870 and 1884, tell us
more about its author than does *Præterita,* his autobiography. But
much of it is obscure, however Ruskin strives to make himself understood: and perhaps *Fors* was fully comprehensible only to those who
had an intimate knowledge of his life.

Præterita, whose composition began with extracts from *Fors Clavigera,* did not reach the point in its narrative at which *Fors* itself was
begun; and it is not likely that the exhausted, despondent autobiography could have explained the dramas of Ruskin's life in the years
that the pamphlet was issued. I hope to have written a biography that
does so for him. *Præterita* does not tell us much about Ruskin's
maturity. Nor does it describe his position as a great Victorian. Its
bitter modesty conceals how extensive was his public career. Ruskin
was twenty-four years old when he published the first volume of
Modern Painters. He was immediately recognized as a significant didactic writer. For the next forty years and more he was a force against the
basilisk of the age. His principled critique of the values of nineteenth-
century society, an opposition nobly sustained and richly elaborated,
is one of the most valuable expressions of that society. But his contribution did not become clearer as he published more books, and the
nature of his writing precluded the composition of single, classic
works. Ruskin's criticism of his times might have had more impact if
it had been concentrated in ten years' work rather than forty. His
extended crusade was both familiar and ignored. To be thus, for a
writer of his temper, was to be truly solitary. Ruskin's complaints that
he was alone in the world often appear exaggerated. His books were
famous and he was a professor in the University of Oxford: what
could be more social than that? He was gregarious and people sought
his company; he had wide circles of friends; he had 'disciples'; many
people loved him; in his own way he was a family man. Yet it is true
that he stood alone and that his work was not appreciated. This was
the more so the longer he lived and wrote. *Fors Clavigera* echoes a

voice that found no response in those it most urgently addressed.

I have not found that Ruskin's purposes — let alone the emotions of his brave, unhappy life — have become much clearer as the result of twentieth-century interest. To some extent, he was the victim of the dismissive prejudices of a period. The scorn of Victorian gravity was of course one reason why he was neglected; another was the rise of the modern movement: a third was the triumph of liberal and democratic values. But the study of Ruskin's life was also impeded by the very instrument that seemed to be designed to promote it. The Library Edition of Ruskin's works was published in thirty-nine volumes between 1903 and 1912. It was, at that date, the most elaborate editorial homage accorded to any English writer, even including Shakespeare. But it appeared at the nadir of Ruskin's reputation. It is perhaps not surprising that its assumptions were not examined at that period. Unfortunately, all subsequent biographies of Ruskin have been deficient because they rely on the Library Edition's editorial apparatus and introductions. Its two editors were E. T. Cook, a Ruskinian since his schooldays, and Alexander Wedderburn, a lawyer who had been one of Ruskin's Balliol 'disciples' at the time of his road-building project in 1874, and who remained a friend ever afterwards. We will meet both Cook and Wedderburn in this book, and learn of their attitudes to Ruskin. For the moment it is enough to say that it was Cook's scholarship that formed the Library Edition; and that it was the firm hand of Joan Severn, Ruskin's cousin, that determined its biographical material.

The present biography differs from its predecessors in placing its emphasis on the later rather than the earlier years of Ruskin's life. I believe that Ruskin was a finer writer and, if I dare say so, a better man, in the years after 1860 and especially in the years after 1870. The Library Edition presents many difficulties of scholarship and interpretation to the historian of these later years. Its editors had to be reticent about a number of matters. Just as they had not wished to say much about Ruskin's marriage, they gave only the barest information about Rose La Touche, even though Ruskin's love for her was a major influence on all his writing after 1860. They could not discuss his repeated mental breakdowns, although these could hardly be ignored; and they could not examine the tortured relationship between Ruskin and Joan Severn, for to do so would have revealed the true nature of *Præterita,* a book which was controlled by Joan and was designed, therefore, to relate only those aspects of Ruskin's life that were uncontentious. These omissions are understandable. Some of them have been repaired by later scholarship. But I would add that Cook (and the

biographers who have depended on him) misrepresented Ruskin in
other ways. Cook was an excellent Ruskinian, except that he was not
an art historian, nor a churchman, nor an imaginative political thinker.
He could not understand Ruskin's passions and he was embarrassed by
his subject's religious life. He regretted Ruskin's quarrels and shied
away from the implications of *Fors Clavigera*. Above all, he deliberately softened Ruskin's political views to make them conformable
with his own liberalism. In this biography I have attempted to restore
to Ruskin those aspects of his career and his personality.

Modern Ruskin scholarship may be said to have begun in 1929,
when the late Helen Gill Viljoen, then a graduate student, visited
Ruskin's old home at Brantwood. The house had long since fallen into
disrepair and many of its treasures had been sold. But Viljoen discovered Ruskin's diaries, many packets of family letters and one
manuscript that meant much to her, the autobiography and diary of
Rose La Touche. Helen Viljoen also met W. G. Collingwood, another
disciple of Ruskin who had known him since the 1870s. Collingwood
had subsequently become Ruskin's secretary, and his views on the
honour due to Ruskin's memory significantly differed from Wedderburn's, or Cook's, or Joan Severn's. Viljoen's discovery of original
manuscript, with Collingwood's conversation, turned her away from
the account of Ruskin presented in the Library Edition. She determined to study him afresh. The first fruit of her lifetime of Ruskin
scholarship appeared in 1956, when she published *Ruskin's Scottish
Heritage,* an account of her subject's forebears. This was announced as
the first volume of a biography. My own belief is that its purpose was
to analyse the inaccuracy and bias of the Library Edition: in this way it
was propædeutic. Viljoen (who was never to write more than three or
four fragmentary chapters of her biography) thus laid down a principle of Ruskin scholarship. She insisted that students of his work
should at all times return to the manuscript sources. I have attended to
this advice, and in my own researches have been guided by Helen
Viljoen's friend Professor Van Akin Burd, whose exemplary editions
of *The Winnington Letters* and *The Ruskin Family Letters* have been an
inspiration to all modern Ruskinians. I have also benefited from the
example of James S. Dearden, Curator of the Ruskin Galleries at
Bembridge School. In the many months I spent with Mr Dearden
reading through the Bembridge archive I learnt (as he, Professor
Viljoen and Professor Burd had learnt before me) that knowledge of
Ruskin has been handed down by personal help and generosity.

Helen Viljoen believed that Ruskin scholars should approach their
subject as though the Library Edition did not exist. This was an

extreme position, which she perhaps held because she never worked in Oxford and did not know of the documents that had aided Cook and Wedderburn in their labours. In the Bodleian Library is an archive almost as considerable as that at Bembridge. Its main sequence is in the volumes known to Ruskinians as the 'transcripts'. These are typewritten copies of all Ruskin's correspondence which was gathered for the Library Edition but not published in it. These thousands of letters are accompanied by complete transcriptions of all Ruskin's diaries. Surprisingly, this material was not known to the editor of Ruskin's diaries, Joan Evans, with the result that her edition of these journals (1956-9), which prints less than half of the complete text, is incomplete and only randomly annotated. The full treasures of the transcripts did not begin to enter Ruskin scholarship until 1969, when Van Akin Burd published *The Winnington Letters*. I hope that this biography's use of them will repay the trust with which Alexander Wedderburn bequeathed the documents to his old university.

$$\star \quad \star \quad \star \quad \star$$

Such, in brief, is the history of the main stream of Ruskin scholarship, as it has appeared to me. I have of course benefited from many other scholars and Ruskinians. They are fully acknowledged in the bibliographical notes in the second volume of this biography. I must now thank Messrs George Allen and Unwin, the Ruskin Literary Trustees, for their courtesy in allowing me to publish letters and other manuscripts of John Ruskin. For permission to publish material in their possession I thank The Education Trust Ltd, The Ruskin Galleries, Bembridge School, and its Chairman, R. G. Lloyd, CBE, QC. I am grateful to the Bodleian Library and Ashmolean Museum in Oxford for allowing me to quote from documents preserved in their collections. Permission to quote from published and unpublished letters has been kindly granted by Sir Ralph Millais, Bt., the Beinecke Library at Yale University, the Master and Fellows of Trinity College, Cambridge and the Directors of the John Rylands Library, Manchester. The Syndics of the Fitzwilliam Museum, Cambridge, have given me permission to quote material in their archives. I am grateful to the Trustees of the National Library of Scotland for allowing me to quote from manuscripts in their possession and the Trustees of the Trevelyan Estate have generously given me permission to use letters now deposited in the library of the University of Newcastle upon Tyne. Permission to reproduce illustrative material has been kindly granted by: Sir Ralph Millais, Bt., the Education Trust, Ruskin Galleries,

Bembridge; The Brantwood Trust, Coniston; the Ruskin Museum, Coniston; the Ashmolean Museum, Oxford; the City of Birmingham Museum and Art Gallery; the Fitzwilliam Museum, Cambridge; the Greater London Council Photographic Collection; the Graves Gallery, Sheffield; and the National Portrait Gallery, London.

*   *   *   *

A biographer may be allowed some personal comment in acknowledging help and inspiration. I was introduced to the study of Ruskin in the late 1950s, by a fellow cyclist who was then in retirement from his trade as a second-hand bookseller. I grieve that I have forgotten the name of this self-educated man, Clarion Club member and socialist. I no longer believe that Ruskin had any real connection with the Labour movement: but the questions I was then told to put to myself are still the right ones. What do you think about art? What do you think about the poor? I was not a successful student of Ruskin, however. I found his books puzzling and often incomprehensible. My friend did not give me much assistance. He implied that I might grow up to them. This was true: but young men are vexed by such demands on their patience.

When I was an undergraduate in the early 1960s, I was asked to understand that an interest in Ruskin was as foolish as an enthusiasm for modern art. I wish therefore to record my gratitude to the Courtauld Institute of Art, its then director, Anthony Blunt, and my friends Michael Kitson and Anita Brookner for their kind welcome and interest while I studied there as a postgraduate. Richard and Margaret Cobb helped me in many ways when I began my research. Arthur Crook, John Wain, Nuala O'Faolain, Peter Lowbridge, Anna Davin, Luke Hodgkin, Alexander Cockburn, Peter Carter and Martin and Fiona Green all encouraged me when I decided that I would one day write about Ruskin. The late Tony Godwin gave me excellent advice on writing biography, and Marghanita Laski's generosity allowed me to explore his recommendations. I have always been able to submit my writing to the wise scrutiny of David Britt, while Andrew Best of Curtis Brown has lifted many a care. I have long valued the sympathetic interest of Catherine Lampert and Elizabeth Wrightson.

Most of this book was written in Oxford. I am especially beholden to the Warden and Fellows of St Antony's College for their hospitality during the time I held an Alistair Horne Fellowship there: I am grateful for the friendly interest of Teddy Jackson, Tom Laqueur, Harry Willetts and Theodore Zeldin, Fellows of St Antony's with a wide sympathy for the humanities. The late Frank McCarthy Willis–Bund told me much about the Irish Church in which he was raised, and I had the privilege of conversation with John Sparrow about Victorian Oxford. It has always been a pleasure to exchange views and information with Richard Ellmann. John Owen, 'Senex' of the *Oxford Times,* helped me with matters of Oxford lore and tradition. Godfrey and Peter Lienhardt asked me the sort of questions about my interests that helped me to define my views on those interests. All Oxford men are indebted to the university's librarians. My heartfelt thanks go first to Margaret Miller of the Ashmolean Museum, who enabled me to work with the museum's collection of books by and about Ruskin that were the gift of E. T. Cook: I therefore used the same editions, pamphlets, press cuttings and the like from which Cook fashioned his editorial apparatus. Jane Jakeman, now of the Ashmolean, was at that date the most helpful of all the librarians at the Bodleian — where all the librarians, I hasten to add, are efficient and sympathetic beyond the calls of duty Fanny Stein, Ann Nimmo-Smith and Andrew and Peggoty Graham (all of Balliol families) were my friends and hosts while I lived in Oxford, and my research would not have been possible without their kindnesses to me. David Soskice, Christopher Hill, Tony Kemp-Welch, Frank and Ceci Whitford, Christopher Butler, Andrew Sugden, the late Lesley Smith, Islie Cowan, Joe Masheck, Juliet Aykroyd, Malcolm Warner, Meriel Darby, Deborah Thompson, Raphael Samuel, Mary-Rose Beaumont, John Ryle, Peter Ferriday, W. L. Webb, Eric Hobsbawm, Sheila Rowbotham and Peter Townsend all assisted with the writing of this book, whether they knew it or not.

I was fortunate that, in Oxford in the mid-1970s, there was a group of young scholars working on various aspects of Ruskin. Since there were no older specialists in British universities they were in effect (or so it appeared to me) the avant-garde of the new Ruskin studies. Nobody hoarded their discoveries, and I feel that I must have gained more than anyone else from our discussions. Robert Hewison's thesis on *The Queen of the Air* was a pioneering piece of research: so also was Dinah Birch's dissertation on Ruskin and the Greeks. Tanya Harrod and Nicholas Shrimpton wrote doctorates that stressed Ruskin's public and literary life, while Michael Simmons's examination of *Fors Clavigera* was a truly understanding approach to Ruskin's later years. The most detailed and sensitive work on Ruskin and Italy was Jeanne Clegg's: some of it was published in her *Ruskin and Venice* (1981). She is the Ruskinian to whom I am most deeply indebted, and this biography is dedicated to her. I (and other members of this group) would wish to record our indebtedness to Van Akin Burd, both for his scholarship and his interest in our own work. Of other Ruskinians, I extend my thanks especially to Naomi Lightman, Brian Maidment and Harold Shapiro.

The late Claude Rogers, Professor of Fine Art at the University of Reading, first invited me to examine the collections of the Guild of St George, which at that time (the mid-1960s) were stored in great confusion in the cellars beneath his department. All Ruskinians, and not least myself, are indebted to Catherine Williams for her work in cataloguing this material and for her suggestive comments on the early organization of the Guild of St George. I am also grateful to Peter Fitzgerald and Andrea Finn for inviting me to Reading, and thank the University of Reading Library for giving me access to the book and manuscript collections of the Guild of St George. I thank the Master and Directors of the Guild for a grant that assisted in the research for this book. I acknowledge the financial assistance of the Arts Council of Great Britain, and would add that the Council's Ruskin exhibitions of 1964 and 1983 both helped my work: the first, by its demonstration of the variety of Ruskin's interests, and the second (cogently devised by Dr Clegg) by showing the thematic unity of these interests, and their best expression in Ruskin's 'Guild period', the years of his Slade professorship and *Fors Clavigera*.

During my stays on the Isle of Wight I was made welcome by a number of Bembridge people. I must first of all thank Mr and Mrs Hastings and Ray and Sheila Rowsell for making holiday accommodation available to me in the winter months; and during Bembridge winters I was especially glad to have the company of John and Barbara Arthure, Rosalind Jenkinson and the late General Sir Michael West and Lady West. The best help in the writing of a long book is often of an indirect kind. To be blunt, one needs to be cheered up. My wife, Alexandra Pringle, has sustained me in all ways. So have some 'modern painters'. I owe a personal and intellectual debt to Clement Greenberg: I do not know whether it is apparent in these pages. Lastly, it is a pleasure to me to thank friends who are artists: they must have thought, over the years, that my Ruskinian interests were far removed from their own concerns. My gratitude for their support and patience goes especially to Terry Atkinson, Gillian Ayres, Michael Bennett, Anthony Caro, Barrie Cook, Barry Flanagan, John McLean, Ronnie Rees and John Walker.

*   *   *   *

The spelling and punctuation from original manuscripts has been retained but normalized in quotation from secondary sources.

CHAPTER ONE

1785–1837

John James Ruskin, the beloved father of the subject of this book, was born in Edinburgh in 1785. He was the son of John Thomas Ruskin, whose financial misfortunes, madness and suicide were to darken the lives of both his son and the grandson he never knew. John Thomas had gone to Scotland from London, where he had been born in 1761, the son of the parish clerk of St Bartholomew the Great. As a young man he had been apprenticed to a vintner, but gave up his indentures when, after his father's death, he removed to Edinburgh. There he became a grocer: in later years he described himself as a 'merchant'.[1] Writing *Præterita* a century afterwards, Ruskin claimed that his grandfather had married suddenly and romantically. That was perhaps because his wife came from a more genteel background. Catherine Tweddale was a daughter of the manse, and her forebears had owned land. Her father was the minister of the Old Luce church at Glenluce in Galloway. Catherine was sixteen when she married. With its usual wistfulness about family legends, *Præterita* recounts that when her daughter Jessie was born in the next year, 1783, the young mother danced 'a threesome reel, with two chairs for her partners'.[2]

John Thomas's grocery business was established in only a small way when John James, Jessie's brother, was born. Their situation improved when Catherine Ruskin inherited some money in 1794. The family then moved to a house in a better part of Edinburgh, St James Square in the New Town. Little is known of John James's childhood there. But it is clear that when he entered the Royal High School in 1795 he was an intelligent and serious boy. The school's headmaster was Dr Alexander Adam, a famous figure in Edinburgh society, the author of a Latin grammar and a book on Roman antiquities. John James quickly took to the classical authors and therefore benefited from Adam's stern regime and difficult Latin exercises. He had artistic talent as well: he studied a little under the landscapist Alexander Nasmyth. His ambition in life was to be a lawyer, a common way to advancement for an able Scottish boy without a background. Had he continued at school, in the democratic and competitive Scottish education that the Royal High School typified, John James surely would have risen in his chosen profession. However, when he was sixteen John Thomas insisted that he should go to London to begin a career in trade. John James obeyed, but he never forgot his disappointment: it is

one reason why his own son's talents were so fostered. John Thomas
probably had financial motives for dissuading his son from a legal
career. He was expanding his business but was not doing so prudently.
Acting as an agent for other merchants, he may even have speculated
on his own account with remittances that were not his. At all events,
we know that he did not wish to bear the cost of John James's further
education, and that he wished his daughter Jessie to be settled with a
practical tradesman. In 1804 he seems to have arranged that she should
marry Patrick Richardson, a prosperous tanner from Perth. He was
eleven years older than Jessie, and she did not marry him for love.
'Very submissive to Fates mostly unkind', was John Ruskin's view of
his aunt's sad life.[3] She bore many children, lost six of them in
childhood, was widowed, and died herself in 1828.

John Thomas was often away from Edinburgh. When both her
children had left home Catherine Ruskin felt the need of family
company. She wanted somebody to talk to, who would not be a
servant but would help to run the house in New Town. Her choice fell
on her niece by marriage, Margaret Cock. Margaret was the daughter
of John Thomas's elder sister Mary, who had remained in the south of
England when her brother had gone to Edinburgh. She had married a
publican, William Cock, the landlord of the King's Head in Croydon,
a small public house at the side of the market place, with two little bars
and three rooms upstairs. Margaret Cock was born there in 1781. The
tavern was not too large for her mother to run by herself when
William Cock died. She was probably quite determined. Certainly she
saw to it that her daughter got a dainty education, for a publican's
daughter. Margaret attended Mrs Rice's Academy for Ladies, the best
girls' school in Croydon. This might have led to a position suitable for
a young lady, and the invitation from Scotland was almost such a
thing. Margaret now changed her surname to Cox. In Edinburgh she
probably concealed the lowliness of her background. Her modesty
and carefulness became the tenets of her new life. *Præterita* describes
her at this period as 'a girl of great power, with not a little pride' who
'grew more and more exemplary in her entirely conscientious career'.[4]
She was by nature pious: seriously believing, that is, in the unchanging
laws of her God. Her embroidery was excellent. She read a great deal
in her spare time. She administered the Edinburgh household with
firmness and efficiency, and was to do so for thirteen years. All her
youth and young womanhood was given to this home. In these years
she developed an unswerving love for her cousin, John James. In time
he came to love her too. He was four years younger than Margaret,
dark-eyed, romantic, a poetry lover, living by himself in London.

1. John James Ruskin, father of John Ruskin, by Sir Henry Raeburn, 1804.

There was also much that was exemplary in his character, as Margaret knew with pride. Although he was not often in Edinburgh, their love did not suffer on that account, except in parting. Years later, Margaret recalled 'a night of passionate grief and tears spent upon the floor of her bedroom' after he had gone back to England to return to his counting house in a wine merchant's.[5]

John James Ruskin had discovered that he had the temperament of a businessman. This was what his father lacked. John Thomas was moody and extravagant. Always hot-tempered, he sometimes fell into black rages. It is recorded — from a hostile source, to be sure — that once 'coming home from one of his rounds a day earlier than he was expected, and finding his wife having a tea party, he in a fit of anger swept off the array of china into the fireplace'.[6] No evidence suggests that he was particularly mindful of his family: many letters indicate how tolerant they were of him. He was not always able to meet his financial commitments. Worse, he was not always inclined to do so. His business floundered and then collapsed. In February of 1808 Catherine Ruskin had to write to John James in London to tell him of its failure. The younger Ruskin immediately became the strength of the family. He undertook to pay off his father's debts. It was fortunate that a large part of them was owed to a Mr Moore of London for whom John Thomas had acted in Scotland and the north of England. Moore knew John James and admired him. Proceedings for bankruptcy were avoided.

In 1809, in the midst of this family trouble, John James and Margaret became engaged to be married. The engagement was to last for eight years. They had no prospects beyond those marked by John James's determination, and limited by John Thomas's insolvency. The young people's love for each other was to grow as they themselves grew older. Initially there was not a great deal of joy in it. Theirs was not a splendid match. It was as if John James were getting married to his duties. Cousin marriages were not regarded without unease. Margaret had no money and was the daughter of an innkeeper. Since John James felt that he could not marry until he had paid off his father's debts, the affianced couple had to resign themselves to separation and long labours. John James's industry was remarkable. He went for years without a holiday. Occasional visits to the theatre and to lectures were not enough of a recreation: he worked until his health was threatened. He wrote regularly to his family and, separately, to Margaret. She supervised an enforced move from New Town to a cheaper house at Dysart, on the Fife coast near Kirkcaldy. Later the Ruskins rented Bowerswell, a house on the east bank of the Tay, not far from

2. Margaret Ruskin, mother of John Ruskin, by James Northcote, R.A., 1825.

Patrick and Jessie Richardson in Perth. Margaret also applied herself to
her own improvement. Dr Thomas Brown, later Professor of Moral
Philosophy at the University of Edinburgh, was a family friend. He
had been a mentor of John James's in his younger days and now was
glad to advise Margaret on her reading. She taught herself Latin and
even a little Hebrew. But in her loneliness she found her greatest
comfort in the Bible.

In London, John James had risen to be head clerk of the wine
importing firm of Gordon, Murphy and Co. By his exacting standards, it was not an efficient house. He complained to Margaret of
'their ridiculous stile which has resembled that of princes more than
Merchants'.[7] He had a trusted but not powerful position and was
conscious that the firm was not good enough for him. One other
person thought the same. Pedro Domecq was a young Spaniard with
French nationality. His family owned extensive vineyards in Spain
and he was working in London to extend his knowledge of the wine
business. Placed among the foreign clerks in Gordon, Murphy, 'he
had not exchanged ten words in as many months' with John James
when he decided to approach him with the proposition of a partnership.[8] But he had seen the thrifty young Scotsman at work, and
discerned his qualities. The two men discussed the wine trade outside
the office and found that they got on well. They determined to look
for another partner with some capital. By happy chance they were
both acquainted with Henry Telford. He was a Kentish country
gentleman. His interest in life was horses. He hunted and went to
every race meeting he could. But he never betted; and now he realized
that he would not be risking his money by becoming a sleeping
partner in Domecq's enterprise. Telford owned premises in Billiter
Street, in the old City of London between Leadenhall Street and
Fenchurch Street. Here the firm of Ruskin, Telford and Domecq was
established. The amiable Telford gave advice when he was asked for
it, sat in the office for only one month in the year, while John James
was on holiday, and left matters to his younger partners.

John James had worked hard for his salary at Gordon, Murphy. He
worked even harder now and in the years to come, as his intention was
to build a fortune from his commission. He was helped by the boom in
the wine trade after the Napoleonic wars. But his own industry,
particularly in travelling, brought great rewards. He was entitled to
boast, when he came to look back on the early history of the firm, that
'I went to every Town in England most in Scotland & some in Ireland,
till I raised their exports of 20 Butts wine to 3000'.[9] His finances
improved steadily after the foundation of the new business; prospects

were excellent: but in Scotland there were more troubles with his father. John Thomas began to object to his son's engagement to Margaret. He perhaps thought that his son could now make a better match: but it is possible that his insensitive behaviour was part of the more general misanthropy that was overtaking him. We have hints of these difficulties in a letter home from John James in 1815:

> Oh my own Mother as you have always loved me will you and my dear Father assure Margt that you have both become reconciled to our Union & be happy — or will you see her & me both fall sacrifices to this anxiety. Neither her constitution nor mine are fit for a long struggle. I have already said that if it leads to eternal Ruin I will fulfill my engagement with Margt. I hope my Dr. Father will therefore no longer cause us any uneasiness . . . Oh if you expect me to make some efforts to keep the family united — do not let her on whom my life depends sink under my Father and your displeasure. The state of our worldly matters requires that we should not oppose each other in things to add to that distress . . .[10]

John Thomas was of course in no position to prevent the marriage. His son's letter, pleading yet firm enough, shows what great strains there were on his filial piety. It also shows his forbearance. What Margaret thought is not recorded. In later years she never mentioned John Thomas.

Only a couple of months after this letter, John Thomas broke down. Reports of his melancholia now indicate that he had fallen into madness. Six hundred miles to the south, John James wrote anxiously to his mother, to enquire how much money his father had been spending and how much the neighbours knew of what had happened. He asked her to forbid drink to him and to take over the family purse. It seems that John Thomas was raving and did not recognize his surroundings. His family did not know what to do with him. John James wanted him to be at home. He could not bear the thought of his father being committed to an asylum: 'If there be any possibility of the disease subsiding or if his intervals of reason are frequent I cannot endure the thought of his being altogether among strangers . . .'.[11] It was a tenderness that other members of the Ruskin family, sixty years later, would extend to his own son. Yet it was of a necessity compassion at a distance, and it was given to Margaret to nurse the man who had opposed her marriage. John Thomas did not fully recover, and was never able to carry on business again.

Two years after this breakdown, the whole family was broken by a series of deaths. In September 1817 old Mrs Cock of the King's Head

died in Croydon. Margaret travelled south for the funeral. She had not
been there long when the news came that Catherine Ruskin had died of
apoplexy. John James went up to Edinburgh with Margaret to attend
his mother's funeral, then returned to London. He left his fiancée,
stunned by the deaths of her mother and her aunt, with a horror to
face. Ten days later John Thomas Ruskin committed suicide. Margaret Cox was alone in the house with him: most accounts agree that
he cut his throat.

★   ★   ★   ★

Three months later, as soon as was decently possible after such
bereavements, John James and Margaret were married in Perth. There
were no celebrations. Margaret had come to loathe the house at
Bowerswell, as well she might. She wanted to leave Scotland as
quickly and as quietly as possible. She never would re-enter Bowerswell, the house in which she had known so much unhappiness, not
even when her own son was married there thirty years later. Margaret
Ruskin was not a young wife. She was thirty-seven when she wed: she
had waited long and suffered much. Nor were John James's financial
troubles now over. John Thomas left debts of £5,000 behind him,
money that would not be finally paid off for another ten years. But
John James had bought and furnished a comfortable house for his
bride. No. 54 Hunter Street, Brunswick Square, was a solid bourgeois
building. It was part of a fairly recently built terrace. Each house had
three storeys as well as an attic and a basement. There were areas in
front and small gardens behind. In this house, quite near to Gray's Inn
and the British Museum, near the open spaces in front of the Found-
ling Hospital, their only son was born on 8 February 1819.

John Ruskin remembered little of the Hunter Street house, and
never revisited it in adult life. *Præterita* recalls the excitement of a very
small boy watching the dustmen and coalmen. One London view
stayed with him always, 'of a marvellous iron post, out of which the
water carts were filled through beautiful little trap-doors, by pipes like
boa-constrictors'. [12] He was less than five years old when the Ruskins
moved from Hunter Street to a house outside London. This move
accompanied not so much a change in status as a desire for a different
domestic life. No. 26 Herne Hill, the Ruskins's home for the next
nineteen years, was bought on a 63-year lease for £2,192. Four miles
from 'the Standard in Cornhill', [13] the old coaching station from which
distances from the capital were measured, it was a semi-detached

3. 54 Hunter Street, Brunswick Square, where John Ruskin was born in
1819. Photograph c.1950.

house of three storeys and a garret. Herne Hill is in fact part of the
Norwood Hills, a ridge of the North Surrey Downs. This wooded
country was watered by two streams forever dear to Ruskin, the
Wandle and the Effra. From John James's new house, one of a group of
four right at the top of the hill, one could see to St Paul's, to sailing
boats on the Thames at Greenwich, to Harrow in the north and to
Windsor Castle in the west. Below the hill were the rural villages of
Walworth and Dulwich. The house itself was comfortable. Margaret
Ruskin took most delight in the gardens. Ruskin recalled how she
tended the lilac and laburnum at the front gate. At the back of the
house she had the best pear and apple trees in the neighbourhood. The
orchard was seventy yards long, a whole world to the small child who
followed his mother while she planted and pruned, plucked the
peaches and nectarines, and in the spring gathered almond blossoms,
the first flowers after the snowdrops.

In this house Margaret Ruskin had the happiness of youth when she
was forty. The long years of loneliness and waiting, the madness and
the deaths, could all be forgotten. All her life Margaret was silent
about those years. She had earned her happiness and there was no
reason why she should dwell on the way in which she had earned it.
She delighted in her child and in running her own home: she delighted
in her love for her husband. The family letters from Herne Hill,
written while John James was away collecting orders, seem often to be
the messages of lovers twenty years younger than themselves: 'at
night I go to bed saying tomorrow I shall hear from my beloved I rise
in the morning rejoicing that I shall soon have your letter the rest of the
day I delight myself with reading it and the thoughts of it . . .', writes
Margaret to her husband.[14] Their intimate affection grew within the
years of their marriage. Ten years after their wedding, twenty years
after their engagement, John James is writing,

> My Dear my Lovely Margaret how do you contrive to inspire me
> with unfading Love to light up flames of passion that neither age
> nor familiarity can extinguish. I see you forever as young as sweet &
> oh I think each year still sweeter, decked anew in some fresh
> Beauty, in some new graces to hold me to charm me to stir my very
> soul with fiercer and warmer Emotions to make me think I am
> come into possession of some newly discovered Treasure. Such is
> the power of Innocence of pure womanly love & affection as they
> exist and adorn the sweetest the gentlest the most feminine of her
> Sex. If I began to love coldly I have come to love warmly & to feel
> every year something added to the force of my love & my admira-
> tion . . .[15]

4. 27 Herne Hill, Ruskin's home in south London, 1823–42.

There are thousands of Ruskin family letters, since it was the Ruskins's habit to write every day when separated from any member of the family. John James was often away from home selling sherry, his firm's speciality, and other wines. He acted as his own salesman and as the only traveller for the firm. He would have no business with agents, but took all responsibilities on his own shoulders. This he continued long after he could have deputed work. John James had not come to the firm with capital, as Telford had with his bonds and Domecq with his Macharnudo vineyard. He contributed unwearying drive. Every night, from the commercial room of the best inn or coaching house in the town, he wrote home to his wife. This correspondence consists mainly of love letters, with talk about their son. There is little about the wine trade, and the part of the business John James must have hated: the deference to customers, the bonhomous negotiations with hoteliers and landlords, the long coach trips and the company he did not wish to keep.

John James was usually on the road for a fortnight to three weeks. Some of his itineraries can be reconstructed from the letters. In 1822, for instance, staying for one night in most places but for two or three in the cities, he went from Stamford to Newark, Leeds, Bradford, Kendal, Liverpool, Chester, Manchester, Warwick, Coventry, Leicester, Huntingdon, and thence back to London. This kind of tour did not change as the firm prospered. Fourteen years later his schedule was just as demanding. On 15 December 1836, he wrote to Margaret from Ipswich. In the next few days he was in Norwich and Yarmouth, returned to Norwich, then went on to King's Lynn. On Christmas Day he was in Lincoln — the Ruskins, being Scottish, did not celebrate Christmas — and on Boxing Day in Leeds. After that he visited Rochdale, Liverpool — staying at a hotel he detested, the Adelphi — Manchester and Birmingham. Again, the last of the sequence of letters is from Huntingdon, before reaching London and the 'head of all my possessions and heart of all my joys'.[16]

This hard-working, loving, rather proud man, stern but romantic, returned to Herne Hill from these exhausting trips, or from the long routine of the counting house, as one returns to peace, to order and love. Dinner was at half-past four, always. In summer the Ruskins took tea in the evening under the cherry tree, or in the parlour in winter, and John James would read aloud from Shakespeare, or Pope's *Iliad,* or his favourite Dr Johnson, or *Don Quixote*; classical books that were supplemented by the romantic poets of the day, in particular Byron and Scott.

A pillar of the household was Anne Strachan, young John's nurse, who had come from Bowerswell with the newly married couple and remained in their service all her life. She was a sharp-tongued, difficult person whom John Ruskin adored. Her endless disputes with Margaret Ruskin, about anything, were an accepted part of Herne Hill life, sometimes to the surprise of visitors. Perhaps she and Margaret quarrelled a little over John. Anne was a spinster; Margaret Ruskin, deeply attached to the son she had been lucky to bear at her age, spent more time with her child than was common in a similar 1820s household. Margaret would do anything for him, but she was totally unyielding in matters of right and wrong. She wrote to his father,

Were he Son to a King, more care could not be taken of him and he every day gives proof of possessing quickness memory and observation not quite common at his age with this however I fear he will be very self willed and passionate — he has twice alarmed me a good deal by getting into such a passion that I feared he would have thrown himself into a fit this will I trust be cured by a good whipping when he can understand what it is for properly.[17]

Such disciplines were probably exaggerated in *Præterita*. Certainly Ruskin's claim in his autobiography that he lacked toys is incorrect. *Præterita*, or rather *Fors,* called the Herne Hill garden an Eden where '*all* the fruit was forbidden'.[18] This was not so. John Ruskin had toys, a rocking-horse, dogs, a pony, all the books and drawing materials he could wish for. *Præterita* is correct, however, to insist on the importance of the Bible in Ruskin's young life. Herne Hill was a paradise where Scripture was read every day. The Bible, Margaret's great solace in the years of her unhappiness, became the first principle of her son's serene childhood. Through it, he was taught to read and to remember. When John was three, his mother wrote, 'we get on very well with our reading he knows all the commandments but the second perfectly and the Lords prayer his memory astonishes me and his understanding too'.[19] This biblical teaching informs all Ruskin's later writing. The volumes themselves are familiar to the student of Ruskin. First of all was the old family Bible of the English Ruskin family, inscribed with the dates and hours of all their births, from John's great-grandfather's 'John Ruskin, Baptised Aprill 9th 1732 O.S.', to all his children and grandchildren; then the Baskett Bible of 1741 in which John James wrote his own birth and baptismal dates; and the Edinburgh Bible of 1816, which Ruskin opened when writing *Præterita* — noting then how the eighth chapter of first Kings and the thirty-second of Deuteronomy were worn dark, for they were his mother's favourite reading.[20] He learnt from this volume every morning, when his mother took out her own Bible from its silk bag with purple strings to begin the day and the day's learning.[21] Every single day of every week, from the time he began to read until he left home to go up to Oxford, Ruskin read two or three chapters a day with his mother and learnt some verses by heart. He wrote,

> She began with the first verse of Genesis, and went straight through, to the last verse of the Apocalypse; hard names, numbers, Levitical law, and all; and began again at Genesis the next day. If a name was hard, the better the exercise in pronunciation, — if a chapter was tiresome, the better lesson in patience, — if loathsome, the better lesson in faith that there was some use in its being so outspoken.[22]

In these morning sessions Ruskin also learnt by heart the Scottish paraphrases, the psalms rendered into eighteenth-century verse that

were the hymns of the Church of Scotland. He learnt to speak them
resonantly and rhythmically, giving as much attention to meaning as
he would when reading from Scripture. Some literature seemed also
sacred to the childish Ruskin. In *Præterita*, recalling that Walter Scott's
Waverley novels were 'a chief source of delight' and that he could 'no
more recollect the time when I did not know them than when I did not
know the Bible', Ruskin nonetheless felt it right 'with deeper gratitude
to chronicle what I owe to my mother for the resolutely consistent
lessons which so exercised me in the Scriptures as to have made every
word of them familiar to my ear in habitual music'.[23]

Contemporary romance and the Bible could co-exist. So could
assiduous attendance at church and a cheerful home life. Letter after
letter speaks of the high spirits and the happiness of Ruskin's childhood. An early one came about because John was full of things to say
to his father and pretended to write them on his slate. Margaret invited
him to dictate what he could hardly write: only the signature is in his
hand:

> My Dear Papa I love you — I have got new things Waterloo Bridge
> — Aunt brought me it — John and Aunt helped to put it up but the
> pillars they did not put right upside down instead of a book bring
> me a whip coloured red and black which my fingers used to stick to
> and which I pulled off and pulled down — tomorrow is sabbath
> tuesday I go to Croydon on Monday I go to Chelsea papa loves me
> as well as Mama does and Mama loves me as well as papa does — I
> am going to take my boats and my ship to Croydon I'll sail them in
> the Pond near the Burn which the Bridge is over I will be very glad
> to see my cousins I was very happy when I saw Aunt come from
> Croydon — I love Mrs Gray and I love Mr Gray — I would like you
> to come home and my kiss and my love JOHN RUSKIN.[24]

This Richard Gray and his wife Mary were a Scottish couple who
lived not far away in Camberwell Grove. Richard Gray was also a
wine merchant. Without children of their own, the Grays enjoyed
spoiling young John Ruskin. The cousins in Croydon mentioned in
the letter were of another Richardson family, for Margaret's sister
Bridget had married a baker of that name. They all lived over the shop
in Croydon High Street. For the four boys and two girls who were the
Richardson children Ruskin had 'a kind of brotherly, rather than
cousinly, affection'.[25] In his early years they were much together. On
at least one occasion Margaret expressed a fear that their rougher ways
might be bad for John, but this does not seem to have become an issue.
The Ruskins were not over-troubled by questions of social class.

Prœterita gives a quite misleading picture of people living 'magnificently' on Herne Hill, giving splendid receptions, attended by coachmen in wigs. His parents, Ruskin claimed, could not enter such society because of their plainness and thrift: his father would not 'join entertainments for which he could give no like return, and my mother did not like to leave her card on foot at the doors of ladies who dashed up to hers in their barouche . . .'.[26] This is nonsense: there was no such society on Herne Hill. The visitors who did come to Herne Hill were numerous, and they were more interesting. John James's diaries show that he entertained practically every night, including Sundays. His friends and social circle we shall shortly examine. For the moment we can think of the Croydon Richardsons, who might come up to borrow the pony; friends of Margaret's who would have tea and play with her precocious, talkative son; a number of Scottish people; and friends who shared John James's literary and artistic tastes and belonged to the fringes of the literary world. They were the ones who would take up John Ruskin when he was fourteen or fifteen and introduce him to the excitement of meeting literary men and writing for publication.

Ruskin did not go to school until he was fourteen, and to this extent his childhood was sheltered. But there was no want of instruction. He had his mother's lessons, his father's reading and his own curiosity. From the age of ten he had tutors. He learnt to read and write early on. He copied maps and read the standard children's authors. He began Latin, at first with Margaret and then with John James, who often corrected his exercises by letter. There was much respect for learning in this Scottish household. John James was concerned for his own self-improvement. He had been denied the opportunity for study in his youth, and he wished to make up for it in his independence. In only a few years' time, his own reading and his son's would often coincide as they discovered books together. In the early '30s (as we may discover from his accounts) John James was buying such books for family use as Lindley Murray's *English Grammar,* a Hebrew grammar and a Greek grammar (the Ruskins used Dr Adam's Latin one, kept from Royal High School days). John Burke's *General and Heraldic Dictionary of the Peerage* was bought, along with works by Tacitus, Homer, Cicero, Cæsar and Livy. There was a Homer done into French, Chateaubriand (that was rather daring), and *Anecdotes of the Court of France.* John James bought a set of Scott's novels, Dr Johnson's *Dictionary*, and his *Lives of the Poets*. He subscribed to *Blackwood's Edinburgh Magazine* and every year bought a number of annuals. Maria Edgeworth's novels were there, and Bulwer Lytton's *Last Days of Pompeii*. The radical Hazlitt (whose lectures John James might have heard) was in this library, and so was Byron.[27]

Such books were the staple of Ruskin's childhood reading. We shall hear of many others, lesser known today, such as Bernardin de Saint-Pierre's *Paul et Virginie,* which had a minor effect on his later writing. The literary atmosphere of the Herne Hill parlour was felt through all Ruskin's life, for he felt that books given to him by his parents were peculiarly authoritative. John James was determined that his son would not enter trade and Margaret mentally dedicated her child to God, and wished that he might have an ecclesiastical career. They absorbed themselves in literature because they enjoyed it. Nonetheless, the cultivation of John's evident intellect and talents was somewhat forced. John James occasionally recognized that there was absurdity in the way he encouraged his son to great things, but that did not deter him from letters such as this:

> . . . the Latin being somewhat difficult I am astonished at your understanding it so well & writing so like a Classic Author. You are blessed with a fine Capacity & even Genius & you owe it as a Duty to the author of your Being & the giver of your Talents to cultivate your powers & to use them in his Service & for the benefit of your fellow Creatures. You may be doomed to enlighten a People by your Wisdom & to adorn an age by your learning. It would be sinful in you to let the powers of your mind lie dormant through idleness or want of perseverance when they may at your maturity aid the cause of Truth and Religion & enable you to become in some ways a Benefactor of the Human Race. I am forced to smile when I figure to myself the very little Gentleman to whom I am addressing such language . . .[28]

In fact, the 'little gentleman', ten years old when he received this communication (and there were others like it), was scarcely in need of encouragement. In this same year he wrote to John James,

> I do believe that the last year of my life was the happiest: and shall I tell you why? Because I had more to do than I could do without cramming and cramming, and wishing days were longer and sheets of paper broader . . . I do think, indeed I am sure, that in common things it is having too much to do which constitutes happiness, and too little, unhappiness.[29]

This now reads as a prophetic remark. All his life Ruskin felt that time was wasted, and worse than wasted, if any day had not been used for study. At the unhappiest times of his life he worked the harder, often then returning to those subjects which had brought him joy in childhood. Foremost among these was geology. Ruskin's lifelong dedica-

tion to the analysis of the materials of the earth began at about this
time. John James was fond of saying that his son had been an artist
from childhood but a geologist from his infancy.[30] He encouraged and
perhaps initiated John's hobby when he brought home a collection of
fifty minerals bought for five shillings from a local geologist in the
Lake District. 'No subsequent passion had had so much influence on
my life', Ruskin wrote in *Deucalion,* his collection of geological
studies.[31] These golden pieces of copper ore from Coniston and
garnets from Borrowdale were the more exciting in that they came
from the romantic Lakes. But, like the cheap Bristol diamonds (transparent rock-crystal found in Clifton limestone) which John James
brought from that centre of the wine trade, Ruskin valued his stones
first of all for their visual particularity, for the way that they needed to
be closely examined, pored over. They appealed to that love of detail
which was so marked a feature of his visual sense. He liked to see how
small, bright things stood against a background. On a family holiday
in Matlock he was struck by the New Bath Hotel and

. . . the glittering white broken spar, speckled with galena, by
which the walks of the hotel were made bright, and in the shops of
the pretty village, and in many a happy walk along its cliffs, I
pursued my mineralogical studies of fluor, calcite and the ores of
lead, with indescribable rapture . . .[32]

Ruskin began a mineralogical dictionary at the age of twelve. His
first boyhood ambition was to become, as the famous Charles Lyell
then was, the President of the Geological Society. In four or five years'
time Ruskin progressed from making collections and classifications:
he began to study the broader aspects of geology, its feeling for the
great sweep and variety of the earth and its questioning of universal
history. It led him early to intellectual life. He was attending meetings
of the Geological Society, in those days a most animated institution,
before he went to university.

★   ★   ★   ★

In 1828 there was an addition to the small Ruskin family. For some
time Margaret and John James had been thinking of having John's
cousin Mary Richardson, of the Perth Richardsons, to come to live
with them after the death of her mother Jessie. It was a sad time. Jessie
had been a comfort to Margaret in her years of exile. John had loved
the visits he made as a little boy to the Richardsons' house by the Tay
where the river ran just outside the back door, swift and sparkling, 'an

infinite thing for a child to look into'.[33] John James wept bitterly at the
thought of his sister's wasted life. But he now acted swiftly and
generously to help the family. He settled one of the sons in business,
gave money to the other two and brought Mary into his own home.
She lived with the Ruskins until 1848 when, like John, she married.
Mary was fourteen when she came to Herne Hill; from that time on
John Ruskin had in effect an elder sister. They did not grow closer
together as the years passed, but that was not through any lack of
affection. In childhood they shared everything, from the Bible reading
and drawing instruction to shared projects, expeditions and holidays.
If John was the cleverer by far, Mary had four years' advantage of him.
All in all, they made a contented pair. John James could not be as proud
of Mary as he was of John, but he wrote to a friend, 'Mary Richardson
is another treasure . . . she has an excellent understanding, & is really
pious and withall possesses a Spirit & a naivete a Joyousness combined
with the most perfect Innocence that makes her all we could desire.'[34]
On Mary the Ruskins lavished the tuition that Perth had been unable
to provide. With private tutors and at a day school in the neighbourhood she studied music, drawing, French, geography, dancing, writing, arithmetic and Italian.

A great event in the Ruskin family was the annual summer tour,
wonderful holidays that opened vistas of exploration and romance. In
a carriage lent them by Henry Telford, and later in one that they hired,
the Ruskins toured all the parts of the British Isles that were picturesque or had literary associations. They went to Scotland, where they
stayed at the Richardsons', in 1824, 1826 and 1827; to Wales in 1831;
to the west of England in 1828; to Derbyshire in 1829, and to the Lake
District in 1824, 1826 and 1830. Usually they set off after a ritual
family feast, John James's birthday on 10 May, and were often touring
for a matter of months rather than weeks, especially when their tours
were extended to the Continent. 'I saw all of the high-roads, and most
of the cross ones, of England and Wales,' Ruskin claimed.[35]

The Lake District, where he was to live after his parents' deaths, was
from the first particularly dear to Ruskin. His earliest real memory
was of being lifted up by his nurse Anne Strachan on Friar's Crag
above Derwentwater. That was in 1824. In 1830 the Ruskins decided
to make an extended stay in the Lakes. In the party were the three
Ruskins, Mary Richardson and Anne. It took them five weeks to reach
Kendal from Herne Hill, since they stayed in Oxford for a little while,
lingered in the Midlands and made a detour to Manchester so that John
James could do some business. Once among the Lakes they made
excursions from the Low Wood Inn at Windermere and the Royal Oak

at Keswick. John and Mary collaborated on a journal of the tour. One entry is of especial interest. It is one of the very few times that Wordsworth is mentioned in the early years of Ruskin's life.

> We went to Rydal Chapel in preference to Ambleside as we had heard that Mr Wordsworth went to Rydal . . . We were in luck in procuring a seat very near to that of Mr Wordsworth, there being only one between it, & the one that we were in. We were rather disappointed in this gentleman's appearance especially as he seemed to be asleep the greater part of the time. He seemed about 60. This gentleman possesses a long face and a large nose with a moderate assortment of grey hairs and 2 small grey eyes . . .[36]

From this journal, in the months after the tour, the un-Wordsworthian John wrote a poem entitled *Iteriad, or Three Weeks among the Lakes*. It contains 2,310 lines in rapid rhymed couplets and is a remarkable production for a boy of eleven. It is doggerel, of course; but a doggerel that nicely recaptures the excitement of Ruskin's picturesque explorations.

It was in 1829 that the Ruskins decided to find their son a tutor. John Rowbotham, who ran a little school near the Elephant and Castle and wrote simple textbooks, came to Herne Hill twice a week to teach him mathematics. A more important teacher was the Reverend Edward Andrews. The Ruskins worshipped in his church, the Beresford Chapel, Walworth. We must now consider the Ruskins's religious background. They gave their religious (though not necessarily their political) allegiance to the Evangelical party of the day. They appreciated Evangelicalism's fervour, its insistence on the authority of the Scriptures, its stress on salvation in the atoning death of Christ, its belief in the importance of preaching and its lack of interest in liturgical worship. Since the Ruskins believed in the inspiration of Scripture they tended to be suspicious of authority within the Church. They were openly hostile to Roman Catholicism and high church practices and doctrines. To some extent, their religion was formed by their Scottishness. John James's mother, we recall, was a daughter of the manse. Her minister father and other relatives were from Galloway, where there was a strong covenanting tradition: the National Covenant of the Scottish Presbyterians of 1638 was still real to the Tweddales. The Ruskins (and Anne Strachan) had respect for this heritage but were not bound to it. They were not rigid in religious matters, though Margaret was more conservative than was John James. Between their removal from Scotland to London and John Ruskin's matriculation at Oxford we may observe a number of shifts of

allegiance. To place their son at the centre of the Anglican establishment, Christ Church, and to hope that he might become a bishop, was
hardly to adhere to the Church of Scotland. No doubt the Ruskins
changed their churches and their views in accordance with their own
elevation in the English social scale. But this is to over-simplify, and
ignores the effect of the peculiar ministers to whom they were
attached.

Some of these matters became obscure in later years. The matter of
the Ruskins's first London church is a case in point. Where did they
worship when they lived in Hunter Street? We know that John was
baptized in the Caledonian Chapel, Hatton Garden, by a bilingual
minister who preached in both Gaelic and English. Only a little
afterwards this chapel became famous and fashionable, for it was here
that Edward Irving, Carlyle's friend, arrived from Scotland in 1821
and immediately became the most celebrated preacher in London. But
the Ruskins did not attend his services.[37] *Præterita* speaks of 'The Rev.
Mr Howell', whose preaching was imitated by the infant Ruskin. This
mystified Ruskin's editors. They were unable to identify him because
Ruskin had forgotten his real name. The Reverend William Howels,
minister of the Episcopal Chapel, Long Acre (which was not very far
from Hunter Street) was a Welshman. A contemporary description of
Howels as a man 'of extraordinary inability & not a little eccentricity'
is typical of much that was said of him at the time.[38] His preaching
style was apparently ludicrous: perhaps this is why Ruskin's infant
sermon in imitation of him, 'People, be good', was 'a performance
being always called for by my mother's dearest friends'.[39] It is less
surprising that the Ruskins should have been attending a chapel within
the Church of England than that they should be sitting under a
laughing stock. Be that as it may, it is worth considering that they
preferred not to go to the Scottish revivalist sermons, with their
emphasis on conversion, that Irving was currently giving at the
Caledonian Chapel.

Edward Andrews, John Ruskin's first tutor, was an Evangelical
Congregationalist. He may also have been a fabulator. He was famous
for his ornate sermons, his energy, and his ambition.[40] He was
described, not very flatteringly, as 'a sort of Pope' among his co-
religionists. His position was apparently symbolized by his chapel in
Beresford Street. Ruskin's recollection was this:

> Dr Andrews' was the Londinian chapel in its perfect type, definable
> as accurately as a Roman basilica, — an oblong, flat-ceilinged barn,
> lighted by windows with semi-circular heads, brick-arched, filled

by small-paned glass held by iron bars, like fine threaded halves of cobwebs; galleries propped up on iron pipes, up both sides; pews, well shut in, each of them, by partitions of plain deal, and neatly brass-latched deal doors, filling the barn floor, all but its two lateral straw-matted passages; pulpit, sublimely isolated, central from sides and clear of altar rails at end; a stout, four-legged box of grained wainscot, high as the level of front galleries, and decorated with a cushion of crimson velvet, padded six inches thick, with gold tassels at the corners . . .[41]

This is accurate but satirical, and Ruskin does not mention that this memorial to suburban Congregationalism was more expensive than most of its type. Its cost led to Andrews's embarrassment, and nearly his downfall. He himself had put up some of the money to pay for it, but much more had been borrowed on a mortgage. This meant debts which could not be paid. Andrews finally had the humiliating experience of having his church doors shut against him by the mortgagee. He had to welcome his flock in the assembly room of a nearby public house, the Montpelier Tavern. This disaster occurred after the Ruskins had left the Beresford Chapel for a more established church. But they had known for some time that Andrews was no grave and steady pedagogue. One of Margaret's letters reports how the minister arrived at the house, uninvited, at eight o'clock in the morning:

He came he said to ask me about Mrs Andrews state she had another child about three weeks ago and has continued getting weaker ever since . . . he gave me a long acct. of her complaints in the hope I am certain that I should say there was no chance of her living long the Drs say there is no hope of her he also enlarged much on the torment she had been to him for the last ten years . . . I think the Dr has wonderful talents the way he ran on while giving John a little insight into the Hebrews on monday . . . but he is certainly flighty not to say more and in many respects his habits manner of conducting his secular affairs tho' with the best and kindest intentions must to any woman with so numerous a family have caused much serious and distressing apprehension . . .[42]

Although the elder Ruskins spoke of Andrews's 'unwise indulgence of every caprice' they evidently did not consider him too little sedate to be their son's tutor.[43] They thought he had brilliance in him, and liked his popularity and energy. Crowds came to his sermons, and he toured his parish at a run. He had advanced views about women's education: he favoured the sort of liberal instruction that Mary was now receiving. The children of both families were friends. One of Andrews's daughters, Emily, was to marry Coventry Patmore and become the model for *The Angel in the House*: this was the family connection through which Ruskin was first to be introduced, by Patmore, to the Pre-Raphaelite Brotherhood. Emily and John went blackberrying in the summer when the latter was first taught by Andrews. He evidently was delighted with her, his tutor, and his tutor's sermons. He wrote to John James:

> Dr Andrews delivered such a beautiful sermon yesterday I never heard him preach one like it we were putting it down as well as we can for you to look at when we come home We that is Mary and I were so delighted with the sermon that we went out on a hunt for Dr Andrews . . .[44]

The summaries of the sermons that John and Mary made are preserved in some nine notebooks. Although they were often the work of Sunday afternoons in Herne Hill, they were not imposed on the children, and Ruskin says that he was eager to 'show how well' he could record the addresses.[45]

The Ruskins's Sunday indicates that they had abandoned the strict Sabbatarianism of Scotland. They went to church only once on the sabbath and there was no family worship at home. As so often, *Præterita* is slightly contradictory and tends to exaggeration. Ruskin wrote that 'the horror of Sunday used to cast its prescient gloom as far back in the week as Friday'.[46] But elsewhere in the autobiography he was eager to point out that his mother was not like Esther's religious aunt in *Bleak House,* who 'went to church three times every Sunday, and to morning prayers on Wednesdays and Fridays, and to lectures whenever there were lectures; and . . . she never smiled'.[47] John James invited friends to supper on Sunday evenings. The reading was devotional — Bunyan's *Pilgrim's Progress* and *Holy War,* Quarles's *Emblems,* Foxe's *Book of Martyrs,* and Mrs Sherwood's *Lady of the Manor* (borrowed no doubt from Mary), 'a very awful book to me, because of the stories in it of wicked girls who had gone to balls, dying immediately after of fever' — but that was hardly exceptional in a middle-class household of the day.[48]

*   *   *   *

When John Ruskin reached the age of twelve his parents decided that he should be introduced to some more adult interests. A child of the early nineteenth century, in a house like the Ruskins's, would not normally dine with its parents; but on special days young John would now be allowed out of the nursery — his own room at the top of the house, which was kept for him until 1889 — to sit with John James and Margaret. At these meals, John James would read aloud from 'any otherwise suspected delight', literature that was not really for children.[49] A favourite was Christopher North's *Noctes Ambrosianæ*, then appearing in *Blackwood's Magazine*. This robustly tory column, full of coarse wit and savagery, John James read 'without the least missing of the naughty words'. More important than the *Noctes* was the enthusiasm for Byron. John James was passionately fond of his poetry. It is a mark of the independence of his taste that it did not notice any religious prohibitions. In many a home like the Ruskins's, this radical and libertine would have been prohibited. But John Ruskin soon came to know most of Byron. Margaret Ruskin made no objection. *Præterita* goes so far as to associate a shocking feature of Byron's life with Margaret Ruskin's literary tastes. Ruskin is discussing La Fornarina, Byron's mistress, the illiterate wife of a baker. Margaret Ruskin, he said 'had sympathy with every passion, as well as every virtue, of true womanhood; and, in her heart of hearts, perhaps liked the real Margherita Gogni quite as well as the ideal wife of Faliero'.[50] Twenty years later, in her sixties, Margaret would be an enthusiastic reader of Elizabeth Browning's 'Aurora Leigh'. She was not a prude, and in some respects she was a liberal mother.

At this time John Ruskin was first allowed to take wine and to accompany his father to the theatre. John James, a boy actor when at school, loved any kind of dramatic spectacle. His letters often reminisce about theatrical experiences: such things as

> . . . my first play — the *Fashionable Lover* & first afterpiece the *Maid of the Oaks* — I have never seen real Oaks with the pleasure I had in the painted Oaks in that piece. Then for greater excitement we had Lewis's *Castle Spectre* for which I waited an hour before the doors opened . . . Kemble was heroic in voice & person — but a few words of Mrs Siddons Lady Macbeth & Keans Othello dwell in my memory for ever . . .[51]

Margaret Ruskin would not go to the theatre herself, but although she thought that he ought not to contribute to theatrical charities, her husband's reactions were not a matter of contention. Nor did she object to her son being introduced to such pleasures. Ruskin was ever afterwards a lover of the popular theatre.

The freedom to enjoy the romance and excitement of contemporary literature was willingly granted to Ruskin in his boyhood. John James

also indulged his son's taste in art, such as it then was. The elder
Ruskin had kept up the artistic interest he once had when at school. He
now, in 1831, readily agreed that John should follow Mary Richardson in taking drawing lessons. Ruskin's first instruction in art came
from Charles Runciman. He was not a particularly good artist but was
competent to show young people the elements of formulaic water-
colour landscape. John Ruskin enjoyed these lessons and was good at
them. With or without Runciman's encouragement, he soon felt the
eagerness to make art as a splendid construct out of his paint box.

> I must say I was delighted when [Runciman] inquired for my colour
> box, and that not merely for the purpose of splashing colours over
> paper, but because I think that there is a power in painting, whether
> oil or water that drawing is not possessed of, drawing does well for
> near scenes, analyses of foliage, or large trees, but not for distance,
> or bare & wild scenery, how much superior painting would be, if I
> wanted to carry off Derwent Water, & Skiddaw in my pocket, or
> Ulles Water, & Helvellyn, or Windermere, & Low Wood, Oh if I
> could paint well before we went to Dover I should have such sea
> pieces, taken from our windows, such castles & cliffs — hanging
> over the ocean, And ships on those waters, in heaving commotion.
> There would be a night scene, with the waters in all the richness, of
> Prussian blue & bright green, having their mighty billows created,
> with Reeves best white, & the sky above, a very heaven of indigo,
> with the moon, & attendant stars pouring their bright rays upon the
> golden waters, in all the glory of Gamboge, with the moon shining
> out over the waters of Dover.[52]

*   *   *   *

In 1832 John James's partner Henry Telford gave John a copy of
Samuel Rogers's *Italy* for his thirteenth-birthday present. Rogers's
poem is not now much read, but became greatly popular in its day.
John James already had a copy in the house: the significance of this new
book, the edition of 1830, was that it contained illustrations. They
were vignette engravings after Prout, Stothard and, most of all,
Turner. Rogers's first works had been published in the 1780s: his
best-known poem, *The Pleasures of Memory*, is of 1792. *Italy*, whose
first part was issued in 1822, its second in 1828, is in some ways a
Byronic poem, though evidently the production of an older man. The
1830 edition, by virtue of its illustrations, has a place in the enlarge-
ment of the picturesque tradition that developed after the Napoleonic

wars. The picturesque mode became less provincial, less conventional. Turner's imagination and new standards of naturalism were
important in this change. In literature, the picturesque tourist who
visited familiar sites was replaced by a traveller in search of personal
fulfilment. This image was most potent in the third and fourth cantos
of Byron's *Childe Harold*. Ruskin was slightly too young in 1832 to
appreciate a connection between Byron and Turner; he had never yet
been to the Royal Academy, and so did not see Turner's *Childe
Harold's Pilgrimage*, exhibited with a quotation from the fourth canto,
when it was shown there three months after he had received Telford's
present. But Turner's steel engravings in *Italy* fascinated him: and
soon he would set out to find the actual sites from which the drawings
had been made. Now, in the spring of 1833, he went with his father to
a printseller's in the City to look at the specimen plates for Samuel
Prout's *Sketches in Flanders and Germany*. John James subscribed, the
book was brought to Herne Hill, the family looked at it together. It
was Margaret Ruskin who suddenly suggested that their summer tour
this year should follow Prout's route: why should they not go to see all
these wonderful places themselves?

John James had taken them on a short trip abroad in 1825, to Paris
and Brussels, with a visit to the field of Waterloo. This was to be a
longer tour. Their route was from Dover to Calais, and thence to
Strasbourg by following the Rhine. The detailed itinerary, the choice
of hotels, payment for horses and the like along the road were made by
a courier named Salvador. The Ruskins's routine was that they would
breakfast early and start early, travelling forty or fifty miles a day.
They would reach their destination in time for dinner at four o'clock.
After dinner John and Mary would go exploring, sometimes with
Anne Strachan, sometimes by themselves. They had tea at seven in the
evening. John then spent two hours writing and drawing before bed.
When they drove up to Schaffhausen, however, on the eve of one of
the great visual experiences of Ruskin's life, this routine had been
upset. They had arrived after dark, the next day went to church, and
were occupied in the town until late afternoon. Ruskin wrote:

> It was drawing towards sunset, when we got up to some sort of
> garden promenade — west of the town, I believe; and high above
> the Rhine, so as to command the open country across it to the south
> and west. At which open country, far into blue, gazing as at one of
> our distances from Malvern of Worcestershire, or Dorking of Kent,
> — suddenly — behold — beyond!
>   There was no thought in any of us for a moment of their being
> clouds. They were clear as crystal, sharp on the pure horizon sky,

and already tinged with rose by the sinking sun. Infinitely beyond
all that we had ever thought or dreamed, — the seen walls of lost
Eden could not have been more beautiful to us; nor more awful,
round heaven, the walls of sacred Death . . . Thus, in perfect health
of life and fire of heart, not wanting to be anything but the boy I
was, not wanting to have anything more than I had; knowing of
sorrow only just so much as to make life serious to me, not enough
to slacken in the least its sinews; and with so much of science mixed
with feeling as to make the sight of the Alps not only the revelation
of the beauty of the Earth, but the opening of the first page of its
volume, — I went down that evening from the garden-terrace at
Schaffhausen with my destiny fixed in all of it that was to be sacred
and useful . . .[53]

And this was so: Ruskin to the end of his days never ceased to study the
Alps and to associate them with the broad principles of his teaching,
even his political economy. The experience at Schaffhausen was as
immediate as a revelation, and as subsequently haunting. As the
family tour went on through Switzerland and to Italy, more and more
of Ruskin's future work seems to be adumbrated. At the castle of
Chillon, where Byron and Shelley had been before them, the Ruskins
found Byron's name cut out by himself on a pillar. Salvador scratched
out John's on the opposite side of the same pillar; and John James
wrote in his diary that night, 'May he be the opposite of his lordship in
everything but his genius and generosity.'[54] The Ruskins entered Italy
by the most dramatic of passes, the Via Mala, and saw at Lake Como
the very scene that Turner had illustrated in Rogers's *Italy*. They went
on to Milan, then to Genoa and Turin; turned round, and entered the
Alps again by the St Bernard Pass, thence driving to Vevey, Interlaken
and Chamonix, the home of so much of Ruskin's mature work.

This rather odd party — how unlike the aristocratic youths who
made the Grand Tour before them — travelled back to England
through Paris. Here John first met the young woman to whom, soon
enough, he would lose his heart. Pedro Domecq, John James's partner, was splendidly prosperous. He had inherited fine vineyards, his
English business was successful, and so was his trade on the Continent. He proudly wore a royal crown over his arms, for in 1823 he had
been appointed wine merchant to the king of Spain. The eldest of his
five daughters, Diana, was engaged to be married to the Comte
Maison, one of Napoleon's marshals. Domecq's other daughters, all
much younger, were at home on holiday from their convent school.
John Ruskin, at fourteen, was out of his depth. The adults were too
sophisticated for him: at dinner the talk was of the recent death of

Bellini, whose *I Puritani* was then playing at the Italian Opera. His French was not as good as Mary's. He was a failure at the games the girls played: in '*la toilette de madame*' he had to impersonate parts of a woman's clothing. Dancing lessons that he had occasionally attended in Herne Hill disappeared from his mind when he was taken to the floor. The girls concluded that he was of no interest. All this was embarrassing enough. In two years' time, when he fell in love with Adèle-Clotilde, the second of the sisters, it would be torment.

★   ★   ★   ★

The Ruskins had left London in May and did not return to Herne Hill until late September. During the months they were abroad Ruskin had written constantly. He now began to write an account of the tour, illustrated by himself, in both prose and verse. Mary, previously his collaborator, was relegated to a copyist. Ruskin envisaged a finished work of 150 pieces of poetry and prose. He did not write as much as that, but his labours were prolonged. His prose, which relied on over-ornate models, was less successful than his verse.

A low, hollow, melancholy echoing was heard issuing from the recesses of the mountains, the last sighing of the passing-away tempest, the last murmurs of the storm spirit as he yielded up his reign; it past away, and the blue rigidness of the transparent cavern of the glacier woke rosily to the departing sun.[55]

The poems are better. Often they imitate Walter Scott:

> Bosomed deep among the hills,
> Here old Rhine his current stills,
> Loitering the banks between,
> As if, enamoured of the scene,
> He had forgot his onward way,
> For a live-long summer day . . .
> — No marvel that the spell-bound Rhine,
> Like giant overcome with wine,
> Should *here* relax his angry frown,
> And, soothed to slumber, lay him down,
> Amid the vine-clad banks, that lave
> Their tresses in his placid wave.[56]

Ruskin was attempting to convert his experiences in Switzerland and Italy into the conventions established by the literature he knew. This was also the case with his art. His drawings are rather accomp-

lished. They imitate not so much Turner as steel engravings after
Turner. Perhaps more important than these artistic experiments was a
piece of scientific work. The tour produced his first published prose. It
is entitled 'On the causes of the colour of the Rhine' and was to appear
in September 1834 in *Loudon's Magazine of Natural History*.[57]

In the autumn after his first continental tour the ebullient Dr
Andrews was replaced. John Ruskin started to go to school, walking
down the hill to Dr Dale's small establishment in Grove Lane, Camberwell. Thomas Dale is sourly recalled in both *Fiction Fair and Foul*
and *Præterita*, but these memories ignore Ruskin's debt to him. Dale
had a hard mind and liked argument. While Andrews had been easy to
please, Dale was a continual challenge to Ruskin. He disliked polite
learning and believed in the moral force of literature. Dale was older
than Andrews and further on in his career. In 1833 he was the incumbent of St Matthew's Chapel, Denmark Hill: he had been successively
a curate at St Michael's, Cornhill, and St Bride's, Fleet Street, where
he was to return as vicar in 1835. Dale had made a verse translation of
Sophocles and had issued his own poems as well as more purely
devotional books. He was a Cambridge man and was involved with
the new foundation of the University of London. The wonder is that
he bothered with such a school as the one in Grove Lane. Ruskin was
not prepared for his reception on his first day there. He had taken
Alexander Adam's Latin grammar with him

> . . . in a modest pride, expecting some encouragement and honour
> for the accuracy with which I could repeat, on demand, some
> hundred and sixty close-printed pages of it. But Mr Dale threw it
> back to me with a fierce bang upon his desk, saying (with accent and
> look of seven-times-heated scorn) 'That's a *Scotch* thing!'[58]

Ruskin attended, in the mornings only, the school run by 'my
severest and chiefly antagonist master' from September 1833 to the
spring of 1835, when he broke down with a severe attack of pleurisy.
For the first time in his life he mixed with a number of other boys. He
seems to have ignored his schoolfellows, or at any rate to have stood
apart from them.[59]

> Finding me in all respects what boys could only look upon as an
> innocent, they treated me as I supposed they would have treated a
> girl; they neither thrashed nor chaffed me, — finding, indeed, from
> the first that chaff had no effect on me. Generally I did not under-
> stand it, nor in the least mind it if I did, the fountain of pure conceit
> in my own heart sustaining me serenely against all deprecation.[60]

However, some boys at Dale's school remained friends for years. There was Edward Matson, son of a Woolwich colonel who took them to see army exercises; Edmund Oldfield, interested in Gothic architecture, of which Ruskin knew nothing; and Henry Dart, a clever and literary young man whom Ruskin was to meet again at Oxford. His closest boyhood friend, however, was not at Dale's but at Shrewsbury. Richard Fall was the son of a Herne Hill neighbour. In the holidays he often spent the mornings in John's room at the top of the house, now known as his study rather than his nursery. In the afternoons the two boys would go out with their dogs, animals for which Ruskin had great fondness, now and thereafter. Richard was practical and good-humoured, some kind of capitalist in later life. He seems to have had a robust attitude to Ruskin's poetry. He 'laughed me inexorably out of writing bad English for rhyme's sake, or demonstrable nonsense either in prose or rhyme.'[61]

However, Ruskin's feelings that he had a poetic vocation was encouraged by many around him. John James carried his son's poetry with him as he went about his business. Richard Fall's mockery was a kind of encouragement. Thomas Dale, a poet himself, was more interested in English literature than in the classics. Now, in Ruskin's teens, the possibility of publication arose. Charles Richardson, the eldest of the Croydon cousins, was apprenticed in the publishing company of Smith, Elder. Charles used to come to lunch every Sunday, often bringing with him new books that his firm had published. Smith, Elder would have seemed an estimable firm to John James. He knew their offices in Fenchurch Street, just around the corner from his own premises. He knew that the successful business had been built up by ambitious, hard-working, cultivated young Scotsmen. George Smith came from Elgin, Alexander Elder from Banff. Smith, John James's near contemporary, had begun in publishing by working for John Murray: on one occasion he had delivered proofs to Byron himself. Smith, Elder had been founded in 1816. By the time that Charles Richardson came to them in the early '30s they had developed an interesting list and were vigorously promoting their books. They were especially proud of the quality of the steel engraving in expensive art books, views by Clarkson Stanfield, or 'the Byron Gallery'. Another speciality was the keepsake annual. These books appeared every autumn and contained verse, some short pieces of prose and a large number of engravings. They were popular Christmas presents, especially for women, and the phrase that was often used in advertising them, that they presented 'sentiment refined by taste', is a good indication of their style.

Smith, Elder's annual, *Friendship's Offering,* was edited by Thomas
Pringle. A superannuated poet, he had once mixed in the great Edinburgh circles of Scott and Lockhart but had been put out to grass after
the failure, for which he was responsible, of the first issues of *Blackwood's Edinburgh Magazine.* Pringle it was who now in 1835 printed
Ruskin's verse. The young man was proud enough to have his poetry
in such a place as *Friendship's Offering.* Between 1835 and 1844 he
published some twenty-seven pieces in the annual, as well as contributing to similar productions such as the *Amaranth*, the *Keepsake*,
and the *Book of Beauty.*

Pringle took Ruskin to visit Samuel Rogers at his home in St James's
Place, a signal honour. Ruskin was sufficiently inattentive to his
manners to warmly congratulate the poet on the quality of the illustration of *Italy.* This was a rudeness, for the accurate jibe against Rogers
was that the success of his poem, unnoticed when it appeared, was
solely due to the format in which its second edition was published. As
they left the breakfast party, Pringle warned Ruskin that he must be
more deferential to great men. Another acquaintance of Pringle (and
of Alexander Elder) was James Hogg, the 'Ettrick Shepherd', the
contributor to *Blackwood's* and friend of Scott. When Hogg made his
last visit to England he drove out to Herne Hill and was struck with
Ruskin's talents. A little later on, while writing to John James, he
enquired about the young poet's progress. The elder Ruskin replied in
a proud but guarded manner:

> I will venture to say that the youth you were kind enough to notice,
> gives promise of very considerable talent. His faculty of composi-
> tion is unbounded, without, however, any very strong indication
> of originality . . . I have seen productions of youth far superior, and
> of earlier date, but the rapidity of composition is to us (unlearned in
> the ways of the learned) quite wonderful. He is now between 14 and
> 15, and has indited thousands of lines. That I may not select, I send
> his last 80 or 100 lines, produced in one hour, while he waited for
> me in the city . . .[62]

Correspondence ensued, more verses were sent. Hogg wrote to
Ruskin with advice, told him that he was leaning heavily on Scott and
Byron, and invited him to come to stay in Scotland. The invitation
produced a peculiar response, one that says much for the self-
sufficiency of the Ruskin family:

> I cannot sufficiently thank you for your kind, your delightful
> invitation, one which it would have been such a pleasure, such an

honour for me to have accepted. Yet I cannot at this period make up my mind to leave my parents even for a short time. Hitherto I have scarcely left them for a day, and I wished to be with them as much as possible, till it is necessary for me to go to the university . . . I love Scotland, I love the sight and the thought of the blue hills, for among them I have passed some of the happiest days of my short life; and although those days have passed away like a summer-cloud, and the beings which gave them their sweetness are in Heaven, yet the very name of Scotland is sweet to me . . . But it is best not to think of it, for as I before said, I do not wish to leave my parents, and they are equally tenacious of me, and so I can do little but thank you again, again, and thrice again . . .[63]

To refuse such an invitation from a famous poet was perhaps over-reticent. But the literary ambitions of the young Ruskin were well served by a kind of society that existed between Herne Hill and the City of London. Its members were enthusiastically bookish, though often connected with commerce. They were Scottish or Irish, liberal in their interests but tory in every matter of principle. They inclined towards the Evangelical party in the Church but they distrusted enthusiasm. They opposed reform. They were bluff, hearty and convivial. These are the people we find at John James's dinner table, at parties which he might give three or four times a week. Here a minor literary world mingled with friends in the wine business. These backgrounds often overlapped. The Ruskins were good friends with Mr and Mrs Robert Cockburn, the first of whom *Præterita* describes as 'primarily an old Edinburgh gentleman, and only by condescension a wine-merchant'.[64] His wife was the Mary Duff of Lachin-y-Gair, a distant cousin of Byron's and reputedly the first of his loves. Another favourite guest was the Reverend George Croly. This Orange Irishman was renowned for his wit. John James thought him the most amusing man he had ever known, and wrote of his contribution to one party — at which the Cockburns were also present — 'Our table holds only Ten else there was fun for thirty if we could have had them.'[65] Croly was the rector of St Stephen's, Walbrook, in the City of London. He was not known for his piety, but rather for the zeal with which he held the ultra-Tory position that the constitution of 1688 was perfect and that England was the 'fortress of Christianity'.[66] He also had literary standing. He was a contributor to *Blackwood's Edinburgh Magazine* and was the author of poetry, fiction and expensively illustrated travel books: these last were published by Smith, Elder. Croly was of John James's age, and his poetry was now dated. In truth it had never been very fresh, and its derivation from Byron had earned him a derisive assault in *Don Juan*. [67] About this matter Croly cared not one fig.

Although he never wished to admit it, Ruskin owed much to Croly's belligerent opinions: they appear, for instance, in *The Stones of Venice*. As he grew up, the clergyman's acquaintances were to expand John Ruskin's knowledge of men of the world. This happened at an earlier age than *Præterita* would lead us to believe. Through Croly Ruskin met, for instance, Sir Robert Harry Inglis, an amateur of the arts and steadfast Tory Member of Parliament for the University of Oxford. Again through Croly, he touched the outside circle of those raffish Orangemen who organized the Tory press of the 1830s. They were people like William Maginn and Stanley Giffard, who had a background in *Blackwood's* and whose political views were identical with those of the Ruskins. Maginn had been a founder of *Fraser's Magazine,* which was read with appreciation in Herne Hill. But he was known for his intemperance and for his debts. Such a person could never be acceptable at the Ruskins's table.

A tory *littérateur* who was acceptable, and admirably so, now entered the family circle. After Thomas Pringle's death, Croly had a hand in the succession of the editorship of *Friendship's Offering*. It went to W. H. Harrison, who lived near to the Ruskins at Camberwell Green. This conservative-minded man spent his time between commerce and letters. He worked for the Crown Life Office and was registrar of the Royal Literary Fund. Now began a long-standing literary relationship, for Harrison not only went through Ruskin's poems with him, word for word, but looked after every detail of his manuscripts and saw them into press until 1870. In 1878, after his death, Ruskin wrote in 'My First Editor' an account of *Friendship's Offering,* Harrison's 'Christmas bouquet', in which he would assemble

> . . . a little pastoral story, suppose, by Miss Mitford, a dramatic sketch by the Rev. George Croly, a few sonnets or impromptu stanzas to music by the gentlest lovers and maidens of his acquaintance, and a legend of the Apennines or romance of the Pyrenees by some adventurous traveller who had penetrated into the recesses of these mountains, and would modify the traditions of the country to introduce a plate by Clarkson Stanfield or J. D. Harding . . . [68]

This was a slightly mocking description of the publication, for it was written at a time when Ruskin was inclined to deride his own early pretensions. He had forgotten, or chose to forget, how exciting those pretensions once had been.

★   ★   ★   ★

The first poems that Pringle printed in *Friendship's Offering* were inspired by the tour the Ruskins made in the summer of 1835. In the next year their route was through France to Geneva and Chamonix. From Innsbruck they crossed the Stelvio to Venice, which Ruskin now saw for the first time. They were in Venice in October, then came home through Salzburg, Strasbourg and Paris, reaching London on 10 December. Since they had left England on 1 June this was more than a holiday. For Ruskin it was an extended period of pure delight, perhaps the most important of the early family tours and a model for those long sojourns on the Continent which produced so much of his writing.

Ruskin now began to keep a diary. It was a practice he continued for the next fifty-four years, until he could write no longer. One or two of these diaries were lost, and occasionally pages were cut out of them. But they exist almost in their entirety and in many ways are an invaluable record of Ruskin's personal and intellectual life.[69] They say less about his private feelings than do his letters: nor do they tell us more about his mind than do his published writings. But in them we can often trace the origins and progress of his books, or sense the various moods of determination, or boredom, or sometimes exhilaration, that belong to the solitary work of a writer. This first volume of the diaries was clearly bought to make a serious record of the travels of 1835. In its 172 pages (nicely bound in red leather) there is no mention of any other member of the family party. Ruskin's aims were scientific. They were mostly inspired by his fifteenth-birthday present. This had been Horace-Bénédict de Saussure's *Voyages dans les Alpes* (1779-96). The Swiss geologist had expanded Ruskin's interests into landscape. Before, he had collected stones. Now he was interested in the orographic, the study of whole mountain ranges. Ruskin was always to feel that de Saussure was a kindred spirit. He 'had gone to the Alps, as I desired to go myself, only to *look* at them, and describe them as they were, loving them heartily — loving them, the positive Alps, more than himself, or than science, or than any theories of science.'[70] The diary is nonetheless dry. It begins with the 'stiff white clay containing nodules of radiating pyrites' he found at the bottom of the cliffs of Dover;[71] notes the sandstone tract in which lies Fontainebleau and the limestone, quartz and ironstone at Bar-le-Duc. At Poligny he began to study how the Jura mountains rise from the plain; and in the Alps he makes notes on glaciers and snow. By the time the Ruskins reached Chamonix there are diary entries three thousand words long describing mountain formations. These entries are accompanied by drawings and geological maps.

Another book carried on this tour contained a different form of expression. Ruskin was writing poems about what he saw. But he found his verse to be inadequate, too much bound to his stylistic models.

> I determined that the events and sentiments of this journey should be described in a poetic diary in the style of Don Juan, artfully combined with that of Childe Harold. Two cantos of this task were indeed finished — carrying me across France to Chamonix — where I broke down, finding that I had exhausted on the Jura all the descriptive terms at my disposal, and that none were left for the Alps.[72]

And so only 'Salzburg' and 'Fragments from a Metrical Journal' found their way into *Friendship's Offering*. The geological diary was sent whole to John James's friend J. C. Loudon to see if there was anything in it that might be extracted for his *Magazine of Natural History*. Loudon had already published Ruskin's short piece on the colour of the Rhine but seems not to have been attracted by the diary. He was nonetheless encouraging to his would-be contributor: he would print two long letters from Ruskin in 1836 and was soon to publish his first adult work, *The Poetry of Architecture*.

Ruskin's drawing became more interesting during this six-month stay on the Continent. Some sheets are scientific *aides-memoire,* or were meant to accompany putative geological articles; but others, especially of Unterseen, Fribourg and the Jungfrau are of artistic competence. A view of the Ducal Palace, though out of perspective, shows a talent for architectural drawing. He had probably benefited from a change of drawing master. In June 1834 he had left Runciman to study under Copley Fielding, the President of the Society of Painters in Water-colours, often called the Old Water-colour Society. This was a trade association and exhibiting society of minor artists who, by reason of their medium, were excluded from the Royal Academy. They were very largely landscapists, and had no interest in the large historical and mythological *machines* demanded by Academy taste. Their patrons were to a great extent middle class. They gave drawing lessons and supplemented their income by illustrating keepsake annuals and travel books. John James and his son were exactly of their time and class in their appreciation of Fielding, of Prout's picturesque views of the Rhine, of David Roberts (whom Ruskin was to copy), of James Duffield Harding (who was to be the last of his drawing masters).

Ruskin remembered them, in 1879, with the same affectionate and slightly satirical tone that he had used the year before in his memorial of W. H. Harrison and *Friendship's Offering:*

What a simple company of connoisseurs we were, who crowded into happy meeting, on the first Mondays in May long ago, in the bright large room of the Old Water-Colour Society; and discussed, with holiday gaiety, the unimposing merits of the favourites, from whose pencils we knew precisely what to expect, and by whom we were never either disappointed or surprised. Copley Fielding used to paint fishing boats for us, in a fresh breeze, 'Off Dover', 'Off Ramsgate', 'Off the Needles' — off everywhere on the South Coast where anyone had been last Autumn; but we were always pleasantly within sight of land, and never saw so much as a gun fired in distress. Mr Robson would occasionally paint a Bard, on a heathery crag in Wales; or, it might be, a Lady of the Lake on a similar piece of Scottish foreground — 'Benvenue in the distance'. A little fighting, in the time of Charles the First, was permitted to Mr Cattermole; and Mr Cristall would sometimes invite virtuous sympathy to attend the meeting of two lovers at a Wishing-gate or a Holy Well. But the farthest flights even of these poetical members of the Society were seldom beyond the confines of the British Islands . . . It became, however, by common and tacit consent, Mr Prout's privilege, and it remained his privilege exclusively, to introduce foreign elements of romance and amazement into this — perhaps slightly fenny — atmosphere of English common sense. In contrast with our Midland locks and barges, his 'On the Grand Canal, Venice' was an Arabian enchantment; among the mildly elegiac country churchyards of Llangollen or Stoke Poges, his 'Sepulchral Monuments at Verona' were Shakespearian tragedy; and to those of us who had just come into the room out of Finsbury or Mincing Lane, his 'Street in Nuremburg' was a German fairy tale . . .[73]

*   *   *   *

At the beginning of 1836 Pedro Domecq came to England with his four younger daughters, Adèle-Clotilde, Cécile, Elise and Caroline. John James invited him to leave the girls at his home while he travelled to call on some of his English customers. John Ruskin was now sixteen, and approaching his seventeenth birthday on 8 February. When he had met the Domecq daughters in Paris two years before, he had been socially at a loss. Now he was old enough to fall in love. The four extraordinary girls took possession of the house in Herne Hill.

John Ruskin thought all the sisters beautiful, but Adèle-Clotilde the most beautiful of them all. She was fifteen, fair-haired, graceful. She had been born in Cadiz but educated in France. She spoke French, Spanish and a peculiar broken English. She was accustomed to society in Paris; and her clothes, all Parisian cuttings and fittings, were from another world. Many years later, and in guarded terms, Ruskin confessed what had happened to him. He had never been 'the least interested or anxious about girls — never caring to stay in the promenades at Cheltenham or Bath, or on the parade at Dover; on the contrary, growling or mewing if I was ever kept there, and off to the sea or the fields the moment I got leave'.[74] Romantic love he knew only as a literary convention. That illusion was now shattered. He had never felt a great desire that was unfulfillable. But now the certainty, the safety and happiness of his young life all suddenly vanished. Adèle reduced him 'to a mere heap of white ashes in four days. Four days, at the most, it took to reduce me to ashes, but the *Mercredi des cendres* lasted four years.'[75]

Most youths desire girls before they first fall in love. John Ruskin, sheltered and innocent, experienced his sexual awakening like a blow. Ruskin said that it took him four years to recover, but it may have been very much longer than that. His first love was hopeless, as was to be the great love of his life. Adèle was physically near and in every other way remote. He could hardly converse with her, and she — through sophistication, or embarrassment — would have nothing to do with him. 'I endeavoured', wrote Ruskin, 'to entertain my Spanish-born, Paris-bred, and Catholic-hearted mistress with my own views upon the subjects of the Spanish Armada, the Battle of Waterloo, and the doctrine of Transubstantiation.'[76] It was a mistake to try to impress Adèle with his writing. He read aloud from his prose romance *Leoni: a Legend of Italy* and she laughed at it. All his attempts to please brought only 'rippling ecstasies of derision'.[77] She was not old enough, or perhaps nice enough, to have handled the business with whatever tact or kindness was demanded. Ruskin was made to feel that he was despised. The whole household was in chaos. John was besotted, Mary discomfited. The girls' French maid was in dispute with Scottish Anne Strachan. There had to be special arrangements for meals, there were difficulties about church services, and the girls were amazed at the morning Bible readings. All this incompatibility increased the bewilderment with which Ruskin met his humiliation. To make matters worse, his parents failed him. For they too had been living in a kind of innocence of his adolescence. One would have expected more from John James, especially when the obtuse Pedro Domecq raised the idea of a marriage, blithely going to his partner and 'offering to make his daughter a protestant'.[78] Such discussions were not precisely cut off; and John James and Margaret Ruskin merely waited for Adèle to go away and for it all to pass over.

Præterita tells us how, fifty years later, Ruskin could remember nothing more of what happened after Adèle's departure from Herne Hill. Benumbed by love at seventeen, he did not like to recall his suffering at the age of sixty-seven. In fact he had turned to literature. Under a mulberry tree in the Herne Hill back garden he set up a desk and wrote some of a Venetian tragedy, *Marcolino,* in which Adèle appears as the heroine Bianca. Several poems addressed to her, like 'The Mirror', 'Nature Untenanted', and 'Remembrance' went to *Friendship's Offering*. But love, though it prompts adolescents to write, does not teach them how to do it. Fortunately Ruskin now found a new kind of literary instruction. He now began to attend lectures and tutorials at King's College in the Strand. He was following an old schoolmaster. Thomas Dale was rising in the Church and had become the first Professor of English Literature and History in the new university foundation. His new incumbency was of St Bride's, Fleet Street. This was regarded as a significant position in the hierarchy of the Church of England. The professorship was also an important post. It had been offered to Southey, then Poet Laureate, before Dale was approached.

In this way, the lovesick Ruskin became one of the very first university students of English Literature, for Dale in King's College was the originator of English as an academic discipline. A letter to John James describes the beginning of the course.

> Four lectures on this subject have spoken of four celebrated authors of old time — Sir John Mandeville, Sir John Gower, Chaucer, and Wickliffe. We are made acquainted with their birth, parentage, education, etc; the character of their writings is spoken of, and extracts are read as examples of their style . . .[79]

After the lectures Ruskin, with two other students, went for tutorial discussions with Dale in his rooms in Lincoln's Inn Fields. Ruskin felt some antagonism towards his wholesome pedagogy. For he and Dale were in fact literary rivals. Dale too had a hand in keepsake annuals. He was the editor (and his wife's father was the publisher) of an annual called the *Iris*. This publication was in competition with *Friendship's Offering*, which Dale attacked in one of his prefaces, scorning such a 'Gorgeous Gallery of Gallant Inventions, or a Paradise of Dainty Devices, or a Phoenix Nest, or even a Garden of the Muses'.[80] Dale's own version of the keepsake format was dreary. The poems and tales were all religious, and were mostly by himself. His illustrations came not from the contemporary romantics of the Water-Colour Society but were engraved after Poussin, Correggio and Benjamin West.

After Dale's death one of Ruskin's essays was found among his papers. It was a heated defence of some contemporary authors. One of Dale's publications was an edition of the Reverend John Todd's classic *Student's Guide,* to which, in 1836, he contributed a foreword. Todd's manual contains a section entitled 'Beware of Bad Books' which condemns, among others, Byron, Scott and Bulwer. The essay Dale had set Ruskin was 'Does the perusal of works of fiction act favourably or unfavourably upon the moral character?', a title which gave the young author his first opportunity to write polemic. Ruskin began by attacking the censors of literature, first 'the old maid of jaundiced eye and acidulated lip, whose malice-inwoven mind looks on all feelings of affection and joy as the blight looks on the blossom . . . and makes amends for the follies of her youth by making her parrot say "Amen" to her prayers', and then the 'haughty and uncharitable sectarian' as well as 'home-bred misses who had set up for being pious because they have been set down as being ugly'. Most of the rest of this spirited essay is devoted to the proposition that Scott's fiction humanizes and polishes the mind, and that its effect is moral. Straying from fiction, Ruskin then attacked those who are 'filled with such a horror of Byron's occasional immorality, as to be unable to separate his wheat from his chaff' and concluded, 'We do not hesitate to affirm that, with the single exception of Shakespeare, Byron was the greatest poet that ever lived . . . His mind was from its very mightiness capable of experiencing greater agony than lower intellects, and his poetry was wrung out of his spirit by that agony.'[81]

Thus was dismissed Ruskin's English Literature tutor. His first writing on art dates from these months: it is rather like the essay he wrote for — against — Dale. This was an equally vigorous defence of Turner. Ruskin's admiration for the engravings after Turner in Rogers's *Italy* had not at first encouraged him to find out more about the artist. He copied them, but he did not seek out more examples. He had seen original Turners from 1833, when he first went to the Royal Academy exhibitions, but he had received mixed impressions from them. In 1835, before going on the continental tour, he was even nonplussed. *Keelmen Hauling in Coals,* for instance, which is a night piece, contrasted too oddly with Turner's version of Virgilian romance in *The Golden Bough.* The extravagant *Burning of the Houses of Parliament* Ruskin simply could not grasp: he was silent about the painting for the rest of his life. In 1836, however, Turner exhibited *Juliet and her Nurse, Rome from Mount Aventine* and *Mercury and Argus*. At seventeen, full of love and poetry, intellectually provoked by his new studies with Dale, he now had a new kind of æsthetic encounter. It was not passive: it was critical. It was the knowledge of being convinced by excellent painting. As he later explained, it was 'not merely judgement, but sincere *experience*' of Turner that he had now found.[82] When, therefore, in October of 1836, he read the review of the pictures in *Blackwood's Edinburgh Magazine* he was aroused not only by its wrongness but by its insincerity. The notice of the Royal Academy exhibition was by the Reverend John Eagles, an amateur artist and regular reviewer for the paper. He wrote of 'confusion worse confounded' in *Juliet and her Nurse*; in the Roman picture he found 'a most unpleasant mixture, wherein white gamboge and raw sienna are, with childish execution, daubed together'; while of *Mercury and Argus*, he pronounced,

> It is perfectly childish. All blood and chalk. There was not the least occasion for a Mercury to put out Argus's eyes; the horrid glare would have made Mercury stone blind . . . It is grievous to see genius, that it might outstrip all others, fly off into mere eccentricities . . .[83]

Ruskin's angry reply was in championship of the wronged. It was also elevated. He immediately made the highest claims for Turner. His imagination was 'Shakespearian in its mightiness'. For the first time we hear the voice of that extravagance in prose that would subsequently be an effortless attribute of his writing. He could now describe a painting like this:

> Many coloured mists are floating above the distant city, but such mists as you might imagine to be ætherial spirits, souls of the mighty dead breathed out of the tombs of Italy into the blue of her bright heaven, and wandering in vague and infinite glory around the heaven that they have loved. Instinct with the beauty of uncertain light, they move and mingle among the pale stars, and rise up into the brightness of the illimitable heaven, whose soft, and blue eye gazes down into the deep waters of the sea for ever . . .[84]

In such a way Ruskin's defence went beyond the inadequacies of Eagles's article. In its assertions of mightiness and attempts to write exalted descriptions of paintings we find the beginning of Ruskin's lifelong endeavour to celebrate Turner above all other artists.

John James thought that the reply ought to be shown to Turner before it was sent to *Blackwood's*. His son's writing was accordingly

forwarded to the painter through Smith, Elder. This meant that there
was a kind of contact between Turner and his champion. Soon Ruskin
received a letter from him. It read:

> My dear Sir,
> I beg to thank you for your zeal, kindness, and the trouble you have
> taken on my behalf, in regard to the criticism of *Blackwood's
> Magazine* for October, respecting my works; but I never move in
> these matters, they are of no import save mischief and the meal tub,
> which Maga fears for by my having invaded the flour tub.
>
>   P.S. If you wish to have the manuscript returned, have the
> goodness to let me know. If not, with your sanction, I will send it
> on to the possessor of the picture of Juliet. [85]

This characteristic letter closed the episode. The manuscript, the germ
of *Modern Painters,* was not returned, and was not discovered for
another sixty years. This was no great disappointment to Ruskin. He
had not really thought that he would appear in *Blackwood's.* And he
now had other things to think about, for a week after receiving
Turner's letter he went up to Oxford to matriculate.

CHAPTER TWO

1837–1840

At the beginning of 1837, when John Ruskin left his family home to go into residence at Christ Church, he was just eighteen years old. A rather tall — five feet eleven — and slight young man, he had blue eyes, a thin face, a prominent nose and reddish hair. His hands were long and nervous. There was a scar on his lower lip where a dog had bitten him in childhood. His courteous manner was a combination of formality and attentiveness. There was something deliberate in his speech, however casual the conversation. The manner of rounding off his sentences was the legacy of the Bible readings and his mother's insistence on correct and meaningful pronunciation. From his father's Scottish accent perhaps came his burring way of pronouncing his 'r's. He was slightly dandyish. He enjoyed dressing up for special occasions. His clothes were not fashionable, usually, but they were distinctive. Two items of his dress were not to be altered throughout his life. He always wore a slim greatcoat with a brown velvet collar and never appeared without a large, bright blue neckcloth. Interested in other people, young Ruskin nonetheless had a certain conceit in himself. He was quite ambitious: he had started to think of winning the Newdigate prize for poetry before he matriculated. He was eager to learn but already preferred to go about learning in his own way. He was sufficiently sure of himself not to be put out by differences of social class, though he was certainly aware of such differences. He was kind, but self-willed. People noticed him, and he quickly made friends: nonetheless there was something about Ruskin which discouraged the hearty friendships of youth. In some ways he was simple and innocent, compared to his public school–educated contemporaries. But he was more advanced than they in other of the world's sophistications. He was an accomplished draughtsman, a published geologist and a published poet. He knew people in the London literary world: he was much travelled, and he was in love with a *Parisienne*. All in all, it is little wonder that few people understood this talented, complicated young man as he began his university career.

* * * *

Readers of *Præterita* will recall how 'Christ Church Choir', the chapter of autobiography devoted to Ruskin's Oxford education, invokes the regular morning worship of that collegiate body,

> . . .representing the best of what England had become — orderly, as the crew of a man-of-war, in the goodly ship of their temple. Every man in his place, according to his rank, age and learning; every man of sense or heart there recognising that he was either fulfilling, or being prepared to fulfil, the gravest duties required of Englishmen.[1]

The whole passage is more a vision than a memory, for these were the sentiments of a much older Ruskin. The Christ Church Ruskin knew at the end of the 1830s was not orderly, and duties were not much thought of. The buildings were dirty and dilapidated. Learning was perfunctory, undergraduates idle and riotous as often as not. The very choir of which Ruskin speaks was used to store beer, and dogs had to be chased from the chapel before services could begin. As elsewhere in Oxford, the customs of the eighteenth century lingered in Christ Church. An antique learning prevailed, and a sedentary Anglicanism hardly touched by the fresher piety of Evangelicalism. Wines, gambling and hunting were the undergraduate amusements. There were good men and conscientious students, of course: Christ Church was even then, as much as Oriel or Balliol, nurturing the first generation of great Victorian dons: but it was not an inspiring environment for such an eager young man as Ruskin.

Writing *Præterita*, the distinguished honorary student of Christ Church felt that he ought to say something positive about his undergraduate days in the college. Ruskin found this extremely difficult. He had not greatly enjoyed his Oxford career and he knew that his formal higher education had not been a significant part of his life. Ruskin had already had experience of a more liberal university course, one more suited to the future author of *Modern Painters*, at King's College. The routines of the classical curriculum at Christ Church were by comparison dull. Ruskin exaggerated when he said that he could only just grasp Greek verbs and that his Latin was 'the worst in the University'.[2] But the Christ Church Collections Book indicates that his attainments were little more than average. Perhaps he was too independent: he instinctively approached the ancient authors as he would read modern literature, liking some books and dismissing others. A cancelled passage of *Præterita* reveals that

> Both Virgil and Milton were too rhetorical and parasitical for me; Sophocles I found dismal, and in subject disgusting, Tacitus too

hard, Terence dull and stupid beyond patience; — but I loved my Plato from the first line I read — knew by *Ethics* for what they were worth (which is not much) and detested with all my heart and wit the accursed and rascally *Rhetoric,* — which my being compelled to work at gave me a mortal contempt for the whole University system.[3]

Learning by rote was unwelcome to the young poet. The classical authors did not fit a sensibility that had already been formed by more modern literature. Even Ruskin's genuine love of Plato did not emerge for another twenty years. The learning that filled and inspired his earlier books came from the Herne Hill library, from architecture and painting and from a half-scientific observation of nature. At Oxford, therefore, his emergent powers are most to be seen in his letters to friends; in his poetry and drawing; and in the beginning of such independent prose writings as *The Poetry of Architecture.*

Of all Oxford colleges Christ Church is nearest to the Anglican establishment of Church and State. So numerous are its ties with government and the throne that the college, especially to its members, seems almost a part of the British constitution. Its undergraduate body is aristocratic: on occasion it is royal. The Visitor of Christ Church is the reigning monarch: the college's chapel is Oxford Cathedral. Its own constitution, with a dean, eight canons and subordinate officers, dates from its foundation by Cardinal Wolsey and Henry VIII. To enter this society was to renounce the nonconformist heritage of the Ruskin family. Moreover, John Ruskin entered Christ Church at the summit of its own hierarchies. He was a gentleman-commoner. This was a rank, which John James purchased, and was generally the province of sons of the nobility. Gentlemen-commoners had special privileges, the best rooms, sat together at separate tables, and were given distinctive gowns and mortar-boards (Ruskin preserved his, and wore it when he was Slade Professor). The social incongruity of a merchant's son among this aristocratic class was obvious. Yet Ruskin took his place without embarrassment. His contemporaries were tolerant young men. He was derided when he unwisely mentioned Adèle's aristocratic French connections: but there is otherwise no record at all that he was treated as a parvenu. Such friendliness was remarkable: G. W. Kitchin, later Dean of Durham, who was at Christ Church only five years later than Ruskin, had to become ingenious to explain it. He wrote in his *Ruskin at Oxford* that Christ Church was 'very like the House of Commons in temper; a man, however plain of origin, however humble in position, is tolerated and listened to with respect, if he is sincere, honest and "knows his subject" '.[4] This was

not true of Christ Church, and did not cover Ruskin's case. The fact is
that he maintained himself socially — as he would do all his life — by
being exceptional.

John Ruskin cared next to nothing about what appeared to others as
his peculiarities. To wish for his mother's company might seem
unusual in a young man in a male society. Yet when Ruskin went into
residence in Christ Church, his family came to Oxford with him.
Margaret Ruskin and Mary Richardson moved into lodgings in the
High Street, where John James joined them at weekends. Every
evening, as his student life allowed, Ruskin went after hall to sit with
his mother and cousin until Great Tom, the bell of the college, called
out that its gates were closing. This arrangement continued throughout his three years as an undergraduate. What could more demonstrate
the unity of the Ruskin family, and their disregard of other social
forms? The naturalness of the Ruskins's dependence on each other was
soon accepted by other students. Often enough, young men of the
nobility came to the lodgings to meet Margaret Ruskin. There was
something so frank and powerful in her, this innkeeper's daughter,
that snobbishness was beside the point. The same was true of John
James. For their part, the elder Ruskins took a lively interest in their
son's friends, whether they met them or not. They were especially
gratified that he got on well with such aristocrats as Lord Kildare,
Lord March or Lord Somers — this last, Charles Somers Cocks, a
friend with whom Ruskin was to have a lasting acquaintance. John
Ruskin's social success was the triumph of the whole family: it represented the culmination of all that Margaret and John James had
done together since the dark days, never mentioned, in Scotland.

Ruskin knew few people from other colleges, but within Christ
Church the range of his acquaintance was wide. He belonged to none
of those 'sets' which for G. W. Kitchin define college life. He would
certainly not have allied himself to an 'idle or vicious set'; yet he was on
terms with the gamblers, 'men who had their drawers filled with
pictures of naked bawds — who walked openly with their harlots in
the sweet country lanes — men who swore, who diced, who drank,
who knew *nothing* . . .';[5] on terms too with the sportsmen, for we find
him one day in an alehouse over Magdalen Bridge with Bob Grimston
(later famous on the turf),

> . . . to hear him elucidate from the landlord some points of the
> horses entered for the Derby, an object only to be properly accomp-
> lished by sitting with indifference on a corner of the kitchen table,

5. Ruskin's Rooms at Christ Church, Oxford, by John Ruskin, 1839.

and carrying on the dialogue with careful pauses, and more by winks than words.[6]

These people were not really his friends, and those who were closer to Ruskin were still unlike him in temperament. Thus it was at Christ Church, so it would be all through his life. Ruskin became friendly with two of his tutors. The Reverend Osborne Gordon would remain a mentor to Ruskin until his death in 1883. He was the Censor of Christ Church and University Reader in Greek. His classical knowledge was more up-to-date, if less magisterial, than that of Thomas Gainsford, the Dean of Christ Church. The Dean was famed for his Greek scholarship yet knew no German, the language of all modern contributions to the knowledge of Greece. But it was not Gordon's more alert attitude to the study of the ancient world (it was not that much more alert) that made him important to Ruskin, but rather his deft, conscientious way of bringing a spirit of enquiry to his students. Gordon was a dry, rather amusing man, not too likely to be impressed; not so much argumentative as disinclined to be taken by other people's certainties. He was very sharp, almost cynical. But his personal kindness was not disguised by his quizzical ways. Ruskin learnt much from Gordon, and John James was delighted with him.[7]

Osborne Gordon was first among the people who knew the Ruskins socially in Oxford and also became visitors at Herne Hill. His earlier visits to south London were made to give Ruskin extra tutorials in the vacations. He was not paid for this help, but John James's account books show that in 1862 he gave the college the almost extravagant sum of £5,000 in Gordon's honour: it was to be used for the augmentation of poor college livings. The extra tuition indicates both that Gordon felt Ruskin's talent and that he feared that he would fall at the hurdles of the examination system. Side by side, in the Herne Hill parlour as in the rooms of the Peckwater quadrangle, they worked through the texts in which the older man found so much more pleasure than did Ruskin. Afterwards, as they walked in the familiar paths to Dulwich and Norwood, or from Oxford to Shotover and Forest Hill, Ruskin would expatiate on his religious beliefs: he was young enough to think that fervour would impress his tutor. Gordon, though, addressed himself on these walks 'mainly to mollifying my Protestant animosities, enlarge my small acquaintance with ecclesiastical history, and recall my attention to the immediate business in hand, of enjoying our walk, and recollecting what we had read in the morning'.[8] Ruskin found a similar attitude in another of his tutors. The Reverend Walter Lucas Brown was stimulating to Ruskin because he had an interest in aesthetic discussion. Like Gordon, he taught

Ruskin Greek (possibly a more wearisome task because of his charge's belief — reiterated in early volumes of *Modern Painters* — that a pagan civilization could produce nothing to compare with Christian art), and tried to win him from an inclination towards extreme Protestantism. He made Ruskin read Isaac Taylor's *Natural History of Enthusiasm* (1829), a now forgotten classic of Anglican moderation and caution against millenialism and suchlike notions: ideas which were greatly unwelcome in Christ Church but common enough in south London chapels which Ruskin knew well.

It is possible that Brown and even Gordon might have felt themselves a little under scrutiny when in the company of John James Ruskin. The wine merchant commanded any social gathering. His complete self-assurance, candid manner and outspoken opinions gave the impression of a man with whom one contends; but what made people yield to him was his good nature, however rough, and his desire of that fellowship which exists between people who love books. Evidently a man of the world, he still retained, even in his fifties, some of the ardours of his youth. John James was good company for younger men, and his enormous pride in his son was so unadorned as to be infectious: people thought more of Ruskin himself through knowing his father. His weekends in Oxford gave John James new opportunities to test his views on men and manners. He did not feel amiably towards eccentrics and he disliked lazy people in privileged positions. For these reasons he was likely to be taken with undergraduates. A contemporary of his son whom he especially liked was Henry Acland. This well-meaning medical student breathed outdoor virtues. He was not a sportsman but was brave at sailing and riding. Acland came from the Devon baronetage but had decided to stay in Oxford, where he also had family connections, to promote the study of the medical sciences. These plans had come to him early in life: he was the sort of man who plans his life. His association with Ruskin, who by comparison was quicksilver, was in many ways unlikely. It probably began because the slightly older Acland took Ruskin under his wing. But the friendship was permanent: more than forty years later *Præterita* recorded that it 'has never changed, except by deepening, to this day'.[9] While they were undergraduates, Acland guided Ruskin in the ways of Christ Church, discussed science with him, but most of all listened to him. Thereafter, Acland's more pedestrian mind was often exercised in keeping up with Ruskin. This had far-reaching consequences for them both, and for Oxford: it was Acland who first realized that Ruskin had the makings of a great teacher.

What Acland saw in Ruskin, Henry Liddell saw too, but his interest was to turn to suspicion. Liddell, whose name was once known to

every schoolboy for his Greek lexicon, was to become the Dean of
Christ Church. At this time he was a young tutor there, about to be
ordained, and was already discussing with Henry Acland the changes
they expected to make in the university. From a letter he wrote in 1837
we have a glimpse of Ruskin as he appeared to Liddell:

> I am going to . . . see the drawings of a very wonderful
> gentleman-commoner here who draws wonderfully. He is a very
> strange fellow, always dressing in a greatcoat with a brown velvet
> collar, and a large neckcloth tied over his mouth, and living quite in
> his own way among the odd set of hunting and sporting men that
> gentlemen-commoners usually are . . . [He] tells them that they
> like their own way of living and he likes his; and so they go on, and I
> am glad to say they do not bully him, as I should have been afraid
> they would.[10]

Liddell's appreciation of Ruskin's drawing was genuine, and he
made sure that Dean Gainsford saw the numerous architectural and
topographical studies with which Ruskin was engaged. He probably
introduced Ruskin to the great collections of old master drawings
which belonged to Christ Church and were then stored, in no particular order and with inexact attributions, in the college library. Liddell
knew rather a lot about classical art, as Ruskin had to recognize. But
his cool and Olympian manner did not encourage Ruskin to seek him
out: he merely provided Ruskin with a minor lesson in growing up,
his first experience of disliking someone without having good
grounds for doing so.

It is clear that Ruskin lacked a friend who would be a comrade to
him in the romantic discovery of literature and art. There could have
been such a person — many of them, perhaps — in London, but they
were not to be found in Christ Church. Here is one of those cases in
which an 'advanced' taste belongs not so much to a younger generation as to a different class. Ruskin's outlook on art had more in
common with his father, who was now in his late fifties, than with his
peers at Oxford. In this connection the Ruskins's long and friendly
acquaintance with Charles Newton is of interest. Newton, most
famous today for his excavation of the Mausoleum at Halicarnassus,
one of the wonders of the ancient world, was three years Ruskin's
senior at Christ Church. He left the university to take a post in the
rapidly expanding British Museum at the end of Ruskin's first year.
They scarcely had the opportunity to become intimate, therefore, but
they maintained a friendship for many years. The great difference
between the classicist Liddell and the archæologist Newton was in

temperament. Newton was entirely jovial. His opposition to Ruskin's picturesque, romantic and naturalist views was always cast in the form of a joke. This was often exasperating to Ruskin, though it was good for him to be laughed at; and so they concealed their differences in jests until, in the late 1860s, they simply drifted apart. At Oxford, Newton gave a shock to what Ruskin called his 'artistic conceit' when he asked him to draw a Norman arch to illustrate a talk at the local architectural society. The result, full of Proutian mannerism, was not adequate as illustration. It was salutary, Ruskin later reflected, to realize that his drawings had shortcomings. They might be admired elsewhere in Oxford, but that was not good enough. His progress as an artist had of course been halted during the time he attended the university.

Another person who found a use for Ruskin's ability with pen and brush was Dr William Buckland, the geologist and mineralogist who was a canon of the cathedral and the college. For Buckland Ruskin made diagrams. He was probably the only don at Christ Church that Ruskin had heard of before matriculating at the university, for he was a geologist of considerable repute. Ruskin had almost certainly studied his work at about the time that he was going to Dale's classes in English Literature. Buckland was perhaps as eccentric as any don in the annals of Oxford: at any rate, his eccentricities are amply recorded in those annals. In his house at the corner of the great quadrangle of the college he kept a bear, jackals, snakes and many other beasts and birds. These he ate. He claimed to have 'eaten his way through the animal kingdom'.[11] He also served his pets to his guests. It is not surprising that there are many stories about Buckland and his menagerie. They became Christ Church legends; and some of them were later transformed by Charles Dodgson into scenes in *Alice's Adventures in Wonderland* and *Through the Looking-Glass,* stories first told in the 1850s to the Alice Liddell and Angie Acland who were the daughters of Ruskin's contemporaries. Henry Liddell despised 'poor Buckland' and considered that he had not the intellectual calibre to occupy a chair in the university.[12] That is as may be. What is certain is that Ruskin's acquaintance with Buckland expanded his geological knowledge, and that this was an intellectual inspiration at a time when such inspiration was not easily found. At his table (where Ruskin managed to miss 'a delicate toast of mice') the undergraduate met 'the leading scientific men of the day, from Herschel downwards',[13] and was introduced to Darwin, thereby initiating a respectful debate between the two men that would last for decades.

We should remember that geology in the 1830s was a new and exciting science. The Geological Society, whose meetings Ruskin

eagerly attended, was in the intellectual vanguard of early Victorian
London. The science's dependence on field-work, its interest in
natural phenomena and demand for close observation were suited to
one part of Ruskin's temperament. His ambition to become President
of the Geological Society was perhaps not unrealizable. For in this
company the contributions of amateurs could be as valid as those of
professionals, and a young man would be heard alongside seasoned
practitioners. Ruskin's experience in geology later on gave him confidence to approach another new science in which he was an amateur,
economics. The difference was that he did not expect to enjoy the
study of political economy. Geology was pleasure, a wonderful combination of discovery and recreation. For this reason we should be
wary of the theory that geological work now made progressive
attenuations of his Christian faith. The bearing of geological research
on the literal interpretation of Genesis did not trouble Ruskin at this
stage. It might well have distressed his Calvinist mother, but both
Ruskin and his father were skilled at avoiding the issue when they
spoke with her about such matters. In any case, she could see nearer
enemies. Her son's days as an undergraduate coincided with the
headiest time of the Oxford Movement. Romanism was claiming
many a young man. Margaret Ruskin greatly feared that her son
might be touched by the scarlet attractions of this foreign religion.
And yet we find that Ruskin, who already had a relish for theological
controversy, had no interest whatsoever in the Tractarian debate.
While Newman was preaching his famous sermons in the university
church opposite Margaret Ruskin's lodgings, her son scarcely knew
who he was. It was not that Ruskin considered the position taken by
the Tractarians and then rejected it. He ignored them completely. A
great religious current simply passed him by.

There was a Ruskin family tradition that Margaret, like the biblical
Hannah, had dedicated her new-born son to the service of God. While
he was at Oxford it was still her hope that he would enter the ministry.
John James was non-committal on the subject, and kept quiet about
his heart's desire, that his son should become a poet. Ruskin thought
about the Church, but not as much as he thought about Adèle and
poetry. He wanted to win the Newdigate. If Ruskin were to take a
university prize it would not be in the classics. The prize for English
verse therefore had to be his aim. When he looked at the previous
winners he could see fair hope of success. The problems were that the
subject was not of his own choosing and that the required length was
greater than the lyric to which he was accustomed. But fluency and
'correctness' were highly regarded, and here Ruskin's experience of

polishing verses with W. H. Harrison would no doubt help. Nonetheless, he failed to win the prize in the first two years that he entered the competition. He was beaten in the first year by another pupil of Dale's, J. H. Dart (in later life a translator of the *Iliad*), and in the second by Arthur Penrhyn Stanley, later Dean of Westminster. It is interesting to note that the second place in the year that Ruskin won the Newdigate was taken by Arthur Hugh Clough. The two men were never to become friends despite some shared interests. Their common task in 1840 was to write about 'Salsette and Elephanta'. These are Indian islands which were converted to Christianity. The obscure subject required research, some of which was undertaken by John James. Of the completed and victorious poem there is not much to say, except that the translation of recondite material to literary form was doubtless a useful exercise for the future author of *Modern Painters* and *The Stones of Venice*.

Ruskin's Newdigate poems are not interesting. Nor, in truth, are the verses from Oxford which are to be associated with Adèle. But we should not confuse their conventional sentiments with the real feelings of their author. Ruskin's love for Adèle was genuinely painful. It was also long-lasting. The new environment of Oxford did not help him to forget her. And if he lived a more adult life there, it did not equip him to control his despondent and yearning emotions. When Ruskin wrote his autobiography he looked back on those days with horror. Some passages which refer to Adèle were cancelled because of their bitterness. It is significant that they associate her with his ambition to carry off the Newdigate. Both were desired and both desires were vain. 'To be a poet like Byron was no base aim, at twelve years old,' Ruskin wrote, 'but to get the Newdigate at nineteen, base altogether.' So it was with his love: 'The storm of stupid passion in which I had sulked during 1836 and 1837 had passed into a grey blight of all wholesome thought and faculty, in which a vulgar conceit remained almost my only motive to exertion.'[14] Unfortunately, during Ruskin's second Oxford year Pedro Domecq sent his daughters to England for their further education. They were placed in a convent school at Chelmsford. John James had been asked by his partner to assume their guardianship and the girls were therefore brought into the Ruskin family. They came again to Herne Hill and stayed for weeks over the Christmas of 1838. Once again Ruskin was put on the rack. *Præterita* cannot conceal the feelings of waste evoked by the memory of that Christmas.

> Every feeling and folly, that had been subdued or forgotten, returned in double force . . . and day followed on day, and month

to month, of complex absurdity, pain, error, wasted affection, and rewardless semi-virtue, which I am content to sweep out of the way of what better things I can recollect at this time, into the smallest possible size of dust heap, and wish the Dustman Oblivion good clearance of them.[15]

Relations with the Domecqs were further complicated when Pedro Domecq died in an accident at the beginning of the next year. We do not know how John James's guardianship then stood. But it is unlikely that he was involved in the negotiations which now took place for the betrothal of Adèle to a Baron Duquesne. She had never met the man, but appears to have readily acquiesced in her arranged marriage. Perhaps she was spiritless: one cannot tell. John James's concern for his son's sufferings appears in a letter to Margaret Ruskin:

I wish John could have seen enough of Adèle to cure of the romance & fever of the passion. I trust my Dear Child will not suffer an Injury from the violence of feeling. I am deeply affected for him because I cannot bear that he should by anything have his feelings wounded. Please not to say anything until we know more.[16]

Thus John's parents adopted the policy of telling him nothing of what was happening. He did not know of the marriage plans for many more months. During this time he imagined that there was still hope that he might, some day, win some affection from her. When at last he discovered the truth the shock was brutal. There is only the bleak note in his diary, 'I have lost her'.[17] Two years later, on the anniversary, the diary records 'that evening in Christ Church when I first knew of it, and went staggering along down to dark passage through the howling wind to Childs' room, and sat there with him working through innumerable problems'.[18]

These 'problems' were from Euclid: as he would do all his life, Ruskin sought solace from love in work. He used study to drive out thoughts of Adèle. The official routines of a Christ Church education now seemed even more divorced from the real concerns of his life. His parents' hope that he would excel at the things that are highly regarded in Oxford meant that neither he nor they thought highly enough of the best achievement of his undergraduate years. This was the collection of papers known as *The Poetry of Architecture*.

Although it was not published within two covers until many years later (in an American pirated edition in 1873, and in England in 1893, when it was issued under W. G. Collingwood's supervision), we will say that Ruskin wrote a book when an undergraduate. It is a bold

rumination on the picturesque. The origins of the book are in the first
summer tour Ruskin made with his parents after matriculating. Between June and August of 1837 they drove together through Yorkshire, the Lake District and the Derbyshire Dales. The cottage scenery
suggested a piece of writing to him: so also did the domestic architecture he noted when on a tour through Scotland and England the
following year. The papers were written up in Oxford and were
immediately printed in J. C. Loudon's *Architectural Magazine*. Ruskin
signed them with the pen-name 'Kata Phusin', or 'According to
Nature'. They attracted some attention, and the notice taken of them
ought to have been gratifying. *The Times* wrote that the author 'has
the mind of a poet as well as the eye and hand of an artist, and has
produced a series of highly poetical essays'.[19] That was indeed so: *The
Poetry of Architecture* is distinctively a poet's book, even though much
of its prose style derives from Johnson's essays in the *Idler* and the
Rambler, the Ruskins's favourite reading while on tour.

The *Poetry of Architecture* appears significant today because of its
place in the picturesque tradition and because it announces the themes
of such later writings of Ruskin's as, most notably, *The Seven Lamps of
Architecture*. At the time of its composition, however, only the Newdigate seemed important, and Ruskin had little interest in his prose
publication. When Ruskin took the Newdigate, in the summer of
1839, the prize was handed to him after a public recitation by none
other than Wordsworth. Margaret Ruskin did not dare attend this
ceremony, so splendid was it. John James wrote to Harrison, 'There
were 2000 ladies and gentlemen to hear it: he was not at all nervous,
and it went all very well off. The notice taken of him is quite extraordinary.'[20] Ruskin did not enjoy his triumph, for he was inconsolable
about Adèle. Back at Herne Hill in the vacation his parents made
uncharacteristically worldly attempts to put other girls in his path.
Ruskin was polite to them. He seemed to be progressing in the world's
honours, but his spirits were very low. On a family tour in Cornwall
he spent hours looking at the sea. He was made a Fellow of the
Geological Society: this was no comfort. In February 1830 he came of
age, was given an income of £200 a year by his father and also received
from him Turner's *Winchelsea*. The gift contained a dark augury,
Ruskin later thought: 'The thundrous sky and broken white light of
storm round the distant gate and scarcely visible church, were but too
true symbols of the time that was coming upon us; but neither he nor I
were given to reading omens, or dreading them.'[21]

Ruskin was referring to his first experience of breaking down after a
prolonged spell of work: and he writes thus sombrely because he was

reminded of more recent failures of his health and mind. In Ruskin, as in other literary people, overwork was usually self-imposed, almost self-willed. He seems almost to have courted its outcome. The breakdowns followed a rising pattern in which long hours of concentration were accompanied by nervous tension which in the end, straining and tightening, could not sustain the labour. Since Ruskin always filled his waking hours with mental activity, only those most sensitive to him could tell when danger was approaching. Nobody around him now realized how close he was to collapse. They were interested in the possibility that he might take a first. Soon after his twenty-first birthday, after consultations with Walter Brown, all parties agreed that Ruskin should not spend a further year at Oxford but should try to graduate with a splendid degree at the end of the next academic term. Ruskin, now living in rooms in St Aldate's, returned to his classical texts, his work coming 'by that time to high pressure, until twelve at night from six in the morning, with little exercise, no cheerfulness, and no sense of any use in what I read, to myself or anybody else: things progressing also smoothly in Paris, to the abyss'. By this Ruskin means Adèle's marriage. Three weeks after she was wed to another man, Ruskin was troubled late one evening by 'a short tickling cough . . . followed by a curious taste in the mouth, which I presently perceived to be that of blood'.[22] He immediately walked round to his parents' lodgings in the High Street; and the next day he was in London, with doctors.

CHAPTER THREE

1840—1841

Although he returned there eighteen months later to complete his residence and take his degree, this was the abrupt and slightly inglorious end of Ruskin's first career in Oxford. The doctors did not agree about his condition. He might seem tubercular: but there was no more blood. Certainly he was in a state of nervous exhaustion. Everyone thought that he should rest, and that he should winter abroad. At Herne Hill, feeling the empty relief that comes after prolonged intellectual exertion, Ruskin quietly obeyed medical advice. Occasionally he went into town. Then, at the dealer Thomas Griffith's home, on 22 June 1840, there was a momentous meeting. Ruskin's diary records:

> Introduced to-day to the man who beyond all doubt is the greatest of the age; greatest in every faculty of the imagination, in every branch of scenic knowledge; at once *the* painter and poet of the day, J. M. W. Turner. Everybody had described him to me as coarse, boorish, unintellectual, vulgar. This I knew to be impossible. I found in him a somewhat eccentric, keen-mannered, matter-of-fact, English-minded — gentleman: good-natured evidently, bad-tempered evidently, hating humbug of all sorts, shrewd, perhaps a little selfish, highly intellectual, the powers of the mind not brought out with any delight in their manifestation, or intention of display, but flashing out occasionally in a word or a look.[1]

'Pretty close, that, and full, to be seen at a first glimpse, and set down the same evening', Ruskin later added when he copied out the entry.[2] So it was: but of course he had thought many times about the probable character of the artist. He had also been studying Turner at the home of one of his connoisseurs, B. Godfrey Windus. In the light and airy library of his villa on Tottenham Green this retired coachbuilder had collected some fifty Turners, as well as work by such artists as J. D. Harding, Clarkson Stanfield, J. B. Pyne and Augustus Calcott. Ruskin had obtained from the benevolent Windus *carte blanche* to visit the collection at any time he liked. From Windus he learnt not only about the pictures, their dates and subjects, but also about Turner himself. He heard many stories about the labyrinthine ways of selling work that were habitual both to the painter and his dealer. As the Herne Hill collection of paintings expanded, this was useful knowledge to the Ruskins. *'Be on your guard'*, said Windus of Griffith, Turner's agent, to John James at a private view, 'He is the cleverest & the deepest man I ever met with.'[3] This kind of talk seemed to make it the more difficult to approach Turner. Windus was not the sort of man to talk about the deep significance of Turner's art: Ruskin was left with the feeling that there were many great mysteries behind the evident beauties of his work. When he met Turner he did not suddenly realize anything about the man. The meeting told him what he had already suspected (and was well placed to know, with a father like John James) that rough and half-educated men can be as full as anyone of tenderness and imagination. So he observed Turner without venturing much conversation: certainly he did not tell him that it was he who had written the defence of his pictures three years before.

Ruskin had written the reply to the *Blackwood's* article just before he went up to Oxford: now he had met Turner immediately after leaving the university. These coincidences might have helped to persuade him that he had been wasting his time there, but since 'many people, including myself, thought I was dying, and should never write about anything', he was too preoccupied with his own health to think of Turner in connection with his literary career.[4] The annual continental tours had also been interrupted by Oxford: for three years the Ruskins had driven only through England and Scotland. As a winter in a Mediterranean climate had been prescribed, John James decided that the family should tour through France, rest in December on the Italian coast, and then tour home again the next spring. When autumn approached the Ruskins prepared to leave the Herne Hill house to the servants and the Billiter Street business to the clerks. They crossed the Channel in September of 1840 and did not return to England for ten months.

★ ★ ★ ★

In 1883, when Ruskin wrote down that rather dramatic reminiscence, that 'many people, including myself, thought I was dying', he happened to be travelling through France with his young friend, W. G. Collingwood. Their discussions often concerned universities, and his companion caught a sense of the bitterness Ruskin could still feel about his departure from Oxford. His biography of Ruskin used a poem of 1838–40, 'The Broken Chain', as 'a fit emblem of the broken life which it records'.[5] The poem, which appears to be derived from Coleridge's 'Christabel', was indeed begun in Oxford and finished on the Italian journey. But it is not especially autobiographical, whatever its deathly themes, and no public or private writings indicate that Ruskin was now afraid of dying. His diaries of that date are of some interest. Ruskin did not keep a journal in Oxford, but in his last days there began a new notebook on whose first page we find the declaration:

> I have determined to keep one part of diary for intellect and another for feeling. I shall put down here whatever is worth remembering of the casual knowledge that we gain so much of every day, in conversation, and generally lose every to-morrow. Much is thus lost that can never be recovered from books.[6]

This proposal has led some commentators to believe that somewhere there must be another diary with 'feeling' in it. But the existence of such a manuscript is unlikely. Ruskin closed his notebook of conversations after he had written the entry recording his first meeting with Turner. He then bought a new, red leather volume in which to write up notes on his foreign tour. The first thirty-four pages of this book have at some stage been cut out, and it begins now at Pontgibaud on 7 October 1840, as the party made their way through France to the Riviera. It describes weather, landscape and antiquities: the writing is almost entirely dry and factual.

The journey through France took six weeks. In Italy their route lay through Pisa, Florence and Siena. References to works of art in the diary now become more frequent. But there is little sense of engagement. At Florence,

> I still cannot make up my mind about this place, though my present feelings are of grievous disappointment. The galleries, which I walked through yesterday, are impressive enough; but I had as soon be in the British Museum, as far as enjoyment goes, except for the Raphaels. I can understand nothing else, and not much of them. At English chapel, and mass in the palace; fine music as far as execution went, but of German school . . . English sermon very good, a little slow. Walked after dinner, but weather very cold for Italy, and windy, and streets strangely uninteresting.[7]

From such entries, which are quite free of pretended appreciation, we would not expect a display of 'feeling' written down in another book. Ruskin's more formal writing at this date consists of letters to Edward Clayton, a Christ Church contemporary, and to Thomas Dale. The letters to Clayton were published with Ruskin's acquiescence in 1894, as *Letters of a College Friend,* when their sharper comments on theological subjects were omitted. Those addressed to Dale were found with the essay on Byron Ruskin had written at King's

College. They were edited and published by Dale's granddaughter in 1893. The letters are carefully composed and express conventional Protestant views. On architecture, however, Ruskin becomes more vehement. Writing from Rome, he comments,

> St Peter's I expected to be *disappointed* in. I was *disgusted*. The Italians think Gothic architecture barbarous. I think Greek heathenish. Greek, by-the-bye, it is not, but has all its weight and clumsiness, without its dignity or simplicity. As a whole, St Peter's is fit for nothing but a ballroom, and it is a little too gaudy even for that . . .[8]

Neither Rome nor Naples, at this date or any later date, were to win one word of approval from Ruskin. It was not merely that they contained so little painting or architecture that he liked: he felt an exaggerated revulsion from what he imagined to be the spirit of their civilization. To Dale he wrote of Rome:

> There is a strange horror lying over the whole city, which I can neither describe nor account for; it is a shadow of death, possessing and penetrating all things . . . you feel like an artist in a fever, haunted by every dream of beauty that his imagination ever dwelt upon, but all mixed with the fever fear. I am sure this is not imagination, for I am not given to such nonsense . . .[9]

Given such attitudes, it is not surprising how closely the Ruskins held to the English colony in Rome and Naples. They seem to have made no attempt to meet any Italians. In their letters, and in the diary of Mary Richardson, there is one repetitive theme: foreign disease and morbidity is contrasted with English health, Protestant honesty compared to Catholic superstition. Mary's diligent diary provides many reports of the sermons in English churches. In Turin she gives an account of a sect who were to be rather important to Ruskin's religious attitudes. There the family went to

> . . . a French Protestant service at the Prussian ambassador's . . . there were many of the poor Waldenses present, nearly all the women of the poorer class (who wore caps only) were of that interesting race who have suffered so much from Popish persecution . . . their church is said to be the purest of all Christian churches, but they are miserably poor . . .[10]

In Rome, 'I have today witnessed one of the grandest Church Ceremonies to be seen in the world — with the Pope in St Peters,' John James wrote home to W. H. Harrison. 'How infinitely I would prefer a sermon from Dr Croly.'[11] His son was in correspondence with

Croly (who, like Harrison, had never been in Italy) during this sojourn in Rome, and was exchanging views with him on these patriotic and anti-Catholic matters. The seeds of *The Stones of Venice* were being sown.

The English colony encouraged (as is the way in such communities) expatriate sentiments to harden into prejudice. Mary Richardson often reports on social evenings with such leading figures of the colony as

> Mr Rugg, quite a character, been in Naples for 11 years, was a martyr to rheumatism until he came here . . . a great admirer of Pitt whom he used to go and hear debate almost every night. Quite a man of the old times, a great Tory . . . does not approve of the High Church principles prevalent at Oxford . . .[12]

There were many like Mr Rugg, snobbish, curious to meet visitors, patriotic though an emigré, clinging to the politics of a previous generation. The colony was just large enough to have its own social stratifications. The Ruskins did not quite enter the height of English society in Italy. They took apartments in the same building as the aristocratic Tollemache family but were not on visiting terms. One of the Tollemache daughters, the beautiful Georgina, was greatly admired by Ruskin. He looked at her in church and later confessed that he followed her through the streets: but he could not meet her. The Ruskins inclined towards the artists. Mary tells us of studio visits they made, mostly to painters and sculptors now forgotten, but also to 'another English artist's, a Mr Lear, also young and promising . . .'.[13] One of these meetings was to be so significant as to reverberate through the rest of Ruskin's life. He had a letter of introduction to Joseph Severn (given to him by Acland), the painter friend of Keats, who twenty years before had brought the poet to Italy, and who himself had remained there ever since:

> I forget exactly where Mr Severn lived at that time, but his door was at the right of the landing at the top of a long flight of squarely reverting stair . . . Up this I was advancing slowly, — it being forbidden me ever to strain breath, — and was within eighteen or twenty steps of Mr Severn's door, when it opened, and two gentlemen came out, closed it behind them with an expression of excluding the world for ever from that side of the house, and began to descend the steps to meet me . . . One was a rather short, rubicund, serenely beaming person; the other, not much taller, but paler, with a beautifully modelled forehead, and extremely vivid, though kind, dark eyes. They looked hard at me as they passed, but

in my usual shyness . . . I made no sign, and leaving them to descend the reverting stair in peace, climbed, at still slackening pace, the remaining steps to Mr Severn's door, and left my card and letter of introduction with the servant, who told me he had just gone out. His dark-eyed companion was George Richmond . . .[14]

As they passed him on the stairs, Ruskin had heard Severn say to his companion of him 'What a poetical countenance!'[15] The remark recalls us to Ruskin's artistic life, and his precarious health. Severn's friend was George Richmond, also a painter and one who many years before had known a great poet. With Samuel Palmer and others, Richmond had been a disciple of Blake: he had attended his deathbed and closed his eyes.[16] Two new acquaintances such as Richmond and Severn — they all met a day or two later — could not but prompt thoughts of the lives and deaths of poets. John James went with his son to the Protestant cemetery to visit Keats's grave. He afterwards reflected that young John Ruskin was made of 'sterner stuff' than the poet.[17] But when his symptoms returned and Ruskin coughed blood for three successive days the comparison with Keats was inescapable. The Ruskins's new friends were entirely sympathetic: Richmond especially showed a tenderness for the young and worried man. Thus, in grave circumstances, was born a friendship that would bind the Ruskins, the Severns and the Richmonds for years and decades to come. Joseph Severn's son Arthur would marry Ruskin's cousin Joan Agnew: his daughter Mary would be the bride of Ruskin's college friend Charles Newton. Generations of the Richmonds, neighbours of the Ruskins in Clapham and the Lake District, were always to be family friends: and when Ruskin was old and insane, Joan Severn would look to them for understanding and comfort.

It was the strain of writing the Oxford chapter of *Præterita* that brought about Ruskin's attack of madness in 1885. The autobiography alternates sour memories of the university with pleasing portraits of friends from these Roman days. Its composition was confused by Ruskin's mental breakdown, and this perhaps is why it does not dwell on the change that came over his spirits, and his health, when the Ruskin party left the south of Italy in the spring of 1841 and drove to Venice. Here he found a glad excitement such as he had not experienced before in a city. He was old enough now to feel connections between the buildings of Venice and a world of imaginative literature, romantic history and Turnerian art. What before had been only a foreign place, however picturesque, now sparkled with cultural implication. *Præterita* could not quite recapture the feeling. But an almost contemporary letter to Ruskin's Venetian friend Count Zorzi is eloquent of his rapture:

> Of all the happy and ardent days which , in my earlier life, it was granted me to spend in this Holy Land of Italy, none were so precious as those which I used to pass in the bright recess of your Piazzetta, by the pillars of Acre; looking sometimes to the glimmering mosaics in the vaults of the Church; sometimes to the Square, thinking of its immortal memories; sometimes to the Palace and the Sea. No such scene existed elsewhere in Europe, — in the world; so bright, so magically visionary, — a temple radiant as the flowers of nature, venerable and enduring as her rocks, arched above the rugged pillars which then stood simply on the marble pavement, where the triumphant Venetian conquerer had set them . . .[18]

Many long hours were spent in exploration of Venice, in drawing and note-taking. The diaries take on a different tone. Ruskin was on the mend: he had been rescued by his feelings for Venice's beauty. His convalescence seemed to be over. He became more active, even energetic, and the family set off for England. Their route on this return journey was through the Alps. The first day that they spent among the hills was a turning point in his life:

> I woke from a sound tired sleep in a little one-windowed room at Lans-le-bourg, at six of the summer morning, June 2nd 1841; the red aiguilles on the north relieved against pure blue — the great pyramid of snow down the valley in one sheet of eastern light. I dressed in three minutes, ran down the village street, across the stream, and climbed the grassy slope on the south side of the valley, up to the first pines. I had found my life again; — all the best of it. What good of religion, love, admiration or hope, has ever been taught me, or felt by my best nature, rekindled at once; and my line of work, both by my own will and the aid granted to it by fate in the future, determined for me. I went down thankfully to my father and mother and told them I was sure I should get well.[19]

CHAPTER FOUR

1841–1844

After this tour, Ruskin writes in *Præterita*, 'a month was spent at home, considering what was to be done next'.[1] He felt that to be 'free in mountain air' would restore him, and sought leave from his parents for an independent expedition. He planned to tour Wales with Richard Fall. They would be attended by a new family servant, the resourceful John Hobbs (known always as George to distinguish him from his master). Ruskin's parents asked him to call on the renowned Leamington physician, Dr Jephson, on his way to Wales. This he did: but his report of the interview persuaded his father that he should immediately return from his rendezvous with Fall in the Welsh Marches to place himself, until further notice, under Jephson's care. Thus began an odd six weeks in Ruskin's life, most of it spent in a lodging house near the Leamington medicinal wells. Jephson's regimen stipulated many glasses of these spa waters, a slender diet and regular hours. Ruskin observed these routines without interest. He took walks to Stratford and to Warwick Castle. His father came to visit him, as did Osborne Gordon. Ruskin scarcely considered preparations for the Oxford schools, which he now thought to sit the following Easter, but read Walter Scott, drew, and studied Louis Agassiz's *Recherches sur les poissons fossiles*. Out of boredom, he now wrote what was subsequently the most popular of his books, the short tale for children called *The King of the Golden River*. This story, 'a fairly good imitation of Grimm and Dickens, mixed with a little true Alpine feeling of my own', was written in fulfilment of a promise to a little girl, Euphemia or 'Effie' or 'Phemy' Gray, who had visited Herne Hill earlier in the year.[2] She was the daughter of George Gray, a Perth lawyer who administered the trust which controlled the affairs of Jessie Richardson's children. In seven years' time she would become John Ruskin's wife, and *The King of the Golden River* was published in 1850, in the second year of their marriage.

One detects an irresolution in Ruskin in Leamington. But he left Dr Jephson's care with a serious purpose in mind. He went to visit his tutor of two years before, the Reverend W. L. Brown. Now in his mid-thirties, Walter Brown had recently married. He had therefore been obliged to leave Christ Church for a college living at Wendlebury, a grey, distressed village, often flooded, nearer Bicester than

Oxford. His position there was no advertisement for a career in the Church, as Ruskin must have noted. For he had come to talk to Brown about his religious vocation. As he approached the end of his Christ Church career, the question of whether he should take orders was pressing. Certain of his contemporaries had entered the Church. His admired Osborne Gordon was just about to do so. His college friend Edward Clayton, to whom he was now writing long and serious letters, was ordained in this year: and Clayton, like many others, expected that Ruskin would follow him into the ministry. Margaret Ruskin would have been delighted to see her son in orders. But John James had reservations. He could not feel that his son's ardent temperament was fitted for the Church, for ardour in religion he mistrusted. He had written to Ruskin at Leamington, 'It sounds paradoxical but these Heavenly subjects require to be approached in the most worldly way. We must hold to the anchor of Rationality, stick to our Humanities.' Again — prophetically — he warned that 'too much enthusiasm in Religion ends in Selfishness or Madness'.[3] Ruskin's own views were not dissimilar. And Brown himself was a man of some caution in religious matters: he was the tutor who had made Ruskin read that dampening book, *The Natural History of Enthusiasm*. We know less than we might wish about the movements of Ruskin's mind in thinking of a religious vocation. No doubt he discussed the matter in prayer, and perhaps he was affected by a pleasure he took in disputing with Brown: however that may be, their subsequent correspondence shows that he left Wendlebury much doubting his suitability for a life in the Church.

His commitment to poetry also weakened in these few months. He began to realize that for him it had been an adolescent preoccupation. John James, tactfully, allowed his son time to sense that his real ambitions lay elsewhere. At no time did his father urge Ruskin towards any particular career. To say, as he now sometimes did, that he longed for his son to be a poet was scarcely to guide him towards professional opportunities. Nobody imagined that Ruskin's aspirations would lead to art criticism. But the notion of a principled attachment to art was growing in him. He would never be a professional artist, but at the same time he was determined to be more than a gentleman amateur. After his return to London in the autumn of 1841, Ruskin began drawing lessons with a new master. This was James Duffield Harding. To seek his tuition represented an æsthetic and almost a political decision. First, Harding brought Ruskin nearer to Turner. His current practice was to some extent based on Turner's art. Harding knew Turner: Ruskin had met his idol only once since their introduction more than a year before. Decades later, considering this, the writer of *Præterita* lamented that he had not known even a hint of instruction from Turner himself after their first meeting: 'If he had but asked me to come and see him the next day! He would have saved me ten years of life, and would not have been less happy in the close of his own . . .'[4] The older Ruskin knew how mechanical Harding's interpretation of Turner was. In 1841, however, his instruction seemed apposite. It also had a didactic element which, for a time, commended him to the Ruskins. Harding held an ideological view of post-Renaissance painting. His taste had a nationalist and Protestant bias. His beliefs may be crudely stated since they were themselves crude. He believed that nature and 'truth' were available only to contemporary Englishmen. He associated falsity in art with Catholicism, falsity in religion. He despised Claude's classical landscape and thought the Dutch schools ignoble. Such opinions, belligerently stated, had an effect on the young Ruskin.[5] Amplified and expanded, they would soon reappear in the first volume of *Modern Painters*.

*   *   *   *

Today, it seems an absurdity to speak of Turner and Harding in the same breath. One we know to have the grandeur of a major artist: the other is a drawing master, who draws like a drawing master. But the first volume of *Modern Painters* is full of such juxtapositions. Ruskin's book rises to heights of appropriate eloquence in describing Turner and the old masters; then, immediately, we are in the company of Clarkson Stanfield, David Roberts, Copley Fielding, Samuel Prout, the minor domestic artists Ruskin saw on the walls of the Old Water-Colour Society. From his knowledge of art one would not anticipate a poetic or a magisterial book. *Modern Painters* was not written from great galleries, print-rooms and libraries: it was written from suburban south London. It is remarkable how *Modern Painters* can soar away from Ruskin's personal experience of art. It strikes great chords; but in it one finds still that boyish greed for painting and talk about painting that now began to overtake Ruskin, that made him haunt those places where he could see pictures, that directed him more and more to the Richmonds's in Clapham, where the talk was of nothing but art, that made him listen with more respect to Samuel Prout (often a visitor at Herne Hill), that sent him to Tottenham and Camberwell to call on Mr Windus and Mr Bicknell, collectors who liked to show off their treasures to this eager young man.[6]

Of course, it was Turner's acquaintance that Ruskin most desired.

The old painter was not easily approached. But he seems to have shown kindness on the earlier occasions when he met his admirer. The diary entry which records their second meeting is of 6 July 1841, just before Ruskin left town for Wales and Leamington. He writes, 'Dined with Turner, Jones and Nesfield at Griffith's yesterday. Turner there is no mistaking for a moment — his keen eye and dry sentences can be the signs only of a high intellect. Jones a fine, grey, quiet, Spectator-like "gentleman".'[7] Thomas Griffith, who that evening entertained not only Ruskin and Turner but also the water-colourist William Nesfield and the Royal Academician George Jones, attracted many an artist and connoisseur to his home at Norwood.

John James Ruskin was never among them, however: nor did he ever invite Griffith to Herne Hill. Probably the sherry merchant disliked the commercial style of the picture dealer. 'My father could not bear him,' Ruskin simply records.[8] As Ruskin's appetite for Turner grew John James's hostility to Griffith caused many difficulties. Griffith was Turner's sole agent, and John James was for that reason the less inclined to spend his money on Turner's paintings. This soured as nothing else could the tender relations Ruskin enjoyed with his father. One incident in particular remained with him all his life. It somehow grew in his imagination, filling him with resentment, a feeling that he had been thwarted in more than material possessions; a feeling that was replaced in later years by the sadness with which, in 1886, he set down the story:

> In the early Spring of [1842], a change came over Turner's mind. He wanted to make some drawings to please himself; but also to be paid for making them. He gave Mr Griffith fifteen sketches for choice of subject by any one who would give him a commission. He got commissions for nine, of which my father let me choose at first one, then was coaxed and tricked into letting me have two. Turner got orders, out of all the round world besides, for seven more. With the sketches, four finished drawings were shown for samples of the sort of thing Turner meant to make of them, and for immediate purchase by anybody.
>
> Among them was the 'Splügen', which I had some hope of obtaining by supplication, when my father, who was travelling, came home. I waited dutifully till he should come. In the meantime it was bought, with the loveliest Lake Lucerne, by Mr Munro of Novar.
>
> The thing became to me grave matter for meditation. In a story by Miss Edgeworth, the father would have come home in the nick

6. *Turner on Varnishing Day*, by S. W. Parrott, 1848.

of time, effaced Mr Munro as he hesitated with the 'Splügen' in his hand, and given the dutiful son that, and another. I found, after meditation, that Miss Edgeworth's way was not the world's, nor Providence's. I perceived then, and conclusively, that if you do a foolish thing, you suffer for it exactly the same, whether you do it piously or not. I knew perfectly well that this drawing was the best Swiss landscape yet painted by man; and that it was entirely proper for *me* to have it, and inexpedient that anyone else should. I ought to have secured it instantly, and begged my father's pardon, tenderly.

He would have been angry, and surprised, and grieved; but loved me none the less, found in the end I was right, and been entirely pleased. I should have been very uncomfortable and penitent for a while, but loved my father all the more for having hurt him, and, in the good of the thing itself, finally satisfied and triumphant. As it was, the 'Splügen' was a thorn in both our sides, all our lives. My father was always trying to get it; Mr Munro, aided by dealers, always raising the price on him, till it got up from 80 to 400 guineas. Then we gave it up, — with unspeakable wear and tear of best feelings on both sides.[9]

Ruskin exaggerated the loss of the 'Splügen'. However, like all his many exaggerations, this one has the truth of being heartfelt. The 'Splügen' meant more than it ought to have done. All his life Ruskin was liable to confuse his personal history with the history of art. He was able to take certain works — like this Turner drawing, or della Quercia's Ilaria di Caretto tomb at Lucca, or Carpaccio's painting of St Ursula — and give them a private value that over-emphasized their cultural importance. This was usually in looking back over his life. In years to come, Turner's late Swiss drawings were to signify everything that he owed to his father. But in the spring of 1842 they were revelatory. Elegiac though they are, Ruskin could not now feel that they were the sunset of Turner's career, for he was gripped by the realization that they belonged to the dawning of his own. So strong was this feeling that it persisted long after Turner's own death in 1851, when Ruskin was still inclined, against all the evidence, to interpret the drawings as the beginning of a new stage in Turner's career, his 'third period', and would even force them on painters younger than himself, the Pre-Raphaelites, as a progressive example for their own art.

In Pre-Raphaelitism, again, Ruskin found the significance of an experience which *Præterita* recalls as of this time, the spring before he began to write *Modern Painters*.

One day on the road to Norwood, I noticed a piece of ivy around a thorn stem, which seemed, even to my critical judgement, not ill 'composed'; and proceeded to make a light and shade pencil study of it in my grey paper pocket book . . . When it was done, I saw that I had virtually lost all my time since I was twelve years old, because no-one had ever told me to draw what was really there! All my time, I mean, given to drawing as an art; of course I had the records of places, but had never seen the beauty of anything, not even of a stone — how much less of a leaf![10]

Two pages further on in *Præterita*, Ruskin writes of how he came to draw an aspen tree in the forest of Fontainebleau a month or two later:

> Languidly, but not idly, I began to draw it; and as I drew, the languor passed away: the beautiful lines insisted on being traced, — without weariness. More and more beautiful they became, as each rose out of the rest, and took its place in the air. With wonder increasing every instant, I saw that they 'composed' themselves, by finer laws than any known of men. At last, the tree was there, and everything that I had thought before about trees, nowhere . . .[11]

Præterita attaches great importance to these experiences. But this section of the autobiography was written in 1886, after Ruskin's fourth mental breakdown, and without the *aide-memoire* of his diary. 'To my sorrow and extreme surprise,' he then noted, 'I find no diary whatever of the feelings or discoveries for this year. They were too many and bewildering, to be written.' Ruskin had forgotten that in 1872 he had given the diary in question to Charles Eliot Norton.[12] Had he been able to consult it, he would have found no reference to this moment in Fontainebleau. Nor can we now trace any drawing of an aspen, or of ivy, that would correspond with these reminiscences. Ruskin in old age was describing (as is not uncommon in *Præterita*) a gradual change of mind as a sudden conversion. The development of Ruskin's drawing from the picturesque towards naturalism was steady rather than dramatic. Certainly it cannot have been effected by a revelation while actually drawing. But it is clear that he was developing a theory of naturalism. Perhaps this contributed to a dissatisfaction with his rather artificial verses, though he nowhere says as much. He usually discussed naturalism in terms of his drawing. He wrote to Edward Clayton this year, 1841,

> Time was (when I began drawing) that I used to think a picturesque or beautiful tree was hardly to be met with once a month; I cared for nothing but oaks a thousand years old, split by lightning or shattered by wind . . . *Now*, there is not a twig in the closest-clipt hedge that grows, that I cannot admire, and wonder at, and take pleasure in, and learn from . . . Now this power of enjoyment is worth working for, not merely for enjoyment, but because it renders you less imperfect as one of God's creatures — more what He would have you . . .[13]

That is distinctly the voice of *Modern Painters*, the book that Ruskin could now have been considering, were he not distracted by his final Oxford examinations.

Ruskin returned to Oxford to take schools in the spring of 1842. He was far past his undergraduate life. Not even the proud John James cared much about the examination results. Ruskin took a peculiar degree. It was an honorary double fourth, which indicated success and failure in about equal measure.[14] John James brought the Dean of Christ Church a hamper of wine and took his son back to Herne Hill. Ruskin this spring seems pointedly the 'Graduate of Oxford', the pseudonym with which *Modern Painters* was to be signed. There were many things that he wanted to do in London. His examinations interfered with the Water-Colour Society opening, the Royal Academy opening, a Wilkie private view. His interests more and more inclined him towards such events and the kind of company he would find there. Although it is tricked out with Oxford learning, the first volume of *Modern Painters* has the flavour of Ruskin's return to early Victorian London; and its hero, the barber's son from Covent Garden, is lauded for wisdom and imagination quite beyond the cramped instruction of the university.

*   *   *   *

The Ruskin family, now reunited, were looking forward to their annual summer tour. Their destination in 1842 was Switzerland. The diary Ruskin kept as they travelled from Calais through Rouen, Fontainebleau, Sens and Auxerre to Geneva, reveals a conscientious tourist. It is not an artist's diary. It is the notebook of a natural scientist, a geologist, a student of the Bible. But Ruskin had not forgotten English art. He left England with Turner's Swiss drawings in his mind, and had seen Turner's work at this year's Royal Academy exhibition, two Venetian subjects together with *Snow Storm, Steamboat making Signals, Peace – Burial at Sea* and *War: The Exile and the Rock Limpet*. A parcel of English newspapers sent on to Switzerland now inflamed his memories of the paintings. In one of them was a review which attacked Turner's contributions. The same morning that he read the review, in the Protestant church in Geneva, Ruskin knelt to pray. There he resolved to write a reply. This was to have been a pamphlet. Hot for battle, Ruskin thought to write it at Chamonix the next day. But an immensity of theme came between him and his task. It was nature. Among the rocks and the pines and the great mountains, Mont Blanc above and the green valleys below, Ruskin found that he could not confine what he had to say to a few pages. That *Modern Painters* was begun among the Alps has its significance. As from a vantage point, there spread out before him the whole length of Europe, its cities and long rivers, its seas and the island kingdom in the

North. Such vistas, which reappear ever afterwards in his writing,
were early on imagined by the 'cockney cock-sparrow', as Ruskin
later described himself at this age. Perhaps feeling a little shy of his
resolution, he said nothing about his new writing to Osborne Gordon,
who had now joined the Ruskins. Not until *Modern Painters* was
actually published did he confess to his tutor how his holiday work
had developed as they turned for home through Germany.

> I meditated all the way down the Rhine, found that *demonstration* in
> matters of art was no such easy matter, and the pamphlet turned
> into a volume. Before the volume was half way dealt with it
> hydrized into three heads, and each head became a volume. Finding
> that nothing could be done except on such enormous scale, I deter-
> mined to take the hydra by the horns, and produce a complete
> treatise on landscape art. [15]

★   ★   ★   ★

Modern Painters was written in a new home. John James Ruskin had for
some time been looking for another house. He wanted one more
appropriate to his social standing, a home in which he could entertain
the friends his son had made at Christ Church. At the same time there
was a lack of pretension in his choice. After inspecting properties in
Tooting, Penge and Fulham, he bought the lease of a house less than a
mile from Herne Hill. It was No. 163 Denmark Hill, situated on the
crest of this northern outcrop of the Surrey Downs, looking down to
Dulwich in one direction and Camberwell in the other. John James
had never aspired to own land, as one might have expected in a
self-made tory of his temper. Nor had he ever wished for a town
house. But he was well suited in Denmark Hill, the 'Belgravia of the
South'. The Ruskins's new home was three storeys tall. There was a
lodge, and the house itself was set among seven acres of land, half of it
meadow, the rest divided into flower gardens, kitchen gardens,
orchard. There were cows in the meadow, pigs and hens in the
out-houses. Margaret Ruskin delighted in her farm management. She
was also pleased to increase the number of servants. We will come to
know them well, for these servants' lives became more and more
interwoven with the Ruskins's, ever afterwards. David Downs, for
instance, a Scotsman who came to Denmark Hill as head gardener and
in later years was a factotum for all Ruskin's outdoor schemes —
crossing-sweeping, road-building, moor-draining — died in Ruskin's
service, as did the Tovey sisters, who were to manage Ruskin's
teashop; while some, such as George Allen, married other Denmark

7. 163 Denmark Hill, Ruskin's home from 1842 to 1871, by Arthur Severn.

Hill servants, in his case George Hobbs's sister Hannah, and thus became part of the extended family network. No-one was ever cast off. At Denmark Hill they now settled into the routine of life that was to last, with disturbances, for thirty years, while in his study above the breakfast-room, looking over a view 'inestimable for its help in all healthy thought', Ruskin began the series of books that would take him from his writing apprenticeship to the Slade chair in Oxford.[16]

Ruskin said nothing to people outside his immediate family about his resolve to write on Turner. Only his parents and Mary Richardson knew what he was doing. The first volume of *Modern Painters* was composed privately, in effect secretly. Osborne Gordon, one of the first guests at Denmark Hill, was still kept in ignorance. Acland, Newton, Liddell, intellectual Christ Church men Ruskin occasionally met in the months when he was writing the book, had no idea that what was passing through his mind was being committed to paper. W. H. Harrison and all mutual acquaintances of the Ruskins and Turner were equally unaware of his labours. A consequence was that *Modern Painters* was written without any kind of professional advice.

This perhaps helped Ruskin to find his own originality: certainly it meant that nobody counselled him to be cautious. Reticent about his own large ambitions, Ruskin now listened to people but did not seek instruction from them. We have a fair idea of his life at the time when he was preparing his book. He had much talk with Richmond about art, for he was now sitting for a portrait which John James had commissioned. Richmond's son Willie recalled Ruskin at this period as a 'gaunt, delicate-looking young man, with a profusion of reddish hair, shaggy eyebrows like to a Scotch terrier, under them the gleaming eyes which bore within them a strange light, the like of which I have never seen except in his',[17] a description not very like his father's water-colour portrait, later entitled 'The Author of *Modern Painters*', which shows a rather stiff, formally-dressed person, pen in hand, sitting at a desk in the middle of a field. Ruskin was occasionally with Harding, but the lessons were more like conversations. He read Coleridge. He often called on Windus and Griffith. He took many a walk over the fields to Dulwich College picture gallery, whose collection of baroque and Dutch art is therefore much discussed in *Modern Painters*. He listened attentively to the Reverend Henry Melvill's sermons: he was the incumbent of Camden Chapel in Walworth Road, Camberwell. In Richard Fall's company he was often at the Geological Society. As his twenty-fourth birthday approached in February of 1843 he ventured to invite Turner to the celebratory dinner. His diary records, 'Turner happy and kind; all else fitting and delightful — but too late to sit writing.'[18] A few days later he 'called at Turner's . . . Insisted on my taking a glass of wine, but I wouldn't. Excessively good-natured today. Heaven grant he may not be mortally offended with the work!'[19]

This is one of the few references to *Modern Painters* in the diary. By March of 1843 the journal peters out, and we understand that Ruskin is in the final stages of his book. It resumes on 1 May. 'Couldn't write while I had this work for Turner to do; had not the slightest notion what labour it was. I was at it all April from 6 morning to 10 night, and late to-night too — but shall keep on, I hope.'[20] The completed manuscript now required a publisher. John James, who until his death in 1864 was to act as his son's literary agent, first of all approached John Murray. Without looking at the book, Murray gave as his opinion that a volume on the Nazarenes would be more popular. 'He said the public cared little about Turner,' John James wrote to W. H. Harrison, 'but strongly urged my son's writing on the German School, which the public were calling for works on.'[21] John James, not a man to be thus slighted, took the book immediately to Smith, Elder and Co. A bargain was quickly struck; George Smith changed the title from Ruskin's *Turner and the Ancients* to *Modern Painters: Their Superiority in the Art of Landscape Painting to the Ancient Masters*; edited it, as far as one may judge, hardly at all; sent it to press: and in the first week of May of 1843 the book itself was in the shops.

The reaction to *Modern Painters,* by 'a Graduate of Oxford', was not immediate, nor did the book at first sell widely. But in the first year of its life it won a distinguished audience. Wordsworth (from whose *Prelude* its epigraph was taken) thought it the work of 'a brilliant writer', and recommended it to visitors to Rydal Mount.[22] In other literary circles, we find Tennyson writing to the publisher Moxon:

> Another book I very much long to see is that on the superiority of the modern painters to the old ones, and the greatness of Turner as an artist, by an Oxford undergraduate, I think. I do not wish to buy it, it may be dear; perhaps you could borrow it for me out of the London Library, or from Rogers. I saw it lying on his table.[23]

Samuel Rogers may have pressed the book on readers other than the thrifty Tennyson. It was perhaps he who had sent a copy to Robert and Elizabeth Browning in Italy. To Mary Russell Mitford, who had also told them of it, Elizabeth Browning wrote,

> The letter in which you mentioned your Oxford student caught us in the middle of his work on art. Very vivid, very graphic, full of sensibility, but inconsequent in some of the reasoning, it seemed to me, and rather flashy than full in the metaphysics. Robert, who knows a great deal about art, to which knowledge I have of course no pretence, could agree with him only by snatches, and we, both of us, standing before a very impressive picture of Domenichino's (the 'David' — at Fano), wondered how he could blaspheme so against a great artist. Still, he is no ordinary man, and for a critic to be so much of a poet is a great thing. Also, we have by no means, I should imagine, seen the utmost of his stature.[24]

This was a more independent view than that of other literary women. Mrs Gaskell and Charlotte Brontë read Ruskin together, and Charlotte Brontë (also a Smith, Elder author) could write to W. S. Williams at the firm,

> Hitherto I have only had instinct to guide me in judging of art; I feel now as if I had been walking blindfold — this book seems to give me eyes. I *do* wish I had pictures within reach by which to test the new sense. Who can read these glowing descriptions of Turner's works without longing to see them? . . . I like this author's style

much; there is both energy and beauty in it. I like himself, too, because he is such a hearty admirer. He does not give himself half-measure of praise or vituperation. He eulogizes, he reverences with his whole soul.[25]

And from George Eliot we have the first occasion on which Ruskin is referred to as a prophet. 'I venerate him', she wrote, 'as one of the great teachers of the day. The grand doctrines of truth and sincerity in art, and the nobleness and solemnity of our human life, which he teaches with the enthusiasm of a Hebrew prophet, must be stirring up young minds in a promising way.'[26]

These opinions were all privately expressed. Ruskin himself had no notion of them. The public reaction to the book, when it came, was not from such notable pens. John James, now pasting his son's reviews into a large ledger, was satisfied. They were unanimously flattering. They were not however of much intellectual weight.[27] The Ruskins were gratified by the *Britannia*'s notice, which they rightly guessed to be by Dr Croly, but the major journals gave no space to the book. Neither the *Athenæum* nor *Blackwood's* seemed to be aware of its publication. Turner was once again maligned for his contributions to the Royal Academy exhibition that May. And the painter himself said not one word to Ruskin about what he had written, about his 'labour for Turner'. Ruskin was not comforted to reflect that it was quite in Turner's character to say nothing on such an occasion, for the rest of his artistic acquaintance were slow to speak well of the book, whether or not they knew that it was his. *Præterita*, exaggerating somewhat, says,

> The sympathy of the art-circles, in praise of whose leading members the first volume of *Modern Painters* had been expressly written, was withheld from me much longer than that of the general reader . . . Taken as a body, the total group of Modern Painters were, therefore, more startled than flattered by my schismatic praise; the modest ones, such as Fielding, Prout, and Stanfield, felt that it was more than they deserved, — and, moreover, a little beside the mark and out of their way; the conceited ones, such as Harding and De Wint, were angry at the position given to Turner; and I am not sure that any of them were ready to endorse George Richmond's consoling assurance to my father, that I should know better in time.[28]

A personal effect of the appearance of *Modern Painters* was that it revealed to Ruskin his power as a writer. He now knew, as he had not quite known before, that writing was to be his instrument, his sword.

His desire to be valiant had found its expression. That so many people thought of his book as literature was welcome indeed to a young man who was now abandoning his poetic ambitions: he knew that there would have been no reaction to a book of his verses. To some extent this compensated for the moderate admiration of the artists he knew. Ruskin now began to find that to be known as an author gave him a special position. For a time, as it became an open secret that *Modern Painters* was his, he was a literary celebrity. He entered the world where fashion and culture were one. Under chandeliers, we find him in the company of Sir Robert Inglis, Richard Monckton Milnes, Samuel Rogers — it now was ten years since Henry Telford had given him Rogers's *Italy* — dining here, breakfasting there, leaving cards, accepting and returning invitations. This phase did not last long. As was to be the pattern throughout his life, a spell of party-going was followed by a return to his study, where he felt most at home. In any case, he was not perfectly suited to this company. He was not at ease with the women he met at such gatherings. Rogers was jealous and quarrelsome, Milnes a dilettante. There were tories 'of the old school' and Evangelicals around the dinner table at Sir Robert Inglis's. But the sentiments Ruskin heard there were somehow too worldly, too close to Parliament. Partly in reaction, he developed a hostility towards the book that had given him the *entrée* to such a world. In it, he told Liddell, 'there is a nasty, snappish, impatient, half-familiar, half-claptrap web of young mannishness'.[29] More publicly (and perhaps *Modern Painters*'s anonymity helped him here) he defended his book. Ruskin replied to the criticism which was published in the October number of *Blackwood's*. He also prepared a preface to the second edition of *Modern Painters*. But he had already realized that what was needed was a second book. With commendable self-discipline he now ignored his success and began to think again about his real, lonely, career as a writer.

★   ★   ★   ★

A book as various as *Modern Painters* could give its author a variety of suggestions for a sequel. Ruskin's first book is in a grand sense miscellaneous. It is philosophy and æsthetics, and much more than that. It is poetry. It is prose. It is a treatise. It is a great pamphlet. It is a defence, or rather a vindication. It is a sermon. It is art criticism, art history, a commentary on recent exhibitions, or an introduction to certain collections. It is a meditation on landscape, or an exercise in how the eye may examine nature. Ruskin did not think to choose between his various interests: hardly any book of his belongs to a *genre*. The second volume of *Modern Painters* was to be a more compact book than the first, but he prepared for it by a wide range of studies. To his irritation, the 'Graduate of Oxford' had to return to the university after the publication of his book. This was to keep the term he had lost through illness. Ruskin stayed in rooms and, he improbably claimed, 'learnt a great deal of Raffaele at Blenheim'.[30] There was more stimulus in London than in Oxfordshire. Now began Ruskin's lifelong association with the British Museum, its collections and their keepers, for he went there to talk to Charles Newton, now a member of its expanding staff. Newton's passion for classical archæology, so little in accord with Ruskin's developing tastes, gave them plenty to argue about. His knowledge of painting was growing in these quiet months after the appearance of *Modern Painters* I, yet there was something that was not quite fresh about his studies. He took notes from two books which he felt would give him a firmer knowledge of the schools of European art and, perhaps, their relevance to English painting of the day. Both were by foreigners. The first had not yet been translated. Alexis Francis Rio's *De La Poésie Chrétienne* (1836) became well known after 1854, when it appeared in England as *The Poetry of Christian Art:* it was probably the widely read Liddell who introduced it to Ruskin at this early date. Ruskin also studied G. F. Waagen's *Works of Art and Artists in England* (1838). Waagen was Director of the Berlin Gallery, and his book was written with authority. It was not sufficiently appreciative of Turner, however, and Ruskin's diary noted, 'I have had the satisfaction of finding Dr Waagen — of such mighty name as a connoisseur — a most double-dyed ass.'[31]

With Turner himself Ruskin's relations were increasingly cordial, although the old man's moods and crotchets often baffled his admirer. The relationship between the Ruskins and their favourite painter was in large part commercial, the more markedly so since Turner had still not acknowledged Ruskin's writing. John James's account book reveals that the new house on Denmark Hill was being filled with Turner water-colours of the larger and more finished sort. In that year he bought the *Llanthony Abbey, Dudley Castle, Land's End, Constance* and *Derwent Water,* for prices ranging from fifty to one hundred guineas. They were not enough for his son. Towards Christmas of 1843, when the Grays from Perth were once more staying with the Ruskins, John took the fifteen-year-old Phemy (as she was generally called) to see Windus's much larger collection. There, as usual, he was struck with an acquisitive jealousy. Two days earlier, his diary had recorded a meeting with Turner:

Very gracious: wanted me excessively to have some wine, but ambiguous as to whether he would or would not part with any of the works in his gallery. Couldn't make him out, and came away in despair. Says he fears there will be no sketches this spring; I shall be sadly disappointed. Phemy is a nice creature; played all the evening for me . . .[32]

Ruskin was perhaps attempting to buy directly from Turner without going through Griffith and without consulting his father. John Ruskin and John James Ruskin could not be in accord when thinking of buying Turners. If they talked together about possible purchases, it seemed always as if the father were making half-promises to the son. Neither of them, ever, dealt in half-promises. The discussions were painful to them both, and each feared the possibility of the other's resentment. Thus it was that John James now kept his own counsel in meditating a major acquisition. It was to be a congratulatory present. *The Slave Ship,* shown at the Royal Academy in 1840, was available through Griffith. Since he had the authority of his own son's book John James could not doubt that this was the right choice. *Modern Painters* said of the picture that it was 'the noblest sea that Turner has ever painted, and, if so, the noblest certainly ever painted by man'; and, further, that 'if I were reduced to rest Turner's immortality upon any single work, I should choose this'.[33] The price was only 250 guineas. Negotiations with Griffith went smoothly enough. The painting was brought out to Denmark Hill and, in Scottish fashion, was presented to Ruskin on New Year's Day.

The painting's full title was 'Slavers throwing overboard the dead and dying — typhon [*sic*] coming on', a theme probably suggested by an incident recounted in Thomas Clarkson's *History of the Abolition of the Slave Trade* (1808). One would look far to find a less domestic subject, and the painting appeared strangely in the entrance hall at Denmark Hill. Ruskin came down to it every morning on his way to the breakfast-room, then went upstairs past it on his way to his study. Perhaps its presence was a constant reminder to him that he should pitch high his writing. The passage in *Modern Painters* that described the picture had a kind of fame. Samuel Prout, who had seen the painting when it was still with Griffith, stood before it for some time and then exclaimed, 'by heaven all that Mr R[uskin] said of it is true!'[34] What Ruskin had in fact said (while relegating the overt subject of the picture to a footnote) was this:

It is a sunset on the Atlantic, after prolonged storm; but the storm is partially lulled, and the torn and streaming rain-clouds are moving in scarlet lines to lose themselves in the hollow of the night. The whole surface of sea included in the picture is divided into two ridges of enormous swell, not high, nor local, but a low broad heaving of the whole ocean, like the lifting of its bosom by deep-drawn breath after the torture of the storm. Between these two ridges the fire of the sunset falls along the trough of the sea, dyeing it with an awful but glorious light, the intense and lurid splendour which burns like gold, and bathes like blood. Along this fiery path and valley, the tossing waves by which the swell of the sea is restlessly divided, lift themselves in dark, indefinite, fantastic forms, each casting a faint and ghastly shadow behind it along the illumined foam. They do not rise everywhere, but three or four together in wild groups, fitfully and furiously, as the under strength of the swell compels or permits them; leaving between them treacherous spaces of level and whirling water, now lighted with green and lamp-like fire, now flashing back the gold of the declining sun, now fearfully dyed from above with the undistinguishable images of the burning clouds, which fall upon them in flakes of crimson and scarlet, and give to the reckless waves the added motion of their own fiery flying. Purple and blue, the lurid shadows of the hollow breakers are cast upon the mist of night, which gathers cold and low, advancing like the shadow of death upon the guilty ship as it labours amidst the lightning of the sea, its thin masts written upon the sky in lines of blood, girded with condemnation in that fearful hue which signs the sky with horror, and mixes its flaming flood with the sunlight, and, cast far along the desolate heave of the sepulchral waves, incarnadines the multitudinous sea.[35]

The passage prompts declamation: and like many another set piece in *Modern Painters* had been written aloud, as Ruskin paced the fields and gardens of his neighbourhood. Its literary background is not only dramatic — from, of course, Macbeth's

> This my hand will rather
> The multitudinous seas incarnadine,
> Making the green one red[36]

— but is also to be found in an amount of English poetry from Thomson to Coleridge, a type of verse that includes Turner's own epic 'The Fallacies of Hope'. Self-conscious about the passage, worrying over the connections between poetry, 'truth', and the factuality of painting, Ruskin was to defend his description to Walter Brown. 'If I had been writing to an artist in order to give him a clear conception of the picture, I should have said':

> Line of eye, two–fifths up the canvass; centre of light, a little above it; orange chrome, No 2 floated in with varnish, pallet-knifed with flake white, glazed afterwards with lake, passing into a purple shadow, scumbled with a dry brush on the left, etc. Once leave this and treat the picture as a reality, and you are obliged to use words implying what is indeed only seen in imagination, but yet what without doubt the artist intended to be so seen; just as he intended you to see and feel the heaving of the sea, being yet unable to give motion to his colours. And then, the question is, not whether all that you see is indeed there, but whether your imagination has worked as it was intended to do, and whether you have indeed felt as the artist did himself and wished to make you . . .[37]

The letter reflects a more practical interest in oil painting. Ruskin's own few experiments with the medium belong to the period after the publication of *Modern Painters* I. They came to nothing, or next to nothing, for he did not fully enjoy the medium. Like many other excellent critics and teachers, Ruskin was only half a creative artist. He responded to art, he could urge art on, but he did not like to fashion things. With Edmund Oldfield, he had a scheme to design stained glass windows for Camberwell Church. But this gave him no more real pleasure than did oil painting. He liked to draw; and a pen or fine pencil line, supplemented by body-colour or water-colour, was always to be his true medium. Drawing was closer to his instincts for recording, measuring and classifying. It was drawing that linked his love of geology with his love of art. Geology had the feeling, for Ruskin, of a science in its youth, a science in which all might be discovered. The foreign tour of 1844 was in essence an expedition to Chamonix and the Simplon. Ruskin's diaries witness his studies in the Alps, and an autobiographical chapter in *Deucalion,* his book devoted to geological matters, records a memorable meeting that summer. The Ruskins were staying at an Alpine inn:

> . . . my father and mother and I were sitting at one end of the long table in the evening; and at the other end of it, a quiet, somewhat severe-looking, and pale, English (as we supposed) traveller, with his wife; she, and my mother, working; her husband carefully completing some mountain outlines in his sketch-book. Whether some harmony of Scottish accent struck my father's ear, or the pride he took in his son's accomplishments prevailed over his own shyness, I think we first ventured word across the table, with view

of informing the grave draughtsman that *we* also could draw.
Whereupon my own sketch-book was brought out, the pale traveller politely permissive. My good father and mother had stopped at
the Simplon inn for me because I wanted to climb to the high point
immediately west of the Col, thinking thence to get a perspective of
the chain joining the Fletschorn to the Monte Rosa. I had brought
down with me careful studies . . . of great value to myself, as
having won for me that evening the sympathy and help of James
Forbes. For his eye grew keen, and his face attentive, as he
examined the drawings; and he turned to me instantly as to a
recognized fellow-workman, — though yet young, no less faithful
than himself . . . He told me as much as I was able to learn, at that
time, of the structures of the chain, and some pleasant general talk
followed; but I knew nothing of glaciers then, and he had his
evening's work to finish. And I never saw him again.[38]

To James Forbes's position in Alpine exploration and geology we
will return, as did Ruskin. He knew his fellow guest in the Simplon
inn as the author of *Travels through the Alps of Savoy and other parts of the
Pennine Chain* (1843), which had extended the studies of the Louis
Agassiz Ruskin had read in Leamington. Forbes was to be a controversial figure for thirty years yet, and Ruskin his distant ally, for indeed
their paths were not to cross again. Now, the Ruskins hired an Alpine
guide who became much more than a servant to them, and who
remained a family friend until his death in 1874. Joseph Couttet,
whom Ruskin called 'the captain of Monc Blanc', was of the race of
guides who were becoming famous in these early years of the English
conquest of the high peaks. His father had been de Saussure's guide.
Joseph himself, a veteran of the Napoleonic armies, was fifty-two in
1844. Reliable, thrifty, avuncular, he soon had all the Ruskins's confidence. 'For thirty years he remained my tutor and companion', says
Præterita. 'Had he been my drawing master also, it would have been
better for me . . .'[39] Osborne Gordon joined them at Zermatt, and
under Couttet's guidance the party became even a little adventurous,
supping on black bread and sour milk under the Riffenberg, and then
'my mother, sixty-three on next 2nd September, walking with me the
ten miles from St Nicholas to Visp as lightly as a girl. And the old
people went back to Brieg with me, that I might climb the Bel Alp
(then unknown), whence I drew the panorama of the Simplon and
Bernese range . . .'[40]

It is in *Deucalion,* Ruskin's compendious geological volume, that
one quarries further reminiscences of this summer in the Alps and its

steady, joyful work; for instance, above the gorge of the Aletsch torrent — making some notes on it afterwards used in *Modern Painters,* 'many and many such a day of foot and hand labour having been needed to build that book'.[41] He kept Cary's Dante by him as he worked: he was using it to elevate his thoughts. He was full of love for the mountains and after long weeks among them was depressed by the thought of dustier work that lay before him in the Louvre on the way home. From Paris he told George Richmond, 'I have been on the hills some ten hours a day at the very least' and 'in this garret at Meurice's, the memory of snow and granite makes me testy'.[42] He was writing to Richmond to ask which pictures he should study in the Louvre. There are some notes on Venetian art in the travel diary that Ruskin had begun in Geneva on 1 June and was to close on his return to London on 20 October. One senses how perfunctory were his visits to French galleries and palaces. But the last entry in the journal is a happy one:

Have not written a word since returning from Chamouni, for my days pass monotonously now. Only I ought to note my being at Windus's on Thursday to dine with Turner and Griffith alone and Turner's thanking me for my book for the first time. We drove home together, reached his house about one in the morning. Boylike, he said he would give sixpence to find the Harley St. gates shut, but on our reaching his door, vowed he'd be damned if we shouldn't come in and have some sherry. We were compelled to obey, and so drank healths again, exactly as the clock struck one, by the light of a single tallow candle in the under room — the wine, by the bye, first rate.[43]

CHAPTER FIVE

1845–1846

Just as some events in life, however unexpected, seem to confirm or explain what had preceded them, so Ruskin's tour to Italy in 1845 gave a shape to what had only been stirring in his mind. The first purpose of the tour, a reaction from his disappointing visit to the Louvre in the previous year, was to study Italian painting *in situ*. But he learnt more, and more about himself, than he imagined he might. He was to be away from home, and from his parents, for seven months. It changed him. Interests became convictions. His taste became active, and with added historical understanding. But some experiences of art this summer touched him so vividly that they had the effect of precluding further modulation of his taste. It was one of the ways in which his opinions on art became frozen. Inflexibility was already a danger to his sensibility. He half realized this, but explained it away by saying that he had to learn more. George Richmond attempted to make him look for good qualities in painting he instinctively disliked. But Ruskin was too impatient. He would listen to Turner, of course, but the painter was scarcely concerned to train young art critics. He often told his eloquent champion that 'all criticism was useless'.[1] He told Ruskin of his disapproval of the strictures in *Modern Painters* on his lesser contemporaries: 'You don't know how difficult it is.'[2] It was true that Ruskin knew little about working in oil. But he had a fair idea about drawing and water-colour. In the winter of 1844-5 he was working from Turner's own *Liber Studiorum*. Although the diaries are sparse, one has the impression that he saw Turner quite often. The conversations between the two men are unimaginable. What Ruskin records of them hints that they were approaching the mysterious slight on Ruskin's integrity for which, he later told Carlyle, 'I never forgave him'.[3] On the other hand, there is such a quantity of Turnerian lore in Ruskin's later writing, and of such a type, that one feels that it must derive from conversations in the studio. Ruskin later said that these were intimate. Certainly Turner was enough of a friend of the Ruskin family to give family advice. He knew how alarmed Ruskin's parents would be at the thought of their son travelling abroad without them. He constantly attempted, Ruskin later recalled, to dissuade him; and so, 'When at last I went to say good-bye, he came down with me into the hall in Queen Anne Street, and opening the door just enough for me to pass, laid hold of my arm, gripping it strongly. "Why will you go to Switzerland — there'll be such a fidge about you, when you're gone." '4

This of course was the first time that Ruskin had travelled abroad — or scarcely anywhere — without the company of John James or Margaret. He was twenty-six. Perhaps with reason, his parents were concerned about his safety, for which they made arrangements. He was to travel with George Hobbs and with Couttet. They would meet the Swiss guide at Geneva, and he would act as courier and watch over Ruskin's health. To travel apart from his family did not trouble Ruskin: geographical separation from those he loved never meant much to him. For his parents, however, it was painful. His eager and vital presence in Denmark Hill brightened their lives. It did more than that. For the son's constant activity had an invigorating effect on the father. When Ruskin was away from home John James was a lesser man. Margaret Ruskin felt this in her turn, for she was far more responsive to her husband's moods than to her son's. John James was hypersensitive to the movements of Ruskin's opinions. The old lady usually ignored what he was thinking. She now packed Bunyan's *Grace Abounding to the Chief of Sinners* in his bag, though he had told her often enough of his dislike for the book. Mildly and subserviently he remonstrated with her. It made no difference. This was often how theological matters were left to rest. Had she known them, she would have been alarmed at Ruskin's religious opinions this winter. Just before Christmas of 1844 he had spent a couple of days in his parish with the recently ordained Edward Clayton. His Christ Church friend's rather grim religious views prompted Ruskin to write to Henry Acland as follows, for Acland had many friends and relatives in the high church party:

I have been in the country — for a day or two — with Edward Clayton . . .
    . . . Now you know — Acland, that I wish as far as may be in my power — to keep with the highest Church supporters — but I hope to heaven this is not their general doctrine . . . For — I am no ultra Protestant — on the contrary — I am far too much inclined the other way — I dispute not transubstantiation — I refuse neither to fast nor to confess myself — I would not check at praying to the Virgin — I abhor not the invocation of saints — I deny not the authority of the Church — But there are two things that I *do* deny — yea, I will deny — so long as I have sense — the first — that man can forgive sins — the second — that God can behold iniquity — i.e. — the doctrines of

a purchased absolution — and a *merited* redemption. In these two — & in them only — it seems to me the power & poison of the Papacy rests — and as soon as the priest becomes the arbiter instead of the Performer of our righteousness — then and there I think the axe is laid to the root of our religion — and the way opened for all manner of blasphemy & sin.[5]

These remarks are so startling that the letter was suppressed by Ruskin's first editors. Those who best understood him, like Acland, knew that he would say something quite different to the next friend. To Ruskin, religious belief was often a matter for argument. Many men in holy orders were to rue his delight in being contentious. If he felt falseness in another man's God, he was capable of arguing a different view with a strange, pitiless gusto. But he had a sense of divinity in others. His feeling for George Herbert — not all that common in the earlier part of the nineteenth century — is one example. He had discussed his poetry with Clayton at Christ Church. He now used Herbert to try to show his mother how *Grace Abounding* suffered from the narrowness and inflexibility of its conviction. She took no notice, but George Hobbs probably did. Their life abroad had one constant feature. Every morning young Ruskin would read with his young servant a chapter or two of the Bible, and the English service. They would then talk about the meaning of the Scripture. We must imagine them in a Paris hotel room, taking the purity of English religion with them, in chapters and verses. As they drove south, Ruskin approached the papist Continent as though he bore St George's own banner. That did not prevent him from travelling luxuriously. His coach was a marvel, a *calèche* drawn by two horses, shining black and gilt. There were good coach-builders in Camberwell, before the railways ruined everything. The roof opened to the sun, the springs were buoyant, here was the buggy and here was the rumble-seat. Inside were any number of pockets and drawers and little bookcases; a place for his writing-case (the only part of his luggage Ruskin ever packed for himself) and clever leather frames to hold the selection of Turner water-colours he took with him wherever he went. Who could not be happy as the day is long, to travel in a vehicle such as this? At Champagnole Ruskin had two trout from the river, a woodcock, then soufflé, with a bottle of Sillery *mousseux*.

Meanwhile the sun was sinking gradually, and I was warned of something equally perfect in *that* direction & way, by seeing my champagne suddenly become *rose*. And a beautiful sunset it was — glowing over the pinewoods, and far up into sky, long after the sun went down. And as I came back to my souffle & sillery, I felt sad at thinking how few were capable of having such enjoyment, and very doubtful whether it were at all proper in me to have it all to myself.[6]

* * * *

The changing urgencies of the tour were only half understood by Couttet and George, compelled by their young master to linger in some places and flee from others. Sometimes there was a relaxed halt, but not often. One such produced the interesting drawing of the Italian maritime pine, done at Sestri as they passed from the French and Italian rivieras and approached the Carrara hills (Plate 8). Thence they sought Lucca, 'where I settled myself', *Præterita* says, 'for ten days, as I supposed. It turned out forty years.'[7] Ruskin meant that he found his life's interests there. His stay at Lucca was for little more than a week. But it gave a vivid prelude and direction to his studies of mediæval painting and architecture. Lucca also gave him the contrast between the old Italy and the new, between mediæval order and restive modern conditions. In 1845 the city was governed as a duchy. Soldiers lounged outside the ducal palace; a military band played. Beggars were everywhere. And in the church of San Frediano,

Such a church — so old — 680 probably — Lombard — all glorious dark arches & columns — covered with holy frescoes — and gemmed gold pictures on blue grounds. I don't know when I shall get away, and all the church fronts charged with heavenly sculpture and inlaid with whole histories in marble — only half of them have been destroyed by the Godless, soulless, devil hearted and brutebrained barbarians of French — and the people here seem bad enough for anything too, talking all church time & idling all day — one sees nothing but subjects for lamentation, wrecks of lovely things destroyed, remains of them unrespected, *all* going to decay, nothing rising but ugliness and meanness, nothing done or conceived by man but evil, irremediable, self multiplying, all swallowing evil, vice and folly everywhere, idleness and infidelity, & filth, and misery, and desecration, dissipated youth & wicked manhood & withered, sickly, hopeless age . . .[8]

In San Frediano Ruskin first thought to trace and copy frescoes before they rotted or fell to pieces, or were simply destroyed to make way for new tombs, new monuments. At the same time he worried that this might waste his time, that paintings in the next church might be desecrated even at that moment. In search of a general knowledge of Italian art, he now found two works that kept a symbolic meaning

8. *Stone Pine at Sestri*, by John Ruskin, 1845.

for him all through his life. One was a painting, the other a recumbent statue. In the Dominican church of San Romano he stood before the Fra Bartolommeo *God the Father with Mary Magdalene and St Catherine of Siena*. This is not a picture of the first quality, and was not in fact what he called it: 'the first example of accomplished sacred art I had seen'.[9] But it gave him a serene, lofty ideal: it was a token that there had been a whole realm of art, centuries of it, that had belonged to God. A similar realization, only a day or two later, came from a piece of sculpture. This was Jacopo della Quercia's tomb of Ilaria di Caretto (Plate 9). It dates from the early fifteenth century and is perhaps more Gothic than early Renaissance in feeling. Ruskin was enraptured. It seemed to him that he had never experienced sculpture before. Nor, it seems to us, was he ever to have any feeling for sculpture that surpassed this early delight. It became a touchstone, and perhaps too much of a touchstone. The young wife lying in death had a haunting impression on Ruskin. In years to come her image would be confounded with that of Rose La Touche; and as one reads the description of the monument that Ruskin now sent to his father, one senses not only the tone but also part of the inspiration of later, desolate, marmorial writing.

This, his second wife, died young, and her monument is by Jacopo della Querce, erected soon after her death. She is lying on a simple pillow, with a hound at her feet. Her dress is of the simplest middle age character, folding closely over the bosom, and tight to the arms, clasped about the neck. Round her head is a circular fillet, with three

9. *Tomb of Ilaria di Caretto*, by Jacopo della Quercia, at Lucca, by John Ruskin, sketched in 1874.

star shaped flowers. From under this the hair falls like that of the Magdalene, its undulation *just* felt as it touches the cheek, & no more. The arms are not folded, nor the hands clasped nor raised. Her arms are laid softly at length upon her body, and the hands cross as they fall. The drapery flows over the feet and half hides the hound. It is impossible to tell you the perfect sweetness of the lips & the closed eyes, nor the solemnity of the seal of death which is set upon the whole figure. The sculpture, as art, is in every way perfect — *truth* itself, but truth selected with inconceivable refinement of feeling. The cast of the drapery, for *severe natural* simplicity & perfect grace, I never saw equalled, nor the fall of the hands — you expect every instant, or rather you seem to see every instant, the last sinking into death. There is no decoration or work about it, not even enough for protection — you may stand beside it leaning on the pillow, and watching the twilight fade over the sweet, dead lips and arched eyes in their sealed close. With this I end my day, & return home as the lamps begin to burn in the Madonna shrines; to read Dante, and write to you.[10]

In Ruskin's response to the Fra Bartolommeo and the della Quercia there was a feeling for their location, their placing in quiet holy places of the town. Lucca itself, Ruskin noted, had within its rampart walls 'upwards of twenty churches . . . dating between the sixth and twelfth centuries'.[11] His short stay included some drawing of these churches. He afterwards believed that this marked the beginning of his architectural studies. *The Poetry of Architecture,* since its stance was both English and picturesque, had to be forgotten. The change is marked by a different kind of drawing, especially of façades. Ruskin's graphic style became more notational as he looked at the church of San Michele (Plate 10). The drawings were scarcely composed and there was no attempt to finish them once the detail had been caught. In this respect they closely correspond to the visual experience of looking at a Gothic church with a will to consider it in part rather than in whole. In Pisa, where the party travelled next, he used his notebooks more fully and the study of such churches is accordingly more complete. He was teaching himself how to grasp architecture, preparing for those wonderful notebooks from which he was to write *The Stones of Venice.*

Ruskin was surprised to find how much his reactions had changed since he was last in this part of North Italy in 1840. Lucca then he had reckoned 'an ugly little town'. Pisa 'as *town* is very uninteresting'.[12] The Campo Santo in Pisa he had been 'thoroughly disappointed in: it is very narrow, not elegant, and totally wanting in melancholy or in

10. Part of the façade of S Michele in Lucca, by John Ruskin, 1845.

peace, the more so for being turned into a gallery of antiquities'.[13] In 1845 it was the Campo Santo above all that moved him: 'My mind is marvellously altered . . . everything comes on me like music.'[14] The simile had to do with the way that *quattrocento* art had displayed itself to him. It was grave sometimes, sweet sometimes, seraphic always. Ruskin gave himself up to the frescoes. Yet he was almost equally stirred by his conviction that they were all threatened. His letters are alternately filled with ecstatic descriptions of the paintings and expressions of rage at their probable fate. In his more meditative moments he found that he could make an alliance between his Protestant mind, his searching in antiquity, fresh enthusiasm, and a kind of realism he found in the pictures. The Campo Santo was a graphic Bible. In it there was an ancient truthfulness. He wrote to his father,

> I never believed the patriarchal history before, but I do now, for I
> have seen it. You cannot conceive the vividness & fullness of
> conception of these great old men . . . Abraham & Adam, & Cain,
> Rachel & Rebekah, all are there, the very people, real, visible,
> created, substantial, such as they *were,* as they must have been —
> one cannot look at them without being certain that they have lived
> — and the angels, great, & real, and powerful, that you feel the very
> wind from their wings upon your face, and yet expect to see them
> depart every instant into heaven . . .[15]

Most of these impressions are taken from paintings by Benozzo Gozzoli, but he passed swiftly to others. On 18 May he could report of his progress, 'Benozzo I have done, & Giotto I am doing, then I have Simon Memmi, Antonio Veneziano, & Andrea Orgagna [*sic*].'[16] Some of Ruskin's attributions were wrong, and remained wrong. This scarcely mattered. He had found a new way of looking at the world.

Art historians of Ruskin's and later generations knew what tact, guile, patience and willpower are needed to have a scaffolding erected in an Italian church. Ruskin, with his money, charm, and servants, somehow managed it immediately. He soared above difficulties. Couttet and George sorted things out at ground level. He drew and traced from the frescoes, aware as he did so that the whole shape and the whole subject of the next volume of *Modern Painters* was now quite changed. What the book would contain he could not foretell: but in some way he changed his plans and his itinerary in accordance with his feelings for it. A few more days, he imagined, and he might get to the end of 'my *resumé*' of Pisa: it was as though (as writers and lecturers sometimes can) he was able to feel already the further end of his peroration. The relationship between this tour and *Modern Painters* II is obvious and can be demonstrated in one hundred details. Behind that, there is a similarity in the pace and the vision of the book and the tour. There were high points and more high points, and scarcely more than breathing spaces between them. In Lucca and in Pisa, as everywhere else in Italy, he found that there was more to be done, more to be understood, than ever he had imagined. Probably it was now that he realized that *Modern Painters* would have more than two volumes. He also realized that he had thrown away parts of his past life. The first volume of his book was effaced from his mind. So was his poetry: he had no time for it. Oxford he had no thought for: he was learning more in a few months than he had in years at the university. He wrote to Osborne Gordon to say that he did not wish to meet him. Suddenly, Rogers and his *Italy* seemed beside the point. He quoted Rogers to his father, but he no longer believed in him. John James, reading his daily letters (that took the place of Ruskin's diary entries) in Billiter Street, could not keep pace with his son's discoveries. This disturbed him so much that he redoubled his warnings about health. Ruskin told his father that he would eat no figs, that he drank clean water, that his scaffold was safe. He sent him accounts of what he spent, and scarcely ever failed to be dutiful, entertaining and reassuring.

In Florence, where he arrived at the end of May, he had most need to tell his parents of his safety. There were signs of strain which could not be kept out of the letters home. Neither of his servants had any control over his mental activity. He was often at work in the churches at five o'clock in the morning and did not cease until mid-evening. Nor was this merely a tourist's long day. Only by taking the notebooks and drawings in one's own hand, and then by attempting to cover the same ground, can one appreciate the ferocity of his study. But this is to simplify. He had a different pace for different uses of the pen. Script, one can tell, is extraordinarily rapid. One gathers this not so much from the handwriting as by taking any lengthy sentence and then by discovering how its subordinate clauses, as one transcribes it, take one beyond the point where one can recall its initial impetus. Meanwhile, we note of his drawing in 1845 that it tends to be more cursive in landscape subjects such as the Sestri pine, while the study of architectural detail and outlines of paintings are of necessity drawn more slowly. They are not, however, laborious; and many personal recollections of Ruskin when drawing indicate that his pen and brush were more fluent than most people's.

In Florence, much of his time was spent in drawing. He wrote his last poem, 'Mont Blanc Revisited', feeling that his time was being wasted. 'I haven't time if I draw to see half the things — and I must draw too, for my book,' he wrote to his father,[17] adding next day that 'there is so much to be read and worked out that it is quite impossible to draw, except the little studies for my book. I regret this the more because unless I draw a bit of a thing, I never arrive at conclusions to which I can altogether trust.'[18] Thus it went on, Ruskin now adding to his labours by borrowing books from the library of Santa Croce. For relaxation he sometimes helped the monks at their haymaking, on the hill of Fiesole. But for two months, almost without remission, he was absorbed in Giotto studies, in the Ghirlandaio chapel of Santa Maria Novella, finding Masaccio and Fra Filippo Lippi in the Brancacci Chapel and Fra Angelico in the Convent of San Marco.

★   ★   ★   ★

Ruskin was tired by this effort. Advised by Couttet, he decided not to remain in Italy in midsummer. 'I begin to feel the effects of the violent excitement of the great art at Florence — nothing gives me any pleasure at present, and I shall not recover spring of mind until I get on a glacier.'[19] The party went up through Milan to Como and finally to Macugnaga in the Val Anzasca. Here, high in the mountains, Ruskin rented a chalet, little more than a hut. It was next to a torrent, approached by a stony path and a pine bridge, rocks and waterfalls to one side, pines and 'stunted acacias' on the other. In Switzerland they again found haymaking. Ruskin walked on the mountains from dawn and gave his hand to the peasants in the evening. The valley was his. He conceived the idea of asking Turner to stay with him there. Affecting the casual, he enclosed the invitation in a letter to John James, saying 'is the gentleman doing anything — if he isn't, tell him he may as well come here & catch fish and climb hills with me . . .'.[20] In truth, he wanted to stand at Turner's shoulder to see how he drew mountains. But the artist would not come; and Ruskin buried himself in Shakespeare.

In all Ruskin's books there are more references to Shakespeare than to any other writer, excepting only Dante. Like other great Englishmen, Ruskin learnt Shakespeare early and knew ever afterwards that he was part of his own mind: one does not often find occasions when Ruskin deliberately sat down to study him. Nor did he often write directly about the plays. The dispersion of his comments has the effect of obscuring how complete a Shakespearian he was. In 1886, looking back on his days in Macugnaga, and writing in sadness and defeat, Ruskin observed:

. . . the writer himself is not only unknowable, but inconceivable; and his wisdom so useless, that at this time of being and speaking, among active and purposeful Englishmen, I know not one who shows a trace of ever having felt a passion of Shakespeare's, or learnt a lesson from him.[21]

Thus the despairing *Præterita* recalls but slightly perverts what indeed was Ruskin's experience of the weeks in Macugnaga in 1845: that there were no *lessons* to be drawn from reading Shakespeare that summer. And while he knew that he needed to relax, Ruskin had still a desire for books that would cut a path for him. 'Formerly I hated history, now I am always at Sismondi,' he now told his father. 'I had not the slightest interest in political science, now I am studying the constitutions of Italy with great interest . . .'[22] Jean-Charles-Leonard Simonde de Sismondi's *Histoire des républiques italiennes au moyen age* (1838), whose three volumes Ruskin carried with him, can be added to Rio's *Poésie Chrétienne* as a book which shaped Ruskin's growing mediævalism. He had an instinct and a desire for such writing. Shakespeare was put away, and study resumed.

Before he left the Alps Ruskin spent much time in that kind of work, half scientific and half artistic, which he had invented for himself, pursuing observations of sky or granite, glacier or woodland. One day 'I stopped 5 hours, watching the various effects of cloud over the plains of Lombardy, after getting the forms of the mountains that I wanted above the valley of Saas.'[23] A day or two later, from Faido, St Gothard, he writes of his location of a Turner site: 'I have found his subject, or the materials of it, here; and shall devote tomorrow to examining them and seeing how he has put them together.'[24] Ruskin was on his way to Baveno, where he had a rendezvous with J. D. Harding. They met: and sketching as they went, attended still by Couttet and the exhausted George, the two water-colourists went by Como, Bergamo and Verona to Venice. Ruskin was drawing now in genuine rivalry with his former master. But the interest they took in each other's work was brought to a halt by the experience of Venice. Ruskin's first reaction was negative: it was one of horror at modern improvements. Approaching the city, deliberately, from the pictures-que angle that he recalled from 1835, he suddenly found the new railway bridge from Mestre 'entirely cutting off the whole open sea & half the city, which now looks as nearly as possible like Liverpool at the end of the dockyard wall . . .'.[25] Everywhere he seemed to find neglect of the Venetian treasures, and signs that it would shortly become even like an English manufacturing town. It wrung from him the cry that would be repeated in the first sentence of *The Stones of Venice* a few years later: 'Tyre itself was nothing to this.'[26]

For a few days, Ruskin could not settle to the study of painting, beyond noting how he could find 'among the wrecks of Venice, authority for all that Turner has done of her'. He told his father, 'I have been in such a state of torment since I came here that I have not even thought of Titian's existence.'[27] He would not much do so. Nor would he much consider the Bellinis, nor look as he had intended for Giorgione. He was to have the revelation of a quite different artist.

I have had a draught of pictures today enough to drown me. I never was so utterly crushed to the earth before any human intellect as I was today, before Tintoret. Just be so good as to take my list of painters, & put him in the school of Art at the top, top, top of everything, with a great big black line underneath him to stop him off from everybody — and put him in the school of Intellect, next after Michael Angelo. He took it so entirely out of me today that I could do nothing at last but lie on a bench & laugh. Harding said that if he had been a figure painter, he never could have touched a brush again, and that he felt more like a flogged schoolboy than a man — and no wonder. Tintoret don't seem to be able to stretch himself till you give him a canvas forty feet square — & then, he lashes out like a leviathan, and heaven and earth come together. M Angelo himself cannot hurl figures into space as he does, nor did M Angelo ever paint space itself which would not look like a nutshell beside Tintoret's. Just imagine the audacity of the fellow — in his massacre of the innocents one of the mothers has hurled herself off a terrace to avoid the executioner & is falling headforemost & backwards, holding up the child still. And such a resurrection as there is the rocks of the sepulchre crashed all to pieces & roaring down upon you, while the Christ soars forth into a torrent of angels, whirled up into heaven till you are lost ten times over. And then to see his touch of quiet thought in his awful crucifixion — there is an *ass* in the distance, feeding on the remains of strewed palm leaves. If that isn't a master's stroke, I don't know what is. As for *painting,* I think I didn't know what it meant till today — the fellow outlines you your figure with ten strokes, and colours it with as many more. I don't believe it took him ten minutes to invent & paint a whole length. Away he goes, heaping host on host, multitudes that no man can number — never pausing, never repeating himself — clouds & whirlwinds & fire & infinity of earth & sea, all alike to him — and then the noble fellow has put in Titian, on horseback at one side of

11. Copy after the central portion of Tintoretto's *Crucifixion*, by John Ruskin, 1845.

one of his great pictures, and himself at the other, but he has made Titian principal. This is the way great men are with each other — no jealousy there . . .[28]

Experiencing the physicality and great size of the paintings in the Scuola di San Rocco, Ruskin was so overwhelmed that he could not make the correct comparisons with Titian. In truth there is not much that is essential to Tintoretto's art that had not been more beautifully expressed by Titian. But Ruskin was not able to think in such terms. All life long he overrated Tintoretto, as if in honour of this experience. Now as ever afterwards his response was personal and partial, and in expression overstated. His judgements on painting were scarcely ever tempered by the local and comparative methods of the art historian. And he now began to pit himself — as always he would — against the founders of this new intellectual discipline. The tour of 1845 produced some writing that was never collected, Ruskin's additional notes to Murray's *Handbook for Travellers in North Italy*. This material appeared in the 1847 edition signed only as '(R)'. Sir Francis Palgrave, the compiler of the original work, is bitingly criticized in his own book.

Ruskin now met another classifier and recorder, Mrs Anna Jameson, who was working on the Venetian sources of her *Sacred and*

Legendary Art. He also made the acquaintance of the English connoisseur, William Boxall, who was later to be Director of the National
Gallery. The three made expeditions together. Boxall knew Wordsworth, and Ruskin rather admired him. Mrs Jameson, however,
'knows as much of art as the cat'.[29] She was older than Ruskin and had
much determination. But he found that his understanding of the
Italian schools was way beyond hers. Boxall was to remain a friend,
though a distant one, for many years. *Præterita* remembers Mrs Jameson kindly. *Sacred and Legendary Art,* however, is a poor thing in
comparison with the truly spiritual second volume of *Modern Painters,*
just as her book on Shakespeare's heroines falls limply beside only two
pages of comment on Shakespeare which Ruskin incorporated in the
Alpine passages of the fourth volume of his earliest great work.

There is a touch of arrogance in Ruskin's dealings with Mrs Jameson. This is only to be expected. The revelations of the past few
months had demanded something from Ruskin's sensibility and from
his personality: he had responded with the kind of effort that a man can
perhaps only make in his twenties. He had matched his own potential
against his discoveries. A young man can learn, and become more
learned. He can find things in life of which he was unaware. Ruskin
had done these things, and had done more than that. He had enlarged
himself. This could not protect him from the consequences of his
overwork. Couttet, with a gentle care that Ruskin could often inspire
in other men, had warned him of the reaction that might come.
Harding left, Boxall left, but Ruskin stayed on to make further studies
in the city. For the first time he used daguerrotypes to record buildings, but most of his labour was in drawing and making voluminous
notes. Almost feverishly, he sought to capture as much of Tintoretto
and Venice as he could. On the way home, after seven months abroad,
he succumbed. He was ill at Padua and again, after bidding farewell to
Couttet, on the journey to Paris. He did not visit the Louvre but
hurried straight home, arriving at Dover on 5 November.

*   *   *   *

Much of the tension that Ruskin felt during his tour concerned his
obligations to his parents. His dutiful letters to Denmark Hill give
almost daily reassurances about his health and safety. Towards the end
of his long stay the messages from his parents often asked him to come
home. One letter in particular made him think of his mother and her
grief: it told him of two deaths, of his cousins Mary and John, of the
Croydon Richardsons. When he opened his next year's diary, half-

12. *Corner of St Mark's after Rain*, by John Ruskin, 1846.

way through the composition of *Modern Painters* II, Ruskin wrote an honest analysis of his feelings at the time:

I ought to note one circumstance — a series of circumstances — connected with the past year which ought to be as important, as any that ever happened to me. From about the close of September at Venice, to the 26th of October, or thereabouts, at Vevay, I had been kept almost without letters, except one or two at Brieg full of complaints of my stay at Venice. I was much vexed at Vevay by finding no letter of credit there and the next day I received the news of my cousins' deaths (Mary and John) — Sufficiently uncomfortable in these several respects and not very well. I received in passing through Lausanne (and that by chance, having doubted whether I should send George to post a letter half way down the town, and only let him go because I was busy drawing some figures at a fountain and couldn't interrupt myself) a short letter from my Father, full of most unkind expressions of impatience at my stay in Venice. I had been much vexed by his apparent want of sympathy throughout the journey, and on receiving this letter my first impulse was to write a complaining and perhaps a bitter one in return. But as I drove down the hill from Lausanne there was something in the sweet sunshine between the tree trunks that made me think better of it. I considered that I should give my father dreadful pain if I did so, and that all this impatience was not unkindly meant, but only the ungoverned expression of extreme though selfish affection. At last I resolved, though with a little effort, to throw the letter into the fire, and say nothing of having received it, so that it might be thought to have been lost at Brieg, whence it had been forwarded. I had no sooner made this resolution than I felt a degree of happiness and elation totally different from all my ordinary states of mind, and this continued so vivid and steady all the way towards Nyon that I could not but feel there was some strange spiritual government of the conscience; and I began to wonder how God should give me so much reward for so little self-denial, and to make all sorts of resolves relating to future conduct. While in the middle of them we stopped to change horses at Rolle, and I got out and sauntered down, hardly knowing where I went, to the lake shore. I had not seen Mont Blanc all the journey before, and was not thinking of it, but when I got to the quay there it was, a great and glorious pyramid of purple in the evening light, seen between two slopes of dark mountain as in the opposite page [where there is a drawing] — the lake lying below as calm as glass. In the state of mind in which I then was it seemed a lesson given by my own favourite mountain — a revelation of nature intended for me only.[30]

Further notes in this diary reveal how Ruskin then devoted himself to spiritual exercises, 'continuing in earnest prayer and endeavour, or determination to do right',[31] while fighting the physical effects of what was surely a nervous illness. His sense that he was called to do great work was never in perfect concord with what his parents expected of him. There is for this reason a slight element of expiation in *Modern Painters* II, which was written in London in the winter of 1845–6 and published the following spring. If the whole of *Modern Painters* is Ruskin's great gift to his father, then its second volume is a subsidiary gift to his mother. More formally religious than the first volume, and much more like her religion than like John James's, it reads as though its intention was to gladden her. At the same time, the book could not quite present an explanation to John James of how his son had stepped away from him. Both of them knew that this had happened, and neither could do anything about it. Ruskin promised his father that the next year they would all travel together and he would show them the wonderful things that he was now writing about. But there was still a gap between them. *Modern Painters* II is in some respects a solitary book, for it is the record of one young man's pilgrimage and the formation, by revelation, of a most personal taste. What the book has to say about this is of importance. 'True taste is for ever growing, learning, reading, worshipping, laying its hand upon its mouth because it is astonished, lamenting over itself, and testing itself by the way it fits things.'[32] It is a bold image, the more so for being active and physical, a youthful thought that belongs (as Ruskin himself belongs) to the period between Romanticism and the beginnings of a modern apprehension of art. Ruskin cultivated the self-awareness of such taste. Of necessity, it was his alone.

But the reading that contributed to *Modern Painters* II was a different matter. This was shared and discussed. Osborne Gordon had recommended Hooker to him, Ruskin later recalled. He ascribed to Hooker an ornateness of language in the book. Perhaps this was to exaggerate the influence. A nearer and more potent example would be in the sermons of Henry Melvill. These were read, listened to, and discussed in Denmark Hill. They had so much effect on Ruskin that he could dream about them forty years later, and their combination of artificial language and religious fervour was surely present in the young art critic. In the early 1880s, when he looked back on *Modern Painters* II,

Ruskin thought that the book might be of interest to 'the literary student' as well as to an art lover.[33] W. G. Collingwood, whom Ruskin probably had in mind, was inclined to think that the book was 'really a philosophical work' and wished to place it 'as a reflex of the great movement of German philosophy and as the completion of the English school of æsthetics begun by Coleridge'.[34] However that may be, it is certain that much of Ruskin's university reading, which he discussed with Acland and Newton as well as with Gordon during the composition of *Modern Painters* II, finds a place in his æsthetic system. His formal æsthetic was always to be of more interest to Ruskin than anyone else, however; the popularity of *Modern Painters* II was mostly in 'passages' that were known, for a time, as glories of English prose. Such extracts rather annoyed the later Ruskin, who did not like to be famous for mellifluous sentences. He believed, rightly, that the importance of the book was in its introduction of a taste for early Italian art and for Tintoretto. Ruskin was neither the first nor the sole discoverer of early Italian art. But he was by far the most persuasive, as the respectful reviews of his book (excepting still the *Athenæum*'s notice) indicate. At the age of twenty-five he had established an artistic authority that was crusader-like. This could excite his contemporaries. Acland, writing to Liddell as another young don who hoped to change Oxford, now for the first time suggested that Ruskin be brought back to the university. Ruskin himself had no such desire. He was eager for other things. As soon as he had finished the second volume of *Modern Painters* he began the studies of architecture that were to absorb him until the end of his marriage in 1854. Not waiting to see the publication of his book but entrusting all to W. H. Harrison, Ruskin left with his parents for the Continent. This was in April of 1846: they would not return to England until six months later.

*   *   *   *

When looking back on those days in *Præterita* Ruskin quite accurately stated:

> I had two distinct instincts to be satisfied, rather than ends in view, as I wrote day by day with higher-kindled feeling the second volume of *Modern Painters*. The first, to explain to myself, and then demonstrate to others, the nature of that quality of beauty which I now saw to exist through all the happy conditions of living organism; and down to the minutest detail and finished material structure naturally produced. The second, to explain and illustrate the power of the two schools of art unknown to the British public, that of Angelico in Florence, and Tintoret in Venice.[35]

Only by forcing arguments could Turner be introduced to such a scheme, and he makes only a minor appearance in this second volume of *Modern Painters*. Ruskin did not write again publicly about Turner until 1851, when the painter was dying. In some other ways Turner seems now to have lost his place in Ruskin's life. We hear next to nothing about the relations between the artist and the critic. Ruskin made no record of any of his conversations with Turner, nor any record of their meetings. So distant do the painter and critic seem that one cannot imagine how they corresponded; and in fact it is likely that many of their exchanges by letter were conducted through the medium of John James Ruskin. Evidence of Turner's visits to Denmark Hill is in John James's correspondence and diary rather than in his son's diary. It seems that the painter was at the Ruskins's on New Year's Day of 1846, when according to Finberg's biography of Turner he might have discussed his will with John James;[36] and was there again on 8 February, 'Mr John's' birthday. John James's diary reveals that he dined at Denmark Hill on 19 March of 1846, just before the publication of *Modern Painters* II, with Mrs Colquhoun, a Mr Young, William Boxall, George Richmond and Joseph Severn. He next visited (it appears) at Ruskin's birthday party the following 8 February, when the other guests were Charles Newton, W. H. Harrison and Mrs Cockburn; then again on 3 June of 1847, when he met William Macdonald, the son of an old Scottish friend of John James's, the water-colourist Joshua Cristall, George Richmond, C. R. Leslie, Samuel Palmer and Effie Gray; and just before Ruskin's marriage to this last, at his 1848 birthday dinner, Turner sat down with Richmond, Boxall, Sir Charles Eastlake and the Reverend Daniel Moore who had succeeded Henry Melvill as incumbent of the Camden Chapel. It will be seen that these were hardly intimate meetings. Of Ruskin's more personal relations with Turner in these years, we have little idea. He would have seen something of him at Griffith's, and we know that he had — at times — access to Queen Anne Street. But when the snatches of evidence for such meetings are accumulated, it is noticeable that Ruskin had far less to do with the artist he most admired than would have been expected.[37]

The reasons for this lack of contact might be the obvious ones: the difference in age and temperament between the two men. But one other piece of evidence suggests that their relationship had been damaged. Twenty years after this time Ruskin found himself estranged from an older man whom he revered. This was Carlyle. A dispute between them lasted for some weeks. At the height of their quarrel, Ruskin wrote to Carlyle in the hottest anger: wildly, almost, but with the anger of a man whose personal honour has been damaged. In this letter Ruskin tells Carlyle that Turner had once called his honour into question, and that he had never forgiven him. Ruskin gave no further explanation and we cannot know what had happened. But it is significant that the matter should have come to the surface at this emotional point. As long as he lived Ruskin never again mentioned that something had come between himself and Turner. One can only guess at what it was. It could have been something to do with purchasing: here was an area of Turner's life where goodwill could often fail. It could have been to do with Ruskin's writing. Turner's extraordinarily reserved attitude to Ruskin's heartfelt books cannot but have been a psychological difficulty to the writer who claimed to understand his art. Ruskin never had much to say about Turner's interest in him and his writing. But for five years of his life this must have mattered to him far more than any kind of public success. Later, Ruskin was to make an unusual and rather sinister claim about Turner's health in these years. He felt that the painter had then been not merely in physical decline but suffered from 'mental disease', whose onset he could date: 'The time of fatal change may be brought within a limit of three or four months, towards the close of the year 1845.'[38] This was the period when Ruskin was back in London and writing the text of the second volume of *Modern Painters*. Something may have passed between them then. At any rate, Ruskin felt that he could not hope for the painter's affection during his declining years. After Turner's death, Ruskin was in correspondence with Griffith. Turner's agent had gone out of his way to let Ruskin know that the painter did have some regard for the writer. Ruskin wrote back that he was 'deeply gratified . . . by what you say of Turner's having cared something for me. My life has not been the same to me as you may well imagine since he has gone to his place — nor will it ever be to me again what it was — while he was living . . .'[39]

From 1845 onwards, or after he had finished writing *Modern Painters* II, Ruskin might have thought of putting his knowledge of Turner into manageable form, with the aid of notebooks, drawings, reproductions and the like. But this approach was never congenial. The classical methods of the art historian (such as they were, at this date) found no adherent in the young art critic. He disliked systems and when he made catalogues they tended to the eccentric. Furthermore, he believed that to understand Turner it was more important to study nature than old oil paintings. At the same time, Ruskin was liable to find new enthusiasms outside art, or to return to his old pursuits in the geological sciences. When *Modern Painters* II was published in April of 1846, he was already on a different intellectual tack. The notices were almost overwhelmingly flattering. One of them brought a new friend, a doctor and writer who for the rest of his life would attempt to keep up with Ruskin's imagination. This was John Brown of Edinburgh,[40] who had reviewed the book for the *North British Review* and had written privately to its author. Ruskin received Brown's letter on the Continent, for he had taken his mother and father away from England before publication day. One part of him wanted to show his parents what he had been writing about. But he was also in search of knowledge that as yet was undefined to him: historical, religious, sculptural, architectural, or some combination of these things. Landscape art became less interesting. No further volume of *Modern Painters* would appear for ten years.

CHAPTER SIX

1846–1847

Between 1846 and 1856 Ruskin was mostly concerned with architectural studies. These are the years which saw *The Seven Lamps of Architecture* (1849), the three volumes of *The Stones of Venice* (1851-3), various lectures and occasional writings on building, and the collaborative venture of the construction of the Oxford Museum. Ruskin's interest in architecture was lifelong, of course: it extends from *The Poetry of Architecture,* written when he was an undergraduate, to the last of his Oxford lectures in the 1880s. But this decade gave him his central position in the Gothic Revival. He was led to architecture by his reading of mediæval history, by his increasing concern with the history of the Christian Church, and by a study of architecture in Turner's water-colours. His own increased ability to draw buildings also played a part in his new interest. Ruskin was now confident enough of his own drawing to show some water-colours this year, 1846, in a mixed exhibition at the Graphic Society. It is recorded that 'a member of the Royal Academy, after examining the subjects with much attention, exclaimed in our hearing — "The man who can draw like that may write anything he pleases upon art"'.[1] Ruskin might not have taken this as a compliment. His drawing had direct connections with his writing. The ability to grasp architectural subjects by the process of recording them in drawing now began to give a new kind of authority to his connoisseurship of building. His studies of architectural details, mouldings, doorways, arches, pinnacles, far outnumber the drawings he made from paintings, or sculpture; and they gave him an apprehension of building that seems to have a unique combination of the optical with the tactile.

Ruskin benefited from the scholarly attention to mediæval architecture that, in England, had preceded the analysis of earlier schools of painting. His serious introduction to Gothic building was made with the help of a book that had been published as long before as 1835, Robert Willis's *Remarks on the Architecture of the Middle Ages, Especially of Italy*. When he bought this book is not known: but many notes and drawings in his current diary testify to a careful interest in Willis. As the Ruskins travelled down the Continent towards the goal of their tour, which was Venice, we may see how he attempted to apply the method of Willis's *Remarks* to French and German buildings. In 1880, in a supplementary footnote to a new edition of *The Seven Lamps of Architecture,* Ruskin acknowledged that Willis 'taught me all my grammar of central Gothic' and that in his book on the flamboyant style he had anticipated Ruskin in the 'grammar of the flamboyant I worked out for myself'.[2] As usual, Ruskin's reading had been extensive but piecemeal. If this was to his disadvantage as an architectural historian, the lack was more than balanced by his industry before the *motif* of the buildings he studied. Nor should we underestimate the value of his distance from the architectural profession, for this allowed him to ignore all the practical problems of architecture. Ruskin made the literature of the Gothic Revival inseparable from the general revival of the arts in mid-nineteenth-century England, and gave it a spiritual inspiration that in many other writers and architects was sectarian or merely perfunctory.

John James Ruskin had not anticipated this new involvement with architecture and the effective abandoning of Turner studies. He had trouble in following his son's enthusiasms. One purpose of the tour of 1846 was for Ruskin to be able to show his father all that had excited him in his great expedition the previous year. There is no doubt that Ruskin felt guilty that his long absence abroad had distressed his parents. This loving and dutiful son could not feel content with himself until he had once again made a sort of comrade of his father. To this end he wished to show him the main subjects of his newly published book, the 'angel choirs' of *quattrocento* painting and the turbulent visions of Tintoretto. Many English travellers would go to Italy with Ruskin's famous book as their guide. John James, in Venice and Pisa, was the first but not the most appreciative of them. There is some humour in the way that Ruskin later described his reactions:

> We had been entirely of one mind about the carved porches of Abbeville, and living pictures of Vandyck; but when my father now found himself required to admire also flat walls, striped like the striped calico of an American flag, and oval-eyed saints like the figures on a Chinese teacup, he grew restive . . .[3]

In fact John James was distressed. It was becoming apparent to both father and son that Ruskin's first tour without his parents had erected a greater barrier between them than either had realized. John James now swung back to his old longing for his son to be a poet. W. H. Harrison, still editing *Friendship's Offering,* had written to Venice to ask if there were any lines — a song, perhaps, or a picturesque description — that he could publish in his annual next Christmas. Ruskin was far beyond such things. John James had to reply:

I regret to say there is no chance of this; my son has not written a line of poetry and he says he cannot produce any by setting himself to it as a work — he does not I am sorry to say regret this — he only regrets ever having written any. He thinks all his own poetry very worthless and considers it unfortunate that he prematurely worked any small mine of poetry he might possess. He seems to think the mine is exhausted and neither gold nor silver given to the world. He is cultivating Art at present searching for real knowledge but to you and me this knowledge is at present a Sealed Book. It will neither take the shape of picture or poetry. It is gathered in scraps hardly wrought for he is drawing perpetually but no drawing such as in former days you or I might compliment in the usual way by saying it deserved a frame — but fragments of everything from a Cupola to a Cartwheel but in such bits that it is to the common eye a mass of Hieroglyphics — all true — truth itself but Truth in mosaic . . .[4]

This 'mass of Hieroglyphics' was the notebook in which Ruskin was making his architectural studies. As his father lamented, he had no interest in making frameable and finished drawings of whole buildings or scenes: he wanted to avoid settings and the picturesque. Instead, he concentrated on the details of individual forms. Here was born the knowledge of Venetian architecture that was the strong foundation of *The Stones of Venice*. However, the epic history of her building was not yet in Ruskin's mind. He was thinking of making his new studies into a chapter or section of the next volume of *Modern Painters*. The integrity of his sequence was a problem at Venice in the summer of 1846. Ruskin was now revising his text for the third edition of the first volume, and found it awkward to accommodate Titian and Tintoretto. Writing from Lucerne on the way home, he confessed to George Richmond that 'I have got some useful bits of detail . . . especially in architecture — though in Italy I lost the greater part of my time because I had to look over the first volume of *Modern Painters,* which I wanted to bring up to something like the standard of knowledge in the other . . .'.[5]

The party returned to England at the end of September 1846. The elder Ruskins would never go to Italy again. Their son had garnered much information in the summer months, but it felt miscellaneous. It took another year and more for his architectural feeling to gell into the extended essay which is *The Seven Lamps of Architecture*. Ruskin had not yet realized a simple truth about himself: how easy it was to write a book on anything that interested him at the time. For this reason, his literary production in the next two years was comparatively meagre.

The autumn of 1846 was taken up with studies in the British Museum. We might note here that this great institution was Ruskin's best-loved museum. He always enjoyed his visits to Bloomsbury more than those he made to the National Gallery. He did not neglect the country's foremost painting collection, and was often there for professional reasons. But it was too much associated with the Royal Academy and with the traditions of baroque painting. For this reason he often urged the National Gallery to buy examples of earlier Italian art. He did so with a novel and urgent authority, and often by speaking directly to the gallery's trustees and other interested parties. The identity of the 'Graduate of Oxford' had still not been revealed on Ruskin's title-pages, but there can have been few people in art circles who did not know that he was the author of *Modern Painters*. He had renown, and for that reason was invited to many a drawing-room. Ruskin's regular complaints about evenings in society no doubt tell us of his dislike of fashionable salons: they also show that he kept accepting the invitations. This pleased his parents. It also gave relief from another kind of social life which he undertook and of which he never complained. His parents entertained a great deal but never themselves dined away from home: Ruskin went to other people's houses on their behalf. Thus, many a night and for many a year, he spent hours with family friends who were a generation older than himself. They were Scottish, or in the wine trade, or were clergymen. This circle included Dale and Croly, whose conversation — if not their sermons, for Ruskin went to hear Dale preach every Tuesday until 1848 — he might well have found repetitive. Society in great London houses off Hyde Park was in comparison tinsel. That was why it was sometimes welcome.

A house Ruskin sometimes frequented was Lady Davy's, in Park Street. She was Sir Humphrey's widow: garrulous, well-connected on the Continent as well as in London, quite near to the court. But her receptions, Ruskin tells us, also 'gathered usually, with others, the literary and scientific men who had once known Abbotsford'.[6] There Ruskin met a young woman who attracted him. She was Charlotte Lockhart, Sir Walter Scott's granddaughter and the daughter of James Lockhart, the novelist's biographer. Ruskin had met the father and daughter before, in 1839, when he had dined at the Cockburns's.[7] Charlotte had been scarcely more than a child then, and Ruskin an undergraduate. Now the 'little dark-eyed, high-foreheaded' Charlotte was of age, and Ruskin looked at her with interest. His later recollections of their meetings at Lady Davy's are confused, and it is not now possible to estimate the relations between them. They were, in an empty kind of way, romantic. But they had nothing to say to each other. 'I could never contrive to come to any serious speech with her,' says *Præterita*.[8] He wrote to Charlotte instead, in letters which have not survived. Some of them were probably sent from Ambleside, where Ruskin went with George Hobbs in March of 1847. At the Salutation Inn he sat down to write a book review that had been commissioned by Charlotte's father. Lockhart was eminent in what Ruskin called 'the old Scott and John Murray circle' not only by virtue of his biography but also by his editorship of the *Quarterly Review*.[9] He had asked Ruskin to write about Lord Lindsay's *Sketches of the History of Christian Art*. The invitation was somehow confused with the young critic's feelings for his daughter; and so, as *Præterita* sardonically records, Ruskin 'with my usual wisdom in such matters, went away into Cumberland to recommend myself to her by writing a *Quarterly* review'.[10]

Lord Lindsay's book had been on Ruskin's mind. He had heard of it long before its publication. In 1845 he had written to his father from Florence asking him to enquire of George Richmond what it would contain, 'for the artists here talk very much about what he is going to do & write about old art . . .'.[11] Ruskin had thought that Lindsay's plans 'may in some degree influence me in the direction I give to parts of my book'.[12] Richmond had replied to John James that he liked Lord Lindsay, admired his scholarship and that his book was to be 'a history of Christian art from the revival of paintings up to the time of Raphael'.[13] But *Modern Painters* II was not affected by Lindsay's plans. We should not think of the two authors as being in competition. Ruskin had already become so individual a writer that the question of rivalry simply did not arise. He and Lindsay had similar interests. Lindsay is referred to in Ruskin's books, always favourably, for years to come. They met occasionally at meetings of the Arundel Society and the like, but struck no sparks from each other. Ruskin's review is rather prophetic of their relationship. It is flat, measured, and anonymous. It strikes the manner of the current reviewers only too successfully. Were it not that the sentiments were so accordant with *Modern Painters* II one would hardly know that it was by Ruskin. It is significant that Lockhart asked him to 'cut out all my best bits'.[14] The editor also excised a hostile reference to the architectural writer Gally Knight, who was a John Murray author. Ruskin tells us that 'this first clear insight into the arts of bookselling and reviewing made me permanently distrustful of both trades': and though he was to notice Sir Charles Eastlake's writing for the *Quarterly* he never thereafter reviewed a book in his life.[15]

Ruskin chose the romantic setting of Ambleside for the mundane task of his book review to separate himself from distractions in London. He also, consciously or half-consciously, went there to test his feelings for Charlotte Lockhart. As things turned out, any burgeoning love or distant contemplation of her 'harebell-like' beauty was swept away by a deadening depression of his spirits.[16] *Præterita* records: 'I fell into a state of despondency till then unknown to me, and of which I knew not the like again till fourteen years afterwards.'[17] Ruskin's autobiography, pledged to avoid painful memories, says no more. But the cause of his depression in the Lake District, where he balanced sentences in the mornings and rowed every afternoon amidst 'black water — as still as death; — lonely, rocky islets — leafless woods — or worse than leafless — the brown oak-foliage lying dead upon them; gray sky; — far-off, wild, dark, dismal moorlands', was the thought of Adèle Domecq.[18] His parents knew of his interest in Charlotte. But they simply feared the effect Adèle still had on him. Ruskin could only speak of her to his parents in broad hints. 'It makes me melancholy with thinking of 1838,' he told his mother.[19] That was when he had last been at Ambleside, when he had most suffered from love nearly ten years before. Just as he had decided to recommend himself to Adèle by his writing, so he had recently sought to impress Charlotte. But the memory of the waste and futility of his love for the French girl now made Charlotte appear trivial. When he returned to Denmark Hill from the Lakes John James realized what was wrong with his son and saw how long-lasting had been the effects of Adèle's disastrous intrusion into their lives. He wrote frankly to a friend that 'the passion however was powerful and almost threatened my son's life — various journies abroad have scarcely dissipated his chagrin nor repaired his health . . .'.[20]

The recipient of this letter was George Gray, John James's old business friend from Perth; and the subject of his son's affections was particularly in his mind because a guest at Denmark Hill was Gray's daughter Euphemia, 'Effie', the girl Ruskin would eventually marry. John James had immediately sensed that the presence of the most attractive Effie might add a further complication to Ruskin's desolation over Adèle and uncertain attitudes towards Charlotte. His early suspicions turned out to be correct, as in the three or four weeks to come the two young people came to know each other. It is important that the three affections of Ruskin's young days — Adèle, Charlotte, Effie — were present in his mind concurrently during these weeks. For her part, Effie did not at first think that John's affairs of the heart had anything to do with her. The letters she sent to Perth afford amused

glimpses of the (to her) bizarre household at Denmark Hill together
with overawed accounts of Ruskin's visits to town:

> I am enjoying myself exceedingly although in a quiet way, Mr
> Ruskin is as kind as ever and as droll — Mrs Ruskin is the same but I
> think she is beginning to feel old age a good deal, she sleeps so badly
> during the night that she falls asleep in the evenings. She is always
> saying that she is afraid I will weary with her but we get on
> admirably and she is always giving me good *advices* which I would
> repeat had I not so much news to tell you. John I see very little of
> excepting in the evening as he is so much engaged but he seems I
> think to be getting very celebrated in the literary world and to be
> much taken notice of. On Saturday he was at a grand reunion of Sir
> R. Peel's where everyone was, the Duke of Cambridge was there
> boring everybody with his noise. Sir Robert Peel and Lady Peel
> were there the whole time and extremely affable. On Friday John is
> going to a private view of the Royal Academy, the ticket is sent to
> him by 'Turner' who is one of the 30 Academicians who have a
> ticket at their disposal so that it is the highest compliment paid to
> any man in London. They have got home a very fine Picture by the
> above artist yesterday of Venice which is the largest they have and
> must have cost *something* . . . The Cuisine here is conducted admir-
> ably . . . Mrs Ruskin approves most graciously of my toilette, she
> says I am well dressed without being at all fine or extravagant . . .[21]

Since her London holiday in 1841, when little 'Phemy' had challenged Ruskin to write the fairy story that became *The King of the
Golden River,* he had met her only twice, and then briefly. The first
occasion was in 1843, when Effie was fifteen, and stayed at Denmark
Hill with her brother George. The second was a visit she had made in
the previous year, just before the publication of *Modern Painters* II, and
probably before the time when Ruskin had met Charlotte at Lady
Davy's. Now, in this spring of 1847, she presented a more adult charm
and confidence. She had left her school, Avonbank, near Stratford-
on-Avon, quite well-read and with musical accomplishments; she had
helped her mother to manage a large house and family; she knew she
was attractive and she knew what it was to have admirers. From
Effie's lively letters to Perth we see that she was inclined to laugh a
little at John's evident lack of interest in Charlotte:

> Mrs Ruskin told me of John's affaire the first night I came but I did
> not tell you as I thought she perhaps did not wish it to be known but
> she did not tell me who the Lady is and John never hints of her. He is

13. Euphemia Ruskin, by John Ruskin, 1848 or 1850.

the strangest being I ever saw, for a lover, he never goes out without grumbling and I fancy the young lady cannot be in London . . .[22]

This was written on 4 May, shortly after Effie arrived at Denmark Hill. She could not at first decide about Ruskin. On the one hand she thought of him as 'such a queer being, he hates going out and likes painting all day';[23] on the other, she was impressed by his fame and brilliance. It took her only a little time to become relaxed in his company. She then saw his charm and came to welcome his attentions. For Ruskin also relaxed. Pleasing Effie was a pleasure to him. He put aside his objections to poetry in order to present the stanzas *For a Birthday in May* on her nineteenth anniversary. He drew her portrait.

Together they went to the opera to hear Jenny Lind. Charlotte Lockhart did not exist. John and Effie's fate was being cast. They slipped into romance because they enjoyed each other but also because there was an atmosphere of betrothal all around them. Mary Richardson had just left her adopted home in Denmark Hill to marry the lawyer Parker Bolding, a connection of the Scottish Richardson family. Ruskin's near contemporary at Christ Church, Henry Liddell, came out to dine. He brought with him his bride Lorina: she, like Effie, was nineteen years of age. Suddenly the atmosphere at Denmark Hill was youthful. Charles Newton came for the night and delighted Effie: 'He amuses us beyond expression and went on with John this morning, he is a great genius.'[24] Another guest was young William Macdonald, who is tantalizingly described in *Præterita* as 'the son of an old friend, perhaps flame, of my father's, Mrs Farquharson'.[25] Ruskin hardly knew Macdonald, but he now arranged to go to stay with him at his hunting lodge in the Highlands later that summer. Ruskin was no sportsman, but his journey to the Highlands would inevitably take him past Effie's home in Perth. It was almost a rendezvous, almost a declaration. Macdonald was later the best man at their wedding.

Effie was due to return to Scotland. John would go there later in the summer, but he first had an engagement at a meeting of the British Association in Oxford: he was to attend the geological section of this learned conference. We do not know how the two young people parted, but it seems that Ruskin was agitated by something that was not love. One querulous and unhappy letter survives from this date. Writing to his friend Mary Russell Mitford, the gentle author of *Our Village,* he announced that

> I have most foolishly accepted evening invitations, and made morning calls, these last four months, until I am fevered by the friction. I have done no good, incurred many obligations, and suffered an incalculable harm. I know not what is the matter with me, but the people seem to have put a chill on me, and taken my life out of me. I feel alike uncertain and incapable of purpose, and look to the cottage on Loch Tay not as an enjoyment, but a *burrow*.[26]

This does not seem the mood of a man who is optimistically in love: more the opposite; and when Ruskin arrived in Oxford the pall of his Ambleside depression once again settled on him. His pleasures with Effie were forgotten, replaced with the sense of failure and frustration, the twin memory of his disappointment with his university career and his love of Adèle. He now wrote to his parents:

I am not able to write a full account of all I see, to amuse you, for I find it necessary to keep as quiet as I can, and I fear it would only annoy you to be told of all the invitations I refuse, and all the interesting matters in which I take no part. There is nothing for it but throwing one's self into the stream, and going down with one's arms under water, ready to be carried anywhere, or do anything. My friends are all busy, and tired to death. All the members of my section, but especially Forbes, Sedgwick, Murchison and Lord Northampton — and of course Buckland, are as kind to me as men can be; but I am tormented by the perpetual feeling of being in everybody's way. The recollections of the place, too, and the being in my old rooms, make me very miserable. I have not one moment of profitably spent time to look back to while I was here, and much useless labour and disappointed hope; and I can neither bear the excitement of being in the society where the play of mind is constant, and rolls *over* me like heavy wheels, nor the pain of being alone. I get away in the evenings into the hayfields about Cumnor, and rest; but then my failing sight plagues me. I cannot look at anything as I used to do, and the evening sky is covered with swimming strings and eels . . .[27]

Practically all the period of Ruskin's courtship was one of neurasthenic depression, of great worry about his health and his future. This return to Oxford threw him into an illness that seems as much nervous as physical. He felt no better when he returned to London. Quiet pursuits at Denmark Hill failed to restore his spirits. Eventually it was decided that he should return to Dr Jephson's establishment at Leamington Spa. Once again Ruskin submitted himself to the regime that had seemed helpful after his breakdown in 1841. At that time he had written *The King of the Golden River* for Effie; during this stay he found no comparable amusement. The diary reveals that he drew, botanized, and worked on his second commission from the *Quarterly Review,* an account of Charles Eastlake's *Materials for a History of Oil Painting.* But the diary now gives the impression of boredom rather than of agitation, and only once among its flat descriptions do Effie's initials indicate that Ruskin was, perhaps, a lover.

I have spent a somewhat profitless day; owing, as I think, to coldness and wandering of thought at morning prayers. I must watch if this be always the case. After drawing at Warwick Castle, I went over there again in the afternoon, and walked some distance on the road beyond, past the sixth milestone from Stratford (thinking much more of ECG than of Shakespeare, by the bye). There was much most beautiful in the fresh meadows on each side of the

road; and a little divergence from it, once, brought me to the side of
the Avon, a noiseless, yet not lazy stream, lying like the inlet of a
lake between shadowy groups and lines of elm and aspen, quiet and
something sad. [28]

At some point in the months that Ruskin spent at Jephson's he was
joined by William Macdonald. His later recollection was that the
young Scotsman had also come to take a cure. It is more likely that he
had called on his way from London, and was encouraging Ruskin to
come up to his shooting lodge at Crossmount. From this point Macdonald began to have a kind of presiding influence over Ruskin's
courtship. Without him, Ruskin probably would not have gone to
Scotland to woo Effie in her own home. Eventually Jephson dis-
charged him and he travelled north. At Dunbar, where he arrived on
18 August, he made a remarkable drawing of seashore rocks that
(together with his review of Eastlake's book) is a significant part of the
early history of Pre-Raphaelitism. But art was not on his mind. After
finishing the drawing he felt 'dispirited and ready to seek for any
excitement this evening'. [29] A day or two later he was in Perth, where
he called on Effie's father at his office but made no attempt to see her.
That night his journal records,

> I have had the saddest walk this afternoon I ever had in my life.
> Partly from my own pain in not seeing E.G. and in far greater
> degree, as I found by examining it thoroughly, from thinking that
> my own pain was perhaps much less than hers, not knowing what I
> know. And all this with a strange deadly shadow over everything,
> such as I hardly could comprehend; I expected to be touched by it,
> which I was not, but then came a horror of great darkness — not
> distress, but cold, fear and gloom. I am a little better now. After all,
> when the feelings have been so deadened by long time, I do not see
> how the effect on them can be anything else than this. [30]

In the days to come many letters were exchanged between Ruskin,
his father, his mother, and Mr Gray. The letters between Ruskin and
his parents discuss Effie's character and suitability: they also dispel
some lingering doubts about Charlotte Lockhart. At the Crossmount
shooting lodge, high in the hills above Lochs Rannoch and Tunnel,
Ruskin made one or two dispirited efforts to join in the sport. Soon he
gave up following the guns in favour of drawing thistles. Thus he
occupied himself for more than a fortnight before he wrote to the
Grays proposing to visit them at Bowerswell. They replied immediately; and at the beginning of October, three and a half months after he
had parted from Effie, Ruskin presented himself to her at the house
which once had belonged to his grandfather.

CHAPTER SEVEN

1847–1849

'A man should choose his wife as he does his destiny,' Ruskin later wrote, at the time when he was begging to marry Rose La Touche.[1] His marriage to Effie was to cast a shadow over all his later life, and indeed over all his biographers' attempts to explain that life. In October of 1847 that destiny was unimaginable. He had no conception of himself at the age of fifty, or sixty, no thought of himself as a man in the prime of life or in old age. No doubt he did not differ, in this, from any other young man who is about to wed. But there was nonetheless an element of calculation in his approach to a proposal. This he owed to his parents. He could not imagine his own marriage without thinking of the most perfect marriage known to him, that of his father and mother. Nor could John James and Margaret believe that the mould of his marriage might differ from their own. For this reason the atmosphere became charged with the difficulties of a union between two families. It was as if the young people were being asked to take more responsibility than they had thought of. When John arrived at Bowerswell Effie did not quite know what was going on. Her reaction was to be cool to the man who had not declared himself as her suitor. It was a difficult few days, in which everything was left unsaid. When Ruskin left to go back to London nothing had been clarified, for of course he wished to talk to his father. Back at Denmark Hill, with John James's blessing, he must have decided to be firm, to take his destiny in his own hands. Characteristically, he did so by writing. About a week after returning home he sent a letter to Effie that contained an offer of marriage. He was immediately accepted.

> It would be doing dishonour to my own love — to think that — when I had leave to express it — it was not intense enough to deserve — to compel — a return — No — I cannot doubt you any more — I feel that God has given you to me — and he gives no imperfect gifts — He will give me also the power to keep your heart — to fill it — to make it joyful — Oh my treasure — how shall I thank *Him*?

wrote Ruskin shortly afterwards.[2] Such letters that have survived from the engagement maintain, when they can, a religious tone and a pure, literary passion. It was in the nature of John and Effie's union,

unconsummated as it was, that the engagement should be as important as the marriage itself; and in their searching for higher things at
this time there was a happy seriousness they were not to know again.
However, there were times when Ruskin became worried and querulous. Unconsciously or not, he wished Effie to feel the same anxieties
for him that his parents felt. He may have been right to believe that his
intellectual labours had an effect on his second book review, a long and
thoughtful account of Charles Eastlake's *Materials for the History of Oil
Painting*. The effort he put into the research and writing was considerable, and when it was finished he felt the need to recuperate by the sea.
At Folkestone, slightly depressed, he wondered whether he had lost
the feeling for nature that had so possessed him in past years, when he
was writing *Modern Painters*. As the date of their wedding approached
more problems arose. The political revolutions on the Continent
greatly disturbed Ruskin. Effie's father's finances suddenly took a
sharper turn for the worse. He had speculated in railways, which in the
Ruskins's view was the height of imprudence. But Ruskin's real fear
was about himself: the belief that he was not well, and that in his
marriage he had to hold himself away from any kind of excitement.
Only a month before the wedding he addressed his fiancée in these
terms:

> There are moments when I think you have been a foolish girl to
> marry me — I am so nervous, and weak, and — dreamy — and
> really ill & broken down — compared to most men of my age, that
> you will have much to bear with and to dispense with — my father
> was for many years in the same state, and it ended in his secluding
> himself from all society but that which he sees in his own house I
> inherit his disposition — his infirmities, but not his power — while
> the morbid part of the feeling has been increased in me by the very
> solitude necessary to my father. At this moment, the dread I have of
> the bustle of Edinburgh is almost neutralizing the pleasure I have in
> the hope of being with you — it amounts to absolute *panic*. And —
> above all — in speaking of me to your friends, remember that I am
> really not well. Do not speak of me as able (though unwilling) to do
> this or that — but remember the real frets — that late hours — &
> excitement of all kinds are just as direct and certain *poison* to me as so
> much arsenic or hemlock and that the *least* thing excites me. From a
> child, if I turned from one side to another as I slept, the pulse was
> quickened instantly and this condition has of late years been aggra-
> vated by over work — and vexation. I have been four years doing
> the mischief — and it will be two or three at any rate, before, even

with the strictest care, it can be remedied.— Take care that you make people understand this as clearly as possible.[3]

*   *   *   *

Neither of Ruskin's parents wished to attend his wedding. Margaret Ruskin's horror of Bowerswell had not been dispelled by her son's engagement to the daughter of the house.[4] Nor did John James wish to return there. He wrote to Mr Gray,

> You expect that Mrs Ruskin and I should come to Perth and nothing can be more reasonable — I at once acknowledge we ought to come; but with Mrs Ruskin's feelings and prejudices I scarcely dare contend — for my own part, I am sincerely desirous of coming, but on the best consideration I can give the subject — I have decided to keep away . . . I can only exist in the absence of all excitement — that is by leading a quiet life — it is just 30 years this 1848 since I slept in a friend's house. I take mine ease at an inn continually and I go on with my business pretty well — I have thought I might come to Perth but if I were unwell — I should only be in the way — a marplot and a nuisance . . .[5]

There was some lameness in these excuses; and John James's attempts to be tactful to the Grays would always be at odds with his native bluntness. But as the wedding approached the elder Ruskins and Grays were content with their children's obvious contentment with each other. The celebrations in Perth were not spoilt by the absence of John James and Margaret Ruskin. To Effie, it made the occasion seem more like a family party for the Grays. None of John's old friends went to the wedding. One would have expected him to have asked Henry Acland or Richard Fall to be best man. Instead, William Macdonald performed this duty. Ruskin never saw him again after the wedding day. The ceremony itself was Scottish, and not elaborate. John and Effie were married in the drawing-room at Bowerswell on the morning of 10 April. The guests sat down to the wedding dinner after the couple left in the late afternoon. A letter from Mrs Gray to Margaret Ruskin describes how happy they looked as they drove off to Blair Atholl, where they were to spend the first night of their honeymoon.

The marriage was not consummated that night, nor ever afterwards. Both John and Effie wrote down why this was so at the end of the marriage six years later. Effie said in a letter to her father of 7 March 1854,

> I had never been told the duties of married persons to each other and knew little or nothing about their relations in the closest union on

earth. For days John talked about this relation to me but avowed no intention of making me his Wife. He alleged various reasons, Hatred to children, religious motives, a desire to preserve my beauty, and finally this last year told me his true reason (and this to me is as villainous as all the rest), that he had imagined women were quite different to what he saw I was, and that the reason he did not make me his Wife was because he was disgusted with my person the first evening April 10th.[6]

Ruskin's statement was written out for his lawyers at the time of the annulment. He states, no doubt correctly, that Effie had been upset by her father's financial problems, and that the fortnight before the wedding had been particularly harrowing for her.

Miss Gray appeared in a most weak and nervous state in consequence of this distress — and I was at first afraid of subjecting her system to any new trials — My own passion was also much subdued by anxiety; and I had no difficulty in refraining from consummation on the first night. On speaking to her on the subject the second night we agreed that it would be better to defer consummation for a little time. For my part I married in order to have a companion — not for passion's sake; and I was particularly anxious that my wife should be well and strong in order that she might be able to climb Swiss hills with me that year. I had seen much grief arise from the double excitement of possession and marriage travelling and was delighted to find that my wife seemed quite relieved at the suggestion. We tried thus living separate for some little time, and then agreed that we would continue to do so till my wife should be five and twenty, as we wished to travel a great deal — and thought that in five years time we should be settled for good.[7]

Thus, early in the honeymoon, something was decided between them. Effie's letter to her father further relates, 'After I began to see things better I argued with him and took the Bible but he soon silenced me and I was not sufficiently awake to what position I was in. Then he said after six years he would marry me, when I was 25.'[8] John's deposition says:

It may be thought strange that I *could* abstain from a woman who to most people was so attractive. But though her face was beautiful, her person was not formed to excite passion. On the contrary, there were certain circumstances in her person which completely checked it. I did not think either, that there could be anything in my own person particularly attractive to *her*: but believed that she loved me, as I loved her, with little mingling of desire.[9]

It is not clear from these accounts when it was that Ruskin said he would consummate the marriage when Effie was twenty-five: her phrase 'after I began to see things better' surely refers to some time later than the honeymoon. She probably began to argue with Ruskin about their sexual life after she and her husband visited France that summer: only then did she realize the extent to which he was bound to his parents rather than to her. The matter of Ruskin's 'disgust' with Effie's body is mysterious. There is no evidence, apart from his, to suggest that Effie was in any way malformed. The doctors who examined her at the time of the annulment reported, 'We found that the usual signs of virginity are perfect and that she is naturally and properly formed and there are no impediments on her part to a proper consummation of the marriage.'[10] Later in life, she bore Millais eight children. One must enquire what deficiencies there might have been in Ruskin himself, or whether he held ignorant or even fantastic notions of femininity. He might have been impotent. Or he might have been rendered impotent by something which he, in his ignorance of women, found shocking. It is possible that Effie was menstruating on their wedding night. But is it possible that Ruskin could still believe menstruation to be abnormal after six years of marriage? He and Effie shared a bed during all this time. We cannot now expect to know what Ruskin's sexual feelings were. But it is fair to say that on his wedding night his sexual impulses were in some part limited, or directed, by his ignorance of sexual matters. One wonders what John James had ever told him. Ruskin's father was a direct man, and there is ample evidence that he was no prude. Ruskin must have heard discussion of sex at university, if not at school. And would he not have gathered something of what girls are like from Mary Richardson, who came to Herne Hill when she was fourteen, and he ten?

Ignorance and shyness affected John and Effie's honeymoon. This was no exceptional thing in many young married couples. But in the Ruskins's marriage the things that were misunderstood, or never said, hardened into the unpleasant principles of the union. We know of one thing that was vehemently stated. When Effie's letter to her father mentions 'hatred to children' she was speaking of her husband's aversion to babies. After middle age Ruskin liked babies as much as people normally do: but in his earlier years he found them repulsive. Sometimes he describes his dislike with a humorous note that makes one suspect that there was pretence in his hatred of the newly-born. More often one is struck by the weirdness of his attitude. He refused to go to see his cousin Mary's child. Effie then wrote: 'I tried to enforce on John that we ought to call on her, but he won't as he says he can't

bear lumps of *putty* as he terms babies . . .'[11] Effie later reported
when she finally prevailed,

> John allows it to be passable for a baby because it has eyes like rat's
> fur and he likes it a little because it is not like a baby at all, but has a
> black face like a mouldy walnut, which is a great deal for him as it is
> quite against his principles to admire any of them at all . . .[12]

Ruskin claimed that it made him sick to be in the same room as Henry
Acland's baby. It is possible that the revulsion he felt was connected in
his mind with sexual intercourse. And other interpretations are possible. But Effie was unable to help Ruskin out of his psychological
difficulties. She was baffled: and as the marriage went on, her baffle-
ment was transformed to a bitter sense of the injustice and unnaturalness of her own sexual unhappiness.

*   *   *   *

John and Effie toured in the Highlands for a few days. It was early in
the season and the inns were empty. From Scotland they went to
Keswick, whose vicar's sermons Ruskin admired.[13] As his father was
in Liverpool on business, Ruskin invited him to come to the Lakes.
This John James declined. The young couple returned to London three
weeks after their wedding day. A splendid reception awaited them at
Denmark Hill. The head gardener was at the gate with a bouquet of
orange blossom for Effie: he, Margaret Ruskin and all the other
servants welcomed the bride to her new home. A German band (John
James's favourite music) played in the garden. There was a celebration
dinner. Effie, John James wrote to Mr Gray, was

> . . . very well and in her usual spirits or way which we never wish
> to see changed — my son is stouter and better than we have ever
> seen him in the whole course of his Life — They are in appearance
> and I doubt not in reality extremely happy and I trust the union will
> prove not only a source of happiness to them but of satisfaction and
> comfort to us all . . .[14]

Effie was able to write to her mother that Mrs Ruskin 'bids me say
how happy she is to have me here and she hopes I will feel quite a
daughter to her'.[15] In the next few days old Mrs Ruskin gave Effie so
many presents, mainly household treasures, that the girl became
embarrassed. Their purpose was functional. Mrs Ruskin said that she
might as well have them now since they would in any case be left to

her. The young Ruskins were now using the top floor of Denmark Hill while John James was looking for somewhere they could live. This was not to be in the Denmark Hill area. John James was conscious that his son was famous, would become more famous, and that he would now need to entertain in some style. He accordingly searched for properties in the most fashionable parts of London.

Effie was a social success. She first appeared in public at the private views in May of the Royal Academy summer exhibition and the exhibition of the Old Water-Colour Society. The first people she met as a married woman were artists: Copley Fielding, Clarkson Stanfield, David Roberts, Landseer and Prout. One day she and John went to breakfast at Samuel Rogers's, where the old poet introduced her to those knowing, witty and well-known *littérateurs* whose company he most enjoyed. Ruskin took her away from the party quite early. On an impulse he decided to call on Turner. From Rogers's elegant rooms in St James's Place they went to the painter's dirty, shuttered house in Queen Anne Street. The door was at length opened by Turner himself. Effie was taken aback by his bare and miserly accommodation: but warmed to him as he produced wine, drank her health, then took her to see his painting of *The Fighting Téméraire*. A few days later Lady Davy, in whose house Ruskin had met Charlotte Lockhart, gave a dinner in honour of the newly married couple. Lockhart himself was there, and the rest of the company was no less distinguished. Around the table were Lord Lansdowne, a member of the Cabinet and a trustee of the National Gallery; Walter Hook, the famous vicar of Leeds, now half-way through the eight volumes of his *Dictionary of Ecclesiastical Biography*; and Henry Hallam, the mediæval historian for whose son Tennyson had written *In Memoriam*. Effie was not in the least over-whelmed by such men, and they found her charming. Invitations multiplied. John James Ruskin was pleased with the way that John and Effie had begun to spend their evenings. He told Mr Gray, 'I am glad to see Phemy gets John to go out a little. He has met with some of the first men for some years back but he is very indifferent to general Society and reluctantly acknowledges great attentions shown to him and refuses one half . . .'[16]

*   *   *   *

Months before the wedding, it had been decided that John and Effie, together with Mr and Mrs Ruskin, would go on a continental tour in the summer. The plan was abandoned as the news came to England of the 1848 revolutions in Europe. Republican movements were so widespread that it seemed as if the whole of Europe would soon be at war. At the beginning of March, Ruskin had thought that he should marry as quickly as possible and set off for Switzerland immediately. Since Savoy, with other parts of Charles Albert's kingdom, Piedmont and Sardinia, was at war with Austria, it was now dangerous to travel to Chamonix, the place Ruskin most wished to show Effie. The earlier part of their marriage was overshadowed by political uncertainties. On their wedding day, the Chartists had marched to Westminster in demand of reform. The Bourbon monarchy had collapsed. The streets of Paris were barricaded by revolutionaries: Louis-Philippe and his queen had fled to England. By the summer, Hungary and all of the Lombardo-Veneto had revolted against Austrian rule. Manin's republic had been declared in Venice. All this was greatly disturbing to the Ruskins. It was republicanism, therefore evil. And what would be the consequences for the wine trade? Ruskin feared that it might be ten years before they could travel freely in Europe again. He was aware, of course, that the Napoleonic wars had kept Turner at home for just as long. And so, with much political foreboding, the Ruskins decided to take their summer tour in a calmer atmosphere, visiting the cathedrals of southern England.

Now began the period when Ruskin was most absorbed in architecture, the years of *The Seven Lamps* and *The Stones of Venice*. It was a time of deepening religious and political consciousness, but it coincided with his marriage, a time of human and personal failure. During his marriage Ruskin was thoughtless and insensitive to others as at no other period of his life. It was as though he had entered some strange second adolescence, learning rapidly but failing to be adult. Effie Ruskin now had to follow her husband as he pursued what to her were eccentric interests. Before going on the family tour round the English cathedrals, John and Effie spent a fortnight in Dover. Thence they proceeded to Oxford, calling on Miss Mitford on the way. They had been invited to stay at the Aclands's house in Broad Street. There, Ruskin took the liberties allowed to an old friend. He ignored the Aclands's baby, argued vehemently against Henry Acland's high church leanings, and read a book while they were at a concert. From Oxford John and Effie went on to a rendezvous with the elder Ruskins in Salisbury. The weather was bad. Salisbury Cathedral was damp. John began coughing badly and was annoyed at his drawings. A family expedition to see a new church at Wilton was not a success. John grumbled, his mother scolded and his father fussed and interfered. Effie was astonished to see how all three Ruskins behaved. Finally John took to his bed, where he remained for a week while Effie slept in a different room. Mrs Ruskin also had a cold and John James was suffering from stomach upsets. Effie became irritated and lost her temper with her mother-in-law. For this outburst Ruskin gravely rebuked her. The holiday became grimmer and it seemed best to go home. Very soon the whole party returned to Denmark Hill.

In such circumstances Ruskin had been meditating his work on building. He had not been engaged on a book since the spring of 1846, when he finished the second volume of *Modern Painters*. That summer's continental tour had produced many architectural notes, probably as a relaxation from his labours on the Italian primitives and Tintoretto. From that time until his wedding the thought of an architectural book had remained with him. His notes were of a practical and visual type, but in a current diary we find an undated passage that indicates the themes that also occupied him:

> Expression of emotion in Architecture as Monastic — peaceful — threatening — mysterious — proud — enthusiastic.
> Expression of ambition — Difficulty cutting, vaulting, King's College, etc., raising of spires, etc.
> Consider luscious architecture: How far beautiful.
> General style. What constitutes its greatness. First, mere labour; patience, skill and devotion (Sacrifice). Then labour of *thinking* men; if nothing be lost, nothing valueless; consider if under this head one might not have a 'Spirit of Husbandry' (consider also, awe and mystery and their spirit under head of Power). Yet it is fine to see work for work's sake, or rather for completion of a system sometimes.[17]

Readers of *The Seven Lamps of Architecture* will recognize that in these jottings lie the first thoughts of that famous book, and may reflect on the ability of Ruskin's architectural writings to make numinous notions rather specific. Perhaps this was because much of what he now wrote on architecture was derived from urgent personal experience. While preparing the second volume of *Modern Painters*, he had been appalled by the destruction of ancient buildings. A long note to the second volume's chapter on the 'Theoretical Faculty' — which Ruskin later, in 1883, cancelled in despair that his warnings had not been heeded — lists some of the recent losses. All had personal associations for him. The old houses at Beauvais, the wooden loggias at Geneva, mediæval houses at Tours and the church of St Nicholas at Rouen had all gone. Ruskin recounts how the 'restoration' of the old Baptistery at Pisa had been done so clumsily and cheaply that the building was ruined.[18] His discovery of ancient art brought with it a furious realization that the modern world had no regard for its safety. In Pisa, he saw bricklayers knocking down a wall in the Campo Santo on which frescoes had been painted. In Florence, he found that the old street running towards the cathedral had been torn down: in its place was a row of kiosks selling knick-knacks and souvenirs. The old refectory of Santa Croce was being used as a carpet factory. Ruskin saw rain beating through the windows of the Arena Chapel in Padua and dripping into buckets in the Scuola di San Rocco. It filled him with a literally religious horror. In a letter to his father in 1845 he broke into a quotation from Revelation:

> I think verily the Devil is come down upon earth, having great wrath, because he knoweth that he hath but a short time. And a short time he will have if he goes on at this rate, for in ten years more there will be nothing in the world but eating-houses and gambling houses and worse . . . the French condemned the Convent of San Marco where I am just going, and all the pictures of Fra Angelico were only saved by their being driven out . . .[19]

A part of Ruskin's hatred of republicanism was that he felt that it would bring with it the destruction of art and of ancient buildings. In such a frame of mind *The Seven Lamps of Architecture* was written, and painting for the moment abandoned. The preface to its first edition explains that *Modern Painters* could not yet be concluded

> . . . owing to the necessity under which the writer felt himself, of obtaining as many memoranda as possible of mediæval buildings in Italy and Normandy, now in the process of destruction, before that destruction should be consummated by the Restorer, or Revolutionist.[20]

Ruskin was so anxious to get on with *The Seven Lamps* that he decided that he and Effie should go to France. This they did, attended by George Hobbs, almost as soon as they came home from the dismal holiday in Salisbury. John James Ruskin accompanied them to Boulogne, then crossed the Channel back to England. The French port was full of rumours of war. An Englishman, going home, told them that Paris was full of soldiers. It was said that France had declared war on Austria, and that an army had marched over the Alps. John and Effie went by rail from Boulogne to Abbeville. Here Ruskin began work. 'I was dancing round the table this forenoon', he wrote to John James,

. . . in rapture with the porch here — far beyond all my memories
or anticipation — perfectly superb, and all the houses more fantastic, more exquisite than ever; alas! not all, for there is not a street
without fatal marks of restoration, and in twenty years it is plain
that not a vestige of Abbeville, or indeed of any old French town
will be left . . . I got into a cafe and have been doing my best to draw
the cathedral porch; but alas, it is not so easily done. I seem born to
conceive what I cannot execute, recommend what I cannot obtain,
and mourn over what I cannot save.[21]

Effie was delighted with her first visit to France. Like Ruskin, she
enjoyed being abroad: unlike him, she took pleasure in practising
foreign languages. She was a little upset to attend her first mass, but
enjoyed the attentions given to them at the best hotel, where they were
the only guests. Most of her time was spent idly. Ruskin worked
assiduously on Norman architecture. She sat on a camp stool while he
drew, measured, and took notes of buildings. In the evenings she was
entrusted with making a fair copy of these notes. The political situation and the threat of war seemed real, yet distant. Ruskin began to
think that he might venture further into Europe, and even take his
parents to Italy. As he now wrote to John James, 'I trust the negotiations which France and England have together undertaken will pacify
all and that we may have another look at Venice yet before the Doge's
palace is bombarded.'[22]

From Abbeville John and Effie went on to Rouen. Here was one of
those cities, 'tutresses of all I know', that Ruskin believed governed his
life's work, and should always be approached with reverence. To a
student such as himself, Abbeville was therefore 'the preface and
interpretation of Rouen'.[23] Ruskin had been to the Norman capital in
1835, 1840, 1842 and 1844, on the summer tours with his parents that
had formed his taste. All through his life Ruskin would reminisce
about his walks through the city in 1842 in search of the Turnerian site
for a plate in The Rivers of France, and how in 1857 he had been able to
buy the original drawing. Rouen Cathedral he loved more than any
other northern church: there and in the churches of St Nicholas, St
Maclou, St Ouen, St Patrice and St Vincent, he nourished the non-
Italian part of his architectural sensibility. This belonged to his youth
as much as to his maturity, and he associated Rouen as much with
Prout as with Turner. It was with Prout in mind that he wrote of it as

. . . a city altogether inestimable for its retention of a mediæval
character in the infinitely varied streets in which one half of the
existing and inhabited houses date from the fifteenth or early six-

14. John James Ruskin, by George Richmond, 1848.

teenth century, and the only town left in France in which the effect of old French domestic architecture can yet be seen in its collective groups.[24]

The greater, therefore, was his rage when he and his wife arrived there in 1848. Effie reported to her parents:

John is perfectly frantic with the spirit of restoration here, and at other places the men actually before our eyes knocking down the time worn black with age pinnacles and sticking up in their place new stone ones to be carved at some future time . . . John is going to have some daguerrotypes taken of the churches as long as they are standing . . . he says he is quite happy in seeing I enjoy myself and if it were not for my gentle mediation he would certainly do something desperate and get put in prison for knocking some of the workmen off the scaffolding.[25]

In these trying conditions, in Rouen, at Falaise, Avranches, at Mont St Michel, Bayeux, Caen and Honfleur, sometimes patiently but more often urgently, Ruskin filled the eight notebooks and hundreds of sheets of drawing paper that were the basis of *The Seven Lamps of Architecture*. Absorbed in his work, he took little notice of Effie. It was some time before he noticed that she had become bored with sitting in churches. He was not sufficiently interested in her family problems. While they were in France, John James had been unhelpful with the problem of finding her brother a commercial position. Her father's affairs had not improved, and now she learnt that her Aunt Jessie was seriously ill. Of all this, Ruskin wrote to his father with the honesty of the totally self-engrossed:

Even when poor Effie was crying last night I felt it by no means as a husband should — but rather a bore — however I comforted her in a very dutiful way — but it may be as well — perhaps on the other hand, that I am not easily worked on by these things.[26]

Effie was tired of France. She wanted to go back to England and then go to Scotland to see her family. Ruskin said that his own health would not permit a winter journey to Scotland, but that she ought to go there with a companion. There the matter rested, for Ruskin now made an impulsive decision to visit Paris. It might be dangerous, and he had no love for the city, but he felt that he should compare Notre Dame with the northern churches. The Ruskins arrived in Paris in the aftermath of fighting. Their trunks were opened and searched for weapons. Few shops were open, the Tuileries deserted. There were marks of fighting in the street. The republican government had reorganized the Louvre in a manner which infuriated Ruskin. Paris was, he found, as a result of the recent 'slaughterous and dishonest contest', a society plunged in 'gloom without the meanest effort at the forced gaiety which once disguised it'.[27] A week later the Ruskins were back in Denmark Hill.

CHAPTER EIGHT

1849–1850

The house which John James Ruskin had found for John and Effie, and which he had taken on a three-year lease, was in Mayfair. No. 31 Park Street was three doors away from Lady Davy's and looked out over the gardens of the Marquess of Westminster's Grosvenor House. Effie was excited by her new home and the smart brougham that her father-in-law had provided for her. Ruskin was less interested in these fashionable surroundings. He organized a study for himself in Park Street, but did not move all his books and effects from Denmark Hill. Nor was he ever to do so. He could not think of Park Street as his home, and often used to drive out to Denmark Hill to dine and stay the night. However, a good number of the Ruskins's evenings were spent at London social occasions of one kind or another. This could often be a point of contention. But there was not a simple contrast between a bookish husband and a gay young wife. There was an intellectual élite among these Mayfair gatherings which welcomed the Ruskins. It consisted of statesmen, writers, public personages connected with the fine arts and senior members of the Church of England. The Ruskins met, for instance, Henry Milman, now a canon of Westminster but shortly to become Dean of St Paul's, previously Professor of Poetry at Oxford and author of the scholarly *History of the Jews*. Milman was friendly with the historian Henry Hallam, whom Effie and John had met at Lady Davy's; and another friend of Milman's was Thomas Macaulay, the first two volumes of whose history of England had just appeared. The Ruskins met Macaulay at a party given by Sir Robert Inglis at his house in Bedford Square, where literary and political figures, both liberal and tory, met on friendly and slightly competitive terms.

In such houses Ruskin's acquaintance among the 'leading men', as his father termed them, might have been greatly increased. But he made little attempt to win friends in this society. He was rude to Milman, scorned Hallam and took no notice of Macaulay. He thought they were worldly, that they loved neither nature nor art. At Park Street he entertained old friends from Christ Church days like Lord Eastnor and Osborne Gordon. One night the Richmonds came to dinner to eat snipe from Mr Telford's estate. It was the sort of evening

Ruskin would have enjoyed, if only it had been at Denmark Hill.
Towards the end of 1848 he began to press Effie to spend more time in
his old family home. While they were staying there for Christmas and
the New Year of 1849 Effie's relations with her parents-in-law suddenly worsened. She fell foul of Mrs Ruskin. She became ill, lost her
appetite, and felt miserable. One day Mrs Ruskin found her in tears
when she should have been getting ready for dinner, and scolded her.
Soon she developed a feverish cold and began coughing badly. The
elder Ruskins treated her illnesses as self-indulgences. They held it
against her that she did not come downstairs to attend their New
Year's dinner party, when Joseph Severn, Tom Richmond (George's
brother), and Turner were among the guests. Try as she might, Effie
could not get better. Her own doctor and the Ruskins's family doctor
gave her contradictory advice. Then her mother came to stay. Effie
suddenly saw a way to recover her spirits. She decided to return to
Scotland with her mother, leaving her husband behind in London.
Ruskin, hard at work on *The Seven Lamps of Architecture*, was not at all
displeased to be left in peace. He immediately moved out of Park
Street and returned to Denmark Hill. As things turned out, he was not
to see his wife for another nine months.

*   *   *   *

While Ruskin was living in Park Street he was invited to join the
council of the newly founded Arundel Society. Its originators were
C. H. Bellenden Kerr, Sir Charles Eastlake, Edmund Oldfield and
Aubrey Bezzi. We may think of them as the kind of men with whom
Ruskin had sporadic professional rather than social relations. Kerr was
a deaf and eccentric lawyer with artistic tastes. Edmund Oldfield was
Ruskin's schoolfriend at Dr Dale's who knew so much about Gothic
architecture: he now worked in the British Museum. Bezzi was the
Society's secretary. He had republican sympathies and had fled from
Italy with Panizzi, the future librarian of the British Museum: later on
he would become a member of the government of the kingdom of
Sardinia. Eastlake, a busy man, made little appearance at Arundel
Society meetings. The wary respect he and Ruskin felt for each other
had not yet been transmuted into open hostility.

The Society was begun with a didactic and æsthetic purpose. Its
founders had a partial model for their enterprise in the Society for the
Diffusion of Useful Knowledge, but their intention (so their prospectus announced) was to serve a revived interest in art by copying and

publishing reproductions of Italian paintings. Connoisseur-collectors who had assembled engravings after old masters in previous years had not had such an educational purpose. Nor had such connoisseurs commissioned engravings. The Arundel Society was to do this because it was their intention to concentrate on early painting rather than on the classical masters. The prospectus points out that

> . . . the materials for such instruction are abundant, but scattered, little accessible, and, in some instances, passing away. Of the frescoes of Giotto, Orcagna, Ghirlandajo, much of which has never been delineated, nor even properly described, is rapidly perishing.[1]

Other knowledgeable people who were asked to join the council of the Society at the same time as Ruskin were Samuel Rogers, Charles Newton, Lord Lansdowne and Lord Lindsay. They were Ruskin's natural colleagues. But he was in some measure the inspiration of the Society. A good number of its projected publications were taken from works described by Ruskin in the second volume of *Modern Painters*, such as Benozzo Gozzoli's frescoes of the *Journey of the Magi*, the Tintorettos in the Scuola di San Rocco, Fra Angelico's frescoes in San Marco and Ghirlandaio's in Santa Maria Novella. The Arundel Society was variously active until 1897. Ruskin was to write two monographs for it, *Giotto and his Works in Padua* (1853-60) and *Monuments of the Cavalli Family in the Church of Santa Anastasia, Verona* (1872); while its occasional publications in pamphlet form were to give him many ideas for the stream of pamphlets, illustrations and part-publications that he issued via Smith, Elder and, later, through his own publishing company.

★   ★   ★   ★

When Effie Ruskin went back to Bowerswell with her mother at the beginning of February 1849 she was still suffering from the illness that had come on her at Denmark Hill. She was tired, she suffered from feverish colds, her stomach was upset and she had blisters on her throat. We may believe that some of her complaints were generated by the strain of living with such a husband: but Margaret Ruskin knew that the girl had brought the illness on herself. Margaret was now beginning to think of the contrast between her own marriage, so immensely satisfying to her, and her son's. In one letter to John James she openly mentioned her disappointment, though to Ruskin himself

she as yet said nothing. At Bowerswell, the Gray family were suffering from bereavement. Effie's Aunt Jessie had died: now Effie lost her
seven-year-old brother Robert. She was still unwell herself. In these
circumstances she decided to stay with her family at Bowerswell and
not return to accompany the Ruskins on the continental tour they
planned to take that spring. This seemed sensible, if in some ways
unsatisfactory. Ruskin wanted to work in Switzerland. Effie needed
rest. And, as John James wrote to Mr Gray, it was not necessarily
relaxing to be with Ruskin when he was working.

> It may be his pleasure but to be with him is other people's toil — out
> of doors at any rate. They must however arrange their comings and
> goings with each other. They will no doubt settle down very
> delightfully at last pleased with some house at home and I hope
> allow you and me to come to hear them in chorus singing dulce
> dulce domum.[2]

Ruskin was finishing the last pages of *The Seven Lamps of Architecture* as he and his parents set off for the Continent in the middle of
April. He posted them to W. H. Harrison from Folkestone. Two of
the etchings for the book were bitten in his hotel bedroom at Dijon.
This year, the Ruskins were to be away for five months. The tour
provided material for the next volume of *Modern Painters*, though the
book would not appear for another five years. Ruskin dutifully wrote
to his wife during their separation. One is struck by the artificial
adoption of a romantic tone. The first letters emphasize how unreal his
marriage was, not based on any physical or emotional fact.

> Do you know, pet, it seems almost a dream to me that we have been
> married: I look forward to meeting you: and to your *next* bridal
> night: and to the time when I shall again draw your dress from your
> snowy shoulders: and lean my cheek upon them, as if you were still
> my betrothed only: and I had never held you in my arms. God bless
> you my dearest.[3]

It is hard to imagine what Effie might have made of such a declaration.
Was it a letter that announced physical intentions, or merely a flourish
by someone who had been reading poetry? The assurance that 'I look
forward to meeting you' was clearly untrue, since Ruskin was about to
spend some months in his favourite places with his parents, his favourite people. The more Effie thought about her situation the less it
seemed to her that she was truly married, in any way. She had strong

feelings for her own family yet the Ruskins tugged her away from them. She was too much put upon by the Ruskin parents and yet John Ruskin, her husband, in all ways eluded her. Ruskin himself could not understand this, nor begin to imagine what it might be like to be in Effie's position. Only a few days later he was writing to her in these terms:

> I often hear my father and mother saying — 'poor child — if she could but have thrown herself openly upon us, and trusted us, and would have made her ours, how happy she might have been: and how happy she might have made us all'. And indeed I long for you my pet: but I have much here to occupy me and keep me interested — and so I am able to bear the longing better perhaps than you, who have only the routine of home: I hope next summer I shall be able to make you happy in some way of your own.[4]

One explanation for Ruskin's behaviour toward Effie at this time is that like many artists he became withdrawn and egotistical when nurturing his responses to nature, or to art, in preparation for some creative effort. A curious piece of self-examination is recorded in his diary the day after he sent this letter to Effie.

> It is deserving of record that at this time, just on the point of coming in sight of the Alps, and that for the first time in three years — a moment which I had looked forward to, thinking I should be almost fainting with joy, and should want to lie down on the earth and take it in my arms — at this time, I say, I was irrevocably sulky and cross, because *George had not got me butter to my bread at Les Rousses*.[5]

Whatever else we may feel about this confession, it is important to realize that Ruskin was in pursuit of his previous Alpine experiences. He believed that he was at a nexus of his imaginative life. 'The sunset of today', he recorded on 3 June, 'sank upon me like the departure of youth.'[6] This was not merely a grandiose remark. Not for the first time, Ruskin was thinking of Wordsworth's *Immortality* óde.[7] Following the poem, he also considered whether the intensity of his earlier feelings for nature could not be recaptured. Ruskin's diary this spring and summer tells us time and again how he went back to places where he had been deeply moved in previous years. He sought out the same paths, the same resting places that he had last visited three years before and, more significantly, had known as a boy in 1835. The exercise was not only to observe the landscape and weather. It was also to observe his own responses, to try to stand outside himself as an æsthetic being.

Sometimes he used personal inducements to bring his mind to an artistic state. At Blonay, amid 'lovely scenes', he

> . . . required an effort to maintain the feeling — it was poetry while it lasted — and I felt that it was only while under it that one could draw or invent or give glory to any part of such a landscape. I repeated 'I am in *Switzerland*' over and over again, till the name brought back the true group of associations — and I felt I had a soul, like my boy's soul, once again. I have not insisted enough on this source of all great contemplative art. [8]

Such self-explorations are the source for the discussion of the æsthetic emotion found in the tenth chapter of part four of the third volume of *Modern Painters*. In that volume, as also in the fourth, there are many passages which derive from Ruskin's studies in 1849 at Vevey, Chamonix, the Rhone Valley and Zermatt. The books were not published until 1856, seven years later, and were written in 1855: but they take the experiences of 1849 as their starting point. A passage on grass in *Modern Painters*, quite famous in the nineteenth century, may be taken as an example. The 1849 diary entry at Vevey reads:

> I looked at the slope of different grass on the hill; and then at the waving heads near me. What a gift of God that is, I thought. Who could have dreamed of such a soft, green, continual tender clothing for the dark earth — the food of cattle, and of man. Think what poetry has come of its pastoral influence, what happiness from its everyday ministering, what life from its sustenance. Bread that strengtheneth man's heart — ah, well may the Psalmist number among God's excellencies, 'He maketh grass to grow upon the mountains'. [9]

Five years later, in the course of a discussion of mediæval landscape, and just after some suggestive remarks about grass in Dante, Ruskin's diary note becomes a set-piece:

> Go out, in the spring-time, among the meadows that slope from the shores of the Swiss lakes to the roots of their lower mountains. There, mingled with the taller gentians and the white narcissus, the grass grows deep and free; and as you follow the winding mountain paths, beneath arching boughs all veiled and dim with blossom, — paths that for ever droop and rise over the green banks and mounds sweeping down inscented undulation, steep to the blue water, studded here and there with new-mown heaps, filling all the air with fainter sweetness, — look up towards the higher hills, where the waves of everlasting green roll silently into their long inlets

among the shadows of the pines; and we may, perhaps, at last know
the meaning of those quiet words of the 147th Psalm, 'He maketh
grass to grow upon the mountains'.[10]

In such ways, this fruitful tour of 1849 was the first stimulus of
writing that would occupy Ruskin for the next decade. If he could
strike his mood in these months he was beautifully alert to all he saw:
mountains, wood anemones, the darkness of pine forests, or the flight
of the grey wagtail. To return once again to the diary:

Friday 4th May. — Half breakfasted at Chambery; started about
seven for St Laurent du Pont, thence up to the Chartreuse, and
walked down (all of us); which, however, being done in a hurry, I
little enjoyed. But a walk after dinner up to a small chapel, placed on
a waving group of mounds, covered with the most smooth and soft
sward, over whose sunny gold came the dark piny precipices of the
Chartreuse hills, gave me infinite pleasure. I had seen also for the
third time, by the Chartreuse torrent, the most wonderful of all
Alpine birds — a grey, fluttering stealthy creature, about the size of
a sparrow, but of colder grey, and more graceful, which haunts the
side of the fiercest torrents. There is something more strange in it
than in the seagull — *that* seems a powerful creature; and the power
of the sea, not of a kind so adverse, so hopelessly destructive; but
this small creature, silent, tender and light, almost like a moth in its
low and irregular flight, — almost touching with its wings the
crests of waves that would overthrow a granite wall, and haunting
the hollows of the black, cold, herbless rocks that are continually
shaken by their spray, has perhaps the nearest approach to the look
of a spiritual existence that I know in animal life.[11]

On many occasions during the summer of 1849 Ruskin chose to be
solitary among the Alps. But he was enlivened by the arrival in
Switzerland of his boyhood friend Richard Fall. Together with Couttet and George Hobbs, he and Fall went out on climbing expeditions.
At other times Ruskin left his parents for a few days and went with
George to draw and take daguerrotypes. He made notes on the angles
of various peaks, examined the flora, analysed the geology, ascertained the movements of glaciers, watched the streams and clouds.
Some of this material was gathered into the diary, but many other
notebooks were used. Apart from sketched memoranda Ruskin made
forty-seven drawings which were highly enough finished for him to
catalogue, a rare procedure with his own work. This was the last time
that he was to draw landscape consistently for a number of years. The

15. *La Cascade de la Folie, Chamouni*, by John Ruskin, 1849.

best known of the drawings is *La Cascade de la Folie, Chamouni* (Plate 15). It is highly detailed, dramatically unfolding a vista of mountain scenery beyond and high above the plunging waterfall. These drawings were used a few years later to write the chapter on aiguilles in the fourth volume of *Modern Painters*. A number were executed during a memorable few days, full of difficult climbing, when Couttet took Ruskin on *le tour de Mont Blanc*. The young Englishman and his guide went by St Gervais and Contamines over the Col du Bonhomme to Chapui: thence ascended to the Col de la Seigne, 8,000 feet high, where Ruskin drew, before proceeding to Courmayeur. They then went over the Col Ferret to Martigny, and from Martigny to Zermatt, where Ruskin made the study of the cliffs of the Matterhorn that enabled him to write the chapter 'On Precipices' in the fourth volume of *Modern Painters*. He then spent three days in Montanvert, where after a day's Alpine note-taking he wondered if he had ever enjoyed an evening so much in his life, sitting 'at the window quietly today watching the sunset and the vast flow of ice, welling down the gorge — a dark and billowy river — yet with the mountainous swell and lifted crests that the iron rocks have round it'.[12]

This summer among the Alps also set Ruskin to consider peasant economy and culture. In a diary entry at St Martin's we find the origin of the great chapter in *Modern Painters* IV, 'The Mountain Gloom'. Ruskin was thinking then

> . . . what a strange contrast there is between these lower valleys, with their ever-wrought richness mixed with signs of waste and disease, their wild noon-winds shaking their leaves into palsy, and the dark storms folding themselves about their steep mural precipices — between these and the pastoral green, pure aiguilles, and fleecy rain-clouds of Chamouni . . .[13]

Natural life both intermingled and contrasted with the social order in the Alps. The peasants were poor, wretchedly so. There was much goitre and cretinism. How could there be such human misery in such divinely fashioned surroundings? It was this 'melancholy knowledge', Ruskin confessed in *Præterita*, 'of the agricultural condition of the great Alpine chain which was the origin of the design of St George's Guild'.[14] But that was far in the future, and in 1849 Ruskin could not quite bring himself to think independently about social problems. He was so absorbed by nature that even the evidence of war left him only a cool observer. Chamonix is in Savoy. At this date Savoy, with Piedmont, was part of the kingdom of Sardinia. In the 1848 revolutions Charles Albert, the King of Sardinia, had fought against the Austrians. He had been defeated, had abdicated, and had given up his throne to his son Victor Emmanuel. The Ruskins saw the remains of Charles Albert's defeated army at Chambéry. John reported to Effie:

This place is full of soldiers, returned from the last battle: shabby fellows the Savoyard troops were always and look none the better for their campaign: and as the government cannot afford them new clothes, though it is getting them into some order again as fast as it can, they look slovenly and melancholy: more beggars on the road than ever, and the people seeming hard put to it — but a quiet and gentle people, and one that with a good religion, might be anything . . .[15]

In June, when John James Ruskin thought that he had never seen his son in better health, trouble started between the Ruskins and the Grays. Effie's illnesses were still troubling her. She decided to consult Dr James Simpson, Professor of Midwifery at the University of Edinburgh. It is possible that Simpson advised her to have children: he certainly did so later on. But when Effie wrote to Ruskin to tell him about the consultation she did not report to him what Simpson had thought. Ruskin was annoyed by this, and so were his parents. John James's letters to Perth changed from concern to condemnation: 'About your daughter Mrs Ruskin and myself must continue to be anxious and as I use no reserve I will confess to you that the feeling is mixed with sorrow and disappointment.'[16] Grievances were aired about Effie's clothes, housekeeping, and the like. For a little while, as this unpleasant correspondence continued, Ruskin was markedly kinder to his wife than his parents were. But it is plain that practically all his attention was given to the mountains, not to Effie's well-being. In the circumstances, Mr Gray showed great patience. He wrote to John James Ruskin,

If I may be permitted to hint a word by way of advice it would simply be that Mrs Ruskin and you should leave John and Phemy as much as possible to themselves — married people are rather restive under the control and supervision of parents tho' proceeding from the kindest and most affectionate motives.[17]

If this was generally so of married people, it was not so of John Ruskin. While he exchanged quite pleasant letters with his wife he made no attempt to calm the increasingly angry tone adopted by his father. Behind the whole quarrel was a simple question. Why was Effie not happier? Ruskin kept silent. One of John James's pleas was for complete frankness. Mr Gray wrote of how his daughter hated hypocrisy. But the sexual position of the young couple was unsuspected by the parents. Had Ruskin ordered Effie not to tell her mother that he refused to make love to her? A great deal was not discussed. As far as one can gather from the many letters now exchanged, neither family mentioned children. But they said many other things to each other, and on the Ruskins's side said them harshly. Towards the end of his stay in Switzerland Ruskin was writing to Effie's father with an extraordinary interpretation of her unhappiness:

> The state of her feelings I ascribe now, simply to bodily weakness: that is to say — and this is a serious and distressing admission — to a nervous disease affecting the brain. I do not know when the complaint first showed itself — but the first I saw of it was at Oxford after our journey to Dover: it showed itself then, as it does now, in tears and depression: being probably a more acute manifestation, in consequence of fatigue and excitement — of disease under which she has long been labouring . . . an illness bordering in many of its features on incipient insanity. [18]

Ruskin had not seen his wife since February. When, in late August, the Ruskins started to make plans to go home, the Grays were anxious that John should go to Perth to collect Effie. There was a simple reason for this. There was much gossip in Perth, as well there might be, about Effie's marriage. The Grays wanted John to be seen there with his wife. The elder Ruskins objected to this proposal and Effie, once more, received a most un-uxorious letter.

> As for your wish that I should come to Scotland — that is also perfectly natural — nor have I the slightest objection to come for you: only do not mistake womanly pride for womanly affection: You say that 'you should have thought the first thing I should have done after six months' absence, would have been to come for you'. Why, you foolish little puss, do you not see that part of my reason for wishing you to come to London was that I might get you a couple of days sooner: and do you not see also, that if love, instead of pride, had prompted your reply, you would never have thought of what I *ought* to do, or your *right* to ask, you would only have thought of being with me as soon as you could . . . [19]

In the event, however, Ruskin did go to Perth. He arrived there towards the end of September, thin, sunburnt, slightly distracted. Relations were bound to be difficult. There was embarrassment in the air, though Ruskin did not feel it. Now Effie made a suggestion that was both bold and sensible. She asked Ruskin to take her to Venice. It was perfectly possible. Nothing stood in their way. The bombardment of the city was over, Manin's republican government had fallen, and Venice was once more in Austrian hands. For Effie, the great advantage of going to Venice was that she could have John on her own. For Ruskin, too, there were good reasons for going there. He could continue his architectural studies at a time of relative political stability. He might never have another such opportunity. Dr Simpson was in favour of the plan. John James Ruskin wrote a sensible and generous letter giving them his blessing: he would, of course, be paying all their expenses. In this way the Ruskins's marriage was rescued for a time.

★   ★   ★   ★

Ruskin had scarcely been back in England for three weeks before setting off with Effie en route for Venice. Effie took a companion with her. This was Charlotte Ker, a Perth neighbour. In London, Effie got on perfectly well with the elder Ruskins. She busied herself with the exciting task of getting their two carriages ready, while Ruskin and George Hobbs packed books and daguerrotype equipment. From Boulogne, sometimes posting and sometimes travelling by rail, they travelled quickly towards Switzerland. Ruskin was at his most kind and charming. Effie wrote home with the news of her

> . . . first view of the Alps, the Plain of Geneva and the Lake seen from an elevation of 3,000 feet the most striking Panorama I ever beheld but curious to say I was not in the least surprised by the magnificence of the view as it was exactly like what I had always supposed it would be . . . John was excessively delighted to see how happy we were and went jumping about and executing *pas* that George and I agreed Taglioni would have stared her widest at.[20]

In the Alps, Effie and Charlotte were shocked by the condition of the peasantry. To have observed poverty in rural Scotland was no preparation for this. They saw children with no arms, women with huge goitres that had necklaces and crosses draped over them. The men were filthy and toothless. Chamonix was a cleaner village than most: it was one reason why the Ruskins stayed there so often. An arrangement had been made with Couttet to meet them there. He was delighted to see Ruskin again so soon, and even more delighted to meet Effie. Ruskin, alone, climbed up the Breven to a favourite site and took notes on the aiguilles across the valley. But he was conscious that his *Modern Painters* work would have to be put aside for architectural research in Venice. Abandoning his aiguilles, he took up a local ghost story instead. Some Chamonix children had been frightened by the apparition of a woman dressed all in black. Ruskin, who derived from Anne Strachan an interest in ghosts that would remain with him all his life, sought out these children. He talked to them, interrogated the local priest, and even organized the digging of a large hole at the place where the spectre had been seen.

The party had paused in Switzerland to allow time for Venice to recover from the cholera epidemic that had spread through the city during the siege. As they moved on to Milan the effects of war became apparent. Roads were closed, churches had been commandeered, provisions were scarce. Austrian and Croatian troops were everywhere. Ruskin's diary now becomes filled with architectural notes, while Effie's letters home are packed with social detail. In Milan she and Charlotte were hoping to set eyes on Field-Marshal Radetzky 'as he is a *decided* lion'.[21] Radetzky was the Civil and Military Governor of the Lombardo-Veneto, an elderly soldier who had commanded the Austrian army which suppressed the Italian nationalist revolts. In Milan, Effie was not sure of her political feelings. She declared, 'I am a thorough Italian here and hate oppression.'[22] Very soon, however, she took the Austrian side, as did her husband. Ruskin was only slightly less vehement than his father in expressing dislike of republicanism. As English tories, they were without sympathy for nationalist aspirations. Ruskin's view was that the Italians, unhappy as they no doubt were, had brought the occupation on themselves by their past sins and follies, and that the Austrian government was probably as wise as one could hope for from a Romanist administration. He saw the suffering, but it did not engage him. He had, he confessed, 'no heart nor eyes for anything but stone'.[23]

The railway to Venice had been destroyed, so the party had to leave their carriages outside the city. George arranged the transfer of their luggage to the Hotel Danieli on the Riva degli Schiavoni. The hotel was only a hundred yards from St Mark's Square: from the windows of their suite they could see the Campanile and could hear the Austrian band that played in front of St Mark's every night. Ruskin immediately toured the major Venetian buildings to make sure they were still standing. To his relief, the damage was not as extensive as he had feared. Quite soon he left Effie and Charlotte, with their Murray's guide, to go exploring on their own. Effie searched for the Venice of Titian and Veronese. She was pleased with the *festa* of the Madonna della Salute, held every year since 1662 as a thanksgiving after the plague. She was never to see the many festivals and holidays that commemorated Venice's proud past: the Austrians had suppressed them. The English party, since they sided with the Austrians, necessarily had a foreigner's view of the city's life, and hardly a sympathetic one. They were cut off from the proud Venetian nobility, except the collaborators, and also from most intellectuals. Effie now learnt the differences between the *italianissimi*, the patriots, and the *austriacanti*, Italians with Austrian politics. She saw how they never mixed, never went to the same social occasions, frequented different cafés. She learnt that the Austrian band in St Mark's Square was a symbol of Austrian supremacy: that was why all patriots left the square as soon as it started to play. One day she witnessed the burning of all the paper money, the *moneta patriottica*, that had been issued by Manin's government. It was an action designed to humiliate the Venetians. The city's economy was at a standstill. Thousands had no employment and nowhere to live. On the way back to the hotel at night Effie passed the homeless lying packed together at the end of bridges. 'The lower population here are exactly like animals in the way they live,' she wrote, 'and the fishermen's families live in rooms without an article of furniture and feed in the streets.'[24]

Ruskin was eager that Effie and Charlotte should go into Austrian society so that they would be safely occupied while he worked. He wrote to Lady Davy asking her to arrange some introductions. He had one contact of his own. John Murray had given him an introduction to a man who would be able to help him among Venetian archives. This was Rawdon Brown, who became a lifelong friend. Brown, ten years older than Ruskin, had lived in Venice since 1833. He was eccentric, quarrelsome, quite out of sympathy with his homeland and full of a detailed love of his adopted city. He had bought and restored a palace on the Grand Canal which he filled with Venetian art, documents and curiosities. When the Ruskins arrived in Venice he was practically the only English person there: the others, like most of the Venetian aristocracy, had left the city before the siege began. Brown's curiosity and eclectic mind had some effect on Ruskin, perhaps even beyond the writing of *The Stones of Venice*. For that book he was a guiding influence. Ruskin's researches were continually helped by him, both intellectually and practically. Brown had access to state papers and to the library of St Mark's and could show Ruskin how to use them. He also, shortly, introduced Ruskin to another English antiquary, Edward Cheney. This Shropshire landowner had a house in Venice which he visited every year. Cheney rather distrusted Ruskin's tastes — he was himself an admirer of the baroque — but opened his library

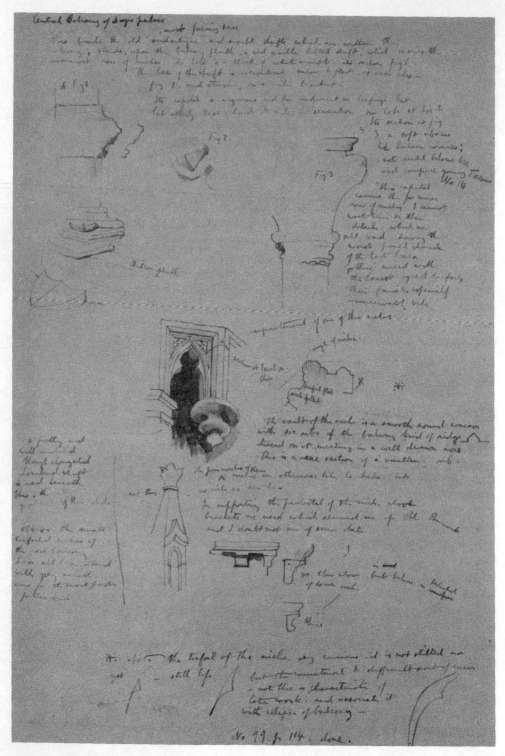

16. Worksheet no. 99. In preparation for *The Stones of Venice*: notes on the Ducal Palace, December 1849, by John Ruskin.

to him and sometimes sent a servant round to the Danieli with suggestions that he thought might be useful.

As Effie and Charlotte began to meet people in Venetian society, Ruskin became more deeply absorbed in his researches. They had some shared diversions: a picnic, improvised games of shuttlecock, trips to the islands, dinner with Brown. But they usually spent their days separately. 'I could hardly see less of him than I do at present with his work,' Effie wrote, 'and think it is much better if we follow our different occupations and never interfere with one another and are always happy . . .'[25] Effie was the centre of attention. She had beauty and high spirits. Eager to meet people, unabashed in foreign languages (she had to speak French, German and Italian), she made many friends, and certainly some admirers too. It seems that she attended parties and balls practically every night. Charlotte was a good chaperone, but Effie was not thereby the less noticeable as a woman who appeared everywhere without her husband. In the society in which she moved — enclosed, rich, cosmopolitan, full of intrigue — this could have been misunderstood. But Effie had cool feelings for propriety. She knew how to be charming without being flirtatious. Other women liked her. Mrs Gray was a little concerned, but Effie rejected her worries.

> I hope I have inherited a little of my father's sense and your discretion to some purpose. In fact John would require a wife who could take [care] of her own character, for you know he is intensely occupied and never with us but at meal times, so that we can do anything we like and he does not care how much people are with us or what attention they pay us. I understand him perfectly and he is so kind and good when he is in the house that his gentle manners are quite refreshing after the indolent Italian and the calculating German, but we ladies like to see and know everything and I find I am much happier following my own plans and pursuits and never troubling John, or he me.[26]

Effie loved Venetian society. She mixed with the officers of the occupying forces and their ladies, with the *austriacanti* nobility and with the visitors to Venice who moved in such circles. The very names that we find in her letters home are eloquent. There was the Madame Taglioni who once owned the palace in which Rawdon Brown now lived, Count Wimpffen, the Count and Countess Minischalchi, Baroness Hessler, the Countess Mocenigo and the Duc de Bordeaux. At a private musical performance attended only by Italians she met Prince Joseph Giovanelli. At balls she talked to the Baroness Wetzler, danced

with the young officers Holzammer and Montzig, but mostly with
Prince Troubetzkoi, whom she later decided not to see in London. She
chatted to the Saxon consul Herr Becker, to the Baron Urmenyi, 'my
handsome old friend who lives here in the hotel',[27] and to the Marquis
Selvatico, the President of the Venetian Academy. One might not
think that a twenty-year-old girl from Perth would mix naturally in
this society. Yet Effie did so with great success. Her vivid personality
carried her over her lack of sophistication. She had much Scottish
feeling for morals. She criticized the Baroness Gras du Barry, 'a Scotch
woman married to a Frenchman, just from Paris, a dashing woman
attended by a handsome young French count, the kind of person I
particularly dislike to see any countrywoman of mine become'.[28] Effie
would not call on Marie Taglioni, the ex-dancer, because her mother
felt it would be an impropriety (though she saw much of her in other
people's houses); she went to German Protestant services, read her
Bible in St Mark's, and refused invitations for Sundays.

Effie reported to Perth that Venetian society could not decide
whether her husband was mad or very wise. Ruskin took no notice of
anyone and would let nothing disturb him from his work. His
activities called forth comment. In crowded squares he could be seen
bent over his daguerrotype equipment, with a black cloth over his
head. He climbed up ladders and scrambled over capitals. He lay full
length on the floor to draw some awkwardly positioned detail. His
tape measure (which he kept until he died) was constantly in play. On
descending from climbs over buildings he would stand musing, or
attending to his notebook, while his gondolier dusted him down. He
became a figure of fun for 'the blackguard children who hinder me by
their noise and filth and impudence' as he paced around their favourite
playgrounds, the bombed and ruined churches.[29] Beggars followed
him everywhere. Much of his work was so laborious and irritating
that he was liable to fall out of love with the city. 'I went through so
much hard, dry, mechanical toil there', he wrote a few years later,

> . . . that I quite lost, before I left it, the charm of the place . . . I had
> few associations with any building but those of more or less pain
> and puzzle and provocation: — pain of frost-bitten finger and
> chilled throat as I examined and drew the window-sills which didn't
> agree with the doorsteps, or back of house which wouldn't agree
> with the front; and provocation from every sort of soul or thing in
> Venice . . .[30]

One person who did not provoke him was his wife. He was indifferent
to Effie's social occupations. After supper he went into his room to

write while Charlotte and Effie practised waltzes and polkas with friends. If he was obliged to go out in the evening he took a book with him, or wrote. The description of champfered edges that appears in the first volume of *The Stones* was written at the opera. Ruskin, normally a theatre-lover, now wrote to his father that

> . . . operas, drawing rooms and living creatures have become alike nuisances to me. I go out to them as if I was to pass the time in the stocks and when I am in the rooms, I say and do just what I must and no more: if people talk to me I answer them, looking all the while whether there is any body else coming to take them away. As soon as they are gone I forget their names and their faces and what they said and when I meet them the next day I don't see them. When I walk with Effie she is always touching me and saying that is so and so — now don't cut him or her as you did yesterday . . .[31]

When Effie was practising polka steps her partner was an Austrian officer, a first lieutenant of artillery named Charles Paulizza whose expertise had directed the final bombardment of the city. Paulizza seems to have been a romantic type of officer. He was fair, with long moustaches. He swirled his grey military coat lined with scarlet. He was a poet, he could play the piano, and he drew. Ruskin quite liked him, but as he could not speak English and his Italian was weaker than Ruskin's, the two men found conversation difficult. Ruskin must have summoned all his politeness when invited to admire Paulizza's drawings, which appear to have been plans and diagrams for his attacks on the city: but he was glad to use his influence to gain entrance to buildings under military occupation. Effie and Paulizza conversed in German. Soon he came to escort her everywhere. Her letters home are full of him. Descriptions of his charm and his accomplishments alternate with assurances that she is in no moral danger. A great friendliness had sprung up between them. There may have been more than that on Paulizza's side, but he behaved always with courtesy. Effie's letters, so frank are they, bespeak that if she were not so content with Ruskin — as, at this period, she was — she might have loved this man. She wrote to her mother,

> He is very fond of me, and, as you say, were John unkind to me and not so perfectly amiable and good as he is, such excessive devotion might be somewhat dangerous from so handsome and so gifted a man, but I am a strange person and Charlotte thinks I have a perfect heart of ice, for she sees him speaking to me until the tears come into his eyes and I looking and answering without the slightest discom-

posure, but I really feel none. I never could love anyone else in the
world but John and the way these Italians go on is perfectly disgusting to me that it even removes from me any desire to coquetry,
which John declares I possess very highly, but he thinks it charming, so do not I . . .[32]

Effie's position was plain. But she knew what gossip was like, and she
knew more about Perth gossip than Venetian gossip. She asked Charlotte not to mention her friendship with Paulizza in her letters home.[33]

Ruskin's work preparatory to the first volume of *The Stones of
Venice* was coming to an end by March of 1850. Effie was not happy at
the idea of returning to London. She could not imagine any life that
could be as pleasant as was hers in Venice. The end of their stay came
quickly, and Effie felt that they must soon come back to the city she
had grown to love. While Ruskin finished off some work in St Mark's
she looked forward to seeing Radetzky, and perhaps even meeting
him. The military governor was due to make a short visit to Venice
from his headquarters in Milan, and Effie knew that she would be
invited to the same functions as the famous old soldier. The Ruskins
had a farewell lunch with Paulizza. An embarrassment was that Ruskin's Italian bankers came to say goodbye at the same time. Patriots,
they would not speak to an Austrian. Rawdon Brown gave Effie a
brooch as they went by gondola to the railway. The next night the
Ruskins were in Padua, and in Vicenza the night after that before
staying for a few days in Verona. By 9 April they had reached Paris,
where Effie made a visit that gave her much to think about. Ruskin
took her to call on the Domecqs. Adèle was now twenty-nine, and
married to Baron Duquesne. Effie thought her the least attractive of all
five sisters. But she looked with a special interest at Adèle's young
daughter, who spoke excellent English and was playing with a doll
that Mrs Ruskin had sent her. A few days later John and Effie Ruskin
were back in Denmark Hill.

CHAPTER NINE

1850–1852

When the Ruskins once more moved back to Park Street in the early summer of 1850 their life fell into a predictable pattern. Effie busied herself with her friends and her entertaining. Ruskin worked on his book and occasionally, grudgingly, accompanied her to parties. Most of his writing was done at Denmark Hill. He left Park Street after breakfast and did not return there until the evening. If he did not see his parents for a day or two, he wrote to them, and these letters often express his dislike of the society in which he moved:

> My dearest mother — horrible party last night — stiff — dull — large — fidgety — strange — run-against-everybody — know-nobody sort of party. Naval people. Young lady claims acquaintance with me. I know as much of her as of Queen Pomare. Talk. Get away as soon as I can — ask who she is — Lady Charlotte Elliott — as wise as I was before. Introduced to a black man with chin in collar. Black man condescending. I abuse several things to black man, chiefly the House of Lords. Black man says he lives in it — asks where I live — I don't want to tell him — obliged. Black man asks — go away and ask who he is. Mr Shaw Lefevre — as wise as I was before. Introduced to a young lady — young lady asks if I like drawing — go away and ask who she is — Lady Something Conyngham. Keep away with back to wall and look at watch. Get away at last — very sulky this morning — Hope my Father's better — dearest love to you both. Ever, my dearest mother, your most affec. son.[1]

There were many aspects of politics and public life of which Ruskin was simply ignorant. His 'black man' was Charles Shaw-Lefevre, the rather famous Speaker of the House of Commons. Effie, on the other hand, did not make mistakes of this sort. While she knew little of politics she was interested to know who was important. She had much talent as the mistress of a fashionable house. All the same, she longed to go back to Venice. One day in May she burst into tears as she and Ruskin were looking over some of Prout's sketches of the palaces and lagoons. Ruskin then promised her that they would return as soon as he had finished the first volume of his history of the city.

It was at this time that John and Effie met Sir Charles and Lady

Eastlake. Sir Charles had recently become the President of the Royal Academy. He had also married the formidable Elizabeth Rigby. Forty years old, six feet tall, she was the only woman contributor to the *Quarterly Review*, in whose pages she wrote pugnacious articles on art and other topics. She took to Effie at once, found Ruskin 'improving on acquaintance', but was soon to come to hate him.[2] Her husband and Ruskin knew that they were opposed on all aesthetic matters but managed to be polite to each other. Lady Eastlake sensed the hollowness of the Ruskins's marriage. She went out of her way to be kind to Effie, aware that kindness to one partner in a marriage can sometimes express malice towards the other. Effie could not always see why Ruskin distrusted people like the Eastlakes, for she had little understanding of his intellectual loyalty to his tastes. But she was sure that his artistic obsessions disturbed her social arrangements. They had an invitation to the country seat of Edward Cheney, whom they had met in Venice. Ruskin did not want to go: he knew the house would be filled with the wrong sort of art. Effie could not see that this mattered at all. And when Ruskin took her out of town to visit people with whom he wished to talk she was not properly entertained.

In April of 1851, they went together to Cambridge to stay with Dr Whewell, the Master of Trinity. The two men ignored her while they discussed architecture and theology. For many reasons Effie wanted to see her family in Scotland. She took the opportunity presented by another of her mother's pregnancies to leave London for Bowerswell. While she was there she went once more to see Dr Simpson, and it was after this consultation that she began to state publicly that she wished to have children but that her husband was opposed to her desire. She might have told Lady Eastlake: certainly she wrote to Rawdon Brown about it. She declared to him,

> I quite think with you that if I had children my health might be quite restored. Simpson and several of the best medical men have said so to me and your gracious permission to me against your prejudices amuses me not a little, but you would require to win over John too, for he hates children and does not wish any children to interfere with his plans of studies. I often think I would be a much happier, better person if I was more like the rest of my sex in this respect.[3]

This was speaking quite openly: it was close to confessing to the shrewd old man the real circumstances of her marriage.

*   *   *   *

The first volume of *The Stones of Venice* was published in March of 1851. While there were some objections to it in the architectural press, several accusations of bigotry and an attack in the *Athenæum*, the book was on the whole well reviewed. That is perhaps because it was treated as literature. It is indeed literature: but, as Ruskin was to discover and lament, many people were so beguiled by his prose that they took little ✓ notice of what he was saying. In the book's mixture of history, politics, æsthetics and theological polemic, two things stood out most clearly to the average reader. They were Ruskin's style and his elevated conception of the importance of art. Charlotte Brontë was typical in her response. She wrote to a friend that

> *The Stones of Venice* seems nobly laid and chiselled. How grandly the quarry of vast marbles is disclosed! Ruskin seems to me one of the few genuine writers, as distinguished from bookmakers, of the age. His earnestness even amuses me in certain passages; for I cannot help laughing to think how utilitarians will fume and fret over his deep, serious, and (*they* will think) fanatical reverence for art.[4]

Ruskin had to resort to the less literary form of the pamphlet to convey the reality of his political views. Three days after the publication of *The Stones* he issued *Notes on the Construction of Sheepfolds*. This is an expansion of 'Romanist Modern Art', the twelfth appendix to the first volume of the parent book, which attacks the Roman Catholic A. W. N. Pugin. The latter was the architect who had done most to associate the English Gothic Revival with the Catholic revival and the Oxford Movement. Ruskin wished to dissociate his own work from any taint of Catholicism. But he went further than this: he wished to claim that his own establishment Protestantism was an active spiritual force, and could be the inspiration of true modern art.

Conservative Protestant politics after the 1848 revolutions give the background to both *The Stones of Venice* and *Notes on the Construction of Sheepfolds*. An immediate stimulus was the 'Papal Aggression' and the Anglican response. In 1850 Pope Pius IX appointed Cardinal Wiseman to be Archbishop of Westminster, placing twelve English bishops beneath his authority. This restoration of the Catholic hierarchy led to an outcry quite beyond its political importance. All Ruskin's associates, and he himself, believed that it was not only the constitution that was therefore threatened: the spiritual life of the island nation had been put at risk. George Croly thought that he saw the work of Antichrist:

> England, the Archiepiscopal Province of Rome! Does not the blood of every man in England boil at the idea? England cut up into

quarters like a sheep, for the provision of twelve Papists! England, mapped out like a wilderness at the Antipodes, for the settlement of the paupers of Rome! England, the farm-yard of the 'lean kine' of Rome![5]

Osborne Gordon was part of a deputation from Oxford which went to Windsor to protest to the Queen. While Ruskin and Effie had been at Cambridge the question had been discussed, Whewell assuring them that his undergraduates were even 'violent about the Papal aggressions'.[6] Ruskin's own views were much the same as Croly's. But they were given a far more cultured expression in the form of parallels with the history and art of Venice. *The Stones of Venice*, its appendices, and the *Sheepfolds* pamphlet all show how entangled were his political views with his literary ambitions. *The Stones* is an admonitory epic and a romantic spiritual journey. We can say with justice that it is inspired by Milton and Byron. At the same time it expresses the last vestiges of the toryism that had been defeated in 1829 and 1832 by Catholic emancipation and the Reform Bill.

Many of Ruskin's political views were inherited from his father and his father's friends. However fiery, they could have seemed quaint to men of his own age. But Ruskin was never interested in learning about politics from his own generation. He looked to older men. To John James Ruskin, Croly, and the like, we must now add the influence of Thomas Carlyle. In later years Ruskin could not remember how his knowledge of Carlyle had grown, so interwoven was his own thought with that of the man whom he liked to call his 'master'. He believed that it was George Richmond who first put a copy of *Past and Present* in his hands. In 1850 and 1851 it is probable that he was most affected by Carlyle's *Latter-Day Pamphlets* and especially the chapter on 'Parliaments'.[7] There he would have found an extremism which much of his own writing was concerned to refine and elaborate. Ruskin would never abandon such views as these. He reissued *Notes on the Construction of Sheepfolds* as lately as 1875. He had then long since thrown off his anti-Catholicism, but he still believed in many other aspects of his pamphlet. Its notions of wise monarchical government and Church discipline are a constant preoccupation of *Fors Clavigera* and would be a principle of the constitution of the Guild of St George.

Notes on the Construction of Sheepfolds resembles much of Ruskin's later writing in that it seems designed to force its readers into principled positions. There were a number of replies to *Sheepfolds*, among them another pamphlet by the painter William Dyce. It was also the occasion of some correspondence between Ruskin and F. D. Maurice.

The two men did not know each other. Maurice was at this date the Professor of Theology at King's College in the Strand, and was active in the Christian Socialist movement. Christian Socialism was so anti-pathetic to Ruskin's temperament that an intermediary was needed. This was F. J. Furnivall, the first of the many conciliatory messengers that Ruskin would require in his later career. Furnivall was a serious young man. He was in the chambers of Bellenden Kerr, the lawyer who had been among the founders of the Arundel Society. Furnivall one evening had met Effie, and she had invited him to Park Street. His description of Ruskin at this first meeting is interesting:

> Ruskin was a tall slight young fellow whose piercing frank blue eyes lookt through you and drew you to him. A fair man, with rough light hair and reddish whiskers, in a dark blue frock coat with velvet collar, bright Oxford blue stock, black trousers and velvet slippers — how vivid he is to me still . . ! I never met any man whose charm of manner at all approacht Ruskin's. Partly feminine it was, no doubt; but the delicacy, the sympathy, the gentleness and affectionateness of his way, the fresh and penetrating things he said, the boyish fun, the earnestness, the interest he showed in all deep matters, combined to make a whole which I have never seen equalled.[8]

Furnivall was always abjectly devoted to Ruskin. He became a regular visitor not only to Park Street but also to Denmark Hill: there, he was given hearty treatment by John James, who liked him despite thinking him a fool. He was one of the few people who took Ruskin's side at the time of the annulment of his marriage, when Effie described him, accurately enough, as 'an amiable weak young man, a vegetarian, Christian Socialist and worshipper of men of genius . . .'.[9] The letters which Furnivall carried between Ruskin and Maurice came to nothing, theologically. But they had a social effect. Quite soon, Furnivall was to bring to Denmark Hill the invitation to join the Working Men's College.

★   ★   ★   ★

Ruskin's protestations that he disliked going into society were exaggerated. While he disliked the glittering occasions which so excited Effie, he was no hermit. He was often at the Carlyles's in Chelsea and he kept up with his many acquaintances from the circle around Samuel Rogers. He made such new acquaintances as Dickens, Thackeray, and the painter G. F. Watts, from whom he commissioned a portrait of

Effie. Although he did not often go there he was a member of the
Athenæum. Ruskin maintained his father's practice of inviting literary
and artistic acquaintances to dinner three or four times a week. He
preferred to do this at Denmark Hill rather than Park Street, for the
atmosphere was less formal and he could show off his Turners. A
frequent guest was Coventry Patmore. He was a family friend, for he
had married the daughter of Ruskin's old Camberwell tutor Dr
Andrews. At this time — between the Ruskins's first and second stays
in Venice — Patmore held a lowly position in the British Museum. He
mixed with artists as much as with his fellow writers. He was admired
by the painters who formed the Pre-Raphaelite Brotherhood. William
Michael Rossetti recorded that he and his brother bought Patmore's
first book of poems soon after it appeared in 1844, and urged it on
William Holman Hunt, Thomas Woolner and John Everett Millais,
other members of the Brotherhood. In 1849 Millais had begun *The
Woodman's Daughter*, a painting which illustrates a poem from this
volume; and soon he would paint Emily Patmore. As he was on easy
terms both with these artists and with Ruskin, Patmore was the ideal
person to introduce them to each other.

Ruskin's contact with the Pre-Raphaelites was not inspired by pure
camaraderie, although his influence on their fortunes made it appear
that he was almost one of their number. He was to be intimate with
Millais and Rossetti and, later on, with Holman Hunt. He knew
William Michael Rossetti slightly in later years. Since Ruskin was
older than the members of the Brotherhood by a decade and more, it
was difficult for him to mix with them on equal terms. Furthermore,
he mixed with them separately, and consecutively. He saw much of
Rossetti in the 1850s when he was no longer on terms with Millais, and
he had no real contact with Hunt until his friendship with Rossetti
ended. At the time when the Brotherhood was most cohesive Ruskin
was abroad, or absorbed in other matters. He may even have contributed to the break-up of the Brotherhood by championing Millais to
the exclusion of his comrades. However, Ruskin's writing had certainly given some inspiration to the PRB in its early days. In the
summer of 1847 William Holman Hunt had read *Modern Painters*. He
later claimed that 'of all its readers none could have felt more strongly
than myself that it was written expressly for him . . . the echo of its
words stayed with me, and they gained a further value and meaning
whenever my more solemn feelings were touched'. [10] On the basis of
what he had read in *Modern Painters* Hunt urged Millais towards a high
sense of purpose and naturalistic principles. This crucial resolution had
an effect on the first Pre-Raphaelite pictures, Hunt's *Rienzi* and Mil-

lais's *Lorenzo and Isabella*. However, when they were exhibited in the
Academy exhibition in 1849, Ruskin was in Venice. He first saw
Pre-Raphaelite painting in the Academy exhibition of 1850, where
there were hung Millais's *Christ in the House of his Parents, Ferdinand
lured by Ariel* and a portrait of James Wyatt, together with Holman Hunt's
Claudio and Isabella. At the private view he did not at first notice
Millais's picture. 'My real introduction to the whole school', he wrote
many years afterwards, 'was by Mr Dyce, R.A., who dragged me,
literally, up to the Millais picture of the *Carpenter's Shop*, which I had
passed disdainfully, and forced me to look for its merits.'[11]

Whatever Dyce made Ruskin see in Millais's paintings, the critic
then showed no particular interest in Pre-Raphaelitism. He did not
particularly like *Christ in the House of his Parents*: it is never mentioned
in his writings without great reservations as to, for instance, its
dwelling on 'painful conditions of expression, both in human feature
and in natural objects'.[12] No writing of Ruskin's ever mentions Millais's other work of that year, the Shakespearian illustration *Ferdinand
lured by Ariel*. It was not until 1851 that he looked at Pre-Raphaelite
painting carefully, three years after the formation of the Brotherhood.
At the Royal Academy that May Millais showed *Mariana, The Return
of the Dove to the Ark*, and *The Woodman's Daughter*. The newspaper
critics were hostile, as they had been the previous year when the
meaning of the initials 'PRB' had slipped out. The subject of *The
Woodman's Daughter* was from Patmore's poem 'The Tale of Poor
Maud'. Millais knew that Patmore was acquainted with Ruskin, and
boldly asked the poet to ask him if he would write something about
Pre-Raphaelite painting. Ruskin went back to the Royal Academy to
look again at the paintings, then sat down to write the first of two
letters to *The Times*. The journals were already full of comment on the
first volume of *The Stones of Venice* and *Notes on the Construction of
Sheepfolds*. Ruskin, the controversialist of the moment, now entered
another fray.

He did so with caution. Signing himself 'The Author of *Modern
Painters*', Ruskin put the case for Pre-Raphaelitism. His first letter,
though it ends with a large claim for the movement, is not at all
vehement and is careful not to be laudatory. He began by saying,

> I believe these artists to be at a most critical period of their career —
> at a turning point, from which they may either sink into nothing-
> ness or rise to very real greatness; and I believe also, that whether
> they choose the upward or downward path may in no small degree
> depend upon the character of the criticism which their works have
> to sustain.[13]

This might seem an ordinary remark, but it has its significance. The Pre-Raphaelites, in appealing to Ruskin, were conscious that public rejection was close to professional failure. They looked to Ruskin for promotional reasons. They were all of them eloquent young men, and they all wrote: two of them, William Michael Rossetti and F. G. Stephens, already had access to the press as writers on art. They were quite able to speak for themselves, but wished to exploit Ruskin's authority. But Ruskin's view of his authority was of a different sort. It was also original. For it had not been said before that new artists, in relating their work and their ambitions to the circumstances of the time, should be directed by art criticism rather than by their professional teachers. Nor had it previously been assumed, as Ruskin now did, that the critic's function was to inspire good art by unrelenting public didacticism. And this is the first time that one meets the modern notion of a young artist, or group of young artists, at a turning point: a point that could be a 'breakthrough' in a career. On all these matters, Ruskin was convinced of his own rightness. Now, in the year when the aged Turner no longer had the strength to exhibit, he suddenly became the arbiter of a new generation.

The Pre-Raphaelites were known to be a coterie bound by a common programme. Ruskin's defence therefore insisted that he was not their friend and did not share their tastes.

> Let me state, in the first place, that I have no acquaintance with any of these artists, and very imperfect sympathy with them. No one who has met with any of my writings will suspect me of desiring to encourage them in their Romanist and Tractarian tendencies . . .[14]

But he approved of their evident desire to avoid academic history painting and their naturalistic techniques:

> These Pre-Raphaelites (I cannot compliment them on common sense in choice of a *nom de guerre*) do *not* desire nor pretend in any way to imitate antique painting, as such. They know little of ancient paintings who suppose the work of these young artists to resemble them . . . They intend to return to early days in this one point only — that, in so far as in them lies, they will draw either what they see, or what they suppose might have been the actual facts of the scene they desire to represent, irrespective of any conventional rules of picture-making; and they have chosen their unfortunate though not inaccurate name because all artists did this before Raphael's time, and after Raphael's time did *not* this, but sought to paint fair pictures rather than represent stern facts, of which the consequence has been

that from Raphael's time to this day historical art has been in acknowledged decadence.[15]

Ruskin defended the Pre-Raphaelites against the charge that they made 'errors' in perspective drawing and closed by offering to find a larger number of errors in work by recognized academicians. A week later he wrote a further letter to *The Times*. It was to some extent modified by John James, but ended, as the first had not, with a ringing declaration of the Pre-Raphaelites' importance:

> I wish them all heartily good speed, believing in sincerity that if they temper the courage and energy which they have shown in the adoption of their system with patience and discretion in pursuing it, and if they do not suffer themselves to be driven by harsh and careless criticism into rejection of the ordinary means of obtaining influence over the minds of others, they may, as they gain experience, lay in our England the foundations of a school of art nobler than the world has seen for three hundred years.[16]

The Times was not convinced by Ruskin's two letters. Under the second they published an editorial rejoinder. It raised what would subsequently be the most common criticism of Ruskin's appreciation of Pre-Raphaelite painting: 'Mr Millais and his friends have taken refuge in the opposite extreme of exaggeration from Mr Turner; but, as extremes meet, they both find an apologist in the same critic.'[17]

Holman Hunt and Millais composed a letter to Ruskin in which they thanked him for his interest. The address given was Millais's; probably because he lived in Gower Street at his parents' house, while the other Pre-Raphaelites were in cheap lodgings. Very soon John and Effie Ruskin drove round from Park Street to call on Millais. The painter was twenty-two years old, a year younger than Effie and ten years younger than Ruskin: and he seemed younger than his age. With his curly fair hair, handsome profile and intense manner, Millais made an immediate impression. He always had. He had been a child prodigy, and his abilities had been recognized by the then President of the Royal Academy, Sir Martin Archer Shee. Thus Millais had become the youngest student ever to have been admitted to the Royal Academy Schools, at the age of eleven. Since then he had won every prize and distinction. A person as clever and as personable as Millais had found it quite easy to be a rebel: it was as easy as being a prodigy. He was proverbially lucky. In the next few weeks, he became good friends with the Ruskins. He visited them both at Park Street and at Denmark Hill. And there was a further invitation, although he may

not have seen its significance. Millais reported to his earlier patron
Thomas Combe that

> I have dined and taken breakfast with Ruskin, and we are such good
> friends that he wished me to accompany him to Switzerland this
> summer . . . We are as yet singularly at variance in our opinions of
> Art. One of our differences is about Turner. He believes that I shall
> be converted on further acquaintance with his works, and I that he
> will gradually slacken in his admiration . . .[18]

It was this connection between Turner and Pre-Raphaelitism that
Ruskin now attempted to elucidate, or rather to claim, in a further
pamphlet. It was entitled *Pre-Raphaelitism*, and was published in
mid–August, before the Royal Academy exhibition closed. It
occasioned more argument than had his letters to *The Times*. They had
been judicious. The pamphlet was eccentric, and its title was misleading. It was not about Pre-Raphaelite painting: Ruskin had scarcely
seen more than half a dozen examples of the school. It was largely
about Turner, and was the result of Ruskin's meditations on a visit he
had made to Farnley Hall that spring. This Yorkshire country seat had
been the home of Turner's friend and patron Walter Fawkes: it contained around two hundred water-colours by Turner, including the
fifty-one drawings of the Rhine, and a number of oils. The house now
belonged to Walter's son Francis Hawkesworth Fawkes, to whom
Ruskin's pamphlet was dedicated. The treatise is prefaced by a quotation from *Modern Painters*, the famous injunction to young artists to
'go to nature in all singleness of heart, and walk with her laboriously
and trustingly, having no other thought but how best to penetrate her
meaning; rejecting nothing, selecting nothing, and scorning
nothing'.[19] It seemed to Ruskin that Pre-Raphaelite painting was
inclined to follow this path: if it did not, then it should do so.

The pamphlet must have seemed beside the point to the Pre-
Raphaelites themselves. No painting by any member of the Brotherhood is mentioned in it. And while fidelity to nature was a Pre-
Raphaelite principle, they were not landscape painters and had no
interest in Turner. Years later, Holman Hunt claimed that their neglect of Turner was simply because they did not know much about him:
'Turner was rapidly sinking like a glorious sun in clouds of night that
could not yet obscure his brightness, but rather increased his magnificence. The works of his meridian days were then shut up in their
possessors' galleries, unknown to us younger men.'[20] But in fact
Turner had seemed irrelevant to the making of the new art. Millais and
Hunt wanted paintings of social action and emotion: they wanted

great detail, meticulous drawing, high-keyed colour, a minimum of modelling and a minimum of aerial perspective. Little in Turner could help this kind of painting. A desire to convert Millais into a Turnerian landscapist lay behind Ruskin's *Pre-Raphaelitism* pamphlet, as it lay behind the invitation to a holiday in Switzerland. But the plan rested on many kinds of misconception.

Ruskin would have been more attentive to Pre-Raphaelite art had his mind not been occupied with his Venetian history. There is a prayerful resolution in his diary on 1 May, the morning after he had been to the Royal Academy and had first seen the paintings he would write to *The Times* to defend: 'Morning. All London is astir, and some part of all the world. I am sitting in my quiet room, hearing the birds sing, and about to enter on the true beginning of the second part of my Venetian work. May God help me to finish it to His glory, and man's good.'[21] London was busy that morning because it was also the opening day of the 1851 Great Exhibition. Effie went to the celebrations, alone, with a ticket that had been procured for her by John James. She was not discontented with her life in Park Street, and at the moment she was on quite cordial terms with her parents-in-law. But she still longed for the day when she would leave for Venice. As controversy gathered over Ruskin's recent writings she was supervising household preparations for a six-month stay in Italy. They set off for the Continent at the beginning of August, leaving behind them the Park Street household (to which they never returned), leaving the Pre-Raphaelites busy about their own business, and all England marvelling, in Paxton's glass and iron sheds, at the exhibition of industrial and material progress.

★   ★   ★   ★

Millais had declined the invitation to accompany the Ruskins as far as Switzerland because he had planned to spend the summer painting with Holman Hunt. The holiday party might or might not have suited him. Charles Newton travelled with the Ruskins, for he had been appointed vice-consul at Mitylene and was on his way to take up his post. Also of the party were the Reverend Daniel Moore, of the Camden Chapel, and his wife. In Switzerland other friends joined them, a Mr and Mrs Pritchard. He was the Member of Parliament for Bridgnorth: she was Osborne Gordon's sister. An art critic, an intelligent Anglican, an archæologist rising in the consular service, an MP, all together with their ladies; here was a group of people thoughtful and cultivated beyond the ordinary. That is why they seem so out of place when we see them in Switzerland. For here was no culture, here was no society, no religion: poverty had made the people themselves into monsters. At Aosta, one in five of the population were goitred. Effie saw two funerals of children, their small coffins 'covered over with wedding-cake finery and little boys as bearers. A fat priest led the way with the Cross and was followed by a quantity of cretins and horrid looking men and women, all looking as happy and good-natured as could be and laughing like anything . . .'[22] At the Hospice of St Bernard the beds were flea-ridden and the food disgusting: it was what the peasants ate. As if to complete their contempt for the Catholicism of the valley, all the party listened while Effie played an old piano and made the monks sing merry, secular tunes. The experience disturbed people in different ways. Ruskin pretended at the time that in Aosta he soon forgot cretinism and everything else in the fields outside the walls where he and Newton walked through vineyards to the chestnut groves and looked up at the Matterhorn and Mont Velan. But in fact he did not forget; and years later the origin of the Guild of St George would be in his 'great plan' to bring health and revive agriculture in these benighted Swiss valleys.

*　　*　　*　　*

An important aspect of the *Pre-Raphaelitism* pamphlet is its interest in human happiness: a theme that always afterwards would haunt Ruskin's writing. In Switzerland and Venice he now began to think seriously about the ways in which society — whether Venetian, Swiss or English — ought to be concerned with human felicity. His thoughts were prompted by the miseries he saw around him. But he also began to consider something that he now knew about himself: that he was happy only when he was working, and working towards some noble end. The question also troubled Ruskin because he had to wonder whether the happiness his wife craved was not ignoble. When they arrived in Venice they heard of the death of Effie's admirer Paulizza. Ruskin perhaps was more distressed than she. During this visit to Venice one senses — almost daily, on reading the letters home — that there was a part of Ruskin's mind that was both darker and kinder than heretofore. Of his wife, one notices her invitations. Effie had decided that they would be more a part of Venetian society if they were not lodged in a hotel. Their new home was to be in the Casa Wetzler, at the side of the Grand Canal. They had a drawing-room and a double bedroom, a dressing-room, a dining-room and a study. Underneath were three servants' rooms and the kitchen. In this accommodation

John and Effie could entertain in a manner grand enough for most social ambitions. Once again Effie's letters home are full of the names of the aristocracy. She was thrilled and proud to meet the Infanta of Spain and, at last, Radetzky: he found her charming. Ruskin had little to do with these people. He was more interested in English visitors to the city. This year they were arriving in greater numbers, and practically all of them were in Venice for what might be called cultural purposes. Ruskin used them to test the arguments of the book he was writing, shifting his ground between English politics and art to his Venetian surroundings. With Sir Gilbert Scott, newly appointed surveyor to Westminster Abbey, he could have professional architectural conversations. With Thomas Gambier Parry, now just beginning to collect *quattrocento* paintings, he could talk about fresco techniques. David Roberts came to drink sherry. He and Ruskin understood each other rather well, and Ruskin was pleased to hear how this minor master of architectural painting had turned down Queen Victoria's request that he should paint the Crystal Palace for her. Some people fared badly in these discussions. One became an enemy. This was Henry Milman, the Dean of St Paul's, quite unable to defend Wren's building while Ruskin made comparisons with the Venetian Gothic around them.

Ruskin's letters give only bald accounts of these conversations, but provide a daily guide to his feelings as he plunged into the writing of the second volume of his Venetian cultural history. As always, he pointed out to his parents that he was not overtaxing himself. But sometimes he fails to reassure: and in Denmark Hill there were worries about his health. John James especially was pained to find how much he missed his son. He also worried that Ruskin's views of the world might be diverging from his own. Ruskin himself was no less worried that this might be so. For this reason some of his letters are full of the strident tones of the *Britannia*, John James's favoured political reading. Of the scene in St Mark's Square where the band proclaimed the Austrian supremacy he wrote,

> Round the whole square in front of the church there is almost a continuous line of cafés, where the idle Venetians of the middle classes lounge, and read empty journals: in the centre the Austrian bands play during the time of vespers, their martial music jarring with the organ notes, — the march drowning the miserere, and the sullen crowd thickening round them, — a crowd, which, if it had its will, would stiletto every soldier that pipes to it. And in the recesses of the porches, all day long, knots of men of the lowest classes, unemployed and listless, lie basking in the sun like lizards; and

unregarded children, — every heavy glance of their young eyes full of desperation and stony depravity, and their throats hoarse with cursing, — gamble, and fight, and snarl, and sleep, hour after hour, clashing their centesemi upon the marble ledges of the church porch . . .[23]

Readers of *The Stones of Venice* will recognize how Ruskin could transform such observations into more stately political sentiments. Especially when writing in retrospect, he would always idealize politics. In 1859, thinking about the Habsburg imperial rule, he wrote of Paulizza:

One of my best friends in Venice in the winter of 1849-50 was the artillery officer who directed the fire on the side of Mestre in 1848. I have never known a nobler person. Brave, kind and gay — as playful as a kitten — knightly in courtesy and in all tones of thought — ready at any instant to lay down his life for his country and his emperor. He was by no means a rare instance either of gentleness or of virtue among the men whom the Liberal portion of our daily press represent only as tyrants and barbarians. Radetzky himself was one of the kindest of men — his habitual expression was one of overflowing *bonhommie* . . . For a long time I regarded the Austrians as the only protection of Italy from utter dissolution . . .[24]

Effie's politics, on the other hand, tended towards the personal. She found that British foreign policy had an effect on her position in Austrian society. In February of 1852 she wrote,

The Austrians are crowing over us finely just now at the brilliant figure England is making of herself after her paltry, mean foreign policy these last three or four years, and now she is without a foreign friend with the Caffir War, the French panic, the impertinence of the Roumanians, and last, not least, a Cabinet full of old women to trouble her, and she will find out perhaps at some cost what Lord Palmerston has in store for her. The feeling is so strong against the English and their position on the continent. It is a very different thing to what it was. Before, the English were all My Lords and their word was law and every respect was paid to them before any other nation. Now we are all considered traders and if politeness is shown it is only to individual merit.[25]

Thus Effie on individual merit. It is now of interest to know how she interpreted her husband's views. Ruskin told his father,

Effie says, with some justice, — that I am a great conservative in France, because there everybody is radical — and a great radical in Austria, because there everybody is conservative. I suppose that one reason why I am so fond of fish — (as creatures, I mean, not as eating) is that they always swim with their head against the stream. I find it for me, the healthiest position.[26]

The first public occasion when Ruskin decided to swim against the tide came towards the end of this second stay in Venice. It gave his father much alarm. In March 1852 Ruskin wrote to Denmark Hill, 'I am going for three days to give the usual time I set aside for your letter to writing one for the Times — on Corn Laws, Election and Education . . . If you like to send it, you can; if not, you can consider it all as written to you, but you must have short letters for a day or two.'[27] These letters were written, but John James did not send them on to *The Times*. Some parts of them are preserved. The third letter, which is missing altogether, was probably the foundation of the 'Notes on Education' which is the seventh appendix to the third volume of *The Stones of Venice*. From the first letter and a portion of the second we may see that Ruskin criticized Disraeli, at this date Chancellor of the Exchequer, supported free trade, advocated direct taxes, taxes on luxuries and a property tax. He felt that income tax ought to be '10 per cent on all fortunes exceeding £1000 a year, and let the weight of it die away gradually on the poorer classes'. His electoral schemes were complicated, giving more votes to the property-owning and educated classes than to others. Ruskin thought of a radical coachman who might have fifty votes, which he would then swamp with his own 'four or five hundred'.[28] The letter on education is coloured by Ruskin's experiences at Oxford. In the appendix to *The Stones of Venice* which derives from this letter — it is one of the appendices that have no relevance to Venetian history — Ruskin advocates the study at university of natural history, of religion and of politics. By religion Ruskin had in mind 'the "binding" or training to God's service' rather than the study of theology. Politics is understood as 'the science of the relations and duties of men to each other'.[29]

All this was distressing to John James Ruskin. He did not forward the letters and he wrote back in strong terms about their contents. But in fact — except in the matter of income tax — Ruskin's views did not differ very widely from his father's, and they must often have talked together about just the same problems that he wished to raise in the newspapers. Ruskin's proposals on the franchise, for instance, might seem eccentric today: but such schemes were not uncommon among

tories of the Ruskins's type in the years after the Reform Bill. It was
not exactly a matter of political principle that most stirred John James's
apprehensions. It was his suspicion that there was a dangerous connection between his son's thinking about the national exchequer and his
inability to keep down his personal expenses. The Guild of St George,
in later years, would most amply prove the justice of these fears. But in
1852 the immediate problem was his son's reputation:

> My feelings of attacks on your books and on your newspaper
> writing differ from yours in this way. I think all attacks on your
> books are only as the waves beating on Eddystone lighthouse,
> whereas your politics are Slum Buildings liable to be knocked
> down; and no man to whom authority is a useful engine should
> expose himself to frequent defeat by slender forces.[30]

There was already quite enough trouble in England about Ruskin's
artistic writings. *Pre-Raphaelitism* had been unfavourably reviewed.
The effect of the pamphlet had been to divert public debate away from
Pre-Raphaelite painting and towards the peculiarity of Ruskin's opinions. The Pre-Raphaelites were now at the end of the short period
when they were most criticized and least able to sell their work; and
the abuse formerly directed towards them now fell on Ruskin. Many
publications apart from *The Times* accused him of inconsistency. The
Daily News and the *Builder* both spoke of contradictions. The *Art
Journal* attacked the pamphlet as a 'maundering medley', and the
Athenæum wrote of its preface that 'Rarely has any oracle's *ego* been
stretched further in the demand for blind faith and acquiescence than in
this pamphlet; — rarely has *ego* been more vain-glorious . . .'.[31]
Ruskin wrote from Venice, considerably upset: 'When I read those
reviews of *Pre-Raphaelitism* I was so disgusted by their sheer broad-
faced, sheepish, swinish stupidity, that I began to feel, as I wrote in the
morning, that I was really rather an ass myself to string pearls for
them.'[32] John James had a vague idea that adverse reviews of his
pamphleteering would be good for his son and would make him
concentrate on his book. He may have been right. At all events, the
matter of the letters to *The Times* was allowed to rest.

Since the publication of the second volume of *Modern Painters* Ruskin had occasionally been caught up in public arguments about the
national collections. One of these had been an attack on the National
Gallery conducted in 1846 and 1847 by William Morris Moore. Signing himself 'Verax', he had issued pamphlets criticizing the gallery's
director, Sir Charles Eastlake, on the grounds that his cleaning policy
was mistaken. Ruskin had entered this controversy. He did not do so

as an opponent of Eastlake on restoration, but with a plea that paintings of the earlier Italian schools should be purchased. He wanted the
paintings by *trecento* and *quattrocento* masters to come to England.
Now, in Venice, Ruskin was anxious that the National Gallery should
acquire more paintings by the great Venetians. He had already
approached Eastlake suggesting that he should buy pictures for the
nation, and when he saw a firm opportunity of buying two Tintorettos he wrote to him again. He also wrote to Lord Lansdowne, a trustee
of the National Gallery whom he knew slightly from the council of
the Arundel Society, and used Edward Cowper-Temple as an intermediary in approaching Lord Palmerston, the Prime Minister. Here,
one might think, was the way to get things done: but in obscure
circumstances Ruskin's recommendations were rejected, and the
paintings were not bought.

Ruskin's belief that the governing classes were not fit to be entrusted
with the artistic soul of the nation was now strengthened. He was to be
even more disillusioned by the affair of the Turner bequest. Turner
died in London on 19 December 1851. The news reached Venice as
Ruskin worked among the tombs of Murano, in the cemetery whose
long purple walls Turner once had painted. 'Every thing in the sunshine and the sky so talks of him,' Ruskin wrote to his father, 'their
great witness lost.'[33] He immediately began to think what might be
preserved from Turner's vast production. His thoughts were of something he had long dreaded, that the painter might have destroyed his
own work. Ruskin knew that the condition of the paintings would in
any case be perilous. He worried what mildewed canvases might be in
the cellars in Queen Anne Street, or locked away in rooms that he had
never seen opened. At the same time, he feared that many treasures
would immediately come onto the art market. He therefore wrote to
his father with instructions about possible purchases. But when
Turner's will was published these apprehensions were largely
banished. England's greatest artist had left everything to the nation.
At the same time Ruskin heard that he was to be one of the executors.
Turner's will was characteristic of the man. It was eccentric, blunt,
generous, miserly, and whole-hearted. For such a one as Lady Eastlake, 'It is a very stupid will — that of a man who lived out of the world
of sense and public opinion.'[34] She was wrong that it was stupid, but
the rest of her sentence is worth pondering. All the contents of the
Queen Anne Street house now became the nation's property. Turner
stipulated that the paintings were to be kept together and were to be
seen without charge. *Dido building Carthage* and *Sun rising through Mist*
were left to the National Gallery on condition that they were to be

hung next to two paintings by Claude. Ignoring his next-of-kin, who subsequently disputed the will, Turner left money to build alms-houses for painters, for the establishment of a professorship of land-scape in the Royal Academy schools, and for a dinner to be held annually in his memory.

Ruskin was left nothing except nineteen guineas to buy a mourning ring. This provoked John James to the sardonic comment 'nobody can say you were paid to praise'.[35] Ruskin's father had given considerable sums for the purchase of Turners over the last fifteen years, and he knew that his son's writings had helped to raise the artist's prices. But this kind of resentment was rather swept away when he found what was in the house. John James was one of the first people to go through Queen Anne Street, which he did with Turner's dealer:

> I have just been through Turner's house with Griffith. His labour is more astonishing than his genius. There are £80,000 of oil pictures, done and undone. Boxes, half as big as your study table, filled with drawings and sketches. There are copies of Liber Studiorum to fill all your drawers and more, and house walls of proof plates in reams . . . Nothing since Pompeii so impressed me as the interior of Turner's house; the accumulated dust of forty years partially cleared off; daylight for the first time admitted by opening a window on the finest productions of art for forty years. The drawing room has, it is reckoned, £25,000 worth of proofs, and sketches, and drawings, and prints . . . I saw in Turner's rooms, *Geo Morlands* and *Wilsons*, and *Claudes* and *portraits* in various styles, *all by* Turner. He copied every man first, and took up his own style, casting all others away. It seems to me you may keep your money, and revel for ever and for nothing among Turner's works . . .[36]

It is interesting that John James was so struck to find there the early works that reminded him of Morland and Wilson. Conceivably, Ruskin had talked so much of the 'truth to nature' and the imagination of his hero's work that John James scarcely realized that Turner had long painted in borrowed styles. Ruskin's letters home are slightly reserved at this point: and we do not know much about the way that he reviewed his responsibilities as executor. He started to make plans for a Turner gallery. His ideas were progressive. He wanted it to be top-lit, with all paintings hung on the line and given their proper immediate environment by using flats to subdivide the rooms. He also thought, for a short time, of a biography of Turner. This would have been a deeply interesting book, no doubt. But Ruskin thought that *Modern Painters*, in the course of time, would fulfil the proper part of such a biography's function. There were things about Turner's life and his household that could not be told. As Lady Eastlake gleefully recorded, 'His life is proved to have been sordid in the extreme, and far from respectable.'[37] Effie Ruskin was opposed to a biography because 'what is known of Turner would not be profitable to any lady . . . the sooner they make a myth of him the better'.[38] It is not likely that Effie's views on books had much effect on her husband. But this remark about making a myth of Turner is relevant. Ruskin thought that he would best serve Turner's memory by a critical assertion of his genius. The quotidian drudgery of the biographer was not for him, and

> . . . there might be much which would be painful to tell and dishonest to conceal — and on the other hand — apart from all criticism of his works, probably little to interest — and all criticism I shall keep for *Modern Painters* . . . if I were not going to write *Modern Painters* I should undertake it at once, but I will make *that* so complete a monument of him, D.V., that there will be nothing left for the life but when he was born and where he lived — and whom he dined with on this or that occasion. All of which might be stated by anybody.[39]

Ruskin's position as executor seemed at first to offer him the means to make a full study of the work of the artist he admired above all others. But his commitment to Venice had grown so intense that he did not even make a quick trip to England to see what extraordinary treasures might be in Queen Anne Street. Soon, matters became even more confused. Turner's will was disputed by his next-of-kin. The legal complications indicated that there would be a long suit in Chancery. Ruskin felt that he could not become involved in legal matters.[40] As also did Samuel Rogers, he set about resigning his executorship. His immediate work was in Venice. He genuinely believed that the Ducal Palace would not stand for many more years. He could see no guarantee that the relative political stability of the Austrian occupation would hold. The revolutions of 1848 could be repeated, and with far more terrible results. But while it was necessary for him to save Venice, as far as he could, by writing of her architecture, he could also feel that to write of Gothic was to prepare for his praise of Turner's genius. So he explained *The Stones of Venice* as follows:

> I see a very interesting connection between it and *Modern Painters*. The first part of the book will give an account of the effects of Christianity in colouring and spiritualising Roman or Heathen

architecture. The second and third parts will give an account of the
transition to Gothic, with a definition of the nature and essence of
the Gothic style. The fourth part of the decline of all this back into
Heathenism: and of the reactionary symptoms attending the course
of the relapse, of which the strongest has been the development of
landscape painting. For as long as the Gothic and other fine architec-
tures existed, the love of Nature, which was an essential and peculiar feature of Christianity, found expression and food enough in
them . . . when the Heathen architecture came back, their love of
nature, still happily existing in some minds, could find no more
food there — it turned to landscape painting and has worked
gradually up into Turner.[41]

This was a grand design, and perhaps it is one that is not fully spelt
out in Ruskin's more formal writings. For such a connection was in
the first place emotional. *The Stones of Venice* is written out of knowledge, out of archæological research and some acquaintance with the
city's archives. But it is bound together by passions. Ruskin did not
write it with a historian's deliberation, but let himself be carried by
his emotions. He knew that he had to guard himself against the
nervous excitement that accompanied such efforts: at the same time
his book was fashioned by such excitement. 'The thing I have to
watch', he told John James, 'is the tendency to excitement and sleep-
lessness — the aggravation of that excitability of pulse which my
mother so often used to notice when I was a boy: the least overwork
any day causing a restless feeling all over — and exhaustion afterwards.'[42] Ruskin's letters from Venice pay so much attention to his
own health that they have sometimes been described as hypochon-
driacal. We may also believe that they record the urgent ministrations
of his creative self.

> I found first — that every hour of thought or work of any kind, but
> especially writing, was just so much acceleration of pulse — with
> slight flushing of cheeks and restless feeling all over — That I never
> was healthily sleepy at nights — and often could not sleep more than
> four or five hours, even if I went to sleep at a proper time. That any
> violent exercise would make me restless and excited for hours
> afterwards, instead of wholesomely fatigued — and that the sligh-
> test plague or disagreeable feeling in society would do the same — I
> got into a little dispute with Mr Cheney about some mosaics one
> day — and was quite nervous the whole day after — merely a
> question of whether the colours were faded or not . . .[43]

Day after day, while often he trembled with the strain, Ruskin went on writing. Every evening George Hobbs made a fair copy of his text to send home to Denmark Hill. All this was done as though in a race against time. A strange bond of tension existed between Ruskin and his father as they both sought for the book's expression. Effie knew nothing or little about this, and probably did not wish to understand what was happening between the two men. But she was now being even further excluded from the union of the Ruskin family.

Years later, writing in his diary on 3 March 1874, and thinking over past books, Ruskin wrote, 'And yet the Venice work was good. Let me make the best fruit of it I can, since he so suffered for it.'[44] That was on the tenth anniversary of his father's death. Ruskin still then felt guilt that *The Stones of Venice* had been fashioned out of his father's pain. They needed many kinds of companionship. It was important to them that they could talk freely together about religion, especially since Margaret Ruskin's faith was so inflexible. John James knew that Ruskin had not believed absolutely in the authority of the Bible since he was at Oxford. He also knew that even when he was writing the second volume of *Modern Painters*, whose religious bias seems very close to Margaret Ruskin's, his faith had been confused by 'the continual discovery, day by day, of error or limitation in the doctrines I had been taught, and follies or inconsistencies in their teachers'.[45] Ever since 1845 there had been a difference between the theological confidence of Ruskin's writings and his private misgivings. One would not think that the author of *Notes on the Construction of Sheepfolds* had any difficulties of belief. But just after its publication Ruskin had written to Henry Acland,

> You speak of the flimsiness of your own faith. Mine, which was never strong, is being beaten into mere gold leaf, and flutters in weak rags from the letter of its old forms; but the only letters it can hold by at all are the old Evangelical formulæ. If only the geologists would let me alone, I could do very well, but those dreadful hammers! I hear the clink of them at the end of every cadence of the Bible verse . . .[46]

It was as well that Ruskin could feel like this. For it enabled him to understand how John James Ruskin, now in his old age, could fall into religious despondency as he contemplated his death and his life after death.

Ruskin's religious thinking changed during this second extended stay in Venice, as did his own character. To use crude terms, he became less 'Evangelical' and more considerate of other people's religious feelings: but this is not necessarily to say that his faith became attenuated, nor that (as his mother was to fear) he became closer to the

Roman Catholic Church. Rather, he began the true development of
his own faith, which in the years to come would range widely between
such positions, yet at no time give the impression of compromise. The
spirit of the *eirenikon* was not natural to Ruskin, but he would always
wish to assist another person's piety. There is little justice, at this point
in the two men's lives, in the notion of John James's 'domination' of
his son, for Ruskin was now enabled to act as a spiritual pastor to his
own father. He offered John James an especial comfort when his father
wrote to him about his doubts of the after life. We do not know much
about the nature of Ruskin's own doubts because we do not have
much direct evidence of his prayers. We know that in prayer he made
resolutions: that is how he began *Modern Painters*. In *Modern Painters*
we find his capacity for adoration, which is another component of
prayer, and we assume that his petitions would not greatly differ from
those of other thoughtful men. But of his contemplative prayer we are
in ignorance, except that we may say that in his understanding of God,
Ruskin's doubting was akin to a spiritual exercise, that it led to a
deepening of feeling and a realization that the boundaries of faith are
distinct from the nature of faith.

Ruskin's notes on his Bible reading help us to understand him at this
time. During his second stay in Venice his devotional thoughts were
dominated by study of the Book of Job, which he began in September
of 1851. By the beginning of December he had completed a commentary on Job which occupied ninety pages of manuscript. This has
disappeared, but we should consider what was in his mind. Job is
about innocent suffering, wisdom and the acceptance of God's ways.
It is wise not to strain for a knowledge of God beyond that available to
human speculation. But we also wish to know about revelation,
which is both what God shows of Himself and the manner in which
His nature is disclosed. Thinking of Venice, but much more of the
Alps and of Turner, Ruskin enquired:

> . . . it seems to me that from a God of Light and Truth, His
> creatures have a right to expect plain and clear revelation touching
> all that concerns their immortal interests. And this is the great
> question with me — whether indeed the Revelation *be* clear, and
> men are blind . . . or whether there be not also some strange
> darkness in the manner of Revelation itself.[47]

He was beginning to think of those things that in the fifth volume of
Modern Painters he would write about in the mysterious chapter entitled 'The Dark Mirror'.

Ruskin now felt himself prepared to look at Roman Catholicism with some sympathy. Before, he had scarcely considered the matter. The appendix to the third volume of *The Stones of Venice* which deals with education mentions that four out of the twelve young men who had been his close friends at Oxford had converted to Catholicism. He himself had been quite untouched by the Oxford Movement as an undergraduate. But another Christ Church man, William Russell, now arrived in Venice. They had not been intimates at the university, and Ruskin was surprised to find that both Russell and his wife had become Catholics. Russell's wife died while they were in Venice. Ruskin saw something of him after his bereavement and they talked about religion. John and Effie had other acquaintances in Venice who were in a rather similar situation. They met Viscount Feilding and his wife. She was dying of consumption; he had been estranged from his family since becoming a Roman Catholic. Feilding was not much older than Ruskin and his wife was the same age as Effie. Ruskin felt sympathy for them, and discussed matters of doctrine with Feilding with more interest than he had with Russell. His curiosity was such that it led Feilding to believe that Ruskin might himself convert. It was in part due to conversations such as these that a change of tone occurs in the second volume of *The Stones of Venice*. The passage on the Madonna of Murano, for instance, with its enquiry into the spirit of Mariolatry, would not have been written a year earlier: nor would the appendix entitled 'The Proper Sense of the Word Idolatry'. The details of Ruskin's interest in Catholicism at this time are obscure. Who wrote, in Ruskin's private diary, Hail Marys in English and Latin? The writing is in pencil, not in Ruskin's hand, nor in Effie's. All this is not to say that *The Stones of Venice* is anything but a vehemently Protestant book. The trajectory of its argument could only have come from a background such as Ruskin's. Yet a broadness of spirit characterizes its well-known chapter 'On the Nature of Gothic'. As he began to think about that chapter, in February of 1852, Ruskin told his father, 'I shall show that the greatest distinctive character of Gothic is in the workman's heart and mind.'[48] The author of *Notes on the Construction of Sheepfolds* could not have said this. For the pamphlet's intolerance implied a denial of spiritual grace in others. It was this grace that Ruskin was now anxious to discover in the workmen who had built Venice, or in those who might build Gothic architecture in England.

*   *   *   *

As the time approached when the Ruskins were to return to England, the many problems of their marriage came into sharper focus. On

Ruskin's birthday his father, fretting for his homecoming, gave a
dinner party in his honour. From Venice on that same day, Ruskin
wrote a long account of his health to Denmark Hill, and Effie wrote to
her mother complaining about the elder Ruskins. She claimed that
'both he and Mrs R. send the most affectionate messages to me and all
the time write *at* or *against* me and speak of the hollowness of worldly
society and the extravagance of living in large houses and seeing great
people . . .'.[49] This was true, and Effie probably felt that she would
need some allies when she left Venice for London. She remembered a
slightly indiscreet conversation she had had with Charles Newton
during the holiday in Switzerland the previous year. Newton and Effie
were genuinely fond of each other: and the clever, iconoclastic
archæologist had not concealed from Effie that he found the old
Ruskins rather absurd. He also warned Effie against their influence.
Recalling this conversation, Effie wrote to her mother:

> They are so peculiar that, as Newton said to me when we were
> travelling together, he could not understand how I got on so well —
> he thought two days at Denmark Hill with Mrs Ruskin without
> prospects of release would really kill him and yet he thought her a
> very good woman but very queer — but he advised me never to let
> John away again so long with them without me. He said it did us
> both a great deal of harm and he knew the effects it had on all our
> acquaintances . . .[50]

Newton was of course right. For Ruskin to be truly married meant
that he had to be separated from his parents. But neither Newton nor
Effie fully realized that such a separation, for Ruskin, would be a
separation from his own self.

   Ruskin was determined not to go back to Park Street. It was too
near to London society, which he had now decided made him physically ill. John James was perfectly happy to give up the Mayfair house.
He was less pleased now than once he had been to see his son in the
company of the great. Besides, the house was expensive. It had not
been much used, and three servants were paid all the time that John
and Effie were abroad. Ruskin wanted to live somewhere near his
parents: not necessarily in the same house, but in a house within a short
walking distance of them. Letters between all three Ruskins now
became even more full of devotion for each other, while John James's
letters to Perth relentlessly attacked Effie for extravagance. Effie was
amazed to find a poem from Mrs Ruskin to her son, 'in a style almost
of amatory tenderness, calling John her beloved and Heart's Treasure
and a variety of other terms which only, I believe, a lover would do in

addressing a Sonnet to his Mistress . . .'.[51] At the same time, Effie was spoken of in Ruskin's letters to his father as if she were a difficult child. Perhaps this was because he was personally incapable of helping her make the transition from a fashionable hostess in Venice to a house-wife in Camberwell:

> I do not speak of Effie in this arrangement — as it is a necessary one — and therefore I can give her no choice. She will be unhappy — that is her fault — not mine — the only real regret I have, however is on her account — as I have pride in seeing her shining as she does in society — and pain in seeing her deprived, in her youth and beauty, of that which ten years hence she cannot have — the Alps will not wrinkle — so *my* pleasure is always in store — but her cheeks will: and the loss of life from 24 to 27 in a cottage in Norwood is not a pleasant thing for a woman of her temper — But this cannot be helped.[52]

The prospect of her future London life made Effie all the more loath to leave Venice. She was so filled with foreboding that she became frankly hostile to her parents-in-law. She felt that the Ruskins would all be much more happy and comfortable if they could simply exclude her from any of their plans. The conclusion was inescapable. She now wrote frankly to her father, 'I wish that I had been the boy and never left you — which I believe in the end might have been better for all parties.'[53]

The Ruskins's last weeks in Venice were filled with work and with a peculiar kind of social unreality. John and Effie went twice to Verona to attend Radetzky's balls. These were enjoyable occasions, in contrast to the Venetian carnival which Ruskin must have decided to attend because of its antiquity. But this pre-Lenten feast had long since fallen into corruption. The Ruskins put on 'dominoes', black and white masks, and wandered around Venice late in the evening. The squares were full. People were throwing things, men approached Effie and said things she could not understand. Ruskin went before her to the masked ball which once had been attended by all the great people of Venice. They were not there now, and he saw that the dancing was lewd. They walked further through the streets looking for entertain-ment that did not exist, until Effie became frightened that 'the canaille, not the masks' had surrounded them.[54] Shortly after this slightly disturbing evening came the news that two Austrian officers had fought a duel over Effie after her appearance at the ball in Verona. The Ruskins took no notice. But the dangerous side of Austrian military honour was now to touch them very closely. Just as they were packing to leave Venice, Effie found that some of her jewels had been stolen. Suspicion fell on an English acquaintance of theirs, a Mr Foster. He was not precisely a soldier but had a position as an aide-de-camp to Radetzky. He was sufficiently close to the military establishment, therefore, for honour to be at issue. Foster's closest friend, a Count Thun, was under the impression that Ruskin had personally accused his comrade. He challenged the art critic to a duel. Ruskin mildly declined. Scandal grew. There was trouble in the Austrian garrison. The police were inefficient: Effie was hysterical. They found that they could not leave Venice. Edward Cheney came to their aid and smoothed the matter over. But it made an unpleasant end to their stay. Ruskin did not tell his father about it until they were back in England. John James Ruskin was horrified: all the more so when the story, wildly exaggerated, began to appear in the English newspapers. On 2 August 1852, Ruskin was obliged to write to *The Times* explaining as best he could the facts of the case. It is the only one of his public letters that was not subsequently collected and published. For Effie, the ludicrous aspects of the affair — augmented as they were by much gossip — made all the more bewildering her new life: a housewife, four years married and still a virgin, in a suburban villa to the south of London.

CHAPTER TEN

1852–1854

The new house that John James had found for his son and daughter-in-law was very close to his own. It was No. 30 Herne Hill. The property was next door to the house that the Ruskins had moved to when John was four, and was its duplicate. Although John James did not expect John and Effie to remain there for long he had spent much money on fittings. In doing so he acted with a thoughtlessness which often overcame him in matters concerning his son's marriage. He gave an interior decorator £2,000 and *carte blanche* to furnish the house as he thought best. The result was modern and vulgar. Ruskin, horrified, said that the house was only fit for a clerk to live in and that he would be ashamed to invite his friends there. Effie was also upset, and not comforted by the thought that it was in any case unlikely that London society would come out to Herne Hill. She made only one or two attempts to entertain in this new home. The guests there were usually Ruskin family friends like the Richmonds. To them, soon cheerfully reconciled to the suburbs in which he had grown up, Ruskin wrote in invitation:

> Ours is a most difficult house to direct anybody to, being a number-less commonplace of a house, with a gate like everybody's gate on Herne Hill — and a garden like everybody's garden on Herne Hill, consisting of a dab of chrysanthemums in the middle of a round O of yellow gravel — and chimnies and windows like everyone's chimnies and windows . . . all I can do is to advise you that some half mile beyond my father's there is a turn to the left, which you must *not* take, and after passing it we are some ten or twelve gates further on . . .[1]

More formal entertainment was carried on at Denmark Hill, as it always had been. But life there was not calm in the weeks after the long stay in Venice. There was trouble about the new house. John James was angry about the challenge to duel. He was not concerned with thoughts of physical danger: what upset him was that anyone might call his son's honour into question. Old Mrs Ruskin had taken fright after hearing about John's conversations with Catholics. As had the Feildings, she had somehow gained the impression that he was on the point of conversion. Her fears were greater because Ruskin was now

seeing Henry Manning, the most recent and spectacular of prominent
Anglicans who had turned to Catholicism. Manning and Ruskin (who
were to remain lifelong friends) had much to talk about. Manning was
a friend of Gladstone's: his book, *The Unity of the Church* (1842),
resumed many of the topics of Gladstone's *State in its Relations
with the Church* (1838). These matters had been the underlying concern
of *Notes on the Construction of Sheepfolds*. It was natural that Ruskin
should now wish to discuss them in the light of his recent study of the
history of Venice. John James could see the point of such discussions:
Margaret Ruskin and Effie could not. Effie's religious views, such as
they were, seem now to have become more pronounced. She too
believed her husband to be in some danger, but not from Catholicism.
She believed that it lay in pride. Effie disapproved of his

> . . . wish to understand the Bible throughout — which nobody in
> this world will ever do — and unless they receive it as a little child it
> will not be made profitable to them. He wishes to satisfy his
> intellect and his vanity in reading the Scriptures and does not pray
> that his heart and mind will be improved by them. He chuses to
> study Hebrew and read the *Fathers* instead of asking God to give
> him Light. His whole desire for knowledge appears to me to
> originate in Pride and as long as this remains and his great feeling of
> *Security* and doing everything to please himself he is ready for any
> temptation and will be permitted to fall into it.[2]

For a short period Effie found herself in the unaccustomed role of an
ally of her mother-in-law. Lady Eastlake, who now began to look at
the Ruskins with much curiosity, was able to report to John Murray
after dining at Denmark Hill that 'the old people are much kinder to
their pretty daughter-in-law than they were and look to her to keep
their son from going through some Ruskin labyrinth to Rome'.[3]

Margaret Ruskin's continual derogation of Catholicism eventually
began to irritate her son. To Mrs Gray, who also had expressed her
disquiet, he wrote a sharp, sensible letter:

> I simply set it down as something to the discredit of Protestantism
> that my mother is afraid after having bred me up in its purest
> principles for thirty four years, to let me talk for half an hour with a
> clever Catholic: but I shall certainly not permit this fact to tell for
> more than its simple worth — and that worth is really not much —
> for my mother's anxiety about my religion is much like that which
> she shows with respect to my health or safety — rather a nervous
> sensation than a definite and deliberately entertained suspicion of

danger in this or the other circumstance. Only I see that I must not blame Catholics for illiberality in refusing to argue with, or listen to Protestants.

The beginning of these perilous speculations of mine was only this — that one evening in St Mark's Place — getting into an argument with Lady Feilding — I was completely silenced by her — had not a word to say for myself — and out of pure shame, I determined at once to know all that could be said on the subject — and fit myself better for battle another day: as well as to look into some statements made by Protestant writers, which I had hitherto accepted undoubtingly, but which I found the Catholics denied just as indignantly as the Protestants affirmed them positively. And this I must do before I write any more against the Catholics — for as I have received all my impression of them from Protestant writers, I have no right to act upon these impressions until I have at least *heard* the other side. But I do not see why this should make either you — or any of my Protestant friends anxious. I can most strongly and faithfully assure you that I have no hidden leanings or bias towards Popery: that on the contrary I hate it for abusing and destroying my favourite works of art: my name and what little reputation I have, are entirely engaged on the Evangelical side, my best friends are all Puritans — including my wife — and all my life has been regulated by Protestant principles and habits of independent thought — I am as cool headed as most men in religion — rather too much so: by no means inclined either to fasting or flagellation: — past the age of Romance — and tolerably well read in my Bible: And if under these circumstances — you are afraid when you hear that I am going to enquire further into points of the Romanist doctrines of which I am ignorant — it seems to me that this is equivalent to a confession that Protestantism is neither rational nor defensible — if fairly put to the proof — but a pasteboard religion . . .[4]

No doubt it annoyed Ruskin to have to explain to his family that he needed his intellectual peers. But he had found a fruitful new regime for his writing. Every morning after breakfast he left his new home to walk the few hundred yards to Denmark Hill. There, in his old study, he worked all day on the second and third volumes of *The Stones of Venice*. It was to be a book that scarcely resembles anything else in Victorian literature. Yet it has a literary context. Ruskin was now expanding his acquaintance among contemporary writers. Manning's themes have a bearing on Ruskin's epic history. So have books by Carlyle. So also have a number of poems by Robert and Elizabeth

Browning. Ruskin first made Browning's acquaintance at Coventry Patmore's house at The Grove in Highbury. Effie was curious to know what the Brownings were like. She had no great interest in poetry. But she had noticed how Samuel Rogers, always jealous of other poets, had abused Ruskin when he saw that he was reading Elizabeth Browning's 'Casa Guido Windows'. Mrs Browning did not appear at Highbury that night, but Ruskin got on rather well with her husband. The talk was mostly of Italy. Ruskin had to acknowledge that, despite his liberal views, the poet knew much about the country that he did not. A few days afterwards John and Effie went to call on the Brownings at their lodgings in Welbeck Street. No record of the conversation remains. But it seems that Elizabeth Browning was not inclined to be appreciative of Effie. She wrote to a friend, 'Pretty she is and exquisitely dressed — *that* struck me — but extraordinary beauty she has none at all, neither of feature or expression.'[5]

Effie was beginning to realize that in London literary circles there was a competitive element she had not foreseen. She now came under the scrutiny of another intelligent woman who had formed an exceptional partnership with her husband. Jane Welsh Carlyle was no more impressed with her than Elizabeth Browning had been. Ruskin and Carlyle probably first met in 1850. On 6 July of that year, Mrs Carlyle's cousin John Welsh recorded in his diary that he had seen the Ruskins at the Carlyle home in Cheyne Walk, and that Ruskin had endeavoured to draw Carlyle out on the subject of religion. In December of 1850 Carlyle wrote that he had entertained 'Ruskin and wife, of the *Seven Lamps of Architecture*, a small but rather dainty dilettante soul, of the Scotch-Cockney breed'.[6] Carlyle was probably more appreciative of John James and Margaret Ruskin than he was of John and Effie. 'He used to take pleasure in the quiet of the Denmark Hill garden, and use all his influence with me to make me contented in my duty to my mother,' says *Præterita*.[7] In a few years' time Margaret Ruskin became convinced — and with justice — that Carlyle was responsible for some of her son's errant religious beliefs. But there was no feeling of distrust in the early 1850s. And Ruskin went out of his way to please the Carlyles. Cigars were produced after dinner: for no-one else but the author of *Past and Present* would such an infringement of the Denmark Hill rules be countenanced. In 1854, after Effie had run away, Jane Carlyle recalled how well they (and their dog) were entertained, when Ruskin

. . . twice last summer . . . drove Mr C. and me and *Nero* out to his place at Denmark Hill, and gave us a dinner like what one reads of in

the *Arabian Nights*, and strawberries and cream on the lawn; and was indulgent and considerate even for Nero! I returned each time more satisfied that Mrs Ruskin must have been hard to please . . .[8]

That was of course a misreading of Effie's situation. It was quite a common one. Perhaps only Lady Eastlake among Effie's London acquaintances was inquisitive enough about her to guess at the truth. Effie kept her problems to herself. In Venice it had been easier not to think about them. But in the new Herne Hill home she had the apprehension that her life would be irremediably unhappy. There were some questions to which she could give no answer, and which she could not discuss with Ruskin. If she could imagine herself happy as a mother, could she imagine her husband as a father? If sexual relations began, would he come to love her more, and be less bound to his parents? Did he love her at all? Did she love him? Would sex be enjoyable, or not? While she thought about these matters she came to admit to herself not only that she disliked living where she was but also that she did not like Mr and Mrs Ruskin. There was a kind of comfort in realizing this. At the end of September of 1852 she went to Bowerswell for seven weeks while Ruskin stayed in London to work at *The Stones of Venice*. She then told her parents in detail about the difficulties of living with the Ruskins. As she did not dare to tell them of her sexual problems she emphasized the niggling disputes over accounts. Here was almost daily evidence of the Ruskins's unreasonableness, for she was pursued by letters from Herne Hill accusing her of extravagance. These complaints were almost certainly unjust: in any case they were insensitive. Ruskin himself had been spending freely on his own pleasures. He had brought back many works of art from Venice. He was forming a collection of missals. In six weeks he had spent £160 on plates from Turner's *Liber Studiorum* while Effie was attempting to economize in the house that had been so lavishly over-furnished. 'How is one to please them?' she wrote despairingly.[9]

★   ★   ★   ★

Effie's personal history now became intertwined with the public triumph of Pre-Raphaelitism. In the New Year of 1853 (as usual, changing his mind on this topic) Ruskin announced that he had decided to 'go into society' that coming season: he thought that he would have finished *The Stones of Venice* by then. This was in part for Effie's sake, but also because he wished to meet people who might possess either missals or paintings by Turner. Effie was pleased, the more so when Ruskin rented a house in Charles Street, Mayfair. She did not know it, but this was to be her last appearance as a worldly success. The fashionable London season lasted from May until July, and its traditional opening was the private view of the Royal Academy exhibition. Here Effie shone both in person and portrayal, for she was seen to be the model in the painting of the year, Millais's *The Order of Release*.

Millais had become a most popular artist. In the previous year's exhibition there had been crowds all day long in front of his *Ophelia* and *The Huguenot*. Afterwards he wrote to the wife of his patron Thomas Combe that 'the immense success I have met with this year has given me a new sensation of pleasure in painting'.[10] His next picture, *The Proscribed Royalist*, was designed to be equally pleasing. Millais had begun to discuss his subjects with an agent before embarking on them: this painting of a hiding cavalier visited by a Puritan girl was not entirely his own invention. It was near completion when John and Effie returned from Venice in the autumn of 1852. Millais was then casting around for another subject. Finally he devised *The Order of Release*, in which a proud young wife meets her Highlander husband as he is released from jail. The painting is subtitled with the date 1746, the year of Culloden. Millais must have told the Ruskins about the painting: Effie described it as 'quite jacobite and after my own heart'.[11] Around Christmas or the New Year of 1853, probably when Effie returned from Bowerswell, Millais asked her to sit for the Highlander's wife. Etiquette demanded that he ask Ruskin first, and it is likely that Millais thought that the Ruskins might buy his picture. Determined to make a better portrait of Effie than those by Watts and George Richmond hanging in Denmark Hill, Millais began to paint her face in competitive mood. He took the picture from his own studio in Gower Street and worked on it in Herne Hill. He may sometimes have stayed the night, for Ruskin mentions in a contemporary letter that his house was crowded, had only one spare room and two attic rooms, and that he had 'promised one of these garrets to Millais, the painter, at all times when he chooses to occupy it'.[12]

One must imagine, then, that Millais moved his canvas, easel, brushes, paints, varnishes and so on into the best-lit room in Herne Hill. Effie sat to him from immediately after breakfast until dusk. Ruskin was meanwhile writing *The Stones of Venice* in his study in his parents' house. The question of chaperonage was not raised (in fact Effie was never chaperoned except when travelling) and the question of whether she should appear in a picture at all was smoothed over. It was not strictly decorous. The only acceptable way to appear in painting was as the subject of a commissioned portrait. Effie was not

quite in this position. She took her place in the Academy rooms beside
professional models such as the Miss Ryan — Irish — who had posed
for *The Proscribed Royalist* and the half-professional Westall, who sat
for both the Highlander and the jailer in her picture, and who recently
had been arrested for desertion from the army. Models were regarded
as loose women: so they often were. The Ruskins did not mention the
belief that 'the woman who was made an Academy model could not be
a virtuous woman' until Effie had run away.[13] This shows their
independence from the conventions of society. But there was nonetheless some strain. Effie thought that some of John James's remarks went
beyond banter. After the painting was finished she wrote to her family
that

> . . . he said he had taken pen in hand to John to expatiate on my
> perfections of appearance and manner, that in his life he had never
> seen anything so perfect as my *attitude* as I lay on the sofa the night
> before and that no wonder Millais etc etc, but it sickens me to write
> such nonsense as I could spare such writing and excuse it from a fool
> but from Mr R it sounded, to say the least, I thought, unnatural and
> rather suspicious.[14]

She had begun to wonder whether the Ruskins thought that her
husband's protégé was not a dangerous young man for her to know.

If these were real social difficulties, they were quite swept away by
the success of the painting. A Millais family tradition relates that a
policeman had to be posted in front of *The Order of Release* to keep the
crowds at a distance. Effie found herself and her portrait the centre of
all attention. She wrote home to Perth that 'Millais's picture is talked
of in a way to make every other Academician frantic. It is hardly
possible to approach it for the rows of bonnets.'[15] Effie was everywhere complimented on her part in the picture, as though she had
given Millais some active assistance. She had not: but she looked
forward to being painted once again, and she liked to further Millais's
social career. She talked of him to her friend Lord Lansdowne, who
said that he would invite the painter to dine. A few days later, when
she looked in at a party given by the Monkton Milnes at their home in
Upper Brook Street, she was able to introduce both Millais and
Holman Hunt to this aristocratic patron of the arts. In such gatherings
Pre-Raphaelitism now flourished. What Ruskin thought of this social
life, apart from the fact that it bored him, is not known. But at just the
time that Millais was being lionized in Mayfair, he was finishing the
third volume of *The Stones of Venice*, in which we may read his opinion
that an artist 'should be fit for the best society, *and should keep out of
it*',[16] explaining in a footnote:

Society always has a destructive influence on an artist: first, by its
sympathy with his meanest powers; secondly, by its chilling want
of understanding of his greatest; and thirdly, by its vain occupation
of his time and thoughts. Of course a painter of men must be *among*
men; but it ought to be as a watcher, not as a companion.[17]

★   ★ *(follower)* ★   ★   *(reader)*

The Order of Release is nowhere mentioned in Ruskin's published
works. We do not know what he thought of it, but we do know that he
hardly discussed it during the time that it was painted. He was
absorbed in *The Stones of Venice* and Millais had said that he did not
wish to show his picture to anyone until it was completed. But Ruskin
had some thought of improving Millais's art when, once again, he
invited the artist to go on holiday with him. Ruskin wanted to journey
north, to see Farnley Hall once more, and to stay with some new
friends, Sir Walter Trevelyan and his wife Pauline. He thought that he
and Effie, and perhaps Millais too, would tour in the Highlands and
visit Perth. The Edinburgh Philosophical Institution had invited Ruskin to give some lectures there that November. It occurred to Effie
that she might be able to keep Ruskin in Scotland all summer and
autumn. That would separate him, and her, from the maddening life
between Herne Hill and Denmark Hill. The Ruskins decided to extend
their invitation to Millais's brother William and to William Holman
Hunt, whom they hardly knew. Effie's father was asked to find a
house in the Highlands that they could rent. She wrote:

> John and the two Millais and Holman Hunt will be very busy
> sketching and walking over the mountains, and I shall accompany
> myself in trying to make them all as comfortable as I can, for we
> shall not have a very extensive establishment and there seems no
> certainty of anything to eat but trout out of the Tummel or the
> Garry, but it would amuse you to hear the Pre-Raphaelites and John
> talk. They seem to think they will have everything just for the
> asking and laugh at me for preparing a great hamper of sherry and
> tea and sugar which I expect they will be greatly glad to partake of in
> case of returning home any day wet through with Scotch mist . . .[18]

Effie liked the idea of looking after a household of artists as much as
she liked the prospect of going to balls. Her husband prepared for the
journey by idealizing his relationship with Millais and Hunt. He told
his old tutor W. L. Brown:

> We shall stay for a couple of months with the young painters of
> whom perhaps you may have heard something under the name of

'Pre-Raphaelites'. I fought for them as hard as I could when most people were abusing them — and we have a kind of brotherly feeling in consequence, and shall be very happy, I believe, painting heather together. We are going to study economy. Effie is to cook, and we are to catch trout for Cook — and we are to count for dinner and breakfast on porridge and milk. [19]

However, Holman Hunt, who admired Ruskin without feeling 'brotherly' emotion, now decided that the course of his art should lead him to Syria rather than to Scotland. He had long wished to paint in the Holy Land. Nobody else thought this a good plan. Ruskin tried to dissuade him, but to no avail. Millais was particularly upset to bid farewell to his comrade. Hunt hesitated, then left hurriedly. The rest of the party lingered in London and cancelled the house that Mr Gray had rented. Now their plans were even more fluid. Finally, on 21 June 1853, they left for Wallington by train. In the party were John and Effie Ruskin, the two Millais brothers and Crawley, the Ruskins' new servant.

*   *   *   *

So familiar were they that Ruskin was unable to recall, in later years, when he had first met the Trevelyans of Wallington. This strange couple were perhaps the dearest friends of the first half of his life. He now visited their home for the first time. It is a very large house. Much of it was at that date empty. Suites of uncarpeted rooms presented cheerless vistas. There was a Wallington ghost. It was said that if one found a corner and brought furniture to it one could be comfortable enough at Wallington. Otherwise, the best room in the house was Sir Walter's study. Here he kept his natural history collections, his fossils and stuffed animals, books and topographical pamphlets. He was tall, with drooping moustaches and fair hair that fell to his shoulders. He was reputedly a miser: in fact he gave large sums to charities and concerned himself with the condition of his tenantry. Sir Walter was a teetotaller, and some said that he had never been known to laugh. Yet not all of the many artists and literary people who visited Wallington preferred the company of his talented wife. There were those who found him fascinating. Staying at the house, Augustus Hare, the anecdotalist, wrote:

He knows every book and ballad that ever was written, every story of local interest that ever was told, and every flower and fossil that ever was found . . . His conversation is so curious that I follow him about everywhere, and take notes under his nose, which he does not seem to mind in the least, but only says something more quaint and astonishing the next minute . . .[20]

Scientific and antiquarian interests, social concern, a liking for story and romance: these of course were common components of the Pre-Raphaelite æsthetic. Sir Walter had no particular views about the future of contemporary painting. But he shows how easily and naturally one might join Pre-Raphaelitism. Ruskin's advocacy was powerful. His writings and personal interest were inspiring. But it took no great change of sensibility to like the new painting, for that sensibility was already in existence. As Pauline Trevelyan's house guests assembled at Wallington one observes how different from each other — in age, interests and background — were the champions of Pre-Raphaelitism. We may also see that it was not accepted that Ruskin was its sole arbiter. The Edinburgh physician and man of letters John Brown, with whom Ruskin had corresponded for years, greatly admired the critic. But he disliked his tone and rejected his historical arguments. When Ruskin had published *Pre-Raphaelitism*, Brown wrote to Pauline Trevelyan:

> I am glad John Ruskin is coming back to his first and best love. I read the *Stones* carefully last week; it is a great work — in some respects his greatest — but his arrogance is more offensive than *not* ever, and his savage jokes more savage than ever, and than is seemly or edifying, and his nonsense (and his father's) about Catholic Emancipation most abundantly ridiculous and tiresome. I once thought him very nearly a God; I find we must cross the river before we get to our Gods . . .[21]

Brown passed on to Pauline Trevelyan the *Pre-Raphaelitism* pamphlet: he did not feel like reviewing it himself. Pauline had Tractarian sympathies and was quite happy to take issue with Ruskin over his religious bias. Her notice was generally enthusiastic: she nonetheless pointed out:

> Mr Collins may not paint lilies in a convent garden, but the serpent is supposed to be hid under the leaves: and Mr Millais cannot decorate Mariana's room in the Moated Grange, with some indications of the faith of her country, but the author of *Modern Painters* finds the Pope behind the curtain.

Ruskin probably accepted these criticisms: Pauline Trevelyan was able to scold him, often in jest but sometimes in earnest. She had met Millais in London the previous year and was eager to talk to him again, for her writings had supported the fortunes of Pre-Raphaelitism north of the border. When *Christ in the House of his Parents* and *Mariana* had appeared at the Royal Scottish Academy she had declared most positively for the religious subject, of which she wrote, 'It is about the most wonderful and daring picture that ever appeared on the walls of an exhibition room.'[22]

Millais, the painter of romantic Scottish history, had never been in Scotland. Here, in the Cheviot border country, he heard much of Scottish lore and legend. He felt welcome, and stirred. Ruskin was content. He wrote to his father,

> This is the most beautiful place possible — a large old seventeenth century stone house in an old English terraced garden, beautifully kept, all the hawthorns still in full blossom: terrace opening on a sloping, wild park, down to the brook, about the half a mile fair slope; and woods on the other side, and undulating country with a particular *Northumberlandishness* about it — a far-away look which Millais enjoys intensely. We are all very happy, and going this afternoon to a little tarn where the seagulls come to breed.[23]

On another day the party drove over to Capheaton, the home of Sir Charles Swinburne: his nephew Algernon, a boy at school at this date, was a devoted friend of Pauline Trevelyan. Everybody sketched. Millais drew both Trevelyans, then started on some portraits of Effie. He wrote to Holman Hunt, 'Today I have been drawing Mrs Ruskin who is the sweetest creature that ever lived; she is the most pleasant companion one could wish. Ruskin is benign and kind. I wish you were here with us, you would like it . . .'[24] Millais, Ruskin and Sir Walter walked the hills and discussed the world. One afternoon Effie borrowed a pony and rode by herself over the moors back to the tarn. Hundreds of gulls were just learning to fly.

From Wallington the Ruskins and the two Millais brothers moved on to Edinburgh. Both Millais — Everett, as they now called him, to distinguish him from Ruskin — and Effie were suffering from colds and a painful inflammation of the throat. They went together to see Effie's doctor, the distinguished Sir James Simpson. The party then set off for the Highlands. At the beginning of July they arrived at Glenfinlas, Brig o' Turk, some miles above Stirling. In this remote, beautiful, rather inhospitable spot Millais was obliged to make crucial decisions about his art. These concerned his relations with the Ruskins. John James Ruskin, back in London, would no doubt have been satisfied to hear that

> Millais . . . has been more struck by the castle of Doune than anything and is determined to paint Effie at one of its windows —

18. John Everett Millais, by C. R. Leslie, 1852.

inside — showing beyond the window the windings of the river and Stirling castle. He is going to paint *me* among some rocks — in a companion picture. I thought you would be glad to know he is doing something for you, though he does not seem up to a *composition* . . .[25]

The nature of companion pictures is now relevant. They are usually made in celebration of marriage, and in betrothal or wedding portraits are commissioned by the bridegroom's father. They are domestic: they are made to go on either side of a fireplace or door and their composition is therefore complementary, the figure in the left-hand picture inclining towards the right, and vice versa. Millais thought this would be simple. But when he sketched Effie in the castle of Doune he saw that the complementary picture would be awkward to invent. The particularity of the naturalistic Pre-Raphaelite style tended to preclude such designs. He abandoned the idea and ordered only one canvas to be sent from London. On it he was to paint Ruskin rather than Effie. Suddenly the project had become quite different. Ruskin wrote triumphantly to his father:

> Millais has fixed on his place — a lovely piece of worn rock, with foaming water, and weeds, and moss, and a noble overhanging bank of dark crag — and I am to be standing looking quietly down the stream — just the sort of thing I used to do for hours together — he is very happy at the idea of doing it and I think you will be proud of the picture — and we shall have the two most wonderful torrents in the world, Turner's St Gothard — and Millais's Glenfinlas. He is going to take the utmost possible pains with it — and says he can paint rocks and water better than anything else — I am sure the foam of the torrent will be something quite new in art.[26]

The difference of ambition is clear. The painting would need to involve the 'utmost pains', as it would extend the range of Millais's art. He was not a landscapist, and never before had painted rocks or flowing water. This aspect of the picture would bring him into direct competition with Turner. Nobody had more to say about such matters than the critic whose portrait Millais now had to accommodate within a landscape setting. Ruskin's mention of the St Gothard drawing is significant. It was the water-colour that Turner had painted for him in 1843. In 1845, preparing for the second volume of *Modern Painters*, Ruskin had visited the site 'that I may know what is composition and what is verity'.[27] He had then taken stones, gneiss coloured by iron ochre, out of the torrent. For years he had meditated on what Turner, in conversation with him, had called 'that litter of stones which I *endeavoured* to represent'.[28] He had been back to the site the previous year, on his way home from Venice, to study the light there at different times of day. He sketched the same scene, drew, traced, and etched from the Turner original. At Glenfinlas Ruskin made drawings of the gneiss rocks in the stream. They are very like the background in the Millais picture. But they also resemble Ruskin's studies from Turner. This was the point of his increasing interest in his portrait. It was his opportunity to enforce, rather than merely assert, his old view that Pre-Raphaelitism was Turnerian.

Millais took some time to start the painting. He spent days on a smaller, more relaxed picture of Effie sitting on some rocks further down the stream. Amid the general *camaraderie* of the party an especial friendship was developing between the painter and the critic's wife. At first it was disguised by standing jokes. Millais adopted a chaffingly chivalric attitude towards Effie, referring to her always as 'the Countess': she fussed over him as though he were a great boy. On walks together they could be more straightforward. When not in the open air it became difficult. Millais, Effie and Ruskin, as they passed their evenings and as they slept, were very close to each other. For in their pursuit of economy they had moved out of the inn where they had at first lodged and had rented a small cottage. There was very little room in it. Millais and Effie slept in two boxed-in beds at either end of the parlour in which Ruskin made up his own bed. Effie described their arrangements:

> Crawley thinks Mrs Ruskin would be awfully horrified if she saw our dwelling. John Millais and I have each two little dens where we have room to sleep and turn in but no place whatever to put anything in, there being no drawers, but I have established a file of nails from which my clothes hang and John sleeps on the sofa in the parlour.[29]

In the daytime Millais and Effie were always together outside the house, while William Millais (who had remained at the inn) was happy with his fishing. Ruskin sat alone, making an index of *The Stones of Venice* and preparing the lectures he was to give in Edinburgh. One day Millais crushed his thumb when bathing in the stream: Effie bound it up for him. A little later, greatly daring, she sat him down and cut his hair. Millais began to find their physical proximity quite disturbing. Soon it would render him hysterical with longing.

★   ★   ★   ★

Millais was on the brink of a quite novel, utterly illicit experience. At the same time he was longing to express himself. His painting was in abeyance, for his canvas had still not arrived. In any case he was bursting with creative desires quite unconnected with the projected portrait. Ruskin was puzzled by his protégé's thwarted hyperactivity. He wrote to his father:

> Millais is a very interesting study. I don't know how to manage him, his mind is so *terribly* active — so full of invention that he can hardly stay quiet a moment without sketching, either ideas or

19. John Ruskin, by Sir John Everett Millais, 1853.

reminiscences — and keeps himself awake all night planning pictures. He cannot go on this way. I must get Acland to lecture him.[30]

Henry Acland was on holiday in Edinburgh at the time and was to
spend a few days in the Glenfinlas hotel. He did not find that Millais
needed medical advice but he was fascinated by his activity. What he
found at Glenfinlas he wrote in daily letters to his wife. We should pay
particular attention to these reports. For while it seems clear to us that
the relationships at Glenfinlas were speeding towards a ruinous conclusion, Acland saw there one beautifully unifying bond. It was art.
The doctor first of all explained to his rather strict, Evangelical wife
that in this highly irregular household there was yet an especial propriety. This he could not quite define, but he felt that it had to do with the
way that Millais appeared

> . . . a very child of nature — and oh! how blessed a thing is this. And
> that is just what Mrs Ruskin is — nothing could be more wholly
> unintelligible to my mother (and perhaps even to you) than her way
> of going on here with the boys as she calls the two Millais — but it is
> just like a clever country girl. Thoroughly artless, witty, unsophis-
> ticated to the last degree and tho' I cannot say I should like brought
> up as I have been to have you so! yet there is a certain charm in it in
> her which will presently delight me. It unites the company. Millais
> is a grown up Baby — and does and says in mere exuberant
> childishness now just what a very [illegible] and boisterous child
> would do & say . . .[31]

Rather pleased with his discovery that they were 'children of
nature', a formulation which he repeats, Acland could make many a
parallel with Pre-Raphaelite art as Ruskin taught it. He himself had
given his hand to the diligent naturalism so much enjoined that summer.

> Ruskin I understand more than I have before: truth and earnestness
> of purpose are his great guide, and no labour of thought, or work is
> wearisome to him. He has knocked up my sketching for ever. I was
> quite convinced that the hasty drawings I have been in the habit of,
> are most injurious to the doer, in his moral nature. What I can try to
> do is to draw *correctly* really well. I hope to be well enough to try
> tomorrow a bit of rock & water . . .[32]

Such sentiments are pure Ruskinism. Acland felt that he too could
become a Pre-Raphaelite. It was an effect that Ruskin had on many
amateur artists. But it was not possible for Millais to think in these

terms. He knew in his heart that such talk simply did not apply to him. In truth, he did not care much about either God or Turner. And the more he felt attracted to Effie the less inclined he was to feel virtuous when painting her husband's portrait to his satisfaction. At the end of July, Acland held the canvas while Millais, 'on his highest mettle' according to Ruskin, put down the first marks of the painting.[33] Ruskin's diary records his progress over the next seven weeks.[34] It went on inch by inch: technically, realist Pre-Raphaelitism was a very slow way of making a picture. In the first fortnight Millais was often painting for six hours a day with nothing much to show for his labour. Soon he decided to move to the hotel. The tension of sleeping in the tiny cottage was too much for him. He wanted to paint for Effie, but could not. The time he could spend alone with her became more and more precious, and the hours he spent at his easel more like toil.

Henry Acland was not the only visitor to Glenfinlas that summer. The Millais brothers had lunch one day with the picture dealer Ernest Gambart and the French painter Rosa Bonheur, whose work Gambart promoted in England. Millais was soon to form a profitable relationship with Gambart, and it may have been now that it was spelt out to him that his Pre-Raphaelite painting was being sold for the third or fourth time without commanding the price Gambart would give immediately for a slightly different kind of work. Millais was innocent about the rewards that painting might bring, but he did not wish to be innocent. He suspected that there was little worldly profit in the struggle to please Ruskin. But when he could interest the critic without making an effort he was delighted. On 17 August Millais wrote to his friend Charles Collins,

> You will shortly hear of me in another art besides painting. Ruskin has discovered I can design architectural ornament more perfectly than any living or dead party. So delighted is he that in the evenings I have promised to design doors, arches and windows for Churches etc etc. It is the most amusing occupation and it comes quite easily and naturally to my hand . . . Ruskin is beside himself with pleasure as he has been groaning for years about the lost feeling for Architecture. When I make a design he slaps his hands together in pleasure.[35]

There is some record of these activities in Ruskin's Edinburgh lectures. More heartfelt drawings are those in which Millais depicted Effie with natural ornament. He adorned her not with jewellery but with corn-ears, acorns and flowers. They went on long walks together over the hills, often not returning until after dark. Ruskin and William Millais stayed behind at the cottage. According to William, writing

20. Dr Henry Acland, by Sir John Everett Millais, 1853.

years later, Ruskin should now have been more firm about the proprieties of the situation:

I may say that I think that Ruskin did not act wisely in putting JEM and ECG continually together — Every afternoon by way of exercise Ruskin and I spent our time with pickaxe and barrow and spade to try to cut a canal across a bend in the river — whilst he preferred that ECG should roam the hills with JEM & presently they did not return until quite late — Ruskin's remark to me was, 'how well your brother and my wife gets on together'! — a very dangerous experiment & had it not been *for their integrity* evil consequences must have ensued. I may add that JEM returned home helplessly in love with ECG . . .[36]

This is confused, perhaps because the Millais family liked to believe that Ruskin was so wicked that he deliberately put his wife in the way of temptation. The truth was that he was oblivious of the fact that Effie and Millais were falling in love. When William left Glenfinlas in the middle of August Ruskin took even less notice of them. They occupied themselves and he got on with his work. All through September the three were alone together and yet were strangely separated. The weather was bad. Progress on the painting was ever more slow. Millais was coming to hate it. He continued his long walks alone with Effie. We do not know what declarations they made to each other, but we do know that she told him the truth about her marriage. This was a new intimacy between them which filled Millais with a confused sense of outrage: there was a sense in which he was glad that she had never had a physical relationship with her husband. In these weeks Effie seems to have remained calm enough, but Millais was shaking with tension. Ruskin was still blind to the situation. He wrote to his mother,

I wish the country agreed with Millais as well as it does with me, but I don't know how to manage him and he does not know how to manage himself. He paints till his limbs are numb, and his back has as many aches as joins in it. He won't take exercise in the regular way, but sometimes starts and takes races of seven or eight miles if he is in the humour: sometimes won't, or can't, eat any breakfast or dinner, sometimes eats enormously without seeming to enjoy anything. Sometimes he is all excitement, sometimes depressed, sick and faint as a woman, always restless and unhappy. I think I never saw such a miserable person on the whole. He is really very ill tonight, has gone early to bed and complains of a feeling of complete faintness and lethargy, with headache. I don't know what to do with him. The faintness seems so excessive, sometimes appearing almost hysterical.[37]

Three days later Millais's condition was worse. Ruskin thought that he should do something drastic to restore his spirits. Characteristically, perhaps, he assumed that the cause of the trouble lay in the dissolution of the Pre-Raphaelite Brotherhood. He believed that Millais was suffering because he could not bear the idea of Holman Hunt going abroad. He therefore decided to write to the other Pre-Raphaelite. One cannot read this letter without feeling that Ruskin's concern was genuine.

> My dear Hunt,
> I can't help writing to you tonight; for here is Everett lying crying on his bed like a child — or rather with that bitterness which is only in a man's grief — and I don't know what will become of him when you are gone — I always intended to write to you to try and dissuade you from this Syrian expedition — I suppose it is much too late now — but I think it quite wrong of you to go. I had no idea how much Everett depended on you, till lately — for your own sake I wanted you not to go, but had no hope of making you abandon the thought — if I had known sooner how much Everett wanted you I should have tried. *I* can be no use to him — he has no sympathy with me or my ways, his family do not suffice him — he has nobody to take your place — his health is wretched — he is always miserable about something or other . . . I never saw so strange a person, I could not answer for his reason if you leave him. Instead of going to Syria, I think you ought to come down here instantly: he is quite overworked — very ill — has yet a quarter of his picture to do in his distress — and we must go to Edinburgh — and leave him *quite alone* — next Wednesday. Think over all this.[38]

Hunt did not go to Scotland but delayed his departure for the Holy Land. Millais did not know what to do or where to go. He was tortured by the thought of Effie going to Edinburgh with her husband and leaving him in Glenfinlas alone. Every thought of her increased his confusion. What could he do? What could he say to her if she left? In the event, he announced that he would leave the painting until better weather the following March, when he would return to his place by the stream and the rocks. The artistic household was dismantled. Millais left with the Ruskins and accompanied them to Edinburgh. It was while they were there that, blunderingly and almost inadvertently, he broke up the Ruskins's marriage.

★   ★   ★   ★

Ruskin's forthcoming Edinburgh lectures had been almost as much a part of the background of the Glenfinlas holiday as Millais's portrait. The four lectures had been written in the cottage, or in the open air outside the cottage, and their themes had been explored in conversation with Millais and Acland. Their delivery in the Philosophical Institution was to be the culmination of Ruskin's summer's work. That they were to be given in his father's home town was calculated to feed John James's pride, and thus allay his misgivings about appearances on public platforms. By contrast, Millais's picture was unfinished, and pretty clearly would not be finished in time to hang in the next year's Royal Academy exhibition. There was also the possibility that he might have to abandon it. The distraught Pre-Raphaelite seemed hardly in charge of his own destiny. Perhaps, if he had gone straight back to London, had gone abroad with Holman Hunt, he might have been more decisive about his life. He reflected that his best plan would be to forget about Effie and have nothing further to do with the Ruskins. This might also have been the honourable course to take. But he could not bear to distance himself from the woman he loved, and remained in the Scottish capital all the time that Ruskin was lecturing. The four addresses were on Architecture, Decoration, Turner and his Works, and Pre-Raphaelitism. They were afterwards collected into a book, *Lectures on Architecture and Painting*, which is a clear and balanced introduction to Ruskin's thinking at this time. Their success was gratifying. Over a thousand people filled the hall each time that Ruskin spoke and the press comment, comparing his message to that of a preacher, was exactly what the older Ruskins would have desired. But Ruskin himself was a little uninterested in the stir he was making. He was more concerned to take stock of his relations with Effie and with Millais. He wrote to his father, hearkening back to childhood reading:

> It is curious how like your melancholy letter — received some time ago, about our staying so long away, is to the 176th letter in Sir Charles Grandison. I wish Effie could write such a one as the 177th in answer. But I have had much to think about — in studying Everett, and myself, and Effie, on this journey, and reading Sir Charles Grandison afterwards — and then reading the world a little bit — and then Thackeray — for in 'The Newcomes' — though more disgusting in the illustrations than usual — there are some pieces of wonderful truth. The grievous thing that forces itself upon my mind — from all this — is the utter *unchangeableness* of people. All the morality of Richardson and Miss Edgeworth (and the longer

I live — the more wisdom I think is concentrated in their writings)
seems to have no effect on persons who are not *born* Sir Charles's or
Belindas. Looking back upon myself — I find no change in myself
from a boy — from a child except the natural changes wrought by
age. I am exactly the same creature — in temper — in likings — in
weaknesses: much wiser — knowing more and thinking more: but
in character precisely the same — so is Effie. When we married, I
expected to change *her* — she expected to change *me*. Neither have
succeeded, and both are displeased. When I came down to Scotland
with Millais, I expected to do great things for him. I saw he was
uneducated, little able to follow out a train of thought — proud and
impatient. I thought to make him read Euclid and bring him back a
meek and methodical man. I might as well have tried to make a
Highland stream read Euclid, or be methodical. He, on the other
hand, thought he could make me like PreRaphaelitism and Men-
delssohn better than Turner and Bellini. But he has given it up, now
. . .[39]

   Such things Ruskin might say to himself, or to his father: but they
were rationalizations of an emotional deadlock that could not be
discussed. Effie and Millais could not speak together of their love.
Ruskin now suspected that Effie had beguiled Millais, but he did not
say this to his parents; and the etiquette did not exist which would
allow him to warn his protégé of his wife's charms. Those charms were
in any case no longer apparent to Ruskin. Effie sulked in his company.
Ruskin could not resolve this situation: that is why he wished only that
people were other than they were, and preferably like characters in
Miss Edgeworth's improving novels. He rather badly wanted to be left
alone. He was relieved when Effie went to Bowerswell and Millais left
for London. With the lectures over and these troublesome young
people departed he could begin to think once again about *Modern
Painters* and the Ruskin family tour in the summer. The 'habits of
steady thought' and the like, so often enjoined by Ruskin, had not
been easy to maintain while the shallow-minded Effie and the headstrong young painter had been behaving so peculiarly. Millais, back in
London, now heard that he had been elected an Associate of the Royal
Academy. What Ruskin thought of this distinction is not recorded: he
probably scorned it far more than did Millais's Pre-Raphaelite brethren. John James Ruskin, who entertained Millais at Denmark Hill
while John and Effie were still in Scotland, was full of praise for him.
'What a Beauty of a Man he is and high in intellect but he is very thin,'
he wrote to Ruskin.[40]

Millais had gone out to Denmark Hill because, once invited, he could not see how to refuse the invitation. In many ways he was still much indebted to the Ruskin family. He could think of many reasons for disliking and resenting Ruskin, and now had those feelings about him without looking for reasons. But the bluff, generous, honest John James could not be hated. There was talk of a portrait drawing of him, and no doubt Millais and the elder Ruskin discussed 'The Deluge', the proposed major painting that John had spoken of in his letters home from Scotland. However, these genial exchanges soon ended. For Millais took the bold step of writing to Mrs Gray, Effie's mother. He had met her only once, in Edinburgh, but now felt free to express his views on the marriage and on 'such a brooding selfish lot as these Ruskins'. About Effie, he wrote,

> The *worst of all is the wretchedness* of her position. Whenever they go to visit she will be left to herself in the company of any stranger present, for Ruskin appears to delight in selfish solitude. Why he ever had the audacity of marrying with no better intentions is a mystery to me. I must confess that it appears to me that he cares for nothing beyond his Mother and Father, which makes the insolence of his finding fault with his wife (to whom he has acted from the beginning most disgustingly) more apparent . . . If I have meddled more than my place would justify it was from the flagrant nature of the affair — I am only anxious to do the best for your daughter . . . I cannot conceal the truth from you, that she has more to put up with than any living woman . . . She has all the right on her side and believe me the Father would see that also if he knew all.[41]

Millais 'knew all' about the circumstances of Effie's marriage, but could not mention sexual matters to her mother. Nonetheless, in his correspondence with Mrs Gray he made it clear that there was a youthful, healthy intimacy between himself and Effie that contrasted with an unnaturalness in Ruskin. He hinted that Ruskin was a homosexual: this he may have believed. It cannot be said that Millais in this correspondence wrote naïvely or impetuously. If a break was to come, it had to be of Effie's own doing. But Millais carefully made it plain that he was not a neutral observer of the Ruskins's marriage. Effie knew this in her heart, and knew it the more surely because her mother told her what was in Millais's letters. When she and John returned to London she had another family link with Millais, for little Sophie, her ten-year-old sister, came south with them. Millais drew this sensitive, clever child in his studio in Gower Street. From her he gathered how tense the atmosphere was in Denmark Hill; and Effie gathered from Sophie something of her lover's movements. When

Ruskin came to Gower Street for work on the portrait he talked, as usual. But in truth he and his portraitist were scarcely on speaking terms, for Effie's behaviour at Herne Hill had at last made it plain to Ruskin that she had come to loathe her husband and that she had fallen in love with the artist.[42]

John James Ruskin now wrote what turned out to be his last letter to Mr Gray, complaining of Effie's 'continual pursuit of pleasure', while the unhappy girl found a *confidante* in Lady Eastlake. On 7 March, surely not before time, after weeks of agonized life between Herne Hill and Denmark Hill, she sat down to write to her father to tell him the truth about her marriage:

> I have therefore simply to tell you that I do not think I am John Ruskin's Wife at all — and I entreat you to assist me to get released from the unnatural position in which I stand to Him. To go back to the day of my marriage the 10th of April 1848. I went as you know away to the Highlands. I had never been told the duties of married persons to each other and knew little or nothing about their relations in the closest union on earth. For days John talked about this relation to me but avowed no intention of making me his Wife. He alleged various reasons, Hatred to children, religious motives, a desire to preserve my beauty, and finally this last year told me his true reason (and this to me is as villainous as all the rest), that he had imagined women were quite different to what he saw I was, and that the reason he did not make me his Wife was because he was disgusted with my person the first evening 10th April. After I began to see things better I argued with him and took the Bible but he soon silenced me and I was not sufficiently awake to what position I was in. Then he said after 6 years he would marry me, when I was 25. This last year we spoke about it. I did say what I thought in May. He then said, as I professed quite a dislike to him, that it would be *sinful* to enter into such a connexion, as if I was not very *wicked* I was at least insane and the responsibility that I might have children was too great, as I was quite unfit to bring them up. These are some of the facts. You may imagine what I have gone through — and besides all this the temptations his neglect threw me in the way of . . .[43]

After this revelation it became clear that Effie would have to escape. Her parents' first thoughts were that Mr Gray should go to London to confront John James. But what would be the profit in that? In the event both Mr and Mrs Gray came to London to consult lawyers. They then made clandestine plans with Effie, Lady Eastlake and Rawdon Brown, who was in England to arrange publication of a book with Smith, Elder. The flight was neatly arranged. Ruskin imagined, to his satisfaction, that Effie was to take Sophie back to Scotland and stay there while he and his parents took their summer tour of the Continent. He accompanied her to King's Cross and put her on the train to Edinburgh. At Hitchin, the first stop, Effie's parents joined the train. At six o'clock that evening court officials arrived at Denmark Hill to serve a citation on Ruskin, alleging the nullity of the marriage. Effie's wedding ring, keys and account book were delivered in a packet to John James. There was a fortnight before the Ruskins were due to go abroad. John James managed the legal side as best he could. There was not much to do. The Ruskins intended no defence. They wanted to end the matter as quickly and privately as possible. They determined to behave in public as they normally would. Both John James and his son attended the annual exhibitions of the Water-Colour Society and the Royal Academy, after which Ruskin wrote two letters to *The Times* outlining and praising the symbolism of two paintings by Holman Hunt, *The Light of the World* and *The Awakening Conscience*. These rather eloquent letters were widely regarded, especially among the Eastlake circle, as proof of Ruskin's hypocrisy. Thus the marriage ended, in bitterness and enmity, but with both partners glad to be free once more. Millais managed to finish his portrait, but rejected Ruskin's offers of continued friendship and artistic collaboration. The annulment was granted in the summer, while the Ruskins were abroad; and in July of 1855, a little more than a year later, Millais and Effie were pronounced man and wife.

CHAPTER ELEVEN

1854–1857

Long before Effie's departure, Ruskin had proposed to spend the summer in Switzerland. What reason had he now for changing his plans? A fortnight after his wife's flight he set out for the Continent in the company of his parents. As they left Dover, Ruskin opened a new vellum-covered notebook and diary for the year's fresh work.[1] Its first date is at Calais, on 10 May, John James Ruskin's birthday and the traditional family feast. The opposite right-hand page has been cut out. On it was the drawing of the jib of 'the old Dover packet to Calais'. Since this was reproduced in *Præterita* it is probable that Ruskin extracted it when looking up old diaries to write his autobiography. The illustration is puzzlingly undistinguished, and in *Præterita* is placed next to Ruskin's description of the tours of 1845 and 1846. But its personal meaning is clear. Departure from England in that spring of 1854 meant liberation. Still confusing the dates, *Præterita* confesses

> The immeasurable delight to me of being able to loiter and swing about just over the bowsprit and watch the plunge of the bows, if there was the least swell or broken sea to lift them, with the hope of Calais at breakfast, and the horses' heads set straight for Mont Blanc to-morrow, is one of the few pleasures I look back to as quite unmixed . . .[2]

This summer on the Continent was happy and productive because of the absence of Ruskin's 'commonplace Scotch wife', as he now called her: it was as though, with Effie gone, he could joyously return to *Modern Painters*, the book he owed his father but had abandoned during the years of his marriage.

'I never knew what it was to possess a father and mother — till I knew what it was to be neglected and forsaken of a wife,' Ruskin now wrote to Charles Woodd, an old family friend.[3] With different emphases, he also sent letters that were specifically about his marriage to Henry Acland (asking him to send the letter on to the Trevelyans), to Furnivall, to John Brown, and no doubt to others. Later this year, after his return to England, we find an especially revealing confession to Walter Fawkes.[4] None of this correspondence concerns us at the moment: how was Ruskin to know what issues it would raise when, a

decade later, he was a suitor for the hand of Rose La Touche? On 15
July his legal tie with Effie seemed to be cut. On that day she received
her decree. It read that the marriage 'or rather show or effigy of
marriage . . . solemnized or rather profaned between the said John
Ruskin and Euphemia Chalmers Gray falsely called Ruskin' was
annulled because 'the said John Ruskin was incapable of consummat-
ing the same by reason of incurable impotency'.[5] When Ruskin heard
of this annulment — a decision later to be of such emotional and legal
significance — he probably was only glad that the business seemed to
be over. We do not know what he and John James thought about the
legal aspects of his case, nor how they were advised by the family
solicitors. But it must always have been obvious to them that to
dispute such a decision would not only be unpleasant. For to vindicate
one's own honour in such a situation might mean that Effie would
remain bound to the Ruskins: or, worse, would come back.

   The Ruskins's itinerary was from Calais through Amiens and
Chartres to Geneva; they then spent three months in Switzerland
before returning to England via Paris at the end of September. If this
seems by now a familiar route, we should note that to follow old paths
had a purpose. Ruskin was enabled to restart *Modern Painters* by
revisiting the country in which he had first found its inspiration. In the
years in which Effie and Venice had occupied him he had been lost to
his mountain places. He had not studied nature in his old way since
1849, the year when he had travelled abroad with his parents and
without his wife. These intervening years were now swept aside.
Ruskin's work in this summer of 1854 was glorious, as we may find in
every chapter of the third and fourth volumes of *Modern Painters* that
issue from his meditations in the Alps. In those chapters there is a
Christian spirit that is not at all like the darker, programmatic religious
undertow of *The Stones of Venice*. Happiness and prayer enabled his
love for natural creation to take precedence over his interpretations of
European culture. One would wish to know more about the manner
in which Ruskin generated this revival of an old mood of worship.
Perhaps it is significant that (as his diary reveals) his main devotional
reading was in the Beatitudes and in Revelation. The diary tells us that
at Lucerne, on 2 July, 'I . . . received my third call from God, in
answer to much distressful prayer. May He give me grace to walk
hereafter with Him in newness of life, to whom be glory for ever.
Amen.'[6] This 'call' means a joyous resolution about his writing. We
will remember that Ruskin had known such an answer to prayer on
two previous occasions. The first had been in the church in Geneva in

21. *South Transept, Rouen*, by John Ruskin, 1854.

1842, before he embarked on the writing of the first volume of *Modern Painters*. The second was in 1845, coming home from the Italian tour with the second volume in his mind. Now, in July and August of 1854, at Chamonix, Sallenches, Sion, Martigny and Champagnole, Ruskin took the notes that gave us the noblest passages in the continuation of his great work.

To say this is to admit that few of the most achieved parts of *Modern Painters* are directly concerned with painting. Ruskin's reaction to the Louvre is interesting. As so often, the party stopped in Paris on the way home: as so often, Ruskin gave the great picture collection only a cursory visit. His diary records,

> The grand impression on me, in walking through Louvre after Switzerland, is the utter *coarseness* of painting, especially as regards mountains. The universal principle of blue mass behind and green or brown banks or bushes in front. No real sense of height or distance, no care, no detail, no affection . . .[7]

During the next eighteen months, while he wrote the third and fourth volumes of *Modern Painters* and prepared their fifty plates, he returned time and again to the major intellectual difficulty of his earlier life: the fact that nature is one thing and art another. But there was much else to occupy him. Nature alone could not take up all his attention. Even in the Alps he had written a pamphlet on the preservation of ancient buildings, *The Opening of the Crystal Palace*, and had contemplated an illustrated book on Swiss towns and their history. In Paris, feeling that his work in England was only a week away, he quite suddenly became full of ideas. A letter to Pauline Trevelyan lists them:

> I am going to set myself up to tell people anything *in any way* that they want to know, as soon as I get home. I am rolling projects over and over in my head: I want to give short lectures to about 200 at once in turn, of the Sign painters — and shop decorators — and writing masters — and upholsterers — and masons — and brick-makers, and glassblowers, and pottery people — and young artists — and young men in general, and school-masters — and young ladies in general — and schoolmistresses — and I want to teach Illumination to the sign painters and the young ladies; and to have the prayer books all *written* again; (only the Liturgy altered first, as I told you) — and I want to explode printing; and gunpowder — the two great curses of the age — I begin to think that abominable art of printing is the root of all the mischief — it makes people used to have everything the same shape. And I mean to lend out Liber Studiorum & Albert Durers to everybody who wants them; and to

make copies of all fine 13th century manuscripts, and lend *them* out
— all for nothing, of course, — and have a room where anybody
can go in all day and always see *nothing* in it but what is *good*: and I
want to have a black hole, where they shall see nothing but what is
bad: filled with Claudes, & Sir Charles Barry's architecture — and
so on — and I want to have a little Academy of my own in all the
manufacturing towns — and to get the young artists — preRaphael-
ite always, to help me — and I want to have an Academy exhibition
— an opposition shop — where all the pictures shall be hung on the
line; in nice little rooms, decorated in a Giottesque manner; and no
bad pictures let in — and none good turned out and very few
altogether — and only a certain number of people let in each day —
by ticket — so as to have no elbowing. And as all this is merely by
the way, while I go on with my usual work about Turner and
collect materials for a great work I mean to write on politics —
founded on the Thirteenth Century — I shall have plenty to do
when I get home . . .[8]

Romantic and utopian as these ambitions might seem, there yet
were ways in which Ruskin's schemes could be tested. One was
presented to him almost as soon as he came home from Paris. F. J.
Furnivall, loyal to Ruskin throughout the time of the public furore
over his marriage, now approached him with the news of a proposed
Working Men's College. At a meeting to discuss its foundation Furnivall had distributed a pamphlet which reprinted the 'Nature of
Gothic' chapter from *The Stones of Venice*. He was especially eager that
the experiment should have Ruskin's blessing. The other founders of
the college had probably not anticipated the critic's response to Furnivall: he immediately offered to take a regular drawing class. Ruskin's outlook differed sharply from that of the college's establishment.
He was distant from its principal, F. D. Maurice, and from other
founders like Charles Kingsley and Thomas Hughes. He had nothing
to do with their Christian Socialism. However imaginative Ruskin's
view of politics, he was a tory of his father's type, opposed to democracy and liberal reform. His Christianity was certainly not of the 'sane,
masculine Cambridge school' favoured by Christian Socialism and by
such guiding spirits of the college as Llewelyn Davies.[9] Ruskin might
therefore have brought contention into the new foundation. But this
did not happen, especially since nobody of Maurice's or Kingsley's
type was likely to think that art lessons were important. Ruskin
conducted his drawing class on his own terms, avoided his colleagues
and took little part in the management of the college. Thus he was able
to participate in the educational experiment quite contentedly, teach-

ing regularly from the autumn of 1854 until May of 1858, in the spring
of 1860, then sporadically for one or two years after that.

Ruskin's absorption in the classes in a house in Red Lion Square
might have had a rather personal motive. It is possible that he felt — as
he often would in years to come — that it was time to cease from
vanity and to work quietly at an elementary level, far from public
renown. In this way, the drawing class was a reaction from the fame of
his books and the glittering social life he had led with Effie.[10] A slower
pace and a less excited notion of what he might achieve were also
forced on him by the nature of his students. Before he began teaching
workmen he told Sarah Acland that he was considering 'whether I
shall make Peruginos, or Turners, or Tintorets, or Albert Durers of
them'.[11] Wiser and more limited ambitions soon prevailed, and Ruskin began to think in other terms. He now looked only for a skill in
drawing which might simply allow his pupils to enjoy looking at
natural objects. This became the official policy of his class. He expressed it often, and in varying ways. A succinct summary of his programme was given to a Royal Commission in 1857: 'My efforts are
directed not to making a carpenter an artist, but to making him
happier as a carpenter.'[12] But the contemporary existence of a drawing
class and much theoretical writing about drawing should not lead us to
believe that the former was an expression of the latter. For what really
happens in a class is that individual students manage different things
differently, and the master encourages or corrects them as best he
may. Ruskin was obviously good at it. Here are the recollections of
Thomas Sulman, a wood engraver, who attended the Working Men's
College from its earliest days:

> How generous he was! He taught each of us separately, studying the
> capacities of each student. For one pupil he would put a cairngorm
> pebble or fluor-spar into a tumbler of water, and set him to trace
> their tangled veins of crimson and amethyst. For another he would
> bring lichen and fungi from Anerley Woods. Once, to fill us with
> despair of colour, he bought a case of West Indian birds unstuffed,
> as the collector had stored them, all rubies and emeralds. Some-
> times it was a Gothic missal, when he set us counting the order of
> the coloured leaves in each spray of the MS. At other times it was a
> splendid Albert Durer woodcut . . . One by one, he brought for us
> to examine his marvels of water-colour art from Denmark Hill. He
> would point out the subtleties and felicities in their composition,
> analysing on a blackboard their line schemes . . . He had reams of
> the best stout drawing-paper made specially for us, supplying every

convenience the little rooms would hold. He commissioned William Hunt of the Old Water-Colour Society to paint two subjects for the class, and both were masterpieces . . .[13]

All this is genial; and Ruskin's appointment of the unskilled Rossetti to conduct a life class makes one further suspect that art education at the Working Men's College was as much light-hearted as it was theoretical. Of course, Ruskin's deep instinct for taking matters seriously could not be long suspended. Thus there was a variable relationship in the college between grave purposes and what Rossetti called 'fun'. Rossetti's presence helped to create a contradictory and exciting atmosphere. So did the students. Some were solemn, while others were simply happy to be dabbling with water-colours. All of them seem to have responded to Ruskin, especially at his improvised lectures. Ford Madox Brown, an occasional visitor at the college, reported that 'Ruskin was as eloquent as ever, and wildly popular with the men'.[14] That popularity accounts for numerous reports of the speeches in students' reminiscences. 'We used to look forward to these talks with great interest,' writes 'One who was often present'. 'Formless and planless as they were, the effect on the hearers was immense. It was a wonderful bubbling up of all manner of glowing thoughts; for mere eloquence I never heard aught like it.'[15]

These were some of the first occasions when Ruskin spoke spontaneously in public. As such, the lectures have an important place both in his life and also in his writing. John James had been hostile to the invitations to lecture Ruskin often received. He considered lectures vulgar. 'I don't care to see you allied with the platform', he wrote, '— though the pulpit would be our delight — Jeremy Taylor occupied the last & Bacon never stood on the former . . .'[16] The 'notion of a *platform* & an *Itinerant Lecturer*' offended John James's notions of the dignity of his son's books. Recently, Ruskin had dutifully declined to contribute to a series of lectures in Camberwell: the lectern was also to be occupied by a self-educated workman to whom the Ruskins charitably gave old clothes. In Red Lion Square, there were no similar problems. There, Ruskin found a way of lecturing that depended on a difference in social class. He also expressed himself more extravagantly than his father would have thought wise. This anticipates the pamphleteering of the later Ruskin. His manner to his students was improvised and freely expository; his thoughts were paradoxical and returned upon themselves in apparent contradiction; he employed anecdote, aphorism, and dramatic questions; the tone was both rhetorical and intimate. It was a style that Ruskin would explore in print in years to come, in works that were nominally addressed to working-class audiences: to Thomas Dixon, the cork-cutter of *Time and Tide*, and then to all the 'workmen and labourers of Great Britain' in *Fors Clavigera*.

*   *   *   *

The cold autumn of 1854 was followed by months of bitter weather, long afterwards remembered as 'the Crimean winter'. In the new year, for weeks on end, London was covered by ice and snow. That spring the hawthorn blossoms in the Herne Hill garden were perished by frosts as late as June. Ruskin was unwell. He was tired, feverish, and continually coughing. A short trip to Deal to look at ships and shipping — a visit which later produced *The Harbours of England* — failed to restore him. In late May of 1855 he went to his doctor cousin William Richardson at Tunbridge Wells. Richardson put him to bed, cured him in three days and told him not to be a fool. Perhaps Ruskin simply needed a change. Since the tour abroad the previous summer he had been trying to develop a fresh impulse for the next volume of *Modern Painters*. It was now nearly ten years since the last instalment had been published. Ruskin wanted to find a continuity with what he had then written: he also wished to clarify his experience of architecture and contemporary art during the past decade. But his plans for the book, always liable to modification and expansion, now became merely disparate. The third volume of *Modern Painters*, written at intervals between the summer of 1854 and January of 1856, is entitled 'Of Many Things'.

Ruskin lacked a direction in his life. It was now that he should have left the family home. But he did not: he could not see the point of such a personal emancipation. His writing had something to do with it. *Modern Painters* represented his continuing obligation to his father. Even if Ruskin had thought of independence, the fact that he was writing this book for John James would have discouraged a departure. The way in which he remained his parents' child now became all the more marked. Anne Strachan, his childhood nurse, still treated him as an infant. Little Sarah Angelina Acland, who came to visit Denmark Hill with her brother Harry, Ruskin's godson, tells us how 'Mrs Ruskin made us boats with walnut shells with which we had races in his bath. Anne the old maid who kept Mr Ruskin in great order, came in and said that he had no business to have water in his bath, and that as he had he must see to emptying it!'[17] Many other visitors remarked how close the Ruskin family was. The painter James Smetham, writing to a friend after an evening at Denmark Hill in February 1855, recounted that Ruskin 'has a large house with a lodge, and a valet and a footman and a coachman, and grand rooms glistening with pictures, mainly Turner's . . . his mother and father live with him, or he with them'. Smetham noticed how Ruskin deferred to parental authority, how 'Mrs Ruskin puts "John" down and holds her own opinions, and flatly contradicts him; and he receives all her opinions with a soft reverence and gentleness that is pleasant to witness'.[18]

Ruskin's dependence on his parents had a particular use after Effie's departure. Their protectiveness and pride upheld him. He had no need to consult his conscience and no reason to consider his self-respect. He now faced London and the world of what men were saying about him with equanimity. Mr and Mrs Ruskin had given their son a self-assurance in which there was a mixture of innocence and arrogance. But Ruskin's arrogance was seldom foremost. People were most struck by his openness. All through his life, in whatever circums-tances, he very seldom showed signs of embarrassment. On only one occasion does he claim to be shy. This is in a letter of December 1853, written after he had inadvertently said something rude to the solicitor Bellenden Kerr at a council meeting of the Arundel Society. Asking Frederick Furnivall to help patch the matter up, Ruskin remarked, 'People don't know how shy I am, from not ever having gone into Society until I was seventeen. I forget who it is says that the mixture of hesitation and forced impudence which shy people fall into is the worst of all possible manners. So I find it.'[19] But usually Ruskin was without social inhibitions. It made him a more friendly man. His sensitivity to other people was interested and honest. This was not merely a charm of manner, though he had that. It was an appealing ability — in a man so egotistical — to deal with people on their own terms.

★   ★   ★   ★

A moving aspect of the personal history of Pre-Raphaelitism, so full of desperate and disappointed love, is the record of its friendships. 'True friendship is romantic, to the men of the world', Ruskin had declared in his Edinburgh lectures in 1853.[20] It was an idealistic view, given his current relations with Millais. But there are such friendships, and one may not consider Ruskin's life without regretting, as later he did himself, that in his youth and early manhood he had never known a fellow spirit of his own age and with his own enthusiasms. He had experienced nothing like the young *camaraderie* of the Pre-Raphaelite

Brotherhood. He was separated from the Brotherhood by his age and background. He knew its members only at the time when they were beginning to disperse. But he was able to sense the importance of their fellowship, and he tried to enter it. His attempts to maintain some cordiality with Millais had been rebuffed. Now, in the year after his alienation from Millais, he first became acquainted with Dante Gabriel Rossetti.

Two years after he had defended Pre-Raphaelitism in his letters to *The Times*, Ruskin had still not seen the work of one of the Brotherhood's foremost members. He became aware of Rossetti's art only in the new year and spring of 1853, just before he left for the fateful holiday at Glenfinlas. Ruskin soon found himself recommending Rossetti's drawings to Thomas McCracken, the Belfast shipping agent who was an early patron of Pre-Raphaelitism. In a letter written to Thomas Woolner in Australia, sent with the parcel of Pre-Raphaelite portraits that had been made at the very last meeting of the Brotherhood in 1853, Rossetti explains:

> M'C sent me a passage from a letter of Ruskin's about my Dant-esque sketches exhibited this year at the Winter Gallery, of which I spoke to you in my last. R. goes into raptures about the colour and grouping which he says are superior to anything in modern art — which I believe is as absurd as certain objections which he makes to them. However, as he is only half informed about art, anything he says in favour of one's work is of course sure to prove invaluable in a professional way, and I only hope, for the sake of my rubbish, that he may have the honesty to say publicly in his new book what he has said privately — but I doubt this. Oh! Woolner — if one could only find the 'supreme' Carlylean ignoramus, — him who knows positively the least about art of any living creature — and get *him* to write a pamphlet about one — what a fortune one might make. It seems that Ruskin had never seen any work of mine before, though he never thought it necessary to say this in writing about the PRB . . .[21]

The evident desire for success is quite understandable. Woolner had left England because he could not make a living from his art. Rossetti, in the five years since the formation of the Brotherhood, had sold next to nothing. His painting *Ecce Ancilla Domini* had waited for three years before attracting wary interest from McCracken, who was offering only £50 for it. Millais, on the other hand, at this moment painting *The Order of Release* in Ruskin's own home, had been guaranteed eight times that amount before he even began his picture. Rossetti knew well by now that the fortunes of Pre-Raphaelitism, in the more material sense, would not be his; that the triumphs would be in the Royal Academy, where he had never shown; that success would belong to Millais first, and then to Hunt, but not to him. He might well have been piqued that neither Millais or Hunt had never brought Ruskin to his studio; and in the earliest days of their acquaintance he had to call on the generosity of his nature to avoid such pique.

Rossetti was surprised that Ruskin was favourably disposed towards his art. It could not have seemed likely that the author of *Modern Painters* would appreciate either his vision or his means. Rossetti's drawings are awkwardly managed, out of perspective, and contain no landscape. They have not the technical command that Ruskin believed essential: nor do they have the appearance of seeking such a command. Rossetti's work was not that of an artist willing to 'go to nature, selecting nothing and rejecting nothing'; and his style could never be construed as that of a natural successor to Turner. In short, he was a living refutation of Ruskin's programmatic theories about Pre-Raphaelitism. Here was a contradiction. But Ruskin now gave his blessing not only to Rossetti's art but that of his associates and followers; the mystic unrealism of his wife Elizabeth Siddall; his friend Smetham (whose work Ruskin first saw in November 1854); and his disciple Edward Burne-Jones, whom Ruskin met two years later and who was to be his lifelong friend. Ruskin's support of these artists was largely private. He did not write about them until late in life. When he did so, his impulse was less critical than autobiographical. His memory of their painting was then wound into strange relations with his own youth. For the strain of English symbolist art was not new to Ruskin when he met Rossetti. His early acquaintance with the Richmonds had introduced him to those few people, like Samuel Palmer, who in the 1830s had kept alive the Blake tradition. George Richmond, he who had attended Blake's deathbed, had acted as intermediary when, in 1843, Ruskin had tried to buy a very bold selection of Blake's, 'the Horse, the owls, the Newton, and the Nebuchadnezzar . . . the Satan and Eve, and the Goblin Huntsman, and Search for the Body of Harold'.[22]

Forty years later, when sometimes he thought of himself as Nebuchadnezzar, Ruskin would associate his own madness with Blake. Now, in 1854, when he first went to Rossetti's rooms in Blackfriars, he was surely shown Rossetti's great treasure, the manuscript notebook containing writings and drawings by Blake that the Pre-Raphaelite had bought in 1847 from Samuel Palmer's brother. The similarities between the art of Blake and Rossetti are clear. It is passionate, unnaturalistic, illustrational, made by a poet; it is religious, private, amateur, small in scale and avowedly symbolic. Ruskin quite understood its impulses, and was therefore well prepared for the second, non-naturalistic phase of Pre-Raphaelitism. He could talk to Rossetti in a way that left the young man stimulated as he had not been stimulated by certain of his Pre-Raphaelite brethren. Rossetti pretended at first that he was only interested in getting money out of Ruskin. This was not so: he was excited by him. This had nothing to do with what Ruskin wrote. When a large parcel came from Smith, Elder containing the eight volumes, three pamphlets and book of large folio plates that then constituted Ruskin's *œuvre* he did not really want to read them. But he was glad to make Ruskin a water-colour drawing in return. So began an unlikely partnership (in which Lizzie Siddall was included). Each man found the other exasperating beyond endurance, and yet the relationship was of great value to both. By May of 1855, Rossetti was writing of Ruskin, 'He is the best friend I ever had *out of my own family*.'²³ Although he did not say so, and perhaps would not have liked to admit it, Ruskin's friendship had given him a confidence in his art that he had not experienced in his years in the Pre-Raphaelite Brotherhood.

⋆   ⋆   ⋆   ⋆

The four or five years between the end of Ruskin's marriage and his first meeting with Rose La Touche seem to be dominated by public and social interests. He taught at the Working Men's College, collaborated with architects, scientists and reformers, encouraged the building of the new Oxford Museum; he periodically issued *Academy Notes*, his commentary on new painting, and he worked at the National Gallery in cataloguing the Turner bequest. However, this was also the time — between 1854 and 1858 — when he was closest to poets. His literary acquaintances were many: they always had been. But the likes of Miss Mitford and W. H. Harrison were the minor writers of a previous generation. So were the two poets Ruskin had previously known best, George Croly and Samuel Rogers. They were behind him now, as he began to associate with those writers in the first major wave of Victorian poetry. The Rossettis, Coventry Patmore, Tennyson, William Allingham and the Brownings were all his acquaintances: so were less distinguished poets than these. Ruskin worked hard to keep up with their production. There was a special shelf in his bookcase for verse he was currently considering. He lost no opportunities to discuss their work with the poets themselves: for he could

admire them more easily than he could admire artists, and he believed
that there were bright truths to be found in their company. Perhaps
there were: in any case Ruskin learnt more in these years from poets
than he did from reformers.

His attitude to his own verse was diffident. He was thinking of
himself when he wrote,

> There are few men, ordinarily educated, who in moments of strong
> feeling could not strike out a poetical thought, and afterwards
> polish it so as to be presentable. But men of sense know better than
> so to waste their time; and those who sincerely love poetry, know
> the touch of the Master's hands on the chords too well to fumble
> among them after him . . .[24]

He was silent about his own early attempts as a poet. Probably only
Coventry Patmore, as a family friend, would have seen the collection
of Ruskin's own poems. This privately printed edition had been
projected by John James Ruskin when, in 1847, he finally became
reconciled to the idea that his son would write no more verse. It
appeared in 1850. The book was not circulated, and Ruskin is said to
have destroyed some of the edition of fifty copies.[25] Nonetheless,
Ruskin felt able to criticize such a one as Patmore as a fellow practitioner. This was reasonable, given the prose he could write and the
years he had spent in polishing diction and versification. Such matters
he discussed with Patmore, telling him confidently, 'You have neither
the lusciousness nor the sublimity of Tennyson, but you have clearer
and finer habitual expressions and more accurate thought. For finish
and neatness I know nothing to equal bits of the Angel.'[26] Ruskin was
talking about 'The Betrothals', the first part of The Angel in the House,
which had been published in 1854. He had an interest in this poem-
sequence that was more than technical. He had known the person to
whom it was addressed, Emily Patmore, since his boyhood. Patmore's poem concerns emotional and spiritual satisfaction in marriage. Ruskin's congratulatory letter regretted that 'the circumstances
of my own life unhappily render it impossible for me to write a
critique on it'.[27] Privately, he found the poem's attitudes rather con-
solatory. The more Ruskin sympathized with the ideal of The Angel in
the House the less his own marriage seemed real to him. Patmore's
Angel is an abstract of feminine docility, and could be easily fitted into
Ruskin's idealized view of the marriage bond. Ruskin did not write
about Patmore's poem until 1860. In that year a further instalment was
published, 'Faithful for Ever'. A negative review in the Critic drew a
response from him. He wrote to the editor to defend Patmore as 'one

22. Coventry Patmore, from a drawing by J. Brett, R.A., 1855.

of the truest and tenderest thinkers who have ever illustrated one of the most important, because, commonest states of human life'.[28] Five years later, *The Angel in the House* would reappear in *Sesame and Lilies*, the book written expressly for Rose La Touche at the height of Ruskin's love for her. It is a poem that contributed to his disastrous assumptions about the girl he wished to wed.

It was through the Patmores that Ruskin had first met Robert and Elizabeth Browning; and we hear of memorable evenings at the Patmore home in Highbury. The poetaster Sydney Dobell stumbled into one of them. Patmore wrote:

We once had a small party consisting of Ruskin, Tennyson and Browning only. Sydney Dobell came in late in the evening, and sat down by my wife, and began talking cleverly and very predominantly, laying down the law about many things. Hearing my wife address Mr Ruskin by name, he asked in a whisper, 'Is that *the* Mr Ruskin?' and became a little less authoritative. After making similar enquiries when he heard the other names, he became quite shy . . .[29]

The question of authority was indeed an issue in this Olympian company. Ruskin's place there, and in the wider circles of Victorian literary life, was mostly as an art critic who had written wonderful books. Not everybody believed that he was always as wise about literature as he was reputed to be about art. These questions worried the Brownings a little. In the summer of 1855 they were often at Denmark Hill. On one occasion they brought Frederick Leighton with them, a young artist they had met in Italy: a month or two earlier Ruskin had given high praise to his *Cimabue's Madonna carried in procession through the Streets of Florence*. But was he as good a painter as they were poets? The Brownings could see that there was much that was immoderate in Ruskin's enthusiasms, and they were to find him unpredictable. His appreciations were evidently the judgements of a noble contemporary mind, but they lacked measure. 'I am going to bind your poems in a golden binding,' Ruskin wrote to Mrs Browning, 'and give them to my class of working men as the purest poetry in our language.' Not long afterwards, he was complaining about her 'designs on the English language'. The Brownings sensibly decided to enjoy his praise and to remain equable in the occasional storms of his criticism. When, in 1855, Browning sent a complimentary copy of *Men and Women*, Ruskin worried at the poems. He decided that he found them intellectually awkward. He made Rossetti, Browning's great champion among the younger poets, sit down with him and read them line by line. Still he could not feel their rightness. They were, he told Browning, 'absolutely and literally a set of the most amazing conundrums that ever were proposed to me'.[30] Browning took no offence, but explained his verse to Ruskin at great length. The critic was not convinced, but the episode gave him a valuable lesson in coming to terms with a sensibility unlike his own.

Ruskin knew Tennyson less well then he knew the Brownings, although their acquaintance extended over many years. Tennyson had been an admirer of Ruskin since 1843, when he first picked up *Modern Painters* from Samuel Rogers's library table. In 1855, the year in which

he succeeded Rogers as laureate, he expressed a desire to see Ruskin's
famous collection of Turners. Thomas Woolner arranged an invitation to Denmark Hill. There was subsequently some correspondence
between Ruskin and Tennyson. It consists mostly of polite notes, but
Ruskin made occasional comments about Tennyson's poetry. He was
interested in the reception that year of 'Maud' and 'The Charge of the
Light Brigade'. Both poems were in Ruskin's mind as he brought the
third volume of *Modern Painters* to its conclusion. This volume ends
with some eloquent pages on the subject of the Crimean War. The
Ruskinian prose is not unlike Tennyson's contemporary verse. Ruskin's thoughts about the war, which occur in a section entitled 'On the
teachers of Turner', seemed to have little relevance to a book that was
nominally about art. But Ruskin was extending his writing to include
anything that currently concerned him. Much of this third volume is
in fact about poetry. It can be regarded as his major contribution to
that community of interest which existed between the artistic and the
poetic worlds during the 1850s. And its thoughts about the politics of
the Crimean War indicate that Ruskin — like Tennyson — was
seeking a larger and more public stage for his writing.

★   ★   ★   ★

It was common in all these poets (and this is an unremarked aspect of
Victorian literary life) to take an interest in American literature. Ruskin too was welcoming to transatlantic writing. At one point in 1855
he had on his poetry bookshelf Dante, Spenser, Keats, Wordsworth,
the two Brownings, Hood, George Herbert, Young, Shenstone ('By
the bye, if Mr Browning would be a little more Shenstonian in *flow*, it
would be all I want,' he wrote to Elizabeth Browning[31]), and beside
them Longfellow and Emerson. He was also prepared to consider the
possibility of American art. In 1851 he had been approached by the
American artist and journalist W. J. Stillman, who had been impressed
by Pre-Raphaelite painting on his first visit to Europe the previous
year, had met Turner and had studied the first two volumes of *Modern
Painters*. These were impressive credentials, and after some initial
hesitation Ruskin encouraged Stillman's ambition to found a native
school of art in America. If its inspiration was Turnerian and Pre-
Raphaelite, and if it was true and thoughtful, then perhaps art might
flourish wonderfully in a new country. Ruskin assured Stillman in
1855 that 'nothing gives me greater pleasure than the thought of being
useful to an American',[32] and helped such travellers as J. J. Jerves, a
Bostonian friend of the Brownings, and the collector Daniel Magoon,

though he was alarmed that Magoon was buying Turners to take to the New World. Stillman had founded an art magazine, the *Crayon*, of which eight volumes were published before it disappeared in the Civil War. Ruskinian æsthetics were its main inspiration. Ruskin did not contribute to the magazine , but he looked on the publication with benevolence. He recommended William Michael Rossetti to Stillman: Rossetti wrote for the magazine and introduced his fellow Pre-Raphaelite writer F. G. Stephens to its pages; and thus two contributors to the *Germ* found themselves proselytizing for the new art in a different continent that neither of them would ever see.[33]

It was at this time that Ruskin became acquainted with an American who was to be greatly important in his later life. Charles Eliot Norton was not an influence on Ruskin, but he was his confessor; and it was in that capacity, or his conception of it, that he came to act as Ruskin's literary executor. In *Præterita* Ruskin recounts that he met Norton in Switzerland in 1856. His memory was slightly at fault: Norton first went to Denmark Hill, with a letter of introduction from J. J. Jervos, in October of 1855. Here was a contrast with Stillman. The editor of the *Crayon* was the son of a redneck tradesman. One senses in him the vigour of an American without background who wished to make art his own. Norton was nothing but background. His family had been in New England since the seventeenth century. His father was the biblical scholar Andrews Norton, the 'unitarian Pope'. The family home was at Shady Hill, Cambridge, Massachusetts, only one mile from Harvard Yard. The young Norton, after his Harvard education and a period as a businessman, first approached the artistic and literary world of London in 1850. In Florence that year he met the Brownings. Arthur Hugh Clough became a friend, and lived at Shady Hill during his American years: Norton was staying with the Cloughs in London when he first went out to Denmark Hill. Such acquaintances confirmed Norton's literary interests. In further visits he met artists. Ruskin introduced him to Rossetti; and from Rossetti, and from friends of Ruskin's like William Allingham, he solicited contributions to a new American magazine. This was the *Atlantic Monthly*, founded by James Russell Lowell and others. Through Norton, Ruskin became acquainted with the work of Lowell, and later with the poet himself. In the last volume of *Modern Painters* he is referred to as 'my dear friend and teacher',[34] rather in the same way that Norton, in *Præterita*, was to become 'my first real tutor'.[35]

*   *   *   *

Matthew Arnold was a mid-nineteenth-century poet and critic who lived at some remove from Ruskin and the circle of Pre-Raphaelite poets. Neither his tastes nor his aspirations were at all like Ruskin's. Their mutual interest in Oxford underlines both their temperamental and cultural differences. In the autumn of 1854 the poet of 'The Scholar-Gipsy,' was staying in Balliol, where he had been an undergraduate thirteen years before. He wrote to his mother of his reactions to the contemporary university:

> I am much struck with the apathy and poorness of the people here, as they now strike me, and their petty pottering habits compared with the students of Paris, or Germany, or even of London. Animation and interest and the power of work seem so sadly wanting in them . . . the place, in losing Newman and his followers, has lost its religious movement, which after all kept it from stagnating, and has not yet, as far as I see, got anything better. However, we must hope that the coming changes, and perhaps the infusions of Dissenters' sons of that muscular, hard-working, *unblasé* middle class — for it is this, in spite of its intolerable disagreeableness — may brace the flaccid sinews of Oxford a little.[36]

Ruskin had found no particular excitement in the Oxford Movement, nor would he have believed that the *'unblasé* middle class' were potential reformers. But while Oxford, as a symbol of culture and educational purpose, seemed inert to Arnold, for Ruskin it began to appear as a city in which many of his hopes might be realized. This was not a matter of the university reforms of the 1850s, Arnold's 'coming changes'. In Oxford, Ruskin now came to believe, masters and workmen, students and artists, might have a common purpose; art and nature might be brought together, wonderful architecture built, God served and glorified.

Such ambitions were stimulated by his old friend Henry Acland. As a doctor and a scientist, Acland had campaigned for some years for the extension of the study of natural history at Oxford. As an amateur artist and, after the Glenfinlas holiday, an aspirant Pre-Raphaelite, he also wished to introduce the study of art to the university. Since 1847 he had been asking for a new University Museum that would house the materials necessary for an honours school in the natural sciences. There were principled Tractarian objections in the way. Dr Pusey told Acland that he, Keble and others felt that the study of natural science was liable to engender 'a temper of irreverence and often of arrogance inconsistent with a truly Christian character'. Acland replied with Ruskinian arguments. In 1848 he used the second volume of *Modern*

Painters in his *Remarks on the Extension of Education at the University of Oxford*: he cleared his proposed academic discipline of any supposed impiety by advancing the Ruskinian notion that 'if the teacher of Natural Knowledge fulfil his mission as he ought, he is striving to lift up the veil from the Works of the Creator, no less than the Christian preacher from His Word'.[37] Acland's idea of a Gothic university museum that would serve both scientific and artistic purposes was created by his reading of *The Stones of Venice* and the Edinburgh *Lectures on Architecture and Painting*. Although he had left Glenfinlas by the time that Ruskin and Millais had started to design architecture, it is likely that he knew something of their collaboration. Ruskin, naturally, had been sympathetic to Acland's campaign. The appendix on 'Modern Education' at the end of the third volume of *The Stones of Venice* was a clear declaration of support. But he was slow to propose a specific type of building, even when the University Commissioners, in 1852, had finally agreed that a museum should be erected. In July of 1854 he sent Acland some copies of his pamphlet *On the Opening of the Crystal Palace*, adding, 'You don't want your museum of *glass* — do you? If you do — I will have nothing to do with it.'[38] Ruskin felt that the time had not yet come for the battle of the styles to be won. On 19 October 1854 he wrote to Acland's wife Sarah,

> . . . as for the plans, it is no use my troubling myself about them, because they certainly won't build a gothic Museum and if they would — I haven't the workmen yet to do it, and I mean to give my whole strength, which is not more than I want, to teaching the workmen: and when I have got people who *can* build, I will ask for employment for them.[39]

He did not become enthusiastic until the end of Acland's labours was in sight, when the entries to the competition to design the building had been reduced to two. One of these designs was Gothic, the other Palladian. The Gothic design, submitted under the motto *Nisi Dominus Aedificaverit Domum*, was championed by Acland in a pamphlet and by personal canvass among the members of Convocation; and when the verdict was given for Gothic, by only two votes in a poll of 132, he telegraphed the result to Ruskin, who wrote back that night

> I am going to thank God for it and lie down to sleep. It means much, I think, both to you and me. I trust you will have no anxiety, such as you have borne, to bear again in this cause. The Museum in your hands, as it must eventually be, will be the root of as much good to others as I suppose it is natural for any living soul to hope to do in its earth-time.[40]

*   *   *   *

The architects who had won the competition to build the new
museum were Irish: they were the Dublin firm of Deane, Woodward
and Deane. The artistic spirit among the partners was supplied by
Benjamin Woodward, a civil engineer from Cork whose mediævalism
had led him to take up architecture. Ruskin may have heard of him, for
Woodward had already begun to design on Ruskinian principles. The
library of Trinity College, Dublin, which Woodward began in 1853,
was directly based on *The Stones of Venice*. William Allingham wrote
to Rossetti that it was

> . . . after Ruskin's heart. Style, early Venetian (I suppose), with
> numberless capitals delicately carved over holly leaves, shamrocks,
> various flowers, birds, and so on. There are also circular frames
> here and there in the wall, at present empty, to be filled no doubt
> with eyes of coloured stone . . .[41]

Ruskin thought that *Nisi Dominus* was 'though by no means a first-rate
design, yet quite as good as is likely to be got these days, and on the
whole good'. The great advantage to it was that Woodward, already a
Ruskinian, was malleable. 'Mr Woodward', Ruskin remarked to
Acland, 'is evidently a person who will allow of suggestion.'[42] His
enthusiasm was growing. Woodward's plans could be modified; more
money could be raised, and Pre-Raphaelite artists could be attracted to
the project.

> I hope to be able to get Millais and Rossetti to design flower and
> beast borders — crocodiles and various vermin — such as you are
> particularly fond of — Mrs Buckland's 'dabby things' — and we
> will carve them and inlay them with Cornish serpentine all about
> your windows. I will pay for a good deal myself, and I doubt not to
> have funds. *Such* capitals as we will have![43]

*   *   *   *

Ruskin's pamphlet *On the Opening of the Crystal Palace* has one or two
passages that are not so much concerned with architecture as with
public health. In the latter part of 1854, at the time when he was
beginning his drawing classes at the Working Men's College and
corresponding with Acland about the Oxford Museum, Ruskin
attended a committee of eminent men organized by Arthur Helps, the
author of *Friends in Council* (1847), a book in dialogue form on the
nature of wise government. Their purpose was to organize relief from

the cholera epidemic that had broken out that summer. Ruskin's pamphlet has an interpolated question that was surely derived from the misery in the East End:

> If, suddenly, in the midst of the enjoyments of the palate and lightnesses of heart of a London dinner-party, the walls of the chamber were parted, and through their gap, the nearest human beings who were famishing, and in misery, were borne into the midst of the company — feasting and fancy-free — if, pale with sickness, horrible in destitution, broken by despair, body by body, they were laid upon the soft carpet, one beside the chair of every guest, would only the crumbs of the dainties be passed to them — would only a passing glance, a passing thought, be vouchsafed to them?[44]

The arrival of cholera could be predicted: one of Helps's pamphlets on the subject is entitled *Some Thoughts for next Summer*. The epidemic would strike slum districts with inadequate drainage in hot weather. Another member of Helps's committee, whom Ruskin now met for the first time, was John Simon. This intelligent, liberal-radical doctor, Medical Officer of Health for the City of London since 1848, had stated with horrible accuracy in which streets and courts people were likely to die.[45] Simon would soon begin to work with another man who also became a friend of Ruskin's, William Cowper. This future trustee of the Guild of St George was now beginning his political career at the Board of Health. Henry Acland, too, had been much concerned with cholera that summer, for the epidemic had visited Oxford. Like Ruskin's dinner guests, the Oxford slums had forced themselves upon the attention of the university. One might live in London and never visit the East End: the slums of Oxford are only at the other side of the garden walls of the colleges. St Ebbe's began immediately behind Pembroke and the Christ Church house in which the undergraduate Ruskin had lodged. Jericho is built against the walls of Worcester College. These districts were not served by the same water system as the university, and cholera raged in their undrained streets. Acland worked unceasingly to limit the number of deaths. But he lacked assistance and facilities. Families were lodged in compounds on Port Meadow: corpses were placed in hastily erected sheds: clothing was burnt or fumigated. Acland's experience that summer, with his analysis of the causes of the epidemic, appear in a short work he entitled *Memoir on the Cholera at Oxford in the Year 1854, with Considerations Suggested by the Epidemic*.

A remarkable feature of Acland's book, which is largely concerned with provisions for sanitation, is that it ends with a plea for art. 'The Physician and the Philanthropist must desire the success of Schools of Design, and Schools of Art,' he argued, adding that Oxford needed a Professor of Art and that 'a new page of nature and of art has been opened to us through the works of Ruskin'.[46] Acland had been taught to feel that naturalism in art had something to do with the fight against disease. The study of natural science must lead to an ameliorated public health, and natural science should be studied in the same spirit that a Ruskinian artist looks at the world. Ruskin's and Acland's joint publication, *The Oxford Museum* (1859), indicates that for them both Pre-Raphaelitism and Gothic architecture were signs of spiritual health; that this was the root of good government; and that the university could

> . . . become complete in her function as a teacher of the youth of the nation to which every hour gives wider authority over distant lands; and from which every rood of extended dominion demands new, various, and variously applicable knowledge of the laws which govern the constitution of the globe . . .[47]

Now, in the summer of 1855, Rossetti came to Oxford to look at work on the museum. He complained that he was bored by Acland's constant topic of conversation, drainage, and perhaps was dissatisfied with other matters. For Ruskin had brought Lizzie Siddall to Oxford to be under Acland's care. After his second meeting with Lizzie (whom he then rechristened Ida, after the heroine of Tennyson's 'The Princess') Ruskin had decided that something had to be done about her health. His mother's home-made medicines, prepared to complicated recipes, had been urged on the listless beauty. But they had not been effective: and so Ruskin had turned to Acland. In May of 1855 he announced to him that 'I am going to burden you still with other cares on the subject of Pre-Raphaelitism, of which you have already had painful thoughts enough', and explained the relation between her and Rossetti as best he could. 'She has a perfectly gentle expression', he wrote, 'and I don't think Rossetti would have given his soul to her unless she had been both gentle and good. She has more the look of a Florentine 13th Century lady than anything I ever saw out of a fresco.'[48] Ruskin's plan was that Acland would examine her, and then perhaps send her to some cottage on the Acland family's Devon estates. Instead, Acland invited Lizzie to come to stay in Oxford.

The visit was not a complete success. Lizzie felt social apprehensions. The girl from the Elephant and Castle had coped with being taken up by the Pre-Raphaelites: to cope with people who had taken up the Pre-Raphaelites was more difficult. Rossetti's letters from Oxford to his mother are at pains to emphasize Lizzie's social success. He reports that Acland

> . . . said he would introduce her into all the best society. All the women there are tremendously fond of her — a sister of Dr Pusey (or daughter) seems to have been the one she liked best. A great swell, who is Warden of New College, an old cock, showed her all the finest MSS in the Bodleian Library, and paid her all manner of attentions . . .[49]   *lavished attent. upon*

Acland examined the mysterious and silent Miss Siddall, but could find little wrong with her. His vague diagnosis was that she was feeling the effects of 'mental power long pent up and lately over-taxed'.[50] She met many people, in the normal rounds of Oxford hospitality. But she was not able to feel at home at the Aclands's. Her ways were not theirs. Mrs Acland complained of the untidiness of her room, and perhaps of other things. She may have been asked to leave: for one letter from Ruskin offers to recompense the Aclands for their expenses on her behalf, and continues 'it is provoking that she can't be reasonable and take proper lodgings when she is bid'. In another letter Ruskin apologizes and makes excuses for her. The excuse is that she is a genius. 'I don't know how exactly that wilful Ida has behaved to you,' he wrote to Mrs Acland.

> As far as I can make out she is not ungrateful but sick, and sickly headstrong — much better, however, for what Henry has done for her. But I find trying to be of use to people is the most wearying thing possible. The true secret of happiness would be to bolt one's gates, lie on the grass all day, take care not to eat too much dinner, and buy as many Turners as one could afford. These geniuses are all alike, little and big. I have known five of them — Turner, Watts, Millais, Rossetti, and this girl — and I don't know which was, or is, wrongheadedest.[50]

There is little sign of genius in the drawing which Lizzie left behind her as a gift, and which the Aclands regarded as a curiosity. It is an incompetent illustration to Wordsworth's poem 'We Are Seven'. Ruskin wrote loyally that 'It is quite childish in comparison to what she *can* do. She will show you one day — if she gets better.'[51]

It is possible that a strained atmosphere between Rossetti and Lizzie and the Aclands explains why Rossetti made no contribution to the Oxford Museum, although some of his art was left in Oxford: for he now became friendly with Woodward and was to work with him on his other Oxford building, the Union, two years later. On Ruskin's, Woodward's and Acland's behalf, Rossetti delivered an invitation to Millais, but his Pre-Raphaelite brother would have nothing to do with such a scheme. Ruskin himself took the Pre-Raphaelites' place in making plans for the museum's ornamentation. He produced many drawings and was in constant communication with Woodward. The architect often went to Denmark Hill, where he met Rossetti and other artists. He also had serious talks with F. J. Furnivall, the most favoured of Ruskin's colleagues at the Working Men's College. Illustrative material from Ruskin's own collection was urged on Woodward: a direct link exists between Ruskin's Venetian sketchbooks and the new building in the meadows north of Wadham. Neither Woodward's ground-plan nor his elevations were changed, but he was flooded with ideas for detail. One of Ruskin's gifts to the Gothic Revival was the lesson that ordinary designs might be wonderfully enlivened by decoration. This decoration could be carved, painted, or introduced by differently coloured brickwork and masonry. All these expedients were important, and Ruskin's help all the more necessary, because the university would pay for only the shell of the building. The problem of funds, and perhaps of wages, was raised in other ways. Acland, Woodward and Ruskin were all eager that workmen should be able to express themselves as artists while they were engaged on the building. But they knew nothing of problems on site. Woodward had brought a number of workmen with him from Ireland. Two of them, the O'Shea brothers, were talented. One brother carved a complicated window from a drawing by Ruskin. They also invented their own designs from nature. Tuckwell's *Reminiscences of Oxford* tells us how 'Every morning came the handsome red-bearded brothers Shea, bearing plants from the Botanic Garden, to reappear under their chisels in the rough-hewn capitals of the pillars.'[52] The O'Sheas were not in all respects obedient to Acland's authority, and they provide a number of amusing stories which have found their way into a type of Oxford lore. One of them seems to have been dismissed by Acland, then reinstated. This was James O'Shea; and in his case the line that separated the professional artist from the labourer was not distinct. This may have caused the friction. Or O'Shea (who significantly is not granted a Christian name in Acland's account) may simply have rebelled against the man who could write of 'the humour, the force, the woes, the troubles, in the character and art of our Irish brethren'.[53]

Ruskin, who liked O'Shea, preserved a scrap of one of his letters. It indicates that the Irishman was scarcely literate. What culture could be shared by the different classes? The museum began to teach Ruskin how difficult this question was: the Working Men's College, on the other hand, seemed to have only facile answers to the question. A note from Ruskin's new valet Crawley (for George Hobbs had emigrated to Australia) to the Christian Socialist Furnivall has also been preserved. In this year, 1855, when Furnivall was most often a Denmark Hill guest, he gave presents of books to the servants. Crawley wrote to his benefactor:

> I am asshamed [sic] of miself for not writing by return of post to thank you for your kind present — which I feel deeply grateful for — I am reading Ruth to my fellow servants we are all delighted with it. The language is beautiful and deeply interesting and the morals it sets forth are very good and i trust that all who reads it will view it as a lesson and profit by so doing . . .[54]

Not all men of the working classes would be as acquiescent as Crawley. John James Ruskin was not opposed to his servants having books, but he wanted to know where it would all end. He had even heard mad talk of a Working Women's College. John James's approval of his son's ventures was in any case tempered by the large sums of money he was expected to contribute to them. But it was the sheer giddiness of the idea of a further Working Men's College at Oxford that now prompted him to write to Henry Acland:

> . . . the subject of a Working Mans College at Oxford . . . I trust no such absurdity will obtain a footing at Oxford. Mr Furnivall, a most amiable Radical & Philanthropist seems to have nothing to do but to start projects for others to work & he may have an Eye to Oxford — but I sincerely hope neither you nor my son will take any trouble about it. I think both your father and Mrs Acland must have been saddened to see the weight of work thrown on you by the Museum. That must be at least quite enough . . . My Son has enough to do with his writings and his London college. I became reconciled to the latter because he seems to do good service to some good and true men but neither kindness or charity require all plans to be made the scene of these amiable exploits — I should like these experimentalists to feel their way to go along gently and discreetly. It may be lack of enthusiasm in me makes me feel a lack of discretion in them. I hope in trying to drag up the low they will not end in pulling down the high . . .[55]

The 'absurdity' of such a college at Oxford was avoided for another half a century. When it was founded, three years after Ruskin's death in 1900, it would bear his name. Ruskin would not have approved of that college; and it is an irony of his reputation that as his political and educational beliefs became more distinct from the ordinary they also were less understood. In the late 1850s, the condescending good will one associates with F. D. Maurice has an echo in the classes given to workmen on the museum site. Ruskin's personal difficulties may be found in an unpublished address he gave there in April of 1856. It is fluent, but his unease is nonetheless discernible. The political problems raised by the museum may have guided Ruskin towards a firmer expression of views that were increasingly isolated from those held at the Working Men's College. *The Political Economy of Art*, a book which alarmed the Christian Socialists, was written while Ruskin was helping at the museum in the summer of 1857. It is probably significant that in that long vacation there was a further decline in Ruskin's belief in the social power of Pre-Raphaelite art. He had always been reserved about the Pre-Raphaelite ambition to paint frescoes. He now distanced himself from an independent Pre-Raphaelite venture, the decoration of the interior walls of the Oxford Union. This was another new Woodward building. When Ruskin visited it he found Rossetti and many another young artist heartily at work. He thought of paying for another painting in the spandrels above the debating hall. But he did not: neither did he give advice about fresco technique.

In that summer of 1857 the young Pre-Raphaelite spree in the Union was evidently a more successful collaboration than had been achieved in the museum. Both Acland and Ruskin had to note that the artists had joined forces to adorn a monument to adolescent self-importance. These same artists had not been inclined to help with Acland's underfinanced cathedral of the natural sciences. The doctor gave beds to some of them, in his rabbit-warren of a Tudor house in Broad Street. But Ruskin may have recognized apostasy. He never in his life, neither in writing nor, apparently, in conversation, mentioned Woodward's Union building. He also developed his aversion to staying in Oxford. In 1857 he lived in a rented cottage in Cowley, three miles outside the city; in 1861 he stayed at Beckley, six miles away; and when he was elected Slade Professor in 1871 he took up lodgings in a public house in Abingdon, six miles away in the other direction. He also distanced himself, in this summer of 1857, from Dean Liddell's plan to have Woodward design model cottages for workers living on land owned by Christ Church. He was learning that since one must expect disappointments in Oxford it is better to maintain one's own position than to compromise with a powerful person you distrust. At some point in the 1850s Ruskin gave away his drawings for the unfulfilled museum windows to Acland's small daughter Angie. He had already hinted to the museum workmen that the only satisfaction they might find in their labour might be the vague one that they were 'laying the foundation of a structure which was calculated to exercise a very beneficial influence on succeeding generations'.[56] For his part, he might as well give his contribution to a child. Only one piece of writing came out of the museum project. The pamphlet, *The Oxford Museum*, was issued jointly by Ruskin and Acland in 1859. Its purpose was to raise more money. By this time Ruskin felt even further from the museum. But some of its lessons settled in his mind. In fifteen years' time, when he took hints from Acland for his road-mending project with undergraduates, it would be recalled. Then, he would attempt to give the experience a symbolic value: one that had no practical application, as it turned out, and which was executed by the amateur workmen who became (as no real workmen ever did) his 'disciples'.

CHAPTER TWELVE

1855–1857

During the 1850s Ruskin was often confronted by the kind of questions raised by O'Shea's artistic ability, or what there was of Lizzie Siddall's artistic ability. At the Working Men's College they could scarcely be avoided, except by saying (as Ruskin did) that he was not training professional artists. The real difficulty was in the definition of an amateur. But there were also problems concerning the status of fine art and its relation to those who might wish to own it, who would be wealthy, and those who ought to study it, who would often be poor. Ruskin, especially when addressing such an amateur artist as Lady Waterford, was inclined to hint that he did not believe that there should be a distinction between 'high' and 'low' art.[1] But he was wise not to enter this territory. It was enough that he recognized that such problems existed. His interest in the wide distribution of art came from his study of the social forms of architecture, its openness for all to see and use. At the beginning of his first letter in *The Oxford Museum*, Ruskin made some criticisms of private ownership of art. Many purchases, he argued, came about through 'acquisitive selfishness, rejoicing somewhat in what can NOT be seen by others', while he and the Gothic Revivalists hoped 'to make art large and publicly beneficial, instead of small and privately engrossed or secluded'.[2] But this was to compare painting (in this instance, two small Meissoniers) with an architectural project. The argument was hardly viable, and was not much pursued. Nonetheless Ruskin's mind was edging around the idea of a democratic art, and in *Academy Notes*, his series of criticisms on the Royal Academy summer exhibitions, it appeared that he looked to Pre-Raphaelitism for an art that would be for all men. 'The old art of trick and tradition', he argued, 'had no language but for the connoisseur; this natural art speaks to all men: around it daily the circles of sympathy will enlarge; pictures will become gradually as necessary to daily life as books . . .'[3]

Direct, immediate appreciation of 'this natural art' was not always possible for Ruskin, since he was not a contributor to magazines. But his letters to *The Times* on Pre-Raphaelitism had been successful enough for him to wish to repeat them. In the summer of 1854, while artistic London was full of the scandal of Effie's departure, Ruskin had written again to the newspaper. His two letters concerned another member of the Pre-Raphaelite Brotherhood, William Holman Hunt, who was on distant but mutually appreciative terms with Ruskin. Hunt had sent *The Light of the World* and *The Awakening Conscience* to the Academy. Of the first, Ruskin wrote,

> Standing by it yesterday for upwards of an hour, I watched the effect it produced upon the passers-by. Few stopped to look at it, and those who did almost invariably with some contemptuous expression, founded on what appeared to them the absurdity of representing the Saviour with a lantern in his hand. Now, it ought to be remembered that, whatever may be the faults of a Pre-Raphaelite picture, it must at least have taken much time; and therefore it may not unwarrantably be presumed that conceptions which are to be laboriously realised are not adopted in the first instance without some reflection . . .[4]

Evidently enough, the picture required elucidation, which Ruskin then proceeded to give, concentrating on the symbolic iconography. Of Hunt's second picture he did much the same. 'I am at a loss to know how its meaning could be rendered more distinctly, but assuredly it is not understood. People gaze at it in a blank wonder, and leave it hopelessly . . .'[5] Ruskin was discovering that even the 'natural art' of Pre-Raphaelitism was often obscure to its audience; and for this reason his *Academy Notes* is often simply exegetical as well as critical.

Ruskin published *Academy Notes* annually between 1855 and 1859, and once more in 1875. The origin of the pamphlet, within Ruskin's own work, is in the *addenda* to the second edition of the second volume of *Modern Painters*, which was written in 1848. In this section of his book Ruskin commented on some works in the Royal Academy exhibition of that year which 'either illustrate, or present exceptions to, any of the preceding statements'.[6] Works by Linnell, Mulready, Stanfield and others are then examined within the context of the main theories of the book. The rise of Pre-Raphaelitism demanded publicity for paintings more important than these; and the effect of his letters on Hunt gave Ruskin the idea of a pamphlet published at the beginning of May every year that would pick out the best paintings and make claims for the art that he supported. No doubt this form of criticism appealed to the campaigner and reformer in Ruskin: that side of his which made a contemporary, in the *Saturday Review*, describe him as 'a Luther in the world of art, protesting against the errors of its teachers, and claiming for all the right of individual reading and understanding of its scripture — the book of Nature — unshackled by the arbitrary interpretation of others . . .'.[7] But it also appealed — and

this is not the same thing — to Ruskin's satisfaction in wielding his
personal authority. Convinced that his own abilities were superior to
those of other reviewers, he found a way of stating that his judgements
were above debate. 'Twenty years of severe labour, devoted exclusively to the study of the principles of Art, have given me the right to
speak on the subject with a measure of confidence,' he claimed.[8] But
the growing number of his enemies suspected that he considered
himself infallible.

In comparison with other art criticism of the day, Ruskin's pamphlet is splendid. In no way 'impartial', it carried the banner for the new
realist painting of the Pre-Raphaelite school. It divides artists into
those who belong to the movement, those who by greater effort
might join it, and those who are irremediably benighted. The first
Academy Notes, of 1855, opens with a hostile notice of a Pre-Raphaelite
enemy, Maclise, who had submitted *The Wrestling*, an illustration of
As You Like It. Ruskin commented, 'Very bad pictures may be divided
into two principal classes — those which are weakly and passively bad,
and which are to be pitied and passed by; and those which are energetically or actively bad, and which demand severe reprobation . . .'[9]
Maclise's picture fell into the second class. It was nothing new for art
reviewing to be so completely dismissive of paintings, by Academicians or not. But Ruskin's moralism was new: so was his professional-
ism, for he assumed an understanding of art far above that of its actual
practitioners. Confidently, Ruskin's pamphlet prefers a marine scene
by J. F. Lewis to the Maclise picture, then passes to Sir Charles
Eastlake. Ruskin had learnt much since the time, just before his
engagement, when he had reviewed Eastlake's *Materials for a History of
Oil Painting*, and had respectfully applied himself to understanding
Renaissance ways with pigment. Now, looking at Eastlake's
Titianesque *Beatrice*, Ruskin remarked cuttingly, 'An imitation of the
Venetians, on the supposition that the essence of Venetian painting
consisted in method: issuing, as trusts in Method instead of Fact
always must issue, — in mere negation'. Ruskin found that Eastlake
'ends, as all imitators must end, in a rich inheritance of the errors of his
original, without its virtues'.[10] There was much justice in these
remarks. But Sir Charles Eastlake — and Lady Eastlake, who soon
would seek revenge — had no doubt that this was a personal attack:
especially since Ruskin blandly commended another portrait, scarcely
a better painting, by a Ruskin family friend, George Richmond, of a
man much admired by the Ruskin family, Sir Robert Inglis.

Academy Notes is much dependent on concepts, not of failure and
success, but of good and bad. A minor painting with minor intentions

might be good: the Lewis is better than the Maclise. Painters who have good in them can be corrected and put on the right path. J. R. Herbert and William Dyce, both artists of the high church, are now examined. Ruskin places Herbert's *Lear recovering his Reason at the Sight of Cordelia* in the category of 'passively bad' paintings and recommends that he 'limit his work to subjects of the more symbolic and quietly religious class, which truly move him'.[11] For Dyce (who, one recalls, had made Ruskin look again at his first Pre-Raphaelite painting, Millais's *Christ in the House of his Parents*), Ruskin had a dismissive comment. His *Christabel* was 'an example of one of the false branches of Pre-Raphaelitism, consisting in imitation of the old religious masters. This head is founded chiefly on reminiscence of Sandro Botticelli . . .'[12] Ruskin had always preferred contemporary realism in Pre-Raphaelitism. For that reason, probably, he gave surprising praise to Millais's *The Rescue*. This painting of a fireman taking a child from a blazing house was Millais's first appearance since he showed *The Order of Release* in 1853. It was also the first time that he had showed since Effie had left Ruskin. Perhaps Ruskin was, by praising this work, attempting to show his impartiality. For one cannot imagine that in a previous year he would have said, as he now did, that 'the execution of the picture is remarkably bold — in some respects imperfect' while defending this with the argument that 'there is a true sympathy between impetuousness of execution and the haste of the action'. His final judgement was that *The Rescue* was 'the only *great* picture exhibited this year; but this is *very* great. The immortal element is in it to the full'.[13]

In Ruskin's criticism of Millais, the 'greatness' of the picture is not elucidated. Neither here nor elsewhere did Ruskin give to contemporary artists the full power of his writing. There is no comparison between the sweeping rhetoric of *Modern Painters* and the clipped remarks in *Academy Notes*. In truth, Pre-Raphaelitism did not mean to Ruskin what Turner meant to him. In 1855 it was already beginning to fail his hopes for the movement. One picture this year was an indication that the future of English art might not lie with Pre-Raphaelitism. It was Frederick Leighton's *Cimabue*, the picture of the year to most people. William Richmond, George's son (who, then a schoolboy, had an ambition to become a Pre-Raphaelite) thought it 'so complete, so noble in design, so serious in sentiment and of such achievement, that perforce it took me by the throat'.[14] Rossetti wrote to William Allingham about the art politics of this hugely successful painting: 'The R.A.s have been gasping for years for someone to back against Hunt and Millais, and here they have him.'[15] Millais must have looked nervously at this painting. He had already heard of Leighton: Thackeray had told him that there was a young artist in Rome who would be President of the Royal Academy before him. And we can imagine that Millais had felt some trepidation when opening *Academy Notes*. But Ruskin still awarded him his best praise, and was in comparison tepid about Leighton's picture. It had not

> . . . care enough. I am aware of no instance of a young painter, who was to be really great, who did not in his youth paint with intense effort and delicacy of finish. The handling here is much too broad . . . It seems to me probable that Mr Leighton has greatness in him, but there is no absolute proof of it in this picture . . .[16]

The first number of *Academy Notes* must have sold more copies than Smith, Elder had expected: for there was a second edition and then a third. To this third edition Ruskin added a supplement, in which he discussed or mentioned other paintings in the exhibition (none of them distinguished) which had been pointed out to him by friends — Rossetti was one — or which he had noticed on subsequent visits to the galleries of Burlington House. However, most of this supplement is taken up by a reply to the *Globe* newspaper, which had criticized some of Ruskin's remarks about local colour in a painting by David Roberts. Ruskin now stated, ominously, that in writing against a painting he never said 'half of what I could say in its disfavour; and it will hereafter be found that when once I have felt it my duty to attack a picture, the worst policy which the friends of the artist can possibly adopt will be to defend it'.[17] In the face of such arrogance, what would any artist's friend do? People now began to openly dislike Ruskin. Ford Madox Brown, to whom Ruskin talked in Rossetti's studio, and who answered, 'Because it lay out of a back window' when the critic asked him why he had chosen to paint Hampstead Heath,[18] now began his lifelong hostility, as did some others, especially if they had been noticed in *Academy Notes*. For Lady Eastlake, Effie's confidante and the wife of the painter whose work had been so denigrated, the time seemed right for an attack on the man she had come to loathe. She began to consider the whole of Ruskin's output, in preparation for a refutation. In the winter of 1855 she laboured over this extremely lengthy article. It was finished at the end of January 1856, after the third volume of *Modern Painters* had been published, and appeared anonymously in the *Quarterly Review* in March of that year.

Lady Eastlake's hate-filled article was the most complete and damning account yet given of Ruskin's writings and his position within the world of art and letters. Unfortunately, it is not illuminating. 'Mr

Ruskin's intellectual powers are of the most brilliant description, but
there is, we deliberately aver, not one single great moral quality in
their application.' And again, 'Mr Ruskin's writings have all the
qualities of premature old age — its coldness, callousness and contradiction.' And again, 'his contradictions and false conclusions are from
the beginning those of a cold and hardened habit, in which no
enthusiasm involuntarily leads astray, and no generosity instinctively
leads aright . . .'. And again, of *Academy Notes*, 'Nothing can be more
degradingly low, both as regards art and manners, than the whole tone
of this pamphlet, calculated only to mislead those who are as conceited
as they are ignorant.'[19] Ruskin was not much troubled by this attack:
he only observed, in the preface to his next year's pamphlet, that he,
unlike Lady Eastlake, signed his name to his criticisms.

★   ★   ★   ★

Early in 1855 the dealer Ernest Gambart had approached Ruskin with a
commercial proposition. Gambart was in possession of twelve Turner
plates. His plan was to publish them in an expensive limited edition
with an explanatory text by the author of *Modern Painters*. This was the
origin of the book we now know as *The Harbours of England*. Ruskin
might not have agreed to lend his pen to such a scheme. But it offered
him a rare and possibly unique opportunity to complete a part of
Turner's own work with one of the artist's own collaborators. For the
plates were in the charge of the engraver Thomas Lupton, and the
project was a revival of a plan he had made with Turner, as long ago as
1825, to issue a series entitled *The Ports of England*. Ruskin was further
tempted by Gambart's offer of two fine Turner drawings in way of
payment. The bargain was made: and he wrote the descriptions of
plates of Sandwich, Sheerness, Falmouth and other seafaring towns
while recuperating from illness at Deal in the spring of 1855.

The Harbours of England was not published until the next year, a
month or so after the third and fourth volumes of *Modern Painters* had
appeared. Not surprisingly, it has a number of affinities with them. It
also harks back to the sections on sea painting in the first volume,
while its remarks on the 'Dover' and 'Scarborough' bear on much that
is said of Turnerian topography and composition in the fifth and final
volume of Ruskin's great exposition of landscape art. *Harbours*, the
only book that Ruskin wrote to fulfil a commission, is both serious
and an occasional piece whose intention is to captivate the reader. It
contains magnificent things, thoughts that could only be Ruskin's,
and sentences that he alone could write. However, some of the com-

mentary is almost light-hearted. In such a text one might overlook
references to Ruskin's most personal experiences of Turner. Yet they
are there. At one point, for instance, he mentions the studies of
shipping that he had found in one of Turner's drawers. Ruskin had
come upon these sheets after the artist's death, on one of the occasions
when he had been to Queen Anne Street to look through the quantities
of art that had been left there. Of these expeditions he was mysteri-
ously silent: not until old age, and then in the delirium of his madness,
did he speak of what he had found. Nor did he ever write directly of
how he had searched the house. Only occasionally, in the privacy of
his diary, do we stumble on the memory of his thoughts when he
uncovered *The Fighting Téméraire*, lurid amid the dust and darkness of
the abandoned studios. In *The Harbours of England*, the *Téméraire* is
clearly and confidently judged as the last of Turner's paintings
'executed with perfect power'.[20] Ruskin thought more about the
picture than that: *The Harbours of England* reminds us — as *Modern
Painters* does not — how Ruskin was reluctant to relate all he knew
about the painter he most admired.

When *The Harbours of England* was published Ruskin might have
been gratified to read in the *Athenæum* that

> Since Byron's 'Address to the Ocean' a more beautiful poem on the
> sea has not been written than Mr Ruskin's preliminary chapter. It is
> a prose poem worthy of a nation at whose throne the seas, like
> captive monsters, are chained and bound. It is worthy of the nation
> of Blake and Nelson, of Drake and Howe, and true island hearts
> will beat quicker as they read . . .[21]

Ruskin's patriotism was not as simple as this, however, and much else
in this favourable review would have annoyed him. From about the
time of *Harbours* Ruskin (unlike his father, who still kept a book of
press cuttings) paid less and less attention to his reviews. The history
of his relationship with the press becomes increasingly an account of
misunderstanding. But Ruskin probably felt benevolently towards
one review which appeared in 1856. It was by two young men whom
we may count not only as admirers but as followers of Ruskin.
William Morris and Edward Burne-Jones, recent graduates of Exeter
College, Oxford, had written enthusiastically in the *Oxford and Cambridge Magazine* about the third volume of *Modern Painters* in reply to
Lady Eastlake's hostilities in the *Quarterly Review*. Out of a slough of
conventional criticism, the authors wrote, 'this man John Ruskin rose,
seeming to us like a Luther of the arts'.[22] This is the second time we
have encountered the phrase; and it is to be found elsewhere in the late
1850s. It is as though those who valued the temper of Ruskin's

criticism were hard put to find a parallel, though they wanted to make
a mighty and valiant comparison. Those without an extravagant
admiration for Ruskin, a class which would include most regular
reviewers, did not know what to make of him. But they did not lack
reports of his current opinions. In 1856 much of Ruskin's thinking was
expressed in lectures rather than in books; in addresses to the Working
Men's College; to workmen employed in the building of the Oxford
Museum; and in a lecture at the Society of Arts on 'The Recent
Progress of Design as Applied to Manufacture'. These were fully
reported in newspapers.

*   *   *   *

From May until October of 1856 the Ruskins were on the Continent.
This was the last time but one that they travelled abroad together. The
tour itself was not particularly memorable. It is most marked by the
cementing of the unusual friendship with Charles Eliot Norton, who
for many years afterwards received some of Ruskin's most intimate
letters. The Ruskins's outward route from Calais was familiar: they
were met there by Couttet, who escorted them along the old road
from Amiens to Senlis, to Rheims, and thence to Basle. They then
spent nearly two months in the lakes of northern Switzerland and the
Bernese Oberland. There Ruskin's parents rested, while he began
work on a project that had been in his mind, vaguely, for some years.
This was to be a Swiss book. Ruskin had much feeling for the subject,
but he could not decide how to express himself. The most obvious
course was to write a history of Switzerland. He had recently been
rereading Sismondi: and one can imagine a romantic Swiss version of
his *Histoire des républiques italiennes*. But Ruskin was more attracted
by the idea of a portfolio publication. This would consist of engraved
drawings of Swiss towns with a commentary. The inspiration for such
a work was clearly Turnerian. The format would no doubt have been
based on that of *The Harbours of England*. Perhaps the thought of
matching his own drawings against Turner's example dissuaded Ruskin from his project. In any case, nothing came of it.

   Evidence of Ruskin's work on the history and topography of Switzerland is to be found in some annotated books, in a handful of
drawings — sketchy, not at all suitable for engraving — and in a new
diary. This vellum-covered volume was opened when Ruskin left
England in May: he used it for journal and notes for the next two years
and more. It gives the impression of desultory and sporadic labour.
Ruskin later told Lady Trevelyan that he had done little more than ten

days' work all summer. He was no doubt tired after completing the middle volumes of *Modern Painters*. It was wearisome to have to look after both his parents and Anne Strachan, who had travelled with them. As usual, Ruskin indulged his father. John James showed little interest in the Swiss illustrations. Once more he asked his son when *Modern Painters* would be completed. This is probably why the party now moved on to Geneva and Chamonix, the original homes of the book. Here Ruskin resumed geological and cloud studies. But he also had to conduct family outings. It was on a steamer in Lake Geneva, at a cabin table 'covered with the usual Swiss news about nothing, and an old caricature book or two' that Charles Eliot Norton reintroduced himself to the party.[23] In his present, rather bored mood he found Norton interesting. He was both eager and polite; an American certainly, but a gentlemanly American. Norton talked of literature and art, as he imagined he was obliged to do, and the Ruskins listened to him. Slightly puzzled that he had not been engaged in debate, Norton wrote of his new acquaintance: 'He was apt to attribute only too much value to a judgement that did not coincide with his own.' Ruskin had let him talk on, feeling himself an older and wearier man. For his part, Norton had decided that Ruskin was 'one of the pleasantest, gentlest, kindest, and most interesting of men', adding, however, 'He seemed to me cheerful rather than happy. The deepest currents of his life ran out of sight.'[24]

We will come upon these 'deeper currents' in the vellum diary. Norton was right to realize that they existed. But he would never give them enough credit. He always afterwards relied too much on his first impressions of Ruskin. He believed him directionless, a man he could himself direct. Norton had attached himself to Ruskin at a watershed in the critic's life. Ruskin was thirty-seven now, just at the beginning of the crisis of his middle age. In Switzerland he was affected with indolence and something near to depression. He was slightly indecisive, in a state of not knowing, of waiting to be persuaded. Neither people nor literature greatly affected him: and in Switzerland there was no art to be seen. He met Harriet Beecher Stowe this summer: he did not admire *Uncle Tom's Cabin*, and was not impressed by its author. He read George Sand novels, one after the other, then read them aloud to his mother for entertainment. He realized they were bad, but what of that? Ruskin raised himself from his lethargic mood, or at any rate attempted to combat it, by considering his father's age and energy. John James was now seventy-one. Ruskin, considering how his father had passed the three-score years and ten of the biblical life span, decided to calculate how the 'perfect term of human life' applied to himself.[25] This was in Geneva, on the Sunday morning of 7 September, in the same town — and perhaps on the way to the same chapel — where he had knelt to pray and vowed to write the vindication that became *Modern Painters*. The sums in the diary revealed that Ruskin could expect to live for 11,795 days. Thenceforward he wrote the diminishing figures in his daily entry, not abandoning the practice until (day 11,192) 8 July 1858: significantly, perhaps, at a time of religious uncertainty.

Quietly, (he did not announce his 'signal-word or watchword' until 1876[26]) Ruskin now replaced the *Age quod agis* on his father's coat-of-arms with a new personal motto. It was the single word 'Today'. He thought of it always with a corollary, the verse from the gospel of St John, 'The night cometh, when no man can work'. On the way home from Switzerland Ruskin gathered his forces, made sure to take notes in the Louvre, began to make new plans. Back in England, the diary suddenly indicates how full was his social and professional life. On 21 October (day 11,753) is the entry 'visit Morris and Jones'.[27] Guided no doubt by Rossetti, Ruskin had visited his young Pre-Raphaelite admirers at their lodgings in Red Lion Square. Edward Burne-Jones was simply overjoyed, especially since Ruskin proposed to call there regularly on his Thursday visits to the Working Men's College: 'Tomorrow night he comes again', wrote Burne-Jones, 'and every Thursday night the same — isn't that like a dream? think of knowing Ruskin like an equal and being called his dear boys. Oh! he is so good and kind — better than his books, which are the best books in the world.'[28] Ruskin made many other visits that autumn. We find him at the Prinseps's, where he 'heard sad report of poor Watts',[29] with Furnivall, with John Lewis; and dining at Gambart's with the celebrated French *animalier* Rosa Bonheur. In such company Ruskin was relaxed and garrulous. One might imagine him at ease with the world, were it not that the shadow of the Turner bequest had once again been cast over his mind. The National Gallery had organized a small exhibition of Turner's oil paintings. This was the first public appearance of any of the work that had been left in Queen Anne Street. The exhibition had a dramatic effect on Ruskin, with consequent damage to his health. By 28 November (day 11,716), he was ill. The diary notes 'curious illness attacking me in the afternoon of Saturday, before dinner, with shivering, weakness, loss of appetite, as if the commencement of a serious illness; feverish night with heat and quick pulse, but perspiration. Heavy headache and disgusted, incapable feeling all Sunday, going gradually off towards evening'.[30]

★   ★   ★   ★

The involved story of Ruskin's dealings with the Turner bequest is examined below. For the moment we should look at a book that was written in this winter of 1856–7, *The Elements of Drawing*. The book issues in part from Ruskin's Turner studies, in part from the activities at the Working Men's College; but its procedures come from Ruskin's correspondence with his admirers. Since the mid–1840s he had taught drawing by letter. The first of his pupils by correspondence were Henry Acland and the daughter of his Christ Church tutor Walter Brown: the most recent was Harriet Beecher Stowe's daughter. Whole sequences of these letters relating to drawing have survived, and such collections (lovingly mounted in albums, often enough) throw some light on *The Elements*. For of course they show how impractical and laborious such a method of instruction must be. They also indicate that the teaching was not progressive: it always returned to first principles. *The Elements of Drawing* reflects the way in which these lessons often ended in discouragement. The book was designed to relieve Ruskin from the many demands that were made on him, now that he had a class. It also had a remedial purpose. It opposed the numerous drawing manuals that demonstrated quick ways of composing picturesque landscape. In one way, the book is as near as we know to a Pre-Raphaelite manual. But its insistence on painstaking drawing from nature still meant only exercises. That they were of stones, flowers and leaves was refreshing. But they would not have taken a pupil very far. Certainly there is no intention of helping a reader of the book to become an artist. Ruskin was a better teacher (as all drawing masters must be) when he sat down side by side with someone. Then his instruction could be both efficient and inspiring. But he could not project teaching into independence and individual style. Here was one aspect of his confused and contradictory relations with Rossetti — and also with Burne-Jones, for the younger artist was now also brought into the Working Men's College. They were at one and the same time Ruskin's comrades, his colleagues and his pupils. But neither of them had anything to do with *The Elements*, and it is doubtful whether either of them could have performed its exercises. Ruskin still badgered Rossetti to correct his drawing. But he never criticized Burne-Jones, whose art was dependent on Rossetti's: not now, when Burne-Jones was in his novitiate, nor ever afterwards.

Given the principles of *The Elements of Drawing*, it is strange that Ruskin brought Rossetti and Burne-Jones to teach at the Working Men's College. He must have given them the duller or the quirkier students. He could not have let them plant bad habits or bohemian ways in the aspirant artist-workmen who were destined for duty in Denmark Hill. This is only one of many ways in which his notion of a democratic art fell down. After their dinner at Gambart's, Rosa Bonheur spoke of Ruskin from the point of view of a French professional artist. 'He is a gentleman,' she said, 'an educated gentleman; but he is a theorist. He sees nature with a little eye — *tout a fait comme un oiseau*.'[31] She had seen that, being a gentleman, he was an amateur; and that his social position had made him insensitive to the ambitions of easel painting. This combination infuriated a critic nearer home. Ruskin's theories were bitterly scorned by an art educationalist who was near to Pre-Raphaelitism. William Bell Scott was a painter who was Principal of the School of Design at Newcastle. Despite their common friends at Wallington he and Ruskin could scarcely be polite to each other, let alone agree about art. Bell Scott visited the Working Men's College drawing classes and was appalled.[32] He too taught working men. He knew how to encourage artists to make paintings. Ruskin, he was convinced, did not. And it is true that Ruskin was of most use when talking to women amateur water-colourists. Many technical matters confirm this judgement. One is the problem of perspective. In 1859 Ruskin added *The Elements of Perspective* to *The Elements of Drawing*. This was supposed to explain and demonstrate eternal rules. But the problem for a realist painter in 1859 was that the more 'correct' his perspective, the more his pictorial space looked like Renaissance space, perhaps even like that of the despised Raphael. This is the kind of painterly problem Ruskin did not enter. *The Elements of Perspective* was not a help to contemporary painters. Significantly, it is based on the exercises in Euclidean geometry that had pleased Ruskin when he was a Christ Church gentleman-commoner.

In these earliest days of avant-garde culture, it is not surprising to find great optimism for the future of art combined with the collapse, or confusion, of traditional teaching practices. We would also expect to find the most variable assessments of the worth of new art. Ruskin's comments in *Academy Notes* show how alert he was to the merits of contemporary painting. But these detached paragraphs, the most direct art criticism he ever wrote, are scarcely important when we think of the great flood of experience that formed his sensibility. That experience was not modern: it was 'of the old school'.[33] It was also provincial. As *Academy Notes*'s additional observations on the 'French Exhibition' remind us, there is little profit in reading Ruskin on modern foreign painting. He rather disliked German art, the first nineteenth-century continental school he was aware of. He would not come to dislike the Nazarenes until he looked at them in 1859, but he knew before that there must be something wrong with the school: had not John Murray asked him to write a book on them rather than on Turner? His attitude to French painting was negligent. He never in his life visited the *Salons*, the Parisian equivalent of the Royal Academy exhibitions. In Pall Mall, Gambart showed French paintings every year from 1854. Ruskin occasionally noticed them. In these years he most admired Edouard Frère, for his sentiment and his invaluable record of peasant life. French peasants were important to Ruskin, and his distrust of new French art was usually mixed with his attitude to vicious republican Paris. He loved France for its provinces and their architecture. In 1857, giving an address at the Working Men's College, he spoke of French 'manners' and cathedrals: these indeed were his real interests. But he also knew a surprising amount of modern French literature. In a few years' time, with help from Swinburne, he would acknowledge that there was talent in Baudelaire. He could not be so tolerant about art. Paintings always made him angrier than books: they as it were blinded him; and no help from Swinburne in the next few years could make him understand the French background of the most challenging artist he encountered in the years after Pre-Raphaelitism, who was of course Whistler.

CHAPTER THIRTEEN

1855–1858

Not far from the Royal Academy of Arts lay the Olympic, a public house with some music hall entertainment. Here, in June of 1855, George Butterworth had spent the evening after a visit to the annual exhibition. In his pocket was a copy of *Academy Notes*. Butterworth was a young carpenter. He had come to London from Lancashire and was living in lodgings in south London. He had enrolled at the Working Men's College art classes the previous year. His diary tells us much about the life of an artistically inclined young workman who had come under Ruskin's influence. One of its entries records the birth of the idea of the *Notes*:

> Went up to see Mr Ruskin who I heard had been to the Academy once more to look at Millais's picture, and had come back too unwell to go to college — he however would see me but for a few minutes as he said he had something on his mind which he intended to have [illegible] some criticisms of the pictures at the Academy which he intended to have [illegible] and sold at the doors along with the catalogues — the idea so tickled his fancy that he laughed aloud, he was in such good spirits that I not only got him to have two of the Turners home to work upon but his permission to take out of the frame the Carisbrooke . . .[1]

Butterworth framed for Ruskin and therefore had a good personal experience of the Denmark Hill collection. He also gave Ruskin woodworking lessons: the critic 'wanted it for exercise to keep him from thinking'.[2] Thus Butterworth came to carry away wine, money and pictures from Denmark Hill. Perhaps it is true, as Ruskin believed, that he was feckless. *Præterita* speaks darkly of him, or rather of 'the deadly influence of London itself, and of working men's clubs as well as colleges'.[3] When Butterworth's diary notes how he and a friend, another carpenter, had spent a Sunday afternoon discussing designs for an altar-piece and then reading aloud from the Working Men's College pamphlet of *The Nature of Gothic*, we might recognize a workman-artist cast in the perfect mould of the Ruskinian labourer. But the instinctive and relentless high tone of Ruskin's contact with the world prevented him from understanding the relaxations of working-class youths, particularly if they were artists. To one such,

J. J. Laing, he wrote at this time, 'The great lesson we have to learn in this world is to *give it all up*.'[4] Butterworth was too eager to experience the world to command Ruskin's good opinion. He felt it presumptuous in the young man to go on a painting holiday in Wales, or indeed to visit in his native Middleton the Turner patron John Hammersley. Butterworth thought to go up to Denmark Hill and please Ruskin with Hammersley's tales of the painter. But he was in error. He had mistaken his place.

At the Working Men's College, Butterworth had a slight acquaintance with George Allen, another northerner. Allen, a native of Newark, was already a highly qualified joiner, good enough to attract the best employment that his trade offered. Butterworth wrote in his diary that he had seen how Ruskin had an especial interest in him. 'I think he intends to make Allen into something.'[5] This indeed was so. George Allen's new career as Ruskin's *factotum* and, eventually, his publisher, began at the Working Men's College. In old age he looked back on his other opportunities with particular nostalgia. 'In the early days of the renaissance of industrial art,' he told J. W. Mackail, 'when the movement was first projected, Dante Rossetti asked me to join him and William Morris in the practical carrying out of their plans . . . I was obliged to forgo all thought of doing so having just then accepted Mr Ruskin's offer . . .'[6] In fact, Allen had himself made an offer which bound him to Denmark Hill. On Christmas Day of 1856 he married Hannah, Margaret Ruskin's maid and George Hobbs's sister. Ruskin now set Allen to learn new skills. He paid Thomas Lupton and J. H. Le Keux to teach him mezzotint techniques and line engraving. Le Keux was from an old family of engravers. Lupton had worked for Turner. Ruskin's intentions were obvious. In this way he established a direct artisanal link between Turner's work for engravers and the superb plates that illustrated his own books.

Thus, as Ruskin sensed his disillusionment with the Working Men's College, he more and more used it to recruit his personal labour force. Partly to mock the Christian Socialists, he now occasionally talked of a 'protestant convent', whose inmates would be engaged in art work and supervised by himself.[7] In practice, this meant that artists became Denmark Hill servants of a special sort. To Allen and Butterworth (who was sporadically employed until the '80s) we must now add the names of William Ward, Arthur Burgess and John Bunney. All three came from the Working Men's College and remained in Ruskin's employment until they died. Burgess was a wood–engraver who had been, according to the obituary notice Ruskin wrote, 'variously bound, embittered and wounded in the ugly prison-house of London labour'.[8] Ward had been a clerk in the City. Ruskin turned him into a

Turner copyist and drawing master, using him to teach pupils he had
no time for. Bunney also was a clerk. He was employed by Smith,
Elder. His contact with Ruskin therefore took him out of the commercial side of the firm and into the direct artistic employ of its most
celebrated author. It was a foreshadowing of Ruskin's eventual decision to take all his publishing into his own hands.

*   *   *   *

Letters of instruction and encouragement to these men are numerous.
Ruskin had been teaching people to draw by letter since the time of the
composition of the first volume of *Modern Painters*. It was a practice he
maintained all his life. Recipients of such letters must be numbered in
dozens, and some of these pupils must have received up to a hundred
separate missives. A feature of these letters is their relative uniformity.
Little or no account is taken of an individual's artistic predilections,
nor much of his or her relative advancement. It was all the same to
Ruskin: one and the same will was impressed on all. Of course, it was
only rarely that an independent professional artist would seek instruction from him. This helped Ruskin to maintain the illusion that the
same art should be made by everybody. Early in his acquaintance with
Louisa, Marchioness of Waterford, he declared 'I am not surer of
anything I know, than of this, that there is no real occasion for the
gulph of separation between amateur and artist.'[9] It was a radical,
mistaken view, one of a number of misconceptions that lay behind
The Elements of Drawing.

What purported to be a timeless book turned out to be utterly and
inescapably of its day. How could one expect any book of Ruskin's to
be anything but individual, or to belong to any time other than the
months in which it was written? *The Elements of Drawing* comes from
such concerns as his classes in Red Lion Square, his love of detail in
engravings after Turner, and his correspondence with such eager
amateurs as the Marchioness of Waterford. Embedded though it is in
this tiny corner of the history of drawing, the book still has a significant position in the history of that sub-branch of art education which is
carried by drawing manuals. Such manuals belong to the post-
Renaissance period. *The Elements* is the last one to have relevance to
living fine art, and its terminal position is what confers on it a poignant
importance. For there is no such thing as a drawing manual within the
avant-garde tradition. Nor is such a thing quite conceivable. All
manuals after *The Elements* have been either academic or vulgar in
nature. Ruskin's book is in fact a witness of how fragile a period style
his realism was. It also reminds us of the problems of realism, how it

was troubled by compositional design and had difficulty in continuing the landscape tradition. To another young lady artist Ruskin explained, 'In general, persons who have drawn landscapes have merely blotted — and not drawn anything. And to them the book must imply the entire overturn of all previous thought or practice.'[10] In fact, anyone with serious pictorial ambitions would find in *The Elements* all the problems of becoming a modern painter, and few of the solutions. For schoolgirls and copyists, however, it had its uses. It provided them with exercises.

In the new year of 1857 there was demand for Ruskin the public man. We find him addressing the Architectural Association, then giving a lecture at St Martin's School of Art; making speeches to the committee for a memorial to the painter Thomas Seddon; and discussing plans with the council of the Arundel Society. More important than these activities was the matter of Turner's gift of his work to the nation, for the executors and lawyers had now completed their deliberations over Turner's simple and generous wishes. The question of Ruskin's resignation from his executorship was once more raised. But only a mind as narrow as Lady Eastlake's could still entertain the view that such mechanical duties should have been more Ruskin's concern than the vast spiritual exercise of which *Modern Painters* is the record. Four volumes of that book, and numerous miscellaneous writings besides, were by now the evidence of that endeavour. For those few who read him attentively, it must have seemed that Ruskin's effort to understand Turner was not distinct from his wish to understand everything about the world; its light and knowledge, its destiny. At the same time, however elevated Ruskin's conceptions, he moved in the circles of politics and administration. His bitter remark in the preface to the third volume of *Modern Painters*, that Turner's countrymen had buried 'with threefold honour, his body in St Paul's, his pictures at Charing Cross, and his purposes in Chancery' — a comment quite evidently directed at those who had charge over Turner's *œuvre* — announced that he would turn his attention to public artistic policy.[11]

Disregarding the niceties of an approach to the National Gallery's trustees, within whose purview Turner's legacy now belonged, Ruskin wrote to *The Times*. His letter offered to sort and arrange the whole of Turner's drawings and sketches: all his work, that is, not done in oil on canvas. Neither the trustees nor Sir Charles Eastlake, the National Gallery's director, responded to this letter. Ruskin then repeated his offer by approaching the newly elected Prime Minister, Palmerston. This proved effective. However, more than three months

were to elapse before Ruskin received an official invitation to arrange
the drawings. During this time (and repeating the strategy of *Academy
Notes*) Ruskin issued a rival catalogue to the brief official publication
that accompanied the first exhibition selected from the Turner
bequest. This is known as *Notes on the Turner Gallery at Marlborough
House*. Like *Academy Notes*, it comments on certain paintings in an
exhibition not chosen by Ruskin himself. These were all oils, for the
drawings were still unsorted and, indeed, not yet unpacked. This
catalogue is the shortest single work by Ruskin on Turner, yet contains a wonderful amount of his understanding of the artist. One
notices, first, how much better this pamphlet is than *Academy Notes*.
Its judgements are surer, less wayward, more considered: they are also
loving. One is astonished by the set-piece with which it ends, on the
Téméraire of 1842. And everywhere, as the trustees of the National
Gallery must have seen, there is a complete assurance in Ruskin's
personal knowledge of the artist and in his ability to discriminate
between his works. [12]

This was in early January 1857. Ruskin was soon worrying that he
had made the wrong moves in his negotiations with the National
Gallery. He had perhaps sought too high a level, through over-
confidence and through disdain for Eastlake. An appendix to the
Marlborough House *Notes* had made challenging remarks to the effect
that 'the national interest is only beginning to be awakened in works of
art': this could have irritated the trustees. [13] When, therefore, they
invited him to make a trial selection, the framing to be done at his own
expense, he was pleased to agree. The small private exhibition he now
prepared was cleverly devised. Ruskin took one hundred drawings to
illustrate an imaginary tour (but to places he and Turner knew well)
from England up the Rhine, through Switzerland to Venice and back.
The catalogue he wrote to accompany the show is a curiosity. It is
marked 'for private circulation only' and was directed towards the
trustees, whom Ruskin now addresses as though they were children. [14]
One point of his selection was to demonstrate how much of his
expertise was topographical. The ability to identify Turner's sites
would be crucial to the cataloguing of the collection. But his proposals
for framing, preservation and presentation were also exemplary. He
had his own private work-force, in the persons of George Allen and
William Ward. In short, the trustees could hardly refuse him. There
was no possibility of Ruskin being a happy colleague of Sir Charles
Eastlake. But one can work in a museum without speaking to its
director, and Ruskin struck some kind of relationship with the keeper
of the collections, Ralph Wornum. This was not easily managed:

Wornum had attempted to persuade Ruskin that Lady Eastlake was
not the author of the attack on himself and Turner in the *Quarterly
Review*. But they got on well enough, for Wornum knew that he could
not have done the work himself.

Ruskin had been right: the legacy required his special knowledge
and commitment. Turner was not the first artist to have had an
obscure and private career. But he was the first whose art had to be
brought into the national heritage by a critic working in consort with a
national museum. Ruskin was more aware of the implications of this
situation than were his temporary colleagues. And thus, as the work
he now began gave him a yet deeper feeling for Turner, it also
alienated him from the routines of committees and administration,
meetings and deliberations, that were part of the growing profession-
alism of museums and exhibitions.

Ruskin's involvement with the Turner bequest was much interrupted. *The Elements of Drawing* was concluded in the spring: some of
it was written concurrently with the Turner catalogues. In *The Elements* there are traces of Ruskin's current work on Turner, just as in the
Turner catalogue we will find addresses to students. The 1857 number
of *Academy Notes* now had to be written. It is a little shorter than its
usual length and is dominated by Ruskin's criticism of Millais's *Sir
Isumbras at the Ford*. The critic objected to the new fluidity of Millais's
application: 'The change in his manner, from the years of "Ophelia"
and "Mariana" to 1857 is not merely Fall — it is Catastrophe; not
merely a loss of power, but a reversal of principle.'[15] Ruskin added
some kinder remarks. His beautiful iconographical explanation of the
picture is a little akin in tone to what he had said of Turner in the
Marlborough House *Notes*. Millais was of course unappeased by
Ruskin's suggestive remarks about his themes. The brevity of the rest
of *Academy Notes* almost made it appear that the pamphlet had been
issued with the sole purpose of condemning his painting. Ruskin's
relations with the Pre-Raphaelite movement as a whole were, as usual,
difficult. A further cause of friction and misunderstanding was now
provided by the increased number of independent exhibitions. This
year an exhibition was held in Fitzroy Square. It was in effect the only
Pre-Raphaelite group show. Ruskin might have made the exhibition
more successful: but since the organizing force behind the show was
Ford Madox Brown, he had to keep his distance. When he helped with
the memorial exhibition for Thomas Seddon he was good at raising
money for the widow. But he was more prominent personally than
other friends of the artist had wished. At a *conversazione* held in May of
1857 he delivered an address on the dead artist, whom in fact he had not

known very well. Ruskin's speech is known from a newspaper report. It was rather long, and only a part of it was about Seddon himself. The artists' death (from dysentery, in Cairo, while on a painting expedition) set Ruskin off on a disquisition that introduces the themes of his later political writing. The *Journal of the Society of Arts* reports it thus:

> The simple sacrifice of life had in it nothing unusual — it was, on the contrary, a melancholy thing to reflect how continually we all of us lived upon the lives of others, and that in two ways, viz., upon lives which we take, and upon lives which are given. It was a terrible expression to use — this taking of life, but it was a true one. We took life in all cases in which, either for higher wages, or by the compulsion of commercial pressure, men were occupied without sufficient protection or guardianship in dangerous employments, involving an average loss of life, for which life we paid thoughtlessly in the price of the commodity, which, so far, was the price of blood. Nay, more than this, it was a well-recognised fact that there was scarcely an art or science in the present day, in which there was not some concomitant circumstance of danger or disease, which science had not striven to abate proportionably with the endeavours to advance the skill of the workmen. And thus, though we had abolished slavery, we literally bargained daily for the lives of our fellowmen, although we should shrink with horror at the idea of purchasing their bodies; and if these evils, arising partly from pressure of population, but more from carelessness in masters and consumers, from desire of cheapness, or blind faith in commercial necessities — if these evils went on increasing at the rate it seemed but too probable they would, England would soon have to add another supporter to her shield. She had good right still to her lion, never more than now. But she needed, in justice, another, to show that if she could pour forth life blood nobly, she could also drink it cruelly; she should have not only the lion, but the vampire . . .[16]

Perhaps John James's fear of his son's lectures came from a realization that Ruskin was always likely to say something inapposite. The Seddon address was a case in point. One might agree with these sentiments, or not: one would still doubt that this were the right occasion to express them. Ruskin had also agreed to give two lectures in July at the Art Treasures exhibition in Manchester. He was unconcerned that what he said might not relate to the art that was exhibited. He did not attend the opening of the exhibition. Instead he took lodgings in a farmhouse in Cowley, then a village three miles outside Oxford. There, 'in the middle of a field, with a garden of gooseberries and

orange lilies; and a loose stone wall round it, all over stone-crop', he
began to write the lectures which became *The Political Economy of
Art*.[17] Charles Eliot Norton was in Oxford at the time, and later
claimed that Ruskin discussed his writing with him. If so, this was the
first occasion on which the young Bostonian had ventured to tell
Ruskin what he ought to be thinking and saying. It is more likely that
Ruskin had helpful conversations with Henry Acland, whom he saw
almost daily, for they still had much work to do on the University
Museum. Ruskin tried his hand at building Acland's study: 'I built a
great bit yesterday, which the bricklayer my tutor in a most provoking manner pulled all down again. But this bit I have done today is to
stand.'[18] Ruskin felt the more protective of the museum because it was
just now that Liddell, who had recently become Dean of Christ
Church, was restoring and erecting new buildings there. Pointedly, he
had not asked for Ruskin's advice. The circumstances would be bitterly recalled in an unpublished draft of *Præterita*. Ruskin now parted
company with the college in which he had been educated. In this year
he was elected an honorary student of Christ Church in company with
Gladstone and Acland. He valued the honour in an abstract fashion: he
would not go there. When at last he spent an evening in hall in 1883 he
remarked that he had not dined in his own college for thirty years.

This was the Pre-Raphaelite summer in Oxford. Ruskin was calling
himself a 'PRB' as though he were a member of the defunct
Brotherhood, and addressing Jane Simon, the wife of John Simon, as a
'PRS', a sister in art.[19] He had a little contact with many of the
artists, William Morris among them, who were working in the
Union. He may also have met Swinburne for the first time. But
Ruskin was not close to them and left Oxford in early July to give his
Manchester lectures.[20] He travelled afterwards to Wallington and
thence to Edinburgh, where he had rendezvous with his parents for a
tour of Scotland. In Manchester he left behind him an amount of
consternation. In 1880, when he reissued *The Political Economy of Art*,
Ruskin changed its title to *A Joy for Ever (and its Price in the Market)*.
Keats's phrase and the sardonic addition were employed to reassert a
radicalism that had been somewhat forgotten in the previous two
decades. Much that Ruskin declared in Manchester became common
currency not much later on. But to reread the 1857 lectures is still to be
struck by their vigour and attack. To assert that one can talk of art and
political economy in the same breath, to open an art lecture with
comments on poverty, was to announce, all suddenly, a political
position.

John James Ruskin, so jealous of his son's public reputation, was not dismayed by the Manchester lectures. Nor, when at length it came, was he put out by the generally negative reaction in the press. After publication, when *The Times* criticized Ruskin for speaking on matters that were not the province of an æsthete, his father was still cheerfully of the opinion that there was value in the address. *The Times* had associated Ruskin with Dr Thomas Guthrie, a famous Scottish preacher of the day, a philanthropist and pioneer of the ragged schools, whose *City: its Sins and Sorrows* had recently been published. John James wrote about the matter to Jane Simon:

> Mrs R. named to me your having heard that my Son's meddling with Political Economy might weaken his Influence in matters of Art. I feared this myself, but by his own confession his studies of Political Economy have not encroached much on his time — and on this weary subject a few new ideas will do no harm. The Times couples him with Dr Guthrie and says they are both in a state of helpless ignorance of the first principles of Political Philosophy. I might, perhaps, prefer the Simplicity of Dr Guthrie to the Philosophy of the Times; but, if my Son has so greatly committed himself in his last little book, I trust to the talk of Mr Simon, Mr Helps and Mr Carlyle bringing us an amended Second Edition . . .[21]

And to E. S. Dallas, who was a journalist on the newspaper, he repeated, 'As a City man I am half with *The Times* in believing my Son and Dr Guthrie innocent of Political Economy; but these Geniuses sometimes in their very simplicity hit upon the right thing, whilst your ponderous Economy discusser twaddles on in endless mazes lost.'[22] John James was not quite near the mark in believing that a combination of Simon, Helps and Carlyle would make Ruskin a sounder critic of society. Simon the administrator, Helps the experimental liberal reformer, were both people with whom Ruskin enjoyed an exchange of views. But he took little notice of what they said. It was towards Carlyle's message that his mind tended, towards a visionary conservatism that John James could not understand. For Ruskin as the Master of the Guild of St George, Dr Guthrie's philanthropy made 'all things smooth and smiling for the Devil's work'.[23]

This will plainly appear in *Munera Pulveris* of 1862, the best of Ruskin's middle-period political writings. The book is dedicated to Carlyle. In 1857, however, the relationship between the two men might have seemed rather distant. Carlyle had no interest in art: he even seemed to dislike it. Ruskin was too busy with art work to think of Carlyle. After the holiday in Scotland with his parents (and a brief visit to Oxford to see the Pre-Raphaelite frescoes) Ruskin had to settle down to the long task of the arrangement of the Turner drawings. In some basement rooms in the National Gallery, which Ruskin scornfully called its 'cellar', he began to unpack the tin boxes in which the treasures had been crammed away. Because he had known the house in Queen Anne Street Ruskin was not surprised at the state of the drawings. But the description of their condition which he gave in the fifth and final volume of *Modern Painters* is filled with a sort of retrospective horror at what he now found:

> . . . some in chalk, which the touch of the finger would sweep away; others in ink, rotted into holes; others (some splendid coloured drawings among them) long eaten away by damp and mildew, and falling into dust at the edges, in capes and bays of fragile decay; others worm-eaten, some mouse-eaten, many torn, halfway through; numbers doubled (quadrupled, I should say,) up into four, being Turner's favourite mode of packing for travelling; nearly all rudely flattened out from the bundles in which Turner had finally rolled them up and squeezed them into his drawers in Queen Anne Street. Dust of thirty years' accumulation, black, dense, and sooty, lay in the rents of the crushed and crumpled edges of these flattened bundles, looking like a jagged black frame, and producing altogether unexpected effects in brilliant portions of skies, whence an accidental or experimental finger-mark of the first bundle-unfolder had swept it away.[24]

The first task was to ensure the safety of the drawings. In his cramped conditions, without enough natural light, sending up clouds of chalk and dust, and without the aid of any professional restoration techniques, Ruskin began his protection. He had to work with his sleeves rolled up, washing his hands every few minutes, spreading the drawings out on whatever surfaces were available, measuring and numbering them. Every evening, as George Allen recalled, 'after our day's work at the Gallery Mr Ruskin and I used to take the measurements of drawings to Denmark Hill, where I cut with my own hands about 800 thick passe-partout mounts — they were taken to the Gallery and the drawings inserted there'.[25] Many of them could not have been mounted before they were pressed. Since there were 19,000 separate drawings to deal with the variety of cleaning and cataloguing problems was enormous. At first, Ruskin seemed to be optimistic. Stacy Marks, the genial painter of birds who was to be a friend for many years, found him quite confident when he introduced himself in the 'cellar'. Marks wrote:

I found the eloquent exponent of Turner in rooms in the basement of the building, surrounded by piles of sketch-books and loose drawings by the master, which he was arranging, mounting and framing, — a congenial employment, a labour of love, to which he devoted months of time, with no recompense beyond the pleasure which the occupations afforded him. I can remember little of our conversation except that it was chiefly about Turner and his work. I had gone to the Gallery with an ill-defined feeling of awe of the great man I was about to see, but this was dissipated directly I had shaken hands with him. There was none of the posing of the genius; I found him perfectly simple, unaffected, kindly, and human.[26]

'Every day, and often far into the night,' Ruskin claimed, he worked on. By the end of December 1857 it seemed to him that there were 10,000 drawings which were 'far enough carried forward to give some question as to whether they should be exhibited or not'.[27] In effect, Ruskin was now re-learning Turner's entire career, and more intimately than he ever before had thought possible. He wrote to Ellen Heaton, a water-colourist and collector, of the 'excitement of discovering something precious or learning something new every half minute'.[28] This was almost painful. For as more and more was unfolded of Turner's art Ruskin had the gathering impression that what he had thought of him was only what a young man might think. The drawings recalled to him what he had known of the man. In truth Ruskin had revered him, until their quarrel: and in some measure had still revered him after he had decided that he could not forgive him. But he had never loved the man as he had loved the work, and he now looked sorrowfully on all that had been hidden in the artist's character. Perhaps he had only known Turner personally in his utter decline? Ruskin found that he could not talk of these troubles to his father. He did not even formulate his thoughts until the next summer. Then, far away in Bellinzona, he wrote to his father as follows:

You are quite right in your feeling about the later drawings in this respect, that the power of sight is in a considerable degree diminished, and that a certain impatience, leading sometimes to magnificence, sometimes to mistake, indicates the approach of disease; but at the same time, all the experience of the whole life's practice of art is brought to bear occasionally on them, with results for wonderment and instructiveness quite unapproached in the earlier drawings. There is, however, one fault about them which I have only ascertained since my examination of the Turner sketches. There is evidence in those sketches of a gradual moral decline in the painter's mind from the beginning of life to its end — at first patient, tender, self-controlling, exquisitely perceptive, hopeful, and calm, he becomes gradually stern, wilful, more and more impetuous, then gradually more sensual, capricious — sometimes in mode of work even indolent and slovenly — the powers of art and know-ledge on nature increasing all the while, but not now employed with the same calm or great purpose — his kindness of heart never deserting him, but encumbered with sensuality, suspicion, pride, vain regrets, hopelessness, languor, and all kinds of darkness and oppression of heart. What I call the 'sunset drawings' — such as our Coblentz, Constance, Red Rigi, etc., — marks the effort of the soul to recover itself, a peculiar calm and return of the repose or youthful spirit, preceding the approach of death . . .[29]

One small group of drawings might have epitomized, for Ruskin, Turner's moral decline. Somewhere in the boxes he found work which he was later to describe as 'grossly obscene'. Ruskin had remarked in the Marlborough House catalogue, 'I never know whether most to venerate or lament the strange impartiality of Turner's mind, and the vast cadence of subjects in which he was able to take interest.'[30] At this point, Ruskin was remarking how great mythological subjects might alternate with views of the Isle of Dogs. Such a Thames-side scene might not be fully worthy of its painter, but it was still within the realm of art. These obscene drawings were not. This was also Wornum's view. For the good of Turner's reputation, and in the interests of the high view of the national culture that the bequest was intended to serve, it seemed best that these drawings should not form part of the collection. Ruskin already believed that there was no point in preserving 'valueless' scribbles or scraps. Wor-num was of the opinion that even to possess these drawings was illegal. The National Gallery authorities were in favour of burning them. Ruskin agreed, and watched as Wornum lit the fire. He hardly ever made explicit mention of this episode and it is not easy to estimate what effect it had on him. It was probably only a part of the experience of working with the Turner bequest. But it was around this time that he came to believe not merely that Turner's 'mind and sight partially gave way',[31] as the Marlborough House catalogue states, but that the painter went mad and 'died mad'. Such views were always privately expressed. Just as he never spoke of his quarrel with Turner, so he would not write publicly of his feeling that the artist's mind was diseased. Many years later, when Ruskin's own mind was in pitiful disarray, we occasionally find renewed warnings about a 'passionately sensual character' that would lead to 'a kind of delirium tremens. Turner had it fatally in his last years';[32] and Ruskin's work with Wornum, otherwise forgotten, is suddenly mentioned in his diary's passages of insane free association that were written in the days before his own delirium.[33]

*   *   *   *

> The manual labour would not have hurt me [wrote Ruskin of his work on the Turner catalogue] but the excitement involved in seeing unfolded the whole career of Turner's mind during his life, joined with much sorrow at the state in which nearly all his most precious work had been left, and with great anxiety, and heavy sense of responsibility besides, were very trying: and I have never in my life felt so much exhausted as when I locked the last box, and gave the keys to Mr Wornum, in May, 1858.[34]

The experience would be reflected in the graver tone of the fifth volume of *Modern Painters*: this spring, tired though he was, Ruskin proselytized for the future of art. In the first week of May he wrote *Academy Notes*, and published the pamphlet immediately. He noted with satisfaction that Pre-Raphaelitism had triumphed 'as I stated five years ago it would'.[35] If some of the initial impetus had left the movement, a social gain had become important. Art now had a democratic function. But this was not to be confused with mere popularity. *Academy Notes* dismissed Frith's *Derby Day* — 'It is a kind of a cross between John Leech and Wilkie, with a touch of daguerrotype here and there, and some pretty seasoning with Dickens's sentiment' — and reserved its most hopeful praise for John Brett's *Stonebreaker*.[36] With *Academy Notes* done, Ruskin felt ready for travel. After the traditional family feast on 10 May he set out, alone, for Italy: it is probable that he had arranged to meet Brett there.

In Paris Ruskin visited (a family obligation) the Comte and Comtesse Maison: the Comtesse was the eldest of the Domecq daughters. A week later he was in Basle, where he was joined by Couttet. There and at Rheinfelden he identified the sites of some of the Turner drawings he had recently catalogued. In the letters to Denmark Hill which now replace his diary we often find the themes of the last volume of *Modern Painters*. From Brunnen, in William Tell country, he wrote:

> I am surprised to find what a complete centre of the history of Europe, in politics and religion, this lake of Lucerne is, as Venice is a

centre of the history of art. First, the whole Swiss nation taking its name from the little town of Schwytz, just above this, because the Schwytzers were to the Austrian Emperors the first representatives of republican power, in their stand at Morgarten; then, the league of the three cantons to defend each other against all enemies, first signed and sealed in this little village of Brunnen; followed by the victories of Laupen, Sempach, Granson, Morat, and gradually gained power on the other side of the Alps in Italy until the Swiss literally gave away the Duchy of Milan, the competitors for it pleading their causes before the Swiss Council at Baden; and meantime, the great Reformation disputes in religion making these hills the place of their eternal struggle, till Zwingli was killed in the battle with these same three Catholic cantons, just beyond Zug on the road down from the Albis; whilst, on the other hand, the Republican party at Geneva was Protestant, and binding itself by oath in imitation of the oath of these three cantons, and calling itself Eidgenossen — 'bound by oath' — gets this word corrupted by the French into 'Huguenots', and so to stand generally for the Protestant party in France also.[37]

Some of Ruskin's admiration for the only modern republic he could approve of was worked up from, for instance, André Vieusseux's *History of Switzerland*, translated into English in 1840, but such prosaic sources were imaginatively paraphrased. Ruskin's views of the schisms of European history were romantic and partial, and he felt that art and legend are the heart of a nation's life. Thus, since history, art and nature are intertwined, the history of Switzerland was to be treated in the chapter of the fifth volume of *Modern Painters* entitled 'The Leaf Shadows'. Ruskin was in fact returning to an ambition he had felt since completing *The Stones of Venice*, a book on the culture of Swiss towns. It was never written, partly because it stirred in him disturbing social reflections. The peoples of Switzerland, he explained to his father, 'have sunk and remain sunk, merely by idleness and wantonness in the midst of all blessings and advantages . . . every man always acts for himself: they will never act together and do anything at common expense'.[38]

Ruskin's feelings for Switzerland were to reappear years later in his plans for the Guild of St George. Now, in 1858, they have a relevance to his collaboration with two English painters. This year he met at Fluelen J. W. Inchbold, a painter much commended in *Academy Notes*, and spent some time with John Brett. His praise of Brett's *Stonebreaker* in *Academy Notes* had concluded, 'If he can paint so lovely a distance from the Surrey downs and railway-traversed vales, what would he not make of the chestnut groves of the Val d'Aosta!'[39] Another letter to his father tells us more of his attitude to these two members of the Pre-Raphaelite school:

> I sent for [Brett] at Villeneuve, Val d'Aosta because I didn't like what he said in his letter about his present work, and thought he wanted some more lecturing like Inchbold: besides that, he could give me some useful hints. He is much tougher and stronger than Inchbold, and takes more hammering; but I think he looks more miserable every day, and have good hopes of making him completely wretched in a day or two . . .[40]

There is in existence a notebook of Brett's which dates from this summer. It indicates that he and Ruskin were at one point working side by side, attended by Couttet. It contains portrait sketches of the old guide. Some pages are by Ruskin. They are marked 'JMWT': Turner's initials, for Ruskin, as before, was attempting to force his personal knowledge of Turner into the practice of a younger artist.[41]

★   ★   ★   ★

Towards the end of this summer, in Switzerland and Turin, we find signs that the forty-year-old Ruskin was developing a different interest in the opposite sex. Ruskin's sexual maladjustment is not an uncommon one. He was a pædophile. He is typical of the condition in a number of ways, for pædophilia generally emerges in his age-group, often follows a period of marital breakdown, and in old age is accompanied by (or is a palliative to) a sense of loneliness and isolation. An attraction to young girls was in Ruskin's sexual nature to the end of his life. In a letter to Denmark Hill from Italy, he now wrote, 'One of the finest things I saw in Turin was a group of neglected children at play on a heap of sand — one girl of about ten, with her black hair over her eyes and half-naked, bare-limbed to above the knees, and beautifully limbed, lying on the sand like a snake . . .'.[42] The image remained with him for a quarter of a century and more. The dark Italian girl appears in his diary in later years: she was even mentioned in the disastrous last lectures in Oxford in 1884. In 1865, in *The Cestus of Aglaia*, Ruskin describes her in a manner which is as close as he ever approaches to the sensual:

> She was lying with her arms thrown back over her head, all languid and lax, on an earth-heap by the river side (the softness of dust being

the only softness she had ever known), in the southern suburb of
Turin, one golden afternoon in August, years ago. She had been at
play, after her fashion, with other patient children, and had thrown
herself down to rest, full in the sun, like a lizard. The sand was
mixed with the draggled locks of her black hair, and some of it
sprinkled over her face and body, in an 'ashes to ashes' kind of way;
a few black rags about her loins, but her limbs nearly bare, and her
little breasts, scarce dimpled yet, — white, — marble-like . . .[43]

The sight of this girl was like a landmark for Ruskin, as he afterwards
looked over his life. But pædophilia became a part of his character only
gradually. The turning-points Ruskin identified were often over-
precise. So it was with the history of his religious convictions, which
at just this period underwent a change that Ruskin was later to exaggerate. The account in *Fors Clavigera* of April 1877 tells us:

I was still in the bonds of my old Evangelical faith; and, in 1858, it
was with me, Protestantism or nothing: the crisis of the whole turn
of my thoughts being one Sunday morning, at Turin, when, from
before Veronese's Queen of Sheba, and under quite overwhelmed
sense of his God-given power, I went away to a Waldensian chapel,
where a little squeaking idiot was preaching to an audience of
seventeen old women and three louts, that they were the only
children of God in Turin; and that all the people in the world out of
sight of Monte Viso, would be damned. I came out of the chapel, in
sum of twenty years of thought, a conclusively *un*-converted
man.[44]

We must not believe that Ruskin changed his mind about religion as
abruptly as this. In *Fors*, and in another account of the experience in
Præterita, Ruskin abbreviated the way that he came to reject his
mother's Evangelical beliefs. 'That day,' he claimed, they 'were put
away, to be debated of no more.'[45] That was not true: he spent the next
thirty years debating them. Perhaps it was his hostility to conversion
that made Ruskin write in this way, as if his experience had been
directly opposed to that of so many other Christians. Conversion
experiences are common in Christian, and especially Protestant, cultures: but an opposite experience of shedding a faith as though by
revelation is not known. Nonetheless, something happened to Ruskin's Christianity in these months. It had to do with a solitary life in an
unfamiliar, enlivening place. *Præterita* notes, 'I have registered the
year 1858 as the next, after 1845, in which I had complete guidance of
myself.'[46] In 1845, Ruskin had worked hard. This summer he was

determined to be lazy. He was glad that his father was not with him to urge the completion of *Modern Painters*. He relaxed in the social pleasures of Turin. Looking back at the Alps, and for once rather pleased to have left them, Ruskin diverted himself in what was still the capital of the old Sardinian kingdom, a town of colonnades, orange trees, soldiers, bands, theatres. He rose late, lingered over coffee and *Galignani* (the European English-language newspaper, as full of gossip as of information), sauntered to the picture gallery for an hour until 'I think it time to be idle' and 'see what is going on on the shady side of the piazzas'.[47] He dined well, drank half-pints of champagne and spent every evening at the Opéra Comique. On Sundays, the actors' *riposo*, he read French novels.

A few weeks earlier, on the second Sunday after parting from his parents, Ruskin had made a sketch of some orchises. It was the first time in his life that he had drawn on the sabbath day. There in his diary were the pen outlines of the flowers.[48] Could this be wrong? How could art and nature be ruled by Sabbatarianism? And once he had left Inchbold and Brett behind Ruskin's didacticism vanished. His appetite for art became fixed on one painting. In Turin's indifferent municipal gallery he took to copying a small detail from Veronese's *Solomon and the Queen of Sheba*, the painting mentioned in the account of the 'unconversion'. This he studied with a strange mixture of indolence and fanaticism. Augustus Hare, who passed through Turin that summer, reported of Ruskin's work:

> He was sitting all day upon a scaffold in the gallery, copying bits of the great painting by Paul Veronese . . . One day in the gallery I asked him to give me some advice. He said 'watch me'. He then looked at the flounce in the dress of a maid of honour of the Queen of Sheba for five minutes, and then he painted one thread: he looked for another five minutes, and then he painted another thread. At the rate at which he was working he might hope to paint the whole dress in ten years . . .[49]

It seems that this account was hardly exaggerated. The exercise occupied Ruskin for more than a month, and all that came of it were a few tiny scraps of overworked detail.

Ruskin's insistence that he was disillusioned with Evangelicalism in a Waldensian chapel has significance. It was his practice to read over the English service with his valet if in a foreign town without Protestant churches. In Turin, however, there were chapels of the Waldensian faith. They were newly and cheaply built: religious liberty had been granted to the sect in Turin only in 1848. The Waldensians, or

Vaudois, held a special place in the Protestant mythology of the
Ruskin family, as in English Protestantism as a whole. Milton's sonnet
'On the late massacre in Piedmont', with its prayer 'Avenge, O Lord,
thy slaughtered saints . . .', was inspired by the Waldensians' earlier
persecution. Confined to the Swiss, Piedmontese and northern Italian
valleys, they had there, some believed, preserved an uncorrupted
form of primitive Christianity. Appeals to the Vaudois character may
be found in the most entrenched of Ruskin's writings, in the *Pre-
Raphaelitism* pamphlet and in *Notes on the Construction of Sheepfolds*.
Now, however, he was exasperated by the narrowness of the faith.
How could one love Veronese and believe this preacher? A long letter
to his father now marks this turning point in Ruskin's views. Having
put the view that 'A good, stout, self-commanding, magnificent
Animality is the make for poets and artists, it seems to me', Ruskin
further explained,

> One day when I was working from the beautiful maid of honour in
> Veronese's picture, I was struck by the gorgeousness of life which
> the world seems to be constituted to develop, when it is made the
> best of. The band was playing some passages of brilliant music at
> the time, and this music blended so thoroughly with Veronese's
> splendour; the beautiful notes seeming to form one whole with the
> lovely forms and colours, and powerful human creatures. Can it be
> possible that all this power and beauty is adverse to the honour of
> the Maker of it? Has God made faces beautiful and limbs strong, and
> created these strange, fiery, fantastic energies, and created the
> splendour of substance and the love of it; created gold, and pearls,
> and crystal, and the sun that makes them gorgeous; and filled
> human fancy with all splendid thoughts; and given to the human
> touch its power of placing and brightening and perfecting, only that
> all these things may lead His creatures away from Him? And is this
> mighty Paul Veronese, in whose soul there is a strength as of the
> snowy mountains, and within whose brain all the pomp and
> majesty of humanity floats in a marshalled glory, capacious and
> serene like clouds at sunset — this man whose finger is as fire, and
> whose eye is like the morning — is he a servant of the devil; and is
> the poor little wretch in a tidy black tie, to whom I have been
> listening this Sunday morning expounding Nothing with a twang
> — is he a servant of God?[50]

John James could well have anticipated these sentiments, but Ruskin's mother was in high alarm. She sent him long instructions and
five pounds to donate to the Vaudois church. This Ruskin passed on,

dutifully, reflecting that he had given as much recently to a ballerina at the Opéra Comique. Deference to his mother sent him on an expedition to the Vaudois villages in the hills above Turin. 'I have seldom slept in a dirtier inn, seldom see peasants' cottages so ill built, and never yet in my life saw anywhere paths so full of nettles,' he complained.[51] He sought out an unidentified 'theological Professor' to talk with. But this person could convince him of nothing. Ruskin was conscious of the gap that was opening between him and his parents and found that he did not wish to make an effort to repair it. In one respect this was damaging to his work. He was only laxly engaged with the end of *Modern Painters*, the book that John James so wanted to be a great memorial to a father's belief in his son. There are, to be sure, certain passages in the fifth volume that derive from his summer in Turin. The conjunction of Wouverman and Fra Angelico in one chapter is due to the fact that both were represented in the Turin gallery. But *Modern Painters* would have been better served if Ruskin had spent more time in Venice, as his preface to the last volume admits. On his way back to England he had some intention of working in the Louvre. But he paused there only briefly. He arrived home in London with little done, and a mind greatly changed.

CHAPTER FOURTEEN

1857–1858

Ruskin was increasingly in demand as a lecturer. The success of *The Political Economy of Art* had persuaded him that the lecture was a natural form for his writing. Unofficial addresses at the Working Men's College (which were improvised) gave him a sense of the closeness of the lecturer's audience. From 1857 until his mental collapse in 1878 there was not a year when he did not speak publicly three or four times. Such addresses were usually published soon afterwards. The assumptions of the Working Men's College drawing class were repeated at the opening of the new Cambridge School of Art in 1858. Here again is the realist, democratic argument that 'We must set ourselves to teaching the operative, however employed — be he farmer's labourer, or manufacturer's; be he mechanic, artificer, sailor, or ploughman — teaching, I say, one and the same thing to all; namely, Sight.'[1] Other lectures given in 1858 were published the next year with the title *The Two Paths*. The first of them was organized by Ruskin for his own purposes. He had instituted a competition among the students of the Architectural Museum for the best piece of 'historical sculpture'. At the prize-giving this year the chairman was C. R. Cockerell. He was an opponent, since he was a classicist and Professor of Architecture at the Royal Academy. Ruskin was graceful to Cockerell in his introductory remarks but the rest of his address on 'The deteriorative power of conventional art over nations' was a call to arms. The 'two paths' of the book's title were the clear alternatives before art students, 'whether you will turn to the right or the left in this matter, whether you will be naturalists or formalists; whether you will pass your days in representing God's truth, or in repeating men's errors'.[2] Less tendentious, wider-ranging and more deliberately entertaining was another lecture collected in *The Two Paths*, that on 'The work of iron, in nature, art and policy', given in Tunbridge Wells in February of 1858, probably at the request of his cousin George Richardson.

At the beginning of the next year Ruskin went north to lecture at Manchester and Bradford. His appearances were organized by Gambart, whom he met for breakfast at the home of a local industrialist, Sir Elkanah Armitage. There they discussed the picture market, with enthusiastic schemes 'for buying all Venice from the Austrians —

pictures, palaces, and everything', and 'asked Sir Elkanah to set the project on foot, in Manchester'.[3] 'The Unity of Art', the lecture Ruskin now gave, was milder than his previous address in Manchester at the time of the International Exhibition. It seems to have been designed to point to controversial issues without itself arousing controversy. The whole expedition was friendly. Ruskin called on the novelist Elizabeth Gaskell, his admirer since the publication of *Modern Painters* III, when they had been introduced by Furnivall, and then set off towards Bradford. He told his father that he was studying Turnerian sites at Bolton Bridge and Knaresborough. But he seems to have been excited by a landscape that is Mrs Gaskell's rather than Turner's:

> The drive from Rochdale to Burnley is one of the grandest and most interesting things I ever did in my life . . . the cottages so old and various in form and position on the hills — the rocks so wild and dark — and the furnaces so wild and multitudinous, and foaming forth their black smoke like thunderclouds, mixed with the hill mist . . .[4]

Ruskin's dislike of the industrial north was not at the pitch it would reach a decade later. He could even propose a sensible co-operation between the demands of manufacture and the demands of art. His lecture at Bradford, 'Modern Manufacture and Design', was designed to be useful rather than hortatory. It does, however, contain the first of Ruskin's many direct questions to industrialists:

> If you will tell me what you ultimately intend Bradford to be, perhaps I can tell you what Bradford can ultimately produce. But you must have your minds clearly made up, and be distinct in telling me what you do want. At present I don't know what you are aiming at, and possibly on consideration you may feel some doubt whether you know yourselves. As matters stand, all over England, as soon as one mill is at work, occupying two hundred hands, we try, by means of it, to set another mill at work, occupying four hundred. That is all simple and comprehensible enough — but what is it to come to? How many mills do we want? or do we indeed want no end of mills? Let us entirely understand each other on this point before we go any farther. Last week, I drove from Rochdale to Bolton Abbey; quietly, in order to see the country, and certainly it was well worth while. I never went over a more interesting twenty miles than those between Rochdale and Burnley. Naturally, the valley has been one of the most beautiful in the Lancashire hills; one

of the far-away solitudes, full of old shepherd ways of life. At this time there are not, — I speak deliberately, and I believe quite literally, — there are not, I think, more than a thousand yards of road to be traversed anywhere, without passing furnace or mill.[5]

Ruskin's lecture ended with a direct comparison between Bradford and (in a magnificent description, a *tour de force* for lecture purposes) mediæval Pisa. He admitted, 'I do not bring this contrast before you as a ground of hopelessness in our task; neither do I look for any possible renovation of the Republic of Pisa, at Bradford, in the nineteenth century.'[6] And yet, although he did not realize it, all his instincts would soon lead him to propose just such a renovation. In five years' time he would address the burghers of Bradford with contempt: and in a decade he would come to the conclusion that the only way to save England was indeed to recreate there the conditions of the Gothic cities of the past.

★   ★   ★   ★

Ruskin's description of the 'wretch' who had talked of the election of the Waldensian faithful was followed, that summer of 1858, by further attacks on Protestant services he attended on the Continent. To John James he wrote from Paris of a 'disgraceful' English evensong, the sermon 'utterly abominable and sickening in its badness'.[7] Such outbursts were not unusual. The Ruskins's church-going habits meant that they listened to a great number of sermons, a form of literature they rarely read, and both father and son were given to a violent connoisseurship of the preaching class.[8] As we might expect from these intelligent, curious and prejudiced men, they had some unusual preferences. For about five years, from 1857, their favourite preacher was an uncouth Evangelical Baptist for whom neither felt much doctrinal sympathy. This was Charles Haddon Spurgeon. When the Ruskins first went to listen to him and sought his acquaintance he was scarcely twenty-four years old, yet had become the most popular preacher in London. At the age of sixteen he had been converted by a Primitive Methodist. 'Baptism loosed my tongue,' he said, 'and from that day it has never been quiet.'[9] It was an uneducated tongue. Spurgeon was still an Essex country boy. His early practice in his vocation had been in extempore gatherings in Hackney Fields. He had progressed to the Exeter Hall and the Surrey Gardens Music Hall, working-class venues that could accommodate his audience of thousands. His oratory was interspersed with humorous anecdote and doggerel verse. It made the fastidious wince. Spurgeon was a preacher to whom one sent the servants. 'He is likely to do really good service among the class to which he belongs,' one contemporary remarked, 'though he would be a scandal and a nuisance at St George's, Hanover Square, or in Westminster Abbey.'[10] Many intellectuals could not abide him. Matthew Arnold, for instance, was repelled. Yet Spurgeon's spirit shone beyond his vulgarity, as Lord Houghton — a fair reporter of nineteenth-century devotion — rightly saw: 'When he mounted the pulpit you might have thought of him as a hairdresser's assistant: when he left it, he was an inspired apostle.'[11]

Like Houghton, Ruskin defended Spurgeon to the sophisticated. 'His doctrine is simply Bunyan's, Baxter's, Calvin's, and John Knox's,' he wrote to the Brownings, '— in many respects not pleasant to *me*, but I dare not say that the offence is the doctrine's and not mine. It is the doctrine of Romish saints and of the Church of England. Why should we find fault with it especially in Spurgeon and not in St Francis or Jeremy Taylor?'[12] Between Ruskin and Spurgeon there developed an unlikely, warm friendship. They had next to nothing in common apart from their knowledge of the Bible and a love of its exegesis. Ruskin simply ignored all aspects of Spurgeon's views that would annoy him. The Baptist's fiery hatred of Carlyle he overlooked. He was not drawn by Spurgeon's insistence that all churches should be Greek rather than Gothic. Instead, nightly, at Spurgeon's tiny south London house, tasting wines from John James's own cellar, Spurgeon with a cigar, they would spar over their intimacy with Scripture and their utterly different natures, Ruskin provocative, Spurgeon laughing at him, each capping the other. Spurgeon recalled with amusement how 'Mr Ruskin came to see me one day, many years ago, and amongst other things he said that the Apostle Paul was a liar, and that I was a fool!'[13] But Ruskin had a real attachment to Spurgeon. The preacher's wife records:

> Towards the end of 1858 Spurgeon had a serious illness, and Ruskin called to see him during his convalescence. How well I remember the intense love and devotion displayed by Mr Ruskin, as he threw himself on his knees by the dear patient's side, and embraced him with tender affection and tears. 'My brother, my dear brother,' he said, 'how grieved I am to see you thus!' His sorrow and sympathy were most touching and comforting. He had brought with him two charming engravings . . . and some bottles of wine of a rare vintage . . . My husband was greatly moved by the love and consideration so graciously expressed, and he very often referred to it afterwards in grateful appreciation; especially when, in later years, there came a change of feeling on Mr Ruskin's part, and he strongly repudiated

some of the theological opinions to which Mr Spurgeon closely
clung to the end of his life.[14]

As one or two of their contemporaries recognized, there is something of Spurgeon's fundamentalism in Ruskin's *Unto This Last*. That
influence points to another difference, temperamental as well as intellectual, between Ruskin and the Working Men's College. While his
politics alarmed all the Christian Socialists who gathered there, the
college's principal, F. D. Maurice, on the rare occasions when he met
his drawing master, was taken aback by the restless vehemence with
which Ruskin expressed views on religion. There was that about
Maurice which goaded Ruskin. He preferred to spend time with
Spurgeon, whom Maurice greatly distrusted. Ruskin's ties with the
Working Men's College were slackening. He saw Furnivall still but
was bored by others of the lecturers. The students who most
interested him he had taken away from the college and made his
assistants. Butterworth was still receiving money from Ruskin.
George Allen was taking lessons in line engraving from John Le Keux
and in mezzotint from Thomas Lupton, in preparation for the illustration of the fifth volume of *Modern Painters*. This was a more advanced
and significant teaching than was available at the college, for the
skilled Lupton had worked for Turner himself in years gone by.
Ruskin was pleased by this direct artisanal connection between Turner
and his own book: it had a deeper meaning in it than the elementary
drawing classes he used to give in Red Lion Square. Some of those
classes were now entrusted to Allen, but most of Ruskin's instruc-
tional drawing was carried out for him by William Ward, whom
Ruskin now referred to as both the college's and his own 'under
drawing-master'.[15]

When Ruskin was first asked by an Irish gentlewoman, a Mrs La
Touche, to give advice on her daughters' art education he sent William
Ward to see her, being too busy to call himself. Maria La Touche he
probably met through Lady Waterford, for she too was an
artistically minded woman not quite at home among the Irish aristocracy. She was the daughter of Catherine, Countess of Desart. This
countess had been twice married, first to the Earl of Desart. Their son
was young Otway, Earl of Desart, whom Ruskin had known at Christ
Church. Catherine was widowed in 1820, when in her early thirties.
Four years later she married again. Her new husband was Rose Lambert Price. He came of a baronetcy family in Cornwall which owned
large estates in Jamaica. Rose Lambert Price was much younger than
the still young dowager countess: he was still in his early twenties on

their wedding day. Maria Price, later Maria La Touche, was their daughter and only child, and thus the half-sister of Ruskin's Christ Church friend. She was not to remember her father, for he died two years after his marriage. Catherine, once more widowed, returned with her child to the Desart estates in County Kilkenny. There Maria spent her childhood.

With no memory of her Cornish father, with a background that was a trifle *déclassé*, Maria Price grew up to emphasize her Irishness. Intermittently educated near Brighton, in later life a traveller and the owner of a house in London, she yet had no wish to leave her native land. She was wed into another section of the Irish ascendancy. In 1843 she married John La Touche. The La Touche family had been in Ireland since the revocation of the Edict of Nantes. Huguenot supporters of William of Orange, one had fought for him at the Battle of the Boyne. They had established a silk-weaving factory in the north and a bank in Dublin that later became the Royal Bank of Ireland. In the eighteenth century they purchased a country house at Harristown, County Kildare. Their fortunes became intermingled with the Anglo-Irish aristocracy. John La Touche's mother, for instance, was a daughter of the Earl of Clancarty. John La Touche was sent to England to be educated at Christ Church. He matriculated in 1833 and would have left Oxford just before the young Ruskin arrived there. He succeeded his father as head of the family in 1844, a year after his marriage to Maria Price. They then settled at Harristown, where their three children were born.

Maria La Touche, not in sympathy with the Anglo-Irish society she knew as the mistress of Harristown and the wife of the Sheriff of County Leitrim (as John La Touche became), disliked the hunting and horse racing, the gambling, drinking and crudity of manners of her acred neighbours. She was self-consciously devoted to the life of the soul. With a few other Irish ladies like Louisa, Marchioness of Waterford, Lady Drogheda and Lady Cloncurry, both married to County Kildare landowners, she formed a little society they called the Aletheme: they rechristened themselves with Greek names and discussed art. Lady Waterford was the most cultured of this group but Maria La Touche had more energy, more of a will to be artistic. She was more than merely amateur. She published two novels, *The Clintons* and *The Double Marriage*, both of them set in Ireland, both treating of romance across the divide that separated Catholic from Protestant. She wrote verse and was noted for the vivacity of her letters. She was quick to make friends, eager to travel, a little gushing. She thought a little wildness not a bad thing. She liked to visit London. John La

Touche had banking and government business there and so they kept a house in Mayfair, at first in Great Cumberland Street and later in Norfolk Street. [16]

Maria La Touche was in London in the new year of 1858, with her daughters Emily and Rose, when she first approached Ruskin. The momentous first meeting with Rose is described in the final pages of *Præterita*, an account which is practically the last thing Ruskin ever wrote: He called at Great Cumberland Street,

> . . . and found the mother — the sort of person I expected, but a good deal more than I expected, and in sorts of ways. Extremely pretty, still, herself, nor at all too old to learn many things; but mainly anxious for her children. Emily, the eldest daughter, wasn't in; but Rosie was, should she be sent for to the nursery? Yes, I said, if it wouldn't tease the child, she might be sent for. So presently the drawing room door opened, and Rosie came in, quietly taking stock of me with her blue eyes as she walked across the room; gave me her hand, as a good dog gives its paw, and then stood a little back. Nine years old, on 3rd January, 1858, thus now rising towards ten; neither tall nor short for her age; a little stiff in her way of standing. The eyes rather deep blue at that time, and fuller and softer than afterwards. Lips perfectly lovely in profile; — a little too wide, and hard in edge, seen in front; the rest of the features what a fair, well-bred Irish girl's usually are; the hair, perhaps, more graceful in short curl round the forehead, and softer than one sees often, in the close-bound tresses above the neck. [17]

Ruskin, now in his fortieth year, was taken with the La Touches. He liked the mother and felt that there was something exceptional about Rose. He had never taught a little girl before except by correspondence. There was no reason why he should do so now, except that he wanted to. He corresponded with Mrs La Touche while in Switzerland during the summer and on his return invited her, with Rose, to visit Denmark Hill. They were shown all the treasures: the Turners, the minerals, John Brett's painting of the Val d'Aosta, which Ruskin had just bought. Old Mrs Ruskin provided apples, peaches, a copy of *The King of the Golden River* for Rose. They visited the stables, where Ruskin chaffed Rose about Irish pigs. Soon they were on pet-name terms. Ruskin charmed the child, and she charmed him. Mrs La Touche evidently felt that an extraordinary privilege had been granted her: her letter of thanks was overwritten:

My Dear Mr Ruskin,
I have too long delayed thanking you, in my name and in Rose's, for

23. Rose La Touche, by John Ruskin, c.1860.

the pleasant hour we spent last Thursday — You, who live with and for Art, will not easily guess how much enjoyment you afforded to me, who am wholly unaccustomed to such an atmosphere out of dreamland. The 'Val d'Aosta' and the Rossettis and some of the Turners have been before me ever since — and Rose was very eloquent about them on the way home, she will not forget them, and will refer to them in memory hereafter, with better understanding of their meaning. Altogether we owe 'the immortal memory of one happy day' to Mrs Ruskin's kindness and yours: and more beautiful than all past sunsets was that which we saw on our way home — it was the interpretation, or rather it seemed to me the Apotheosis, of one or two of the Turners you had shown me — one of those skies no-one else ever attempted to paint — and under it, this evil London glorified into a shadowy semblance of the New Jerusalem, a city of sapphire and gold — It is a real consolation to me here, that my windows look towards the sunset: at home there would be a purple tracery of winter trees between me and the sky, and only a glow on the river's face to reveal what *it* saw. I have been wishing ever since, that you could see and tell the world about the Atlantic — I have never seen the Mediterranean — nor the subdued sea that sleeps around the 'Stones of Venice' except as you have shown them . . .[18]

There is much more of this letter, in the same manner. It closed with an invitation. Mrs La Touche wanted Ruskin and his mother to come to her new house in Norfolk Street, off Park Lane. When Ruskin went there he met other members of the family. Emily was grave and sensible, not very like the clever, inventive Rose. 'One never laughed at what she said,' *Præterita* records, 'but the room was brighter for it.'[19] But if the daughters were dissimilar it was their father who seemed almost out of place in the family. He was not the swaggering Irish sportsman that one would expect. He had been, but in a life that he had put behind him. Nor was he interested in the world of affairs and politics that, Ruskin presumed, had brought him to London. For, by fateful coincidence, he had been converted and baptized by Spurgeon. Ruskin knew of, but had not witnessed, Spurgeon's mass baptisms. Had he done so, he would no doubt have found them grotesque. He could not but find something peculiar, unnatural even, in John La Touche, who now professed a strict Calvinism far removed from the commonplace Church of Ireland Anglicanism of his wife. It was a Calvinism not only out of place in Mayfair but also extremist within its Irish context. One might compare (Ruskin was soon obliged to) the Evangelicalism of another branch of the La Touche family planted at Delgany, fifteen miles from Harristown, visited a few years before by the historian J. A. Froude. Of these La Touches, Froude recorded:

> There was a quiet good sense, an intellectual breadth of feeling in this household, which to me, who had been bred up to despise Evangelicals as unreal and affected, was a startling surprise. I had looked down on dissenters especially, as being vulgar among their other enormities; here were persons whose creed differed little from that of the Calvinistic Methodists, yet they were easy, natural, and dignified.[20]

But this could not be said of John La Touche. His religion had not this naturalness. It seems that it could be satisfied only by the severities of the beleaguered Presbyterian church in Southern Ireland and its counterparts among Ulster Orangemen. The man himself was extraordinary. As is common in such converted sectarians, John La Touche believed himself to be — from the moment of his conversion, an experience to which he constantly returned — saved, redeemed, touched by God. He was at once dourly reserved and highly emotional. This was not a man with whom Ruskin could make light conversation about Christ Church. Ruskin's own association with Spurgeon was, for La Touche, no more than frivolous. His guest's standing as an art critic meant nothing to him, for he had no culture. Ruskin's own loss of conviction in the Evangelical faith further separated them. Neither now, nor at any later time, could the two men find anything in common.

Rose and Emily La Touche came out to Denmark Hill on further occasions, sometimes with their mother, never with their father, sometimes with a nurse or maid. Some attempt was made to start the girls drawing. Leaves and flowers were brought in from the garden. Ruskin was surprised at how much Maria La Touche knew of botany. Soon it was decided to transfer the classes to Norfolk Street, where there was a proper schoolroom. Ruskin went there more and more often. Maria La Touche was delighted: she could show him off to her friends. But Ruskin preferred to arrive an hour or two before the children's bedtime and then to take his leave, pleading that he had to work on his book. It was a friendship with the children. And soon enough there came an understanding that there was an especial love between Rose and Ruskin that was not shared by Emily. He was as kind to Emily as anyone, but the sisters were not equal in his affection. In this peculiar way Ruskin became established in the La Touche household, and Rose became established in his life. It was irreversible, not to be ended until Rose died and Ruskin died: 'Rose, in heart, was with me always, and all I did was for her sake.'[21]

This was true, but for the five years after 1858 much of Ruskin's work was desultory. It was almost as though he were waiting for something to happen to him, something that would give a new direction to his life. By 1862 or 1863 he would have to identify his feelings for Rose as love. That did not occur to him now. And in these years he was lionized, even pursued, by a number of women. Ruskin was eligible. Both he and his father had the occasional idea that he might marry again. The pain of his marriage was behind him: so was the scandal. He was handsome, rich, distinguished. At forty, he was in the prime of life. All the same, his close friendships with the opposite sex were all with comfortably, happily married women. They were with people like Lady Trevelyan, with Mrs Simon, now with Mrs La Touche and soon with Mrs Cowper. These are women to whom he writes long, intimate, affectionate letters. He never writes as much to the husbands, sending a greeting only, although he is friendly with them. Within such settled relationships Ruskin could adopt a romantic attitude in which flirtation was not absent. With Jane Simon he had some secrets; to her he dropped heavy hints about women, especially Mrs La Touche, 'a lady who will perhaps be a friend in the course of time, and who is in the stage of friendship which would have been offended for ever unless it had received two notes . . .',[22] and of whom, a little later, he wrote, again to Mrs Simon, 'Yes, I think you are really very jealous. I wonder whether the "other" fault would be brought out if I were to show you what nice long letters I get now — every week or so — without being much troubled to answer them — from the other lady friend who I was fishing for . . .'[23]

Such ponderous flirting, which Ruskin too much enjoyed, had to be set aside on two occasions when women declared themselves in love with him. The first was an American, a Miss Blackwell, who knew the Simons and was a painter. We learn of her through letters to John James Ruskin, to whom Ruskin later revealed this admirer.

The whole affair was so ludicrous and pitiable that I did not want you to be troubled with it — and still more — did not want to be troubled with it myself more than was needful. It appears this young person came from America expressly to see if I should suit her for a husband — and had been trying to get more intimate with me by all sorts of low cunning, until at last in a fit of passion she betrayed herself to Mrs Simon — who had suspected her long: — then the question was how to cut her most decisively — with least offence . . .[24]

Of Miss Blackwell we hear no more. Anna Blunden was for longer
Ruskin's suitor. An artist, she began by sending him poetry, which he
advised her not to publish. His first letters to her were written under
the impression that he was addressing a man: not for some time did
Anna reveal her sex, and not before she had assured Ruskin of her high
regard for his conduct at the time of his marriage. Her importunate
tactlessness Ruskin suffered for years; his patience broke down when
she declared her love, and the letter he wrote then is revealing:

My dear Anna,
Upon my word I believe you are the profoundest and entirest little
goose that ever wore petticoats. You write to me four pink pages
full of nonsense about daisies and violets and 'being nothing but a
poor flower' and then you fly into a passion at the first bit of advice I
give you — declare that you do not want any — but that *I* do — and
set yourself up for my adviser — controller — and judge. You fancy
yourself in love with me — and send me the least excusable insult I
ever received from a human being — it was lucky for you I only
glanced at the end and a bit or two of your long angry letter and then
threw it into the fire — else if I had come upon the piece which you
refer to today — about my being false — I might have burnt this one
as well, without even opening it. You little idiot! fancying you
understand my books — and then accusing me of lying at the first
word that puzzles you about yourself — fancying you love me, and
writing me letters full of the most ridiculous egotisms and conceits
— and disobeying the very first order I give you — namely to keep
yourself quiet for a few days — and talking about suffering because
you have set your fancy on helping a man whom you can't help but
by being rational. Suffering! — indeed — suppose you had loved
somebody whom you had seen —, not for an hour and a half, — but
for six or seven years — who *could* have loved you — and who was
married at the end of those years to someone who didn't love them,
and was not worthy of them. Fancy *that*, — and then venture to talk
of suffering again. You modern girls are not worth your bread and
salt — one might bray a dozen of you in a mortar and not make a
stout right-hearted woman out of the whole set. I suppose you have
been reading some of the stuff of those American wretches — about
rights of women. One of them came over from America the other
day determined to marry me whether I would or no — and amused
herself by writing letter after letter to me to slander my best friends.
By the way, in the end of that long letter of yours — there was
something about 'silencing the *only* tongue that pleaded for me' —
or some such phrase (I wish I could silence it — by the bye, if you

write any more letters, let them be on white paper — or depend upon it the servants will open them — by mistake!) but are you really goose enough to think I have no friends? what do you think of Mrs Browning by way of a beginning — whom I have not written to for nine months — though she loves me truly — while you force me to waste my time writing to you. There again — you are so simply ridiculous in every point that I can't find words for you.

Write to a London Banker in large business and see if you can get *him* to answer love letters — and do you suppose that because my business concerns human souls, and not bags of money — that I am the more willing to interrupt it?

However, here is one more serious word for you — and try to make some proper use of it. There was some nonsense in your long letter about Britomart and Una. Both of them were in love with the man they were to marry, and who loved them. *Every* young women who loves a man who has not asked for her love, or at least if she may not naturally look forward to his marrying her — has lost proper control over her feelings: — praying to God to know whether you are to do it — is the same thing as praying to Him to know whether you are to jump down a precipice. God will not answer such a prayer — and the Devil will.[25]

There was as much pain as anger in this letter. The extremity of Ruskin's exasperation laid bare a longing of his adolescence. The reference to Adèle shows us something that normally was hidden in Ruskin, the memory of an emotion keener than any he had felt for his wife. Anna had uncovered what Ruskin wished to forget: the view that women fall in love at the devil's command refers to the buried subject of the end of his marriage. In conventional social circles, one has the impression in these years of Ruskin as a man with a winning urbanity, even when taken aback. That is the picture given by the account in *Præterita* of a new friendship with a woman he had first seen many years before. It was the beautiful Georgiana Tollemache, whom he admired from afar as a youth in Rome. They were at a party, sitting on a sofa, when he burst out with what must have been a pleasing declaration:

Having ascertained in one moment that she was too pretty to be looked at, and yet keep one's wits about one, I followed, in what talk she led me to, with my eyes on the ground. The conversation led to Rome and, somehow, to the Christmas of 1840. I looked up with a start; and saw that the face was oval, — fair, — the hair, light-brown. After a pause, I was rude enough to repeat her words,

'Christmas in 1840! — were you in Rome *then*?' 'Yes,' she said, a little surprised, and now meeting my eyes with hers, enquiringly. Another tenth of a minute passed before I spoke again. 'Why, I lost all that winter in Rome hunting you!'[26]

Georgiana Tollemache was now Mrs William Cowper. She and her husband were to play an important part in Ruskin's future life. Their names were to change twice in the coming years. They became the Cowper-Temples in 1869 and Lord and Lady Mount-Temple in 1880. That was because of William Cowper's noble birth and, it was said at the time, because of its irregularity. The gossip was so generally accepted that we can use the account of a friend of the family, Logan Pearsall Smith. 'Cowper Temple', he explains,

. . . was in law the son of Earl Cowper, but said to be the son of Lord Palmerston, who had long been Lady Cowper's friend, and who married her when Lord Cowper died. Their son had inherited Lord Palmerston's estates and great house at Broadlands; and the problem of this double paternity, if I may put it so . . . had been successfully regulated by the young William Cowper's adding Lord Palmerston's family name of Temple to that of Cowper in a double appelation. After acting as secretary to his unavowed father, he served in several posts in the governments of the time and was raised to the peerage as Lord Mount-Temple . . .[27]

Those 'several posts', no doubt easily available in the many Whig governments of the mid–century, were as Junior Lord of the Treasury, Junior Lord of the Admiralty, Under-Secretary for the Home Department, President of the Board of Health, First Commissioner of Works, and the like: not the appointments that would be given, one after the other, to an exceptionally ambitious or talented man. People remembered his wife more than him. Georgiana was now in her late thirties. She was vague, sweet-natured, hospitable; a trifle theatrical in her manner, yet not a seeker for attention; she was comforting, rather, a helpful woman who found herself in sympathizing with other people's problems. Later, Ruskin was to find her too bland, a person without an edge. This was when he took many troubles to her about his marriage and about Rose, the girl he wished to marry. Now, in the late 1850s, he was simply pleased to know her and quite interested to know her husband, and enjoyed the first of many visits to the family home at Broadlands.

CHAPTER FIFTEEN

1858–1859

A proud entry in John James Ruskin's 1858 diary reads: 'March 10th Wednesday John began 5th Volume Modern Painters.'[1] Neither father nor son had much idea what the volume would contain, although they had realized that it ought to end the book. As soon became apparent, at least to its author, to approach a conclusion was to magnify the difficulties in making a new start with each volume while also relating new matter to old. To finish *Modern Painters*, now, was not merely to terminate a body of work, nor to finalize a scheme of art. The book represented twenty years of growth, revelation, reconsideration, and to conclude it was to conclude a part of Ruskin's life. It was that portion of his life that he owed to his father. John James was now seventy-five. Ruskin knew as his father knew that this fifth and last instalment would probably be the last thing he wrote for him. These matters were not spoken of.

It is possible to find many an intellectual influence in *Modern Painters* V, and more than one stylistic influence. Despite its grave tone and elevated subject-matter it is also one of Ruskin's books in which we find traces of his daily life in London. They are perhaps the more evident because there was so much in his life that was half decided. He was caught between new experiences and the doubting of old experiences. There was no certainty to drive forward the preparation of the fifth volume, and for this reason Ruskin felt little affection for his book. He looked widely for stimulus, even to James Russell Lowell in America. To Lowell he admitted being able

> . . . only to write a little now & then of old thoughts — to finish Modern Painters, which *must* be finished. Whenever I can write at all this winter I must take up that for it is tormenting me, always about my neck. — If no accident hinders it will be done this spring and then I will see if there is anything I can say clearly enough to be useful in my present state of mystification . . .[2]

Part of Ruskin's problem was that there was no one person with whom he might discuss the contents of his book. This was to be a volume that wandered far from John James's conception of the world. The last gift was the one in which the companionship between the two men was least evident. Instead, we have a book in which we hear the echoes of conversations with schoolgirls, or with the painter John Brett; that recapitulates talk with G. F. Watts, Tennyson, and the Brownings; that at some points seems to bring Ruskin closer to the Richmond family than he had been for years; and in the aftermath of the Crimea is thoughtful of war. *Modern Painters* V is in this sense a contemporary book. But in fact it retreats from the art of the day, from modern painting. It closes Ruskin's writing on Turner as it bids farewell to his committed response to the art of his contemporaries.

The first number of *Academy Notes* had taken up some observations made in the second volume of *Modern Painters*. The last of the series Ruskin published in 1859: the pamphlet is rather unlike his current major work. Some sections of this *Academy Notes* are ordinary. One or two entries have a private background: there is praise of a (probably) unremarkable picture by 'A. Blunden'. As so many people did, every year, one turns first to the verdict on Millais's contributions. In this exhibition they were *The Vale of Rest* and *Apple Blossoms*. But those few who followed Ruskin's thinking with care would have wished to see what he made of the painting he had encouraged, in part supervised, and had now purchased, John Brett's *Val d'Aosta*. Evidently, Ruskin now felt that there was more to Brett than to Millais, if only in potential. The *Val d'Aosta*, he argued, was 'landscape painting with a meaning and a use . . . for the first time in history we have, by help of art, the power of visiting a place, reasoning about it, and knowing it, just as if we were there . . .'. Ruskin then uses the picture to describe the agronomy of the valley. But it is clear that art should have a higher function. Although he does not use the word, Ruskin returned to his theories of the imagination in finally criticizing the painting: 'It has a strange fault, considering the school to which it belongs — it seems to me wholly emotionless. I cannot find from it that the painter loved, or feared, anything in all that wonderful piece of the world . . . I never saw the mirror so held up to nature; but it is Mirror's work, not Man's.'[3]

Thus was dismissed Brett's painting. Soon afterwards his friendship with Ruskin, such as it was, came to an end. *Modern Painters* V, which at one point acknowledges him, is full of longing for a kind of painting that Brett could not provide. His Swiss landscape was the second high point, as Millais's Glenfinlas portrait had been the first, of that naturalism in English painting which Ruskin had done so much to foster. But Ruskin wanted more from naturalistic art. He wanted passion and he increasingly wanted some kind of symbolism. It was not quite in Pre-Raphaelitism, not even in Rossetti's, to provide the satisfaction that comes from such art. But it was there in Turner. Ruskin now found that he could gather more and more from the painter he had first admired, especially if he allowed Turner's thematic implications to settle and grow in his own imagination. Unconsciously or not, Ruskin looked into Turner for themes that were mythological rather than literary. This pleased a cast of his mind which sought a veracity grander and more mysterious than simple fidelity to nature. How thin and contrived, therefore, appeared Millais's invented symbolist painting, *The Vale of Rest*: what depth of meaning that picture feigned to possess already existed, ten times over, in Turner.[4]

Much of this cloudy conviction was found in Turner's Greek painting. The young Ruskin had felt it his Christian duty to attack Greek culture. But for years past he had been thinking more of the spirituality of the pagan world. His thoughts were occasionally expressed in public, in such places as the chapter 'Of Classical Landscape' in *Modern Painters* III, but more often they were kept to conversations with friends. Such friends were usually artists: they were not churchmen. Ruskin's sense of Greece did not move in strict measure with the fluctuations of his Christianity. But he allowed his instincts to find a relationship between the world of the ancient gods and the world that belonged to Christ. His study of myth was not scientific, nor archæological. He had no real feeling for the classical tradition. His Greek preoccupations — so marked in *Modern Painters* V — were more individual than they were akin to Turner's. His dark, emblematic books on Greek themes in the 1860s have no parallel in other literature of the day, though many Victorian intellectuals wrote on Greek culture. The great exponent of this kind of painting was G. F. Watts, and for him Ruskin now felt a sympathy that heretofore had been rather distant. However, Ruskin's appreciation of Watts's art hardly entered his public writings. The most telling comments are in private letters, from which we gather that Ruskin had benefited from discussions with an artist who knew as much about Titian as did the Richmonds and whose themes evoke, if they do not describe, the ancient world.

Ruskin's commendations of Titian are found at all stages of his career, but his feeling for the artist is not easily grasped. In the late 1850s there were people who heard Ruskin talk of Titian and believed his talk to be empty. One of these was probably the visually uneducated Tennyson, with whom Ruskin had a slight, wary friendship. There exists a vignette of Ruskin, by himself, in the company of this other great Victorian. In the spring of 1859 he wrote to a correspondent in the provincial north of England, a schoolmistress:

Any person interested in the art and literature of Young England would have been glad if they could have had a good sketch of one or two bits of scene yesterday.

You must have heard people speak of Watts — He's named with Rossetti sometimes in my things — the fresco painter — a man of great imagination & pathetic power: — he is painting Tennyson's portrait — both staying at the pleasant house of a lady to whose kind watching over him in his failing health, Watts certainly owes his life: — Mrs Prinsep — an old — (as far as a very beautiful lady of about eight-and-thirty can be so injuriously styled —) friend of mine also.

One of the scenes that perhaps you and one or two other people would have liked to have sketched, was this — Watts lying back in his arm chair — a little faint — (he is still unwell) with Tennyson's P.R.B. illustrated poems on his knee. Tennyson standing above him — explaining over his shoulder why said illustrations did not fit the poems, with a serious quiver on his face — alternating between indignation at not having been better understood, and dislike of self-enunciation: — I sitting on the other side of Watts — looking up deprecatingly to Tennyson — & feeling very cowardly in the good cause — yet maintaining it in a low voice — Behind me as backer Jones, the most wonderful of all the PreRaphaelites in redundance of delicate & pathetic fancy — inferior to Rossetti in depth — but beyond him in grace & sweetness — he, laughing sweetly at the faults of his own school as Tennyson declared them and glancing at me with half wet half sparkling eyes, as he saw me shrink — A little in front of us — standing in the light of the window Mrs Prinsep and her sister — two, certainly, of the most beautiful women in a grand sense — (Elgin marbles with dark eyes) — that you would find in modern life — and round the room — Watts' Greek-history frescoes. Tennyson's face is more agitated by the intenseness of sensibility than is almost bearable by the looker on — he seems to be almost in a state of nervous trembling like a jarred string of a harp. He was maintaining that painters ought to attend to at least what the writer *said* — if they couldn't, to what he meant — while Watts and I both maintained that no good painter could be subservient at all: but must conceive everything in his own way, — that no poems ought to be illustrated at all — but if they were — the poet *must* be content to have his painter in partnership — not a slave.[5]

The 'Jones' of this letter had not yet changed his name to Burne-Jones. Still now in his twenties, Jones already had a reputation in just the sort of company Ruskin's letter describes. Indeed, he was hardly known elsewhere. He owed his convenient insulation from the difficulties of an early career to Rossetti and Ruskin. From Rossetti he derived his art, and it was Rossetti who had first introduced him, with his comrade William Morris, to the critic. As undergraduates, not many years before, Jones and Morris had read *The Stones of Venice* aloud to each other. To be taken up by Ruskin himself was wonderful good fortune. William Morris did not greatly interest Ruskin. But for 'Ned' he felt immediate and unshakeable affection. This was partly because they avoided the issues raised by Burne-Jones's art. Ruskin had a feeling that it might represent the next phase of Pre-Raphaelitism. Yet he made no attempt to mould Jones to the form of his own beliefs. He gave him no instruction whatever, only gifts. Nor did he mention him in print. It was to be fully eleven years before he gave public approval to his painting. This was in a lecture at the Royal Institution in 1867. The address he gave was quite important, and fully written out, but Ruskin never published it. Nearly another two decades passed before, in his last Oxford lectures, Ruskin again praised Burne-Jones before an audience. This was in 1883. The man had meant more to Ruskin than his art: and by then the art meant more to him in memory than in reality.

In 1859 Ruskin was not sure what new art he wanted. An appendix to that year's *Academy Notes*, the last of the sequence, gives a couple of pages to two exhibitions of water-colour societies. It is one of the first of the occasions, numerous later on, where we find an important statement in a comparatively minor or sequestered part of his works. He wrote here that English water-colour was 'in steady decline', that it was characterized by falseness and vulgarity, and that art itself, not merely water-colour, now suffered from 'the loss of belief in the spiritual world'. This sentiment was not totally new. But the prescription was startling. Ruskin argued, 'Art has never shown, in any corner of the earth, a condition of advancing strength but under this influence. I do not say, observe, influence of "religion" but merely of a belief in some invisible power — god or goddess, fury or fate, saint or demon.'[6] He was calling for an art of spiritual power which did not exist and could hardly be produced on demand. The difference was in his appeal to invisible powers which might not be Christian. In the context of his previous writings this was little less than impious. When he came to write out similar thoughts in the last volume of *Modern Painters* he rather clothed and obscured them. He wrote in such a fashion as, conceivably, to hide from his mother the loss of the Evangelical thrust with which the work began.

As *Academy Notes* went to press, Ruskin's parents were uppermost in his mind. The old people were as vigorous as ever in the way that they read and argued. Travelling, however, was difficult for them: Margaret Ruskin had scarcely been into London in the last few years. They wanted to spend one more summer on the Continent. It was to be a German expedition. Ruskin felt that he ought to study the Titians in German collections before writing any more about Venetian Renaissance art. Furthermore, at the National Gallery Site Commission in 1857 he had been embarrassed by questions put to him by two enemies, Effie's friend Dean Milman and the academic architect Charles Cockerell.[7] They had made him admit ignorance of German art galleries. And so the last family tour went from Brussels to Cologne, Berlin, Dresden and Munich. Ruskin found that contemporary art was no better in Protestant Germany than in France or Italy. To Clarkson Stanfield, whose abilities had been kindly surveyed in previous volumes of *Modern Painters*, he wrote condemnations of the Nazarene school. None of the party really felt at ease in Germany. Ruskin liked Nuremberg: but he was glad to find his old routes from Schaffhausen to Geneva. Leaving his parents there, he climbed to Chamonix in search of the original inspiration and the original material of *Modern Painters*. When the family reunited they travelled quickly to Paris and thence returned to London. It had not been a particularly exciting tour, and much sadness was mixed with the pleasures the Ruskins could always find for themselves. Nor was the expedition helpful to Ruskin's book. In the end his father had to insist on its completion. Ruskin did not confess how this came about until many years later, in an Oxford lecture. His address to undergraduates on *Modern Painters* was largely unscripted, but among the notes Ruskin wrote is this reminiscence:

> Now the thing which I have especially to thank my father for is that he made me finish my book . . . He made me finish it with a very pathetic appeal. For fifteen years he had seen me collecting materials, and collecting and learning new truths, and still learning — every volume of the four pitched in a new key — and he was provoked enough, naturally, and weary of waiting. And in 1859 he took his last journey with me abroad; and when he came home, and found signs of infirmity creeping on him, and that it were too probable he might never travel far more, until very far, he said to me one day, 'John, if you don't finish that book now, I shall never see it.' So I said I would do it for him forthwith; and did it, as I could.[8]

*   *   *   *

Immediately after this German tour Ruskin left his parents at
Denmark Hill while he went to stay for three weeks at a girls' school in
Cheshire. This was Winnington Hall, near Northwich. He had been
there once before, briefly, in the spring before leaving for Germany.
Ruskin had then found, to his surprise, that he enjoyed the company of
schoolchildren. He wanted to go there again. He was indulged at
Winnington; and after the strain of conducting his parents through
Europe it was a relaxation to talk to young girls. The school was a
retreat, and in some ways it became a second home. For the next ten
years it provided a background for some of the happiest moments of
his adult life.

Winnington Hall lay just outside the growing industrial area of
Manchester. The school had taken over an old manor house, set
among lawns and gardens. Its headmistress was Margaret Alexis Bell.
She had first met Ruskin when he gave his lectures in Manchester in
1857. Their friendship had developed slowly. Neither had met anyone
quite like the other. Ruskin felt that he had to explain himself to Miss
Bell: it was to her that he had addressed the long letter describing his
conversation with Watts and Tennyson. The world of metropolitan
Victorian culture was important to the determined Margaret Bell. In
some ways she wished to join it. She had been born into an unyielding
type of northern Methodism but she now held liberal religious opinions, mostly derived from broad church Anglicanism. She followed
recent literature. She wished to appreciate art. Like many a headmistress who owned her own school, she had a slightly uncertain social
status. But she was not much concerned with the usual appearances of
gentility. Her educational views were progressive, as Ruskin now
came to understand. He had some distant acquaintance with school
education, for he was in a position to give places at Christ's Hospital (a
privilege inherited from his father's City connections). But of girls'
schools he knew nothing. When he found that there were Turners on
the walls at Winnington, that drawing and water-colour were central
parts of the curriculum, that study was mingled with play and that
nothing was learnt by rote, Ruskin was made curious. To see his own
portrait hanging side by side with F. D. Maurice's only emphasized
the differences between this happy place and the Working Men's
College;[9] and Ruskin began to wonder what his influence in it might
be.

*   *   *   *

A life half lived, with so much left to do; a growing sense of being wiser; a feeling that he was witnessing the approach of his father's death; a hardly sentient understanding of what Rose La Touche meant to him: all these things and more were in Ruskin's mind as Christmas of 1859 and the new year of 1860 approached. In February he would be forty-one. He had found much success in the world but had also learnt that public opinion is valueless. His troubles with the Royal Academy, the National Gallery, and indeed the Working Men's College, had all shown him that such institutions were too worldly for the spirit of Turner he had tried to communicate. He had lost hope for architecture when the Oxford Museum was built. He no longer felt that he wanted to make comrades of artists. To one, J. J. Laing, who had written enthusiastically of the spreading influence of Pre-Raphaelitism, he replied bleakly, 'I entirely disclaim all parties, and all causes of a sectarian or special character.'[10] One notices how drawn he was at this time to people whose own concerns were inapposite, nothing to do with his own: Spurgeon, whose vision of heaven was so clear, or little Rose La Touche, or the girls at Winnington, or Americans. Ruskin looked often to Carlyle. But he did not feel the need of him that would come later on, and was not yet writing for Carlyle's approval. He had to finish *Modern Painters* for his father: but he did not know whether John James would like his last volume and he did not know what he would write next, or who it would be for. He had no obligation ever to write a book again. He told the Brownings that he wanted 'to be able to take a few years of quiet copying, either nature or Turner — or Titian or Veronese or Tintoret — engraving as I copy. It seems to me the most useful thing I can do. I am tired of talking.'[11] Ruskin's diaries are empty in these months, and his correspondence is not vigorous. It would take a couple of years, and the realization that he was in love, before he once again found a confident voice in which to address the world.

A SHORT LIST OF THE CHIEF BOOKS CITED

Quotations from Ruskin's published works are taken from the Library Edition, *The Works of John Ruskin*, ed. E. T. Cook and Alexander Wedderburn, 39 vols., London, 1903–12. References are given by volume and page number thus: (XVI. 432). Place of publication of titles referred to in the Notes is London unless otherwise stated. Frequently cited books are abbreviated as follows:

Diaries. *The Diaries of John Ruskin*, ed. Joan Evans and John Howard Whitehouse, 3 vols., Oxford, 1956–9.

RFL. *The Ruskin Family Letters. The Correspondence of John James Ruskin, his Wife, and their Son John, 1801-1843*, ed. Van Akin Burd, Ithaca and London, 1973.

RSH. Helen Gill Viljoen, *Ruskin's Scottish Heritage*, Urbana, Illinois, 1956.

RI. *Ruskin in Italy. Letters to his Parents 1845*, ed. Harold I. Shapiro, Oxford, 1972.

RG. Mary Lutyens, *The Ruskins and the Grays,* 1972.

EV. Mary Lutyens, *Effie in Venice*, 1965.

MR. Mary Lutyens, *Millais and the Ruskins*, 1968.

NOTES

Chapter One

1. On all these matters see RSH and RFL. Both Professor Viljoen and Professor Burd provide information about Ruskin's ancestry. RSH has an appendix covering 'The Edinburgh Ruskins and their descendants and relatives of Croydon'. RFL contains a family tree.
2. XXXV, 62.
3. XXXV, 62.
4. XXXV, 18.
5. Ms *Præterita* Beinecke Library, Yale University.
6. From Sir Albert Gray's papers concerning his family and the Ruskins. Bodley Ms Eng Letts c 228.
7. JJR-Catherine Ruskin, 5 Oct 1812, RFL 54.
8. RSL, 116. See also RFL, 64n-65n.
9. JJR-George Gray, 31 Aug 1848, RG 150.
10. JJR-Catherine Ruskin, 13 Apr 1815, RFL 76.
11. JJR-Catherine Ruskin, 30 Jun 1815, RFL 79.
12. XXXV, 15-16.
13. XXXV, 34.
14. JJR-MR, 23 Jun 1819, RFL 95.
15. JJR-MR, 6 Dec 1829, RFL 211-12.
16. See RFL, 374-413 for this journey.
17. MR-JJR, 10 Apr 1820, RFL 98.
18. XXVIII, 345-6.
19. MR-JJR, 30 Jan 1822, RFL 109.
20. These favourite chapters are discussed by Viljoen in RSH 162.
21. The Bibles are described and illustrated in W. G. Collingwood, *Ruskin Relics*, 1903, 193-213.
22. XXXV, 40.
23. XXXV, 39-40.
24. JR-JJR, 15 Mar 1823, RFL 127-8.
25. XXXV, 88.
26. XXXV, 131.
27. Ms Bembridge 28.
28. JJR-JR, 6 Nov 1829, RFL 209-10.
29. JR-JJR, 10 May 1829, RFL 199-200.
30. To Jane Simon, for instance. Bembridge Ms L 12.
31. XXVI, 294n.
32. XXXV, 75.
33. XXXV, 63.

34. JJR-R. Gray, 17 Jan 1833, RFL 276.
35. XXXV, 16.
36. II, 286-97.
37. XXXV, 25.
38. Howels is identified in a letter from Ruskin to Joan Severn which includes both a letter from Howels and this contemporary comment; JR-JRS, 3 Jan 1876, Ms Bembridge L 41. The *Præterita* passage was taken from *Fors*, but Ruskin evidently did not correct the mistaken name when the autobiography was issued. For Howels see also Edward Morgan, *A Memoir of the Life of William Howels*, 1854.
39. XXVIII, 297-8.
40. For Andrews (and other clergy in the area) see F. G. Cleal, *The Story of Congregationalism in Surrey*, 1908, 105.
41. XXXV, 132.
42. MR-JJR, 10 Mar 1831, RFL 242.
43. MR-JJR, 10 Mar 1831, RFL 243.
44. JR-JJR, 19 Jan 1829, RFL 173.
45. See Van Akin Burd, *The Winnington Letters*, 1969, 60n.
46. XXXV, 25.
47. XXXV, 143.
48. XXXV, 73.
49. XXXV, 142.
50. XXXV, 143.
51. JJR-Mary Russell Mitford, 17 Dec 1853, Ms Bembridge L 11.
52. JR-JJR, 27 Feb 1832, RFL 267-8.
53. XXXV, 115.
54. Ms Bembridge 33.
55. II, 387. See also 359-68.
56. The description of the tour is at II, 340-87.
57. See XXXVIII, 3 *et seqq.* for Ruskin's publications. His first appearance in print was with 'On Skiddaw and Derwent Water', a poem in the *Spiritual Times*, Feb 1830, II, 265-6.
58. XXXIV, 365.
59. XXXV, 395.
60. XXXV, 83.
61. XXXV, 139-40.
62. See J. Garden, *Memorials of the Ettrick Shepherd*, 1894, 273-7.
63. I, xxviii.
64. XXXV, 102-3.
65. JJR-W. H. Harrison, 6 Jan 1839, Ms Bembridge L 5.

66. See George Croly, *Historical Sketches, Speeches and Characters*, 1842, 45 *seqq.*, and 310 *seqq.*

67. *Don Juan*, XI, Cantos 57-8.

68. XXXIV, 95.

69. The majority of Ruskin's diaries are preserved at Bembridge. References are given in this book to the published version (ed. Joan Evans and John Howard Whitehouse, Oxford, 1956-9), but also to the Bodleian Library transcripts, which contain the full text, and to the original volumes, in which there are diagrams and drawings.

70. VI, 476.

71. 3 Jun 1835, Diaries 2.

72. XXXV, 152.

73. XIV, 389-91.

74. XXXV, 179.

75. XXXV, 179.

76. XXXV, 180.

77. XXXV, 180.

78. JJR-George Gray, 28 Apr 1847, RG 27.

79. JR-JJR, 25 Mar 1836, RFL 350.

80. The *Iris*, 1834.

81. The essay is printed at I, 357-75.

82. XXXV, 217.

83. Extracts from Eagles's review are at III, xviii.

84. Ruskin's defence was found among his papers after his death. It is printed at III, 635-40.

85. XXXV, 218.

Chapter Two

1. XXXV, 191-2.

2. XXXV, 193.

3. XXXV, 610.

4. G. W. Kitchin, *Ruskin in Oxford and Other Papers*, 1904, 27-8.

5. JR-JJR, 12 Aug 1862, *The Winnington Letters*, ed. Van Akin Burd, 1969, 369-70.

6. XXXV, 196.

7. For Gordon see G. Marshall, *Osborne Gordon*, 1885.

8. XXXV, 252.

9. XXXV, 198.

10. H. L. Thompson, *Henry George Liddell*, 1899, 215n.

11. A. J. C. Hare, *The Story of my Life, 1896-1900*, V, 358.

12. Liddell-Acland (1854). Bodley Ms Acland d. 69.

13. XXXV, 205.

14. The manuscript of *Præterita* is preserved in the Beinecke Library, Yale University. Some plans, notes and passages are in Ruskin's diaries. For these extracts see S. E. Brown,

'The Unpublished Passages in the Manuscript of Ruskin's Autobiography', *Victorian Newsletter*, 16, Fall 1959, 10-18.

15. XXXV, 229.

16. JJR-MR, 13 Mar 1840, RFL 667.

17. 28 Dec 1839, Diaries 73.

18. 12 Mar 1841, Diaries 165.

19. I, xliii.

20. JJR-W. H. Harrison, 9 Jun 1839. Ms Bembridge L 5.

21. XXXV, 255-6.

22. XXXV, 259.

Chapter Three

1. 22 Jun 1840, Diaries 82.

2. XXXV, 305.

3. JJR-JR, 20 Apr 1842, RFL 734.

4. II, 343.

5. W. G. Collingwood, *The Life and Work of John Ruskin*, 1900, 75.

6. 31 Mar 1840, Diaries 74.

7. 15 Nov 1840, Diaries 110.

8. I, 380.

9. I, 381-2.

10. Mary Richardson's diary, 30 May 1840, Ms Bembridge T 49.

11. JJR-W. H. Harrison, n.d., Bodley Ms Eng Letts c 32 fol 55.

12. Mary Richardson's diary, 7 Feb 1840, Ms Bembridge T 49.

13. Mary Richardson's diary, 3 Apr 1840, Ms Bembridge T 49.

14. XXXV, 274-5.

15. XXXV, 275.

16. For George Richmond and his family, see A. M. W. Stirling, *The Richmond Papers*, 1926, and Raymond Lister, *George Richmond*, 1981.

17. JJR-W. H. Harrison, 25 Dec 1840, Bodley Ms Eng Letts c 32 fol 54.

18. For Ruskin's relations with Zorzi, see Jeanne Clegg, *Ruskin and Venice*, 1981, 183-7.

19. XXXV, 297.

Chapter Four

1. XXXV, 299.

2. XXXV, 304, *The King of the Golden River* was perhaps too long for *Friendship's Offering*, or Ruskin was perhaps unwilling to publish it there. John James wrote to W. H. Harrison that 'I expect in a week to receive manuscript of a Fairy Tale but which I must to follow orders dispatch to Scotland directly. I should like when it comes for you to cast your eye over it . . . if it would do for any monthly

. . .', 27 Sep 1841, Bodley Ms Eng Letts c 32 fol 78.

3. JJR-JR, 25 Aug 1841, RFL 680.

4. XXXV, 306.

5. See, for instance, the similarities between MPI and Harding's *The Principles and Practice of Art*, 1845. There are a number of stories of Harding's later opposition to *Modern Painters*. Ruskin claimed that Harding was jealous of the position given to Turner (XXXV, 401). Henry Holiday describes a Harding drawing class in 1858. Holiday had been drawing a large landscape from nature. '"What", [Harding] said, "are you a Pre-Raphaelite?" "I am." The diplomatic sky darkened and his face was itself a declaration of war. He at once attacked what he assumed to be my main body, viz., Mr Ruskin, and opened fire with two charges. 1st, that the writings of his renegade pupil were a mass of pernicious heresies; and 2nd, that they were merely a re-cook of his (Mr Harding's) own works on art . . .' Henry Holiday, *Reminiscences of my Life*, 1914, 49.

6. Ruskin thought Prout a little staid but always remembered him kindly, perhaps because the artist died after the party John James held for his son's birthday, while Ruskin was in Venice in 1852. W. H. Harrison recalled him 'at dinner at Mr Ruskin's . . in wonderful spirits, and I remember his challenging me in a glass of champagne, and my rallying him on some circumstance . . . He was stepping into his carriage at the door at night, and shook hands very heartily, adding, "Why don't you come and see me?" This was eleven o'clock, and before twelve he was dead.' Harrison, 'Notes and Reminiscences', *University Magazine*, May 1878, 545.

7. 6 Jul 1841, Diaries 209.

8. XIII, 478.

9. XXXV, 309-10.

10. XXXV, 311.

11. XXXV, 314.

12. XXXV, 316.

13. Ruskin's correspondence with Clayton was published in 1894 as *Letters Addressed to a College Friend 1840-1845*. Some additional letters are at Bembridge. See I, 407-502.

14. Ruskin's degree has puzzled historians. The most reasonable explanation is Collingwood's. 'He could not now go in for honours, for the lost year had superannuated him. So in April he went up for a pass. In those times, when a pass-man showed unusual powers, they could give him an honorary class; not a high class, because the range of the examinations was less than in the honour-school. This candidate wrote a poor Latin prose, it seems;

but his divinity, philosophy, and mathematics were so good that they gave him the best they could — an honorary double fourth.' W. G. Collingwood, *Life*, revised ed., 1911, 69.

15. III, 665-6. The letter is dated 10 Mar 1844.

16. XXXV, 381.

17. A. M. W. Stirling, *The Richmond Papers*, 1926, 138.

18. 8 Feb 1843, Diaries 242.

19. 24 Feb 1843, Diaries 245.

20. 1 May 1843, Diaries 245.

21. The circumstances are explained at III, xxxii. A number of John James's letters to Harrison are concerned with the shortcomings of magazines and their publishers. It is the father of *Fors Clavigera* who writes 'I have *used my endeavours* to peruse Blackwood from old associations but in vain . . . you are right in a good monthly being wanted, but to start a new one would require a devotion to the Cause of more than one amateur of large fortune, for *publishers* are the smallest souled merchants in London — hard ignorant blockheads iron hearted pawnbrokers — receiving brains in pawn, doling out the merest pittance . . .' JJR-W. H. Harrison, 16 Dec 1843, Ms Bembridge L 5.

22. See William Knight's *Life of William Wordsworth*, 1889, II, 334, III, 243.

23. *Alfred, Lord Tennyson*, A Memoir by his Son, 1897, I, 223.

24. *The Letters of Elizabeth Barrett Browning*, ed. F. G. Kenyon, 1897, I, 384.

25. *Macmillan's Magazine*, Aug 1891, lxiv, 280.

26. J. W. Cross, *The Life of George Eliot*, 1885, II, 7.

27. John James Ruskin's press cuttings books are preserved in the library of the Ashmolean Museum, Oxford.

28. XXXV, 401.

29. III, 668. The letter is dated 12 Oct 1844.

30. 27 May 1843, Diaries 248.

31. 21 Nov 1843, Diaries 249.

32. 12 Dec 1843, Diaries 254.

33. III, 571-3.

34. 24 Nov 1843, Diaries 250.

35. III, 571-3.

36. *Macbeth*, II, 2, 64.

37. XXXVI, 81. The letter is dated 28 Sept 1847.

38. XXVI, 219-20.

39. XXXV, 329.

40. XXXV, 325.

41. XXVI, 222.

42. XXXVI, 38-9. The letter is dated 12 Aug 1844. The Hotel Meurice, in the rue de Rivoli, was used by Ruskin until his last visit to Paris

in 1881.
43. 20 Oct 1844, Diaries 318.

Chapter Five

1. XXXVI, 406.
2. XX, 25, and see also VII, 453 and XVIII, 148.
3. JR–Thomas Carlyle, 12 Jun 1867, in *The Correspondence of Thomas Carlyle and John Ruskin*, ed. G. A. Cate, Stanford, California, 1982, 136.
4. XXXV, 341-2.
5. JR–Acland, 27 Dec 1844, Bodley Ms Acland 4 b-c.
6. JR–JJR, 10 Apr 1845, RI 13.
7. XXXV, 346.
8. JR–JJR, 3 May 1845, RI 51.
9. IV, 347.
10. JR–JJR, 6 May 1845, RI 55.
11. XXXV, 346.
12. 8 Nov 1840, Diaries 106.
13. 18 Nov 1840, Diaries 108.
14. JR–JJR, 18 May 1845, RI 67.
15. JR–JJR, 18 May 1845, RI 68.
16. Ibid.
17. JR–JJR, postmarked 21 Jun 1845, RI 123.
18. JR–JJR, 22 Jun 1845, RI 124.
19. JR–JJR, 16 Jul 1845, RI 148. This was in Milan.
20. JR–JJR, 27 Jul 1845, RI 163. In fact Turner would never leave England again.
21. XXXV, 369.
22. JR–JJR, 6 Aug 1845, RI 168.
23. JR–JJR, 10 Aug 1845, RI 170.
24. JR–JJR, 15 Aug 1845, RI 172.
25. JR–JJR, 10 Sept 1845, RI 198.
26. JR–JJR, 11 Sept 1845, RI 200.
27. JR–JJR, 14 Sept 1845, RI 202.
28. JR–JJR, 4 Sept 1845, RI 211-12.
29. JR–JJR, 28 Sept 1845, RI 216.
30. 4 Jan 1846, Diaries 321-2.
31. 19 Jan 1847, Diaries 322. The entry is a long gloss on that of 4 Jan 1846.
32. IV, 60.
33. See the 'Epilogue' to the 1883 edition, IV, 343-57, which describes the 1845 tour and 'the temper in which, on my return to England, I wrote the second volume of *Modern Painters*'.
34. W. G. Collingwood, *The Art Teaching of John Ruskin*, 1891, 117.
35. XXXV, 413.
36. A. J. Finberg, *Life of J. M. W. Turner*, 1939, 418.
37. On the other hand, it is clear from his writings that Ruskin had amassed a great deal of Turner lore in the early years of his

involvement with the artist. No doubt this came from other artists, other collectors, and from Griffith. Some of these matters are dealt with in vol. XIII of the Library Edition, but there is no modern book on Ruskin's knowledge of Turner, except for the necessarily partial (but excellent) volume by Luke Herrmann, *Ruskin and Turner: A Study of Ruskin as a Collector of Turner, Based on his Gifts to the University of Oxford*, (1968).
38. XIII, 167.
39. JR–Griffith, 31 Nov 1854, Ms Bembridge T 73.
40. Famous for his *Horæ Subsecivæ* (1858-61 and 1882), which includes the celebrated dog story 'Rab and his Friends'. See *Letters of Dr John Brown*, ed. by his son and D. W. Forrest, with biographical introductions by Elizabeth T. M'Laren, 1907.

Chapter Six

1. *Church of England Quarterly Review*, July 1846, 205.
2. VIII, 95n.
3. XXXV, 418-19.
4. JJR–W. H. Harrison, Venice, 25 May 1846, Bodley Ms Eng Letts c 32 fol 243.
5. XXXVI, 64. The letter is dated 30 Aug (1846).
6. XXXV, 422.
7. XXXV, 249.
8. XXXV, 422.
9. XXXV, 249.
10. XXXV, 422.
11. JR–JJR, postmarked 21 Jun 1845, RI 123.
12. Ibid.
13. Quoted in RI, 123n.
14. XXXV, 422.
15. XXXV, 423.
16. XXXV, 249.
17. XXXV, 422.
18. VIII, xxv. The letter is dated 18 Mar 1847.
19. Ibid.
20. JJR–George Gray, 28 Apr 1847, RG 32-3.
21. ECG to her mother, 28 Apr 1847, RG 32-3.
22. ECG to her mother, 4 May 1847, RG 35.
23. ECG to her mother, 5 May 1847, RG 35.
24. ECG to her mother, 5 May 1847, RG 35-6.
25. XXXV, 423.
26. XXXVI, 71.
27. JJR to his parents, 27 Jun 1847, VIII, xxv-xxvi.
28. 30 Jul 1847, Diaries 351.
29. 21 Aug 1847, Diaries 362.
30. 25 Aug 1847, Diaries 364.

Chapter Seven

1. See XVII, 417-22, 'Of Improvidence in Marriage in the Middle Classes; and of the Advisable Restrictions of it', a letter from *Time and Tide*.

2. JR-ECG, 2 Nov (1847), Ms, Private Collection. This and other letters of the period are discussed in Mary Lutyens, 'From Ruskin to Effie Gray', *Times Literary Supplement*, 3 March 1978.

3. JR-ECG, 6 Mar (1847). Ms, Private Collection.

4. By a coincidence which must later have struck Margaret Ruskin as ominous, the Gray family had moved into Bowerswell in 1829.

5. JJR-George Gray, 23 Feb 1848, RG 90-1.

6. The evidence about Ruskin's wedding night has been collected by Mary Lutyens. See MR, 154-7.

7. MR 188-92.

8. ECG-George Gray, 25 Mar 1854, MR 156.

9. MR 188-92.

10. MR 219.

11. ECG-George Gray, 10 Jun 1848, RG 120.

12. ECG to her mother, 12 Nov 1848, RG 168.

13. He was Frederick Myers, a Cambridge Evangelical. Ruskin wrote to his brother-in-law, Dr Whewell, Master of Trinity College, Cambridge, of 'a day or two I am enjoying here — happy in the neighbourhood of St Johns church — and in the teaching of Mr Myers — an advantage which was indeed the chief motive of my choosing Keswick for our place of sojourn . . . I am especially gladdened by the return of the services and teaching of my own church — after some weeks experimentalising among the Scotch Free churchmen . . .' Keswick, 17 Apr 1848. Trinity Coll Cambridge Add Ms c 90/83.

14. JJR-George Gray, 28 Apr 1848, RG III.

15. ECG to her mother, 28 Apr 1848, RG III.

16. JJR-George Gray, 24 May 1848, RG 116.

17. Quoted and discussed at VIII, xxiii and 278.

18. See IV, 37-41.

19. JR-JJR, Florence, 30 May 1845, RV 89.

20. VIII, 3n.

21. J. G. Links, *The Ruskins in Normandy*, 1968, 14.

22. Ibid., 19.

23. XXXV, 156.

24. XII, 314-15.

25. Links, op. cit., 26-7.

26. Ibid., 41.

27. The letter was to W. H. Harrison. Links, op. cit., 83-4.

Chapter Eight

1. *Prospectus of the Arundel Society*, 1849, 8.

2. JJR-George Gray, 4 Mar 1849, RG 180.

3. JR-ECR, 24 Apr 1849, RG 185.

4. JR-ECR, 29 Apr 1849, RG 187.

5. 30 Apr 1849, Diaries 374.

6. 3 Jun 1849, Diaries 381.

7. Ruskin had a lifelong interest in this poem: he wished to know how far his own experience resembled Wordsworth's. See V, 364, 368, and XXXV, 233.

8. 3 June 1849, Diaries 381.

9. 3 Jun 1849, Diaries 382.

10. V, 289.

11. 4 May 1849, Diaries 375.

12. 22 Aug 1849, Diaries 431.

13. II Jul 1849, Diaries 408.

14. XXXV, 437.

15. JR-ECR, 3 May 1849, RG 195.

16. JJR-George Gray, Chamonix, 13 Jun 1849, RG 213.

17. George Gray-JJR, 22 Jun 1849, RG 218.

18. JR-George Gray, 5 Jul 1849, RG 231-2.

19. JR-ECR, Champagnole, 2 Sept 1849, RG 249.

20. ECR-George Gray, 9 Oct 1849, EV 45-6.

21. ECR-George Gray, 28 Oct 1849, EV 53.

22. ECR-George Gray, 28 Oct 1849, EV 53-4.

23. JR-W. L. Brown, 11 Dec 1849, XXXVI, 104.

24. ECR to her mother, 15 Dec 1849, EV 89.

25. ECR to her mother, 18 Jan 1849, EV 133.

26. ECR to her mother, 24 Dec 1849, EV 99.

27. ECR to her mother, 3 Feb 1849, EV 131.

28. ECR to her mother, 28 Dec 1849, EV 99.

29. See EV, 146.

30. Ruskin did not visit Venice between 1852 and 1869. On 10 May 1862 he told Rawdon Brown of his fear of sadness at returning there. See XXXVI, 408.

31. Effie told her mother that 'The gentlemen here are very goodnatured, I think, for when they come to see me they leave their cards for John and say all manner of Civil things too of him and he cuts them all on the street unless I am with him and make him, and he never calls on anybody.' 14 Dec 1851, EV 229.

32. ECG to her mother, 24 Feb 1850, EV 149.

33. See Robert Hewison, *Ruskin and Venice*, 1978, 54-5.

Chapter Nine

1. IX, xxxi. Queen Pomare of Otaheite (Society Islands) had appealed some years before for British protection.

2. See *Journals and Correspondence of Lady Eastlake*, 1895, 192.

3. ECG–Rawdon Brown, n.d., but written at Bowerswell, EV 170.

4. See IX, xlv. The Ruskins made little attempt to promote John Ruskin's books and were more eager that they should be widely read than that they should be well reviewed, though John James was nervous of his son's reputation. In his diary is an interesting list of the recipients of presentation copies of the first volume of *The Stones of Venice*. They practically all went to family friends and the engravers who had worked on the book. They were sent to 'Rogers, Acland, Brown W. L., Richmond, O. Gordon, Dale, Rev. D. Moore, Telford, Croly, Melvill, Harrison, Richardson, Inglis, Lockhart, Murray, Mitford, Edwardes (the soldier Herbert Edwardes, whose career Ruskin would examine in *A Knight's Faith*, 1885), Prof. Owen (probably the geologist Sir Richard Owen), Lady Trevelyan, Cheney, Eastlake, Mr George (a family friend who was possibly also a geologist), Runciman, Carlyle, Lady Davy, Dickens, Lupton, Armitage (the engraver J. C. Armytage), Boys (another engraver), R. Fall. Ms Bembridge 33.

5. Croly's alliance of political and religious prejudice, and his great interest in the press, were much remarked. See, for instance, James Grant, *The Newspaper Press*, 1871-3, vol. III, 24, on John James's favourite reading, the *Britannia*: 'Its principles were Conservative, but its chief feature was its thorough Protestantism. This will be readily believed when I mention that it was at first under the editorship of the late Rev. Dr Croly . . .' This was so of all the Ruskins's admired clergymen. Grant also reports, in *Travels in Town*, 1839, II, 103, that 'nearly all the clergy of the Church of England, in London, are decided Tories in their political views . . . The Rev. Mr Melville of Camden Chapel, Camberwell . . . is one of the most furious Tory partizans I ever knew, in the pulpit as well as out of it . . . the Rev. Mr Dale, of St Bride's Church, Fleet St; and the Rev. Dr Croly, of St Stephens, Walbrook, do severally now and then indicate their political views in their pulpit ministrations . . .' In *The Metropolitan Pulpit*, 1839, II, 15, Grant claimed of Melville that 'I have heard him deliver sermons in which there were passages of so ultra-political a character, that had a stranger been conducted blindfolded into the place in which he was preaching . . . he would have been in danger of mistaking the sermon of the reverend gentleman, for a speech of the

Earl of Winchilsea in the Lords, or of Sir Robert Inglis in the Commons . . .'.

6. For the 'Papal Aggression', see E. R. Norman, *Anti-Catholicism in Victorian England*, 1968. For the background of the Ruskins's political views see D. G. S. Simes's valuable *Ultra-Tories in British Politics, 1824-34*, Bodley Ms. D Phil c 1442.

7. See Thomas Carlyle, *Latter-Day Pamphlets*, No. VI, 'Parliaments', June 1850.

8. F. J. Furnivall, in his foreword to *Two Letters Concerning 'Notes on the Construction of Sheepfolds' by John Ruskin*, 1890, 8.

9. ECR–Rawdon Brown, 9 May 1854, MR 207.

10. William Holman Hunt, *Pre-Raphaelitism and the Pre-Raphaelite Brotherhood*, 1905, I, 50-1.

11. XXXVII, 427.

12. XIV, III.

13. XII, 319.

14. XII, 320.

15. XII, 322.

16. XII, 327.

17. Quoted at XII, 1n.

18. J. G. Millais, *Life and Letters of Sir John Everett Millais*, 1899, I, 116.

19. III, 624.

20. Hunt, op. cit.

21. 1 May 1851, Diaries 468.

22. ECG–George Gray, 24 Aug 1851, EV 183.

23. See also the letter to W. L. Brown given in Jeanne Clegg, *Ruskin and Venice*, 1981, 81-3. *Centesemi* were coins, the smallest part of the lira.

24. XVIII, 539.

25. ECG to her mother, 24 Feb 1852, EV 283.

26. JR–JJR, 16 Nov 1851, EV 184.

27. JR–JJR, 6 Mar 1852, J. L. Bradley ed., *Ruskin's Letters from Venice*, 1955, 212.

28. For these letters see XII, lxxviii-lxxxv. Some of the letters themselves are given at XII, 591-603.

29. See XI, 258-63.

30. See XII, lxxxiv.

31. See XII, l-lii.

32. JR–JJR, 28 Sept 1851, Bradley, op. cit., 23.

33. JR–JJR, 28 Dec 1851, Bradley, op. cit., 112. Ruskin recorded 'Turner buried' on 30 December 1851, and then abandoned diary entries until 20 July 1853, when he arrived at Glenfinlas.

34. Eastlake, op. cit., I, 273.

35. Collingwood, *Life*, 1900, 136.

36. XIII, xxvi-xxvii.

37. Eastlake, op. cit., I, 273.

38. ECR to her mother, 4 Jan 1852, RV 242.

39. JR-JJR, 1 Jan 1852, Bradley, op. cit., 119-20.
40. See XIII, xxx.
41. JR-JJR, 22 Feb 52, Bradley, op. cit., 191-20.
42. JR-JJR, 5 Feb 1852, Bradley, op. cit., 164.
43. JR-JJR, 8 Feb 1852, Bradley, op. cit., 171. Written on his birthday, this letter is a very extensive discussion of Ruskin's health in recent years.
44. 3 March 1874, Diaries 777.
45. See XVIII, 32 and XXV, 122.
46. XXXVI, 115.
47. JR-JJR, 25 Jan 1852, Bradley, op. cit., 149. This letter was written on a Sunday: Ruskin always gave more space to religious matters when he wrote on the sabbath.
48. JR-JJR, 22 Feb 1852, Bradley, op. cit., 192.
49. ECR to her mother, 8 Feb 1852, EV 263.
50. Ibid., 265.
51. Ibid., 265-6.
52. JR-JJR, 27 Dec 1851, EV 261.
53. ECR to her father, 19 Jan 1852, EV 249.
54. ECR to her mother, 20 Feb 1852, EV 271.

Chapter Ten

1. XXXVI, 142.
2. ECR to her mother, 3 Aug 1852, MR 17.
3. See MR, 15.
4. JR-Mrs Gray, 28 Aug 1852, MR 19-22.
5. Betty Miller, *Robert Browning*, 1952, 172.
6. Cate, op. cit., 1-2.
7. XXXV, 539-41.
8. See Cate, op. cit., 15. Jane Welsh Carlyle was never sympathetic to Effie. On 23 Feb 1856 she wrote to William Allingham '. . . what can be expected from a man who goes to sleep with, every night, a different Turner's picture on a chair opposite his bed "that he may have something beautiful to look at on first opening his eyes of a morning". (so his mother told me) . . . I never saw a man so improved by the loss of his wife! He is amiable and gay, and full of hope and faith in — one doesn't know exactly *what* — but of course *he* does . . .'. National Library of Scotland, Ms 3283 foll 123-4.
9. ECR to her mother, Feb 1853, MR 29.
10. Millais, op. cit., 92.
11. ECR to her mother, 27 Mar 1853, MR 39.
12. JR-W. L. Brown, 31 Mar 1853, Bodley Ms Eng Letts c 33 fol 110.
13. JJR-MR, 15 Dec 1854, Ms Bembridge L 2.
14. ECR to her mother, 15 Apr 1853, MR 42-3.

15. ECR to her mother, 3 May 1854, RG 45.
16. XI, 53.
17. XI, 53n.
18. ECR-Rawdon Brown, 20 Jun 1853, MR 50.
19. JR-W. L. Brown, Jun 1853, Bodley Ms Eng Letts c 33 fol 46.
20. A. J. C. Hare, *The Story of My Life, 1896-1900*, II, 348-51.
21. *Letters of Dr John Brown*, 88.
22. Pauline Trevelyan's review was to appear in *The Scotsman*. See Virginia Surtees ed., *Reflections of a Friendship: John Ruskin's Letters to Pauline Trevelyan 1848-1866*, 1979, for her connections with Ruskin and Millais.
23. XII, xix.
24. Millais-Holman Hunt, 28 Jun 1853, MR 55.
25. JR-JJR, 3 Jul 1853, MR 59-60.
26. XII, xxiv.
27. See RI, 166.
28. V, 122.
29. ECR to her mother, 10 Jul 53, MR 65-6
30. XII, xxiii.
31. Acland to his wife, 27 Jul 1853, Bodley Ms Acland d 9 foll.134-5.
32. Acland to his wife, n.d., Bodley Ms Acland d 9 fol 136.
33. JR-JJR, 28 Jul 1853, MR 75.
34. Diaries 479.
35. Millais-C. A. Collins, n.d., MR 81.
36. Deposition by William Millais dated 9 March 1898, Bodley Ms Eng Letts c 228, fol 62.
37. JR-MR, 16 Oct 1853, MR 97.
38. JR-Hunt, 20 Oct 1853, MR 101.
39. JR-JJR, 6 Nov 1853, MR 107-8.
40. JJR-JR, 8 Dec 1853, Ms Bembridge L 4.
41. Millais-Mrs Gray, 19 Dec 1853, MR 114.
42. JJR-George Gray, 16 Feb 1854, MR 135.
43. ECR to her father, 7 Mar 1854, MR 154-7.

Chapter Eleven

1. For a description of this book, see Diaries 487.
2. XXXV, 415.
3. Bodley Ms Eng Letts c 33 fol 152.
4. A correspondence conducted through Griffith which Fawkes cut off. The two men were estranged for many years afterwards.
5. See MR 230.
6. 2 July 1854, Diaries 497.
7. 27 Sept 1854, Diaries 511.
8. Surtees, op. cit., 88.
9. Charles P. Lucas, 'Llewelyn Davies and the Working Men's College, *Cornhill*

Magazine, Oct 1916, 421 ff.

10. A successful painter at this period would decline to give lessons: this proved that he was more than a drawing master. Philip Gilbert Hamerton records Ruskin's opinion of drawing masters in the year before he began teaching at the Working Men's College. In 1853 Hamerton had asked him to recommend a master. Ruskin replied 'There is no artist in London capable of teaching you and at the same time willing to give lessons. All those who teach, teach mere tricks with the brush, not true art, far less true nature.' *An Autobiography, 1834-1858*, 1897, 128-30.

11. JR-Sarah Acland, 19 Oct 1854, Bodley Ms Acland d 72 fol 39.

12. XIII, 539.

13. V, xl.

14. Virginia Surtees ed., *The Diary of Ford Madox Brown*, 1981, 196, 16 March 1857.

15. See J. P. Emslie, 'Recollections of Ruskin', *Working Men's College Journal*, vol. 7, 180; and, generally, J. F. L. Harrison, *A History of the Working Men's College*, 1954, 16-85.

16. JJR-JR, 1 Dec 1853, MS Bembridge L 4.

17. Sarah Angelina Acland, 'Memories in my 81st Year', Ms notebook, Bodley Ms Eng Misc d 214.

18. *Letters of James Smetham*, 1891, 54-5.

19. XXXVI, 143-4.

20. XII, 55.

21. *Letters of Dante Gabriel Rossetti*, ed. Oswald Doughty and J. R. Wahl, Oxford, 1965-7, 134.

22. XXXVI, 32.

23. Rossetti was writing to his aunt, Charlotte Polidori. *Letters*, 250.

24. See V, 24-34.

25. See James S. Dearden, 'The Production and Distribution of Ruskin's *Poems*, 1850', *Book Collector*, Summer 1968.

26. Basil Champneys, *Memoirs and Correspondence of Coventry Patmore*, 1900, II, 277.

27. Ibid., II, 278-9.

28. *The Critic*, 27 Oct 1860.

29. Champneys, op. cit., I, 130n.

30. See David J. DeLaura, 'Ruskin and the Brownings: Twenty-Five Unpublished Letters', *Bulletin of the John Rylands Library*, 54, Spring 1972.

31. Ibid. Shenstone is commended for his love of nature at V, 360.

32. Ruskin's relations with Stillman are described in his *Autobiography of a Journalist*, 1901.

33. See R. B. Stein, *Ruskin and Aesthetic Thought in America, 1840-1900*, Cambridge, Mass., 1967.

34. VII, 451.

35. XXXV, 520.

36. *Letters of Matthew Arnold*, 1848-88, ed. G. W. E. Russell, 1895, I, 38-9.

37. J. B. Atlay, *Sir Henry Wentworth Acland*, 1903, 140-53.

38. Ruskin-Acland, n.d., Bodley Ms Acland d 72 fol. 37 a-b.

39. Ruskin-Sarah Acland, 19 Oct 1854, Bodley Ms Acland d 72 fol 39.

40. XVI, xliii.

41. XVI, xliv.

42. Ruskin-Acland, n.d., Bodley Ms Acland d 72 fol 43.

43. XVI, xlv.

44. XII, 430.

45. For whom, see Royston Lambert, *Sir John Simon 1816-1904 and English Social Administration*, 1963.

46. See Atlay, op. cit., 192-3.

47. XVI, 221.

48. Atlay, op. cit., 227.

49. Rossetti to his mother, 1 Jul 1855, *Letters*, 262.

50. Atlay, op. cit., 225-8.

51. Bodley Ms Acland d 72 fol 58.

52. Quoted in XVI, xlix.

53. See XVI, 207-40.

54. Ms Bembridge L 17.

55. JJR-Acland 25 Jun 1855, Bodley Ms Acland d 72 fol 54.

56. XVI, 436.

Chapter Twelve

1. Louisa, Marchioness of Waterford, was a rich amateur and patroness. She had mixed in Pre-Raphaelite circles since at least 1853. Ruskin's letters to her are collected in Virginia Surtees ed., *Sublime and Instructive*, 1972.

2. XVI, 213-14.

3. XIV, 152.

4. The letters are given at XII, 328-55.

5. Ibid.

6. IV, 333.

7. See XIII, xxi.

8. XIV, 5.

9. XIV, 9-10.

10. XIV, 13-14.

11. XIV, 18.

12. XIV, 19.

13. XIV, 20.

14. See A. M. W. Stirling, *The Richmond Papers*, 1926, 163 *seqq.*

15. Dante Gabriel Rossetti-William Allingham, 11 May 1855, *Letters*, 252.

16. XIV, 27.

17. XIV, 35.
18. Virginia Surtees ed., *The Diary of Ford Madox Brown*, 1981, 144, for 13 July 1855.
19. XIV, 43-6.
20. See XIII, 41 and 168.
21. *Athenæum*, July 26, 1856.
22. *Oxford and Cambridge Magazine*, June 1856.
23. XXXV, 519.
24. For Ruskin's early acquaintance with Norton, see *Letters of Charles Eliot Norton*, eds. Sara Norton and Mark A. DeWolfe Howe, Boston, 1913; and Kermit Vanderbilt, *Charles Eliot Norton, Apostle of Culture in a Democracy*, Cambridge, Mass., 1959.
25. 7 Sept 1856, Diaries 519.
26. See XXVIII, 517.
27. 21 Oct 1856, Diaries 524.
28. See XXXVI, liii.
29. 16 Oct 1856, Diaries 524.
30. 28 Nov 1856, Diaries 525.
31. See Dore Ashton, *Rosa Bonheur*, 1981, 111.
32. See William Bell Scott, *Autobiographical Notes*, 1892, II, 9-10.
33. A favourite phrase of Ruskin's. The first sentence of *Præterita* begins, 'I am, and my father was before me, a violent Tory of the old school.' XXXV, 13.

Chapter Thirteen

1. From George Butterworth's diary, Ms Bembridge 35.
2. Ibid.
3. XXXV, 488.
4. See XXXVI, 186-7 and 278-9.
5. Butterworth, op. cit.
6. See Brian Maidment, *John Ruskin and George Allen*, D. Phil. thesis, University of Leicester, 1973, 48.
7. See XXX, lv-vi and XXXVI, 186.
8. See XIV, 349-56.
9. Surtees, *Sublime and Instructive*, 8.
10. Ibid., 93.
11. V, 4.
12. See XIII, 161-2.
13. See XIII, 173-81.
14. See XIII, 186-226.
15. XIV, 106-11.
16. XIV, xxxvi and 464-70.
17. XXXVI, 263.
18. Ibid.
19. Ibid.
20. XXXVI, 273.
21. JJR-Jane Simon, 19 Feb 1858, Ms Bembridge L 12.

22. XXXVI, 319n.
23. XXIX, 593. John James's accounts show that he was a regular contributor to Guthrie's charities.
24. VII, 4.
25. XII, xxxvi-xxxvii.
26. H. Stacy Marks, *Pen and Pencil Sketches*, 1894, II, 165.
27. Surtees, *Sublime and Instructive*, 215.
28. Ibid.
29. JR-JJR, 20 Jun 1858, *Letters from the Continent 1858*, ed. John Hayman, Toronto, 1982, 51-2.
30. XIII, 119.
31. XII, 99.
32. This is a problem that underlay Ruskin's writing for the 1878 exhibition at the Fine Art Society. The catalogue was written at a time when his own mind failed. See XIII, 409-10 and 520-1.
33. See *The Brantwood Diary of John Ruskin*, ed. H. G. Viljoen, 1971, 98.
34. V, 5.
35. XIV, 151.
36. XIV, 161-2.
37. JR-JJR, 5 Jun 1858, Hayman, *Letters from the Continent*, 28-9.
38. See *Letters from the Continent*, 14-80, for Ruskin's letters home from Switzerland. Very many of them discuss Swiss character and institutions.
39. XIV, 172.
40. JR-JJR, 26 Aug 1858, *Letters from the Continent*, 147.
41. See Allen Staley, *The Pre-Ruphaelite Landscape*, 1969.
42. JR-JJR, Sept 1858, *Letters from the Continent*, 171.
43. XIX, 83.
44. XXIX, 89.
45. XXXV, 496.
46. XXXV, 493.
47. JR-Lady Trevelyan, 27 Sept 1858, *Reflections of a Friendship*, 132.
48. 23 May 1858. Diaries 535. Ruskin wrote beneath the sketch, 'This drawing of orchises was the first I ever made on Sunday: and marks, henceforward, the beginning of total change in habits of mind. 24th Feb. 1868.'
49. A. J. C. Hare, *The Story of My Life, 1896-1900*, II, 107-9.
50. VII, xli. Although Ruskin sent these views to his father they were not exactly in a letter, but in one of the 'Notes on the Turin Gallery' he was composing with a view to *Modern Painters* V.
51. See *Letters from the Continent*, 141-4.

Chapter Fourteen

1. XVI, 171.
2. See XVI, 259-92n. The whole lecture is a fine statement of Ruskin's views in the latter days of his Pre-Raphaelitism.
3. XVI, lxv.
4. XVI, 336n.
5. XVI, 336-7.
6. XVI, 340.
7. JR-JJR, 12 Sep 1858, *Letters from the Continent*, 170.
8. In 1880 Ruskin looked back on his experience of sermons. 'I am now sixty years old, and for forty-five of them was in church at least once on the Sunday, — say once a month also in afternoons, — and you have about three thousand church services. When I am abroad I am often in half-a-dozen churches in the course of a single day, and never lose a chance of listening . . . add the conversations pursued, not unearnestly, with every sort of reverend person . . .' XXXIV, 217n.
9. W. J. Fullerton, *C. H. Spurgeon*, 1920, 39.
10. Joseph Johnson, *Popular Preachers of our Time*, 1864, I, 613.
11. Quoted in Fullerton, op. cit., 39.
12. XXXVI, 275.
13. XXXIV, 659-61.
14. Ibíd.
15. See XV, 189.
16. For this background, see Van Akin Burd, *John Ruskin and Rose La Touche*, 1979, 23-49.
17. XXXV, 525. Ruskin mistook her age in this passage: she was ten years old. But factual mistakes in *Præterita* were seldom corrected.

18. Bodley Ms Eng Letts c 34 fol 3.
19. XXXV, 526.
20. See Waldo Hilary Dunn, *James Anthony Froude*, 1961-3, I, 64-7.
21. XXXV, 533.
22. JR-Jane Simon, 20 Jun 1858, *Letters from the Continent*, 187.
23. JR-Jane Simon, 9 Nov 1858, Bodley Ms Eng Letts c 34 fol 88.
24. JR-JJR, 26 Jun 1858, *Letters from the Continent*, 59.
25. JR-Anna Blunden, 20 Oct 1858, *Sublime and Instructive*, 98-100.
26. XXXV, 503.
27. Logan Pearsall Smith, *Unforgotten Years*, 1938, 39-40.

Chapter Fifteen

1. Ms Bembridge 33.
2. XXXVI, 338-9.
3. XIV, 234-8.
4. Ruskin would have been the more displeased in noticing that the painting depicts the back garden at Bowerswell.
5. JR-Margaret Bell, 3-4 Apr 1859, *Winnington Letters*, 149-50.
6. XIV, 240-3.
7. XIII, 539.
8. XXII, 511-12.
9. For this background, see Van Akin Burd, *The Winnington Letters*, 1969, 19-54.
10. XXXVI, 324.
11. XXXVI, 331.

INDEX

The following brief index refers only to proper names. A full index will be found at the end of the second volume.

BORN FOR THIS

Maya Comerota

It's Saturday morning in Elkins Park, Pennsylvania. I'm nine years old, and I've just arrived at my friend Jillian's house.

"C'mon, let's go!" I call.

"Coming!" she calls back as she runs down the steps with her sweatshirt and backpack. "I was getting supplies."

She and I were like a female Tom Sawyer and Huckleberry Finn that summer, heading out first thing in the mornings on long adventures that would keep us out until after dark.

We'd fill our backpacks with blankets, Archie Comics, snacks, sandwiches, and apple juice boxes, then take off for the magical wonderland in the woods behind our neighbors' backyards.

We'd climb trees and take turns swinging on the rope above the creek while imagining we were anyone we wanted to be.

We'd play, build castles and forts, then fall over exhausted onto a bed of leaves, panting heavily and giggling from our effort.

When we'd finally come back to Jillian's house, we'd run upstairs to begin our musical escapades.

After dressing up and doing each other's makeup and hair like Madonna and Debbie Gibson, we'd sing "Cherish," "Like a Prayer," and "Electric Youth" at the top of our lungs.

We'd stay up late and then call into the pop radio station, Eagle 106.

"You have reached Eagle 106. What's your name and song?"

"This is Jillian calling from Elkins Park. I want to request 'One More Time' by Timmy T. and give a shout-out to my girl, Maya, who is here with me!"

I would let out a squeal with her as we both jumped up and down. We were on the radio, just like we knew we would be!

There was nothing we couldn't do. No one we couldn't be . . .

Adventurers. Explorers. Pop singers. Broadway stars. Makeup artists. Actresses. Dancers. Teachers. Doctors.

We believed whatever we dreamed, whatever we imagined, we would be.

I was going to live a legendary life full of incredible musical adventures, jet-setting around the world to impact lives *and* have an incredible husband, three kids, a puppy, and a beautiful home.

Twenty-five years later, after following all the rules I thought I was meant to follow, working hard to get good grades, and working even longer and harder at work, I wasn't a singer, Broadway star, or a doctor. But I was making an impact, building billion-dollar brands and supporting hundreds of thousands of patients around the world as the director of Latin America for a Fortune 100 Biotech company.

I was flying first class to Guatemala, Mexico, Colombia, Brazil, and Argentina where I would stay at the St. Regis for weeks at a time with my own personal butler, concierge, driver, and security detail to take me to and from the hotel and office.

I had married James, a gorgeous, adventurous, six-foot-five Australian with long brown hair and an accent that would make any woman swoon.

We knew we'd get married the moment we met. Our beautiful wedding was held in Antigua, Guatemala, in a fifteenth-century monastery, lit by two thousand candles.

It seemed like a fairy tale.

We moved to a beautiful condo in Chicago and later bought a lake house and a boat. We weren't often home at the same time because of our work schedules, but we would meet in different locations around the world. I had recently found out I was pregnant with our first child.

I'm sure from the outside looking in, I seemed to have it all.

But deep down inside, I felt something was missing. I wanted *more*.

I would think, "Maya, how can you possibly be unhappy? You have a great career. You have a gorgeous husband. You get to travel and stay at the most beautiful places. You're going to have a child. You have a dream life."

I could hear how ridiculous it sounded. But the feeling wouldn't go away.

Nine months later, after receiving *another* promotion, I was sitting in my closet on a conference call with my boss at 10:30 p.m., whispering so I wouldn't wake up James who was asleep in the bedroom.

My boss said, "Maya, this launch is huge. We can count on you to get this report to the team by ten a.m. tomorrow, right?"

"Umm . . . sure. Absolutely. Whatever you need!"

What?! I was 225 months pregnant, ten days overdue, and scheduled to get induced into labor in less than twelve hours!

But I *never* let anyone down. Plus my boss had told me she was crazy for hiring me when I was seven months pregnant, and I wanted to prove she'd made the right choice.

So eight hours later, I was on the delivery table, strapped into that contraption that shows how big your contractions are on a video screen, but I was not paying attention. All my focus was on a different screen: my Blackberry.

I felt a little guilty for working right then, but there were things I had to get done before this baby came.

My contractions aren't off the charts yet. I still have time, I thought to myself.

James starts to walk over, I'm sure to take my Blackberry away from me.

"Please. I just need to send these last two emails. You don't understand. I can't let the team down."

I was going to show everyone that I could handle it all. Career. Baby. Family. All of it.

Uh-huh. Right.

After two additional promotions, I was taking Ritalin for ADHD and Lexapro for depression to help me focus through long workdays and to help me feel not so "blue" day after day after day.

One beautiful Sunday afternoon, I was typing away in my office. Hunter was three years old, playing downstairs with his nanny. And I was upstairs working.

I'd been working fourteen-hour days for years. I'd worked every weekend for the last six months.

All I wanted was to go downstairs and play with Hunter, but I felt stuck and chained to my computer.

Bing!

A text from work. I needed to get out of here and clear my head.

"Hunter, Mommy will be home in an hour." I ran out the door and jumped in my husband's truck.

Twenty minutes later, I was stopped at a red light thinking, *How did I get here? I can't even remember driving the last twenty minutes.*

Then *CRASH!*

A huge black SUV crashed into me.

The car started to spin. Everything turned into slow motion. I saw scenes of my life pass before my eyes, both from the life I've lived and the life I had yet to live.

I see my funeral. James and Hunter are so sad.

I see James looking into my eyes with so much love on our wedding day. He hasn't looked at me that way for so long.

I see Hunter's birth and again feel the rush of love I felt when I promised to love him forever unconditionally.

I see all the moments I felt unloved because I compromised myself, apologized for myself, or sacrificed myself.

And I see myself as that little girl running carefree through the woods, climbing trees, singing songs, being anything and anyone she wanted to be.

I knew there was more to life than the one I'd been living.

I knew there was more to *me* than the woman I was being.

There was someone I was created to be, and I hadn't become her . . . *yet.*

But I *wanted* to be her! I *wanted* to feel alive, vibrant, passionate, brave, bold, wild, and free—the way I know each of us is meant to feel. The way we were born to be!

"God, please let me live through this. If I make it out alive, I promise I will be the person you created me to be. I will discover who that is and I will be her."

By the time the police arrived twenty minutes later, I was embracing the woman driving the SUV.

Both our cars were totaled, yet neither one of us had a scratch on us.

Six months later, I handed in my resignation. I was free for the first time. Free to be me, Maya.

Not Maya, director of Latin America, or Maya, global head of innovation. Just Maya.

I wasn't exactly sure who she was yet, but I couldn't wait to meet her and discover why God put her on this Earth.

Slowly I let go of the titles, the roles, the expectations.

I let go of the medications.

I let go of my car, the boat, the lake house.

I let go of my regrets and I started to dream a new dream.

I dreamed of being in love with life and in love with my husband again.

I dreamed of playing and laughing with Hunter.

I dreamed of leading and inspiring women around the world to live the lives they were born to live.

I knew that I had to *become* her first before I could inspire others. I had to first *be* the woman that *I* was born to be.

So I began living that dream.

It wasn't easy. I lost investments. I lost businesses and business partners. I lost some friendships. My relationship with my husband was in turmoil. I even asked for a divorce. But every time things got hard, or I fell down, I would hear the words,

There is someone you were created to be.

You are here for a reason.

You are born for this.

Today, over two million people have been impacted by my messages, events, and programs. I speak on the world's largest and most prestigious stages supporting people to be who they are uniquely created to be and to share their gifts with the world.

But I never forget that before I could share my story and support others to change their lives, I had to dare to dream and first transform my own.

For 2022, I wanted to dream even bigger and bolder and welcome even more freedom, passion, prosperity, joy, and vitality into my life.

My company was poised to double in size, and I am about to expand my team, launch new programs, write another new book, and teach on new stages.

But what I was most looking forward to was doing Everesting 29029 with James. Together we were going to climb twenty-nine thousand twenty-nine feet, the equivalent of Mount Everest, in only thirty-six hours.

We were going to train for six months and cross the finish line together. It was going to be a family vacation with Hunter waiting for us at the finish line. I could already see James giving me a big hug and kiss when we crossed the finish line with our family and friends shouting and cheering for us in the background.

This was going to be especially meaningful because just five years before, I had asked James for a divorce.

We hadn't been happy for many years. We had tried to make it better for so long, and I wanted us both to be happy . . . finally. Even if it meant letting each other go. I knew I needed to let go of our relationship so I could make room for the passionate, joyful, loving relationship we both deserved.

Months later, as James was packing his things in boxes and preparing to move into an apartment nearby, he looked at me and said, "Do you think it's possible we could stay together?"

I paused.

I mean, I believe *anything* is *possible*. That *is* what I teach.

"Dream the impossible dream no matter what."

But this?

We'd been trying to make it work for so long, and it just wasn't. I knew it was time to let it go. I knew that would be the most loving thing for us to do.

"Anything is possible," I said, "but I don't think it's likely."

"I see us together, Maya. That is what I want," James said. "You, me, and Hunter, walking together hand in hand. You're wearing a white dress. I see it so clearly. What do I do with that vision?"

I considered what he was asking.

"Hold that vision then," I said through tears, "but without attachment to me or the outcome."

My vision was of a passionate and loving marriage with a husband who could be my best friend. Someone who would laugh with me and celebrate me being the me I was born to be. I wanted a marriage that would be a true example of what marriage should be, for Hunter and for others. I wanted us to be incredible parents together. I didn't want Hunter seeing two roommates as his parents and believing that was what marriage was. My vision seemed so far from the couple that James and I had become.

But I held on to my vision of the marriage I truly desired and James held on to his.

We leaned into each other, day by day, moment by moment until my dream and his dream merged into one. We didn't force it. We simply became our own dreams. We made choices and decisions in alignment with what we desired and the people we were born to be. I didn't know if we'd stay together and neither did he. But after walking through the fire of difficult conversations, decisions, and actions, we fell in love again and became the couple we both wanted to be.

Doing Everesting 29029 was going to be the culmination and celebration of our journey. The odds of finishing are about 60 percent, but I knew with 100 percent certainty James and I were going to cross that finish line!

Then a few months ago, I was driving Hunter to school. We were belting out songs from Disney's *Encanto* when I began feeling nauseous.

"Mom, what's wrong?" Hunter asked.

"I don't know, little guy. I have never felt this way before."

"I'm sorry, Mom. I hope you feel better! I love you!" Hunter closed the door to walk into school.

When the door banged shut, I remembered . . . there was one other time I felt like this . . . eleven years ago . . . when I was pregnant with Hunter.

I stopped at the Walgreens to grab two pregnancy tests.

Pregnant.

Pregnant.

I stared at them. Uncertain how to feel.

James was working in Virginia.

"We're pregnant," I told him over the phone.

After a slight pause, he said, "Yaaaaaaaay?"

He was trying to sound enthusiastic, processing the news just like I was.

I burst into tears.

This can't be, I thought. *Things are finally back on track. We have big plans this year. The company's growing, I'm speaking all over the country, people are counting on me, we're doing Everest 29029, we are planning on moving and taking vacations as a family. How are we going to do it all if I'm pregnant and have a baby?*

When Hunter was a baby, it was hard! I was working fourteen-hour days and weekends. I did the best I could. I hired help, but my heart broke every time I couldn't play with him and every time I had to travel. The stress of it all came flooding back.

Could James and I survive another baby? We'd talked about it once years ago, but because of our strained relationship, it didn't make sense for us to have more kids.

Will James want to have a baby now?

Over the next twenty-four hours, I experienced every emotion possible, but I couldn't discern how I really felt.

Then I paused and asked, *What would you really love, Maya? If you could dream any dream, what would it be?*

I saw a vision of our family. Of a beautiful baby girl laughing and giggling with us. I saw all the love and joy that she would bring. I saw her gazing at Hunter with her big, beautiful eyes, totally in love with her big brother, and I saw Hunter tickling his little sister. I saw all of us, including our puppy, Coco, going to the beach, the park, and on vacation together. I saw graduations, Thanksgivings, Christmases, weddings, and grandkids. I saw us traveling the world *together* as a family, dreaming our biggest dreams and doing it together. And I saw the impact that this little baby and her big brother would have on the world simply by being who they were born to be.

I called James the next day.

"I think God is laughing at us right now. I think he's saying, 'Maya, James, this is everything you have been asking for. You wanted more love, more laughter, more joy, more fun, more play, more impact, more adventure. Here you go! Your relationship is better than ever, you're in love, you're being who you were born to

be. Everything you desire is coming true in the most miraculous of ways. And it is *easy!*'"

James and I both laughed while sensing the truth in it all.

As I sit here typing, there's a little human growing inside me. She chose us, and we chose her.

One of my favorite authors is Henry David Thoreau. Many years ago, he decided to do an experiment with life. He went into the woods to live for two years, two months, and two weeks because he wanted to learn what life and the woods had to teach him. He wanted to be sure that he didn't come to the end of his life only to discover that he had not yet truly lived.

I didn't want to come to the end of my life and discover that *I* had not yet truly lived.

I started to ask myself the question, *What is my bold, brave experiment with life?*

"James, Hunter," I called, running down the stairs into the kitchen to sit down while James cooked dinner.

"What do you think about going on an adventure and doing a life experiment?"

"Oooh, what kind of adventure?" Hunter asked. James shifted his attention from the pan of vegetables over to me as he put his arms around my growing waist and gave me a big kiss.

"Well, what if once the baby comes, we buy an RV and travel around the world together talking to legendary families about what it takes to make dreams come true? Let's make a documentary and create a television show to share the stories of legendary families who support each other's dreams and aspirations."

I was thinking of people like Oprah, Tony Robbins, Dean Graziosi, Mary Morrisey, Bo Eason, Jesse Itzler and Sara Blakely, Sonia Choquette, Jack Canfield and Jamie Kern Lima as well as my colleagues and students from my Born For This and Living Legendary programs who are also extraordinary people doing extraordinary things.

James winked at me, chuckled, and said, "That does sound like an adventure. Let's do it."

Hunter said, "I'm in!"

Bing!

It was a text message from a mentor, Dean Graziosi.

"Maya, let me know if you have a few minutes to chat today."

He invited me to speak at his upcoming event to thousands of mission-driven entrepreneurs.

"I would love to!" I said, honored and blessed that I got to be me and share my heart with the world without compromising anymore.

Hunter called, "Family cuddle!"

James, Hunter, Coco, and I along with our unborn baby girl gathered in the living room.

Hunter whispered to the little baby growing in my belly, "I can't wait till you get here!"

As I lay there with my family, I closed my eyes and knew that I was finally being the woman I was created to be, living the life I was created to live, feeling more alive and joyful than ever, and knowing that this is still only the beginning of our adventures.

I am born for this.

And so are you.

ABOUT MAYA COMEROTA

Maya is a visionary entrepreneur, transformational teacher, and speaker. Maya spent fifteen years in the biotech industry building multibillion-dollar coaching platforms that impacted over 300,000 people worldwide. After leaving her corporate executive role as global head of innovation, she immersed herself in the study of personal transformation learning from the best of the best in neuroscience, quantum physics, and high performance.

Through her companies, consulting, programs, and live events, Maya has empowered millions of people to achieve new heights of wealth, joy, aliveness, and authentic success.

Maya has been a featured speaker and coach on major media outlets such as NBC, ABC, CBS and has been featured on stages with Dean Graziosi, Mary Morrisey, Bo Eason, among others. Maya was recently invited to train other visionary entrepreneurs on the art and science of turning dreams into reality on Sir Richard Branson's island.

Web: www.mayacomerota.com
Facebook: Maya Comerota
Instagram: @mayacomerota

INTRODUCTION

Kate Butler

I was being interviewed for a podcast last week and the host asked me, "Did everyone in your life think you were crazy when you walked away from a successful company you built to pursue your dream?"

I said, "Yes. Until it worked."

***

I always knew I would do something with writing because expressing myself through words always came innately to me. It was not completely out of the question to believe I would write a book one day, although I did not think I would write twelve international best sellers and go on to publish over 400 #1 best-selling authors as well. This is still, in many ways, shocking to say.

I was thirty years old running a business from my home, based on what I had done in corporate. It made great money. I also got to be home with our children. And I was bored out of my freaking mind. I had an awareness one day that I was selling myself short, that I was not put here to run a staffing and recruiting business, that I was meant for more and I was being called

to do more. And here's the thing about awareness . . . once you know it, you can't unknow it.

If I was going to scrap this business, if I was going to do it all again, if I was going to build an actual dream . . . I was going to do it differently.

When I was working in a business that was out of alignment with my purpose, it always felt like there was something missing, like I could never do enough, like I always had to push to make more happen.

It was constant pressure . . .

What do I need to do this week?

What needs to happen to meet goals this month?

What do I have to do to complete this project?

What does this client need from me now?

Each week, month, quarter, and year, it seemed like a heaviness clouded over me of goals that needed to be achieved and I needed to make happen, but when the goals were met, there was only brief satisfaction. There was never a lightness. It always felt like I was carrying bricks in a backpack and pushing a bolder up a hill. It always felt like no matter what goals were met, I always needed to make more happen. It didn't bring me happiness. It just made me money. It wasn't fulfilling, it just felt like it was what I had to do.

What if I could have both? What if I created from that place?

I was going to build something that ignited a fire inside my belly every time I opened my email. I was going to create something that others wanted to be part of. I was going to start a movement that had me jumping out of bed in the morning. I was going to create a life I was madly in love with.

I wanted to feel like I *get* to do this each day, not like I have to.

And as soon as I decided this, my next thought was, *but how?* And then, *who are you to create this empire that you long for?*

So I had to decide at that moment: which one?

Which one is it going to be, Kate?

Are you going to choose what you've always known? Or are you going to choose the forest with no path, no trails, and no map? Which one?

If you know me, you know I am not much for camping, or forests, or woods. But this was different. This forest was enchanted. I could just *feel* it.

I shared with you earlier that an awareness revealed itself to me. And once you know, you can never unknow it. And so, I *knew*, I knew that although it did not appear that there was a trail or a path or a guide or a map . . . I had this knowing that I WAS THE MAP. I realized I was born knowing the way. I had a deep knowing that I had everything I needed within myself and I always had.

And with this knowing, I then began to ask, so if I have everything I need . . . then why am I waiting for others to give me the green light on my dreams? Why would I let a publisher decide if my story is good enough to tell? Why would I wait for someone to ask me to speak at their event to share my message? Why am I waiting for someone else to give me the opportunity? Why not just create them myself?

And so I did.

I got into action.

The first thing I did was get clear. And I got clear by getting quiet and by getting that pencil to paper.

I asked myself these questions over and over:

What if I stopped waiting to be picked and I picked myself?

What if I stopped waiting for someone else to invite me to their stage and I built my own?

What if I unsubscribed to gatekeepers and just created my own opportunities?

What would that world look like?

I reminded myself it's right now that we get to taste the coffee and bite into pizza and dive into the water and bake the cookies and hold the hand and feel the sand and bask in the sun and walk

in the grass and hike the arch and feel the belly laugh and see the smile of delight and give the kisses goodnight. It's only right now. And even if we have hundreds or thousands of years left, it still won't be enough. Because once we don't have these miracles anymore, we will know, we will *know,* that when we *were* here, we had everything.

The universe had shown me very clearly there was one thing I did not want to be: the person waiting. Because the people who played the waiting game always lost.

So it was time. It was time to dream the dream now. It was time to go for it, to have the journey and allow my God-given map to guide me down my path.

And once I decided, it began to unfold.

The idea for my first children's book came through me, and I felt it right down to my bones. We were on vacation in Aruba, and while sitting on the beach, it all just downloaded. I am not sure where my phone was, but I remember frantically asking my family, "Does anyone have a paper? A pen? I need to write something down right now!" Aunt Penny was back in a flash with a little mini composite book and a pen, which I still have, and I wrote down the entire story of *More Than Mud* right there in that moment.

I had decided I was going to create my dream. My dream was to inspire others to live the life they were meant for. I decided that meant starting with children, my children, my two girls. I wanted to write a book for them, a guide, on how to live a limitless life, but in a language that children could understand. I got into action, and I did this by getting still every morning and connecting into my higher power, and I also did this by journaling each day. And once I got into motion, the rest came. It poured out of me onto the pages. Right there on that beach. And that book went on to be a #1 best-selling book and stayed on the best-seller list for over 100 weeks straight.

This was an opening. I knew it, I felt it, I received it, and I

went for it. We must be ready to walk through the openings when they come.

My next children's book was imagined by my daughter Bella when we were on vacation in Florida. She saw what a phenomenal journey it was to create *More Than Mud,* and she had a dream of creating something too. So she began to bounce ideas around. And then this one day, it was all there, it all came together, and we had our second book. Another divine download, just like the first one, right there in that pool in Ft. Lauderdale. *More Than Magic* was created and at five years old, my daughter Bella became a #1 best-selling author—since the story, after all, was hers.

My daughter Livie is now involved in the writing and illustrations of our books. She started with her first #1 best-seller, *Believe Big.* My husband, Mel, works on the back end of our business. We travel together. My girls and I speak on stages together, we do author readings and book signings, we visit schools and are hired for conferences and events. I have created not only my dream business, but my dream life.

I did not wait. I did not wait for the invitation, I did not wait for permission, I did not wait to be chosen.

I CHOSE ME.

I was born worthy. You were born worthy.

I was born with a dream. We deserve to live out our dreams.

I was born with what I needed to live my dream life beyond measure. We all have our own map inside. We just need to be reminded.

When I decided to create a new business and truly go after creating a dream, it was like coming home to myself. I made decisions based on what felt good, not the way everyone else was doing it. I conducted business based on my moral compass and my soul alignment, not based on what had always been done before. The people I surrounded myself with were more about the vibration they brought to the table, not the résumé. The actions I took each day always involved being still, setting clear intentions,

acknowledging and appreciating things in gratitude, and getting clear about what I was available for and inviting in. In the past, my daily required actions involved a certain amount of calls, emails, follow-ups, and meetings. I now had new non-negotiable actions because I realized that when you combine the foundation of the energetic alignment to the next action you take, it is magnified exponentially.

This is how I explain what has been built over the last twelve years. This is how I explain the wild success of my books, the outrageous success of the Inspired Impact Book Series, being offered my own TV Show, being featured in an award-nominated documentary alongside some of my well-known mentors, speaking on stage next to the greats of our time, and creating millions of dollars, millions of dreams, and millions of lives touched by waking up each morning and being completely head over heads in love with my life.

This is it.

I decided to dream. I decided to choose me. And when we bet on ourselves, we win.

Every
    Single
        Time.

We are just getting started.
We get to do this.
Your dreams are waiting. ALL OF THEM.
I love you.

Kate

ABOUT KATE BUTLER

Kate Butler is a TV Host, Publisher, #1 International Best-selling Author and Speaker. Kate is the host of the TV Show, "Where All Things Are Possible" which streams on Roku. She is also creator of the *Inspired Impact Book Series*, a #1 International Best-selling Series that has published over 300 authors. Kate focuses on taking your story and bringing it to life in a best-selling book . . . this is her specialty!

As a CPSC, Certified Professional Success Coach, she offers dynamic live and digital programs creating transformational experiences to ultimately help clients reach their greatest potential and live out their dreams, including becoming a #1 Best-selling Author through her mentorship. Kate believes in learning the tools to help create those "Made For Moments" in your life. Her passion is teaching others how to activate their authentic mission, share it for massive impact while also creating a lucrative business.

Kate's expertise has been featured on Fox 29, GoodDay Philadelphia, HBO, PHL 17, Roku the RVN network and many more tv and radio platforms.

Kate offers a variety of free tools on her website to help you get clear on what you want and also to show you the path to make it possible. Visit www.katebutlerbooks.com

Connect with Kate:

Facebook: @katebutlerbooks
Instagram: @katebutlerbooks
Website: www.katebutlerbooks.com

YOU ARE WORTHY

Tracey Watts Cirino

Have you ever had a dream sitting silently in you, but you kept pushing it down?

I know I have, and once I was given permission to fully dream and embrace all that is possible, it was like unleashing a never-ending water tower of hopes, dreams, and possibilities just waiting to be brought to life to share with the world.

If you have ever felt like your dreams have been silenced or you didn't feel worthy of having good things happen to you, let alone actually achieving your dreams or you haven't felt safe and supported to share your dreams, and somehow because of not feeling worthy, you silenced your dreams and shoved them all down so deep you were living a lie instead of the authentic life you were born to live, then this story is for you.

I'm a former award-winning salon owner of a salon that has been named one of the top 200 salons in North America seven different times and a #1 international best-selling author, speaker, digital course creator, and business success coach and trainer. I am a loving wife and mother and the friend you want in your corner to help you believe in the power of your dreams and your greatness.

But it didn't exactly start out this way. When I was young, I struggled with so many challenges and struggles and didn't know why I was different or what was wrong with me.

Later on, I eventually was labeled with dyslexia and severe ADHD. I refer to these as my learning differences because they forced me to create what I now call the "go-arounds," a unique path through learning and living with these differences.

Back then, I felt unworthy of love and true belonging. Greatness of any kind felt like it was unattainable, and I was in pain and living in total frustration and anger most days.

Eventually, all that pain and frustration actually led me to achieve my hopes and dreams once I stopped trying to hide all my flaws, trying so hard to be perfect, and realized there was real beauty in being me—flaws and all.

When I was struggling and trying to cover up all my cracks and imperfections, I was miserable. The more I tried to be perfect, the more life was a struggle only leading me on the journey of suffering analysis paralysis. It left me feeling defeated and truly miserable.

I didn't even love myself, and I didn't even know you were allowed or supposed to love yourself. So I really wasn't that much fun to be around back then.

Have you ever felt that way? So much pain and suffering you felt bad for who had to be around you?

Well, if you have or if you have not, that is where I was.

Over time with my go-arounds, I discovered that achieving your dreams is about progress over perfection and done is better than just another crazy idea that doesn't get accomplished. When we stay stuck in a self-sabotaging cycle of pursuing endless perfection, we tend to cause ourselves so much harm under the surface and limit our abilities to achieve our dreams.

Let's get started at one of the moments when I started having big dreams.

There I was at my very first hair show, and I was sitting in the

audience thinking, *Wow, these people are amazing, and they are talking to me directly. Are they living inside my head? Because I have never shared this stuff with anyone. How do they know everything I'm thinking?* I saw so many famous people in the salon industry doing amazing hair on stage, but for some reason, I really connected with Micheal Cole and Geno Stampora on stage, who at the time I didn't know this, but they were teaching us that anything was possible if we just believed. At just sixteen years old, I knew I was born to be on stage and empower people. I didn't know why I felt this way or how it was going to happen. I just knew with every fiber of my being that I was born for that. I remember thinking, *YES, please I want to do that!* Now I wish I could say that it was in this moment everything changed and I knew my calling and everything was smooth sailing from here. But this is real life, and real life is messy, painful, and filled with jagged edges that take us on a real journey of self-discovery. Right?

So let's get into it. At that time I was always told, "Who the F do you think you are? You are so crazy! You can't do that. You are not good enough! You must be crazy! Did you get dropped on your head? How selfish of you to believe you can do anything like that! What is wrong with you? You are not enough! Women are not allowed to do that. Especially women like you who are not that smart."

Have you been told any of these? As a young woman born with a very big dream and huge ambitions, I was often shamed into thinking I was not worthy of my dreams. The truth is, having big dreams made other people uncomfortable.

Fast-forward to a few years later, I was attending yet again another hair show at the Cleveland Convention Center, and I was asked if I had ever thought about being an educator on stage that teaches hair cutting, coloring, styling, and salon business best practices. Guess what my response was. "Yes, absolutely, every day of my life. Sign me up now!"

I practically attacked the man asking me this question.

When I was young, I never had anyone who really understood or even asked about what I was going through or what life was like for me. It felt like I wasn't even worthy of having an idea an opinion or a voice. So I suffered in silence, shoving down my hopes and dreams because I just didn't believe that I was worthy of them.

When I was asked if I had ever thought about being an educator and speaker on stage, I said yes because my intuition had told me years earlier that I was born for this, but I really had no idea what I was getting myself into.

Guess what happened next. They asked me to audition for a spot on the hair design team.

The audition consisted of five intense days of training where they gave you a four inch-thick manual and basically said, "Here, you have to memorize everything in this so you can start presenting on stage and teaching people how to use these products, how to grow their business, and how to do better haircuts and grow their color business. You must memorize this and present it on stage tomorrow."

At the time I had a limiting belief that I was not a good reader because my backward reading had gone undetected for so many years. I was petrified and pretty much shaking in my shoes. Enter the person who changed everything about my belief process. My first mentor and teacher Mr. Cary O'Brian saw me and shouted it out for everyone to hear.

"Hey, Tracey, do you have dyslexia?" *Um, what is happening here?* I was mortified and petrified all at the same time. I had been hiding my little secret forever. A few teachers had mentioned it to my parents, but they were so busy. We had so many kids in my family that they just kind of were like, "Oh, she'll be fine." That was actually a good thing because that's how I discovered the go-arounds that helped me discover how to learn in layers of auditory, visual, and practical application. It forced me to focus on people and really study their behaviors.

However, having Cary say this at this moment in front of a room of twenty-five people was mortifying. I felt like I was dying.

Then what he said next was what was actually most important . . . "Wow, you're doing so great, and I really like how you are presenting the material. Keep it up. Everyone else, do what Tracey is doing." *Wait what? Is he really talking to me?*

Daily, as we had to read out loud in front of this room, Cary would say, "Wow, Tracey, you're the youngest one here, and obviously, we've already talked about your learning struggles, and look how great you're doing." Every day when I made a speech and gave my presentation, he referenced how great my speech was and made a comment about how if I could do it, anyone can do it—which has sort of been my anthem for life ever since.

Trust me when I say if I can do it, you, my friend, can do it too!

Cary was the first person I've ever met in my adult life who saw me and the shameful secret I had buried deep and was hiding from the whole world and still believed in me anyway.

So at that moment in time, the twenty-five of us got narrowed down to four of us, and within just a few months, we were down to just one. And guess who that was. Yup, it was me.

I somehow made it through the dark valley of feeling small and unworthy because one person saw something and believed in me.

So even if the world tells you that you can't do something—because let's face it, if you have failed English in the past as I had or if you have been told your whole life that you're not a good writer, singer, speaker, or aren't worthy of speaking because no one cares what you have to say or you're hoping and dreaming of being a great speaker presenting on stage or being a published author and you kind of shove those down—you'll realize there are Carys in the world who crack you open and help you believe that everything you have been dreaming about is actually possible. In a world filled with noise and often so much judgment, we are constantly told to stop dreaming and be realistic. We are told to get real.

I used to beat myself up or believe something was wrong with me because I was always dreaming and I had big dreams and huge visions for what life could be. I loved fairy tales and truly believed in the possibility of happily ever after.

How about you? I consider it my personal mission to help others believe in their dreams even if everyone around them tells them it is not possible. Even if they have silenced and shoved these dreams down for years and years.

Dreams are the secret ingredient for the magical recipe for us to grow and create a life we love and become the absolute best versions of ourselves. Dreams are the cure that keep us going on our darkest days when it seems like we can't take one more step up the mountain of life—carrying all of our baggage of old hurts, tears, fears, and unkind words, and maybe even years of disappointment and letdowns. Dreams that we hold in our hearts give us the energy we need to take one more step up the mountain. Believing in what is possible or what could be is all we've got.

No matter where you are today on your climb up the mountain of life, just start from where you are. No matter what has happened and what past hurts make you feel like you are not enough. Start from where you are. If you haven't dreamed in a while, think of one tiny little thing, like a wish, you would like to happen. It could be the smallest thing, no matter how big or small, and write it down and start from where you are.

If no one in your life has ever believed in you or your dreams, my friend, that changes for you today because you now have me, and I want to be your Cary. I believe in you and the power of your dreams.

Even if we have not met yet, I want you to know I truly believe in you and your dreams.

It is that simple and I just do! You deserve everything you've ever wanted or dreamed of simply because you do. This is your birthright. Your dreams choose you for a reason and when it

comes to making your dreams come true in your life and in your business, this is my most favorite thing to help you do.

Helping you turn your dreams into your personal reality—whether it is turning that purpose of your dreams into a profitable business or re-clarifying your life so that you can live in better alignment with your dreams—your passion and your purpose is my core genius, and I am just getting started.

Okay, now we have a dream. Now what? Why do you believe in the power of your dreams?

That is the first step that is actually why I was first attracted to the hair and beauty industry because salon and beauty people were always so happy. I had never experienced any other place on Earth like that—better than Disneyland for me. So if you believe that you deserve to achieve your dreams, that's what will happen for you.

Our standards and how things feel are what we truly achieve. I know that things feel right when I am working from my faith and purpose and expanding and growing in the direction of my dream and when I am helping others do this too. It feels as though I'm completely filled with all the god bumps (that is what I call goosebumps) and absolutely exhilaratingly living my absolute best life.

Once Cary showed up for me in a real genuine way and absolutely believed that anything was possible for me, it allowed me to create space and allow so many other hopes and dreams to come to fruition in my life. Accepting that I am guided by God's hand and the universal higher power is always protecting me and leading me in the direction that is best for me and the greater good of all who I have been called to serve is truly me living in pure alignment with my purpose and my mission here on this Earth.

Once I surrender to the idea that things are exactly as they were meant to be, the real magic of dreams coming true actually happens. Even when your current life and circumstances send you on a detour, you will discover more blessings and gifts beyond

your imagination and a whole new way of dreaming bigger than you ever thought possible when you believe that you are absolutely worthy.

When we quiet the mind enough to enjoy our breath and our beating heart, we are guided by divinely trusting our own intuition and inner call to go within and experience life in peace and joy no matter what is happening in the outer world. Everything falls into place when we choose inner peace and wellness. The outside world doesn't matter. Loving your life, what you do and how you contribute to the world, is the path that allows us to achieve our dreams from a place of knowing all is well and good within us and within the world.

When I believed it was possible and had the correct recipe, everything worked out in my life and business. That alone with no action will not help you achieve your dreams. Action without intention and true belief that you are worthy and everything is possible will not produce the result you're looking for. Only when you combine a positive mindset, true belief, and knowing that you are absolutely worthy along with the purposeful action and a success strategy and recipe will your dreams come to be.

Once I realized all of this, I realized I had been dreaming too small, though I had achieved quite a bit of success to the outside world. But I still had been suffering unfulfilled and feeling like part of my heart was missing. Once I realized I was called to serve a bigger purpose to help more people than I could from just inside my salon, that's when I sold it, started the Beyond Common Success Coaching and training company, created the Beyond Common Success method, and started speaking and writing because my dream of helping over ten million women achieve the life and business of their dreams was not gonna happen until I started sharing my passion, my purpose, and my story with everyone.

If you're feeling called to do something bigger and follow your dreams, I would love your help to spread the message so we

can help ten million women together. If you have a dream in your heart that has been silenced and shoved down for far too long, I would love to be your Cary—the person in your corner who really believes in you and encourages you to follow your dreams and pursue your passions. We only have one life to live, and your time is NOW!

A great first step is to sign up for a Beyond Common Success Essentials training to help you get really clear and really present on where you are and where you want to go. I would love to help you believe in the power of your dreams and help you turn them into your new reality.

With love and gratitude,

Tracey Watts Cirino

This story is about my very first mentor, Mr. Cary O'Brien, who believed in me and saw something special in me when I didn't even know what that meant. There were so many times I wanted to quit and give up, and he encouraged me to keep pursuing my dreams no matter what. He has touched my heart and positively impacted so many lives in the hair and beauty industry and beyond, and I just wanted to honor him in this very special way. To pay tribute to his wife Talisa O'Brien and their four beautiful daughters Sydney, Mia, Chloe, and Isabel so that they know that even in passing, his legacy will forever live on because of all the lives he touched. My life and my purpose were positively impacted when I meet someone who believed in me and that is why I believe in you and the power of your dreams with such passion and conviction because knowing that just one person believes in us makes a world of difference that cannot be measured. It can only be treasured and paid forward by the lives that we have the honor and privilege to impact.

It is my hope that Cary's amazing legacy will live on forever by honoring him here forever in my story for Women Who Dream! Keep Dreaming!

TRACEY WATTS CIRINO

#1 International Bestselling Author and Speaker, podcast host of Beyond Common Business Secrets. As a thought leader, and unshakable optimist dedicated to helping you get out of your own way so you can become the person you most want to be. She is a former award-winning salon owner and most sought-after color transformation expert turned business success coach and strategist. As an all-in, no BS, passionate female business success coach and speaker Tracey loves doing keynotes, hosting retreats, training workshops, masterminds, and lighting up the stage to deliver her Beyond Common Success message of Hope & Possibility. She is Certified in the Canfield Success Principles, John C. Maxwell Certified Speaker, Coach, and Trainer as well as Tony Robbins Business Mastery.

She launched her hairstylist career as a stage artist who worked alongside the salon industry's most iconic teachers when she was just 19 years old. Tracey's business, Lavish Color Salon, is a 7-time winner of Salon Today Magazine's top 200 awards. Tracey then sold Lavish Color Salon to follow her passion and focus full-time on helping motivated business owners align their purpose with their passion and business. Beyond Common Success Coaching and Training, Co. was born and now we get to help more business owners and leaders achieve success and live the life of their dreams. Tracey is a Cleveland, OH native who enojys a hike or cooking with her kids and her husband with their dog Rocky right at their heels.

To connect with Tracey:

Web: www.TraceyWattsCirino.com/dreambig
Facebook: Tracey Watts Cirino
Instagram: @traceywattscirino
LinkedIn: TraceyWattsCirino
TikTok: @traceywattscirino

LIVING MY DREAM THROUGH THE FEAR

Ellen M. Craine

"Don't be pushed around by the fears in your mind. Be led by the dreams in your heart."

—Roy T. Bennett

My eighteen-year-old son, Michael, is a pediatric cancer thriver, diagnosed at age eleven. I am not naïve enough to think that we are among the lucky. In the beginning, I felt fear at everything my son endured. I felt fear over whether he would survive the treatments, let alone the cancer. We were fortunate to incorporate integrative medicine, including mistletoe therapy, into my son's treatment plan. I believe, as do his doctors, that it helped him have fewer complications and bounce back more quickly from his chemotherapy. We still have anxiety with every "major" symptom my son has. I am eternally grateful for my son's medical team and their remaining presence to support us on this journey and help us navigate through these challenges.

I do not wish this journey on anyone, regardless of prognosis. I feel the fear and anxiety, but in my heart, I also dream of a world where integrative medicine is available for all pediatric patients and their families as an adjunct to conventional medicine if they

want it. Perhaps this is my way of coming to terms with being a pediatric cancer mom. I do not know. What I do know is that I feel a passion or excitement in my gut and heart when I think about helping other families navigate their cancer journey. I try to focus on this dream and not my fear about my son's potential for relapsing or developing another cancer as we navigate "normal" illnesses or symptoms that may crop up.

I strongly believe families should have integrative medicine available to them without the barrier of finances. Juggling finances when you have a sick family member is a given unless you can afford to take time off work, have a great support system, and the list goes on. It has become a passion of mine to provide resources to my son's outpatient team through education so they can offer these services to other children and their families. To support this dream, my family has established a fund at my son's treating hospital, Beaumont Children's Hospital in Royal Oak, Michigan. Michael's doctor has discretion to use this fund to help children get integrative medicine consultations with the naturopathic oncologist at the hospital. The fund is set up to even help pay for some of the services that may become part of a child's treatment plan.

There are now salt lamps and essential oil diffusers in each outpatient pediatric private infusion room. To my son's doctor's credit, she did fellowship training through a program put on by Beaumont Hospital. I am honored because she has shared that I was a big influence in her decision to take this training and to make some changes in the way things are handled in the outpatient setting for her patients. I was fortunate enough to be a guest lecturer on two different occasions discussing oncology.

It is my dream and passion to continue this work supporting those who want guidance and need help with where to look for a complementary approach to healing emotionally and physically, regardless of prognosis from a pediatric cancer diagnosis. I do not wish this journey on anyone, but having lived through it, and

being a social worker, I am uniquely qualified to provide coaching and support to someone who wants it. I believe it is a higher power within me that allows me to push through and toward this dream of helping others on their journey. I can honestly say that I may not know exactly how someone feels or what their specific journey is like for them, but I can share my experiences and my journey.

About two years after Michael's journey began, and just when we thought we would start to be living a more "normal" life, my husband, Marty, was diagnosed with Stage IV inoperable glioblastoma. He died April 26, 2016, six weeks after his diagnosis. Admittedly, I am not sure I have found my passion or dream around this one. It was definitely harder to navigate the medical system when it comes to integrative medicine. I still struggle to know why the Universe has "gifted" me and my sons with this challenge. I imagine that will eventually come to me. What I do know is that my passion to make the world a better place for my family and others has not died. I am grateful for that. Maybe that passion is enough of a takeaway from Marty's death. Time will tell.

Moving forward five and a half years later, I thought my sons and I were finally gaining some peace in our life. This did not eliminate the grief we each felt with Marty's absence, or the anxiety with every challenge Michael faced, but we slowly started to feel that we could have dreams for our lives and move toward them.

Halloween weekend, 2020, everything started to change. I found a lump in my left breast. Admittedly, I may have felt something smaller a couple of weeks before but minimized the whole thing. Somewhere deep in my gut, I knew it was cancer.

The next week, I saw my gynecologist, had my mammogram and ultrasound, then a biopsy the following Monday. The results came in. I had Stage II breast cancer, invasive ductile carcinoma. I would be looking at a treatment plan that included eighteen rounds of chemotherapy, surgery of some kind, and possible radiation. I was overwhelmed, to say the least, and could not imagine

how I would get through everything. Keep in mind, this was all during COVID, and I had to navigate this on my own—no one could come to appointments. Marty was not there to support me. I have friends, and some excellent ones at that, but that is not the same as having a significant other who can hold and comfort you any time of the day or night.

Additional testing and meetings with a breast surgeon and oncologist followed. Following an MRI, one of the last pieces needed before surgery, a Stage 0 cancer was found in my right breast. By Thanksgiving, I had a port placed in my chest to receive my chemotherapy every twenty-one days until what felt like forever. I could not believe what was happening. The good news appeared to be that there were no lymph nodes on either side that were affected. At this point, I had already had six rounds of chemotherapy with lots of side effects.

I began seeing my treatment in phases. All the testing was one phase. There were a lot of ups and downs throughout this process for me and my kids. I (and we) survived that! My initial six rounds of chemotherapy with the harshest drugs I would be given was another phase. This was very difficult for my twenty-two-year-old, who had already been through so much losing his dad and dealing with his brother's cancer. Matthew now had to be a caregiver for me and his brother while going to school at home, online, during the pandemic.

Surgery was my next phase. My surgeon was recommending a double mastectomy. I was having a hard time wrapping my head around this news. On the one hand, I understood where she was coming from with both breasts being affected by a different type of cancer. On the other hand, a double mastectomy? I hoped I could just have a double lumpectomy and breast reduction at the same time.

One question remained, and it was a big one: did I have any gene mutations that gave me a pre-disposition to breast cancer? This was a concern since my dad had had pancreatic cancer

diagnosed at the age of eighty-two, and his mother was diagnosed with breast cancer when she was sixty-three. There is no known family history of ovarian cancer. I was fearful of finding out I had a gene mutation, not fully understanding the power it would give me if I did. I prayed I was negative and could have the surgery I really wanted. I asked the Universe to guide me to make the best decision for me and my sons.

The genetic testing process included a phone consultation (due to the challenges of COVID) with the genetics counselor and a blood test. After a couple of weeks, I learned that I was BRCA1 and BRCA2 (the most commonly known gene mutations) negative! I was thrilled. Then, the genetics counselor shared that they found I have a newer gene mutation called PALB2. Wait, what? This gene mutation had only been tested for since around 2014–2015. It is linked to pancreatic, breast, and ovarian cancer in women. There is a link with this gene mutation for pancreatic and breast cancer in men as well.

According to the PALB2 interest group, with this gene mutation, there is a 13 to 21 percent chance of breast cancer by the age of fifty and a 44 to 63 percent chance of breast cancer in cisgender females by the age of eighty. For cisgender males, the chance of breast cancer is less than 1 percent by the age of fifty and around 1 percent by the age of eighty. In the cisgender population, there is a 12 percent chance of breast cancer for females over our lifetime. By the age of eighty, people have around a 5 percent chance of getting ovarian cancer and around 2 to 3 percent chance of getting pancreatic cancer with this gene mutation. Cisgender females have an approximate 2 percent chance of getting pancreatic cancer without the gene mutation. At this time, there is no known increased risk for prostate cancer or colon cancer for anyone.[1]

Following my double mastectomy, I learned there was no

1— PALB2 Interest Group, "About the PALB2 gene," PALB2.org, accessed June 28, 2022, www.palb2.org/about-the-palb2-gene/.

cancer in the tissue analyzed. In addition, all of my lymph nodes removed out of an abundance of caution were also negative for cancer. I did not need radiation. So grateful! Finishing my eighteen rounds of chemotherapy December 9, 2021, was the end of another phase in my journey!

It will have been eighteen months since my journey with breast cancer began by the time this chapter is published. One takeaway from this first year of being a cancer patient is that knowledge is power. Getting a cancer diagnosis is scary, but do not give up on your dreams and passions for your life. Learning all you can about your family history and genetic predisposition can be a big help in treatment planning. It may even be lifesaving.

In my breast cancer journey, I incorporate a lot of complementary medicine into my self-care. I learned and did as much as I could before I was diagnosed and continued to do so during treatment. I honestly believe that in spite of all the challenges during treatment, I did as well as I did because of what I did. I am confident that I did not cause my cancer; I was just more susceptible to it because of my genetic makeup. However, I believe in my heart that taking control of my life the best I can is important. It is about even taking just five percent more responsibility each day for my life. For me, this means taking supplements, making sure I am drinking enough water, getting adequate sleep, meditating, exercising, eating as healthy as I can, journaling, asking for help when I need to (something I am learning how to do), having a positive mindset, participating in personal growth training, seeing a therapist, and, yes, giving myself mistletoe injections.

The adult cancer world is harder to navigate than the pediatric cancer world. My dream/passion is to make this world a little easier to navigate by being a coach, educator, and support person for those who want it. I hope by sharing my journey and educating others about the importance of knowing family history and our genetics, I am making a positive impact on at least one person's life.

I am lucky to be looking at my life from the other side of a cancer diagnosis. As I do that, I see helping others on their journey as a piece of my journey moving forward. I believe in the importance of facilitating and having authentic conversations with others on these difficult topics is the key to moving forward in life in a more positive way. I provide individual and family support, so reach out if you need help facilitating these authentic conversations with yourself or with family members or friends. I can be reached at ellen@crainecounseling.com.

I have made an agreement with myself, my children, and others, that I will be around on this earth for at least another thirty years. First and foremost, that is my dream and passion regardless of all the others. I intend to do everything within my power to make that agreement become reality. A good friend of mine shared a message she received from my husband when I was diagnosed, and I still carry it with me today. It said, "I am the captain of my ship." I believe that I am and that we all can be. I look forward to helping you figure out how to be the captain of your own ship.

For more information about mistletoe therapy, visit www.believebig.org.

ABOUT ELLEN M. CRAINE

Ellen M. Craine is in private practice as a licensed clinical and macro social worker in the state of Michigan. She owns Craine Counseling and Consulting Group and has over twenty-five years of experience working with couples, families, groups, and individuals in a variety of capacities. Ellen M. Craine is an effective trainer and educator. She teaches a variety of continuing education classes around ethics for social workers, including informed consent and telehealth, subpoenas, loss and grief, custody and co-parenting issues, and success principles for social workers and others. You can see a full list of her offerings and upcoming events on her website at www.crainecounseling.com.

Ellen M. Craine had her master's degree in social work from the University of Michigan. [CC1] [e2] [e3] In addition, she has a certificate from the Institute of Integrative Nutrition in Health Coaching and is a certified trainer in Jack Canfield's Success Principles.

Ellen M. Craine is a #1 International Bestselling Author in *Women Who Empower*, the seventh book in the Impact Book Series with Kate Butler.

Ellen M. Craine is a co-associate producer of the documentary, *Authentic Conversations: Deep Talk with the Masters.* This documentary is the first in the documentary series and is written, directed, and produced by LA Emmy nominated Dr. Angela Sadler Williamson.

You can learn more about Ellen M. Craine on her website: www.crainecounseling.com

Facebook group: Living through Loss and Grief
Facebook page: Craine Counseling and Consulting Group
LinkedIn: Ellen Craine
Email: ellen@crainecounseling.com

DAYDREAM BELIEVER

Addy M. Kujawa, CAE, DES

"To achieve your dreams, work is required. Suffering is optional."

—Jack Canfield

I grew up in a small, small town. The same town my parents, and their parents, had lived their entire lives. I dreamed of leaving and living in some far-off, distant place. I wanted to be rich and live big and large and loud, and I knew that wasn't going to happen in my little town in Wisconsin.

It was a beautiful, sunny, summer day, and my mom and I were going garage-saleing! I was excited because we were looking for new clothes for my new middle school. I had to move schools, and I was leaving my good friends behind, but it was all right because they were all just a short walk away. The new school was bigger and had art and band and even a real wood shop. I was going to take classes to learn how to cook and bake and sew and make notepads, and I was so excited. We found a beautiful blue dress with flowers and ruffles along with a few other things, and we headed home. I was happy and ready.

Standing at my locker on my first day, I fumbled with the combination. It was the first time I'd had to use a locker, and

I was worried I was going to be late to my first class. I looked around to see kids heading to classes.

To my left, there was a beautiful blonde girl watching me. I smiled quickly and got back to my locker. I heard her call out to me, so I turned to look at her again. She said, "Hey, where'd you get that dress anyway?"

Immediate panic. I was not going to tell her I got it at a garage sale. "Penney's!" I shouted.

She stared at me. Her head tilted and her arms crossed and a smile slowly crept across her face, and she said, "Oh, I don't think so. I think you got that at my garage sale."

And I was crushed. Mortified. Why did I say anything at all? What an idiot! And of course, of course, she had to call me out. Why am I so stupid? Why do I have to be here? I want to go back to my old school. At least everyone there knew what was going on. They knew my family's situation. I went about my day and noticed stares and whispers and laughter. How did everyone hear about it so quickly? There's nothing I could do. I had to keep going, walking through long hallways and sitting through even longer classes. I set my jaw, feeling naked and embarrassed and like I just wanted to hide.

That winter, I was walking home from school one day, and I was so cold and my backpack was so heavy, and on top of that, I was lugging my tenor saxophone home for practice. I walked looking down at the ground for the most part, occasionally looking up when crossing streets. As I crossed the next street, I saw in the distance a thin figure all dressed in black standing at the bus stop. I had a moment to decide whether I was going to turn left or continue on my way which would take me right past him. I looked to my left, and it's uphill. I couldn't do it. I was already loaded down and so tired. I kept going. I thought it would be fine.

As I got closer, I saw he was watching me. And as I got closer, he just kept watching me. *Do I turn around?* I couldn't get any

distance because of the snow piled along the sidewalk. I kept going. Trudging. He started to make comments. "Hey, pretty girl." "Hey, girlie, whatchyou carrying?" "You look nice." "Wanna keep me company?" I kept going. *Why is it taking so long? Why can't my legs move any faster?*

And then I heard it. The worst sound in the world. His throat scraped and then he was spitting, and I felt it land in my hair with a soft but weighty thump. *Ohmygodohmygodohmygod. He. Spit. In. My. Hair. What do I do? What can I do?* I kept going. I hunched over further, hunkering down into my coat even more, hiding as best I could. *Keep going, keep going, keep going, keep going.* I was so angry and so hurt and the tears streaming down my face froze in place and I felt all alone.

Left. Right. Left. Right. And he was hollering at me, but he wasn't coming after me and that's all I cared about. I kept going and eventually I got home. My mom was furious. She wanted to kill him. I just wanted it out of my hair. It was frozen and I didn't want to touch it. I headed to the kitchen, dropping things as I went until I could lean my head into the kitchen sink and run warm water through my hair and keep running warm water until I felt certain it wasn't there anymore and I could scrub and scrub it out. *It's so gross. I'm so gross. Of course I deserve this.* I was bottom of the barrel at my new school. I was the odd duck.

Feelings of worthlessness, fear, loneliness, and desperation for external validation began there and followed me.

The next summer my family went on a trip to Chicago with my aunt and uncle and their kids. We visited a restaurant . . . Ed Debevic's. That was a magical experience for me. Why? Well, at this particular restaurant, the wait staff are rude. Like, really rude. Throwing straws, snarky comments, smart-ass replies to questions. As a kid, to see my parents and my aunts and uncles talked to that way was shocking! And funny! And then, at one point, the entire wait staff got up on all the countertops and the ledges between the seating areas and rocked out—dancing to a song. The entire

restaurant was engaged in the performance, and in that moment, I knew I was going to live there one day. People that lived here lived the way they wanted to; they talked the way they wanted to. At that age, I imagined everyone in Chicago must be like this and so that became my dream. To live in Chicago and be free.

I went back home, went to school, graduated, and got married. I agreed to move to an even smaller town if we would eventually move to a bigger city. After four years and still no move, among other things, we parted ways. I took a year to get myself back to rights, and then I made my first big leap. The first time I really felt like I was showing up for myself, and I was going to do what I wanted to do, and nobody was going to tell me otherwise or get in my way.

I had a month to get everything squared away to attend the University of Madison. Due to my divorce and my own fears and embarrassment, I couldn't get the financial aid to work out. With the prospect of college dwindling and the rent coming due, I applied at all the temp agencies I could find and took any job I could fit into my schedule. My sister suggested a part-time job at her favorite restaurant, Noodles and Company, if they offered free meals to employees like many restaurants did. I applied and began as a busser so I could eat. She was right, a free meal every shift! I worked really hard, and was eventually promoted to manager, and was able to quit my other temporary jobs. Except for Kohl's—the deals on clothes and shoes I was privy to while working returns at the service counter were too good to pass up, so I continued to pick up shifts there.

I worked six days a week at the restaurant, and they were long shifts. I hired so many college kids. I fired someone for the first time and the second time. I caught kids drinking on the job. I started smoking just to get a break. I picked up shifts at the other restaurant that was downtown. I scrubbed the ins and outs of freezers and storage lofts and disgusting coolers. I mopped floors and plunged toilets. I opened up the restaurant so the grease traps could be

emptied. That smell sticks with you; it is beyond anything I had ever experienced up until that time—and I grew up in farm country.

I loved working in the restaurant industry. After about two years, one of my best team members and friend told me she had been offered a job in college after graduation. I bemoaned the fact that I would never get there, sad to be left behind, and she blithely responded with "Why don't you come along? I could use a roommate!"

I canceled my lease and moved in with another friend to finish out my notice. While apartment hunting in Chicago, we found an absolutely perfect unit in a building on the north side. Close to the lake, on the rooftop level with a pool, outdoor access, two bedrooms, and our own patio. Located just a couple blocks from the "L," it was convenient to most anywhere in the city. We put down a deposit, and moving day was set.

I applied to temp agencies and restaurants. The first place I applied? Ed Debevic's of course! I was brought in for two interviews but didn't get the job. Devastating at the time. I was eventually offered an administrative assistant position with a nonprofit and I grabbed it. It wasn't what I wanted at all—the role, the salary, or the location. But it would pay the bills, and I would be able to eat, barely, so I took it.

I had a demanding, visionary boss and a huge workload. I loved what I was doing though. I worked hard. Between being afraid of disappointing or upsetting my boss and wanting and needing validation and the thrill of success, I would sometimes go in at 8:00 a.m. on Monday morning and work all the way through until 5:00 or 6:00 p.m. on Tuesday. Through the night, yes. Exhausted, I would go home and sleep, just to repeat that for Wednesday and Thursday. I knew most of the security guards from arriving early morning, leaving so late at night, and all my weekend treks into the building. I was driven and passionate and wanted more. I was in the Big City, but barely making ends meet.

After several years and two promotions, my manager was let

go. I was already helping out with those responsibilities and helped write the position description for a new hire. Handing in the finished document, the head of the department said to me, "Don't even think about going up for this job. The CEO will never consider you because you don't have a degree." I hadn't actually even considered going up for it, so I was completely blindsided. I turned around, embarrassed, and walked out. During my commute home that evening, my face was hot, tears flowed, and I struggled to shake the embarrassment. Those feelings evolved into frustration, and then anger. Suddenly I was yelling to myself, "Why not me?! I'm already doing a lot of it! I am so good enough!"

At home that night, I opened up my laptop and updated my cover letter and resume to match the position description I had finished earlier that day, and I submitted it to HR. I was sick with anxiety for days, but then my boss interviewed me. And then, I got the job! I continued to work hard and had the longest tenure in the department.

I always had of goal of making, and then continuing to make, twice my age in salary, so when I was thirty, I wanted to be making $60,000 and so on. I was getting close to that not happening, and I knew that any further promotions or career moves would require a bachelor's degree. I had been told often that the manager role I had earned was the last one I would be able to get based on experience only. I had earned my associate's after high school but had opted out of any further education at that time to get into the workforce as quickly as possible. I had taken a class here and there as I could but was still a year and a half away from fulfilling the credits I needed. It was always in the back of my mind, and then I had my first baby, and then my second.

Home with my second baby, on maternity leave, I decided now was the time to jump back into my degree and get it done. I'm not sure why I expected to have extra time while on maternity leave considering I hadn't had any with my first baby and I could

only take seven weeks. I got it in my mind though, and so I filed all the paperwork and started classes.

I took class after class after class with very few breaks to finish as quickly as possible. I did finish and began applying for my next big role: my first lead staff position! I was terrified but determined. I interviewed for many roles and lost many roles. Eventually though, I was offered the lead role for an organization that had three staff, and I was absolutely thrilled. I've been there for twelve extremely rewarding years.

I think back to that young girl often with her big dream and her struggle with her self-worth. A short story allows for only so much to be shared, and I shared two of my most poignant memories out of hundreds that took a toll on me growing up. Just as you have many, I'm sure. All the things that happen in a person's life and the things you have overcome to be where you are. They matter and they are meaningful. And I also feel strongly that while they are meaningful, your past absolutely does not dictate your future.

Whatever dream you are dreaming, let it bloom and blossom in your heart and soul. Napoleon Hill said in his book, "Whatever your mind can conceive and believe, it can achieve."[1] **Your** mind. Not your mom's or your dad's or your sister's or your wife's or your husband's mind. Yours. You are the most important component of that sentence. It doesn't matter what others think or how they feel. It only matters what you believe and think and feel. Believe in you and your dream and work for it. Make them come true. That's what I did. And so can you.

> *"Make a conscious effort to surround yourself with positive, nourishing, and uplifting people—people who believe in you, encourage you to go after your dreams, and applaud your victories."* —Jack Canfield

---

1—Napoleon Hill, Think and Grow Rich (Meriden, Connecticut: The Ralston Society, 1937)

ABOUT ADDY M. KUJAWA, CAE, DES

With over twenty years of executive leadership for professional associations and organizations, Addy is today the CEO of the American Alliance of Orthopedic Executives as well as The Radical Change Group. She is a certified Jack Canfield Success Principles trainer, certified association executive, and certified digital event strategist.

In addition to her job, she has been a frequent speaker presenting on a variety of topics including personal branding, strategic planning, how to sell, how to negotiate, creating your true life destination roadmap, getting from where you are to where you want to be, goal setting that actually works, and much more.

She considers herself a personal and professional development junkie, constantly learning and trying new things.

Addy, as a consummate cheerleader and creator of safe places, has a life purpose to share with others her transformation of her life's events, from tragic and tragedy to appreciation and fulfillment, in hopes of inspiring and motivating them to see new possibilities and to believe in pursuing their own dreams.

To book Addy as a speaker or to work with her, you can contact her directly using the information below.

Web: theradicalchangegroup.com
Email: addykujawa@theradicalchangegroup.com
Mobile: 847-624-2339
Facebook: TheRadicalChangeGroup
Instagram: @theradicalchangegroup

THIS IS *NOT* HOW MY STORY ENDS

Christina Macro

My life began in turmoil, literally. When my mother was eight months pregnant with me, she fell down a flight of stairs into our unfinished basement through the bulkhead door so prevalent of the tiny Cape Cod cottage-style homes of the neighborhood in which we lived. She tossed me around in her belly all the way down ten stairs, then landed on the cold cement floor where she passed out. My father found her when he arrived home from work while my older brother screamed bloody murder in his crib. It was a scene from a tragic movie, thankfully without the tragic ending. My mom told me that story much later in life on one of our girl's week trips to Antigua, and she told me that it was that day that she knew I would be special. When I was born, she said she looked in my eyes and called me her little fighter.

We grew up poor. I mean dirt poor. My mom was a single mother raising four kids on a hairdresser "salary." She survived on tips, her income each year teetered around $16,000 a year. With that, she paid the mortgage, utilities, and fed four kids. With a little over a thousand dollars a month, it is a total miracle that we all survived. We learned to be thankful for the basic things in life like heat and a roof over our head. There were no frills in our

family, and as the only girl, I wore my brothers' hand-me-downs, from their sneakers to their underwear. I would pretend to be sick on gym days because I imagined the self-inflicted horror and embarrassment that would come with my changing into gym clothes in the girls' locker room. I had nightmares every night before gym days that all the girls would discover me sporting my brother's tighty-whities. I remember not being able to participate in class trips or events because my mother just could not afford the additional expense. I would pretend that I simply forgot the permission slip rather than admit that my family was poor and having heat was a higher priority than my taking class field trips. The number of days I spent in the supervised homeroom crying because I could not participate outweighed the number of days that I felt a sense of belonging.

Even in my mother's belly, I experienced firsthand the cycle of being knocked down and dragged through the mud to pull myself up by the bootstraps, dust myself off, and search for ways to see the good, remain positive, and just be happy. I mean, after all, I was a product of a terrible fall in utero and I survived that— what could possibly be worse? I knew that I had this internal strength, and it was inherent in me. It was. It just was.

When I graduated from high school, I had this burning desire to get far away from home to go and conquer the world. I wanted so much for myself, and I knew that the only person who could get me there was the person staring back at me in the mirror. And off I went to the world before me. No matter what lay ahead, I wanted to have a positive impact on my life and in the world. I had big dreams for myself without the means, the tools, the financial support, nor mental capacity to create the path . . . and so it was. Throwing caution to the wind, off I went to conquer my dreams. *Broadway, here I come!*

And not even six years after graduating from high school with a dream in my heart and a skewed vision for sight, there I was stuffed in the bottom of the life barrel of tragic events, failing

miserably while digging my way up and out. I never went to college—I got married young and had a baby instead. Now without my son's father to support me and him, I landed on my own father's doorstep with his new family. With my eighteen-month-old baby and the contents of our life that fit in a rented passenger van, I had not a pot to piss in nor a window to throw it out of. To say that I was at my most vulnerable is an understatement. My father took me in without question. I was in enormous financial debt from mounting medical bills for my son's health issues. I was wet, cold, tired, hungry, and desperate for a way out of the mess I was in at the tender age of twenty-three. I was frantically searching for answers to a life that continued to hand me lemons with no way to make lemonade.

After moving in with my father and his family in Syracuse, I started a career as a waitress in the hotel industry. I worked three jobs when my son was a baby; yes, three. I would take the bus to a law firm during the day and work there opening files and answering phones, get back on the bus home after my day job, kiss my son, have some dinner, and change for my night job as a waitress. And on the weekends, I bartended.

This was not the life I dreamed of. Not in any way, shape, or form. I was living the *furthest* from my dreams. Sad, lonely, alone, longing for love, longing to belong, wishing I fit in, trying to care for a sick child, trying to earn a living. Trying to dig myself out emotionally; I didn't know where I belonged in the world, but I knew it was not at the bottom of that barrel.

I was broken, bruised, lifeless, and living. Barely. But I never stopped believing in me. I knew in my heart that my life experiences at that point were building a foundation for me. A foundation for greatness.

Cesare Pavese once was quoted to say, "We don't remember days, we remember moments."[1] I recall vividly the moment I

1—Cesare Pavese, Goodreads quotes, accessed June 28, 2022, https://www.goodreads.com/quotes/329380-we-do-not-remember-days-we-remember-moments-the-richness.

packed my life in the back seat of my sportscar for a promotion in Washington, DC. This was four years after I had landed on my father's doorstep. I had worked my way up the corporate ladder in the hotel world; I was on my way to an executive position with a hotel in a major metro market. I drove down the GW Parkway from upstate New York and watched with childhood wonder as I drove by iconic monuments like Arlington Cemetery and the Washington Monument. I had arrived. I was in the big city, and my next chapter, filled with hope and expectation, had finally begun. I had picked myself up and brushed myself off. I felt like I was finally advancing my dreams as I had intended. Somehow, in my mind, I knew that my dreams were about creating a life for my son that was in complete contrast to my childhood.

I worked in the hotel industry for ten years, I hit the proverbial glass ceiling set as high as possible for a woman without a degree. I went back to school and earned my network engineering certifications, then off I went to the IT industry; I spent two years working my way up *that* corporate ladder and achieving titles and benefits that small-town girls without a degree could only fathom. We hit the dot-com boom, and I was without a job. I went back to school, this time obtaining my real estate license.

I can clearly recall my first day at my first brokerage. We were in a training class and the instructor asked everyone to go around the room and share their first-year vision in their new career. Each agent stood up and said things like "I want to help people" or "I love houses" or "I want to learn how the industry works." I was the very last person in the entire room of over fifty new agents to speak. I stood up with all the conviction of a seasoned real estate veteran and said, "I am going to sell ten million dollars my first year." I will never forget the look on the instructor's face as her eyes rolled almost completely back in her head. She asked me why I had this particular dream. And with all the clarity in the world, I said, "Look, I don't want to sell real estate for the money. I want to sell real estate because I want to advocate for people and teach

them what the home-buying/home-selling experience should be and what an agent's role is in a real estate transaction. But let's be clear here, I am not independently wealthy, and frankly, I don't even know how I'll afford my first year in business. But I do know this: I have a vision for myself, and I know that if I focus on being the best agent I can be *for* my clients, then the money will follow." Again, she rolled her eyes. I settled almost $10M my first year. I moved on in that industry to earn awards and accolades galore.

Excellence, it seemed, was within my grasp. This financial vision was fostered from my desire to provide a lifestyle for my son that *I* only ever visualized. I finally had the ability to control my own destiny—as my father said to me, "The harder I work, the luckier I get." And I knew in that moment that even without the degrees or the family coat of arms, I *could* get myself places and sail past the industry statistics. I was the one percent.

In my ten years in production, I created financial stability for the first time in my life for me and my son. And then the real estate crash happened. It was about that time that I grasped the reality that I had been living a lifestyle no one could sustain long term. Earning a six-figure income and saving only a fraction meant that when the market crashed, I also faced a financial crisis. And again, I was looking at life through the bottom of the life barrel trying to, once again, dig my way up and out. My 401(k) went from stable to abominable. I started to blow through savings at an alarming rate to maintain my lifestyle. I started to live on credit. And I was sinking quickly. I was crashing hard and fast alongside the real estate market. I had to change course. I found myself once again in survival mode and forging a trail with rewritten dreams consisting of a new career path. I was still focused on my son and ways to build a life for him. My dreams were still about him and ways I could provide for him financially and emotionally.

So, having the foresight to see what was happening in the market, I earned my broker's license and started to hit the streets

to advance my career in leadership. I had missed leadership, so the timing was perfect. I was offered a position as a managing broker with a steady salary, benefits, and a more stable schedule. By this time, my son was in his first year in college and I was paying in full for his education. I got down to brass tacks, built a budget, started selling off things, reduced my lifestyle, gave up the shopping trips, repurposed everything, and paid all my debts. Every last one. And I learned how to live within my means, save, balance, and reduce to a lifestyle focused on needs versus wants while staying committed to supporting my son's almost-adult life.

Once I pieced myself back together from the real estate crash and a terrible divorce, I rebuilt my life, got myself stable, and did everything to continue to focus on my son's stability. It was when he earned his MBA and moved to Chicago with his girlfriend that I began to unravel. And unravel I did, slowly and without any indication of the pain and hurt of being knocked down that was the history of my life experience.

They say that sons are your sons until they marry their wife. This realization hit me hard. It was unfolding before my eyes. I spent my life focused on providing for him. From the moment that child was born, my dreams were actually dreams for his happiness. While this was not necessarily intentional, it was real. Palpable. And who I became. Every day of my life was intensely fixated on ensuring his happiness. Until he left. Without warning and without an ounce of preparation for the thick wall of sadness about to smack me upside the head, he was gone.

When you live your life in a space where your dreams are built around fighting hard every day to provide a lifestyle far removed from your own, it is a fall from grace that can only be described as a poignant and perceptual free fall from a hundred-story building. Sadly, the free fall is one that moves slowly and deliberately in a way that you don't feel until you land on the cement in a million tiny pieces with no emotional glue to put yourself back together.

The year 2016 was the year that began this free fall for me. It was a year. I was fired from my job. Two weeks later, my mom quickly and unexpectedly died. And two months later, my son got married. I suffered losses at the hands of life and God; my coping mechanisms were on overdrive from July of that year. My internal mechanisms were working against me. My body began the debilitating process of dealing with depression and loneliness. I found myself stressed nonstop. I was dealing with the financial burden of my mother dying alongside the emotional trauma of my entire life purpose being stripped from me. All in a matter of weeks.

Just when I got my act together and was ready to heal over the loss of my mother, my father up and died. This went on for another year . . . loss, sadness, depression, grief.

The day after my father died, I laid in bed looking at the ceiling of my bedroom. For the first time in a long time, I cried. I don't cry. I internalize just like my mother. I breathe. I focus forward. I walk, I read. I listen to others. I volunteer. I escape the internal demons. But on this day, I cried. I begged for forgiveness for whatever I had done in my past leading to this intense sadness. I begged karma to back off. I begged my father to stop being mad at the life he chose. I prayed that my mother would not be mad for decisions I made. I cried for the loss of my son. I cried for all the events in my life that required me to be strong. I prayed for strength. I wished for angels to watch over me. I prayed for forgiveness like I had never prayed before.

I wanted clarity and to be whole. For one fucking time in my life. Once. To not deal with being kicked in the teeth. To just have a day without sadness and grief. I was tired of suffering. And tired of suffering at the hands of others.

That very morning, and for the first time in over three years, I stripped myself naked and stepped on the scale. I thought I was seeing things. I had gained almost 100 pounds during the turmoil that was my life. I could hardly breathe when I stepped

on and off the scale a number of times hoping that it was just another event in my life that was unreal.

When they say life is a series of ups and downs, I believed it that morning. I reflected on my life to that point and knew that my life was a series of gut punches that required me to reach deep within to get back up. As I stood on the scale, I realized I had not gotten back up since 2011. I didn't sink quickly to the bottom of the ocean floor; I sank slowly and deliberately over the course of 84 months or 336 weeks . . . slowly eating myself to death. Slowly padding layers of protective fat to keep myself from being seen anymore. I was down for the count. And down for good. That same day, I received an email that changed me forever "Dear Christina, thank you so much for applying for healthcare coverage with our specialized plans designed for the self-employed . . . blah, blah, blah, blah, blah . . . we are sorry to inform you that we cannot underwrite a policy for you due to your weight status considered to be morbidly obese . . ." I stopped at those two words. Morbidly obese. I am morbidly obese? I said it over and over in my head.

The next morning, I awoke with a fire within me that I had not experienced in many years. The flame that breathes life into a decaying spirit and the hopelessness built over years of dejection and grief. I opened my journal that morning and wrote these words: "Things must change." And I then wrote out a list of the things in my life that needed to change starting with my unhealthy relationship with food, my weight, and my stress levels. I knew that I had to start with my weight—I knew that getting my weight under control would positively impact all the other failings of my life.

Finally, I was taking control and succeeding at getting my health back on track and doing all the things that an emotionally healthy person does. Six months later, I was in the hospital with incredible numbness and pain throughout my arms, back, and hands. I was diagnosed with RA, a debilitating autoimmune

disease that wreaked havoc on my body and crushed my spirit. My body was failing me. Suddenly, my diet became the most important focus of my life. And my emotional well-being was at the root of it all. I had to find a way to get back up, but this time I could *not* do it alone. For the first time in my life. I needed help. This time, both my mother and my father were not available to call. Or to lean on. I was truly alone.

By the start of 2020, I had lost eighty pounds. I got the emotional support I needed through a therapist and a business coach. I was working toward the next phase of my life. I had just completed my bachelor's degree in real estate completely online; I graduated Magna Cum Laude and won all the awards. I was accepted in the number two grad school in the country for real estate. I was back in production, just earning enough to cover my monthly nut and also have enough to save. My credit scores were back where they belonged, my savings was back to a respectable level, my 401(k) was growing, and I was doing all the things to reduce stress, sadness, depression while avoiding yet another kick in the teeth. Lord knows I had fought my way through so many in my life. I was over it and wanted a month of pure joy. And then . . . COVID.

With RA, I was that person who did not leave the house. I ordered groceries three weeks in advance, only left the house to walk around my own neighborhood, converted my entire life to Zoom calls, conference calls, and remaining in total fear of catching and dying of COVID. But it was the perfect year to earn my master's degree at a school that was fully online. I mean, we were all stuck inside. I made the best use of my time by studying. And study I did! I graduated top in my class and won all the awards for my cohort. I was selected to compete in a development project competing with schools like Wharton and UNC.

I vividly remember lying in the hospital emergency room in August of 2020. Almost two years had lapsed since I was diagnosed with RA—I was terrified and alone. I was so sick that I

could not get out of bed most days to even walk more than a few feet without my heart racing and my body giving out. I didn't even realize just how sick I was until I had some blood work completed about a month before. I drove myself to the ER. I arrived during the height of the COVID pandemic and immediately was put on every machine, monitor, and IV drip known to humankind. They took vials of blood. A few hours later, the attending doctor came in and said my blood work looked a mess (not in those words, of course) and asked if I had my affairs in order. *My affairs? In order?* Oh my god . . . I went black. My affairs? Like my end-of-life wishes? When he showed me my blood work, it became clear that yes, he was seriously asking if I had my affairs in order. My hemoglobin level teetered somewhere around seven. Just shy of needing a blood transfusion. My C-reactive protein levels had skyrocketed to over thirty-three, and if you aren't aware, that level is a sudden heart attack or stroke just waiting to send me to meet my maker. Every marker of bad health was evident in my lab work. It was the most alarming moment of my life. And I've had many alarming moments. This time was different. This time, I was no longer fighting for my career or my child's well-being. This time, I was fighting for me.

In all my life, I never thought I would face the end in such an in-my-face way. I thought I would die old in a hospice bed with my son by my side whispering that it's okay and I could go knowing that he loved me. Just like the way I said good-bye to my own mother. While I was in the hospital, I reflected on my life. I thought about my childhood. I thought about my mother falling down the stairs and my unlikely survival into the world. I thought about who I wanted to be. I reflected on being knocked down and getting right back up no matter what life threw in my face. I thought about my dreams. I thought about January 19, 2019, and how my father's death impacted my life choices and forced me to face reality and replace my old ideologies for new ones. I thought about the decisions I made and the sheer

determination to be better and do better. I whispered forgiveness. I begged for mercy. I had dreamed at every step of my journey with or without intention. And I wasn't going to stop now.

When I was released from the hospital, it was God who intervened in my life story. I was no longer in control. The diagnosis was hemolytic anemia—a very rare blood disorder in which the body's immune system attacks red blood cells. I was directed to call an oncologist to care for me and prepare a plan for healing. I found the best oncologist in the area and was able to get in the next day, through miracles. This man was truly my hero. My health insurance sucked and covered *nothing*. This doctor was able to place me in a program that provided my medical treatments for free. This treatment was not cheap—$35K per treatment—and I was required to have six of them. I was scheduled for my first infusion mid-October of 2020. I went into the oncologist office, and they brought me back to a room with patients being treated for cancer. Under my mask and sunglasses, I was crying for them. I was crying for myself. I was crying for my inability to control my life anymore. After being seated in my recliner and getting set up with the infusion, I sat staring at the ceiling. The same feeling that I had when my dad died. The same glare. I wanted never for my life to end this way. And once again, I recanted that this was *not* how my story would end. I had begun a healing journey, and healing was it. No ifs, ands, or buts. Healing. Nothing but healing for me.

After a series of infusions and a newfound respect for the medical community, all of my health conditions are in full remission. I've lost 100 pounds. And I refocused my life to one of pure joy and embracing everything that is. I was able to redirect my life in a way that held my dreams within grasp. Through my dreams, I have learned that our dreams are not always about the big vision or how things might unfold. But our dreams are truly about the flame of happiness that we fan with joy, good intentions, and clear vision.

Dreams are born out of the internal strength required of healing—whether we are healing physically, financially, mentally, spiritually, or emotionally. Healing is the process in which we either create and envision our dreams or we fall into the darkest space and cannot get back up. We have the option to choose. I chose to believe that my story would not end there. My story will be one of power and resilience. One of courage and greatness. And one of passion and kindness. It will have an ending that dreams are made of. And I am not done dreaming and in this phase of my life, for me.

ABOUT CHRISTINA MACRO

Christina is a genuine leader, an intellectual, an authentic entrepreneur tapping into her own inspiration to lead others to greatness. As a servant leader, she has succeeded exponentially in her career in real estate, and also personally as a mentor, coach, mother, and friend. Through humor and compassion, she shares her stories in hopes that others discover ways to find and use their voices to dig deep to the core of their being to radiate from the inside out. Christina truly believes that beauty emanates from our souls and we have the ability to build dreams from a centered space using self-respect and self-awareness as the footing. We are all on this planet to support one another, and Christina inherently lives through her generosity of spirit which is unmatched in guiding others to excellence.

Connect with Christina

Email: hi@thebrainybroker.com
Facebook: @thebrainybroker
Instagram: @thebrainybroker
Twitter: @thebrainybroker

NO MORE HIDING

Melissa Malland

The clouded fog. The chaos of guilt running through my head. Keeping busy so I keep repressing the pain and sadness. I suffered in silence for so long. I knew I needed help two weeks after giving birth to my son after suffering postpartum depression with my youngest and realizing some major financial issues were going to hurt my family. My OB-GYN prescribed some anti-depressants and my internist advised me to see a therapist. I was on my way to recovery.

Or was I? Or am I still?

Depression is real. Mental illness is real. Those who say "Get over it" or "It's all in your head" have never suffered with mental illness and, quite honestly, are ignorant. Giving birth to my sons saved me, and going through postpartum after my third child was born saved me. I realized that I had suffered my entire life, but it was never addressed. Going through postpartum depression was a tumultuous time for me, in more ways than one, but it has taught me more about myself, and it finally brought things to light about what I had been suffering from and continue to suffer from even still to this day.

I remember through each of my three pregnancies and deliv-

eries feeling sad and crying. My only solace was my kids. After giving birth to my third son weighing in at twelve pounds, three ounces, that's when it hit me. I was having some blood pressure issues while in the hospital and they kept a close eye on me. I was in the hospital for four days, which is customary after having a C-section. When I arrived home, I was so thrilled to have all of my boys with me under the same roof. I've always dreamed of having kids and a family. I now felt my family was complete, so I couldn't have been more ecstatic to finally be home with all of them.

The next morning I woke up and began taking care of my three sons. My mother lived right down the street from me and would come over to help me as I got "back on my feet." I remember that day she came over, and I just wasn't feeling like myself. She had told me I had this glazed-over look on my face. It was like someone else stepped into my body and I had disappeared. The best way to describe it was that I was functioning, I adored my baby, and I deeply craved spending time with all three of my boys, but *I* was gone. My body was working on robotic mode. I didn't have anything to say, and all I wanted to do was have my baby right next me as I slept.

Despite not having anything to say, I lost interest in things I once enjoyed doing, and I couldn't eat. I was just a body. Nothing more. The feeling of impending doom and the fear I was going to die loomed over me. Later that afternoon, I had ventured outside for the first time since giving birth to walk to the mailbox.

That same feeling started to come over me once again. I felt like I was going to pass out. It was as if God was on my side because my mother had been driving down the street at the same time. I waved her over frantically, and she pulled in my driveway.

My being sick was worrying all those close to me. She was a tad impatient as she was helping me every day since my husband went back to work and she was trying to run errands. I gulped down a glass of orange juice as she thought my blood sugar was

low. That wasn't it. Paranoia along with severe anxiety plagued me as well as this postpartum depression. I felt some pain in my shin, and I was petrified it was a blood clot as a result of my C-section.

My mother gave me orange juice and her daily pep talk as she tried so desperately to get her daughter back. People were starting to get frustrated with me, and they didn't understand why my behavior was so drastic and had changed dramatically. The worst part was I couldn't explain it either. My elation over having a baby was shrouded by some out-of-body experience that had stolen Melissa from her family and friends. The pain in my leg wouldn't dissipate. As my mother burped my baby and my two older boys played in their playroom, I quickly took the phone into the hallway and dialed 911—even though those people who were closest to me thought I was going insane and my thoughts were completely irrational and off base. But they neglected to understand that what was happening to me, both physically and mentally, was real. And as I sat on the steps, I could hear the sirens nearing.

The ambulance had quickly pulled into the driveway with a loud screech and first-aid responders hustled to the door. At that point, my mother had the baby in her arms as she burped him. She thought she had just seen a ghost and was completely perplexed about what was happening, as I had not told her that I called 911. The responders popped up the stretcher as my baby stayed in my mother's arms and my other two babies continued to play in their playroom.

I couldn't stop shaking, I couldn't catch my breath, the last thing I wanted to do was to be away from my babies. They were my only happiness. They were my solace. But no one believed me, no one could handle that my feelings were *real*. I was trapped and I couldn't get out, and those around me held me prisoner as well.

I learned so many years later that if you do not suffer from a mental illness, you can't understand it. There are ignorant people

out there, but I believe most people are simply not educated enough. The stigma centered around mental health/depression needs to be buried and never dug up again. It's ironic, but my husband who thought I was more of a hindrance, said, " I never would have believed anxiety and depression would be like this, but it is tough and it is real" after he had most recently gone through some events that caused his anxiety and depression.

I lay on the stretcher and looked back at my mother. My blood pressure continued to skyrocket as we headed to the hospital. When the ambulance doors opened, my father and husband were there. They looked like deer in headlights and didn't know what to expect. I went through a series of tests to check for the blood clot in my leg, and by the grace of God, I did not have one. Due to impatience, both my father and husband were itching to leave, and once again, I was viewed as a hindrance.

What no one understood was that I didn't feel like myself, but the feelings I did have were real. They were mine and I was almost made to feel humiliated for having any feelings whether they were mental or physical. That has always been the case, and it took almost fourteen years to finally recognize that my feelings are valid. That I don't have to, nor should I, continue to repress and suppress my feelings for the sake of others.

There were many dark days ahead. When I arrived home, my focus was on fixing myself. I began taking medication and seeing a therapist weekly. Thankfully, I was doing those things, because I was going to need the support. It was only two weeks after I had given birth when my husband lost his business. To make matters worse, I also found out that I was going to need major abdominal surgery. Due to having such large babies, my diastasis muscle split in half, and I had two hernias, which made me still look pregnant. I was grateful that I had some tools to use and help me cope with the major issues going on with me personally and my family.

My determination was to get better for me so I could be the best for my sons. Depression can make you question yourself

and feel insecure, less confident, less valued. I felt so many things during this time period. They were so palpable, but I couldn't home in on anything because of that outsider that invaded my mind and body. My mind needed to heal, and I needed to find myself again—or quite possibly, the new me. Quitting was not in my vocabulary, and that invader was going to be kicked to the curb. I wasn't going to allow this to steal my joy or stop my dreams from coming true. I had my teaching career, I was in the middle of completing my master's degree, and most importantly, there were memories to be made with my babies.

Besides taking medication and seeking therapy weekly, there were other things I began doing to help myself. I started walking everywhere and anywhere. I would walk around my neighborhood or find scenic boardwalks and areas near the water. Sometimes I would walk alone and sometimes I'd walk with my sons. The benefits of walking were immeasurable to me on so many levels. I was able to have some mental clarity and peace, and focus on the present while also getting back in shape. There are many people I know who suffer from depression, and I always recommending walking. As of today, fourteen years later, walking is still part of my daily routine and I highly recommend it.

Yoga became a huge part of my life while going through postpartum depression too. It was my outlet; an hour to myself. Yoga helped me focus on the present, the here and now, and most importantly, myself. Let's not forget that I was also meeting new people and socializing. I had been out of work after giving birth, and I was going to remain out of work because I needed to have major abdominal surgery, so socializing with others was important to me. Little did I realize that as each day would pass, all of these things I was implementing into my life was slowly but surely pushing the invader out. It helped me cope with the fact that I was having major surgery, which I've never had before in my life.

Fast-forward to life today. I returned to my teaching career. I

earned my master's degree and passed my state licensure exam to become a principal, all while going through postpartum depression. There was not just one contributing factor that led to my progress, but I can tell you that therapy was so huge for me that I still seek therapy today. The medications did help, along with walking and practicing yoga.

You are the only one who is going to take care of you. No matter how many times people will say they'll be there for you, unfortunately, I learned that during the most difficult time in my life, when I needed those closest to me, my best friend of thirteen years left my side. And I recently had to go through a traumatizing experience within my marriage that taught me so much.

And my sons have taught me so much. I will no longer feel embarrassed or suppress my feelings for the sake of others. I will continue to take care of myself and put myself first. Mental health is my passion, and I have become an advocate for new mothers and all who suffer from depression and anxiety. Don't hide. Don't be embarrassed or afraid. If I can push through and follow my dreams, so can you!

ABOUT MELISSA MALLAND

Melissa Malland has been a teacher for twenty-two years. She is a mom of three boys, ages nineteen, sixteen, and thirteen, and she has been married for twenty-two years. Melissa has a bachelor's degree in education and a master's degree in education administration. She is licensed by the state of New Jersey to serve as a principal in any school within the state. Melissa currently lives in Toms River, at the Jersey Shore, and has since the age of eight. Melissa loves spending her free time with her family, taking walks, spending time at the beach, and reading.

IT STARTS WITH TRUST

Sue Meitner

Beep, beep, beep, beep . . .

Is that my alarm? The noise keeps getting louder and louder. As I finally open my eyes, I realize it *is* my alarm—and it has been going off for the past thirty minutes! How is that possible?

I jump out of bed in a sheer panic. It's only 6:30 a.m., and I am already running behind. Those precious thirty minutes are lost—and as a single working mom, I would do anything to get them back.

I assess the situation and realize I still have enough time to shower and get dressed before waking up my daughter, Allyson. I take a speed shower, throw on my clothes, blow dry my hair, and slap on some makeup. It's days like these that I am grateful my other child is in college. That's one less schedule to juggle.

Okay . . . time to wake up Allyson. I open the door to her bedroom and am accosted by a smell that almost knocks me over. What on earth is that? Oh no. Did Allyson accidentally lock the dog in her room last night? I hit the light switch and Holy Christmas . . . the dog has literally pooped all over the bedroom floor. How is this happening to me, today of all days? I have a

meeting first thing this morning. I close my eyes and think to myself: *Do not lose your mind. Take one thing at a time.*

I gently wake up Allyson, and she instantly notices the smell and then sees the dog mess all over her floor. Before she can freak out, I calmly ask her to go into the bathroom to get dressed. I run downstairs to let the dog outside, and then grab a roll of paper towels and some carpet cleaner. I sprint back upstairs and stare at all the piles of poop. Where do I even start?

I'm going to tackle this one step at a time, as I do everything else in my life. I take off my sweater and start cleaning the carpet. I do the best I can but quickly realize this is a job for professionals. I'll call the carpet cleaner when I get to work. I walk out of Allyson's bedroom sweating from head to toe, smelling a bit like dog poop. It's time to start all over again with another shower.

Allyson and I finally get in the car and off we go. I take a deep breath. It's only 8:00 a.m., and I feel as though I have just run a marathon. Is this how every working mom feels as she grabs her keys and heads off to work? I drop Allyson off at school and realize that I still have time to grab an iced tea from Starbucks. That should get my morning back on track.

On the drive to the office, I sip my iced tea and remind myself how lucky I am, crazy morning and all. I have a career I absolutely love that allows me to help others. I am raising two wonderful children, and I am surrounded by friends and family who love and support me.

When I graduated from college, unaware of what type of job I wanted, fate led me to the mortgage industry where I have spent three decades growing a fruitful career while raising a family at the same time. I've had the luxury of attending my children's basketball games and tennis matches, visiting college campuses and taking family vacations. Admittedly, there were times I worked during a game or two . . . but who doesn't multitask?

Getting to this point in my life has not come easy. There have been many pivots along the way, and I'm sure there will be more

in the future. I am learning to embrace change and accept that it is part of my journey.

Juggling a career as a single mom is not easy . . . and simply not possible without *trust*. I must trust the people around me and my family and be willing to ask for help—whether it's with a load of laundry, preparing a meal, or going on a grocery store run. I can admit that I can't do it all by myself because it really does take a village. I am so lucky to have my parents living nearby and always willing to help. They have been wonderful stand-ins at school events and in times of mini-crises—like the time my son Drew totaled his car while I was in a board meeting.

I must also trust the people I work with. I have found that by surrounding yourself with people who are authentic and who genuinely want the best for you, you can't go wrong. Some of the best advice I've ever received was to identify your areas of weakness and hire people who are strong in those areas. Then trust them to do the job. When you give yourself permission to ask for and receive help at work, you tap into the true power of collaboration. And sometimes that leads you to discover even more about your business and yourself. I tend to be a big-picture person. I love to throw my all into every goal I set, but I sometimes need help determining the steps along the way. I know where I want to go, but I count on my team to help me get there and manage the details.

Admitting that you can't do it all can make you feel *vulnerable*. However, as I reflect on my career, I recognize that embracing my vulnerability is a strength. Being open and honest with others makes me authentic and a better leader. Accepting that I'm not always right and that I make mistakes allows me to pivot and change direction when necessary. It's so important to be open and honest with yourself—especially if you discover you aren't finding joy in achieving the goals you set for yourself. This doesn't make you a failure. It's merely an invitation to follow a new path so you

can continue growing and achieving to your highest potential. The summer of 2018 was my time to be vulnerable and to grow.

It was a hot July afternoon, and as we walked across the University of Alabama campus, my son Drew asked me how I liked the campus. I told him I loved it, and he asked, "How would you know? You've been on the phone with work the entire time." That was my wake-up call. I could not be everything to everyone, and something had to give. I couldn't fake it anymore. I needed to learn how to really be present—especially with my family. It was difficult to admit to myself that I hadn't been present for years and I had lost the happy, fun version of myself. I needed to find her.

Why wasn't I happy? I was the CEO of a successful mortgage company that I started on my own in 2010. I was an award-winning leader in the mortgage industry surrounded by a curated team of talented professionals. I had reached the goals I set for myself. But I was stressed out, overworked, and exhausted—all the time. I still loved building and leading my team, but I wasn't sure I loved owning my own company. It was taking a toll on me, my health, my family, and my friends.

In the past, I had been approached by companies who were looking to join forces. But I always dismissed the idea. I was doing just fine on my own. Or was I? While speaking at a conference in the fall of 2018, a colleague asked if I had considered joining forces with the CEO of another lending company who just so happened to be attending the same conference. He noticed that I had lost my sparkle and thought perhaps this would be a way to get it back. I forced myself to take a closer look. I thought about how it would feel to lose total control of my own independent mortgage company. Would that make me feel like a failure? Would it make me look like a failure in others' eyes? Would I care?

I realized I needed to put aside my ego and be grateful for all the success I had achieved in my career. Now was the time

to pivot. So, at the end of 2018, I trusted my instincts, allowed myself to be vulnerable, and merged with another company. The merger allowed me to continue leading my team of operations and salespeople and gave me the backing and support of a larger company. I gained more time with family and less stress over things like payroll and taxes. It was the best thing to do. We were stronger together and still are to this day. I no longer have my CEO title, and that is okay, although it wasn't easy at first.

I will never forget the day we finalized the company merge, going over each detail of what would stay and what would change going forward. All those years of hard work were being disassembled and rebuilt to work more cohesively with my new team. More than once I found myself choking back tears, needing to excuse myself from the meeting to regain my composure. Thankfully, my new leadership team is made up of truly wonderful, compassionate people who gave me the space and support I needed to take this huge step.

Being vulnerable allowed me to see what I had was not what I wanted anymore. By looking inward and opening myself to consider different opportunities, I gained strength and realized I didn't need a CEO title to be successful. I could find a new measure of success.

Trust and vulnerability have played a key role in my career, but they would be nothing without *confidence* and *determination.* I believe in myself and know that I am one of the hardest workers in the mortgage industry, which has allowed me to be confident in any role I take. I have also learned to be comfortable feeling uncomfortable. This can catapult you to another level of success.

Confidence led me to start my own company, and determination made that company a success. I remember writing my memoir *Crazy Lucky Girl* and feeling so grateful and proud of myself for the journey I have been on. My confidence allows me to speak at large meetings and conferences, run a team of operations and salespeople, and become a top loan originator in

the industry. With confidence also comes the courage to try new things, whether it's filming TikToks, writing another book, or starting a podcast. If you believe in yourself, there is nothing you can't do.

As I look back on the last decade, I believe that having trust, vulnerability, and confidence has allowed me to soar in my career, while still being a role model and rock for my family. By pivoting and trusting myself, I have developed new ventures and friendships that I would have never had the opportunity to explore. The main objective has always been in pursuit of helping people—whether it be in purchasing their dream home or in building their business. I am able to be a confident and passionate leader in the mortgage industry because I trust in myself, and I believe that I am good enough to achieve whatever I want to achieve. I know it's okay to ask for help, and I know I can trust people enough to help me.

I finally pull into my parking spot at the office with just minutes to spare before my morning meeting begins. But before I can even get my car door open, my phone rings. It's the repair man I scheduled to come fix the dryer. He is sitting in my driveway with no access to the house. Are you kidding me? How did I forget about that? I close my eyes, take a deep breath, put my car in reverse, and back to the house I go. Looks like I will be taking yet another meeting in my car.

This is the life of a crazy lucky girl, but it's my life, and I wouldn't have it any other way.

ABOUT SUE MEITNER

Sue Meitner, CMB (certified mortgage banker), is a leader in her profession and community. Her passion is helping to enrich and empower people to identify their vision of success and plot their course to reach it. Sue is an award-winning author, entrepreneur, motivational speaker, mentor, and mortgage expert. She enjoys sharing the ups and downs of her life and career to help others gain a new perspective of their own growth strategies, as exemplified in her book *Crazy Lucky Girl: Do You Have the Keys to Success?*

Sue is a graduate of George Mason University with a degree in communications. She never expected to work with mortgages, but with just the right combination of business, sales, and relationship-building, she discovered this career was the perfect fit for her. She finds helping people buy a home to be extremely rewarding.

Active on social media, Sue offers information on home buying, the economy, mortgage programs, and business growth—plus never fails to applaud the success of colleagues. Sue was recently chosen as correspondent for suburban Philadelphia on the nationally broadcasted show *Financing The American Dream*, airing on CNBC, Bloomberg TV, and several streaming services. Her podcast, *Grab Your Keys,* is her latest initiative in motivating others by discussing keys to success with professionals in various industries.

Do you need help finding your keys to success?

Get started by using the exclusive QR code below to download Sue's free Business Success Game Plan workbook!

Visit SueMeitner.com to follow Sue or purchase her book.

HARNESS THE POWER OF YOUR DREAMS AND LIVE FREE . . . BY DESIGN

Ellie D. Shefi

Have you ever looked around and thought to yourself, *How did I get here?*

Are you living your life on autopilot, doing your best just to get through each day? Is your life dictated by the never-ending items on your to-do list? Or by the demands and expectations of everyone else? Perhaps you are living a life that was determined long ago by someone else—one in which your dreams didn't matter and you never had a say?

I get it. I've lived that life. A life where I was chained to my past. A life where authenticity, abundance, and joy seemed out of reach. A life where I felt pulled along a path by a current beyond my control. A life where I dreamed things would be different but felt powerless to make them so. Then, slowly but surely, I learned the keys to freedom. Through almost five decades of getting back up every time life has knocked me down, I've developed tools to make my dreams come true and live life on my terms. And I'm here to help you do the same.

Who am I to guide you on your journey to living a life that's free by design? I'm Ellie. I'm typically introduced as an attorney,

entrepreneur, #1 international best-selling and award-winning author, featured speaker, strategist, teacher, trainer, mentor, media host, consultant, coach, philanthropist, and publisher— but I haven't always lived a joyful abundant life on my own terms. I've escaped abuse and domestic violence. I've had thirteen major surgeries and survived cancer. I've struggled financially, lived in my car, and eaten the food restaurants were throwing away at the end of the night. And yet, despite those events and circumstances, I've learned to take back my power, dream my biggest dreams, and intentionally create a life I love! I may have been forged by fire, but I choose to live free by design.

And now it's your turn!

With these tools I share, you'll chart your new course and set your GPS toward a life that's free by design. First, you'll identify where you are, where you want to go, and what obstacles lie in between. Next, by learning how to create an impervious mind, embrace the power of gratitude, and master visualization, you'll close the gap to align your current and future lives. Then, you'll be ready to put it all together, intentionally design a life you love in all aspects, and, at last, live your dreams!

So, are you ready? Are you ready to make powerful and lasting changes to your life? Grab your favorite notebook and pen, and let's dive in!

Now . . .

Imagine living a life you love . . .

A life where your dreams come true . . .

A life where you live every aspect on your terms: wealth on your terms, health on your terms, relationships on your terms, courage on your terms . . .

A life of showing up as you want to be in all of your glory . . .

A life free by design!

Step One: Identify

The first step to living a life that is free by design is to identify where you are, where you want to be, and the obstacles in between.

Where Are You?

Let's begin by assessing where you are in your life right now. What's your current reality? Take inventory of your life in a deep and meaningful way so that you're clear about where you're starting. Dig into every aspect of your life: finance, health, relationships, self-care (are you even on your own to-do list?!). You might find some areas of your life are awesome while others need an overhaul. Be honest with yourself about the story of your life as it currently is.

Mirror, Mirror

Play along with an exercise that will help you dive deep into your life—you need a mirror and open mind. Ready?

Look at yourself in the mirror. What do you see? Describe your physical self.

Now, as you look deep into your eyes, describe in detail who and what you see.

Next, describe your life. If you're stuck, consider what you say when you talk to others about your life. How do you describe it to them? How might they describe it to you? Are there any life events that have shaped you; if so, what effect has each had?

Knowing your starting point is the first step in recalibrating your compass and programming the GPS for your new life. After all, when you want to go somewhere, what does your GPS need to know? Just two simple pieces of information: your starting point and your destination! Soon, you'll begin getting clear on your destination, but for now, focus on taking a raw, honest inventory of your life in its current form.

Where Do You Want to Be?

Now that you're super clear on your current reality, ask yourself: Is this what I want? Does my current wealth bring me joy? My health? My relationships with others? With myself?

If you answered no to any or all of these questions, then it's time to identify where you want to be. To approach this question,

let your imagination run wild! It is time to recall and supercharge those past dreams or even create new ones! And now, don't just dream, but dream *big*, dream *free*! This is your chance to see infinite possibilities!

Let's have some fun . . . to dream the ultimate reality, think back to when you were a child and made birthday wishes. In that frame of mind, ask:

What do I want?
What does living life on my own terms look like?
What does my authentic, in-control, joyful life look like?
What does my dream life look like?

Go ahead and describe where you live, what you do, how you feel, who's in your life (and who's not). Describe what financial freedom looks like; what peak health looks like; what amazing relationships look like. Note observations, feelings, events, and accomplishments. Capture every wondrous detail!

Assess Your Obstacles

Now, what's getting in the way of living your dreams?

Identifying your obstacles can be tricky and emotionally taxing. Start by simply asking yourself: Where am I stuck? Finances? Career? Health? Relationships? A combination?

Don't focus on all of them at once. Pick one area and drill down. Be really honest with yourself, and you'll reveal limiting beliefs, bad habits, and disempowering narratives that stop you from living the life you want. Become clear on the obstacles you are creating for yourself.

Now, go even deeper and contemplate *why* you have been creating these obstacles—why you're self-sabotaging, getting in your own way, or limiting your potential. The answer may lie in events and circumstances from your past that have shaped who you are today. It's important to identify those pivotal moments that have created the beliefs and paradigms that brought you to this point

of your journey. Later, I'll show you how to break through these patterns, but for now, simply identify them.

Pick another area of your life and repeat the exercise. Don't be surprised if you find similar obstacles popping up. But take heart. After you've learned to handle them in one area, you'll be set to tackle any other places they might arise.

Step Two: Align

You've reached the next step! This is where the rubber meets the road! It's where you close the gap by using my tools and resources—creating an impervious mind, embracing the power of gratitude, and mastering visualization—to get from where you are to where you want to be.

Create an Impervious Mind

Creating an impervious mind is *the* key to living a life free by design because—let's face it—life happens. And you need to be able to overcome old and new obstacles that stand between where you are and living your dreams. So, how do you create an impervious mind? You master the language that you use and then use those words to write a story that changes your perspective.

Master the Language You Use

Revisit your notes from the Mirror, Mirror exercise. What words did you use to describe yourself and your life when you looked in the mirror? Were they empowering? Or did you go straight to criticism—the wrinkles, the extra pounds, the stalled career, the failed marriage?

Let's try that exercise again. This time, focus on being nice to yourself and use only empowering words. Look at your eyes again, but this time, don't focus on the wrinkles; instead say, "Thank you, eyes . . . You're looking very sparkly today."

While it may seem awkward at first, with practice (yes, consistently using empowering language takes practice!), it'll become the norm, and you'll stop tearing yourself to bits.

Now that you've replaced your disempowering labels and

beliefs with empowering ones, it's time to claim who you are, see your dreams, and create your life that's free by design! Grab your notebook and pen and write down at least half a dozen affirmations (those magical "I AM" statements). Remember to write them in the present tense, as if you're already doing, feeling, seeing, believing, accomplishing, and embracing your dreams and a life lived on your terms!

Next, let's supercharge your affirmations with incantations. With what?!

Incantations are affirmations that get your physiology involved. Take the affirmation "I am strong" and picture someone putting some oomph behind it: saying it out loud, punching the air, beating their chest, whatever makes them actually experience and feel the words they're using. Get your senses involved. Go ahead . . . pick one of the affirmations from your list. Now, say it with power, with emotion, and with a corresponding movement. Really embody it! I bet your incantation let you physically experience your affirmation that time! Powerful, isn't it?!

Change Your Perspective

The words you use, and the meaning you ascribe to them, produce physiological responses and *become* your truth. Have you ever noticed that the more you tell people you're tired, the more tired you feel? The more you tell people you're stressed or overwhelmed, the more stressed and overwhelmed you feel? The words you use and the stories you create about a situation are more powerful than the situation itself! So, using your newfound empowering words to rewrite your stories to change your perspective is the next step in designing life on your terms!

What do I mean? Let me show you:

My friend is a blind woman who was born to a poor family in a village in rural India where it was common for daughters to be sold into marriage for a dowry. Her mother and father knew that she wouldn't attract a high dowry, but without one, feeding her meant that someone else would starve.

One day, her mother led her to a bus stop and left her there. Abandoned. Frightened. Alone.

For years, this was my friend's reality. She told herself the story of how her parents were embarrassed by her, how she brought shame to her family, and how she was such a burden they had to cast her aside in order to be free from the shame and financial burden she imposed upon them.

This story defined her until one day she made a powerful decision. She decided to change her story and change her life. She shifted her perspective and took control of her narrative.

Today, she will tell you that she was born to a loving mother and father in a poor village in rural India. She will tell you that her parents feared her mistreatment by a future husband even if he was willing to pay a dowry. They worried for her future. The only way they could help her have a better life was to let her go.

So one day her mother took her beloved daughter by the hand and led her to a well-lit bus stop near the police station, where she was sure to be found by a policeman. Not wanting to frighten her child or draw attention to what was happening, she sat her daughter on the bench and quietly walked away with tears in her eyes.

As her mother had hoped, a kind policeman found her and took her to the safety of an orphanage, where she was adopted by an incredible family in Canada. She has been more loved by her adopted family than she ever thought possible. She is thriving every single day—all because her loving mother selflessly released her to a better life. Her mother loved her enough to let her go, and for that she is eternally grateful.

My friend's story is a powerful example. Although the events of her life are what they are—her mother left her as a very young blind girl at a bus stop near a police station in rural India—her story reminds us of the power of the words we use and the meanings we give them. As my friend so poignantly demonstrates, you can use the story you tell yourself about events in your life to

80

either keep yourself in an emotional prison, or you can take the key and set yourself free. Changing the meaning she attached to the events of her past set her free. Her shift in meaning didn't change the facts of what happened, but by changing her story, she found a new life, and a new future.

When you change your perspective, everything shifts. You replace chains of the past with gratitude, joy, forgiveness, compassion, and love, and you're empowered to take control, become the architect of your life, and fully live your dreams!

An "Attitude of Gratitude"

Now, let's talk about the power of gratitude. Yes, gratitude. Have you ever noticed that when you allow yourself to feel truly grateful about something, you cannot simultaneously feel angry, anxious, fearful, worried, or frustrated?

Go ahead, try it. Think of something for which you are truly and deeply grateful. Put yourself back in that beautiful moment. Notice how you feel. Notice the warmth. Notice the sense of peace. Notice the love. Notice the joy. Notice the appreciation. Of course, you can feel anger, worry, fear, or frustration before and after you feel grateful, but negative emotions are impossible to feel at the same time as gratitude.

Feeling grateful interrupts whatever negative emotion you're experiencing long enough to help you shift your perspective and fuel your strength to persevere.

I've spent the better part of two decades living in and out of hospitals, fighting for my life, abandoning my dreams. At one point, I grew tired of the pain, tired of the struggle, and tired of the constant fight to survive. I was giving up. I had had enough. I was done fighting the doctors' death deadlines. Then one day, everything changed. It was a day I had to go have another excruciating test. When it was time for me to go for testing, the porter came to get me from my room and wheeled my wheelchair down hallways that he had never taken me through before.

He wheeled me through the hallways of the area in the hospital

where everyone was either paralyzed from the neck down and on a ventilator, or in a coma and on a ventilator. I looked into room after room and realized that any one of those patients would give *anything* to feel the pain I was feeling. In an instant, I realized that my pain was an incredible blessing, and that I was so lucky to be able to feel it travel around my body. In that moment, I made a choice to once again take control of my life. I thanked God that I still had nerves that were connected and synapses that were firing as they should. What a gift! I turned my pity party into gratitude and my weariness became resolve. I became flooded with gratitude for my body and all it provided me.

The ability to find and feel true gratitude is the ultimate mind hack. It is a powerful tool—one that can be learned. Just as you can train your mind to assign empowering meanings to life's events and you can train your mind to frame things in a positive, powerful perspective, you can also train your mind to operate from a place of gratitude. Changing your meaning takes practice. Changing your perspective takes practice. And living in gratitude takes practice. The more work you do in your gratitude practice, the stronger it will be. It's like any other skill you've honed in your life. You can do it!

See It, Achieve It

Earlier, when you dreamed of a life lived on your terms, you got clear on what it is that you want. So, how do you turn that into reality? Through the power of visualization.

Let me demonstrate:

I want you to envision that you are standing in front of a lemon tree. And in front of you is a beautiful, ripe, amazing lemon. Pull it off the tree. Feel it. Squeeze it. Now walk that lemon back into your kitchen and pull out a knife. Cut that lemon in half. Ooh, it's so juicy. Now, lift one half to your nose and smell the lemon. Squeeze some of the lemon juice into a cup and take a sip.

Did you pucker?! Yes, you did! Are you salivating? Yes, you are! But there's no lemon in your hand. You didn't actually smell

a lemon. But your body reacted physiologically because your mind made the association. In your mind, all those steps—from picking to tasting the lemon—were real!

That's the power of visualization! Your mind cannot tell the difference between what's real and what's not. Pretty wild, right?

The same goes for designing your life. If your mind can see it, you can achieve it. Unlike the earlier dreaming exercise, in which you were an observer and you were imagining your future life from an objective point of view, visualization compels you to put yourself *into* the vision and feel it. You sit in it; you taste it; you smell it. You are not just objectively observing from afar. You move out of your head, into your heart.

If you want that Ferrari, smell the leather, feel the steering wheel under your hands, feel your foot hitting the accelerator. If you want to live in that beach house, sit on the balcony listening to the waves with a glass of wine.

So, what are your dreams?

Step Three: Design

This is it! This is your call to action! You took inventory of your life—you *identified* where you are; where you want to be; and what obstacles stand in the way.

Next, you *aligned* your life by learning how to close the gap. You understand the importance of empowering words. You're practicing affirmations and incantations to feel the power of your words. You're on the journey of changing your perspective—of taking ownership of your experiences and attaching empowering meanings to them. You're whole-heartedly embracing the power of gratitude and practicing it until it becomes the default way that you move through the world. And you're learning to master the art and science of visualization. You're dreaming your biggest dreams!

Look at that! You have all the building blocks you need for the final step. It's time to take charge and use these tools to grab hold of your dreams and intentionally *design* a life that you love

in all aspects: life on your terms, wealth on your terms, health on your terms, a career on your terms, relationships with others and yourself on your terms.

You have everything you need to be the architect of your life! Everything you need to show up as the person you design! Everything you need to make your dreams come true!

Now go forward and live them! Live your best life—the joyful, authentic, abundant life you love!

Live a life that's free by design!

ABOUT ELLIE D. SHEFI

Ellie is an attorney, entrepreneur, #1 international best-selling and award-winning author and publisher, sought-after speaker, strategist, consultant, and coach who provides her clients with practical, easy-to-implement tools and strategies that generate results. She helps entrepreneurs to grow their companies; authors to write and publish their books; and speakers to amplify their message so they can scale their impact.

Host of the Free by Design™ television show and the You Are Not Your Scars™ podcast, Ellie is often interviewed in publications and on others' podcasts and television shows, including NBC, ABC, CBS, the New York Times, Forbes, Entrepreneur, Yahoo News, the LA Tribune, and TED Ed, to name a few.

Ellie is also the founder of the Made 2 Change the World™ Foundation (www.made2change.org), a nonprofit that equips and empowers the next generation with the tools, resources, and strategies they need to create the lives, communities, and world they envision.

A member of the National Academy of Best-Selling Authors, Ellie's books include *Unlocking Your Superpower: 8 Steps to Turn Your Existing Knowledge into Income; Sisters Rising: Stories of Remarkable Women Living Extraordinary Lives; The Authorities: Powerful Wisdom from Leaders in the Field; Women Who Shine* and *SuccessOnomics.*

To connect with Ellie and learn more about her work, including how you can get involved with the Made 2 Change the World™ Foundation, please visit ellieshefi.com.

https://www.facebook.com/ellieshefi
https://www.instagram.com/ellieshefi
https://www.twitter.com/ellieshefi
https://www.linkedin.com/in/ellie-shefi/

GOD-SIZED DREAM

Candice Shepard

Through my childhood, my bedroom was a bright, sunny yellow. When my parents switched it over from "little girl" to "big girl," my mom suggested yellow as something fun, positive, and uplifting to wake up in every day. It being the '70s, we had paneling on the walls, so we put up yellow paneling. My bedspread was yellow. We painted the bookcase yellow. Even the carpet was yellow. It was always sunny in my bedroom. It was my safe space. I listened to music, wrote in my journal, prayed, had sleepovers with girlfriends and giggled into the wee hours of the night, did homework, planned my future, and spent hours deep in thought in that bright, sunny room. That yellow tint over everything, akin to rose-colored glasses, shaped my mind in a way that is still very much imprinted in the fabric of who I am.

That was how my mom rolled too. She would never allow anything to keep her down for long. If she was sad, she didn't stay that way. If she was discouraged, she would find a way through. If there was trouble, she found a solution; she would always pick herself up and push through whatever she was facing. Things might get tough, but there was always room for the sun to shine, always a reason to have hope, always something to dream about,

plan for, and work toward. In our house, dreaming was encouraged. But so was planning and working and doing the hard things.

As a little girl, I was headstrong. Okay, that's maybe an understatement. I was bullheaded, determined, tenacious, unstoppable. I would charge through any situation, full speed ahead, and nothing could stop me. In *Women Who Shine*, I shared a story that clearly embodies that full-steam-ahead way of life. I was probably seven or eight when someone tried to deny me the opportunity to play on the boys' baseball team. The main reason I wanted to play on that team—instead of the one I was "supposed" to play on—was solely because of my current abilities and my desire to grow. I was nearly denied because I didn't fit the profile for the players on that team. It was a boys' team, and I was not a boy. End of story. Enter my dad, my hero and champion, who stood strong and said, "She's as skilled at [this thing] as the other kids on this team, boy or girl, and this is where she belongs." I think that was the day I stepped into my potential. My perspective changed in that moment from "some things can't be done" to "anything is possible."

You also know from WHS that I am a high achiever. I've been blessed with a lot of great successes. None of it was luck. It was, and is, prayerful obedience to the will of God and really, really hard work. You also know that where I am now is most certainly not where I began. Sometimes it seems like where I am now is a completely different planet than where I began.

When I was living on the planet of pain and shame and heartache, where hurt and overwhelm was part of my daily life, it was almost impossible to believe there would ever be anything more. I used to lay in that sunny yellow room begging God for something different, something better, something more in line with the calling I knew he had on my life. The sun seemed so dim and out of reach. Some days it seemed impossible to believe the sun would ever come out again. And yet, that sunny yellow room again became my sanctuary, enabling me to dream again.

Confession time . . . I've never been a big "dreamer." I am

- a list maker
- a box checker
- a planner
- a doer
- an achiever (can anyone say Enneagram 3? High D on the DISC? Print 3/8? ENFJ?)
- an outside-the-box thinker
- a *big* thinker

But *dreamer*? Dreamer is not something that has ever been a title particularly fitting for me. That is, perhaps, troublesome from the perspective of writing a chapter in a book called *Women Who Dream*, but hold that thought.

When my parents were redecorating my baby bedroom to a sunny, yellow, big-girl bedroom, a wall hanging seemed to appear out of nowhere that read, "Dreams take time, patience, sustained effort, and a willingness to fail if they are ever to be anything more than dreams." That quote *makes* the title of dreamer fit me. I am very much a dreamer, from a perspective that makes sense to me.

My parents put skin on the idea of what it means to be a dreamer. My mom is very much a dreamer and big thinker, and my dad makes the idea of dreaming, that was still nebulous to me, very practical. My dad makes me laugh all the time; he is so funny. He can take a heavy situation and lighten it up with a joke that will inevitably elicit laughter. For years after I played on the boys' baseball team, my dad used to joke with me, "You can't do that, you're just a girl." Then he'd chuckle with his deep infectious laugh. I knew what it meant. I knew that the world would frequently say things like . . .

"Little girl, step back."

"You're just a girl."

"You can't."

"Stop trying."

"Stay in your lane."

"Who do you think you are?"

And on and on.

But I also knew from that moment on, those expectations would never stop me. I could be both a dreamer and a doer.

But then one day, something stopped me, pulled the rug right out from under me, knocked me flat on my back, and took the wind right out of me. I went from hanging out in the sunny yellow room because it was my safe space to dream, to hanging out in the sunny yellow room because it was my safe space to survive, hide, and escape the awful mess that was going on around me. I stopped dreaming. I stopped planning. I stopped thinking big. I started trying to determine how I could breathe for another day, get myself out of bed, and force myself out of the sun that was my safe haven and into the torrential rains—whether or not I wanted to do it.

Through it all, I prayed. I thought I was merely surviving, but in hindsight, God showed me another perspective. Through the surviving, through the praying, I was also becoming. I was allowing God to take a horrible situation and make it his. To take something unthinkable and make beauty from ashes. I was changing from who I was to who I am. I was allowing him to plant God-sized dreams into my life and my future. It was a time of rest and transformation, although I was too hurt at the time to see that. All I was asking God for was survival. And then I started asking for escape and deliverance from the situation. Eventually, I would ask him for deliverance from the stronghold. But in the middle, in the becoming, the God-sized dreams were evolving and growing and taking root.

Three dreams in particular were being planted into my soul at that time and have finally come to fruition—thirty years later! So often, we fail to ask God for his dream. We fail to recognize that the dream we're meant to chase will always come true if it comes

from him. The dream we're meant to have will always come from him. And even more often, when we ask God for something, we give up before the dream he has planted comes to be reality.

In that time of becoming, God planted three dreams:

1. You will own a law firm one day. This law firm will be used to grow my kingdom and serve my people.

2. You will mother a motherless child.

3. And I will make all of the things you're going through right now . . . all this yuck . . . I will make something amazing from it, and you will help a lot of people with your story. And your story will bring me glory and bring healing to some of my dearly loved daughters.

I do now own that law firm, and we do use it to serve. A law firm that serves the kingdom sounds strange. But God is so good. I am now a mother to a child who was previously motherless. It is beautiful and it is hard. But God is so good. I do now use that horrific season of life to glorify God and help him heal his hurting daughters. I never, ever, ever, ever thought that particular dream was possible. But God is so good.

Y'all, nothing is impossible with God, and God-sized dreams are not only possible but the best dreams you can have. Because if it's from him, you can't stop it. If you're obedient to that God-sized dream, he can use it in a million beautiful and amazing ways.

One day, my family and I were having dinner at my parents' home, and my eleven-year-old daughter started talking about something that she wanted to do. I don't even remember now what it was that she said she was going to do. It was bold, audacious, and really cool. My dad looked at her and said, "You can't do that, you're just a girl." And then he chuckled with his deep, infectious laugh. My daughter had never heard this story, and I

held my breath waiting to see how she would respond. In that split second, I prayed that I had poured enough into her that she wouldn't back down, that had her own internal strength and grit would allow her to stand firm. Under her breath, but just loud enough for the whole room to hear, she said, "Just watch me." The whole room exhaled. My dad said, "That's my girl," and we all went on with our day. I later told her the story and expressed to her how proud I was of this response and my desire that she never lose her determination.

In the waiting and the wondering, in the rising and the falling, in the healing and the hurting, in the becoming, there he is. Make room for your God-sized dream.

ABOUT CANDICE SHEPARD

Candice thrives in many arenas: Jesus-lover, mama, sister, daughter, orphan advocate, friend, attorney, business owner, creator, mentor, speaker, author, encourager, and servant leader, and the list goes on.

Originally from the Midwest, Candice proudly calls North Carolina home now, along with her four children and a bunch of other critters that she loves and cares for. That midwestern pragmatism is still very much present in her parenting style, daily living, and business endeavors.

As the CEO and managing attorney of Shepard Law, PLLC in the Charlotte, NC, metro area; founder and president of the Board of Directors of Tribe 14:18 Ministries, a nonprofit that seeks to care for orphans and the families who love them; and a certified coach, best-selling author, and international speaker with The Athena Tribe, Candice seeks to empower others in all aspects of life, from home to work and everything in between. She is also a legacy author for the Inspired Impact series. You can find out more about her in *Women Who Shine,* and connect with her on the websites below, if you want to work with her or get involved.

Let's connect!

Web: www.ShepardLawPLLC.com
www.Tribe1418.com
www.TheAthenaTribe.com

DREAMS FOR GENERATIONS

Linda Yang

W hy does dreaming about the future come so easily for some people but not for others? The opportunity to dream is free, but for some people, like my parents, the imagination required to dream of something better is only unleashed by significant life-changing events.

Survival

Explosions of beautiful fireworks decorate the night sky, accompanied by the usual loud whooshes, whistles, and bangs. As far back as I can remember, our family has watched America's Independence Day fireworks every year. However, the flashes of light and loud booms sound exactly like bombs exploding during wartime. It's ironic that the way the United States celebrates its freedom and independence reminds my parents of the war they experienced in Laos.

For my parents, war meant death, and survival was the only priority. As refugees of the Vietnam War, my parents and grandparents did not take survival for granted. The Vietnam War created chaos, as did several other wars in the area. During that time, Laos, a small country in Southeast Asia where my grandparents

and parents lived, was the most heavily bombed country in the world.

My parents would often tell me stories of their escape from Laos in the middle of the night, amid heavy gunfire and bombs exploding all around them. They would tell of how they ran from one village to the next, hoping to find some measure of peace and relief from war. Thankfully, my parents made their way to a refugee camp in Thailand and had the opportunity to relocate to America in the late 1970s. Although they did not have any money and were unable to speak English, America gave them an opportunity to dream about a new future—something they did not have the luxury to do in Laos.

Perseverance

When my parents arrived in America, they did not take their opportunity to dream for granted. They held firm to an important, timeless value—perseverance—which helped them achieve their dreams in the face of new challenges in a new country. Perseverance required putting forth constant and relentless effort, despite difficulties and resistance. Determination helped them escape war-torn Laos, and once they arrived in America, persistence helped them learn English and build a life for our family.

Soon after they arrived in America, my parents worked in the farming industry. Farming meant starting the day at 4:00 a.m. every morning to beat the blazing California sun, but they were willing to work hard to support our family. The work provided an income, but it didn't afford proper healthcare for a family with children. My parents' constant and relentless efforts to provide for our family led them to pack everything we had into our car and drive across the country from California to North Carolina in search of better opportunities.

They followed their dreams and were able to secure full-time jobs that provided healthcare coverage. My father worked in a plastic packaging factory, and my mother worked for a textile factory, sewing seams on socks, and was paid according to her

production. The jobs were labor intensive and required long hours. My parents worked relentlessly and saved enough money to purchase two sewing machines, which allowed my mother to sew at home. Their tireless and constant work ethic soon carried over to me. Every weekend throughout our high school years, my twin sister and I sewed seams on socks to help provide for our family and save for our college educations.

Through their actions, my parents taught me that perseverance is vital in accomplishing my dreams. They worked constantly and never gave up despite many difficulties—just so I would have opportunities to realize my own dreams. Perseverance often requires a tremendous amount of sacrifice, but no sacrifice was too great for my parents when it came to their dreams or mine.

Imagination

I believe imagination stretches dreams and inspires one's vision for the future. Especially for those with humble beginnings, the future can be transformational.

From the beginning, my parents did their best to protect me from seeing the harsh realities associated with starting a new life in a new country. At first, I didn't understand the physical and mental toll of working long hours on a farm day after day. I didn't know that my parents' laborious jobs translated to little economic and financial wealth, and I didn't comprehend that my family had to rely on government assistance to help put food on the table.

I do remember clearly that during my early childhood years, I had fun dreaming, imagining, and pretend-playing. I remember daydreaming and wanting to be like my favorite movie stars, musicians, and professional athletes. It didn't matter if the actresses looked different from me. It didn't matter whether I understood what the musicians were singing about or that I didn't have a musical instrument. I didn't care that I couldn't run very fast or that I hadn't found a sport I enjoyed. The only thing that did matter was my imagination, propelling me forward with a belief that I could achieve anything and be anything I wanted. Only

my imagination limited what I could achieve. My twin sister and I shared dreams of all shapes and sizes with each other. My big dreams allowed me to see so many possibilities—nothing seemed out of reach. All I had to do was close my eyes and imagine it.

As I got older, I reached a point when I started to comprehend my parents' struggles. I still recall like it was yesterday when I had to share one egg with my twin sister because my family needed to make a carton of one dozen eggs last the entire week. I started to gain a perspective and understanding of life's harshness, which my parents had tried to keep from me. I gained an appreciation for their sacrifices. Around that time, my dreams also started to evolve and grow bigger. Slowly, my dreams started to not only encompass my own desires; my dreams began to cast a wider net that also embraced my family.

As a first-generation immigrant born in America, my aspirations often reflected achievements I desired as the first in my family. I dreamed of being the first to graduate from college. I dreamed of being the first to own a business and have multiple sources of income. I dreamed of having a high-profile and well-paid professional career in order to provide for my own family and for my aging parents.

Challenges

Accomplishing dreams is an adventure filled with many challenges. My journey has taught me that setting goals and taking measurable actions stretches my capabilities and enables me to realize my dreams.

When I set goals, I set realistic and measurable action steps toward making my dreams reality. I've recognized through my own experiences just how difficult it is to persevere and keep pushing onward in the face of resistance. Even when working smart, it's hard work and there are still challenges to overcome. Taking action requires diligent work, extra effort, sacrifice, and never-ending commitment.

In college, I studied longer hours than most of my peers at

the library because it took me longer to read and understand concepts. Quite often, I had to reread the text and find additional resources to fully understand the materials. After several years of working a full-time job, I decided to go back to school for my master's degree in healthcare administration. At that point in my life, I was married. We were struggling with bills, and I could not return to school full-time. I made the choice to work eight-hour days and attend school part-time in the evenings. Some days I felt exhausted. I often chose to skip social gatherings, and my weekends were filled with reading textbooks and writing essays. Other personal choices I made throughout the years were limiting travels for vacations, emphasizing quality time with my family instead of quantity, sacrificing taking a honeymoon right after my wedding, and saying no to great opportunities that did not align with my dreams. In each circumstance, I chose a path and stuck to a plan that was realistic and measurable.

During challenging times, I reminded myself why I could not take my opportunity to dream for granted. This mindfulness helped me refocus and served as a constant motivator. I've learned that the hardest part of taking measurable action happens internally; sometimes the battle inside my mind made it seem like my dreams were out of reach. Like all of humanity, I also had limiting beliefs about myself. Although I had goals and aspirations, I still doubted my capabilities, and I feared the unknown. However, in the face of that self-doubt and those limiting beliefs, I chose to invest in myself. Throughout the years, I also chose to build upon my strengths, acquire new skills, and confront my weaknesses.

Investing in myself allowed me to overcome challenges, and it stretched my capabilities in ways I could not have anticipated. Investing in myself connected me with other like-minded people, and we cheered each other forward. Working toward any dream takes perseverance, but the wonderful thing is that you get to choose your dreams, and they're only limited by the stretch of your imagination.

Impact

My dreams continue to change, and they're shaped by my perspective of the world and my life. Nothing has impacted my life more than becoming a mother. My children have inspired me and stretched my capabilities in ways I could never have imagined.

My dream for my children is that I'll be able to inspire them to have amazing dreams of their own—without bounds or limits. I hope my children's dreams are filled with visionary goals and aspirations. Just like how I was inspired by my parents, I hope my children will know that they could achieve anything and be anything they want. I remind myself and my children every day to appreciate our opportunity to dream. With this appreciation, I've come to recognize that the impact of achieving my dreams extends beyond me. When I achieve my dreams, it can inspire others to make a difference in their own lives, and it leads to a positive impact in families for generations to come.

ABOUT LINDA YANG

Linda Yang is an experienced, innovative leader specializing in healthcare information technology and analytics. With over fourteen years of experience within many reputable healthcare organizations, Linda also holds a master of health administration in healthcare informatics and comprehensive technical certifications.

Linda continues to lead by example as one of the top experts in the industry. As a mentor, speaker, and author, Linda shares her experience as a first-generation Asian American woman in hopes of inspiring others to pursue their own dreams and passions. Linda enjoys imparting tools that have helped her overcome challenges, gain self-awareness, and find meaningful purpose. She is also an advocate for encouraging women to explore a career in information technology.

Linda lives in North Carolina with her supportive husband, Bee, and their energetic children, Madeline, Meredith, and Jeremiah.

To secure Linda as a speaker or to learn more about mentoring opportunities and inspiring resources, contact her here:

Web: www.PositiveScope.org
Email: LindaYang@PositiveScope.org
LinkedIn: www.linkedin.com/in/lindayang-mha

THE MAGIC OF YOUR INNER TEMPLE

Amalai

Who would have thought that falling, showing my nude body in front of an audience, and getting my home listed in a short sale by the bank would liberate profound and rich meaning into my life?

It was during the month of December in 2016 that I decided to take a tour of Turkey and visit the city of Cappadocia.

I was not used to the cold weather after living in Costa Rica for so many years, so I covered nearly all my body and head in clothing. I remember that only my eyes could be seen.

It was later in the day, as I was coming out from a hand-made-ceramic store and starting to walk into the next adventure for my day, when suddenly I felt a bolt of high-voltage lightning shoot through my whole body. The shock in my body started in my coccyx and rose to my crown; my entire spine was shuddering!

Ouch! I said in my mind as my head started spinning uncontrollably and my sense of equilibrium disappeared.

What could have caused this traumatic event? Well, as I stepped onto the sidewalk, I had slipped on the icy pavement in front of the shop. I found myself sitting down upon that cold and unforgiving winterly place, looking up at the skies—again!

I started laughing. It was the nervous laugh. You know the one where you laugh at a terrible joke that simply isn't funny or when you're feeling anxious.

A hero came to my rescue. The tour guide. His look was one of deep concern. He gently offered me his hand and helped me stand up, returning to the normal world of being vertical.

I said, "Everything is okay." I took his arm and added, "I will walk holding onto you from now on."

That was my second fall that day.

A couple of years later, toward the end of November 2018, I decided to close the door to a successful career in the corporate world and start my journey into entrepreneurship. I enjoyed many years as a leader at IBM, Thomson Reuters, and Cargill, but I could not refuse the continual call of my heart to venture into new freedoms to support others.

I chose to become nomadic and enjoy the freedom to go anywhere in our world. My first destination was Bali, the capital of yoga in Indonesia. This was an easy choice. I had been on a spiritual journey for several years, and Bali seemed like a great place to be again and to start this new chapter in my life.

However, during my last days in Costa Rica as I was preparing to head toward yoga central, disaster hit! Intense pain in my waist and hips started to become unbearable. This was the last thing I wanted to experience in my new life of freedom. Prior to this *incident*, I had visited the doctor several times, and his only suggestion was to inject drugs to help relax my muscles.

As the pain kept appearing and intensifying, the remembrance of *the fall* came to me, and I knew it! I ignored my body, believing I was superwoman, and now I was facing the consequences.

Damn! I said to myself.

Immediately, I headed to the hospital and asked them to take an X-ray to confirm my fears, with the expectation to have an accurate diagnosis and guidance on how to get better. However,

the answer was devastating, and I felt totally frustrated. It felt like I had been given a life sentence.

"Well," said the doctor. "Your coccyx was broken and healed in the wrong way, which is causing the pain. There are many nerve terminations there, and it is impacting some of your main nerves."

I was expecting the hospital to provide a solution to my pain. After all, isn't that what doctors are for? My racing mind kicked in, asking, "Why now? What should I do to get better?" I kept calm and decided not the let panic take over.

The doctor then added, "You need to learn to live with the pain. This is an area of the body that we are not operating on anymore, so just understand that this is part of your life."

As you can imagine, within that moment, I felt abandoned and helpless. I wanted to cry. I was yelling at him in my mind: *Who are you to dictate that life sentence?* His statements were so damning and final! My heart sank.

I was starting to cry. Finally, he added, "Right now, you must go to the physiotherapist to try and control the inflammation. That will reduce the pain. You just must accept in your mind that pain will be an everyday part of your life."

FUCK! FUCK! FUCK! Do you really need to say that? I was yelling at him in my mind.

After beating Hodgkin's lymph cancer at the age of thirteen, I decided that *I* get to decide what to believe. And I decided that I know, from an inner knowing, miracles are possible. But in the medical examination office, I was unable to avoid the power of every word the doctor had said. They had penetrated my body. The spell was thrown. My whole human system just believed it. My understanding that he, and no one else, had power over my life did not feel enough. I felt utterly defeated.

I was less than two weeks from starting my great adventure. My soul was yearning for new freedoms. I was looking forward to

the trip, and I had decided that nothing and no one was going to delay it! So, I carried on as planned.

I did follow the doctor's orders and received some physio-therapist sessions. These did help to reduce the pain. I was able to move better, but the pain was there, lingering on. An ever-present ghost that could not be exorcised.

With all that, I arrived in Ubud, Bali. As I landed, it felt like a huge weight had left my body. The thrill and excitement of being on my adventure filled me completely, encouraging me to keep handling the level of pain and following the complicated instructions I received about the ergonomics and protocol to make life bearable.

I arrived during the rainy season in Bali. My first stop was to stay at a beautiful retreat center located in nature called Yoga Barn. I had decided to enjoy a ten-day immersion-shamanic breathwork and a 200-hours yoga teacher training.

During my stay, there were horrifying moments as I was walking across the wet and slippery floor: thoughts and visions of falling again kept appearing. The ever-present ghost nudging at my confidence.

It felt that I was becoming a car or house uncontrollably swirling in a tornado, subject to its will. But I was able to see the calm within the eye of the tornado. Something was there. It felt like an old memory. But it was too difficult to see clearly, too difficult to get myself there as I had done on other occasions.

Gradually, the memory returned. Yes! I used to meditate and shift energy within my body. I know how to do this! Then the memory was pulled away. It felt it was impossible to return onto that stage. And as if I wanted proof that I could not trust my feet, I slipped once again as I was going down the stairs. It seems that I didn't know how to walk.

Then, I finally made a decision that would change my life.

I was going to freely fall into the whirlwind of the tornado. I was ready to see what it was showing me, so I started to go inside

and observe. I was discovering the act of surrendering to an invitation to heal. As I was swirling, I became aware of three gifts that were going to expand my consciousness:

The Fear of Failing

I was starting to be an entrepreneur. My life/emotional coaching practice (at that time) was up and running. I was doing this in parallel with my corporate job. Self-reflection and natural observation of my life problem helped me to realize that perfection within myself was still there. It had never left and was ever present. A gift. The questions I asked myself were, *What will others say if I fail? What if I am just lying about all this, that I am dreaming to create and share with the world? What if everything I told myself is just bullshit and false promises?* As I was considering these thoughts, I was also encouraging myself by saying, *So what?! It is my life, not other people's lives. And if I fail or fall, well, I will get back up and keep tweaking and creating my dream. I have the gift of persistence, so I will always get up regardless of how many times I fail or fall!*

The Fear of Dying

Nightmares persisted of seeing myself many times a day, slipping and hitting my head on the unforgiving hard ground and dying. I remember there was a point that I told myself, *And if I died, what's wrong with that? I am going to die at some point.*

Am I too attached to my body and this life? I asked myself. Then I responded, *If I die, I die. I will die doing what my heart desires and with no regrets!* "I ACCEPT TO DIE," I shouted to myself, with a new mandate to my ego mind to know *my* decision.

The Lack of Trusting My Feet and Feeling Paralyzed

At the age of nineteen, I had started my career in the corporate world, always having a job, always enjoying the regular paycheck each month. Who doesn't enjoy a regular income! But now, I realized that I was afraid. Yes, I was in Bali, which appeared to everyone on the outside that I had a wonderful new direction in

life and that I knew what I was doing. At some level, probably mentally, I was telling myself that liberating story, but my emotional body and my physical body had yet to catch up and were totally freaked out. The life I knew, keeping me safe and secure, had gone. I was entering into a new life of the unknown. A new charter and destination. I started to realize that I was outsourcing my inner authority. This was the most powerful revelation to understanding self-empowerment, freedom, and consciousness itself.

Revelations were gradually unfolding, as if orchestrated by a benevolent intelligence. Thoughts, energy within my body, behaviors, and confidence started to improve little by little, day by day. I started feeling good, with a new sense of freedom, self-awareness, and a start of evolving into my new self. I finished the 200-hour yoga teacher training. What you might be interested to know is that it was right after my fall in Turkey that I felt directed by the Spirit to study in Bali! Of course, I didn't know the reasons until two years later. "Trust your magic" is a saying that comes to mind.

Of course, while I was in Bali, self-care had become a daily priority. Regular massages helped to heal pain and trauma from my body, and at the same time I was growing stronger—emotionally and energetically. The beauty of my inner world, my inner temple, was introducing itself and aligning with its *human being*. I was becoming whole.

The falling experience taught me how to listen to my body and understand its language. The doctor's spell had been exorcised and the veil to wellness removed. A new world was opening up. The new knowledge and understanding, from past experiences, were beyond the mental or intellectual; rather, it had been embodied within every cell—fully accepting who I am, my potential, victorious over my fears. Miraculously, the pain was almost gone after a few months.

Following the Bali adventure and adding another qualification

to my portfolio, I returned to Costa Rica and then went to Peru to attend a retreat in Puno I was organizing, and to participate in a sexual shamanic immersion. On this retreat, I had the opportunity to focus on activating the second chakra: the sacral chakra and the key to flourishing sexual relationships.

As part of my healing process and personal liberation, it felt important to examine and explore my relationship with sexuality and nudity. A sensitive subject for women.

Being the perfect woman, as Western civilization programs us to be, puts immense pressure on women, a mandate that can become intolerable. Of course, this burden of perfection was programming that I allowed to enter my being, both consciously and unconsciously. I was conforming to people's expectations, or what I thought those expectations were, hoping I could be accepted and do the right thing to receive love.

As I prepared for the retreat, I started to realize how much I feared people would see all the faults that I was feeling within myself, all my imperfections, all my naughty thoughts, all my weaknesses, all my flaws!

You have probably heard of ecstatic dancing: a free experience, where people move their bodies to the rhythm that they are feeling in the moment. During the retreat, I was enjoying an ecstatic dance—with a twist that everyone is naked! *Yikes,* I thought. *This is going to reveal my insecurities!*

So, I mustered as much courage as possible and onto the dance floor I went, joining other naked beings. During this ecstatic dance, I allowed my body to feel the music and to move my body in harmony with those frequencies and sounds. I felt a total connection. I started to relax. Men were dancing. Women were dancing. People were dancing with each other, enjoying the sense of harmony and freedom. So, I decided to be open to dance with another person, vulnerable and showing all my flaws. *No hiding now, Amalai,* I told myself. Someone passed by with whom I connected. We danced together for a bit, not touching

but enjoying each other's presence. *Okay, that went well,* I said to myself. I moved onto another person, and then another person. I felt great. *It's okay to be naked,* I told myself. Then *wham!* I started to dance with this particular guy. Nice looking with a gentle smile. We stared at each other's eyes, feeling the music and dancing rhythmically, in tune, as if we had practiced choreography together since we were children. Then it happened! I felt a sudden shock, I started feeling sick, and my face burned.

I felt I merged energetically with him. We became one. I was able to feel everything he was feeling. He was feeling and seeing everything about myself, beyond my *nudity*. I felt so transparent. I was exposed. I started to feel afraid of this type of profound connection of acceptance and union with another.

Once again, fear started to rise and overwhelmed every part of my body. I backtracked and cut the connection with the man. It was a beautiful experience; one my soul was searching for, and I cut it!

Why? Why? Why? I asked myself. *Why didn't I allow myself to explore this connection of acceptance and union with another?*

I started to realize that another healing of unknown inner trauma was inviting me in regarding my nudity and connection with a man. *Here we go again, Amalai.* I started to ask questions and observe the tornado again from the calm. This is how I started navigating the waters of my sexuality, of my nudity itself, of allowing pleasure in my life. Tons of questions started to arise:

- What is it that I fear about being accepted and connected with another?
- Do I like men or women or both?
- What do I fear the most about being nude?
- What gives me pleasure?
- How can I touch myself with love?
- How do I really want to be fucked?
- How do I want to fuck others?

Questions came thick and fast, like a consuming tidal wave of impending inescapable doom. *Hold on,* I told my brain. *Slow down. Let's take this step by step.* From the tidal wave, tons of questions were uncontrollably washing over me. Some of them were too frightening to even consider.

Memories from my childhood returned. It was time to revisit those locked away and painful moments when I was sexually touched as a child. I felt guilty. But I knew that it was not my fault and that it was not right to be touched and violated by another human being, especially as a child. So, I asked myself, *How can I deal with this conflicted feeling of guilt and pleasure at the same time?*

There were so many emotions. Yet, little by little I faced them head-on. I confronted those memories, the people involved. I made the decision to forgive them, accept that I was *not* guilty, and I forgave myself for holding onto that guilt. *Time to move on,* I told myself. *I am a vibrant sexual being! I deserve pleasure, acceptance, and connection with another!*

Within this raw state, fully exposing myself to myself, I started to feel the rise of love from my heart. My inner being was healing me. I started to feel whole again. It became clear after doing a full immersion in this spiritual sexual shamanism I was liberated. I felt free. I felt myself opening to the world, ready to be seen as I was, embracing myself in all ways and listening to my inner being.

And this is how I understood the role of sexuality in my life, how it reflects in the intimacy of relationships. I kept diving deeper and deeper, experiencing, feeling scintillating sensations that my body wanted to reveal, becoming freer and freer, choice by choice, moment by moment.

An incredible inner transfiguration was underway. A new resurrection was emerging. A new me! Connecting with my body and sexuality was elevating my intuition, my inner knowing. A connection was forming with my inner being, my connection

with the subtle world, my connection with nature—for we came from nature, and we are beings of nature.

And as I was enjoying this connection and dancing with the trees and singing and being myself and daring to become more authentic each day, life was bringing another experience to learn to trust my intuition deeply, not only from the mouth out, but from every atom of my body.

It was early April 2021. I received the news that my dear Uncle Saul passed away. It had been a challenging year as so many other beloved ones left this earth already.

Regardless of knowing that our spirit is eternal and infinite, the pain my human body felt was exhausting. The last couple of months I was receiving messages of so many departures of dear family members that I was still processing. I was continually sighing, knowing that I was still mourning them. I know this last uncle, though, was the last.

Saul was like a father figure, so my foundation of security was crumbling. And two days later, I received a call from my neighbor letting me know that a bank letter arrived saying that my house was going to a short sale for lack of payment.

"What? How so if I have the money in the bank account?!"

A memory from six months back came to me. During the month of June while I was in Costa Rica, I had this intuition to visit my bank where I have my house loan. I put it on my list to go. And of course, just thinking of the queues and all, I kept postponing. My intuition was telling me to go, and I decided to ignore it and prioritize other things.

And now, I was here. The automatic payments stopped working.

From one side, this was for not listening to myself and acting; and on the other side, I felt that another foundation of security, my home, was going away.

I felt insecure, unsafe, abandoned, left behind, ignored, lonely.

I walked the darkest night. And the only light that was coming to me was that the only safe place left, my root, my anchor, my stone, was within.

I realized the material things like my house, the material beings like my beloved uncle and family members were visitors, not permanent. And nothing is permanent; therefore, my foundation can only be what is infinite and eternal in truth, and that was my source.

Learning this lesson of not listening to my intuition, on not paying attention to the small things cost me almost $10K, which was the cost of the bank withdrawing the short sale.

From then on, I listened and acted accordingly, and from then on, my intuition was my best friend.

As you may realize already, life wisdom is always there, creating the opportunities our souls are yearning to free themselves from, the illusion that many times we fall into.

Now let me tell you this: I had the tools, I was ready to see the rawness in myself, I was inviting this rawness and authenticity every day. I believe it was this desire of communion with my inner temple and inner source that allowed me to understand the spiritual meaning of each experience and to embody its wisdom.

And I believe that that journey to the inner temple is waiting for each of you who are ready to meet with your radical authentic self and reclaim your inner authority, your inner goddess, access to the magic of your soul, and feel the radiant love of your inner source.

Remember this:

1. Your body holds an infinite intelligence waiting to emerge if you connect with it. Its power is for you to access and listen to.

2. Only you can choose what to believe about your body.

3. If you fall, it is okay! You always have the capacity

to get up again and again; you did it when you were a child, and many times you laughed when you fell. Other times you cried, but immediately after, you'd get up again. Always!

4. Your sexuality could reconnect you with your wildness within, with the rawness within you, the freedom, and with the permission to be seen, to shine, to be nude, and to be radically untamed and unapologetically yourself.

5. Your intuition has been communicating with you always, and many times you have followed it unconsciously. Your intuition becomes more real and accurate as you start recognizing it. It might be trial and error at the beginning until you recognize with absolute certainty which is your intuition and which your ego.

6. Following your intuition does not mean everything will be rainbows and flowers. It might be difficult sometimes, but it will keep you in full coherence with your soul.

7. And the most important: remember who you are. You are source manifested in a body! You are infinite and radiant love! That is your truth, that is your foundation, and that is the flame living within you, even though you might not be able to see it now. It is there, always, permanently, unconditionally, and lovingly.

I am so grateful that now I facilitate sacred programs for women to reconnect with the magic of their Inner Temple, based on the pillars of body, sexuality, and intuition. As a teacher of mine said to me, "My healing is the training, and the training is

the healing." So, my own healing has become the training that I share from my heart with the world.

Again, you are source manifested in a body, and everything you do is source experiencing itself through you. There is no separation. Separation is only the illusion we are breaking ourselves free from.

Honor your life, as it is the sacred path of remembering who you truly are.

ABOUT AMALAI

Amalai is the founder of Escuela Amalai and Joyful Live Academy and creator of the Dance of Freedom and The Magic of Your Inner Temple.

Amalai accompanies women leaders, entrepreneurs, healers, and lightworkers in their journey of self-exploration, self-healing, and self-mastery so they can live in authenticity, freedom, joy, and fulfillment as well as support others.

She also lives and teaches in Costa Rica, and the USA (Crestone).

Her students said, "Amalai has created a life-changing experience with the program to activate your magic." Amalai is a certified coach by the ICF, NLP, and Timeline Therapy® instructor, HeartMath trainer, yoga teacher, PSYCH-K facilitator, meditation instructor, Angelic Reiki Master, Akashic Records Trainer, a channeler, and past-life regression facilitator. She has worked in the corporate world for twenty years leading regional teams.

To learn more about how you can connect and work with Amalai, please visit her website at www.Amalai.Love, where you can find information about her programs, events, and services.

Download your free five days of self-love from her website today. And if you want to accelerate your self-healing and self-mastery, join her advance programs.

Facebook: YoSoyAmalaiLove
Instagram: Amalai.Love
Instagram: Joyfullife.Academy
YouTube: Amalai Love
Web: www.amalai.love

SELF-DESIGNED DREAMS

Teri P. Cox, MBA

What an amazing and spiritual journey *life* is!

As I embrace this next major chapter in my life, reflecting on the past decades, it feels like a dream. I'm humbled and grateful for it all:

- For the ability to channel my energy and combine my strengths, strategic thinking, and creativity.
- For my family, friendships, and business and personal connections.
- For the deep, loving marriage and soul partnership I shared with my husband Bill for so many years.
- For overcoming challenges and evolving through loss and grief.
- For my power with words, authentically from the heart, and actions for inspiring, engaging, and connecting the golden dots for problem-solving and positive impact.
- For invaluable life lessons worth sharing.

I'm so grateful for those blessings that embody my soul and the woman I am today. Those experiences—the magical

breakthrough moments, the love, the wisdom—are collectively woven together, like golden threads into my life tapestry, protecting and carrying me forward.

The best of those—the golden nuggets—are all about change.

My first critical lesson came from a challenging family situation during my youth in Pittsburgh, PA. I was raised in a middle-class neighborhood in the 1950s by my loving parents who both worked. My father had a hardware store, while my mother worked for the City of Pittsburgh. Education was a priority for my family, so they made sure I was committed to my daily classwork. I excelled as a student, was supported by my great teachers, progressed to an accelerated program, and had lots of friends and fun social activities. All good, right? Except I was emotionally abused by my maternal grandmother who lived on our first floor. An ultrareligious Hungarian woman, bitter from losing most of her family during WWII, she was racist and sexist, felt cursed because she had five daughters and no sons. She took it out on us, except for my older brother, Jack, whom she favored. Her dominant bullying presence was constant with criticism and negativity. I tried to avoid and ignore her as much as I could, but her hurtful messages got to me, damaging my self-esteem and confidence. Some of those messages, now internalized, still haunt me today.

We put up with her for years, excusing her because she was the elder matriarch. Then, during my junior year in high school, she was so offensive to me and my two friends that I finally reached my limit. Overcoming fear to take a stand, given our family pattern, I chose to confront my parents. After serious discussion, we all agreed it was time for a change. My mother and aunts got together and rented an apartment for grandma. She moved out. Such a relief! What an empowering lesson for me and dramatic shift for my family to restore peace and harmony throughout our home!

Yet, what if I hadn't spoken up? Nothing would've changed. It's so important to act beyond fear, against abuse of any kind,

and seek positive solutions, especially during times of emotional upheaval and political divisiveness on a global scale. Since then, I've continued to push beyond fear and self-esteem issues and developed keen protective antennae against abuse of any kind.

I'm a team player, but I learned to be an independent thinker about most things. I don't accept the status quo when innovation is better. It's good practice to think *outside the box* to consider better options. It's wise to be proactive about designing the changes you want for your life, then take action to make them happen.

I recall a conversation I had during a lunch meeting with a dean of the University of Pittsburgh, College of Arts and Sciences. I was his guest during the thirtieth anniversary of the founding of the Women's Studies Program. While at Pitt in the 1970s, I minored in that program. I had a self-designed major in communications and speech, with some of my courses taken at another university near Pitt campus. Knowing much of my story, the dean offered this perceptive insight: "You had a self-designed major and success as a student, then, from what I can tell, you've had a successful self-designed career, marriage—a self-designed life." I hadn't thought about it that way before, but he was right!

While a student, I also led an independent study research project, managing twelve students to gather needed information. Then after graduating, I was hired as editor to produce *HELP YOURSELF: A Women's (People's) Resource Directory for Pittsburgh*, published by the University of Pittsburgh, sold in local bookstores. I handled the PR and media interviews, which launched my career. I became PR director of the local Mental Health Association and hosted an issues-oriented radio talk show, *Impact*, on two local stations as a side gig.

Those experiences and opportunities during and after college built the foundation for a positive, independent, entrepreneurial mindset, igniting my passion for connecting the golden dots to creative solutions, with projects that make a difference.

A defining life-changing event was my interview with a spokesperson for a major oil company headquartered in Pittsburgh. He was on my show to discuss an Arab oil embargo making the news. Afterward, I recruited him to chair my media committee at the Mental Health Association. He also served on our board of directors. We both worked on local United Way campaigns, alongside the Steelers and Pirates of that era. Bill Cox became my mentor and trusted friend. Always encouraging and respectful, he said I was talented and special, but could tell I sometimes doubted myself. I shared the story about my grandmother and how I changed the situation. He applauded my action, but explained that, because of her abusive messages, "my mirror was cracked": I couldn't see the light that others saw in me. His supportive comments bolstered my confidence.

With new courage, two years later, I moved to Atlanta for a new position as the PR director of the Atlanta Merchandise Mart, loaded with demanding, nonstop responsibilities and challenges. I promoted rotating weekly regional markets amid special events and local southern politics. That stretched my skill set at times, requiring me to adapt and learn quickly. I kept in touch with Bill for his advice, as needed. Less than two years later, I moved back to Pittsburgh for a higher-paying marketing job. I reconnected with Bill, and our special friendship evolved into something deeper.

On New Year's Day in 1982, Bill became my beloved husband, soulmate, and partner in all things—and my biggest cheerleader! We were married in Denver and later moved to San Diego because of two transfers by his company. Ultimately, we settled in central NJ, where we both were employed by, then served as strategic communications consultants to, the healthcare and life sciences industry.

We found the perfect center hall colonial house near Princeton and loved sharing it with a family of cuddly fun-loving felines. We worked long hours with great clients, often commuting into New

York City. We also served in leadership positions, volunteering for several organizations with missions that mattered. We enjoyed discovering the great social and cultural activities in the tri-state area—concerts, Broadway plays, fine dining, and dancing. We attended formal events and engaged in PR and advocacy campaigns, sometimes working with celebrities and political leaders, and some became friends. We took long weekend trips and wonderful vacations as often as possible to explore most of the world. Everything meshed perfectly together. We were living the dream!

One of our most memorable vacations was a business trip and visit to Japan when we met Bill's family and saw the key sites in the country. Bill's father was part Japanese, growing up in Yokohama before he moved to the US, and he married and settled in Ohio. He arranged most of our visit with family connections—a personalized way to enjoy the country and its culture. We learned about traditions, such as *kintsugi,* the unique way the Japanese repaired cracks and gouges in broken dishes and pottery by filling them in with gold, transforming them into works of art rather than discards. What a beautiful idea! In many ways, Bill's *golden* messages of love and support over the years helped to repair those old cracks in my self-esteem.

As time went on, my work with corporate clients expanded. I needed to deepen my knowledge about business operations, finance, and marketing. We both were working in New York City, so I began coursework toward an MBA at New York University. That's when our dream life began to unravel.

Keeping up with work and my courses, I also had to take on the responsibility of managing my parents' healthcare. I rearranged my schedule and made regular weekend trips to Pittsburgh for several years to help my mother care for my beloved dad who had Alzheimer's disease. After his passing, the trips continued for years, as I became my mother's support caregiver while she was dealing with congestive heart failure.

During that period, Bill partnered with me in my *virtual*

strategic communications consultancy. We set up offices in our home, working mostly by email and phone with other like-minded, seasoned colleagues across the US, in Japan, and in the EU to help with our healthcare clients. Given my personal experience, and understanding the burdens on family caregivers, I was blessed with the opportunity to recruit organizations such as AARP, National Council on the Aging, Alzheimer's Association, Interfaith Caregivers Alliance, and others on behalf of a client company sponsor. Then, I partnered with them to create *CARING TO HELP OTHERS*, an award-winning user-friendly training program manual to help organizations train volunteers to assist caregivers of older adults. That program helped over 13,000 community organizations across the US and in Japan. It also had a website until 2018, utilized by millions of community agencies and caregivers, setting a new gold standard for programs serving the needs of family caregivers.

My mother passed away from a stroke in 1998. With little time to grieve, three months later, Bill was diagnosed with prostate cancer and other complicated illnesses. That's when we began our convoluted, arduous journey through his challenging eleven-year battle with cancer and more before he lost.

I managed his care and kept it all going in our lives until Bill was gone. Then I still tried to keep going, numb and in denial about how dramatically my life had changed. I resisted the truth until I couldn't any longer. I entered a period of darkness and fear about my unknown future and how to move forward.

With support from caring friends, I took time for quiet contemplation and meditation, a spiritual practice I've used since learning about it at Pitt. Closing my eyes, breathing deeply and going inward, I asked questions of my intuitive wisdom, a deep power we all have within us if we take time to listen. I found the answers I needed to take the first steps. The driven quintessential caregiver, always helping others, I gave myself permission to finally let go. I found the right resources to start learning how to

keep going. With compassion and grace, I began to heal by focusing loving care and attention on *myself*. Stepping out of darkness into the new light of life, I was transformed.

It's been over a decade. I've been on this amazing metamorphic journey through loss, change, and personal growth. I've been enjoying life again with new friends and social groups, dancing to the music of local bands, dating, and traveling to favorite spots to visit special friends and loved ones. I've taken on new consulting projects and partnerships, books to write and coauthor, new courses, public speaking opportunities, and more. I've found new ways to pamper myself and fill my cup with gold.

Since 2020, the entire world has been rocked to the core by the COVID-19 pandemic, growing anger, violence, and divisiveness. Millions of lives have been dramatically impacted. Yet, I remain full of gratitude and hope for the future from the collective good and positive developments I've seen in the world.

I've had some setbacks, felt isolated and fearful at times, postponed projects, and needed much quiet time. Yet, I also seized the opportunity to sell my house of thirty-four-plus years during a rare hot sellers' market. As an agent of change, I've felt blessed, more prepared because of my journey and the powerful lessons I've learned while navigating through change to keep making progress. Here's some of that wisdom for connecting the golden dots that's worth sharing:

1. Change is inevitable. Nothing in life remains the same. You can't control or stop it, and resistance is futile.

2. The more you embrace change, the easier it is to navigate through it. How you respond makes *all* the difference!

3. Be patient and compassionate with *yourself*; give *self-love* during the process.

4. What doesn't kill you, transforms you. *Never give up!*

5. Work through fear by meditating, creating a vision and goals for the future, and continuing to take action.

6. Keep a positive mindset and express gratitude for all of the blessings in your life.

As I embrace a *major* milestone decade this year, I'm focused on maintaining my health, staying positive and connected, and achieving new goals, no matter what is happening in our world. My dreams are about reinvention, new companionship, new experiences, and opportunities for greater abundance, growth, peace, and joy. My vision is about carrying forward the best of my story, and all I bring to the table—my strengths, my gifts as a change agent, and the wisdom I gained from my life journey to inspire and help others navigate through change. With my brand, Teri P. Cox, MBA, I'm building a platform for sharing my story and key messages on social media, writing and publishing new content, public speaking, and consulting with new partners on products and services that support my passion for making a difference both for companies and individuals. Age is just a number! It's *my* time. I've earned my wings. I'm ready to fly!

The two greatest gifts God has given to us are this profound, beautiful journey called *life* and an amazing, resilient human spirit that can transcend beyond any obstacle or darkness, keep shining brightly, and soar to new heights.

Stay positive and keep dreaming! Find golden opportunities to make an impact! Now more than ever, our world needs your special gifts.

ABOUT TERI P. COX, MBA

With passion and creativity, Teri P. Cox has dedicated her life and career to challenging the status quo, connecting the golden dots to better solutions, and transforming through change and loss. An award-winning consultant, strategist, author, and speaker, Teri's provided leadership and expertise serving companies, professional women, those with cancer, and organizations supporting family caregivers across the country. Her projects have made a difference for millions.

Since 1992, Teri has led her firm, Cox Communications Partners, LLC, to position clients for results, helping them build win-win partnerships with aligned stakeholder groups. In 2005, Teri was named one of the *PharmaVoice 100* most inspiring people in the life sciences industry.

Teri is a past-president of the Healthcare Businesswomen's Association and served on the American Cancer Society (ACS) regional board. As advocacy leader, she received the national ACS St. George Medal award.

Teri has an MBA in marketing from New York University's Stern School of Business and a BA in communications/speech from the University of Pittsburgh.

Teri has been featured as a coauthor with Jack Canfield in the best-selling book, *The Recipe for Success*, and guest on podcasts, including *Ordinary People Doing Extraordinary Things* with Keri Roberts.

To learn more, you can connect with Teri P. Cox, MBA at:

Email: tcox@coxcommpartners.com
Linkedin: www.linkedin.com/in/teri-p-cox-mba
Facebook: www.facebook.com/teri.p.cox
www.teripcoxmba.com *(under construction)*

TWO CHOICES

Lori Anne De Iulio Casdia

L ife is about choices. It's actually rather simple. There are truly only two choices: yes or no, up or down, do it or don't do it, right or left, forward or backward . . . stuck or unstuck . . . you see what I mean?

Well I was stuck. So stuck that I lost myself. I got completely swallowed up. There were signs all along the way warning me that I completely ignored.

I had allowed myself to be "justed" to death. Just do this and just do that. It resulted in the greatest loss in my life of myself. I was willingly giving pieces of myself away. One tiny piece at a time until I couldn't even recognize who I was.

It was kind of like gaining weight. You gain a pound here a pound there then one day you look in the mirror or see a picture and wonder what the heck happened. It sneaks up on you, but it was always a choice.

You see, I was in love—truly thought I had a partner. The partner I had always dreamed of, a partnership that would last the ages. I would see myself walking silently down the beach in my eighties holding hands with my man. Like my parents. We were going to be together forever. We were great together.

Complemented each other. We made such a good team, or so I thought.

Little by little, he was telling me, "Don't act this way," "Don't dress that way," "Think this," "Think that."

I would fight myself thinking, *This isn't right. This doesn't feel right. This shouldn't be this way. Life is supposed to be joyous.*

I'd do whatever he said. When I didn't agree, I'd push back, and he'd push back harder. Call me names. Punish me by not speaking to me or just ignoring me. He would refuse to call or text me during the day or communicate in any way like he normally would have. And the ultimate slap of disapproval was that he would become magically too busy and unavailable.

I was stuck. I lost who I was trying to be, what others around me wanted and needed me to be. I didn't like this version of me—what I had become. There were signs all along the way, a nudge here, a sign there from the Universe, God, source (whatever you refer to as your higher power). We are given nudges, signals that tell us something isn't right. Like a flag on the field in football.

When I was growing up, I was taught, similar to the Jack Canfield Success Principles, to take 100% responsibility. Anytime something occurred that was uncomfortable or caused a disagreement or discourse, I looked at it and assessed what I did wrong. *How did I contribute to this event? What action or words did I say or do that created this discourse between us?* I would choose to take it all on . . . 100% responsibility for the discourse. It hadn't even crossed my mind that sometimes it wasn't my issue or responsibility at all. I don't believe he ever said he was sorry or took responsibility at all . . . ever!

So when he was having issues, suddenly I would feel—literally feel—the pain, the heartache, and the depth of his issues. It would feel like a cloud over me. I felt the heaviness from the weight of the issue or event. Even though it wasn't my issue at all, I would take it on as if it were mine to solve. I couldn't separate their issue from my responsibility. I needed to find a way to

separate their "stuff" from mine. But I didn't know this yet. I was still sleeping—walking through life like I was in a dream.

And then one day I looked up and saw this huge pile of hay in front of me. That pile of stuff was everything I was holding here—in my heart and in my head. Each straw of hay represented a different issue. It was staggering, overwhelming, and seemingly something that one person couldn't overcome.

I decided that I must get out from under this huge mountain of hay. If it was all mine, then I would fix or repair each and every straw. But I could see some of the issues and I knew deep down intuitively they weren't really mine, but I owned them anyway. Sometimes just because I was in the room or someone shared their story with me, I would own it.

I had a choice to make. I had an opportunity. I didn't want to be stuck anymore. I wanted to make my own choices. I wanted to *get* to do things, not *have* to do things, and I wanted to find that eighteen-year-old girl who was strong, intelligent, and unstoppable. Where had she gone? Why did I allow her to fade away, get swallowed up?

I was in search of answers. I wanted to get unstuck. I didn't want to feel fearful, helpless, lost, scared.

And then one day, something happened.

I went to an event for work. It was a beautiful ceremony, I was in a peaceful place within myself, and as I surveyed the room, I saw this woman staring at me with sad eyes. As if she were there specifically to speak to me. I had to walk in her direction to leave the auditorium. As I passed her, she stopped me and apologized for disrespecting me. I had no idea what she was talking about. She proceeded to tell me a story, show me pictures, detail every step, move, and maneuver. Yes, he had been cheating on me with her.

I went numb. No emotions. I didn't get upset. I felt nothing. As if I already knew. I asked questions to gauge whether she was telling the truth. She happily proved it with pictures, emails, and

texts. She had it all. It was almost as if she were enjoying telling me her tale. I did and said nothing. I came home and crumbled. I couldn't get the images out of my head. The words she spewed. It was simply awful.

After weeks of weeping and running scenarios over and over in my head, I decided no more! No more tears, no more walls, no more of this nonsense. It no longer served me. I tired of having my grand pity party. I chose to find a way to become unstuck. Whatever that meant.

I searched and searched for answers. I read self-help books, I went to psychics, mediums, had tarot card readings, and watched YouTube videos of astrologists, tarot cards, horoscopes. All in search of the inner peace I was seeking.

I eventually found myself in therapy, trying to figure my way out of this fog of disconnection, of why this was happening. What did I do? Was I not enough? Pretty enough? Smart enough? Didn't I matter? Wasn't I enough to love? Therapy offered help and guidance, but one day something my therapist shared resonated so deeply that I started to read everything I could on the subject.

She said it sounds like these people are all narcissists. I hadn't heard this word before.

Narcissists have an inflated sense of their own importance. They have a need for excessive attention or admiration, always have troubled relationships, and lack empathy for others. They are typically extremely magnetic and charming. They are looking for obedient admirers. A good time. They don't like conflict or dissension. Your sole role is to prop up their insatiable ego. They even tell you what to think and how to feel. They are unapologetic about all of it.

They lie about themselves and others. They are entitled and manipulative, and they take zero responsibility. They are experts at deflection and blame; they blame you for what they are doing

and accuse you of it. It is a mind game that doesn't end well for the receiver.

I found myself making excuses for his bad behavior or minimizing myself for the hurt that I was feeling. I found myself trying to reason and use logic to help him understand the painful effect his behavior had on me. I thought if he understood how much he hurt me, what was hurting me, and why, he'd change. I found out with a narcissist it doesn't matter. He wasn't getting what he wanted or what he needed. That is all that mattered to him, and sadly that is all that will *ever* matter to him. So he moved on.

Months later, I found myself at a friend's spiritual weekend event. My friend, Paul Saladino, a psychic medium, intuitive counselor life coach, certified hypnotherapist, and energy healer located on Long Island, had this event every year. I remember this day so clearly. Little did I know it would change the trajectory of my life.

Paul had hundreds in attendance. I sat in the back alone, sad and weepy as I had been for months, trying to sort out what had happened. I was a little nervous to be there, feeling anxious about being there alone but a little empowered.

Then this speaker came up. Her name, Debi Silber. The words coming out of her mouth spoke directly to me. Truly, at some points, as if in a movie, everyone else blurred and she was looking directly into my eyes and into my heart, talking directly to me. Her confidence was unshakable. Her knowing was innate. She knew me . . . she saw me . . . *Yes, yes, yes, this is what I am feeling, saying, hearing, and thinking.*

I bought her book, the #1 international bestseller, *The Unshakable Woman.* I devoured the words, her stories, and felt compelled to reach out to her. I needed to figure this out. Through working with her, I found out yes indeed, he and others in my life are narcissists. I was calling them into my life and had to learn to stop that. But how?

With Debi's help, I discovered I was suffering from post-be-

trayal trauma. You see, Debi Silber is the founder of the PBT (Post-Betrayal Transformation) Institute, author of *Trust Again (I am one of the fab 14 - part of my story is referenced as Julianna, p.45) and* is a holistic psychologist and a health, mindset, and personal development expert. Through our work, it was so clear to her and now me I had severe trauma from betrayal.

I would take the physical abuse I received years back over the emotional abuse—because wounds heal. Black and blues disappear, but owning all the bad in someone else's life, questioning your every decision, choice, breath, step, questioning one's self-worth predicated on what could not be described as anything less than a selfish narcissistic predator is unquestionably the cruelest, most devastating experience. Not only is your heart breaking, but your mind, body, and soul are too.

In life, there are always only two choices (pulling emotions and ego out): yes or no, go or stay, right or wrong. You can do something or not do something. It sounds so simple, but when you throw the heart in, the game seems to change. The mind almost goes into a drugged state.

Life shouldn't be an emotional roller coaster. It should and will be challenging and a ride but not a daily emotional roller coaster—walking on eggshells, never knowing if Jekyll or Hyde is going to appear.

The betrayal puts every minute of every day of the past with them in question. Healing from the pain caused by another person involves healing our self-esteem, self-worth, trust issues, and more.

Now we have identified what was keeping me stuck and what I was allowing to imprison me. How do I find myself again?

I knew at this point it was time to move on. I never played the victim. Actually I didn't feel like a victim. Okay, maybe when I was having my pity party. Instead, I took responsibility for my actions, and apparently, I was taking responsibility for others as well. I needed to find a way to take this pile of hay—issues,

challenges, unfinished feelings, situations, and interactions—and figure out how much of it was actually mine.

I started the process of taking each straw of hay off the pile and discerning whether it was a *me issue* or a *them* issue.

You may be asking why the delineation. It's about being able to unravel what we need to take responsibility for and what we don't. Sometimes it is partially our responsibility, and sometimes it isn't our responsibility at all. By looking at the issues as they come and being able to identify them, you take the amount of time we dwell on an issue down to seconds. Many times others want us to solve their problem—own their problem merely so they don't have to own it themselves. That's not okay! Say it to yourself, "That's not okay."

That *me issue–you issue* switch is a really important toggle that we all need to learn how to use. I found by being able to recognize what was mine and what was others' enabled me to stay genuine to myself. When you do this, you won't find yourself doing things that don't or no longer resonate with you. You will be a better friend, partner, lover, mother, aunt, teacher, coach, mentor, whatever you are to the people in your life.

You can only imagine what I found on this journey. I had to actually process each piece of hay. It was arduous. It was sometimes painful, regretful, but it had to be done. I was not going to be swallowed up any longer. I had to face my past if I wanted to be free and have a future. I had to learn to trust, in myself and then in others.

Through this process, I found that I had rediscovered myself. I found that I had tried to accommodate so many people that I lost who I was. I was swallowed up and trying to be somebody to everyone as opposed to just being genuinely myself.

I went through a huge transformation between the betrayal and today. Now I seek and find joy every day. I do my power hour of meditation, reading, gratitude journaling, exercise, and affirmations. I get to serve others and help them achieve their vision

and dreams and Soar to Success. I only own what is mine. I know what I want and what I don't want.

After my journey of transformation, I do what I want, when I want. I am completely myself. I have no walls. I allow people to see my vulnerabilities. I embrace my friends, loved ones, colleagues, and clients for all they genuinely are and encourage them to embrace themselves, as they are perfect in every way. I endeavor to always be the best me I can be. Some days I am better at it than others.

Now I know it is all right to be vulnerable. It is human to make mistakes. Before, when I made a mistake, I would beat myself up for days and weeks on end. I would bring it back up years later and be unrelenting to myself. No one could possibly say harsher things to me than I did to myself.

So I practiced differentiating between issues that were mine and others'. Every day I would get better at taking that learning curve down from two weeks to within seconds. I would be able in any circumstance to look at the situation, assess it, and determine what was my responsibility, if any. Now it's just natural and I can make this determination within seconds. Might I even say now it is a habit. A better, healthier habit.

I am so grateful for all of my experiences because it made me who I am today. It made me a better coach. It drove me to learn more about how I could assist and coach others to Soar to Success. I started to study and get certified under Jack Canfield, Tony Robbins, Patty Aubery, Mary Morrisey, Bob Proctor, Brené Brown, Byron Katie, Dr. Joe Dispenza, Dr. Joe Vitale, Ray Higdon, Esther Hicks, Simon Sinek, and many more. My goal was to learn from the best in the industry to serve my clients as best I could—to bring multiple styles and tools to my clients. It morphed into the Lori Anne method of Soaring to Success.

I added to those tools affirmations, gratitude journaling, meditation, essential oils, healing sound bowls, AFT reset, mindset, power hours, and more. I was introduced and certified

as a Ho'oponopono practitioner and Kundalini Meditative Yoga practitioner.

I felt alive. Everything was clearer. I couldn't absorb enough from these experts in the craft.

I am sharing my story to let you know if I can do it, if I can transform into a beautiful butterfly serving others, then you can too. This is to let you know there are tools out there and coaches out in the world ready to guide you through the journey. Be it this simple tool of a *you issue–me issue* or other ones to help you gain clarity and to get you from where you are to where you want to be. To help you navigate the journey so you don't lose yourself but actually grow yourself. To remind you that all of our Success Codes are already within us when we are born. We merely need to look inward to achieve our fullest potential and be able to discern what we will own. To help you get unstuck if you choose to be unstuck. Whatever you choose is the right choice for you.

My final words are yes, it is scary. Yes, it's work. Yes, you will have to jump some hurdles and have some challenges. But aren't you worth it? If you even paused for a second at that question, allow me the liberty of helping you: most definitely you are worth it. I encourage you to try to see the signs at the nudge. I can promise you that transformation will leave you feeling happiness again; you will find joy again. You will reconnect with your higher power and find your purpose. You will be in alignment with who you really are, and you will not have to do it alone. Look inward and follow your dreams. There is a reason why you are here. So you can choose to play a higher role, serve a higher purpose, show up for you, and show up BIG. It might just lead you to your happy ending.

ABOUT LORI ANNE DE IULIO CASDIA

Lori Anne is a life and business transformational success coach, high-performance coach, business and marketing positioner and strategist helping entrepreneurs and business owners who are just starting out or who feel stuck in their life and business to create the business that will sustain the life they desire.

She is the radio host of Healthy Lifestyle with Lori Anne and has been seen on Fox, News 12, Jack Canfield Success TV, and more. With thirty-five-plus years' experience in business and marketing, adding tools as a master mindset mentor, and becoming a life coach, Law of Attraction practitioner, and more, Lori Anne has spent thousands of hours learning from the best in her field to bring you the best tools. Lori Anne is an award-winning coach and speaker, and she believes her life's work is to bring positive creative energy into the world.

Her purpose is to use her love and compassion to illuminate, inspire, educate, and empower people to fulfill their fullest potential, find and embrace their life purpose, live their highest vision, forge a strong foundation, guide them to achieve their vision and dreams, and Soar to Success.

To connect with Lori Anne for speaking engagements; to learn more about her programs, events, retreats, free resources, and coaching services, you can contact her directly:

Web: www.LDCStrategies.com
Email: lacasdia@ldcstrategies.com
FB/IG: LDC Strategies

TRUST YOUR TRUTH

Keri Gavin

My fingers were tightly wrapped around my mom's hand for balance as I hopped from one grocery store tile to the other in the checkout line. A grocery store checkout is the perfect place for a seven-year-old to get fidgety.

I misstepped on one of the orange squares and bumped into the elderly woman behind me. As my eyes glanced up, I was met with a cheery smile from a well-dressed, silver-haired, rosy-cheeked, beautiful blue-eyed elderly woman. In hindsight, she was like a real-life Mrs. Doubtfire. "Oh, no problem, dear," she said as she gently helped me stand upright again.

After a few moments of small talk between her and my mom, the elderly woman leaned forward toward me. Her hat was perfectly placed on her head, and her blue eyes began to widen with wonder. She leaned in closer toward me and asked, "What do you want to be when you grow up, sweetie?"

Hopping back and forth, swinging my skirt behind me with each turn of the squares, I didn't even look up, but I proudly announced without hesitation, "A mom!"

Out of the corner of my eye, I could see her stand tall again,

and she giggled a bit as she responded, "Ohhhh, how cute, but that's not a job, sweetie! What do you really want to be?"

I remember a feeling of confusion. It was as if someone had told me the sky wasn't blue. Being a mom isn't a job? It isn't a thing? My little brain was having a hard time computing what she said.

It was in that split second—with a stranger, who asked a simple conversational question—I quickly learned there were rules of life according to the outside world. Just like that, my own self-trust started to wobble.

Confused, but wanting to respond, I glanced up as she towered over me, my pigtails swinging with each turn of my head as I was trying to make sense of that new information. I politely responded, "Um, well, I think I will be a teacher then!" I replied with a smile beaming across my face!

"Oh, how wonderful!" she answered as her hands clasped in front of her with approval. I felt a sense of confused acceptance. My sweet seven-year-old heart was struggling to reconcile what I truly desired with what the world was telling me was acceptable.

It was the first time I felt a disconnect between what I knew to be true for me and what others wanted for me.

It was technically our senior year at Keene State College, but logistically my best friend Erin and I had one extra semester in the fall after our graduation in May. We had taken our sophomore year off together while the rest of our friends stayed the course. We returned to Keene State the following year, which put us behind the rest of our friends by only a semester since we both had taken some classes at community colleges in that time. Since we were together for that bonus semester, it wasn't a problem—we were actually excited to have one extra semester together before the "real world"! Because we had one extra semester, I made the decision (with her guidance and support!) to do an exchange semester at North Carolina State University for the spring semester so I could live with my then boyfriend.

While I didn't want to leave our off-campus house, we both agreed it was a great opportunity and adventure, and since we'd have a whole extra semester together, just us, why not! We agreed January 1, I would move to North Carolina and return to New Hampshire for the fall. We would live together in the fall to finish the credits needed for our psychology degrees and then be out in the big world with the rest of them.

It was midday on a Wednesday as I was doing some school-work on my computer. An AOL instant message popped up on my computer from one of my closest friends Mikey. "Can you talk?" he asked. My heart skipped a beat, and my stomach felt like it dropped through twenty-seven stories in an instant. It was unlike him to message me like that—I intuitively knew something happened. "Of course," I replied. "Call my cell.'"

I stood up and began pacing the bedroom, looking outside to the parking lot of the apartment as I waited for his call. It couldn't have been more than two minutes, but it felt like one hundred years. Barely hearing a full ring, I answered the phone. "Hey, what's wrong?" I asked in a panic. With a deep sigh and hesitation in his voice he responded, "I don't even know how to tell you this . . . Erin died." The room felt wobbly. My body started to tingle, my eyes were darting back and forth outside looking into the parking lot. My body was processing what he said before my brain could even recognize it.

"What?" I said, "Erin who?"

"Our Erin," he responded.

"What do you mean? Not possible. Wait, what? How? I don't understand?" I choked out.

"We don't know much," he said. "She passed away in her sleep, and we don't know anything else yet."

It couldn't be real. She was twenty-one. Nobody at twenty-one just goes to sleep and doesn't wake up.

"There has to be a mistake," I said. My brain was racing. It had to be someone else. Maybe he was confused.

He wasn't confused. It was real. The poor guy had to keep repeating it to me over and over. My brain would not accept it.

After a whirlwind of flying home, going to our apartment, finally being back with my college framily (friend/family) as well as somehow navigating a funeral I never thought I'd experience, life was moving on. I was angry, I was sad, I couldn't understand how the world was existing without her.

Days turned to weeks, and weeks turned to months, but the heaviness, pain, and sadness stayed. As the end of the summer came, I made one of the most difficult decisions of my life. I knew I couldn't live in our college town without her, without any of our friends, alone. I knew for my mental health and my own well-being, that wasn't an option. But I also knew I was just a few credits away from my degree.

I prayed, I asked for guidance, and I asked for signs, but it wasn't until I turned into my own heart that I got my answer.

I knew I had to finish my semester, but I also knew I had to do it in a way that worked for me. I journaled and asked myself some questions to access clarity. I talked with my therapist and my parents and ultimately decided that the best way for me to do this was to commute the two hours to college, stack my classes back-to-back, sit through six hours of classes, and commute two hours home three days a week. The other two days I nannied full-time 7 a.m. to 7 p.m., and I would manage to keep myself busy.

As I wiped my tears sitting at the beach one afternoon, I knew I didn't go that far to only go that far. I knew she would be so mad at me if I didn't finish! I vowed to her in the moment that I would create a life of memories and moments full of life enough for the both of us.

I also knew it wasn't as simple as everyone was telling me to just "go back and finish it out." I had to do this my way. I had to create a path that worked for me and still got me to the result. That was one of the first monumental moments when I leaned into my self-trust rather than outside approval.

I finished my psychology degree and just a few months later started toward my master's in education in an intensive accelerated program. A few months into that, I got pregnant and three months later got married! Just as I graduated from Lesley University with my masters in Elementary Education in May, my sweet baby boy arrived June first.

This was it. This was what I had been dreaming of all my life. After ten years of nannying for other families and being an elementary school teacher, camp counselor, and babysitter since the age of nine, my dream of becoming a mom was finally real.

From the moment I held him in my arms in the middle of the night, to the sleepless days and weeks to follow, it was everything I dreamed of and more. Sleep deprived for sure, but I was never bothered by the middle-of-the-night feedings, countless hours in the rocking chair, and many nights in the moonlight cuddling this fresh, sweet, new baby boy. I actually quite enjoyed the stillness of these moments while the rest of the world was asleep and it was just me and him.

About three to four weeks into this new role as mom, I sat in the glider chair for a late-night feeding in his room. I found myself staring at his little soft cheeks, his fluttering eyes as he was slowly closing them back to sleep, his tiny arm tucked under my side and his other arm across his chest as his little fingers gripped onto my pointer finger. The full moon poured light into his bedroom so bright it was as if it was daytime. As I sat gliding in the chair studying all his features, tears began streaming down my face. He already looked bigger, fuller, stronger. He was changing so fast, and it was already going so quickly. Even if I didn't know what day it was, every day was spent with him, and yet, I felt like I was already forgetting things.

It was at that very moment I decided I was not going to go back to teaching, and I was going to find a way to work and be with my kid(s). I didn't want to miss anything. I wanted to see it all. I had dreamed about this my entire life, and I knew there was

no way I could not spend my days witnessing this little human explore and discover the world.

I decided I would go back to nannying where my son could come with me. I found an amazing family that welcomed me and my sweet baby Monday through Fridays. At the same time, I had discovered a passion for documenting all these memories I didn't want to miss through photography. Photography had always been a passion of mine, and through all my childhood years you could always find me with a camera. I just wanted to document memories, even from a young age. I was always the one taking pictures with friends, family, and especially if we ever went on trips or adventures.

As I was documenting my own life, my own family, my own memories, I started taking my camera everywhere I went. I started a personal blog that documented our adventures. That quickly turned into taking photos of the neighborhood kids as we all played in the backyards, then friends and family Christmas cards, and before I knew it, people started asking if they could hire me! It was so surprising to me because I never set out to be a professional photographer! I simply didn't want to miss moments from my own life, and I began documenting things through the lens of a mother's love. Being present in the little moments and freezing them in time.

If I'm completely honest, I didn't know that could be a full-time profession! I did have one friend, Melissa, who was a professional photographer, so with these increased inquiries, I reached out to her for some insight. I told her people were asking me to take photographs of their families and she squealed with excitement. "You have an eye for this in a way that can't be taught, Keri. Trust that! You can learn business as you go, but the creative eye is so natural for you!"

In the months and years to follow, I spent late nights and early mornings reading, studying, and learning photography as a craft in online forums and websites as a business. (Pre-Facebook

and online education as it is today!) I began attending workshops and hiring mentors, and before long, I was officially a professional photographer documenting real-life memories for families in the Boston area. Things were really picking up, and I was able to do meaningful work and be with my kids. It felt like a dream come true.

Just a few short years later, I found myself divorced at thirty years old with two small children under the age of four and with a creative business. By identifying something that I loved to create and share with people and making money doing it, I had created an accidental successful business! If you had asked me years before if I could imagine that as my future, I would have said you're crazy.

But despite things going well, as I was newly divorced, I couldn't help but feel like everyone in my world started planting the seeds of doubt in my head. While it may have been coming from a good place and wanting me and my kids to have safety, it was difficult to hear people telling me to go back to teaching because it was "safer." It was difficult to hear that I was "just taking pictures" and it was time to get serious. I was serious. I had been serious for a few years! I had created a business that brought me and others so much joy. While it was amazing, I found myself noticing other people's opinions in my head; just as my business was beginning to grow, doubt was also beginning to creep in.

I decided against all odds and approval to dig deep down into the essence of who I am and remember that even when it's difficult to hear other people's opinions, I trust myself and I know what's best for me. So I continued my photography business and did not get a nine-to-five. The truth is, I never dreamed of being an entrepreneur; I didn't have lemonade stands on the sidewalks or make bracelets to sell in school like many others did. I did always dream of being with my kids as they grew up in the world. I had mostly found my groove of doing work that felt so meaningful and also served my clients!

My business began to grow and expand. With the amazing support of my fiancé, close friends, and family, I was named Best of Boston photographer as well as a few other awards. I was 99 percent referral based; I had created incredible relationships with my clients and colleagues. It was working! The more successful I became, the more questions I started to receive from other creatives asking how I created this successful business. The more I started sharing with them, the more they started creating their own success.

As I continued to grow with photography, I realized I was a great teacher when it came to helping others do the same with their creative work. I was using my (formal) education skills but in a different lens. I was leveraging my psychology background and education skill sets around teaching success to creatives, coaches, and other service-based entrepreneurs.

Once this really started to pick up, I noticed a new fear pop up: What if I don't really know what I'm doing helping other people? I somehow started to believe that I wasn't as good as I should be at the mentoring side of business and I needed to know the real secrets I was somehow missing, despite having created my own success firsthand. I had fallen in love with helping other people create their own success by doing things their own way, but I somehow felt like I was missing a big secret to this next level of success for myself in this new arena outside of photography.

This fear got so big I began going outside of myself and hiring other business-focused teachers and mentors who I thought knew all the answers.

I started implementing and doing things they were suggesting, even though I knew they were against my own beliefs—against what I knew to be true—and before long, my business started to go the other way, the opposite of thriving. Things started feeling more difficult and frustrating, and I wasn't helping and serving as many people as I wanted to. It wasn't true that I wasn't good at

business at all. It was that I was doing things that I didn't believe and didn't feel good about!

The brutal truth is, I spent a few years using various crutches as to why I couldn't fully get back in the game and go after my dreams of fully supporting people to create their own version of success for themselves. I let myself off the hook for a long time, until one day I realized all the excuses I was telling myself were simply just excuses and not the truth. I had been putting myself, my dreams, and my goals on hold simply because my confidence got rocked a bit. And rather than question if it was true, I allowed it to control my dreams.

I had to take an honest look at myself and ask the hard questions.

Was it true I wasn't good at business?

No. I had already created a very successful business. I didn't struggle until I started implementing things I didn't actually feel good about, that were against my grain, that were against what I know for myself.

This is what I know to be true:

Every path to success works. It's choosing the path of getting there in a way that we want to do that creates success. If the destination is the same, it can be as simple as asking, Would you like to take a train or would you like to take a car? You'll end up in the same place, it's just a preference.

This is what has helped me and other people:

Your heart is your compass. What brings you joy and lights you up is not an accident. Remembering that and being reminded of that consistently is one of the most essential parts of reaching your goals.

This is my brilliance:

Navigating the currents of success through a framework that allows you to access your desires and what you naturally enjoy is what allows you to create your own version of success with your

values and priorities. You don't have to choose between making memories with your loved ones and making money—it's an *and*, not *either-or*.

This is my genius:

I help people turn down the volume of self-doubt and turn up the volume of self-trust by changing the way they think about things so they can make the impact and income desired by sharing their heart with the world. Supporting people to go from being a success seeker to a self-trusted CEO (clear empowered operator) of their life and business unlocks anything and everything they desire. I have a unique, simple, and powerful ability to reframe and offer an alternate perspective that allows people to access more relief, more freedom, more grace within themselves.

This Is what I believe to be true:

We must tell ourselves the truth about what we actually want for our lives—not what our parents want, not what our children want, what we want. Then, and only then, can we start to take the microsteps toward that becoming our reality.

- I am here to hold the space and the vision for creatives, coaches, and service-based entrepreneurs, to say that you absolutely can go for this!
- It's okay to pause.
- It's okay to pivot.
- It's okay to lose your confidence.
- It's okay to burn it down and start again.
- It's okay to start over.
- It's okay, and I would assert even essential, to get the right kind of support for the journey. We aren't meant to go it alone.

The most important piece, above all else, is to know how to access what is true for you and then surrounding yourself with people who align with that.

That is the very thing I help people access: the confidence and power within themselves to create their own version of success. Full Stop.

Once I was able to quiet the outside noise and come back to my own self-trust, my own self, my own voice, my own intuition, my mentoring and coaching practice began to grow again. I absolutely love to help people discover it's all part of the human experience, and that it is 100% possible to create whatever is important to you in a way that brings you joy and lights you up.

When we can train our brain and regulate our nervous system and learn the rules to the game, whatever we want to create in this world is available to us.

I knew from a very young age I wanted to be a mom, and I briefly let a stranger question that dream. I started a photography business and almost allowed people to talk me out of it for the illusion of safety. I did allow other people to tell me there are only certain ways to create success even if it compromised what I knew to be true for a little bit. This is the journey of what I call the great remembering and forgetting. This human experience is a roller coaster of emotions—and sometimes we forget what we know to be true for ourselves, and we need to be reminded.

There is no one roadmap to success, but rather a compass that is calibrated to your own heart. Cultivating a practice and the emotional intelligence to come back to self-trust above anything else is our way to success. When we navigate the currents of success, we must always start with the desires in our heart first.

We can chart our own course, align our inner compass, and launch ourselves into the life we imagine when we trust ourselves to know the way. That is my brilliance. That is the magic I help people create for themselves. Remember, your success is inevitable. I believe in you.

ABOUT KERI GAVIN

Keri Gavin is a success and business mentor for creatives, coaches, and service-based entrepreneurs. Keri empowers and educates success seekers to become self-trusted CEOs (clear empowered operators). Self-trusted CEOs create businesses that are centered around their passions, values, and priorities first so they can make the income and impact they desire while actually living the life they used to dream of!

Keri is a former teacher turned successful professional photographer for fifteen years, turned professional success and business mentor. By combining her love of teaching, personal business success, and passion for helping others, Keri supports others to create their success their own way.

Keri is the founder of Rebel Hearts Business Academy and The Heart of Money Experience. These programs are centered around empowering and educating Creatives, Coaches, and Entrepreneurs to make money doing what they love, so they can do more of what they love to do! She is also the host of The Confident Creative Podcast—*Daring for the Dreams*, where you will hear insights and conversations that take lived experiences and turn them into beneficial life lessons for all of us.

Keri's clients and students achieved massive success in their own life and business because the magic is found in creating and sustaining a successful mindset, which leads to a successful life and business. As a mindset expert, Keri has a unique approach to shifting perspectives and helping people access insights for themselves in everything she teaches.

To learn more about how you can connect and work with Keri, please visit her website at www.focusingontheheart.com where you can find her programs, sign up for her weekly newsletter, and purchase her self-study powerful programs.

You can find her on social media here:

Facebook: Keri Gavin Rebel Heart Entrepreneur
Instagram: @keri.gavin
TikTok: @keri_gavin
The Confident Creative Podcast, *Daring for the Dreams*

YOUR HEART KNOWS THE WAY

Mary Gervais

Follow your heart. It knows the way. Follow your heart and open the door to amazing adventures, surprising self-discoveries, and exciting levels of personal empowerment.

When we listen to our inner voice, when we believe in our intuition and innate wisdom, we create new pathways for our heart that can lead to greater peace and joy in our lives.

My own follow-your-heart spirit began when I was very young with treasured childhood books like *Patrick Muldoon and His Magic Balloon* and *The Story of Heidi*. These books opened the door to a world of wonder: the Swiss Alps, Buckingham Palace, the Sphinx, Italy, and Japan. The stories also created the first "pull"—a tug that fed my natural curiosity about the world and where I might fit into it.

When I was ten, I received a gift subscription to *National Geographic Kids* magazine. Every month I devoured the "Go on Safari" and "What in the World" sections. Around the same time, I met a Belgian foreign-exchange student who was staying with family friends. I thought this was super cool, and it ultimately inspired me to apply to Rotary International's Student Exchange program.

I was fifteen when Rotary selected me to go to Johannesburg, South Africa, on behalf of our local club, my community, and the US. I spent a year training for the trip and was excited about my destination. But as the departure date neared, it became increasingly clear that internal resistance to apartheid made travel there unsafe. When Rotary International called to explain this, I had only one question: "Where can I go instead?"

The one country with an opening was Bolivia. I said yes, hung up the phone, and grabbed *The World Book Encyclopedia.* Visions of ancient civilizations, lush jungle vegetation, and soaring Andean mountains swirled around me. I was enthralled; my parents, less so. My mom was more than a bit worried. But *my heart knew* that I was meant to go, and I did.

In Bolivia, I learned to think and converse fluently in Spanish. I developed confidence in speaking before groups. I learned to manage my own finances and make decisions, and gained a greater sense of who I was as a person. I also learned to appreciate and accept other people and cultures.

I was gone for a year. When I returned home and began my senior year of high school, I struggled with reconciling my newfound independence with once again being looked upon as a seemingly "ordinary" teenager in a beautiful but ordinary small town in western New York. Luckily, I had some incredible friends, and our Rotary Club's Swedish exchange student, Helene, and I also became fast friends. We instantly bonded as international travelers with a passion for dreaming big dreams.

In addition to traveling, two early passions that always gave me pleasure were baking and cooking. So when I applied for college, hospitality management and culinary programs were high on my list. On the way home from one college visit, my mom suggested we make an impromptu stop at her alma mater, an all-women's college near Albany, NY. I loved the feel of the school and ended up having an incredible conversation with the admissions team. The school didn't offer hospitality management or culinary arts,

but they did have an international studies program. Eureka! I knew instantly that I would be my best self at this college.

Nearing our high school graduation, Helene said she wished I could go home with her. We looked at each other and said, "Why not?" So, we hatched a plan and presented it to our parents. Everyone was on board and, although gap years didn't exist in 1983, my college agreed to defer my entrance for a year because studying in Sweden fit in with my major. As things fell into place, my dad reminded me that "Where there's a will, there's a way." His advice was important, and such affirmations have always encouraged me.

I also remember my exhilaration when my flight departed JFK in late August. That excitement lasted throughout that year abroad. I studied Swedish in the mornings and attended school in the afternoons. I traveled to Denmark, England, Russia, Finland, and Norway during school breaks, and my best friend from high school joined me for four weeks of backpacking around Europe in the summer. When we couldn't find accommodations in Venice or Pisa, we went with the flow and slept in a Venetian convent and under the Leaning Tower in sleeping bags. Everything aligned that year: friendships, love, self-development.

Meanwhile, things were not so well-aligned at home. My parents had divorced and my childhood home was sold. Mom moved to a nearby city, and Dad moved out of state. Neither was very open to speaking about the family dynamic. It was painful, and although there was a good sense of community and support-ive mentors at my college in New York, it took almost two years since returning before I felt back in the flow.

My college coursework included a junior year semester in Spain, which I extended to a year with an internship at a Seville law firm.

While there, I bumped into a group of fellow American stu-dents on the street who needed directions. I asked them about their travels and discovered they were visiting Spain as part of

a program called Semester at Sea. It's a floating university that travels the world, and it was wonderful hearing about their adventures.

School vacations gave me a chance to explore Morocco and the Iberian Peninsula, which includes Spain and Portugal—countries with a vibrant, alluring, and culturally rich balance of history, culture, food, and incredible people. These trips also forced me to step out of my comfort zone, discover new passions, find my natural rhythm again, and create lifelong friendships.

From the moment I met the students on the street in Seville, the allure of a Semester at Sea beckoned. I called the university that hosted the program and discovered that it included multiple-country study, interdisciplinary coursework, and hands-on field experience. The fall voyage itinerary included stops in Japan, Taiwan, Hong Kong, the Philippines, Malaysia, India, Russia, Turkey, Yugoslavia, and Spain. Serendipitously, they had one spot open because of a last-minute cancelation. There was only one problem. The program cost about $11,000. How could I ever afford this? Would my college even allow me another semester abroad? But the pull was there to keep asking questions. Yes, there was a $2,000 grant still available; yes, I could apply for a $2,000 loan; yes, there was still time to apply; yes, yes, yes.

I was living with my dad that summer, and he said, "If you can pay for it, go for it." Challenge accepted! I called my college and after numerous appointments with the school's administrators, I obtained permission to go.

I worked three jobs from 7 a.m. to midnight, but at summer's end, I was still $550 short. My dad said he'd never seen me work so hard and funded me for the balance. Determination, hard work, and a belief that this could be done allowed me with the voyage of a lifetime.

After graduation, the bright lights beckoned and I moved to Manhattan. As the song *New York, New York* goes, "If I can make it there, I'll make it anywhere."

Naturally, my heart led me to the travel industry. My first job as an assistant manager in a travel company was a good experience, but after nine months, I knew I wanted more than a desk job. Soon after that, I spotted an ad for a sales and marketing position with a Chilean airline that was set to begin flying into JFK. The job description was written for me! I applied, was hired within three weeks, and began pitching Latin America as a destination. I worked with tour operators and travel agencies to create cultural experiences such as winter skiing in July, wine tours, visits to the Chilean fjords, and adventure tours in Patagonia. When the company transferred me to Washington, DC, I built partnerships with the South American embassies, World Bank, International Monetary Fund, and International Development Bank. I traveled for work, and in my free time took trips to Paris, Los Angeles, Iceland, Thailand, Jamaica, and Egypt.

A trip to Puerto Rico added a new trajectory to my life. I fell in love with the island's beauty and its unique culture—a mix of Taíno, Spanish, African, and North American influences. The ocean, the island life, and the people beckoned; I left my job and moved there.

I also fell in love with Bobby. We became friends immediately, but the energy between us was electric, and within three months we were engaged. He made me laugh all the time, and together we found joy in the simple things such as going for walks, seeing foreign films, or exploring new towns on the island. When you know, you know—and it's true, you do.

I insisted on having our wedding in San Juan so my family and friends could experience some of what I loved about the island and its culture.

From the start, Bobby and I supported each other's careers, so when his company offered him a position in Florida, we weighed the pros and cons. The opportunity for his professional growth made it impossible to refuse this offer.

In Florida, I became a sales manager for a cruise line. My

territory spanned the East Coast from Florida to Savannah. A favorite part of my job was my weekly drive to the port and along the coast. It always made me feel alive and grounded.

Our daughter was born in Orlando, and shortly after her first birthday, we made another career move and settled in the Washington, DC area. But after our son was born, I no longer wanted to travel for work, so I took a job in pharmaceutical sales. Life was busy, but I managed to maintain my daily routine of a run or workout. This personal "time out" has always given me the ability to notice when my intuition pings me.

And my intuition was once again pinging me, this time in the direction of that love for baking. I find great joy and relaxation in the process and have many priceless memories of going to my grandmother's house and licking the beaters, enjoying her famous sponge birthday cakes, or coming home after school to my mom's freshly baked cookies. I'm sure those happy moments fed my dream of opening a bakery.

After two years in pharmaceutical sales, Bobby and I talked about making that dream come true. In the evenings after the kids were asleep, I researched franchises and local Maryland bakeries, and began writing a business plan.

When I took my plan to a banker, I realized that it's impossible to get a business loan without solid collateral. My small business adviser also suggested that Bobby and I complete an assessment to determine our tolerance for risk. This was a good exercise, and I definitely won out as the family risk-taker. That being said, we both agreed to use our house as collateral. We felt confident in our professional abilities and believed that if the business didn't work, we would sell the house, cover the loan, and I'd return to corporate America.

The grueling underwriting process at various banks took months, and I still didn't have the money to begin. The turndowns were disheartening. The major stumbling blocks: a lack

of sufficient collateral and the perceived high risk as first-time business owners.

"Where there's a will, there's a way" kept running through my mind, so after rejection number eight, I called my dad. He was an entrepreneur and reminded me that I just needed to find a banker who believed in me and my vision. I kept going. By the time I arrived at bank number twelve, I had my story down, knew all the questions that would be asked and could easily rattle off the projections, use of money, and repayment timeline. The banker and I clicked. He loved my vision and gave me the money I needed.

Finding the balance between being an entrepreneur, mother, and wife took some effort. It was challenging to juggle family, a staff, and the marketing and profitability while also producing a high-quality product at a reasonable price. Bobby helped with the kids and ran the business on Sundays until we could afford a full-time manager.

The sense of pride I felt innovating with new ideas, watching team members grow, and supporting the community was also recognized by the Frederick County Entrepreneur Council as start-up entrepreneur of the year. It was, in short, the best job in the world. Baked goods make everyone happy, and spreading joy is immensely powerful.

Seven years flew by. Bobby was again offered an incredible job, this time in Massachusetts. I was excited for him but I mourned my loss—the idea that I might have to sell my business made me extremely unhappy. But I also recognized that whatever decision I made would have to support our family vision. Family was my priority and I knew that I could always rebuild. The business went on the market. Within two months we had a buyer, but in the midst of moving, the deal fell through. We moved as planned, my assistant manager took charge, and I commuted for six months.

The business did finally sell, but getting to that point was

fraught with unpredictable highs and lows. One of the most important lessons from that experience: Remember to trust and take care of yourself.

Our Massachusetts home in the Holyoke mountain range put us close to nature, which was wonderful for the family's well-being. I was present for my family and felt fulfilled as a mom, but I missed the passion that came from running my business.

How would I find my way back? Informational interviews with community leaders to learn more about the area and their organizations was a start. I read self-development books and met a soul friend and mentor who introduced me to StrengthFinders. This self-development assessment tool helped me identify my natural talents. It lifted my spirits, put me back on track, and guided me to the next leg of my journey—taking me in some positive new directions.

I taught a university class module called "Reinventing Yourself." If you really want to master something, teach it. I became a mentor to young women at a local college and became the annual fund director at a local university. I loved being able to give back to others.

Three years later, we moved again when Bobby was offered a job in Rhode Island. Part of my move-again pact was that I would start work on my MBA since I was interested in teaching at the university level.

Growth comes from change. Reinvention takes planning, and as a family unit, we were getting pretty good at that. Bobby settled into his new job, the kids settled into school, and I networked with local organizations while also enrolled in a full-time online MBA program. In 2013, online education was still in its infancy and when I opted in, it was with the goal of interacting with a global community and engaging with new technologies. I loved the challenge.

When I received my degree, the university hired me as a course evaluator for its MBA program. I also started doing informational

interviews with female leaders, community advocates, and entre-preneurial organizations, and was hired as the director of the Rhode Island Women's Business Center (WBC). The WBC trains and mentors women in business and provides them with many opportunities for growing their businesses. This was soul work!

A brilliant digital designer and former editor from *Better Homes & Gardens* came in with an incredible idea for an e-commerce platform for people who loved old homes. After a few mentoring sessions, she came back with a plan for how the business should be structured. She also explained that she had ADHD and needed a partner to handle the operational and business side of things. When I asked if she had anyone in mind, she said, "What about you?" I was surprised and genuinely flattered and said I'd think about it.

Having been part of renovating my family's cobblestone house for ten years while growing up, the idea fascinated me. But the strongest pull centered on my ongoing desire to start another business. I meditated on this and asked Bobby for his thoughts. Always supportive, he said that it sounded interesting and if I could acquire the start-up funding, I should go for it. Honoring the pull, I wrote the business plan, resigned at WBC, and took the next step in my entrepreneurial journey.

An angel investor provided our initial funding. Creating an e-commerce platform with high-quality content was exciting. But I knew we needed outside mentoring for such essentials as branding, social media development, data collection and metrics, and load time and mobile responsiveness to monitor the first twelve months. So we applied and were accepted in a five-month program at Mass Challenge, a New England start-up accelerator.

The program provided top-notch mentorship in designing ways to produce avenues of growth, funding, and collaboration with strategic partners. We started to scale rapidly, launched our online service directory and marketplace, and built an excellent working relationship with one of our Mass Challenge mentors

who came onboard as our CEO. I pivoted to head of sales and brand partnerships.

That autumn, we pitched to venture capital investors and received a commitment. However, negotiations between them and our angel investor did not go smoothly, and a controlling-interest struggle ensued. Ultimately, after a somewhat-tortured gut check, the CEO and I walked away from the company. Peace, clear boundaries, happiness, and ethical standards are never up for negotiation—even after three years of hard work.

I believe there are no failures, only lessons learned. Challenged and pushed forward, I came away with countless nuggets of knowledge, experience, and wisdom

A few months into COVID, opportunity again knocked for Bobby's career: an offer in Cincinnati would return him to his love of diversity and inclusion. The timing was good. Our daughter had just graduated as an RN, and our son was humming along in his university studies. I started networking with the entrepreneurial community, connected with a wonderful women's service organization, and began co-hosting a weekly Heart-Centered Entrepreneurs Clubhouse room.

COVID quarantine gave me the gift of time to become more spiritually connected with myself. I practiced yoga at home; the mind, body, spirit energy was just what I needed. I also read numerous spiritual enlightenment books, and daily meditation opened my heart.

I began to acknowledge an accumulation of feelings that I didn't know existed: present fears, early childhood pain, even past-life trauma. Inner child work, forgiveness, and heart connection conversations ensued. I learned that I could not fix others or be a people pleaser, which led me to set new boundaries and speak with more clarity.

Forgiveness is freedom, and the heart presents itself for natural healing. By adding mindfulness and gratitude, and letting

everything be a renewal of love, joy, and peace, beneficial energy begins to flow.

Honoring my adventures and intuition, saying yes, showing up for my family and others, and realizing there was more that I needed to explore within myself to be all that I was meant to be has been wild, fun, messy, and marvelous.

We are here to grow, not to be complacent. Trust the adventure and let your dreams guide and inspire you to embrace, express, and embody all that you are. You don't need to know the *how*. It doesn't matter whether the circumstances are perfect or if you are perfect in the circumstances. Just keep moving forward, always follow your heart, and get ready for an unforgettable journey.

ABOUT MARY GERVAIS

Serial entrepreneur and innovator Mary Gervais has helped thousands of women fulfill their dreams of starting, building, and growing their own companies.

Driven by a desire to create more meaningful connections between people and to make the world a more honest and open place, she has also established herself as a leader and guide in co-creation—a form of collaborative innovation where ideas are shared and improved together.

Thriving on new experiences, Mary's love of world travel has led her to live and work in Bolivia, Sweden, Spain, Chile, and Puerto Rico. She has used her marketing savvy and business acumen to create both retail and online enterprises, and she is the former head of Rhode Island's Women's Business Center.

Mary is also a firm believer in the idea that when life hands you a grand idea, embrace it, even if you don't know how to make it happen. Dream big and be bold. Leading by example, Mary continues to show others how to live an abundant, healthy, and joy-filled life.

To learn more about Mary Gervais, you can visit her website at www.maryhelengervais.com.

To connect with Mary, please contact her directly at:

Email: mary@maryhelengervais.com

ONCE UPON A TIME

Tiffany Donovan Green

O nce upon a time there was a young woman who dreamed about a life full of potential and adventure. She was creative, curious, full of youthful charm and vigor. She formulated goals, educated herself, and committed to achieving her dreams. She was confident, determined, and comfortable in her power. Anything was possible.

Then one day, this woman woke up to find herself adrift. She was exhausted, having expended herself in tedium for many years, for she had generously donated her body, mind, and spirit to the needs of others. Suddenly, the benefactors of her labor no longer required her assistance, and she discovered herself bereft of passion and purpose.

Sound familiar? Not all but many women find themselves in this predicament when their children leave the nest. I am one of these women. In my youth, I studied, I traveled, I took full advantage of life. I worked hard and had the good fortune to attend a highly rated law school where I met my prince charming and embarked on what I believed would be a fairytale life.

I was (and still am) a notorious dreamer. But the reality of a demanding career, complicated pregnancies, and the needs of my

family dented my original aspirations. With my husband's career on the rise, I made the decision to leave the workforce. I enjoyed motherhood, but I was surprised by how quickly my confidence and self-worth faded. I panicked and attempted a return to office but did not have the physical, emotional, or mental ability to sustain a professional comeback. I gave up on the pursuit and doubled down on the duties of the devoted mother.

Don't get me wrong—I *loved* raising my boys, and if I could do it all over again, I would make the same (or many of the same) choices. But the experience came at a high cost, a cost that our society does not always recognize or reward. If you give yourself in entirety to another, whether that person is a spouse, a child, or other person of significance, it is often a challenge to find yourself again. And if you do, you might not even recognize yourself. I have casually observed that individuals who give up their careers to take on the full-time at-home parent role are taught to undervalue themselves, surrender their dreams, and sacrifice their power.

And I'm here to say, screw that!

We need to remember who we are, be honored for our service and sacrifice, and be given the chance to fulfill our passions and purpose. But first, we must learn to dream again—without restraint, without judgment, and with the extravagant imagination of a child. Only then can we rediscover ourselves, our youth, and our vitality. And for me, that's where it all began . . . Once Upon a Time.

It was an innocent inquiry: "You're turning fifty this year, what should we do to celebrate?" my husband asked. My expression and demeanor revealed that I was not thrilled. Fifty years. How did that happen? Give birth, blink, and you're fifty. That's how I felt. It didn't seem fair. As a young woman I was going places: I earned a position at a top law firm on Capitol Hill; I was offered a fellowship to study German law at the University

of Heidelberg; I had plans . . . BIG plans. But I couldn't do it all. Did I fail? Sometimes it felt that way.

He tried to cheer me up. "We could go on a trip?"

"Meh . . . " I sighed. "Who would watch the kids?"

Silence.

Reluctantly, he suggested, "What about a party?"

"Party?" I perked up.

Providing Tiffany an opportunity to host a party was like offering bloody remains to a piranha: devoured and digested before the last syllable.

As a creative, nothing gets me going like a themed event. But I had to be original given that many in our community had already celebrated their fiftieth and most of the popular themes had been used previously. Pressure on.

My oldest child, a sophomore in high school at the time, had the opportunity to participate in an educational trip to Europe with his history class. Concerned about his severe nut allergy, my husband and I decided to trail him. We traveled separately to Europe, kept our distance, and did our own thing. We toured Versailles and various castles and palaces in and around Munich. It was regal, it was romantic, almost make-believe, and . . . then it came to me:

An immersive experience that dares imagination, distant in time and tradition, an illusion of artful indulgence, a fiction, a fantasy: a *Royal Fairytale Ball.*

The event was magic—the room twinkled with glittering tiaras and elegant satin gowns, which swirled and swayed to the delicate cadence of the orchestral waltzes. Participants were spell-bound and starry eyed. There was laughter, there was awe, there was wonderment. The fairytale theme provided guests with a sort of freedom, an opportunity to transcend the ordinary, to make believe and become a brilliant star in their own story. It was more than a night to remember—it was an *opportunity* to remember, to

rediscover youth and inspiration, to stretch the mind and wander in the world of the inner child.

That is when things began to change both for me and for many of my guests. A few who had unsuccessful relationships found companionship, some went back to school or started new careers, some packed up and moved on to entirely new adventures, and some, like me, retooled, reinvested, and reinvented themselves.

Since then, every year on my birthday I gather with friends for coffee, lunch, or drinks to celebrate and reminisce about the Royal Fairytale Ball. Naturally, we wore our tiaras. Many of my friends commented on how the tiara made them feel: Pretty. Powerful. Important. Buoyant. Young. There was something magical about these fancy little crowns that seemed to transform the mind and bolster confidence.

A tiara is an ornamental headpiece typically reserved for formal occasions. It's a symbol of power and beauty. Tiaras denote distinguished status and thus could imply elitism. In this light, the tiara might embody a negative connotation since aristocrats and elites are seen throughout history as undemocratic, securing undue privileges at the expense of the majority. But what if the tiara was democratized and rebranded as a symbol of self-love and used to lift individuals up so that they could perceive their unique worth and beauty? I can envision women, and all genders, using this symbol to come together to support each other, to celebrate their strength and potential, and to remember who they are and what they are capable of—at any age.

When my youngest child readied to leave nest and I approached the end of my tenure as a stay-at-home mom, my first thought was *game over*. I was spent, disconnected, and afraid. I didn't recognize myself; I didn't feel like I had an identity outside of the children. When I looked back toward my youthful ambitions, they seemed foreign and unattainable. I had forgotten my passion and my power. But that tiny tin tiara taught me to dream

again. I went back to school to study design and founded my own design firm specializing in green interiors. I started an environmental nonprofit with my children to teach them the values of environmental stewardship and activism like my mother taught me. And most recently, I created a tribute to the tiara, a social and philanthropic society dedicated to self-empowerment: The Tiara Club.

Anything is game, because anything is possible when you reconnect with an unfettered imagination and let yourself dream.

ABOUT TIFFANY DONOVAN GREEN

Tiffany Donovan Green is an entrepreneur, event organizer, and interior designer in Fairfield County, Connecticut. She is the founder of The Green House Interiors, specializing in healthy sustainable design, and a co-founder of The Global Preservation Society, a 501(c)(3) organization dedicated to environmental stewardship and sustainability. Most recently, Tiffany founded The Tiara Club, a social and philanthropic organization dedicated to self-empowerment.

Born and raised in southeastern Michigan, Tiffany earned a BA in history and political science from Albion College; an MA in history at Oakland University in Rochester, Michigan; and a JD/LLM from Cornell Law School in international and comparative law. She lived abroad in Scotland, Germany, and France, and worked at the law firm Jones Day in Washington, DC until she retired to raise her children. She is currently pursuing an MA in interior design from Fairfield University in Fairfield, Connecticut.

Tiffany lives with her prince charming in southwestern Connecticut.

Web:
tiffanydonovangreen.com
tiaraclub.org
the-green-house.com

Instagram:
@tiffany.donovan.green/
@the.tiara.club/
@the.green.house.interiors

Facebook: https://www.facebook.com/tiffany.donovan.10

RECLAIMING WONDER

Linda Gonzalez

In the summer of 2021, a dear friend called me to share a children's book author program offered by Kate Butler Books. She heard me talk about writing a children's book as a gift for my granddaughters and thought I might be interested. While I had talked about writing a children's book for many years, I had never really thought of it as a dream to one day come true. In fact, at this point in my life, I was not sure I had any dreams that I planned to pursue. If I did, they were focused on the life I wanted for my children and, more recently, my grandchildren—not for me. Even my work in higher education, for twenty-five years, revolved around the dreams of my students. This was not intentional. Like so many women, my early adult life focused on a list of to-dos prioritized around children, family, and what society often refers to as work-life balance where there is little *life* and even less *balance*—as if there is a magic script that determines our capacity for knowing how to foster such a balance. When speaking with other women approaching sixty, I learned that we had many commonalities. There was one in particular that started to haunt me. The idea of self-care and how to find it or, in some cases, rediscover it, in a world where so many of our boundaries

get blurred. This thought gave me pause and a reason to dig deeper into the life I am living.

When my friend reached out to share the opportunity of writing a children's book, we were still working our way through the storms of a global pandemic. During some very dark moments, the negative voices in my head told me that there was no way I could do this. At that time, my goal was to do my best to overcome this difficult time so I could enjoy time with family and friends again, continue to support my students working toward earning their college degrees, and start planning for retirement at the traditional age of sixty-five. This was all very important to me. But was there something more? Where was the beautiful sense of wonder about life that often gets lost along the way for so many women? And what is the role of wonder, if any, in my self-care plan that I was encouraged to make part of my fiscal goals this year? Sitting still in a space of reflection about the possibility of writing a children's book for my granddaughters, I became more uncomfortable and scared. Hanging out in this place of uncertainty is what disrupted my life and encouraged me to take the first step. When I dug deeper into my root system, I started to discover that not only was this something that I could do, but it was also something that I had to do. Through these still moments, the words of my favorite author, Parker J. Palmer spoke wonder into my heart: "the God whom I know dwells quietly in the root system of the very nature of things."[1] And this is where my story begins.

When I turned fifty-five, I was very mindful that age sixty was a mere five years away. It was unavoidable. Direct marketing to me about the senior years accelerated at what felt like an exponential pace: emails about planning my financial security for retirement were filling my inbox, and I needed an Excel spreadsheet to keep track of the various "screenings and tests" advised by my healthcare professionals as part of my preventive medicine.

1—Parker Palmer, Let Your Life Speak (San Francisco, CA: Jossey-Bass, 1999).

My positive inner voice recognized the relevance of all of this but knew that for me to truly live out my purpose, the one planted in my root system, I needed to answer a very powerful question: "What else?"

"What else?" became like a broken record in my soul that renewed my sense of wonder. I felt inspired to focus on the *life* part of the equation in that work-life balance that I either lost or never had. Not the bucket list of items that are one and done, although these are important too. Rather, the discovery of dreams that I had either buried or never knew existed in the roots of my soul because I was too busy jamming up my brain trying to multi-task to get stuff done. The conscious and intentional wish list that I ask my granddaughters and students about when we explore their dreams together. The ones that give me an image of a life of victory and purpose. With great determination and practice, I learned to sit in silence, listening to the voice in my root system. The idea of writing a children's book as a gift for my granddaughters became an unwavering thought that bloomed from this daily exercise. With abundant gratitude for this discovery, I signed up for the journey and promised to enjoy the ride.

If Acorns Could Talk is a story that spoke to me during long walks with my granddaughters. They all love to collect bits of nature when we are outside. It is not unusual for us to take home a pocketful of branches, weeds, and rocks to spread around in our rooms as new home décor imagined by young girls with a natural wonder, uninhibited by the grip of perfection. What always struck me most was their fascination with acorns in the beautiful season of autumn. Or was it my fascination with acorns? Giving this question some attention, I discovered that I was not certain. Learning to dig deeper into my root system, I let myself explore the deeper meaning of our conversations on our walks together and began to wonder about the "acorn" and "mighty oak" moments of my life. I noticed that these special moments are not defined by age or experience, not even by ability

or knowledge, but rather by my willingness to try new things that help me to continue to grow into my purpose.

To highlight this point, I think about the joy and gratitude I feel when my granddaughters talk about who they want to become when they grow older. They say it with great purpose and assurance because they completely believe everything is possible. There are no inhibitions or voices of self-doubt—no fears of failing or thoughts about being less than perfect—and the idea of who they want to become is like a mighty oak, growing new branches fed by hopes and dreams. One of my granddaughters at one point wanted to become a superhero. When I asked her how she would become a superhero, she leaped into the air, shouted that she would practice her flying, and fell flat on the floor. What I remember most about this experience is what happened next. She jumped up showing me her muscles, and with the same enthusiasm yelled, "I'm okay!" She was leaning into her purpose. Another granddaughter wants to become a farmer. So last summer she started practicing growing and harvesting her crops. Recently we saw a photo of her lying with a new litter of puppies, like a cultural anthropologist, practicing participant observation among the animals, fully living in her purpose. These acorn and mighty oak moments are in their root systems, and they find them with such ease. They are not stuck by the control of any negative voices. Instead, they keep their sense of wonder that allows them to keep growing into their purpose.

Learning from their approach to fulfilling their dreams about who they want to become, I started to write *If Acorns Could Talk* as a gift to them. It was a sunny summer afternoon in the Northeast when I wrote my first draft. In full joy and wonder, I was overcome by an uncontrollable urge to pour out the words and expressions shared with me through their beautiful voices and little faces on our nature walks together. Leaning into my purpose, I felt a great desire to evoke wonder in others, at every age. The journey of writing this book has reclaimed my sense

of wonder about dreams that I'm yet to discover and eager to explore.

Next year, I will turn sixty. Rather than lean into sixty as if it is a difficult wave to navigate through, I will *dream* into sixty like Lily, the young girl in *If Acorns Could Talk,* and my beautiful granddaughters: Strong! Powerful! Confident! and Resilient! While I am unsure about what lies ahead for me, I am no longer confused about my self-care and work-life balance. The process of becoming an author pushed me to dig into my root system and rediscover the wonder of life that keeps me excited and yearning to explore at every age for as long as I am capable.

Acorns are not a metaphor for age. They are a metaphor for early learners on a journey filled with beautiful dreams. When cared for and loved, they grow into mighty oaks. I am very much an acorn when it comes to playing golf, a sport I started last year as an opportunity to spend time with my husband outdoors. And it is very possible I will remain an acorn in this space for the rest of my life. That still excites me because I know I will meet other acorns and mighty oaks along the journey of playing golf. I am also very much an acorn when it comes to being an author. In less than one year though, I am inspired by the mighty oaks who so freely share their time and talents to help me grow into a mighty oak in this space. When I remain in wonder, I am no longer fearful of mistakes or in search of perfection in the things I want to say and do. Instead, wonder inspires me to pause and listen for the guidance of the voice buried in my root system to teach me more about my purpose. It paves a path and provides a compass for me to lean into my purpose with great passion and enthusiasm. It is a great gift that I have begun to cherish. And I am excited about the learning and discovery, and about the people I am meeting along the way. Perhaps reclaiming wonder is one of the liberating benefits that comes with age—and one we should talk about more often when we contemplate self-care, balance, and purpose.

When I dream ahead, I envision a space where acorns and mighty oaks share life together, teaching and learning from each other. Whether the subject is history, technology, or art, intergenerational acorns and mighty oaks can form communities where learnings and teachings are generously exchanged. In these communities, diversity is valued, and kindness abundantly abounds. Everyone is living in harmony with each other and with nature. The acorns are caring for the mighty oaks and vice versa. There are no preferences and no privileges; just love. If you are reading this, I hope you pause and create the wonder of this image in your mind. What does this vision look like for you?

The journey of becoming an author is in its fledgling phase for me yet has already impacted my life in countless positive ways. For certain, it has stirred up dreams for my senior years that never existed until now. Fueled by wonder, it continues to serve my commitment to my journey of lifelong learning and living with enthusiasm. It is helping me to grow into the purpose destined for me.

Aging with wonder has become something I behold. Now, when I am floundering and in search of clarity about my purpose, I sit in the silence and dig into my root system where the vision of God dwells. What I discover here is infinite possibilities that are unencumbered and ready to be nurtured.

ABOUT LINDA GONZALEZ

There is an entire world community of acorns and mighty oaks with whom I would love to meet and collaborate. If you wonder about the acorn and mighty oak moments in life, please reach out to me on Instagram at @ lindamgonz or send me an email at lindamgonzalez3@gmail.com and let's discover "what else?" together.

Linda Gonzalez is a mentor and coach in higher education. Her passion is working with adult learners working toward fulfilling their dreams of earning their first college degrees. Her twenty-five-year career spans from universities in New Jersey, Arizona, and Utah. She holds a BS in marketing and management and an MA in cultural anthropology. In March of 2022, she became a best-selling author of a children's book, *If Acorns Could Talk* and is enjoying opportunities to read aloud with children. She has recently fulfilled the course requirements for the International Coaching Federation's (ICF) Leadership Coaching certification program through the Doerr Institute at Rice University and is currently completing her practicum as part of this program.

Linda lives in the Pocono Mountains in Pennsylvania with her husband. She is the very proud "Nanny" to five granddaughters ages one to six years old, and she never passes up an opportunity to play a family board game, plan an Easter egg hunt, and engage in healthy competition.

Linda Gonzalez would be thrilled to meet you!

THERE IS MONEY IN YOUR CLOSET

Erin Bonner Hudyma

I wasn't exactly sure how or where to begin my story. Do you know how difficult it is for a Philly girl who loves to talk to try and summarize her life in just a few pages? Well, doll, here I go, trying to fit it all in, including the ups and downs and in-betweens.

When things are going well in our life, those feel-good vibes put a little extra pep in our step, am I right? In those moments, we want to put on our prettiest shoes, get out in the world, and conquer it. But no matter how hard we work on having a positive attitude, sometimes, we just get on the hot mess express and it's beyond our control. And we might cry, scream, curse, or lounge around in sweatpants when it does. Other times, we close our eyes, breathe, and count our blessings—because worse things can happen. And guess what—when we least expect it, they will. At any given moment, our worlds can flip upside down, and we might desperately long to be in a different time, craving bigger and better things.

Think about any moment when you may have felt this way. Did it ever stop you from wishing for more? If anything, I bet it intensified it, right? Even when life seems completely

unmanageable, somewhere inside, tucked underneath all the puffy eyes, empty ice cream containers, and lipstick-stained wine glasses, remain our hopes, visions, and dreams. They might be forced on the back burner for a while as we come up for air, but they really are what keep us going during times of despair.

I want you to know that I see you. I was you. And I am here to tell you, if you look close enough, there are open doors waiting for you to walk through. You will find them because guess what—they are everywhere. They might be disguised or entirely hidden. But even the most damaged entryways can lead us to brighter paths. Just wait until you hear about mine! Our lives are constant peaks and valleys, and it's not about being at the top that matters. It's knowing what to say to yourself during all the in-between moments to shape what happens next.

My life started in southwest Philadelphia. The Bonner family, my family, had eight children. I was number six out of eight. Philip E. "Knute" Bonner, my father, was a World War II veteran, a Philadelphia police offer, and a Pennsylvania state auditor, and my mother, Pat Noone Bonner was a homemaker.

Since I was a child, I was my father's sidekick. He nicknamed me Bedbug. Our personalities, temperament, and the way we talked were so similar. To give you an idea of who my father was, let's just say one of his business cards had, "Teller of Jokes," underneath his name. But what I am most proud of in our likeness was helping others. To this day, I continue his charity, Knute's Angels, and adopt families during the holidays with the help from many people who make donations to, but especially from, Veronica.

In 2003, when I was in my early twenties, I purchased my own home. I was working as a clinical staff member for The Gift of Life donor program, which manages the recovery of organs and tissues for transplant (please register to be an organ donor!). Oddly, my father had become ill with heart issues a few years before, but he aged out as a candidate for a transplant. This never surprised me, though, because no one in the world had a better heart—his was

ageless. Although I was quite young for such a huge responsibility, my mother thought it was best for me to become my father's medical power of attorney. She trusted me since I worked in the medical field, knew the best doctors, and was well informed when it came to such intimidating decision-making.

For the next several years, I continued to help my mother care for my father, scheduling my work and life around his needs. It was in the car, driving my father to appointments, where I would have some of the most important talks of my life. I loved breaking his chops and watching his old-school reaction to everything. He made me laugh so much.

In 2006, I met my future husband, Joe, at the Jersey Shore. I continued to work in the donor program until 2008, when I attempted a career in medical device sales. This was the same time as the stock market and housing crash. Not only was I one of many layoffs almost immediately after I started but my mortgage doubled!

After being unemployed for about a year and a half, I saw a commercial advertising jobs for a local casino. I was never a gambler, but the one thing I was always willing to bet on was myself. I decided to roll the dice and go for an interview. What could I lose? I came back with a job as a table game dealer. Though it wasn't my dream job, it allowed me to earn some well-needed money fast, and although I didn't know it at the time, it happened to be one of the biggest entryways to my future.

At the casino, I met many other unemployed people from all sorts of professional backgrounds and levels in the same situation. I developed a close friendship with another dealer, Margaret, and we shared our stories and pipe dreams in between games. To this day, she continues to be my greatest mentor.

In 2011, Joe and I were married. Six months after we tied the knot, I was diagnosed by our first fertility doctor with stage four endometriosis and had a tumor on one ovary. I come from the most fertile family in the world (each of my parents were one of

seven), and go figure, I have fertility issues! Having a baby was one of my biggest challenges. How was this fair? All my sisters got pregnant when they sneezed! Of course, the problem was me. For being Irish, it sure felt like I was short on luck.

I endured four unsuccessful intrauterine inseminations (IUI) fertility treatments with three different fertility doctors. In between these treatments, I had to have two laparoscopic surgeries to treat the tumors and endometriosis. Though each surgery made the process more painful, it also made my determination to become a mother that much stronger.

On September 25, 2012, as my body was healing, we suddenly lost my forty-seven-year-old brother, Patrick. He passed away from diabetic heart disease. My younger sister, Bridget, then suffered a miscarriage in December. Shortly after, our father died in February 2013. I couldn't help but feel like my entire family was being sucker-punched and that normal life was out of our reach.

A week before my father died, I was taking him to a new doctor when he leaned over in the car and said, "Erin, my time is coming to end. When I get up to heaven, I am going to send you that baby."

One of the first signs my father was watching over me was in February 2013, when the Gift of Life program called me back full-time. My father always loved that I worked for this program, so it was quite fitting. But then on Labor Day weekend 2013, I was rushed to the emergency room with another ovarian tumor. Another laparoscopic surgery had to be scheduled in October.

When I was a bit back to myself, despite recommendations for a hysterectomy, I started the exhausting clinical and financial processes of in vitro fertilization (IVF). On September 25, 2013, exactly one year after my brother Patrick's death, my mother was at his grave site. She looked down and prayed to her son, "Patrick, if you are up there in heaven with your father, please push for Erin to get pregnant, and I'll know that the two of you are together."

Two weeks after my October surgery, I went back to work. On October 24, 2013, a rainy cold fall Thursday afternoon, I was running errands in my typical Philly tuxedo—a velour jump-suit—and felt the need to take a pregnancy test. *Positive?* For real? Later, no lie, Dr. Heinzel told me I got pregnant on September 25, 2013—that day my mother prayed.

Of course, I had a high-risk pregnancy. Did you really expect any different? But nothing else mattered other than becoming parents to our beautiful daughter, Svea, in 2014.

When Svea was nine months old, I had a hysterectomy. I was out of work for about eight weeks and returned to work with a very hectic schedule. I then realized I did not want Svea to be bounced around to my in-laws and sisters, so we made the decision for me to become a stay-at-home mom.

This is when all my experiences sort of bundled into one big vision. I remember sitting in the same spot on my couch, day in and day out, like the movie *Groundhog's Day*. Though I was grateful for the time with my daughter, I would find myself staring at the living room walls while she napped. With twenty-year-old reruns on the TV as background noise, I started to think about all I wanted in life and knew I had to step up my game.

When a great job opportunity was presented to me in 2016 by a well-known local hospital, I was honored. It called for either a master's degree or over ten years of organ transplant experience, and I had the latter. Unfortunately, I was not hired. Though I was let down, I never let it discourage me. I told myself God just had other plans.

The spark I needed came from a close friend, also a stay-at-home mom, asking if I was interested in going into business together cleaning construction sites. I liked the idea of having our own gig, but I knew with being in our forties and getting this off the ground, our bodies wouldn't allow us to keep up with the physical labor for a long time. But it certainly got me thinking about owning a business. The idea that stood out to me was an

adult day care center, after everything I went through with my father. My vision now developed into a goal.

Every day, I sat in the same spot on my couch doing countless Google searches. It's funny how I am now able to value this, because back then, I remember feeling like a bum who did nothing all day. But little did I know with every search on my phone, I was one step closer to the new me.

In 2018, I attended an aunt's funeral. This event was a significant one. While there, I struck up a conversation with her adult caregiver, a local woman who had both a toddler and a newborn. She told me how she worked in the evenings after being with her little ones all day. During the mass, I kept thinking about this impressive woman's spirit, drive, and energy. As the church song, "On Eagle's Wings" played during the procession, what were my fears? Yeah, financial burdens always caused me to worry. But I never once doubted this dream. It never scared me. I always knew I would see the bigger picture, and that day, I did.

I went home and Googled "Homecare Companions—Eagles Wings." No other business had this name! I was off to a good start and felt a sense of inspiration. I held on to every little sign. The next thing I did was shadow my mentor/friend for a day in the life of a business owner. She educated me on capital needs and how to get more experience. The feeling was somewhat overwhelming, but I never once let it intimidate me. I knew I had to get creative financially, especially with concerns from my husband, since he is a "numbers guy." He never expressed doubt, but with a toddler, he naturally wanted to make smart choices for our family. I was reminded of my IVF days when I would stand in the shower and cry, praying for the baby I so longed to have. I took deep breaths and gave myself the same advice I did back then: "Take it one day at a time, Erin." And that's exactly what I did.

Money is probably the number one barrier when it comes to people following their dreams. But remember, this is where you really need to hunt for those secret doors and find opportunities.

The key is to never stop strategizing. My tactic was, "There's money in your closet." So, I began to clean out my unused clothes, home goods, and daughter's toys. And I saved every damn penny, especially the ones from heaven. I cut coupons in the local flyers, digital apps, and online. I had my car payment lowered and tucked the extra money under my makeup tray. Shh! Don't tell my husband. He still thinks the payment was $400 a month.

And here's a shocker. Now before I share this, I'm not trying to tell you to go out and trust this. But always keep the mindset that things are at least worth an inquiry, even just for a lesson learned. You know how you get those email scams about large amounts of unclaimed cash in your name? Well, I figured, let me just check it out. Turns out, I had overpaid on an electric bill years before in my first home and the money was owed to me. I kid you not, my makeup tray was starting to tilt from all the cash I was shoving underneath it.

I quickly learned that besides just equity, you also need countless services to start a business. There's so much paperwork, analysis, and countless hours of computer time involved. And let me tell you, girl, I'm no tech-savvy chick! It was agony for me. Believe it or not, up to this point, I did everything from my phone. I also needed a Tax ID, registration as a Limited Liability Company (LLC), and professional photography for a brochure.

How did I get what I needed without major funds to support it all? I used good old-fashioned bartering just like in the colonial days! Now instead of trading deer skins for muskets, I exchanged fifteen meals for legal services from a close friend's boyfriend Scott. My rock, Margaret, came to my rescue with endless knowledge, and another friend, Kim, was beginning a photography business and offered to take all my pictures. Reaching out to your resources goes a long way. And any time I felt like I was hitting plateaus, for quick reassurance, I would take a trip to a good dollar store for office supplies, even if I was "putting the cart before the horse"— one of my dad's favorite sayings.

I was blessed to have a very large support system, not only with my husband, but with my mother's financial help, my fabulous sisters, and my mother-in-law, Joann, to help with Svea. My mother-in-law retired during this time and I remember her looking me straight in the eyes and saying, "You go ahead and do what you got to do. I got the baby." With that, she took Svea whenever I needed her to and became a full-time MomMom to our little girl and continues to enjoy every second of it.

Before I knew it, I became licensed in June 2019, accepting my first client that August. I went out myself and worked "in the field," with my first employee starting a few weeks later. My goal was now a reality.

Trust me, there were struggles. When COVID hit, I was forced to put the business temporarily on hold, and shift to mainly administrator work. Though the whole world seemed to be in an uproar, I never stopped focusing on my dream. I kept my eye on the prize. On top of the pandemic, my mother became extremely sick, and my sisters, Mary Beth, Bridget, and Deirdre, along with my niece, Tara, had to act as her hospital for weeks. Since I am one to put my money where my mouth is, especially when it comes to caring for my family, we got her through it. We also sold our family home and got our mom settled in a new apartment.

My business started to pick back up in January 2021 and slowly brought my employees back. Shortly after, I got credentialed with Medicaid, thanks to Linda, my office manager, which allowed me to accept other types of insurance. I am proud to say that right now Eagles Wings is now a team with several diverse team members, and we're expanding our client listing.

There's great value and appreciation in taking the smaller steps on the ladder of life, instead of the big ones. We learn from every stage. I feel that my pace allowed me to hold on tight and grasp everything I want to give back to this world.

There's still a lot more stairs for me to climb. I don't even think

I'm halfway there. My chapter in this book might be closing, but it's only the beginning of my story. In addition to physically caring for others, I want to guide others on how to find their path when life goes in, what we believe to be, the wrong way. And who's to say we haven't been upside down the entire time? It's all about perspective and the ability to see things from every angle. Be sure to know and trust there are better things to come, you just got to keep showing up. To that woman who is staring at her walls wondering what her next step is in regard to her next chapter in life, I *see* you, I *was* you, and I *feel* you. Every journey begins with one step, one email, and one phone call toward your dreams. To be continued . . .

ABOUT ERIN BONNER HUDYMA

Erin Bonner Hudyma is the president and founder of Eagles Wings Homecare, LLC. She has a clinical organ recovery transplant background, all while caring for her WWII veteran father, which inspired her to pursue her dream of becoming a business owner in home care. Eagles Wings Homecare helps people remain in their homes and continue to live life independently. She helps them with running errands, watering plants, or attending appointments. Having a heart of gold has always been her one main characteristic.

When she isn't busy tending to her clients and building her dream business, Erin loves being a dedicated mother, wife, family member, and friend. Any free time Erin has, you can find her in the shoe aisle seeking fabulous prices.

If you are interested and ready to become a business owner and eager to start your own homecare business, please reach out to Erin at Eagles Wings about franchising with a start-up homecare company. No special certifications needed, just a heart of gold and compassion. She has staff ready to help you build your new future!

Web: www.eagleswingshomecare.com
Email: erin.hudyma@eagleswingshomecare.com
Phone: 484-540-7586

LISTEN TO THE LIFEGUARD

Erin McCahill

I loved to watch Nanny crochet the most beautiful blankets and could spend hours watching her quickly create masterpieces in single or multiple colors. Each one done with love to be graciously given to someone, expecting nothing in return. As an adult, I think back to those times and the way the yarn created intricate designs with a twist of the needle and different counts. And if it were not right, Nanny would unravel the yarn and start again . This is how my life journey has been. It's been a journey creating a masterpiece with many twists of life and finding the right count that works. It's been an amazing one that has been filled with the most incredible experiences, most devastating experiences, and everything in between.

It has not been easy. So many lessons given were not learned! So many times, I've ignored the universe and its large, red warning flags.

"Why?" you may ask.

It has taken me a while to figure this out.

Just as a blanket starts from a single piece of yarn, so does one's life. Along life's journey, these pieces of yarn will come together

creating your crocheted blanket. You may not realize until later how important that single piece of yarn is in your life.

I am a daughter, sister, niece, aunt, cousin, friend, mentor, leader, innovator, and a personal and professional culture creator. This is what makes me unique and more. My life's design has taken on many different patterns that have been both easy and hard; it is a beautiful, intricate blanket that I've been putting together for years, and I will continue to do so.

I remember the day as if it were yesterday, I was four years old wearing my stylish corduroy pants, blue wind jacket, and of course pigtails with bows, and my favorite saddle shoes. I stood strong at the big sliding glass doors of our townhome in Missouri with my Snoopy suitcase all packed up with my most important possessions. I opened the door, headed out to the big, open field, "that wide-open space," with my parents behind asking, "Where are you going?" I turned around with the utmost confidence and said, "Colorado." And off I went walking into the wide-open field. Never had I been to Colorado before, but somehow, I knew I needed to go there. I have found that this piece of my life has become an integral part of my blanket.

In grade school, we were fortunate and took a family ski trip to Snowmass Mountain in Colorado. I had been skiing since I could walk, but this was different and harder. The fresh-fallen snow each morning was light, fluffy, and deep, which required a new skiing technique. I remember ski school and the challenges it gave me; this yarn was building upon my competitiveness and desire to be the best. As we spent the week there, I fell in love with all the snow, sparkly white lights, and fresh air. It started something in me: it energized me, gave me confidence, let me dream, and felt like home.

Little did I know I would eventually be accepted and attend Colorado State University. Mom and I flew out to tour the campus. I was excited and nervous, not knowing what to expect. We rented a big red Buick, and as we approached campus, we

found out it was College Days, a holiday weekend for the school. My mom stopped at a payphone and called home and said, "We just arrived, and she is coming here. Remember Yankton's College Days?" and she laughed with Dad. This was the start of some of the most incredible and most difficult days of my life. It is also when some of the most important pieces of yarn were brought into my life.

In junior high, my friends and I would assist my neighbor by serving the summer lunch she held for the battered women's association. As a freshman in high school, we catered another battered women association meeting and I vividly remember wearing my white top, black skirt, and red apron, standing in the kitchen with the plantation shutters open, listening to courageous women speak about their situations. I could not understand or comprehend why anyone would put themselves in a situation like they described. I turned and asked her, "Why would they not just leave if someone hit them?" and "How could someone truly lose their self-identity. No one can be brainwashed." She looked at me and she said, "Yes, it happens."

I was taught to always work hard, play hard, and not let anyone see you down. My parents were strong. They instilled strong core values in us, which I'm so thankful for. I am a dreamer, have wildly big goals, and believe in myself and that perfect fairy tale. I look for the best in others, always trying to help others first. These are great attributes until they hurt you.

My parents and brother said good-bye at the end of the summer, and I headed to Colorado early for sorority prep week for my junior year. I'm thankful my dad was persistent and convinced me to rush freshman year and encouraged me to enjoy these four years to the fullest. Many more pieces of yarn started to be entwined into my design. A few days later, in the middle of the afternoon, I got a phone call from my parents to tell me my dad had pancreatic cancer. Immediately I said, "I am coming home," but they said no. They didn't tell me until I was at school

because they needed to keep me living my life, not stopping on the road to my dreams and purpose. I was so lucky and grateful for the network of sisters that were there for me and held me as I cried. At the time, I didn't realize how important this sorority experience would be to me in my blanket's creation. This experience taught me so much, prepared me for my professional career, and introduced me to some of the most important and best friendships of my life.

Dad passed away my senior year. I had gone home in October, as it was time, we were told. I stood outside Dad's hospital room while he was speaking to our priest. He said, "Father, I know it's almost time for me to go home, I want you to do my mass."

I couldn't believe what I heard. I froze, silently cried, and never shared this with anyone. Dad stabilized; I went back to school. I got the call again during our Monday night formal sorority meeting that I needed to come home immediately. Everyone jumped into action to get me home. I was waiting for my late evening flight so there were not many people in the airport. It was lonely and I was scared. I had a layover, and each leg, the crew and passengers were so kind talking me through all the flights and allowing me to make phone calls to make sure Dad was okay. I was taken aback by the generosity of those around me and those giving up a first-class seat for me to be comfortable and make those calls. I called Dad several times along the way—him always asking if I was home yet.

At the layover, coming from all different locations, one of my uncles and some very close neighbors that we considered family ended up boarding that final leg of the flight with me because they too were called home. We had conversations with doctors on next steps and had to decide when it was time to help him be more comfortable on his journey. A decision that was one of the most difficult decisions a family must make. Family and friends were called to say good-bye; he held on until he spoke to everyone. Early in the morning of November 14, 1991, we were all

sleeping best we could, me in the chair by Dad's bed, my mom, brother, uncles, and various neighbors in different places of the hospital. Then we all got a nudge, and everybody came running into the room. I woke up and knew he was going home. I still see his face and how strong he was being, but how scared he was too. I miss him so much!

The universe put me there that October day on purpose—it had more yarn for me. While planning the service, I insisted that our previous priest do mass because that is what I heard. My family and friends kept writing my idea off, but I was persistent and never gave up. It was the longest wake and most beautiful, packed church and celebration. Because I listened to the universe, our previous priest spoke about Dad, and as he described him, his voice cracked, and he became emotional as he thanked me for making sure Dad's wishes of him doing his ceremony came to fruition. Several people turned and looked at me and gave me confirmation and a sign of gratefulness.

I can still hear my dad's final father-daughter talk at the airport. It was a scene from a movie! I had spent the better half of the summer healing from a fractured vertebrae from slipping on cement stairs at my summer job. One of my best friends came to visit, and I'm so thankful she was there to fly back with me. It was difficult. I still see this movie playing out in my head all the time.

Dad's final talk:

"Live life to the fullest. Don't wait go grab your dreams. You can do anything!"

"Take care of your psoriasis, keep it under control."

"Finish school and get your master's."

"Stay healthy and let go of the weight."

I got my MBA, pretty much have my psoriasis under control when I am not stressed, and wow, have I lived life to its fullest!

I know he and Mom are very proud of what I have accomplished. It's been an amazing journey, but I have not let go of all the weight, and life has been tough at times. I had to become an

adult immediately. I met my first husband, who I thought was the love of my life. Though we were from vastly different backgrounds, he turned out to be the start of the unraveling of the yarn.

I could not find the right stitch for my yarn. I was grieving Dad, and the pain was so hard to overcome. I suppressed it all. I wasn't looking at all the signs from the universe—those red flags. While growing up and giving back and servicing those who needed more (remember that piece of yarn from the battered women's association events), I was able to survive a mentally and physically abusive , and non-intimate marriage. I am a survivor of domestic violence. If I didn't service those or hear those women talk at that dinner meeting and ask those questions, I don't think I would have been strong enough to get out. I wouldn't have realized I lost my self-identity and was going through abuse. I'm thankful for the most incredible network of friends in Colorado and Connecticut to help get me out. I was rescued and started my career in sales, but I had to move as it was too close for comfort to my ex. So, everything went into storage. I packed up my Jeep and headed east, confident I would be back in a few months.

As I built my identity and life again, I met so many people, and I'm thankful for them all crossing my path, taking me in as part of their family, helping me grow into the person I am today, and being so supportive.

I put all my energy into my career. I worked hard, played hard, and what resulted were experiences I would never have dreamed of in both the corporate world and my personal life. I was asked to take on positions that challenged me, that helped me grow. Still suppressing the deep hurt of losing my father, I was determined to be the best, and I still held onto that weight. Incredible mentors taught me how to be human, be an innovator, be an influencer, take risks, motivate others, and build the best performing cultures. I built a reputation of taking calculated

risks, failing fast while providing a superior customer experience and building high-performing organizations.

I learned many lessons along the way. Most importantly, I learned how to be who you are, to stand up for yourself and your goals. I realize now looking back that I did what others asked me to do, which might not have been the best for me. Advice from others and mentorship is so important, but what is more important is that you take pieces of yarn from that experience and that advice, and you put it into your blanket of life. Your life blanket is not the same as someone else's, and someone else's yarn and stitch will not fit into your design. I threw myself into my career for so many years and made so many great friendships, but I always put other people first, even if it would hurt me or put me at a disadvantage. I always found the good in others and always will, but there must be a limit. One of the most important life lessons I have learned is that you must take care of yourself first.

I thought I had all the right stitches and pieces of yarn together. A few failed relationships, another failed marriage, toxic relationships, a major career change, and an aging parent my life's journey stretched further than I expected—a crocheted blanket with stiches and yarn in one big, tangled mess.

I went out on my own but missed the corporate world; it's in my DNA. While looking for the right opportunity, I was able to serve others by sharing my story with the world during one of the most historic times, the COVID-19 pandemic. It was there that I finally realized after twenty-nine years that my pain for the loss of my father was so magnificent that I avoided every red flag, literally. The universe gave me so many warnings in so many situations, but the grief was too deep to endure, so I ignored it and didn't want to let go that one last ask from Dad.

But I finally got it! While at the beach setting my goals for the upcoming year and reflecting on the past, I realized the universe is like a lifeguard. If the lifeguard blew the whistle, raised the red flag to get everyone out of the water because of sharks, I would

run away from the water quickly—because I always listen to the lifeguard. Well, I have been running right into dangerous waters, ignoring the red flags from the universe (lifeguard) and not listening at all.

I am a survivor and am excited about the crocheted blanket being built now. There may be some yarn that unravels along the way but not like before. Not focusing on self-worth and confidence will lead to greater pain. So, self-reflect and take care of yourself and serve others. This is where all those pieces of yarn early on in life came back around to help me. Giving back is so important. First, for showing up to serve and help someone else. And second, for your personal self-worth. It builds stronger character, and it puts you on the path of your passion and your journey. It is that next piece of yarn to be crocheted!

So, what does this mean? Focus on the signs the universe gives you, and if it is a red flag, pay attention. That red flag could be anything like seeing messages that unveil the truth, a sign or strong feeling to go left versus right and take a different road to your destination, even actions/reactions of others in situations— these are just a few I have encountered. It has taken me fifty-two years to understand the universe's most important lessons for me:

1. The universe will give you the same lesson over and over until you learn it. Understand it and do something about it.

2. Pay attention! If there is a red flag, back far far away from it. Don't run head-on into it!

If only, I listened earlier!

I have realized it comes down to avoiding the pain of a significant loss. I ignored these warnings both in my personal and professional life in different ways. It has put me in situations I really should not have had to go through.

I always show up to serve for others and now I also show up for myself. This is where I have been able to take my innate ability

in leadership and build things greater than I could ever imagine. I have a greater purpose on this journey in life. I have had so many dreams come true, and having conversations with college friends, acquaintances, and new connections made me take a step back and go, "Wow, I am just getting started!" Everything has come full circle, and it is time to serve more by being a personal and professional culture creator. Amazing things will come along. Marrying together both my personal and professional experiences is how I achieve bigger and bigger dreams in life. This will let me leave a legacy.

I have never taken the easy road to get to where I am today. It has been a journey filled with making difficult choices than others would, standing strong along the way and never giving up. My favorite quote by Robert Frost says it all, "Two roads diverged into a wood and I—I took the less traveled by, And that has made all the difference."[1]

Though some choices may have been right, some wrong, taking the less traveled road has made all the difference in my life's crocheted blanket.

Are you ready to take the road less traveled by?

Come join me and create your personal or professional culture by taking the road less traveled by and making a difference.

1—Robert Frost, "The Road Not Taken," in Mountain Interval (New York: Henry Holt, 1916).

ABOUT ERIN MCCAHILL

Erin McCahill is a corporate leader, entrepreneur, mentor, innovator, a personal and professional culture creator. As a sales and customer experience leader in the telecom, technology, and financial industry, she has built a strong reputation in building new organizations and revitalizing low-performing organizations while providing a superior customer experience. Erin has received numerous awards in recognition of her success. She has found her passion that drives her: helping others build personal and professional cultures. Erin possesses a bachelor of science in business management and an MBA.

Raised in Connecticut and now residing in southern New Jersey, Erin enjoys sports, spending time with friends and family, travel, entertaining, and planning events. She takes you along her journey in life and shows us that when you serve others, life's pieces of crocheted yarn will connect other pieces to help when needed. Enduring tremendous loss as a young adult and as a domestic violence survivor, Erin shares some of the lessons learned in her personal and professional life. She is just getting started, and by putting both experiences together, she is working on bigger dreams!

Web: www.themccahillgroup.com
Facebook: @erinamccahillmba
Instagram: @erinamccahillmba
LinkedIn: @erinamccahillmba
Email: em@themccahillgroup.com

FROM FEAR TO LOVE

Laura Mount

I spent years trying to have children. It was a very dark time in my life. All my young-adult life, I lived under the assumption that one "accident," and you could get pregnant. Well, jokes on me, because that was not true for me. I wanted nothing more than to be a mother. I felt it was my birthright, and my body was deceiving me. I allowed myself to become overwhelmed with the grief and frustration of it. I was trying to control everything in my environment. I was eating only the best of the best. I was taking my temperature every day and trying to find my ovulation—which didn't always come. We were timing sex as best we could. I was on hyper alert, and every time we got a negative test I was devastated. I started acupuncture and Clomid, and doctors and I were holding so tight to the controls. This was the only thing that could make me happy. None of it worked.

At last, we came to the big guns. I said I would never do in vitro fertilization (IVF). I felt this was controlling things too much. It was too sciencey and "unnatural." But here we were, the last stop, the big kahuna. At this point I was desperate. I wanted just one baby, God, just one. I made a vision board, and I put a picture from a magazine of two babies. One girl and one boy to

communicate that I didn't care which one I had. I got my schedule of injections, and I released control. I stopped fighting so hard for it and just did what I was told.

Fast-forward. My egg harvest was ridiculous! Forty-one eggs from one retrieval. We still got four good embryos. Tom had moved to Madison, Wisconsin, from Seattle to start a new job while I stayed back to go through the last stage of the IVF. On the way into the embryo transfer appointment, I called Tom to ask what I should do if the doctor recommended we put two embryos back. He said to do whatever the doctor said. I said, "Are you sure?" He said yes. The doctor recommended we put the two strongest embryos back, so that's what I did. Giddy with the idea of possibly having twins, I went back to my in-laws where I was staying, and every night I spoke to those babies. I put my hand on my stomach, and I told them how much I loved them and how long I had been waiting for them.

I never saw a positive pregnancy test. Never in my whole life. I was too scared to test. I waited for the blood test. When I finally went in a week later, my numbers were through the roof. They called Tom to give him the result because I couldn't bear to hear a negative result from anyone but him. He told me the high HCG number and said, "I bet we are having twins."

Sure enough, a boy and a girl. The perfect mix. One and done. Pink and blue. They came screaming into the world, and our little girl was the girliest of girls and our little boy was the sweetest boy a mom could ever ask for. I was so happy to have a boy and a girl. I would have the best of both worlds. The dirty knees and high energy of the boy and the sweet little girl that would give me grandbabies. I'm not saying these were the right thoughts to have—to put my kids in a box based on their gender assigned at birth—but it is a very natural thing for the mind to do. We start to daydream about our future as a parent the moment we find out we are pregnant, and these dreams contain preconceived ideas based on our lived experience and social cues. My little girl

was surprisingly girlie. I had never been into girlie things even as a small child. She loved princess dresses and anything frilly. Princesses and My Little Pony were the thing of the time. While Lily's outward appearance changed over the years, I never lost the image of the future of her being a mother like me someday.

In March of 2021, we were in the middle of a pandemic, and I was sitting at my makeshift desk in the kitchen in the middle of a workday. My kids were both doing school from home in our tiny bungalow in west Seattle. One of the kids was sitting in the living room about ten feet from me, and I got a text, "Mom, when can we talk about me starting testosterone?"

Um, what? I walked over to the couch and said, "I love you, and we will talk about this, but not over text." I then walked back to my desk, sat down, and dove back into my email and worked the rest of the day to avoid thinking about the conversation we were to have later that day. *What does this mean for the future? Surely this is not real. It's just a phase.* My image of the future was still holding on strong.

That evening, my daughter sat across the table from my husband and I and announced that she wanted to be our son and asked if we would let her go to the doctor to get a prescription for testosterone. She was nervous and struggled to make eye contact with us. I was in such denial. This was a phase, it would pass.

Seven years prior to this conversation at the age of seven, she asked to cut her hair like her brother's—a.k.a. the number 2 guard on the clippers. I questioned her as to why, and she reported that the boys had a book at school that they wouldn't let her look at because she was a girl. She was in the second grade. I told her they would still know she was a girl. At the time I cut the kids' hair. I asked my husband what to do. What if I cut her long hair off and she hated it and was mad at me? Why was I suddenly so attached to her hair? He counseled me to take her to the hair salon and have her tell them what she wanted, and then it wasn't on me. What a genius. She ended up with a short pixie cut at the

hair salon, and when they turned her around to see it, she was so happy. I still have a photo of that big grin on my phone. Then the next time she asked for the number 2 guard, I thought back to that huge smile on her face, and we got the clippers out. Number 2 guard for the win. She loved it.

After this she went back and forth between presenting male (though I didn't have this language then—she wore her brother's clothes) and presenting female. She was happy and well-adjusted, and we never really questioned any of it. I spent approximately zero minutes really thinking or worrying about any of it. She was expressing herself, and as I said, she was a happy, well-adjusted child. I will say that this new haircut did allow her to jump in on boy games at the neighborhood playgrounds where no one knew she was a girl. She loved this.

Let's jump ahead. My son is transgender. This means my son was born with a male brain and a female body. He was born a girl. (I state it this way for your understanding, but the correct terminology is AFAB—assigned female at birth.) We have been on quite a journey. My eyes and heart have been opened in ways I never could have imagined. My son has led the way, blazed a trail, and shown us how it is done.

A lot of trans teens present their gender identity to friends before talking to their parents and family. They may change their pronouns and even their name with their friends and "try things on" for years. By the time they come out to their family, they have had time to adjust to the idea, test the waters, and make up their minds. They are well along the way before the parents are looped in—mentally and emotionally.

This is where we sat on that fateful night. Shocked and not shocked at the same time. I immediately went into denial. I am her mother. I have a gut instinct. Women's intuition or whatever you want to call it, and I was sure it was a phase. It wasn't real. She would turn around the minute she was faced with a needle.

When the words were first uttered, I looked at my husband

before saying anything, and Tom didn't miss a beat. He said, "Of course we support you. Our number one is that you are happy." I was not surprised by his reaction. I often call him Buddha because out of the blue he will just say the right thing. He'll be calm and centered and unfazed. We told our son, of course he can see the doctor. His face lit up. He had our permission to see the doctor and see where it took him—to start a journey to himself. He was over the moon. I thought I was going through the motions, walking a journey with my child that would result in him going back to the status quo, but the key element is that I was allowing him to explore and find his way and keeping my thoughts about the destination to myself and allowing next steps while I was still processing.

Despite the joy on his face, I still didn't see the opportunity that lay in front of me. He had no doubts, and I had to go on my own journey to trust that. Of all of the things I thought I would navigate as a parent, this certainly wasn't on my radar.

As the process moved forward and with each new appointment, I learned new things. These new things often left me with more questions, more anxiety, and more fear. He already knew the process and all of these things and was ready to discuss them. I, on the other hand, was not. I did some of my own research as this was becoming more real. I talked to him candidly about these things. We were learning together as we went, and we continued to learn. I said and did, and still do, the wrong things all the time, and he gives me grace. We keep the lines of communication open, and when I am not sure how to handle something—or rather how he would like me to handle it—I ask.

When we got new photos of all of the grandkids, I really wanted to keep the old photo up to show how much they had all grown, but since the earlier photo was very female presenting, I wasn't sure how he would feel about keeping that photo up, so I asked him. This is very personal child to child. Some embrace all of themselves and see their younger self as part of their identity,

and some completely reject it and don't want to look at photos or have others see photos. I was granted permission to display both photos.

The first step on our adolescent transgender journey is a stop at your primary care doctor. We are lucky to live in a very progressive city that generally is very supportive of the LGBTQ+ community. Some conversation with the doc, and we were off and running with our referral to the gender clinic at Children's Hospital. As a parent I was still freaking out on the inside thinking this wasn't real. *Can't be real. It's a phase. And it is all happening so fast.* I asked my son questions about the validity of his claims (I told you it wasn't easy, and I learned along the way). "The other transgender kid we know came out at like five years old. You're fourteen. Wouldn't there have been signs?" "How can you and other friends of yours also be trans?" "But you wore the pinkest, frilliest stuff when you were young. I didn't pick that out, you did. You wore princess dresses and pink patent leather shoes everywhere." He tolerated my doubt and questioning, and we carried on. I continued to take deep breaths, take the next step, and do more listening than talking.

The change to he/him pronouns was surprisingly difficult. I kept thinking that if he had a more masculine name, it would be easier. His dead name (birth name) was very feminine. I also made the mistake of using this excuse to let other people in his life off the hook. Freshman year of high school he still used his birth name but used he/him pronouns all of high school. He told me that there were a few teachers who still misgendered him, referring to him with she/her pronouns. This felt very disrespectful and intentional to him. He presented male and had done so the entire time he was at the school. I told him that it was hard for people because his name is so feminine, and it made their brains short circuit when they tried to pair it with masculine pronouns. I realized that this excuse was bullshit and said, "You just needed me to say that sucks and tell you I would talk to your counselor at

school, right?" Yes, yes, he did. He didn't need me to support the ignorance of others and leave him to hold that pain on his own. Stepping-stones on the parenting journey. I was slowly seeing life through his lens. He was being outed by people of authority in his life. He had asked them to use the correct pronouns, and they were not.

I know what you are thinking. Will there be some counseling? Therapy? Psychiatrist? Does a kid get to just decide they are a different gender, and we just go with it as parents? How could they know at this age? I mean, the short answer is yes, at least in our program, there is evaluation and a diagnosis of body dysphoria. The long answer is much more convoluted. If you had to choose, would you choose to be in the wrong body? If puberty came along and things started shifting in the wrong direction and you were horrified, would you want to do something about it!? Again, I was ignorant to all of this. "Nobody likes having a period." "Every teenage girl has body dysmorphia when they hit puberty." (FYI dysmorphia is not the same as dysphoria, the feeling of distress or discomfort because of the difference between a person's gender assigned at birth and their gender identity.) Closed-minded, everybody-fits-in-a-box thinking. Again, he answered my questions. He explained the differences between dysmorphia and dysphoria. I was allowing him to carry me and my ignorance and my pain. I was putting him in a position to educate me.

Go back for a moment to your own puberty. I know for me the changes to my body were hard to accept. Now imagine for a moment you see yourself as male and you start to develop D-size breasts, or that you see yourself as female and your shoulders widen, facial hair starts to sprout, an Adam's apple forms, and your voice drops. It would be devastating. You wouldn't be able to hide your gender any longer. It would be there for everyone to see. This is a dangerous time for transgender teens. At best, they hide in baggy clothing and become quiet, shy, angry, and

withdrawn or lean into their gender assigned at birth and live a life that likely is not true for them. At worst, it becomes unbearable, and they cannot stand to be on this earth. According to a survey conducted by the Trevor Project 2021 National Survey on LGBTQ Youth Mental Health, 52% considered suicide and 20% reported attempting suicide. Compared to 32% and 10% in cisgender (identifying as the gender they were born) youth.[1]

There are many things that come with treating body dysphoria. I won't go into the details here except to say they are all terrifying for a parent. Thoughts of future fertility, possible permanent changes, and potential surgeries. It comes hard and fast. Kids don't want to be in this body, and they don't want to be in it stat!

After puberty started, my son had started to retract into himself. He wouldn't speak up anymore. He wouldn't order for himself. We attributed it to standard teenage changes. We discovered that he had been cutting and was feeling very anxious. He was spending more time in his room and not engaging in conversation during dinner. I was very nervous about the cutting and at a loss for how to handle it. He didn't want to talk to us about it and couldn't articulate to us (or didn't want to) why he did it or the relief or benefit he felt he was getting from it. I started to notice the same telltale signs on the arms of his friends.

All through my doubts and fears and skepticism, we kept taking the next step forward. I did a lot of work on myself during this time. I started to see that I needed to get my mind around this. *This is happening!* I had to find a way to work through my thoughts and feelings about what was happening as we were moving forward so I could be there for my child fully and not be in my head about the future and fear of what was happening. I needed to step out of fear and move into love so I could support my child. This couldn't wait until I understood and accepted

---

1—"National Survey on LGBTQ Youth Mental Health 2021," The Trevor Project, accessed June 28, 2022, https://www.thetrevorproject.org/survey-2021.

every facet of it. It couldn't wait until I made peace with it or made decisions around treatments that were four steps down the road. I had to make decisions as they came, I had to work with my spouse and my child and all the therapists, social workers, and doctors to take the next right step. My child needed me, and I needed to step up and out of my mind.

My son was struggling to pick out a new name so I asked if I could help. Imagine my surprise when he said yes. I got baby name books from the library—because I am "old" and apparently forgot about the internet. I picked a list of names and he liked a few. I told my sister-in-law about this list and she said Luke immediately popped into her head when we told her. This was a variation of one of the names on the list. I presented it to Luke, and he loved it. And that is now his name. I love this story because of the support of our family! This was one small step for me to take in showing my son that I love, respect, and support him.

I am lucky to have other amazing parents in my life who helped to light the way on this path for me and keep me focused on what matters. My child. There have been many long walks and tears discussing my fears and what-ifs and commiserating over the confusion of it all. These women helped me process my emotions and see where my thinking may be holding me back. They were my safe place to process all of my feelings and emotions and not burden my child with educating me and making it all okay. This is an absolute must. Burdening our children further and asking them to carry our fears and doubts during this trying time is not fair to them. I needed to find a safe place to process all of this so I could be open and available to hear and support him.

It was the support of these women, the doctors, and social workers that helped us get our minds around hormones. He started taking testosterone about three months into this journey. This was a hard step for us to take. It probably seems like we came to this choice quickly, but it didn't feel that way. We agonized over the possible side effects and the changes this meant—big,

huge, scary decisions for a teenager to make and parents to sign off on. At the end of the day, we had to plug our noses and jump in the deep end of the pool and trust our child, the therapists, and the doctors. The possible side effects of the hormones seemed minimal compared to the other options: anguish for my son and potential loss of life.

When people question our decision to let Luke take testosterone, I am confident in our choice. "You're not going to let him take hormones, are you? I mean dressing as a boy and using he/him pronouns is one thing, but hormones can cause permanent damage." It is not a proven fact that hormones do cause permanent damage. You know what causes permanent damage? Suicide. After presented with all the facts and learning more of other trans journeys, we were able to move past our fears and give our child what he needed to feel better. This is the treatment for body dysphoria.

Just like the social worker said after he started the testosterone, he was back to being his old self—the vibrant and talkative kid we knew before puberty. Luke opened up more to us in general and about his journey. I'm not sure if that is because of the trust we showed him or the confidence in feeling like he was on his own journey and had some control over his destiny.

In retrospect, I can't even begin to imagine the courage it took for him to come forward. In all of this I hadn't considered the courage he was displaying. He was standing in his truth in all walks of his life! This is something a lot of adults I know don't have the capacity for. This was to be celebrated! He was not only being himself, he was supporting other kids along the way.

This is supposed to be a story about me, but there is no story about me without this story. I am a mother. My children are a large part of who I am. My relationship with my children is a large part of who I am. It is the biggest opportunity for me to practice being who I want to be in this world. How I want to treat people. What values I live by. These have all been tested and

continue to be tested along this journey. This has been a grand opportunity for me to pause, take each value and belief, and analyze it and see whether it was truly coming from me or from unconscious programming.

I want to be an open person. I want to be a loving person. I want to be accepting of all beings both similar and different. This is easy to do when all beings "different" are *out there.* When those differences are *in here,* you really get tested. Now the differences (as I am learning) are not all so drastic as gender identity. They can be tidiness, educational acumen, personal interest, intrinsic motivation, desire to please, the list goes on and on. This journey has helped me to look at all of these things and my expectations of myself and others and truly look hard at myself, my actions, my values, and whether or not I am living my values.

My priority is my family. My goal as a parent is to raise loving, happy children whom I have a lifelong relationship with. This takes work. It takes personal reflection and admitting when you react to your past wounds and what you *think* you are supposed to be doing as a parent. To evaluate your motivations. Am I doing this because it is providing the result—a loving relationship with my child—I am after, because it is default parenting based on my childhood, or because I am worried about what *they* (peers, my parents, teachers) may think of me and my family? I now take a long, hard look at what is important to *me*! Does what I am about to say really matter? Does it create confidence and trust in my child, or does it drive a wedge between us? I don't always catch myself, but I always circle back and reconnect. I didn't always do this. I didn't do it because "the parent is always right" or "you can't show weakness or they'll walk all over you."

Well, shit, clearly the parent isn't always right. I assumed I had a daughter!

I have learned to question all the things I previously believed. What boxes am I creating for people? What boxes am I creating for myself? What boxes that others created am I still living in?

I have done a lot of research and it is fascinating to hear stories of other families. It often challenges my default mechanisms. For example, in listening to the story of another family, I saw a pattern in myself that I hadn't recognized. My daughter became my son, and then my son would wear female jewelry and was wearing eyeliner, and my mind couldn't handle it. My mind wanted him to pick a team already. Well, wrong again! There is no team! Male-presenting folks can wear previously labeled female items and vice versa—though let's be honest, ladies, the construct has allowed us to get away with "male" items.

Can you imagine what this might mean for the future? Could this transition loosen the gender inequality? Could nonbinary folks start to really erase that? Could there be an end to getting paid more if you have a penis?

It is time to learn how to think for ourselves. To look at the stories we've been told about the world and ourselves and question them. To really look inside and decide what we think for ourselves. To look at each other and see ourselves reflected back. We have a great resource and example right in our own homes. I am constantly in awe of my children and their peers. They are leading the charge to equality. They are open and accepting, and I feel another shift coming. We can resist this based on their young age and inexperience, or we can help usher it in by listening to our children and supporting them.

I've always wanted to help people improve themselves so *they* could feel better and be successful, but the more I research and see the humanity in us all, the more I really want us to take responsibility for our thoughts and how we show up, not for ourselves, but for each other. For all of our futures.

If you are the parent of a trans teen, you are not alone. Other parents are out there, many of us doubting our choices and fearful of making mistakes. There are resources for you. There are many Facebook groups and in-person support groups. I encourage to you to reach out to these resources, to make connections and

find people you can process with. If you are not finding these resources and you are struggling, please reach out. I am always happy and willing to connect!

ABOUT LAURA MOUNT

Parenting is a journey we don't get a map for. When we first find out we are having a child, we don't know what we are going to get! Boy? Girl? Healthy? We can easily map out different scenarios in our minds as to how our lives together will play out—particularly if we discover the assigned gender of our unborn child. It is a natural thing to do. Hopes and dreams are part of the human experience.

We were thrown a curveball that never appeared in any of the various lives I imagined for myself, my children, and our family. One of my sons is transgender. This was a map I didn't even have in the way back of my closet. There was no file in my brain labeled "transgender" for me to access. This was all new territory.

This is the story of how we created our own map with our child as the cartographer.

Laura Mount lives in west Seattle with her husband, kids, and dogs. She is a full-time working mom of teenage twins. The past year has been transformative for her as a mother as she learns how to support and parent her transgender teen. In this captivating account of this first year, she shares the struggles, challenges, joys, and epiphanies she has had on this journey. This process has helped her evaluate everything she believes and the way she shows up in the world.

Instagram: @laura_mount
Facebook: Laura Mount
LinkedIn: Laura Mount
Web: www.lauramount.com

HOW DO YOU GRAND?

Suzette Perez-Tate

"**N**ana is a grandma?" Charlotte says with confusion as she sees images of grandparents that don't quite match what she is familiar with. This is similar for many families out there. My journey growing up taught me how to face adversity head-on and find solutions. That is exactly what I did with *The Grands*. I am the creator and #1 best-selling author on Amazon of *The Grands Modern-Day Grandparent* children's book series. It wasn't easy getting there because it's not always a straight line to get to where you want to go. This has certainly been my experience in life overall.

I am the youngest of four children with a span of five-, six-, and seven-years' difference from my siblings. At an early age, I never quite felt like I fit in, and I always sought acceptance from others, and I also rooted for the underdog. The two don't always go hand in hand, and they're not always the popular choice.

I didn't see it then but many of my life experiences had prepared me for the journey I am currently on. My parents moved us to a small suburban town with the intention of giving us a better life than they had. They struggled to make ends meet in a community that was middle to upper class. I often would have

homemade or hand-me-down clothes, and there was no money for extras. As kids we knew if we wanted more, we needed to work for it (babysit, mow lawns, yard work, etc.).

As my parents could no longer make ends meet, they moved us from our comfortable cul-de-sac to another part of town. Time to fit into another neighborhood and adjust to my mother going back into the workforce. This was a pivotal change during my junior high years. With both parents working, I had a lot of unsupervised time on my hands, and my siblings were older and doing their own thing or out of the house.

Soon I would start high school and learn to fit in all over again. High school brought on new challenges in trying to stay focused, which was hard for me academically, and keeping up socially. At fifteen I met a young boy at school, and at the young age of sixteen I had my daughter. I stayed at a teenage maternity home for a few months before giving birth to my daughter. I remember crying the first few nights, but I eventually adjusted as I met young girls from all over and from different backgrounds. My mother never shamed me and was so supportive and nurturing through it all.

I eventually had feelings of outgrowing my daughter's father, and he was no longer my future. I moved on and two months later I met my now husband at the age of seventeen. It was late 1987, so we were met with resistance as I am Hispanic, and he is black. My parents did not want me to date him. As much as I strived to fit in and seek acceptance, I always created my own path. Despite my parents' request, I continued to see him, and our bond with each other grew stronger.

Although I was a teen mom (a label I never accepted), I felt strongly about graduating and then going on to college. After high school, I immediately enrolled in a trade school for electronics, and yes, you guessed it, I did not feel as though I fit in. I must have been one of five girls in the whole predominantly male school. After finishing my associate's degree in electronics, it was

time to find a job. I was so motivated to make money to provide a comfortable life for my daughter and me. But doors did not open so easily. Some employers wanted to hire me due to the way I looked rather than the skills I just earned in school. While others rejected me due to my looks, saying that their wife would be mad at them if they hired me. Over the years, I would try my hand at a variety of temporary jobs.

Six years had gone by, and I was still dating my boyfriend from the age of seventeen. I became pregnant with my son, and the resistance to my relationship with my parents was over. They embraced our relationship as though they never had an issue with it.

I remember the day I moved out of my parents' house and moved in with my now husband. Before leaving, my mother asked me if I would leave my daughter with her and my father. I couldn't understand why she would ask me such a thing as I too was close with my daughter and could not imagine ever leaving her. I just couldn't fathom why she would ask me such a question.

Having my daughter at such a young age made my mother a grandmother at the age of forty-two. My mother was such a great example and role model of what it meant to be a modern-day grandparent as she never seemed to fit in the mold. I never met my grandfathers and did not spend much time with my grandmothers. I had a lot of love and respect for my grandmothers but have very few memories with them.

When people saw my mother and daughter together, they often thought they were mother and daughter. The bond my mother had with my daughter was beautiful. She was always her safe place and much like a best friend and personal cheerleader. I was always the youngest parent at back-to-school night and was even mistaken for a high school student during a tryout event for theater. I always felt that I had to grow into being looked at as my daughter's mother.

As my daughter became older, the bond between her and my

mother strengthened. They talked on the phone daily, multiple times throughout the day and night. They enjoyed short trips together and even went to New York when my daughter was in the twelfth grade. They called this their senior trip.

When my mother turned sixty-two, she was diagnosed with breast cancer. She had beat cancer, and then it returned as it metastasized into her lung as Stage IV cancer. My mother showed us what it was like to *live* with cancer instead of dying from cancer. She didn't miss a beat when it came to being a mother or grandmother. She was full of life, something you just don't see represented in stories or images about grandparents.

Soon it would be my turn to experience life as a grandparent—a concept that I just did not see myself embracing as I could not relate to the one-dimensional character often highlighted in stories and images. I mean, have you seen the emoji that represents grandparents?

I have a blended family, and my stepson had our first grandchild. Loren was a beautiful grandbaby. Now, I wasn't being called Grandma or any other endearing nickname just yet as Loren was still too young to speak.

Loren was just born, and my daughter Ashley was pregnant with my second grandchild. Quinn was born the following year. While I still wasn't sure about being called Grandma, my mother was still showing me how grand she truly is. Still, very close to Ashley, she was very involved with Quinn's homecoming and stayed with Ashley while Quinn came home from the hospital, a moment I will always regret not being there for. I may have taken for granted that my mother was always there for my daughter for major life situations. As Quinn was home and looked upon with much love, tragedy was just hours away. I left my daughter, my mother, and my granddaughter with a bit of an unsettling feeling. Early the next morning I received one of the worst phone calls I could have ever received. Ashley pieced together the words "Quinn is dead." Within a year, I had celebrated my daughter's

pregnancy, the birth of Quinn, then a full Catholic mass for my grandbaby's funeral. My heart was crushed for my daughter and mother for the traumatic event they endured together. My mother would always put events in our lives in perspective by saying that they have already experienced the worst thing they could ever experience in their lives.

Another year later came Brooke (Loren's sister). At family gatherings, I was referred to as Grandma Suzette. The name Grandma just had a stigma for me, as it sounded like such an aging reference. I still hadn't quite got my bearings as grandma yet, but I loved the girls so much. When Brooke was born, Ashley was carrying her second child. Come November, Charlotte Rose Smith was born. Being so nervous and unable to forget what happened with Quinn, I stepped into my grandma role as my mother had been showing me all these years. I went to doctor's appointments, smiling from ear to ear over every moment spent with her. I didn't realize that my heart could feel this way. It was truly magic. Everything was about this little girl (as though I had the authority to make any decisions). Here I was for many years trying to just fill my shoes of being called Mom (as many saw me as my daughter's sister) to finally being ready to be called Grandma. It wasn't easy right away, but soon Charlotte was calling me Nana. I light up anytime I hear her call out to me.

But there was still the feeling of not fitting into my role and still remnants of the stigma of being called Grandma, Nana, or anything related to being that one-dimensional character. When reading stories or seeing images about grandparents, I just couldn't relate. I was so actively involved with Charlotte, and I loved being silly without caring who saw me. Over the next few years, my stepdaughter gave us two more grandchildren, Jeremiah and Journey.

Today many grandparents still have a job, career, are active, provide care for their grandchildren, and in some cases live with their grandchildren. I kept telling my mom that I needed to

change the stereotype of grandparents. At times I would joke about it, but then one day I became serious about changing the image of what a grandparent looks and feels like in society. As I became a grandmother, I began to really notice other grandparents and how they showed up in their grandchildren's lives. People I observed were friends, family, coworkers, and even strangers. Our stories were all different in how we showed up in our grandchildren's lives, but the focus remained the same as we all had such a deep love for our grandchildren. No one family is the same, and no one grandparent is the same.

My mother's cancer finally took its toll, and she eventually passed away. A few months later, I was driving home from an out-of-town trip with my husband, and I could not shake the feeling of the modern-day grandparent concept. It was as though my mother was right there with me pushing me toward this endeavor. I pulled out my laptop and began to create a presentation of the concept. I had socialized my presentation with a few people and the concept with others. Immediately I received positive feedback and an understanding of what I was looking to do. This was a feeling of validation anytime anyone understood the concept of the modern-day grandparent.

Later that year I was faced with a career decision to take an early retirement package from a company I had been working at for over twenty-five years. My thought was that I would take the package and begin my writing on a children's book about the modern-day grandparent and start the work I had laid out in my presentation. To be clear, I never set out to be an author. This was more about starting a movement where grandparents would be seen for how they show up in their grandchildren's lives.

I eventually made the decision to continue working and started on my bachelor's degree. Passing up the opportunity to retire gave me the perspective that I didn't have to give up the dream of *The Grands* book series. As you can tell I am very much an "and" person. I can do this, *and* I can do that. When you

believe in something strong enough, you will figure out a way to make it happen. My husband told me a long time ago if I want something I am going to do it. I had a great teacher in my mother as she always went into what I call fix-it mode. She didn't look for excuses or talk her way out of anything; she would immediately figure out a way to make it happen.

I had no idea where to start when creating a children's book, let alone a series. I just knew there was something I really wanted to change, and the series would be the platform for my message. If I overthink a plan or project, I end up talking myself out of it, easily coming up with reasons why I can't do it. I call this action *getting in my own way*. To move forward, I could not get in my own way. Believe me, I had many reasons I could have used as an excuse to get in my own way. I was still grieving my mother's passing, working full-time, attending school full-time, recovering from spine surgery, balancing time with my family, and traveling back and forth to visit Charlotte out of state.

Soon after I found a coauthor to join in on my passion project to coauthor a children's book, it came time to look for an illustrator. This process was all new for me, and I took it all in and learned so much. I went through about five to six illustrators as I needed the grands to be represented just right. COVID restrictions began, and we had to move to work remotely.

When it came to writing, there was so much passion in this project that we had enough content for two books immediately. No one family is the same, and no one grandparent is the same. This was so apparent as I couldn't decide where to limit my characters and family dynamics within the series. We were so green when it came to learning the criteria for children's books and to publishing. Immediately we learned how generous authors and others in the book industry are. I was introduced to Kate Butler who believed in our story and mission. She helped us bring our dream across the finish line and was so enthusiastic throughout the process.

My hope is that many families will see themselves and feel as though they fit in, in this series, concept, and movement. Getting *The Grands Modern-Day Grandparent* series in households around the world to celebrate the relationship between grandparents and their grandchildren is my *dream*. I went from not fitting in or wanting acceptance to being the creator and #1 best-selling author on Amazon of *The Grands Modern-Day Grandparent* series. Tell me, how do you grand? We would love to hear from you and how you grand @thegrandsmdg on Instagram.

ABOUT SUZETTE PEREZ-TATE

Suzette Perez-Tate is a 52-year-old Modern-Day Grandmother and the Creator and Coauthor of the #1 best-selling Amazon children's book: The Grands: The Race and Time With My Grand. Suzette and her husband have been together going on 35 years and have a blended family with 5 children and 5 grandchildren. Suzette has been working for a technology company for 28 years in business operations and recently earned her MBA, proving to herself that it's never too late. She lived most of her life with a feeling of always wanting to fit in or pleasing others, she is finally living life knowing she is enough.

For over 10 years Suzette Perez-Tate struggled with fitting into the one-dimensional image and characterization of how grandparents are highlighted in children's book stories and society. She couldn't ignore that many family dynamics and the way that grandparents show up in their grandchildren's lives were not being represented and she created The Grands Modern-Day Grandparent series. It is important to Suzette to create an experience through her children's books that provides inclusion and diversity celebrating grandparents and their grandchildren where families can see themselves. No one family is the same and no one grandparent is the same.

You can reach out to Suzette Perez-Tate via:

Email: thegrandsmdg@gmail.com
Instagram: @thegrandsmdg
Facebook: The Grands Modern Day Grandparent
Website: www.thegrandsmdg.com

THIS IS *NOT* AS GOOD AS IT GETS

Tracy Richards

I had a whole life. I had built a whole life. I met a man and married him. I had a good job, owned a business, ran marathons and triathlons, had pets, traveled. Over the years, there were some good times and some bad times. To the outside world, it looked like I had it all. My husband and I were the perfect couple, so in sync with each other. How it felt from the inside was something very different. I was suffocating, choking on denial, and convinced that this life was as good as it would get for me. A beginning and an ending would change all of that.

I've never been afraid of beginnings. In fact, they have always excited me. I went to college 2,000 miles from home, I moved across the country two times by myself, and started multiple new jobs. The thrill of something unknown was always fresh. It's the endings that scared me. The finality filled me with fear and made it difficult to embrace the possibilities of a better future. When the chance to begin again was ripe with opportunity, I was always apprehensive.

After fifteen years in the Pacific Northwest, my husband and I moved to northeast Ohio. A job offer for him along with a generous relocation package catapulted us into a new chapter.

We loaded our five dogs and five cats into two cars and made the four-day drive to our new home. I was fearful of the ending that this beginning signified. We were leaving a community and connection behind for a place where I knew no one. The future should have felt wide open, but it didn't.

While our old life had familiarity and safeness to it, it felt lonely. Struggling to find my purpose, I poured all my energy into my animals and my marriage. The only friends I had were those whom my husband and I shared. I gave up my identity long ago, back when we first met, when all I wanted was for him to want me. I gave up my independence when we opened a business that would eventually fail and hurl us into financial crisis. I gave up my peace when we adopted Asha, a dog who was born deaf and blind, with epilepsy and debilitating anxiety. This new location in which we found ourselves would not be able to erase all of that, and so the promise of a new beginning felt empty.

My husband and I were together for seventeen years, married for eleven of those, and through it all, we depended upon each other. I hadn't fallen in love. I had just ended up there and never even bothered to ask myself if that was what I wanted. Our marriage was a partnership, a friendship, a commitment. I believed being married meant stability, affection, and foreverness. My marriage never felt that way to me, instead it was a relentless exercise in bargaining.

I wasn't getting the affection I so desired, but my husband was a solid guy whom I trusted . . . good enough.

I didn't feel passion, but maybe not all relationships were passionate . . . good enough.

I was drowning in our financial struggles, but we were in it together, and how could I ever make my way alone . . . good enough.

I felt overwhelmed with the daily demands of our animals, all of them, but they gave me the love and connection I wasn't feeling anywhere else . . . good enough.

I sacrificed my desires and my dreams, because I worried that if I asked for something more, if I took a chance and tried to find better, I would realize that this was the pinnacle. Then the "good enough" would be a distant memory, replaced by the "remember when" in a life full of regret.

Meanwhile, my husband was making progress in our new environment. He had his job, he found connection in the running community without me, he went back to school for his MBA, he made friends, he found belonging. I stayed at home on the couch with the animals, behind our black curtains with empty walls and old furniture. Our house reflected the way I felt about our relationship. It was sad and dark. No light was able to get in, and I was breaking under the weight of it all.

While I had thoughts of being unhappy and wanting something different, I always pushed them out of mind. Until I couldn't anymore. One day, I collapsed. In one moment, it all changed. I found my voice, and the Universe was ready to match me. It had been waiting patiently all this time. Once I spoke power to my desires, once I imprinted my true feelings on the ether, my whole life shifted.

My husband decided to leave the job for which we had moved to Ohio. He had been there for two years and eight months. Our relocation package required he stay for three years; anything less would result in a financial penalty. I was supportive of his job change because he had been unhappy, and I couldn't tolerate his unhappiness on top of mine. I didn't fully understand the ramifications of the timeline. But I would. Soon enough, I would.

On that day, the day that signaled the line between before and after, I was working in my home office when I got a text from my husband. That text told me that we owed $36,000 in relocation package payback, and we had two months to satisfy that debt. This information literally brought me to my knees. For the first time, I gave myself permission to acknowledge my truth. I had grown tired of living a life of lack, a life of never

having enough of anything, a life of emptiness. At the top of my lungs, through body-consuming sobs, on the hardwood floor of my bedroom, I shook the world with my words. "I don't want to live like this anymore."

"I DON'T WANT TO LIVE LIKE THIS ANYMORE."

That's all it took for there to be a seismic shift. I didn't realize it at the time, but I know it now. The Universe heard me. Loud and clear. Over the next year, I wouldn't live like that anymore, not in any capacity. It would all be different.

Three months later, my husband walked down the stairs, sat on the couch across from me, and much to my surprise, told me we were getting a divorce. There was no discussion, there was no counseling, no chance to reconsider. He had decided and that was it. Three months after that night, our divorce was final. I was left with our five dogs and three remaining cats, a house that was falling apart, tight finances, and no local friends to comfort me. I thought I was lonely before, but this was a different kind of loneliness. There was a glimmer of possibility, but it was over-shadowed by the crippling loss that had preceded it.

The end of my marriage devastated me. I was so overcome with fear, grief, and shame that I was unable to embrace the gift of an empty page. I thought my whole world had closed in on me. Who would ever want all of *this*? Who would want a forty-four-year-old, divorced woman covered in tattoos, with a crappy house, no money, and eight animals? I could not imagine any quality person desiring any of that. And because I couldn't imagine it, it stayed impossible.

I spent the year after my divorce making progress in some aspects of my life. I made my way financially by being scrappy. I said yes to everything, I took every job and contract offered to me until I couldn't keep it straight anymore. I found friend-ships by saying yes to invitations, even when I didn't want them because I knew I had to do something different if I wanted a better future. Yet, in one part of my life, I was treading water. I

entered a relationship with an unavailable man who would never be able to commit to me. I told myself it was the circumstances not my value that kept this connection from becoming more permanent. This affair allowed me to prove to myself that what I had before was actually as good as it was ever going to get for me.

I had shouted out for a different life and now I had it, but I didn't want this one either. I realized I had never asked myself what I did want. I had never formulated my desires, never expressed the exact feelings I hoped for. I had always created my life by default, by saying "okay, this is fine" when I should have been saying "no, I want *so* much more than this." *Fine* is where dreams go to die. I was further into unhappiness than I ever was during my marriage, and that became unacceptable to me. I opened my journal and began to write.

This is how it will be, I started. I went on to detail how my desired relationship would be. How I would feel, what experiences and emotions would abound. It poured out of me onto the pages, and I felt a lightness as if my vision had reached the intended recipient. I realized I had been saying yes to other things in my life, friendships, financial opportunity, a lifetime of lessons from my dog, Asha, but I was saying no to the possibility of romantic love and connection, the one thing I most desired. I needed to find a way to say yes in every part of my life.

This time, I clearly expressed to the Universe what I wanted, and again, it did not disappoint. Shortly after that entry into my journal, the dead-end relationship dissolved. I was overcome with a sense of relief. *Finally.* I no longer had to convince myself or struggle with the impossibility. It just went away. Because it no longer served me. It no longer provided me the feelings I wanted to feel. It no longer aligned with the clarity of my dreams. The fear I had always felt in endings eased. There was an inkling that something so much better was on its way. It had to be because maybe this wasn't as good as it was going to get. I created space for what was meant for me, and it finally showed up.

One April day, as I parked my car and walked down the street to meet a man I had just recently connected with online, I had to convince myself to say yes. We had texted for two days, and now I was on my way to see him face to face for our first date. *Turn around and go home,* I told myself. I was convinced that what I wanted could not be waiting for me. The chance of a beginning was still buried under the bitterness of an ending. Even though it was uncomfortable and scary, I said yes. I decided to move forward toward the life I wanted instead of shrinking back into the one I didn't. That decision changed everything.

"My God, you're beautiful" were the first words he said to me. And every day since, we have built the life that I asked for, the life that I chose, the life that I created through intention and action. This relationship evolved into the "this is how it will be" relationship that I wrote about in my journal. I asked for it, I got it, and I express my gratitude for it every single day of my life.

As other parts of my life grew cumbersome, I remembered that I could formulate my plan. My work situation had become so stressful, at one point I had twelve email addresses because I said yes to everything that came my way, taking no time to consider if it moved me toward my dreams or not. I wanted a single job that would provide me security, purpose, and flexibility. One afternoon, all my work converged into chaos, and I said, "I don't want to do this anymore." Just then, my phone rang and I was offered a job I had been interviewing for that would allow all the things I had conjured. I was onto something.

I always believed that I was limited financially, that I had a certain ceiling I could never break through. I was a spender, not a saver, and my bank account supported this theory. Until it supported a new idea. I again decided what I wanted, how I would feel when my finances were increasing, what it would mean to have that certainty. I wrote it down, I took action every day, and eventually it became so.

The one thing I couldn't seem to tackle, the single issue that

eluded me, was sleep. My dog Asha, the one who was born deaf and blind, the one with epilepsy and anxiety, the one who had stolen my peace . . . she never slept. After years and years of working with veterinarians and all sorts of other practitioners to find a way to ease her restlessness, we still only got three to four hours of sleep at a time. I had gone ten years without a full night of rest. I constantly asked the Universe for sleep. I wrote about it, I dreamed about it, I attempted to move toward it, with no success. Then it occurred to me. It wasn't sleep I wanted; it was the feeling of rest.

I had been asking for something specific, a thing, instead of asking for how I wanted to feel. In all other aspects of my life, in my relationship, my finances, my career, I had created a blueprint for how I wanted to feel. I never asked for the love of my life to look a certain way or have a particular job. I didn't detail what his bank account would hold or what filled his closet. I didn't wonder about investments or think of working for one specific company. All my words, all my visions, all my hopes and actions focused on one thing: how I wanted to *feel*.

I began to approach my relationship with Asha keeping that in mind. I was feeling tired, hopeless, drained, angry, frustrated, and afraid. I thought I wanted sleep, but what I really wanted was to stop feeling these things and instead to be rested and energized, fascinated and in love with this creature who consumed my life. So I did what I had done before. I got my journal and I began to write. It didn't take long for my emotions to transform. Even though my hours of sleep did not increase, I noticed that I felt rested and more loving toward Asha. It became clear. It wasn't the conditions that needed to change, it was me.

There are situations we have control over no matter how much we convince ourselves otherwise. Then there are the things we cannot change. It isn't always the circumstances that need to be different in order for us to realize our dreams. Sometimes it is our expectations, our interpretations, the meaning we assign to

the circumstances that create an unwanted reality. What we think becomes our truth. That is the magic, and once you see that, you can't unsee it.

This wisdom is more powerful than any adjustment of situations, and it helped me overcome the fear of endings. It helped me see that whatever the "this" is in my life, it doesn't have to be as good as it will get if I want something more. I believe this lesson is the main purpose of my life with Asha—so much that I wrote a whole book about it. She approaches her life as if it never occurred to her that anything bad could happen. She interprets the world with hope, and she wants to experience all of life. For more than ten years, I have watched her navigate her surroundings, and finally her messages sunk in.

I now approach all my life through the lens of my feelings. How do I want to feel? I no longer exercise to see a certain number on the scale. I do it because I want to feel healthy and fit, strong and powerful. I'm not writing a book to make millions. I'm doing it because I want the heaviness that comes from keeping it all inside to lift. I want to feel light and free, honest and seen. How I want to feel has become my number one priority, and I am intentional about creating a life to match that.

Four years after the life I had built disappeared, after I was paralyzed with fear, I realize that everything I asked for has shown up just as I intended or *better*. I have a wonderful man in my life, and with him I feel joy and love. I have a job that allows me to feel flexibility and purpose. I feel safe and free in my financial situation. I am a creator and feel growth and accomplishment. My world has transformed from dark and empty to full of light.

Every day I continue to formulate the life I want, I imprint it onto my heart, I take action toward it, I feel as if it already exists. I express gratitude for what I currently have and for all the goodness that I *know* is coming. Because I believe that what I want will be mine, I can afford to be patient. That patience calms any fear.

When you know that you will get what you want, or something

even better, there is no longer any reason to be afraid. The first step is to allow yourself permission to acknowledge that you don't want the "this" in your life, the thing that is "good enough." Only then can you alert the Universe that you are ready for the more you are promised simply by being alive on this planet. Determine how you want to feel, believe in it, and experience life through that lens. Take steps every day to move your story forward. The life of your dreams is there for the taking. So it has been with me, and so, I know, it will be with you too.

ABOUT TRACY RICHARDS

Tracy Richards is an author, speaker, Reiki Master, and energy teacher. She has certifications in Animal Reiki, the Akashic Records, and Positive Psychology. Tracy offers classes in vibration, personal frequency, and Reiki attunements in addition to her life-changing workshops. Her book, *Asha: Lessons in Hope and Life*, is scheduled for publication in September 2022.

Tracy helps clients grant themselves permission to acknowledge the "this" in their life, the realities that are not what they want for themselves, and she guides them through the process of formulating how they want to feel in the life of their dreams. Through workshops and individual sessions, she provides a framework that allows clients to become intentional about the life they want and take action to begin living it. She has a unique way of making others feel seen and empowered. Let her help you step into your own light and love.

To learn more about how you can work with Tracy, schedule a speaking engagement or podcast appearance, and to order her book, visit her website www.tracyrichards.co or email her at tracy@ tracyrichards.co.

Facebook: Tracy Richards
Instagram: @tracyrb226
Author Instagram: @tracyrichards_author
Email: Tracy@tracyrichards.co
Web: www.tracyrichards.co

TAKE YOUR CENTER STAGE

Cori Solomon Santone

I was seven years old and sang "It's a Small World" a cappella to a packed auditorium of my Catholic school. They had themed the entire finale around my performance, which ended with me standing center stage singing the final chorus surrounded by the other forty children in the talent show. The roar of the standing ovation will go down in Catholic school history.

Little did I know at the time, it set the stage for my life.

Since I can remember, my incredible parents have been gifting me with these mantras: "You'll never know unless you try," "You can do anything you put your mind to," "We will love you no matter what." Parents around the world create these safety nets for their kids, but so many people let fears and self-created barriers stop them from doing what they really want to do. Some people stay close to home, comfortable, living out mundane lives, avoiding challenges or heartache.

Believing that I was invincible, I have been jumping out of my comfort zone my entire life. I've moved nineteen times, changed careers four times, and experienced four great love stories. I've been on countless stages now, quite literally and figuratively, and my belief in taking center stage translated into years

of performing arts and taking the lead as a CEO, principal, camp director, fundraiser, consultant, and most importantly, a mom. The inherent problem with putting yourself out there is that it typically comes with a giant spotlight, which invites challenges. New barriers arise and lots of mistakes are made. People judge and criticize, and often, the journey is not all sunshine and rainbows. Like the song says, we live in a world of hope, fears, laughter, and tears. My successes have been clouded with many failures and challenges, but I have honed some valuable coping skills from my experiences that helped me to achieve my dreams.

Some of my coping skills were learned early on. My father was in the US Air Force, so we moved a lot. I learned the value of embracing inevitable change and the power of making friends quickly in new places. My confidence as a young person was unshakable, but like most children, that changed in middle school. In fifth grade, I stopped growing. Not metaphorically, but rather quite literally. Once their equal, I was suddenly different and thus an easy target for the insecure bullies. Short jokes are surprisingly revered as socially acceptable still decades later. After hearing hundreds of these jokes, and enduring three brutally awkward years, I had the opportunity to create a new scene for high school.

With a new setting comes opportunities for new characters and new plot lines. I researched and joined every club possible, sought out new friends, and rediscovered the drama club. On stage, real life didn't exist, and I honed my skills of compartmentalizing and breaking apart people's perspectives. By junior year, I was on top of the world. I was Dorothy in our *Wizard of Oz* production, played varsity soccer, made the varsity cheerleading squad, and fell in love with a star football player. I felt unstoppable, but when you are living life to its fullest, challenges are bound to arise. In the summer leading up to my senior year, my parents separated. It was at a time before people even talked about divorce and certainly before any of my friends' parents were

divorced. My parents were each devastated and going through their own individual turmoil and rebirthing after their eighteen years of marriage. Then, I tore my ACL while in gymnastics practice right before our opening football game. The doctor said there would be a surgery—but no cheer or soccer my senior year. While regaining my strength, I realized I needed to change my setting—create a new scene with room to grow. I revamped my college plans and chose a school three hours away that had an incredible study abroad term built into their curriculum. I finished that senior year as third in my class and with bright plans. I was gifted with the superlative Most Talented. Perhaps it was an odd popularity contest, but to me, it was just the right amount of validation that I had turned things around from my middle school self.

I was going to make the most of the opportunities I had in college. Knowing that a key to being successful is having a strong support network, I sought out friends and joined a sorority. I was flung into a world of diversity, new views, and perspectives that my small, conservative hometown just didn't have. I also joined every club I could including the theater and singing organizations. I realized quickly that though I did love performing, the students set on Broadway careers weren't my people. I gravitated toward the teachers. I quickly committed to a career in education with lots of performing and fine arts electives.

My first summer home, I was shocked back into the reality of my parents' divorce with their split homes and the never-ending drama of high school. Using a summer jobs book from the library, my best friend and I secured jobs at an overnight summer camp in Maine. For the next three summers, I was a Theater Director and then Arts Department Director. I loved camp and camp people. My limited acting talents were able to shine on a rustic stage in the middle of the woods. I saw a world where children were able to be whole—embraced for their individual qualities and thrust into safe opportunities to shine on stage. I

met people from around the world, fell in love again, and found my two closest lifelong friends.

I finished college summa cum laude with a bachelor's in elementary education and mathematics. Now, being from the South, I had some preconceived ideas that I was also supposed to finish with an Mrs. degree (a.k.a. a husband), which at the time, I had no prospects. I was faced with another opportunity to take a big risk. Create a new scene. The obvious choice to move home didn't feel right, but I didn't have much money since I had been student teaching full-time. Being obsessed with Jane Eyre, I researched teach-abroad opportunities and found an agency that would place American teachers at schools in England. My application was accepted, and the agency set up five interviews for late September. Meanwhile, I had spent the summer back at my camp in Maine and fell in love with a windsurfer from England. At the time, I remember feeling confident that I was again creating my position on center stage. Even watching the twin towers come crashing down while I was packing for England wasn't enough to derail me. I flew out the next week with just five people on my international flight.

The first school I interviewed with offered me a job! My first year of teaching was in a small village town with one church, two pubs, and our little school. I taught twenty-seven little English children ages eight to eleven. I was responsible for their traditional subjects and music, art, religion, and British sports. There were no textbooks or teacher manuals. The kids had blank notebooks and a lot of questions about America. I walked to school with my students during the day and drank at the pub with their parents at night. I learned how to drive a stick shift on the opposite side of the hilliest roads I've ever seen and how to corral wandering sheep from the playground at recess. At the end of the year, the school needed a five-year commitment from me to invest the cost of my permanent visa, and I knew in my heart it wasn't the right choice for me. I hadn't found my people and couldn't see a future

where I would thrive. Though it would mean starting over again with so many unknowns ahead, I declined their offer.

I moved back home with my fiancé and found myself an elementary school teaching position. The morale at the school was low, but I found an incredible group of teacher friends, and together, we believed in our power to change things. I always seek out my people. There is no greater bond than those formed by teachers together in the trenches. I also remembered the power the arts had on my learning, so I dove into arts integration and project-based learning. Within just a few years, I was married, leading our district's test scores, and proving to a lot of doubters that through the arts, students could achieve more. For a while, things were okay, but I wasn't finding joy in my life, and I felt a constant pull to make more of an impact in the world. At home, my husband was also feeling lost, so we agreed we needed to make a big change.

Having loved summer camp, I researched and found an arts camp that was based a few states away. We sold our house in just three days at the height of the pre-recession days and made a great profit. Seemed like we were making the right choice. The camp was owned by a couple with two young children, who I thought we would be partnering with for a grand new future. Just a couple of weeks into camp though, I found myself in the middle of a nightmare and realized I had made a terrible mistake. The husband was abusing his wife and children. Our camp nurse taught me self-defense at night in our cabins in case he came after me, and I spent my days running their camp while helping the wife build up the courage to get out of her abusive relationship. Six weeks later, we orchestrated her escape, with great relief and of course police support. I was thinking I must have been meant to come here to help this brave woman. I thought, *This is my path after all*, but the very next day, my husband called me, and before I could share the good news, he said, "I've decided to move back to England. Alone."

Three weeks later, he was gone. I was living back at home and felt like a complete failure. My best friend invited me to Maine so I could get some fresh perspective. I knew I needed to do some research and to reorganize the characters and setting of my world once again to be true to myself and my purpose in the world. I had a dream to work with children in a meaningful way that was authentic to my beliefs. Though I tried and had failed, I wasn't willing to give up.

I did more research and found another arts camp. This time, I researched the camp's history thoroughly, and after my interview, I knew I had found a place I could shine. So, I perhaps did what no other person has done before, and I moved from South Carolina to New Jersey. Alone in this new state, before GPS systems understood Jersey's no left turns/jug handle initiative, I spent a lot of time lost—but only physically, because professionally I had found my place. This camp was eight glorious weeks of children being free to be themselves, having long conversations about their future lives under the stars at night and belting out Broadway tunes on our stage through the day. I trained our staff to work with our campers through an approach I had honed in my many years in the classroom. Rooted in the belief that all children are good, the goal was to form meaningful relationships, establish consistent routines, and use collaborative problem-solving to create equitable and emotionally safe environments for kids to thrive. I spent seven years as a summer camp director, working alongside incredible people, which brought me great joy, not to mention countless plot lines for a TV movie.

One night with a bottle of wine and too many Girl Scout Cookies to count, I created an online dating profile. Online dating is a racket that I embarked upon with a very dear friend, and gratefully, we were both spared by the dating gods from too much suffering by letting both of our first dates be magical men. Picture southern arts ed girl meets Philly music teacher. Tom brought with him two precious little girls (ages three and six), and

I very quickly fell in love with all three of them. He had shared custody of the girls, so we spent half our lives creating the plot of a whirlwind romance novel and the other half making Hallmark-worthy family memories. Of course, there were challenges as I learned about all the ups and downs of being a stepmom, but my relationship with the girls was beautiful, authentic, and full of shared adoration. Tom was my person, and my life's troubled love story had found its magical ending.

Professionally, I was also feeling fulfilled, but the CEO position of my organization opened unexpectantly, and with some encouragement from a generous mentor, I put myself out there. I believed that I could help our nonprofit do more to support children and families. So, I went back to school to get my nonprofit management and financial management certificates, and I was chosen from a national search to be the next CEO.

Little did I know the organization was in dire financial trouble. I had to lay off six people right away, one of whom was a dear friend. Stressful day after stressful day, I worked with a small but talented team to find resources and reinvent the organization. I worked eighty-hour weeks while balancing sleepless nights, crushing pressure, and great unknowns as a young CEO. I made the best decisions I could for the sake of my team and the families we served, but my life was consumed by work.

And then, without sounding cliché, a magical thing happened. None of it felt important anymore; I was pregnant and my perspective shifted. My greatest gift came in mid-September followed by twelve weeks of working from home and processing my new teaching role as a mom. I found myself in an odd position of feeling informed as a mom from having worked with so many children for so many years, including my own stepdaughters, but I also realized what people mean when they say, "You don't really understand until you have your own kids." I was irrationally worrying about everything and wondering how I would teach her

those valuable lessons that my parents taught me. How could I teach all three of my girls to take their own center stage roles?

The return to work was filled with the challenges so many moms know: pumping in weird places, exhaustion you can feel in every fiber of your body, and the constant anxiety of making sure your precious little ones are okay while you are away. But, once I got in the swing of things, I had a renewed sense of purpose in my CEO role. I was an advocate for children, education, and the arts, and I knew I had a responsibility to affect real positive impact for the sake of my three girls and children across the region. I didn't know the opportunity would happen so soon, but as I researched our strategic plans, everything started to crystallize.

The organization's campus had thirty-three buildings that sat empty throughout the school year. Opening a school was not only a possibility, it could be the pillar to stabilize the organization. I started to say it out loud: We should start a school. A dream school. A school that integrates the arts with emotional intelligence and true student-centered decision-making. There were many fans, but there were also people who thought it was a terrible idea. We weren't in a good position to take big risks, but I knew in my heart that this was the right thing to do. Over time, I found a group of smart and talented people who shared my vision, and we banded together.

Three years later, we opened the first STEAM curriculum-focused public charter school of the state in an area with few other options for middle school children. My dream had come true. The school opened with great momentum and a waiting list of over one hundred children. The first year brought a lot of challenges, including ending the year with the COVID-19 shutdown, but I'll never forget those ninety-six children in our first classes and the team who worked tirelessly to create a school like no other.

Over the years, I've had the opportunity to connect with so many different leaders, parents, and children. And I've found that the song is correct: it is a small world after all. We share the same

fears, hopes, and tears. Generationally, we're all worrying about our children overcoming the barriers we've faced and learning the skills we've used to find our successes. People and organizations are figuring out their strengths to create lives that are fulfilling and impactful.

I used to think my gift was my unshakable belief to create any reality I want. I can dream it and make it come true. I can separate my feelings, self-created "truths" and fears from my circumstances to see ways of overcoming barriers of all kinds.

I've realized over the past year that my true gift is helping others approach their life with this same belief. I've found a way of filling in a gap when people and organizations can't seem to create their desired "new scene." I help them identify and then remove barriers that are preventing them from having the outcomes they want. In helping others, I've finally found my center stage role!

So, to all the women and daughters reading this, remember, you also have a safety net. Find the people who believe in you when you have doubts in yourself, and step into the spotlight as the leading role of your life. Use your gifts to overcome the barriers that life will throw at you and the barriers you've created in your own head. I promise you, the standing ovation at the end of the show will be worth it.

ABOUT CORI SOLOMON SANTONE

Cori Solomon Santone is a dreamer with unshakable optimism and passion for living life to its fullest. She is the founder of Center Stage Solutions, a consulting/coaching firm dedicated to supporting executives, women, and youth to overcome barriers that stand in the way of achieving the life, results, and relationships they truly want. She uses her unique skill set, intuition, and humor to guide others through a collaborative problem-solving process that has allowed thousands to achieve success and take center stage.

Her expertise comes from twenty-three years of successful leadership roles in the nonprofit, education, business, and arts sectors where she's served as a regional nonprofit arts ed organization CEO/CFO, charter school founder, residential camp director, sales director, certified teacher, and school administrator. Cori has raised millions of dollars, launched dozens of programs, and changed the lives of thousands of people. Her involvement in the performing and fine arts, and influential teachers and mentors have played an important role in her life.

Cori's heart belongs to her three talented daughters, Cecilia, Abigail, and Isabella, and superhero husband, Tom. She is most grateful to her parents and three brothers for their lifelong support. When she's not giggling with her girls, she loves sharing her southern hospitality through great parties with friends, cooking, and all things creative.

To learn more about Cori's programs or to work with Cori, visit her website at: www.CenterStageSolutions. com or email her at CoriSolomonSantone@gmail.com.

TRANSFORMATIONAL: LOVE, LETTERS, POETRY, AND ART

Ericha Scott, PhD
LPCC917, LAADC, REAT, ATR-BC

People have more grief over unexpressed love than profound trauma.
Tell people you love them!

Meditating on the topic of love through the practice of letter writing, poetry, and art has been the most rewarding and fulfilling discipline of my entire life. Not only have I experienced happier, healthier, and more loving relationships, I have changed. I am more whole and content with myself.

Writing and receiving love letters awakens our consciousness about how much we love and the capacity we have for loving more deeply and selflessly. This is true, even when writing a love letter touches a deep well of sadness inside us and tears flow. One of the gifts of this step-by-step process is that it brings up and releases grief in a very gentle and tender manner. This release helps take down invisible psychological walls, brick by brick.

Psychological issues, such as trauma, abuse, loss, grief, addiction, mental illness, dysfunctional or unconscious attachment styles, and difficulty sustaining long-term relationships in today's

world, all negatively impact our ability to feel and express love fully. Therefore, it is no surprise that unexpressed love has become rampant in contemporary society.

We are busy, if not overwhelmed, with work, family chores, a pandemic, climate change, financial upheaval, and social unrest. In our modern world, we reach for a manufactured greeting card when we want to express love to a cherished person. It is an easy solution, especially since the message provided is typically generic and emotionally nonthreatening.

As a result of minimized love, people suffer with a remarkable amount of unexpressed grief. Unexpressed grief fuels indifference, numbing, and emotional distance from the very people closest to us. In an epoch of "social distancing," people need close, loving emotional connections more than ever.

Researcher James W. Pennybaker, an expert in the lie detector test, "found that keeping secrets makes people sick." He also found that writing about secrets, even for only fifteen minutes, can improve physical and mental health.

It seems ironic, but love can be a secret that you do not know you are keeping.

In other words, just as we might have denial about feelings of jealousy or hate, we may also have denial about feelings of love. Receiving and giving love are essential for well-being, and love can feel very vulnerable.

Martin Luther King Jr. said, "I have a dream!" My dream is to help people all over the world create more compassionate, generous, and harmonious intimate relationships through writing and painting about our love for each other.

During the love letter writing retreats, there is an aura, energy, or a subtle light that fills the room while people are painting and writing. Usually, everyone can feel it.

Here Is Feedback from a Few Past Participants

"My husband began to weep before I finished reading the first

paragraph, in twenty-five years of marriage, I had never written him a love letter."

"My son said, 'Dad, I didn't know you were that deep.' My son has a point, I never knew I could write like this."

"I have told my wife how much I loved her over and over, and it never seemed to stick, but this letter was different. It touched her heart, and she remembered my words."

"My daughter cried when I read my love letter to her. I have been so fearful, critical, and controlling that she did not believe that I loved her. The letter was the beginning of a change in our relationship."

"I had no idea how much poetry and art could heal my relationships."

Who I Am and Why I Developed a Workshop about Love

Throughout my life-span, challenges and transformational mystical experiences—coupled with decades of professional training and teaching experience—have inspired me to find ways to help people remove, or at least bypass, their creative blocks. What intrigues me is that as the creative blocks are removed, it appears as if hidden blocks to our capacity for loving and receiving love are also removed.

This is my greatest joy: helping people express their deepest thoughts, feelings, and perceptions of life, love, and longing with words and paint.

I am Dr. Ericha Scott. Like many of you, my background is diverse. I am an artist, published author and poet, keynote speaker, retreat and workshop leader, and consultant.

But for this love letter writing process and the creative and spiritual retreats I provide to the public, the most potent offering I have is my life experience.

My personal experience that has shaped what I have to offer you is how I overcame significant early childhood challenges with reading and writing via creativity, poetry writing, and art.

Fourth Grade

I remember sitting in class and looking out the window. I had already failed fourth grade once, and I was just about to fail it twice when I overheard my teacher whisper to my mother, "You know, she really likes art, why don't you find her an art teacher?"

I can remember thinking, *That is a* very *good idea!* This was during the early 1960s, and my mother found a long-haired hippie, who wore jeans, flip flops, and one gold earring to teach me how to paint.

Entering the world of art, color, shape, line, and texture in fourth grade enlivened my life. By the end of fifth grade, after a year of art lessons, I was reading at a college level of competency.

With art as my healer, my life changed from a pattern of chronic failure to outstanding success within a very short period.

A few years later, I began writing poetry. Without telling me, my English teacher entered my first poem in a school-wide contest, and I won.

These events significantly changed the trajectory of my life, and they became directional signposts for my future. Even though I was still a child, I knew that I wanted to help other people experience the same kind of success, relief, freedom, and joy I found through painting, reading, and writing.

As I said earlier, I am a trauma expert, and to my surprise, people in the love letter retreats cry as much, or even more sometimes, than in past trauma and abuse workshops.

Yet, at the end of each retreat, people express relief and they appear to feel giddy with joy.

After giving it some thought, I realized people have as much or more grief about unexpressed love than they do about profound trauma. Almost every single person in the retreats has been moved by the beauty of the letters they and other participants have written. One person even placed the love letter he wrote to his wife in the family vault for future generations to read.

Especially with a world in such upheaval, this is a good time

to think about those we love, what we have not said out loud, and what we would like to say.

I hope you will reflect upon the people you have loved throughout your lifetime and select a person who is—or has been—meaningful to you. It could be yourself. It may be a long-time love, someone who remains important to you today. It may be someone who went a different direction in life and you are no longer in touch, and it could be someone who has passed away.

I would like to share another personal experience that is the primary influence for why I have developed this specific retreat. I was inspired by my deceased husband.

In my late forties, I married Bruce Randall Tufts, a NASA scientist, the night before his admission to a hospital for a transplant. Although he was fifty-one years old, he had never been married, and although he was very ill, his joy about our wedding was contagious. Two hundred and forty people showed up to our wedding during a thunderstorm in the desert with very little advance notice.

During our marriage, Randy wrote me a love letter and several cards with handwritten notes. These messages of love and validation sustained and strengthened me over a long period of time, through his leukemia, bone marrow transplant, death, and my grief.

I remain very grateful that this outstanding man outlived his life expectancy prognosis by a year, for the time we were able to be together.

Excerpts From His Love Letter And A Love Note (2001)

In my shaky but loving hand, I must write that I am so profoundly happy that we are married.

You are a wonderful person and wonderful wife. I hope I can approach being as good a person and husband.

So here we are, a year from our loveliest of weddings—what a year of deepening love!

I look forward to continuing strengthening our marriage to each other.

I married you because you are a lovely, intelligent person with a great sensitivity and warmth, and a gleeful inner spark. I love that spark and want to be near it.

I love your ability to come up with good and intriguing ideas and then put them into action. You are one of the smartest and most creative people I know, you truly are unique in this way. You think deeply into an idea and go to the most basic and influential level you can find . . . it is a remarkable quality.

I love your smile, the shape of your head, the curve of your arms, the smooth youthful skin on your face, your graceful bearing and eloquence. Your look can be stunningly beautiful, with your profile like a Greek goddess.

I love your silver hair, and I am glad you did not color it.

I love the light you can bring to a room when you enter.

I love your intuition, your sensitivity to other's needs and thoughts. I love and I am moved by the way others talk openly with you. I love the way you can see many things so clearly yet admit ambiguity.

I love your honesty, your directness, and your diplomacy. (I count on you to talk with troubled friends of ours—you are so much better at that than I.)

I love your creative self, making art so quickly and confidently and beautifully.

I love the you that I see in your baby pictures, so innocent and trusting. I admire the inner work you have done, and respect you greatly for it.

I love your integrity, honesty, and ability to see.

Marrying you is the best thing I have done. I would not miss this for the world.

Love, Randy

Randy became a better husband after writing this letter. It is as if the letter revealed to him how deeply he loved me. I became a better wife because I was able to relax and trust his love.

I hope my story, and Randy's letter, is an invitation for you to join me on a loving and healing journey to deepen the quality of love in any or all your relationships.

Although sometimes it is uncomfortable to speak about, no one escapes illness and death. What if you died, or what if your loved one died suddenly, or what if you have experienced the loss of a loved one already. Do you, or would you, feel confident that you had fully expressed the depth of your love?

You might be surprised by the emotions that emerge while writing a love letter. You might be even more surprised by the emotions your letter will evoke in your recipient or other readers. These emotions are healthy and cathartic. Sometimes people grieve when reading about how much they are loved and why.

I know this sounds confusing. Yet, it is possible for love letters to remind us of periods of time in our lives when we were not loved or truly seen for who we are. It is important to accept love given to us today, regardless of past pain. The old grief will pass as we open our hearts to give and receive love.

To teach you how to write a love letter, I will illustrate a few steps with examples from my personal process of preparing to write a love letter to my husband. You will see that the process is individualized and can be modified to suit your needs.

To help ensure that you are satisfied with the quality of your first letter, please follow my directions below as literally and carefully as possible.

Brief Descriptive Overview of a Few Action Steps

Step 1

Heart-Centered Meditation (Heart Grounding via Somatic/ Sensory Awareness): Please take five to ten minutes to meditate before you start. Allow yourself to notice and feel your heart, and your love, without any judgment. It is very important to feel your heart and your love without trying to ascribe meaning, interpretation, or analysis. There is no wrong way to do this—just notice the sensations of your heart and feelings of love.

Whatever you feel is fine—whether it is warmth, coldness, tingles, pulsing, lightness, heaviness, colors, shapes, symbols, or something else.

Please do not continue this meditation for more than ten to fifteen minutes.

Step 2

Carefully Select Your Letter Recipient (Self, Spouse, Lover, Friend, Parent, Sibling, Child, Mentor): The second step for this process is to select a love letter recipient. It is important to thoughtfully select your recipient, and often, it is the first person who comes to mind. This is true even if that idea is a surprise or it does not make sense to you. The wisdom of the subconscious is not always clear at first.

Feel free to select yourself, or yourself at a younger age. Also, it is okay, in fact it is normal, to have conflicts about the person you select to write to. Please remember, you may write more than one love letter, in fact, I hope you will write many love letters.

Step 3

Make a List of Positive Traits (Positive Traits, Talents, and Strengths): I invite you to write a list of positive traits, talents, or strengths about the person you have selected. Please try to write a minimum of twenty-five to fifty qualities, characteristics, or attributes that you like about the person you are writing. Be sure to be very descriptive and use adjectives and adverbs. These details help

240

your recipient know that the sentiments in the letter are genuine and meant just for them and no one else.

As you write, do so as quickly as you can. Write down everything that crosses your mind, and—for now—do not edit. Following these guidelines will help you bypass the voice of your inner critic and other blocks.

Step 4

Write Out a Shared Vivid Experience with Letter Recipient (When You Felt Loved and/or Loving): I invite you to write via a stream of consciousness or free-association process about one vivid event you shared with your letter recipient. You may select the first event that crosses your mind, or if you think of a more vivid and meaningful event later, go with the more vivid and meaningful.

It helps if you imagine that you are a court reporter and your job is to describe the scene of your event in every detail. Include information about who, what, when, and where, as well as your emotions and loving thoughts. Again, write quickly without editing your thoughts.

Do not use this love letter to slip in a criticism, no matter how well deserved, or even a hint about what behavior(s) you want your loved one to change. That is another type of letter for another time.

Step 5

Haiku Poems: I invite you to write a haiku poem about the event you just described. Haiku poetry is not about rhyming but instead cadence, and so the words and syllables are counted. Haiku poetry is about an actual event, and there is always a reference to nature. The nature referenced might have been true to your experience and therefore literal or it might be symbolic, such as springtime as a representation of new love. But be specific and descriptive instead of just the word "springtime," consider writing, for example, "new buds on the pear tree."

Haiku poems are three short lines. The first line is five syllables long, the second line is seven syllables, and the third line is only five syllables again, and you may change the number of syllables to meet your needs.

It is important to remember that this exercise is about process, and not good poetry or art. When attending a retreat, participants may choose to share their work with the smaller and larger group(s), or not. You may include the poem in your letter or writing a poem may be a warm-up to writing the letter. Notice that this long poem is actually five Haiku, as if the Haiku are stanzas.

LABOR OF DEATH

09/27/2002
The labor of death
brings forth cries of pain and loss,
and winter comes to
the highest point of
the hill. The pinnacle of
his life, hopes, and dreams.
His ash scattered in
the wind, dances before coming
to rest on the sand.
Finally, love lets
go into death, crossing through
a threshold of desire.
Flame turns to ember,
no longer a hot fire
blazing in the desert.

Step 6
Scribble and Doodle Art: I invite you to make a scribble or doodle drawing (which is exactly what it sounds like). You may use any form of crayons, oil pastels, ink pens, colored pencils, watercolors, or acrylic paint. If you have no art supplies, consider making

a magazine photo collage, a sculpture with found objects and super glue, or if you are adventuresome, a blind contour portrait (please see my web page for the directions for portraits, https://www.thesoberworld.com/2019/10/31/self-portraiture/).

What is most important is for you to think about your letter recipient, your love for them, and your positive relationship dynamics while you scribble, draw, collage, or sculpt. There is no need to make anything look like an object. Abstracts are great!

If you have anxiety because of a negative or shameful experience in an art class as a child, use your non-dominant hand. This can liberate you from expectations. Allow yourself to be playful.

The playfulness of a scribble drawing is able to help you relax and focus. If you use both hands, at the same time, it will help engage both sides of your brain for optimal engagement and functioning.

You may or may not include the art pieces or a photo of your art piece with your letter or handmade card.

My painting is not included in this publication, yet the soft rainbow colors, hints of gray rainy days, undulating dancelike forms represent the beauty of our relationship and the tragedy of his illness.

I hope you will make your piece at least 16 × 20 in., but feel free to go small.

Step 7

Share Your Letter and Your Art with a Mentor or Friend: If you are not a participant in one of my retreats, then I invite you to share your letter with one safe person before you read it out loud to your loved one. This is one way to be sure that old resentments or judgments do not inadvertently stain the loving energy of your letter.

Step 8

Read Your Letter Out Loud: I highly recommend reading your letter out loud, face to face, in a private and quiet place, to the

person you love. It is important for the recipient to hear the letter in *your* voice and observe *your* facial expressions. It is also important for you to witness how your words are received.

Prior to reading your letter out loud, please read your letter to a mentor or a wise friend first, then write out your letter in long-hand on good-quality paper. After you have read the letter to your recipient, please give them a handwritten copy to keep.

If you are not able to meet with the person face to face, you may store the letter in a place where you pray or keep your spiritual books. If not there, then possibly in a keepsake box, or another meaningful location until you are able to meet in person or on Zoom.

Summary

For people living and working in our busy modern world, it can seem trivial or even silly to write a love letter. I can imagine how some people might roll their eyes and think, "That is so old fashioned . . . I don't have time, and what is the point?" I understand. I must admit, I underestimated the potential and power of love letters myself. Imagine, a simple love letter can change your life and the quality of your relationships.

Many people have carefully and successfully followed my directions in order to write beautiful letters. That said, it is much, much more powerful to participate in a love letter, poetry, and art-making group.

Therefore, please call me. If you want to take your ability to express love to a deeper level, I am here to help. If you have any questions, call me at 310-880-9761! I have been creating, designing, consulting, and facilitating creative and expressive arts retreats for over thirty-eight years. I work with individuals, couples, families, groups, and businesses of up to eighty people. When you call, we will brainstorm and create exactly what will best meet your needs, and/or the needs of your family, group, or agency.

ABOUT ERICHA SCOTT, PHD
LPCC917, LAADC, REAT, ATR-BC

Dr. Ericha Scott is an artist, poet, and a published author. She is published in professional peer review journals, textbooks, and popular magazine articles nationally and abroad. Dr. Scott is a Licensed Professional Clinical Counselor (LPCC917) in California and a Licensed Professional Counselor (LPC) in Arizona. She is a licensed psychotherapist and addictions counselor. She is certified as a creative and expressive arts therapist, an advanced diplomat addiction counselor, a Reiki Master, and as an interfaith spiritual director. Dr. Scott has been awarded the honorary title of fellow for the oldest professional trauma agency in the world, The International Society for the Study of Trauma and Dissociation. She has also received the Sierra Tucson Alumni Recognition Award for outstanding service to patients in the sexual compulsivity and trauma program. She offered psycho-educational creative and expressive arts retreats for the medical doctors in Andrew Weil, MD's Center of Complimentary Medicine at the University of Arizona for eight years. Dr. Scott designs original and custom educational, psychological, and spiritual creative and expressive arts retreats and workshops. She provides retreats for personal growth or therapy on topics such as love, wellness and physical health, trauma, spirituality, creativity, emotional blocks, compulsivity, addictions, self-harm, family systems, mindfulness, life goals, sleeping dreams and nightmares.

Please view her web site at http://artspeaksoutloud. org or call at 310-880-9761.

- artspeaksoutloud.org
- linkedin.com/in/ehitchcockscott
- facebook.com/ErichaScottPhD

- facebook.com/erichascott
- twitter.com/ErichaScott
- youtube.com/c/ErichaScottPhD

THE PHOTO ALBUM

Abby Steurer

L osing a parent is never easy, but losing a parent at an early
age can take on a whole new meaning. When you are little,
you may not even realize what happened. You may feel sad,
and you may miss that person, but as time passes, you forget what
that person looks like, what they smell like, what their personality
was like. At least, this is what happened to me. What I did not
realize was how the loss of my father would impact my life for
many years to come.

When I was just five years old, my father came down with
pneumonia and unexpectedly passed away days later due to complications. In just days, my mother's world was flipped upside
down and she became a widow with two children. As a mother
myself, I cannot imagine what this must have been like for her.
I can vividly remember being at a family friend's house, which
was across the street from my grandmother's. My friend walked
me back to the house, and as the front door opened, I saw my
entire family sitting in my grandmother's living room. My grandmother let out a cry, and I believe that is when my mom took
my hand, led me into my grandmother's bedroom, and told me
that my dad had passed away. We went back into the living room

where I crawled onto my grandmother's lap. I was so young, but I remember thinking that I had to be strong because everyone was just so sad.

The next memory I have is of my mom, my little brother, and myself sitting on our couch. I was crying, but not about my dad. Maybe I had gotten in trouble? I cannot recall the exact reason, but I do remember looking at my mom and saying, "I miss Daddy!" She cried so hard when I said that and told me she did too. I apologized, and again, I can remember thinking that I could never say those words ever again because it just made her so sad. From that day on, at just five years old, I felt like I could not talk about my father because it was just too painful for everyone else. I guess I wanted to protect her. I definitely did not want to make my mom feel worse or make her struggle more than she already was. I have never liked making others feel angry or sad in any way. So, I rarely brought him up and neither did anyone else.

It is inevitable that death needs to be spoken about, and every family deals with it differently. We created a photo album of all the pictures we had of my dad and me. All five years of memories condensed into one tiny, handheld photo album. Everything I would remember of my father, for the rest of my life, would be from those few pictures. I slept with this album under my pillow for almost my entire life. This album became my lifeline.

My mom remarried when I was seven, and my two beautiful sisters were born. I do not want to go into much detail about my mother's second marriage since it is not my story to tell, but I can tell you what I learned from this situation and what their eventual separation did to impact my life. My mom was a schoolteacher, and when she was not working, we were always with her. She rarely went out. If she did, it must have been quick because I just remember always being with my mom. All of us. Whether it was the grocery store or the movies or anything in between, she had us all with her.

There was a lot of arguing and fighting within our walls for

many years. Most of my childhood. So many nights, I held that photo album of my dad and would dream up stories of what life would be like if only he survived. I became more and more sad about the loss of my father as I became a teenager. I truly do not think I mourned his loss until then. At sixteen, my mom and stepfather separated in what would turn into an extremely messy divorce, and again, I watched my mother struggle. This time with four children. I was sixteen, my brother was twelve, my sister was four, and my baby sister was just an infant. The early days of this divorce were very hard on her. She cried a lot. She worried about shared custody and how she would financially support us, as any mother would. She was very sad and felt like she had failed us.

We left our family home, stayed with my aunt who generously opened her doors for us, and then we moved in with my grandmother. Eventually, my mom was able to purchase the townhouse she is still in today. We moved into our new home with our bedroom furniture, clothing, and lawn chairs for our living room. I can still feel that happiness and excitement, but my mom felt differently. She was nervous, stressed, and sad. I hated watching her go through that. It would take a long time for our mother to regain control of her finances. By the time she was a little more stable, I had graduated from college and was on my way to marrying my husband. I knew that I never wanted to experience even half of what she went through as I started my own family.

My husband and I were married in the fall of 2004. We had our first child, Mackenzie, in 2006 and our son, Nolan, was born in 2008. Before we even became parents, we talked about how much I wanted to be able to raise them. To be home with them as much as I could. I did not want to miss out on any of the special moments. I wanted to be there when they took their first steps. I wanted to be the one to drive them to preschool and to get them on and off their bus, every single day. I wanted to be at the class parties and do all the mom things. But I also wanted to help

provide for my family. I never wanted to be in my mom's shoes if something happened that would make me the sole provider. I already knew that no matter how perfect life looked on the outside, many things could happen out of our control that could uproot the life we had. I wanted to be as prepared for that as I could be. I wanted it all . . . being mom, being a provider for my family, and being Abby.

About six to eight months after our daughter was born, I was filled with anxiety. So badly that at one point, I couldn't leave the house. I became agoraphobic. I was afraid of every movement I made. Every thought I had turned into the worst-case scenario in seconds. I could not walk my baby down the steps without envisioning the worst fall in the world. Bathing her was awful. Instead of enjoying the splashes and coos, all I could see was her drowning and me being unable to save her. I know. Believe me, I know it sounds so awful, but I could not stop the racing thoughts. I was stricken with the need to protect and do everything so perfectly so no harm would come to my family that it sent me into a downward spiral of anxiety and panic attacks.

I had very few friends that had children at this stage, so finding someone that could relate to me was difficult. My husband and family were very supportive, but there was only so much they could do. It was something I had to work hard on to get better. I dove deep into why I might be feeling that way, and it all just seemed to go back to the losses I suffered as a child. I was petrified that my children would go through what I went through, and knowing it was all out of my control, that I could not predict the future, was a scary realization. I always swore that if I could get better, I would be helpful to anyone else suffering with anxiety.

A few years passed by, and I was slowly regaining control of my thoughts. I had to retrain my brain to think in a positive way. Any time I started going down one of those scary-thoughts roads, I would try to redirect myself. I found that keeping busy was the best way to distract myself. Not that having two kids under two

and a half did not keep me busy enough! But I needed something. Something to keep my mind busy. And I remembered that conversation my husband and I had before we had our children. That I wanted to be mom, but also help provide.

As soon as Kenzie was born, I started capturing every detail of her life with my camera. Every facial expression, every tiny finger and toe. I had my camera on hand everywhere we went. It always came back to that photo album of my dad. I felt the need to capture everything, just in case. I did not even realize I was falling in love with the art of photography. I was just making sure my children had memories. The more photos I took, and the more popular social media became, the more others commented on my photos, and eventually, asked me to take photos for them. That is when it hit me! This was it! This would be how I would help provide while I was raising my family. This is what would help keep my mind busy. I spent about a year researching everything I could on the internet. How to start a small business. What to look for in an accountant. What editing software to purchase and how to use it. How to edit. What computer I needed to buy. How to use the big old camera my husband invested in for me to start with. I researched it all! I wanted to be able to capture memories for everyone. I did not want anyone to go through life without gorgeous moments written down on pictures for generations to follow. I did not want anyone to have to remember a loved one from only a handful of pictures. I did not want anyone to have to sleep with a tiny photo album under their pillow and know it is the only thing they have left of their parent. I did not want my own children to feel that way, and I wanted my future grandchildren to see me and remember me at all stages of my life. The good, the bad, the ugly, and everything in between. I wanted to be a memory keeper.

Becoming a photographer gave me a real sense of purpose. I had a passion. I had something to separate myself from being "just Mom" to being a successful business owner. It kept me feeling

motivated and happy and gave me a sense of pride. I noticed I was less and less anxious because I was filtering my energy into photography, and I did not have time to sit and think. The anxiety was still there, but it hovered instead of taking over. I felt so proud of myself for being able to stay home with the kids and bring in that additional source of income. It was a goal I had before even becoming a mother, and I made it happen. I have been a photographer now for over ten years. I went from capturing a few memories for others to winning awards on some of those images. But I was not done.

I began sharing more and more on social media in order to grow. I shared my truth as well as my struggles. I was as authentic as I could be in hopes that it may reach just one person that needed to see they were not alone. I realized the more I shared, the more people felt comfortable sharing their stories back with me. The new connections I made led me to my second business, where I truly feel like I am helping people feel better from the inside out.

Talking to someone about personal struggles can be so important. Sometimes, all it takes is one connection, one conversation, one recommendation. To feel heard and to be listened to is everything. As I get older, I realize that the struggles in my life were there for a reason. I do not allow my personal struggles to get the best of me. Instead, I use them to propel me forward. I try every day to ask myself, "Who am I helping today?" and make an effort to do just that. I feel so lucky to have two businesses that work together seamlessly. I like to tell people that I now get to help people smile on the outside with my photography and on the inside with my hemp wellness business. I would love to talk more with you about hemp and how it can help your body.

Who would have known that a little photo album would have played such a significant role in my life and helped me dream so big? Thanks, Mom and Dad.

ABOUT ABBY STEURER

Abby Steurer was born and raised in the Pittsburgh, PA, area and relocated to southern NJ in 2008. She has been married to her husband, Alex, for seventeen years, and they have two children. Their daughter, Mackenzie, is sixteen and their son, Nolan, is fourteen. Abby has been the photographer and owner of Abby Lynn Photography for ten years. She specializes in family, child, and graduating senior portraits. She has been a finalist in the Shoot and Share photo competition and has had multiple images published in *Shutter Scene Magazine,* including a featured cover artist. Her mission is to capture memories for others with her photographs and to be a listening ear for those struggling with those overwhelming moments in life.

Web: www.abbylynnphoto.com
Instagram: @abby_steurer

PLANTING THE SEEDS OF PASSION

Teja Valentin

Senior year of high school, we were given an assignment to do about where we saw ourselves in ten years. That was so easy, I didn't even hesitate as I wrote out my wishes on my paper!

Graduate from college as a registered nurse, get married to Mr. Talldarkandhandsome, move into a nice house, have two children—a boy and a girl—and adopt a dog.

Did I get all that? Yes, I did! Life seemed so simple back then. I was pondering this as I sat at my desk unhappy with my life. I had a beautiful home, a handsome husband, a sweet four-month-old boy, and no doubt I would have that little girl too! So what happened?! That painless lump on my neck that I swore was nothing became a cancer diagnosis. It felt so surreal. The doctors told me that this was the "good cancer."

As I started getting over the realization of this news, I began to research thyroid cancer. I learned two astounding facts: thyroid cancer is the most common endocrine cancer and affects women three times more than men! How is this good? What I also learned is that the thyroid is considered to be connected to the throat chakra. I had never even heard of a chakra at that point, and I was

immediately intrigued, fascinated. I felt like I was finally putting the pieces together of this incredulous puzzle. What I was reading was starting to make sense to me. Interestingly, the throat chakra is the center of communication. I began recognizing that there was more to me than just my physical body. I was an energetic and spiritual being with a soul. This I believe was a nudge from Spirit. There was a reason this was happening to me. One that I may not have been happy about or understood, but I knew there was a purpose it was showing up.

After six years, multiple neck surgeries to remove my thyroid and affected lymph nodes, and many radioactive iodine treatments, I finally reached a point where the doctors were content to just monitor my thyroid levels and neck ultrasounds. I should have been happy to finally be on the road to better health, except I didn't feel anything. I didn't get angry, sad, or happy. I was flat, numb. Only existing. My husband at the time said it best, "They are basically killing you slowly to make you better." It didn't matter what was happening in my body, my expression to everything was the same. I kept waiting . . . but for what ? I thought, *Okay, when is this going to be over?* It seemed nothing was ever going to change. The light in me seemed to have gone out. Now my only goal was to get my chores done each day, and my reward was to sink into my bed at night and fall into deep sleep.

I felt like such a horrible mom. I never had the energy to play with my children, and my patience was short. My husband was always working twelve-hour shifts or traveling for work and then would be busy on the weekends. I often felt very alone and isolated. My childhood best friend was the only one I could really talk to, and even then, I held back a lot of what was really going on. "I'm fine" was always my automatic response whenever someone asked.

My mother had always told me to shut up. Unable to defend myself or speak my mind, I learned to stay silent. As I grew to an

older child though, it was rude not to respond when adults asked me how I was. My mother told me to just say, "I'm fine."

I couldn't really hide the fact that I wasn't fine anymore. In essence, I felt powerless, helpless . . . just so tired all the time. I had been used to my son being easy to entertain with his blocks or videos or just about anything you placed in front of him. He would be so fascinated with the most minute details. My daughter, however, was my "spirited" child. I could not keep up with her curiosity, and her sense of adventure was endless. She did everything with such gusto. Inside, I was so envious of how she was always fully into whatever she was doing. Passionate. Full of life. I knew something in me had to change if I was to be her mother.

One day, I don't even know how to describe it except there was this shift in my energy. I was feeling sick and tired of feeling sick and tired, and I just got up from the couch, put my sneakers on, walked out the front door, and ran to the corner stop sign! I felt excited and invigorated when I did! Next day, I did it again, and again! Soon I was running one mile, five miles, ten miles. I felt alive! I could feel my heart pumping, my stride taking me further and further from my troubles. On my runs, I could completely detach from all my pain. I could dream, plan, and create. I could be me. Cancer could not define this version of me.

I walked into the house one day after I completed a ten-mile race. Riding on the wave of endorphins from finishing one of the hardest and longest runs, I decided I was going to run a marathon! I joined the Leukemia Lymphoma Society Team in Training to train for the marathon and raised four thousand dollars for the 2008 Walt Disney Marathon in Florida. I couldn't run very fast, but I was there in Disney World, "where dreams come true." I made the most of it as I ran through Epcot, Animal Kingdom, Cinderella's Castle. From the moment the horn blared, I never looked back. Somewhere around mile sixteen, I happened to see my coach. He ran over and, probably seeing how exhausted I was,

he said, "You will cross that finish line if I have to carry you over it." I looked him in the eye and said, "I will cross over that line on my own two feet!"

I did indeed cross that line. This is one of the first times that I became aware of my grit and perseverance. Despite it all, I managed to cross the finish line on my own two feet. My big toes were black-and-blue, and my four-year-old daughter seemed to keep stepping on them the rest of our vacation. In Reiki lore, there is a myth that when you stub your big toe, you are on your way to an awakening . . .

In 2014, I was introduced to gentle yoga, and it was great but I wanted more. A friend recommended that I go for a Reiki session. The Reiki Master saw my spiritual and psychic potential. He gave me much more than Reiki, he gave me friendship, support, hope, and a newfound sanctuary where I was free to be me. There were people there like me!

I had felt like an outcast in my own home. The big flat-screen had taken over, and conversations ceased. The heaviness in the living room was stifling. Still I said nothing.

As I began Reiki Level two, my third eye began to open. I could suddenly see colors so bright, auras and visions. My dreams became even more vivid, and it felt like I was experiencing an awakening. Upon describing my many dreams, especially those with snakes, he explained what I was experiencing was Kundalini energy. Sure enough, a beginner's Kundalini workshop was being offered at the studio. It felt so foreign and weird. I felt so weak and inadequate. My arms and shoulders hurt and were shaking and seemed to weigh a ton. Though, the amazing thing was that after each class, I felt so awesome and pumped; energy was flowing through my body. I wanted to go dancing after each class! The seventh week, our second-to-last week of the Intro to Kundalini course, I shared with my teacher that I had this amazing dream where I was able to destroy a huge dragon-like serpent that was wrapped around my neck trying to choke me. She was horrified,

but I was excited! I had a very good feeling that this was good news coming.

I continued with self-Reiki and Kundalini Yoga on my own every day. The following month after the Intro to Kundalini class was over, I found out that my latest lab work showed the thyroid cancer was undetectable! I felt like my body, spirit, and mind were freed.

Listening to Spirit, I heeded the call to take the Kundalini Yoga teacher training.

I began my training in 2016. Many times I felt like I couldn't keep up, but it was like I had to become undone to put myself back together again. "I'm fine," my mind would echo. I found myself in tears often. This in itself was very healing for someone who always had to hold it in. The support of my teachers and classmates and my "sisters" was unmatched. We were all battling something, mostly ourselves.

During this time, I became my dad's caretaker while he was suffering from Alzheimer's disease. Every time I would go visit him, we would go on our "walk and talks." He always seemed to know what was on my mind. He knew before I did what I was feeling. Four months after Kundalini Yoga teacher training, I had a hysterectomy and I was climbing mountains . . . literally. I had joined a few of my Kundalini sisters in the Women's Hero's Journey. However, there is this thing I have called fear of heights, but these mountains I climb figuratively and physically keep calling me. One day during our walk, my dad said, "You are on a quest." Immediately that resonated. Yes, I was . . . but for what?

The day arrived that I was standing at the base of an almost five-thousand-foot mountain, the highest point in the Allegheny Mountains and Appalachian Plateau. It was very challenging, but I managed to find my next step and pull myself up over and over again. I was staring at the rock in front of me for hours. As we neared the end, we approached the back of the mountain and also the steepest portion, but the top landing was so close. I literally

lost all strength in my arms and shoulders by this point, and I could not gather any more. I started to panic that I was going to end up dangling there forever. Luckily, I had two experienced women with me on that back section—one in front of me and one behind me. They each breathed with me and gave me words of encouragement along with instructions. I was there praying to God and everything holy, especially my father who had crossed over by this time as I begged for strength. Once again, life was flashing before my eyes. The women all before me were at the top and had started to sing to me. In complete surrender, I followed the instructions to clip myself and let myself dangle and rest. Finally, I found my footing and gave it my all, and I made my way to the top. It took some time to process all that occurred on that mountain, but I was astonished that the strength in me had been there all along. On that day, I contemplated the untapped power in each woman. We may not have the physical strength or size, of other experienced climbers but the power of their voices, and their compassion and grace carried me through. I had overcome a lot up to this point, but I still was not living my best life. It was as if I was being kept in this castle with comforts of food, clothing, shelter, vacations, and no worries regarding money, but where did my husband go? Whether he was traveling for work or in the same room as me, he was absent. His lack of presence pierced my heart deeper and deeper. I knew it was time to move on, and I knew that I had to do what I had been putting off for many years. I struggled each day feeling unhappy, not enough, and lonely. My marriage had become a façade. My husband and I became strangers sharing a home and children. Sex was nonexistent.

It was devastating to me to think what it would mean to our kids if I asked for a divorce. There was a fear that I would be burdened with all the blame of wrecking our family. My children would hate me. Fear took over and I kept my mouth shut. After a couple more years of working on myself, noticing the patterns, the stories, the beliefs, and programs that I had, I realized it wasn't

my fault for being afraid. It was a result of my upbringing and inner child trauma. Staying in this marriage meant that I would be safe. The known was better than the unknown. Finally, an intuitive that I confided in about wanting out of my marriage explained that by staying I would actually be doing a disservice to my children because I would be modeling for them it was okay to stay in a loveless marriage. Well, that hit me like a ton of bricks because that is exactly what my parents did. They finally divorced after thirty-six years of marriage and kept it secret from me for five years! Finally, I got the courage to tell my husband what was on my mind and my heart.

One of the most fascinating things I had learned in my discovery of the chakra system was how closely the female sex organs (pelvic floor and uterus) resemble the throat center (vocal cords and larynx). Hence, it is very likely when you have issues in either one of these energy centers, you most likely are having issues in the other as well. This really spoke to me. Not only was my voice and true expression shut down, but my sexuality and passion had been shut down too. Through the divorce, I finally found my voice. I allowed myself to get angry. I made myself heard. I had to be my own advocate and literally speak up for myself. I moved out of the house, and for the first time in a long time I felt I had a purpose. I already knew what my weaknesses were, and now it was time to lean into my strengths.

During COVID, I joined an online coaching program to become a love, sex, and relationship coach. I began going through the motions but still there was some doubt. What will people think? What do I tell my kids? Who am I to talk to others about sex? Can I actually start a successful business doing what I love? Well, it turns out that people are actually fascinated by what I do. It was a scary risk to give up my nursing job, but I am proud of what I do. Proud that my children accept me regardless of what I do. Turns out I am exactly the right person to be talking about sex because most of my clients are just like me!

While on my way to becoming a coach, I helped heal myself of my own disempowered attitude toward sex, love, self-love, and relationships, which I realized I desperately needed. I wanted to learn how to have sex without pain, to be able to relax and enjoy the intimacy, to just receive pleasure, let myself be heard during sex, and of course feel passion! It wasn't until I was in a relationship after my divorce that it was possible to be intimate without any pain, to feel safe to be seen and heard. Connecting with my sexuality felt like a key to this new untapped potential within me. It was truly a spiritual experience. The passion I felt was not just for love but for life. Though the relationship was brief, this beautiful experience gave me the confidence I needed to make some strides in reclaiming my sexuality and liberating the shame and undeservingness I felt in relationships and in myself. I was feeling good with myself even after the breakup with my on-again-off-again partner because this time I was feeling much more secure in myself and realized I had outgrown that relationship.

Now with more time for myself I couldn't deny some discomfort in my mouth. Chewing was very uncomfortable and even painful on my gums. I was shocked when I found out that the treatment was surgery. After feeling devastated, I went inward and decided that I was not a victim and that this was not happening to me but for me. I knew that this occurrence was another manifestation of an unbalanced throat chakra issue. The process was really tough and it almost felt like a joke—coaching clients with a swollen face and a huge gap between my front teeth! I continued to date, and a few men I went out on dates with were kind, but there were a couple who were cruel. I thank these men now because it forced me to really look at myself in the mirror literally and figuratively. If I could not accept myself 100% then how could I expect anyone else to accept me? It was a constant test of self-love, self-confidence, and deservingness. It took me a while to understand that yes, I had learned to express myself but there was still more.

How am I showing up in my life? Am I able to really express my truth to the world? I knew I was still holding myself back. I continued focusing on my coaching program while recovering and healing from the surgery. My healing started to become a metaphor of what was happening in my life. Through the surgery, expander, and braces, I saw that space had to be created, then supported, and finally aligned.

Working through the lessons and practices in my curriculum, I discovered empowered and disempowered parts of myself that I didn't even know existed. I sent love to my wounded inner child, honored my inner feminine and masculine, celebrated my priest-ess energy, befriended my witch energy—all the while using the many integration practices to soothe my nervous system. I feel more whole now. I can now say I love myself and really mean it. The work that I do is life fueling. I didn't know this work would be a dream of mine until I actually just started doing it. I realized that this is where I am meant to shine and share my message.

At the time of writing this story, I again had another health scare. My lab work showed that it appeared the cancer was back. The next few months were a blur with the amount of testing I underwent. The happy ending I had planned vanished just like that. There will be more follow-up necessary, but the good news is that what was found does not appear malignant at this point. I will continue to take matters into my own hands and work with a variety of healers—from modern science to ancient wisdom.

Sometimes the shortest way is through. I followed my intuition to go to Costa Rica and embark on a spiritual retreat to receive healing transmission with plant medicine. I went in the first night of ceremony with Ayahuasca with the intention to see who I had become. I saw that I was a little girl who felt unwanted, unloved, and never enough who then became a woman who still felt unwanted, unloved, and never enough. Mama Aya appeared to me as a beautiful white Flower of Life pattern. In Mama Aya's loving embrace, I could feel her love fill me, and I began

to channel light language . . . until I was told I was too loud by one of the ceremony helpers. The visual ended abruptly and I was upset. I took my blanket and went outside to the hammock under the almost full moon.

I began trying to understand what just happened. I realized I had never been accused of being too loud, but I have always been shut down by people in my life. Interesting! Wrapped up in the blanket, I made myself comfortable and lay in a fetal position. I then started to feel her again, but this time she was the moon and I was in her womb! I felt so cherished, desired, loved, and wanted.

On the second night of plant medicine, my intention was to merge me back to my soul at all costs. It quickly became very scary. It appeared I was having an ego death. I had no choice but to surrender. Mama Aya once again held me as I died over and over and over again. I would see her moonlight streaming in through the window. I would keep adjusting my body to align with her light. She merged me back with my soul. With each death, there was that first breath of life until finally morning came and then I was alive again, filled with such a love for everybody and every-thing including myself. There was a song in my heart and I began to sing. It did not matter how I sounded because I know this was what she was showing me was necessary . . . to flow in love and not hide my song. My song is meant to be shared.

The third night of plant medicine, my intention was to heal my heart. It felt like nothing was happening, but a lot was actu-ally happening behind the scenes. I slept most of the night but still kept insisting I should be doing something or having an "experience." Once again, I realized I was trying to control my fear of the unknown. I welcomed sleep the best I could to allow integration and healing.

The last night was the longest ceremony—and so worth it! It was a beautiful ceremony with many shamans who performed a healing. One shaman in front of each of us and one shaman behind each of us. They fluffed us with their feather wands, their

incantations, holy water and oils, gentle blowing and healing caresses. It moved me to tears knowing that whatever had been showing itself in my body as disease was no longer viable in my body nor welcome because of the vibration of love and light. My heart was healed. I have no proof, but I feel healthy, healed, and whole. We danced and sang and welcomed the morning. No need to sleep.

Once home, I had a wonderful dream where Mama Aya showed me that all my gifts and talents come from the "jewels of my throat chakra." She showed me a beautiful image of blue crystals and gemstones surrounded with light. It was magnificent. This was the confirmation of what I felt all along . . . there will be more to discover on my quest.

The seeds of passion have been planted.

ABOUT TEJA VALENTIN

Teja's thirst for growth and self-actualization fuels the ability to facilitate growth and actualization in others—body, mind, spirit. Through her nonjudgmental and receptive spirit, lighthearted and playful, yet respectful of the serious and sacred, she helps empower you to reclaim your pleasure, passion, and vitality.

Teja Valentin is a proud mom; love, sex, and relationship coach; RN, KRI certified 220-hr. Kundalini Yoga teacher; certified 200-hr. Ayurveda Yoga teacher; certified chair and restorative yoga teacher; certified Usui Reiki Master; sound/energy practitioner; and ordained minister.

In addition to her coaching practice, Teja offers Kundalini Yoga classes, Reiki healing sessions, and Reiki Training and Kundalini/Gong meditations. Words of wisdom that she follows is to "Follow your heart, your One True Teacher." It is her desire and commitment to help plant the seeds of passion in others and guide them on their own path of healing so they may plant their own seeds of passion and bloom hard!

Connect with Teja here:

Web: http://tejavalentin.com
Facebook: https://facebook.com/tejashanti.kaur
Instagram: @teja_valentin

DREAM OF THE FATHERLESS

Jennifer Weaver

"**Y**ou're nothing. You came from nothing. You'll always be nothing!"

No seven-year-old girl should hear those words spat in her face by a frustrated second-grade teacher, but I did. I remember coming in from recess in tears that no one would play with me. I ran straight to my desk, put my forehead down on my folded arms, and sobbed. Snot was running onto the plastic top of my chrome desk, and I was hyperventilating with heaving gasps. My teacher was saying something, but it wasn't anything I could make out over my distress.

She grabbed me under my armpits and yanked me out of my chair, sending it flying out from under me, as she pulled me across the classroom into her office. She threw me in her chair, leaned into my face, and demanded to know why I was crying. I couldn't respond. I was in hysterics and still gasping for breath through sobs and utter shock.

Not responding to her made her even angrier. While red-faced and enraged, those ten words she left me with alone in her office after slamming the door are seared into my brain like a

branding iron leaves on a sixty-day-old calf. They've stayed with me my entire life.

What I wouldn't have given to have my father rescue me at that moment. Upon seeing me being ripped from my desk, dragged, and thrown into a chair, my dad would've burst through my teacher's office and yelled a few choice words and expletives while scooping me up into his arms and storming out of that class full of mean-spirited kids and witch of a so-called teacher. That is if I had a dad. But I didn't.

I was the child of a single mother. My brother was fourteen months younger than me, and we looked very different. He was blond, freckle-faced, and had fair skin with blue eyes. I had a solid olive complexion, dark brown hair, green eyes, and my ears poked out like a little elf.

We both had the same last name as my mother, so I didn't ever question paternity. Why would I? I had no reason to think otherwise. Besides, I looked like my mother with my dark hair, except for my tanned skin and nose, which had a hump and slightly dropped tip that became more prominent with age. But still, something didn't feel right.

I felt out of place as a child. That discomfort was coupled with insecurity and loneliness. There wasn't ever a time in my life that I remember having a dad. My mom was divorced when my brother was two months old, so I wasn't even a toddler when the man whose name is on my birth certificate left.

I only knew him by name as a child. And that name always felt foreign and strange. However, the tall, muscular man who bested all wicked witches I dreamed up in my imagination and always loved and protected me was familiar. He was my hero— whoever he was.

Years passed with me still dreaming about a father I wished I'd had. We moved away from the only stability I had with my grandparents in rural southern Utah to Salt Lake City a few

weeks before my tenth birthday. (If I had a father, we wouldn't be moving away. He'd make sure of that!)

There we were, my brother and I as latch-key kids, home alone as my mother worked double shifts to keep a roof over our heads. But my head was in the clouds with thoughts about what my life would've been—should've been—had I only had a dad.

My dad would go to work in a suit and tie, briefcase in hand, while my mom would help as a teacher's aide at school so I could still see her every day. He'd then come home to our ranch and put on his jeans and cowboy boots, and we'd go outside and ride the horses. That was my dream, but my reality was being in a cockroach-invested apartment, dishes stacked in the sink, and barely any food in the refrigerator. I ached for my father.

Eighth grade rolled around, and I was taking a journalism class. An assignment given was to do an interview with your parents about their marriage and divorce if they had split. With notebook and pencil in hand, I sat at my mother's feet on the floor as she sat on the couch and asked her questions about how she met my dad, when they got married, and why they got divorced.

She explained she'd met my father at the deer hunter's ball in college in the fall of 1969, but she veered off about getting married in March 1970. I was born on June 27, 1970. The accounts didn't add up in my brain, so I asked, "Was I five months premature?"

My mom's outburst of laughter stunned me. Her reply was, "Haven't you figured it out yet?" Dumbfounded, I shook my head no. She continued to explain that my brother and I had different fathers. My father was tall, had brown hair and big hands, was a good dancer, and his name was James, but he went by Jimmy, she said.

Then her demeanor plummeted into sadness, and she looked away, put her hand to her chin, and asked me not to bring it up again because she'd heard that he had gone to fight in the Vietnam War. She didn't know if he was alive or dead. I picked

myself up off the floor, went to my bedroom, crawled into bed, put the covers over my head, and cried.

I kept my word and didn't ask my mom any further questions about my father until I was twenty-one. I had dropped out of college after being told by a communications professor that I was "too ethnic looking" to be a TV anchorwoman, a dream I had since I learned how to write and type. When I was eight, I would use my mom's black typewriter to write stories.

I loved the sounds of the metal slugs with raised letters hitting the white paper. The printed marks on white sheets of words I formulated filled me with glee, so much so that I even squealed with joy as my fingers hit the lettered keys. That is until I made a mistake and had to use the Wite-Out correction fluid. But ultimately, I'd have my story!

I'd take my script and sit in front of my bedroom mirror with a hairbrush in my hand as a microphone to report the latest on the cookie bandit who'd switched out sugar with laundry detergent, destroying any hopes of a successful school bake sale as people burped bubbles after biting into supposed chocolate chip cookies.

The desire to tell stories motivated me to enroll in that eighth-grade journalism class, which also led me to major in communications and broadcast journalism in college. After being told I had no hope of being the next Barbara Walters, I was lost. Another dream of mine had been crushed. I didn't know what to do . . . All I wanted was my dad.

I was in a deep depression, not knowing my identity or what I wanted to do with my life. However, I managed to get myself to work doing inside sales for classified ads. Until one day, I had the strong urge to jump out of the third-story window. My supervisor stopped me and immediately referred me to human resources to get help. I was referred to a counselor who advised me to talk to my mother about my biological father. She thought knowing more about him would help me learn more about myself.

Talking to my mother about my father wasn't easy. But I did

it. She didn't tell me much more about him than when I was thirteen, but she did say that they had a class together, and they recognized each other at the deer hunter's ball. That's how they connected. After the holidays, she never saw him again. She'd heard he'd gone to Vietnam only through other classmates, but she didn't know for sure.

I don't know why that information appeased me for a few more years, but it did. Then, my twenty-fourth birthday was soon approaching. My mom asked me what I wanted for my birthday, and I blurted out, "I want my dad." The dream I had of knowing my father was alive and well. I wondered all the time if I looked like him. Was he a war hero? Did he crinkle his nose like I did when he laughed? Did he work with those big hands that my mom described? I had so many questions, and I wanted them answered.

I got my birthday wish. My mom took a trip back to her college in southern Utah and met with the alumni association president. They reviewed some records and found Jimmy's family's phone number and address. They called, and his father answered the phone.

The alumni association president explained they planned a college reunion and wanted to invite Jimmy. Much to his dismay and my mom's worst fear, Jimmy's father told them he'd been killed in Vietnam. A helicopter he was in crashed from mechanical failure, and he'd died on May 10, 1972.

It was tough waiting to hear from my mom. I was anxious, nervous, and excited all at the same time. That all changed when I finally got the call. He was dead. My dad had died, and so had my dream of ever meeting him. My mom and I decided to write a letter to Jimmy's parents and included some photos of me.

Months later, my mom received a reply from a woman she used to work with, who coincidentally had married Jimmy's brother. She arranged a barbecue, and I met an entire family of

grandparents, aunts, uncles, and cousins . . . and they had dark hair and green eyes like me.

Having another family that I'd never known before was joyous but terrifying and uncomfortable at first. Jimmy's parents, four brothers and sister, and their children were the most down-to-earth, hardworking people I'd ever met. They loved each other and supported each other in everything they did, including a long-standing family business in heating and air conditioning.

They did not shy away from hard labor and loved outdoor recreation like camping and fishing. Though I still felt a loss from being fatherless, I felt more connected to him than before meeting his family. A dream was realized, just not as I had hoped.

Numerous years later, that connection would extend to a man who had fought in Vietnam with Jimmy. He was the chair of the Vietnam memorial that was being erected in my hometown. I had given a classification speech at the Cedar City Rotary Club and shared my story of finding my father only to learn of his sacrifice overseas. Unbeknownst to me, one of the Rotarians shared my story to the memorial committee to ask consent for a paver to be etched in memory of my father as part of the memorial. It was unanimously approved.

As the dedication date of the Vietnam memorial drew near, the chair of that committee, who went by the nickname Doc, visited me at my office. He wore army green and a black baseball cap with the embroidered POW/MIA logo. He explained that his role during the Easter Offensive was to draw out mobile enemy units for ambush since he "had the face of the enemy," being half Chinese and half Japanese.

He talked about a soldier who smoked Camel cigarettes and disobeyed orders, and brought his unit supplies at a volatile time when they were all being asked to surrender during the North Vietnam siege in An Lôc. He said he witnessed the helicopter that soldier was in upon its departure from a supply run get shot down by a PT-76 tank of the Soviet Army.

I was perplexed about why Doc shared this information with me, but I listened. He concluded by extending an invitation to the dedication ceremony of the Vietnam memorial, and he emphasized that I should make sure to bring my children. I accepted the invitation and brought my children to the dedication event that paid tribute to the eight resident soldiers who lost their lives during the war.

The emotional dedication was fitting for the memorial with seven black granite tablets containing information about the war and a five-foot statue in the center of the new Rotary Centennial Veterans Park. After the ceremony concluded, Doc beckoned me to follow him.

With my children in tow, Doc led me to an engraved paver with my father's name, rank, and date of death with the added letters *KIA* (killed in action). My disbelief turned to utter shock when Doc took my hand, put it to his heart, and said, "James Christian Jensen, killed in action, May 10, 1972; I knew your father."

Now Doc's office visit weeks earlier made sense. He was adamant that Jimmy's helicopter didn't crash from mechanical failure but that it was shot down. He was also resolute that from that day forward, he was my father, and I was his daughter. It was the least he could do for the man he said saved his life. That was a dream come true that I didn't even know I had. Since then, Doc has been an integral part of my life. We have shared dinners and lengthy conversations. We've celebrated holidays and birthdays. We've also shared loss when his wife died and renewed hope when he remarried. We were family.

Family doesn't have to be blood related. That truth became even more profound when my cousin and I decided to do an AncestryDNA test. I was forty-nine and wanted to know more about my heritage on my biological father's side of the family because what I knew was that his ancestry emigrated to the

United States from Denmark. They even named the township in Utah that they settled Elsinore after the Kronborg Castle.

The results of that DNA test would change my life forever. I didn't have one drop of DNA from Denmark, Sweden, or anywhere close to those countries. And I didn't match at all with my cousin, whose DNA markers were heavily from Denmark. Devastation does not begin to describe my heartbreak.

I contacted a professional genealogist who analyzed my DNA markers. He said I was clearly Spanish. Hearing those words instantly surfaced a memory of a conversation I had with my grandmother as a teen after I found a wallet-size photo of a man in her projector slides.

On the back of the photo, handwritten in cursive was the name Jose Luis de Dios. I was thirteen and had been told by my mother a few months earlier that my brother and I had different dads but not to discuss it further. My grandmother explained that she'd kept the photo of the foreign-exchange student because she thought he could be my birth father since my mother had dated him.

The same feelings of anxiousness, nervousness, and excitement I had when waiting for that phone call from my mom twenty-five years earlier about my father were coupled with absolute dread. But I did it. My mom cried, "No, no, no, no!" I responded in a whisper, "Yes."

My mom then divulged a relationship with Jose that was not approved of by her father. She corrected what my grandmother had told me and said Jose was from Madrid and had come to the States to do mining and engineering. She said they met at a college party. Their dating consisted of him playing the classical guitar and being intimate.

She went on to say that Jose had asked permission from her father to take her to Lake Tahoe with some friends, which he responded to with disdain and disgust. The answer was obviously no. While Jose was away, my mom encountered Jimmy. She

thought Jimmy was my father. My dreams, once realized, were now shattered.

I picked up the pieces with introspection and prayer. For me to heal, I needed to reveal the truth to people who'd accepted and loved me. My cousin, who did the DNA test with me, accompanied me as I went to my uncles' homes and told them that Jimmy was not my father. Telling my grandfather was the most devastating because he was in a nursing home. I could only talk to him through a window screen amid the COVID-19 pandemic restrictions.

Sharing with him the DNA results were something my ninety-one-year-old grandfather didn't comprehend. I just had to come out and say it. "I'm not Jimmy's daughter," escaped my quivering lips as tears fell down my cheeks. My grandfather put his hand on the screen, so I touched it with mine. He then said, "You're a special girl."

The word *special* is something I fixated on. I was healing, and it made me realize what I longed for in my dreams throughout my life—my father—I already had but in other forms. I did have loving grandfathers and uncles on both sides of my family. I had teachers and mentors. I had Doc. And I always had my father in heaven, who'd been with me my entire life. Divine inspiration told my heart that I was loved and always had been.

Dreams are lovely to have for inspiration, motivation, and in my case, the deliverance of truth. Also, in my case, dreams changed and even came true, but not in the way I thought they would. They also got crushed. But what matters is that you still dream.

My seven-year-old self didn't know it then, but I know it now after a lifetime of dreaming that all of us are not defined by our DNA. My second-grade teacher got it wrong. This is what she should have said: "You are valued. You come from the divine. You will always matter!"

ABOUT JENNIFER WEAVER

Jennifer Weaver is an award-winning journalist and mother to three grown children. She earned a bachelor of science degree in human development and family studies from the University of Utah and a master of management and public administration degree from the University of Phoenix, where she also graduated as a member of the Lambda Sigma Chapter of the International Business Honor Society, Delta Mu Delta. She currently operates her own business, girlcodeandcontent.com, and resides in South Jordan, Utah.

THE LITTLE BARN THAT COULD

Michele Gambone

Abrief introduction is probably in order with the understanding that this story in and of itself is a journey down the road less traveled with myriad choices leading to spiritual awakening and enlightenment. This odyssey has elevated my life beyond what I believed to be my limits and continues to amaze me each and every day.

My name is Michele Gambone, and my life originated in small town Westville, New Jersey, where I still reside with my family. I have always had passion in everything I have done and always believed that my life takes me exactly where I need to be in every moment. I spent many years working in animal rescue and still consider it one of my passions, but a few years back in fall 2014, a new passion came knocking, and it has become an all-encompassing voyage fraught with epic highs and demoralizing lows.

It was just before Thanksgiving in 2014 when I found out about a woman that was eight months pregnant and living in a minivan with her husband and children. We have all heard horror stories about life on the streets, and this story was no different from the countless stories that preceded it—but somehow,

for some unknown reason, I felt compelled to help this family. I believe without a shadow of a doubt it was the Holy Spirit moving me to act and help someone who really needed it. By accident, but absolutely not by mistake, the Unforgotten Haven was born on that day.

The Unforgotten Haven, which today is a nonprofit 501(c)(3) and is now one of the fastest growing charitable organizations in the country, started with extremely humble beginnings with its sole mission statement stated simply as being "the wind beneath the wings of all living things."

I have to take you to the beginning and probably explain the name of this story. As you can imagine, the first family I wanted to help planted a seed deep inside, and the idea and belief started to grow that no one should ever be overlooked or neglected, and each person truly deserves dignity and respect and should always have a safe refuge. The Unforgotten Haven by definition means exactly the idea that was planted that day back in November 2014. It wasn't long before this idea blossomed and donations from angels started to overrun my living room, my kitchen, my porch—well, you get the idea. I found myself needing a space to contain and disperse the blessings we were receiving. In my travels, I happened upon a run-down little barn on the back end of a residential property that was being offered for lease. Now when I say run down, I mean it had no heat, no electric (or none that worked), no insulation to keep out the cold as it was now December, and it had no running water or bathrooms. It was absolutely perfect!

I signed a month-to-month lease, and the little barn had now become my new headquarters. The donations were pouring in. We started with collecting food and toiletries along with clothing by the truckload, and furniture also was fair game. After only eight short weeks, this little barn, which was now packed to its rotted little rafters, was also filling up with volunteers that were fast becoming the life blood to push this growing relief effort

beyond what I was able to do alone. The time spent in this little barn was difficult at best with the winter upon us, and snow often blocked the entrance, and the brutal cold made it almost untenable. I still remember pulling up to the barn after work, using my headlights for light so we could sort donations, and stuffing our gloves with hand warmers as vapor came out of our mouths due to the frigid temperatures. I remember my husband coming to slide open the old, extremely heavy door for us to get inside. It may seem odd to look at this building with fond memories given the physical hardships that everyone endured, but that building helped support an idea and gave hope to a brighter future for everyone. I suppose the symbolism of that building fit right into our mission. It was overlooked and neglected, but it became our refuge, our haven.

The little barn was the springboard for an organization that propelled a belief in helping others.

We, as an organization, had to bid farewell to our beloved barn and move forward to be able to help more people. The next step was at best a leap of faith in which I signed a yearly lease for a much larger and more modern space that could accommodate future growth exactly five months after helping our first family. I say *leap of faith* simply because we had exactly zero funding. If I was to tell you that it was a little scary, that would be a massive understatement. My fears were quelled by my belief that if I put it in God's hands and it was meant to be, we would certainly succeed. I know that there are many nonbelievers, but from where I stand, it's virtually impossible to deny that our survival as an organization was steeped in faith. We have witnessed many miracles and have reached over 1.5 million souls that desperately needed to feel the blessings of a merciful God. This includes people and animals.

The Unforgotten Haven has benefited from the blessings bestowed upon it and thereby has helped more and more people and animals along the way. I am the founder, and yes, that

requires more hours than there are in a day. I have continued to work as a manager of an engineering firm for the past twenty-five years as well and have devoted a minimum of an additional forty to fifty hours per week to this labor of love. Fortunately, as an organization, we have been able to garner corporate as well as private sponsorship from businesses and individuals that can see the value in what we are trying to accomplish. We have amassed a team of volunteers with a passion and belief in helping others and truly have seen this organization bring out the best in everyone. We are now a team of forty individuals that have compassion and love and the belief that we can make the world a better place for all living creatures.

We operate as 100% volunteer based, seven days a week, and the haven is a well-oiled machine. Each supporter and volunteer is the oil to that machine. We are called "The Blessing Hub" as we are the hub filled with donations and we share with churches, schools, and other organizations to spread the love.

The Unforgotten Haven was founded on the fundamental belief that we as an organization can not only make the world a better place but we can elevate those who have lived through some of the most incredibly difficult times ever known. We have seen devastating loss and wept with families that have lost everything and everyone that mattered in their lives.

Each and every day we have seen the best, and yes, the worst that exists in our local communities and all around the world, and we are dedicated to easing the grief and sense of loss from all disasters, man-made and natural.

During this journey, God placed a very special little boy into our lives at the Unforgotten Haven. His name is Nico Cassabria, and he fought Stage IV high-risk neuroblastoma. He fought from age three to age ten. We were the lucky ones to have been able to meet such a hero walking among us here on Earth. Our entire team and the entire community came together despite any differences to embrace Nico and his family through his journey here on

Earth. This is one of our devastating losses, and we still speak of him daily. The work we do is not always rainbows and butterflies. It's often filled with tears and heartache. We often grieve, but we love hard. When you open your heart, it is susceptible to being broken. Nico made everyone want to be a better person during his ten years here. He is part of the Unforgotten Haven family and part of our story. As promised to his family, he will *never* be forgotten. We honor Nico by having his very own project, Nico's Power-Up Packs, which are bags made up with arts and crafts and other items given to children in the hospitals and also to children's infusion centers.

The Unforgotten Haven continues to grow, and with growth we found that we needed even more space to support over twenty individual projects intended to pinpoint specific needs within our communities, such as support for terminally ill cancer patients or for victims of domestic violence as well as our homeless out-reach initiative serving hundreds of homeless in Philadelphia, PA, and Camden, NJ, each Sunday. We found ourselves supporting victims of natural disasters during the Louisiana floods and hur-ricane relief in North Carolina, Texas, Florida, and Puerto Rico. We supported the victims local to New Jersey who lost every-thing in a tornado September 2021. Our most recent support has found its way directly to the Ukraine in an effort to ease the atrocity inflicted on a war-torn nation.

With our rapid growth, we found that we needed a building that would better enable us to support the needs of everyone. Volunteerism is very important to us, and we ran out of space at our current building we rent, so we started searching for a larger building in the beginning of 2021.

We asked and prayed for God to once again provide what we needed, and once again he provided. Our supporters rallied and donated $75,000 toward the purchase of a new building. A family of angels gifted us a half-million dollars. Let me introduce you to the Radwell family! This is the first time the family has

been announced. We wanted it to be special. What better way than to put this miracle into a book. This gift allowed us to purchase a larger building and ultimately gave us the leverage to aid even more people in need.

The Radwell family will never know the impact they have made in this world. Our gratitude can't be expressed in words. As we searched all over South Jersey for a building, many obstacles occurred. It was very difficult to find a commercial property. Then it happened! Directly across from where we rented, a massive building went up for sale for $575,000.

Exactly what we had to the penny.

Who says God isn't listening!

We are expanding, and the building we purchased will be a volunteer headquarters in the near future. The building we rent will remain our pantry where families can stop in anytime we are open for *free* nonperishable food, toiletries, diapers, wipes, formula, baby food, feminine products, and cleaning supplies (depending on what we have donated to us at the time).

Hours and more information can be found on our website: www.theunforgottenhaven.org.

I will leave you with this. When you have faith the size of a million mustard seeds, those seeds spread quickly—just like when you blow on a dandelion. I am thankful every single day that God put faith in my heart and provided me with the best family, team members, and friends a girl could wish for (my dandelion seeds). Without God, my family, and my team, this beautiful organization would not exist.

ABOUT MICHELE GAMBONE

I am happily married with two skin children and six fur children.

I reside in a small town in South Jersey (Westville, NJ) where my family has been rooted for over 100 years!

I have managed an engineering firm full-time for the past twenty-five years (Hydrographic Surveys) and recently went part-time to be more hands-on at the Unforgotten Haven.

I have been a certified colon hydrotherapist for the past fifteen years.

I am a photographer and an animal activist. I enjoy the beach and hope to retire there one day.

I have worked hard since the age of fourteen and would say I am a workaholic. Each day starts at 3:00 a.m. (seven days a week). I enjoy helping others, and it does the soul good.

I am a faithful servant of God, and not a day goes by that I don't pray or give thanks to my father in heaven.

My faith is the size of a million mustard seeds. My favorite quote:

"No one has ever become poor by giving." —Anne Frank

SOUL ANSWERS

Lauren Oberly

Ever since I was a little girl, I've always believed in universal magic and the unseen. From unicorns, imaginary friends, Santa Claus, the tooth fairy—you name it, I believed it. Throughout my childhood years is when these beliefs started to change. I lost a bit of the belief in magic. This is when I started to question everything about myself: my inner truth, my self-worth, self-love, and self-confidence. I always used to think, *How could my parents tell me to believe in anything, when I found out everything I thought was real is a hoax?* Thinking back on this as an adult, it's very clear that my inner child is where my limiting beliefs came from and how I was built as an adult.

I began sitting quietly in contemplation on a daily basis in my late twenties. I began to notice my own thoughts. Many beliefs I held—both negative and positive—came up. One very heartfelt and emotional moment for me was when I made a life-changing decision for my daughter Lily and me. It was Monday morning, October 26, 2020, I experienced one of the scariest and proudest moments I had in my life. I was walking into the courthouse with my sister-in-law to put a stop to the marriage that I knew wasn't serving me any longer. At that moment, I had an overwhelming

number of emotions and thoughts running through my mind. *Can I do this for my daughter and me? Is this the right choice for us? What am I going to do next?* After following my true instinct, a huge sense of calmness came over me. I finally was able to feel and receive the message God was guiding me to see.

Now one of the affirmations I say every single day is, *I am open to the fullness of my power and know that I am perfectly enough exactly as I am.* You have the power to heal your life and I feel that is something everyone needs to believe. We often doubt ourselves and think we do not have the potential to achieve what we want. What people don't realize is we have the power of our minds— claiming and consciously using your power. Trauma is never your fault, but healing is your responsibility. Your ability to love yourself is mirrored in the love you accept from others. If you're seeking a deeper love, look within and seek a deeper love within yourself first. Being true to yourself while loving who you are during the journey is the most courageous thing you will ever do.

I grew up a daddy's girl. I always wanted to be the center of attention, and most of all, I wanted his attention. My dad was born in the 1940s, and back in that time, it wasn't socially accepted to have a voice or express emotions, which means it was all stuffed deep down in his body as trauma. After the passing of his mother when he was seventeen years old, my dad had to grow up fast to help his own father provide for his other siblings, instead of having the freedom of enjoying his teenage years.

It wasn't until about eight months ago that I realized my dad was emotionally unavailable during my childhood. This is where I believe I learned my low self-esteem from. I came to this realization through a coaching session with one of my mentors, Melanie Wilson, an anxiety and trauma coach. I asked myself one day, *Why do I feel a sense of jealousy as I watch my daughter Lily and my dad read books together?* The valuable lesson that I was able to learn in that current moment, was having the ability to look at it

from a different perspective. Shifting from the egotistical version of self, I was able to see this as a blessing in the purest form.

I learned this through my own self-healing and connecting with my intuition. When I feel an emotional trigger, I need to *pause* and identify why I might be feeling this way. What inside of me needs more healing and exploration? If I didn't allow a space for my own healing, I might have missed this pure blessing God put right in front of me. My dad, seventy-three, has been the closest thing Lily has had to a father figure. I am grateful that my dad is able to fill that void for my daughter, as her own father wasn't willing to be present in her life at the time. I've always believed you have children when you need them, not when you want them. God knew I needed change in my life, and Lily is the reason I am the woman I am today. I pray that one day her own father can see how much of a blessing Lily is to us both.

After becoming a mom myself, I felt my relationship with my mom was very important to me. I have always viewed my mom as a caring, loving, strong, independent, hardworking woman. Growing up, I always felt like it was very hard to connect with her. So I prayed about it in hopes of some answers. I needed to get to the root of why I was never able to connect with her. I wanted to learn more about her childhood and her teenage years. So, I was able to come from a place of love and compassion. Just recently, I asked my mom if she would be more open to telling me about her childhood and teenage years. During our conversation, she shared with me her struggles with her own inner peace and past trauma. She also told me she masked all of this for years to make sure my dad, my brother, and I were all taken care of first.

As a child, I saw this as her being controlling, manipulating, and always worrying about everything. In turn, it put a wall between us. I was the type of kid that never liked to be controlled or told what to do. As an adult, this was a hard habit to break and still shows up for me at times. My parents always had very high expectations of me even as a little kid still learning. Knowing this,

I am just the product of my past experiences and trauma, but I am the one who is responsible for healing this. I am responsible for how I show up for myself. I can't blame people for who they are when they are hurt. Just because I was led to believe certain things in my childhood doesn't mean I wasn't safe or protected as a child. If I couldn't believe what my heart and soul believed in, how was I supposed to believe in myself? That's where the limiting beliefs in myself came from.

As a child and teen, I judged others for having big emotions because I couldn't understand how to deal with my own in a healthy way. That is why I was always drawn to codependent relationships. I confused self-sacrifice with self-preservation. Today, my parents are my best friends and my main support system. I am so grateful to have been able to help heal our relationship bond.

Until I had my own daughter, I lived my life just trying to survive day by day. I wanted to get to the root of why I was suffering. I was just a bottomless pit of toxic emotions—fear and shame mainly. I was drowning in my negative emotions about not being enough. This prompted me to start my own shadow work, so I could heal the wounds from my childhood and past relationships. The "shadow" is most apparent in strong emotions. Being able to identify and see what those emotions and sensations are can help you see your life patterns.

Three key parts of starting my shadow work were identifying my life patterns, triggers, and projections with people and relationships in my life. Some of the questions I asked myself while journaling were: *What is the trigger attached to that pattern? What family patterns do I fear I am repeating? How do I present myself to the world?* I did all of this through journaling, self-reflection, and childhood analysis.

After doing my own shadow work, it made me come to the realization I needed to break this generational trend to not subconsciously pass it to my own daughter. I was so sick of what was happening in my life, sick of all the people I let hurt me, so sick

of the pain. I was not going to shrink myself down so someone else was comfortable with me. I would use my voice and be as powerful as I wanted to be. I stopped caring if people thought I was too much. Because I know I am enough. I stopped caring if I asked too many questions, if I seemed too passionate, or if others thought I was too sensitive because I am in touch with my emotions.

I was done ignoring my feelings for the comfort of someone who couldn't handle it. I knew that it was possible to be a misfit in one group and fit in perfectly in another. This is the time I explored my true passion and dreams. Continuing my shadow work, I realized I was the only one who got to decide how I was going to live my life. No one else was going to magically show up and do all the hard work for me. It wasn't until I hit rock bottom, at the darkest and lowest point in my life, that I decided I needed a change, sitting on my kitchen floor packing up boxes alone to move out of the first house I bought on my own. I was so sick and tired of feeling like I had no purpose in this universe. I wasn't strong enough to change for myself at the time, so my daughter became my why. I decided to put in the hard work no matter how hard it felt at times. I chose to believe in the magic you can't see, because this is where my inner belief came from.

Once I chose me, I could not stay in a marriage that wasn't serving my highest good and purpose here on Earth. I have since learned that in a relationship, you either grow together or you grow apart. That doesn't necessarily make you or the another person a bad person. If you don't love yourself, you can't love another person. You're just using that person as a bandage to cover up what you are hiding from yourself.

I started to work through all my trauma and feel my emotions from my past hurt. I had to go through this process alone. I had to show up 100% for myself first to heal so I could show up as a better mother, daughter, sister, friend, niece, and cousin. But

most importantly, God's higher purpose here on Earth was as an energy healer.

As I gained more self-awareness, I learned to trust myself more. I can now even use that introspection in relationships. Starting my self-love journey and becoming whole again, I owe a huge amount of gratitude to my very close and dear friend Tara Lepera. She saw me for what my soul had to offer this world. She walked alongside me, holding my hand and guiding me each step. I wouldn't be the woman I am today if it wasn't for the belief she saw in me. After identifying the negative self-talk, the limiting beliefs, and the ego-driving narrative others projected on me, I changed.

One of the biggest lessons was getting out of my own ego and connecting with my higher self. I started to look at my life from a different perspective. This is the evolution of the journey: the reflection of my childhood, limiting beliefs, and negative self-talk. While also working with Melanie, she helped me realize I had to surrender to myself. I worked with her in a very intense twelve-week program, which was meant to help me rise up from my anxiety and trauma. She helped me develop new beliefs, break the chains to my anxiety, and start to live my life unapologetically. Ultimately, I discovered the only way to fully love myself was to surrender—even though I left a marriage, had to move back home, lost money, had to leave my job, singly provided for my daughter all while building myself back up.

My ultimate lesson was all of these things had to happen in order for me to fully surrender. Honestly, I think it's one of the most helpful perspectives one can cultivate now. I had no idea a passion for spiritual study, creativity, writing, and deeply connecting with nature would be ignited within me. I shifted my focus toward being of service to others. So I was able to walk in my soul's purpose here on Earth. Surrendering isn't about giving up, it's about recommitting. It is not to force the desires of your lower ego mind. It's giving up control for peace. I decided on a

new direction while being gentle with myself as I practiced this new way of being. I am no longer in a mental prison fighting against myself. I am fully living my soul's purpose. In turn, this led me to realize what I had always known my whole life: I am a healed empath. This allowed me the opportunity to tap into my universal energy through Reiki healing, an amazing journey of my soul's destiny for my sacred calling.

Through my own hard work, I found new meaning in my soul's purpose. Your life will change once you discover your passion, spiritual path, and tribe to support you on your journey. If you want to dig deep and uncover your dreams and visions, I invite you to connect with me. I will walk alongside you and guide you to find your own inner light so you can finally live in peace. If you listen to your heart, all things are possible when you are able to dream!

"You can't go back and change the beginning, but you can start where you are and change the ending." —C.S. Lewis

ABOUT LAUREN OBERLY

Lauren Oberly is the founder of Mermaid Light. Lauren is a single mama of a two-year-old girl named Lily. After having her daughter, Lauren always knew there was more to her soul's purpose on Earth than just being a mom. She was tired of working for someone else's dream and decided to stop living in the matrix. Lauren is an energy healer and discovered using her gift as a Reiki master, intuitive life coach, and author. She guides her client's step by step in uncovering their dreams and passions. After becoming the CEO of her own life with the power of prayer and the universe, she helps empower women to find their own soul's purpose on Earth. Lauren believes every human has the power within them to heal. Lauren is just your personal cheerleader to help guide you to see your own inner light.

So I invite you into my world to learn more on how you can work one-on-one with me, visit www.themermaidlight.com or connect with me on social media:

Facebook: Lauren Oberly
Instagram: @LaurenOberly

UNSEEN

Dawn Schimke

My legs dangled, childlike, in midair as I shivered on the examination table at the hospital. It was early December, and I was clad in a skimpy and revealing hospital gown, but it was the words that had just been uttered that sent a chill down my spine. "Prepare for a miscarriage." The doctor standing before me was absent of emotion and barely gave me a second glance when he made the definitive proclamation. The shock of that prognosis silenced me. How does a person prepare in advance for their dreams to be crushed?

The reality of his words hit me on the subway back to my upper Manhattan apartment, and I fought to hold in the storm of heaving sobs until safely away from the dead eyes of the other commuters. A soggily incoherent call to Ken, my fiancé, at his office failed to garner any reassurance. What did *he* know about being the owner of an incompetent cervix and the barbaric threat of having "a stitch" put in place to stave off what seemed like an inevitable outcome.

After three emergency room trips in the six weeks since my pregnancy was confirmed, I was getting used to sharp needles, invasive questions . . . and wild assumptions—was I actively using

crack? For patients who are uninsured and reliant on Medicaid as I was, the medical system often can be a brutal inquiry into their lifestyle and an intrusion on their very autonomy.

Enter Dr. Xu! He was an acupuncturist and well-respected doctor of Traditional Chinese Medicine (TCM) who I had visited occasionally before I learned I was pregnant. Ken was a big fan of so-called alternative medicine and was keen to get me on board. But I knew from my *What to Expect . . .* book that acupuncture is not recommended during pregnancy, so it was with reluctance that I tagged along for my fiancé's Saturday visit. Dr. Xu asked where I had been and beckoned for me to extend my arms so he could listen to my pulses—in TCM there are six, and they each provide information about the systems of the body. A moment later, he flexed his arm triumphantly and said, "I give you strong baby."

His wife, the apothecarist, prepared a bundle of paper packets containing a dusty powder that was to be mixed into hot water every night. My introduction to medical herbalism was via some of the most obnoxiously bitter plants that have ever crossed my palate. I had recently received my diploma in classic pastry arts, and that flavor profile was profoundly offensive. I cried every night before gulping down the potion, but the effects were noticeable in days. The terrifying hemorrhaging that had been happening for five weeks dwindled, then disappeared; the cramps that doubled me over: gone. I finally started to put on weight.

I was feeling better, and my curiosity had been awakened. How did he know what plants my body needed to tune it to the frequency of "baby"? What secrets did he discover by feeling for a barely discernible vibration deep in my wrists? How was this shift even possible? Given the prognosis of my previous doctors, it felt miraculous. Why did they give me the shrug? Why the resignation, the "there's nothing we can do"? Clearly there *was* something to be done, and it was very effective, but how did it work? Over the next several months, I received a different, personalized

formula during each visit, and the dream of baby started to feel like it was going to come true.

During that time, I was added to my husband's excellent health insurance, and I learned something else. Having that coverage makes a massive difference in how people are treated by providers in the allied health professions. I interviewed several OB-GYNs to find the right fit. What a luxury! I had my pick of potential pediatricians, all of whom took a significant amount of time to answer my questions. Would this have happened if I had stayed on Medicaid? Probably not. The system is jammed with people who are not in a position to afford the basic right of healthcare, and there are simply not enough doctors to go around.

In the current medical paradigm, an encounter with the doctor should last fifteen to twenty minutes—this ideal first gained a foothold 1992, based on a complex Medicare calculation.[1] That is very little time to properly assess and diagnose a complex patient with any degree of nuance or accuracy. There is a saying that is heard in medical circles: "When you hear hoofbeats, think horses, not zebras."

In principle, this makes sense—common conditions are prevalent, hence their name. Yet this leaves 3.5 to 5.9 percent of people (approximately 300 million worldwide) who have rare conditions . . . unseen.[2] Beyond that, almost 60 percent of adults in the United States have one chronic condition, and 40 percent have multiple conditions that affect their day-to-day life and functioning.[3] Often, the most complex patients have challenges

1—Roni Caryn Rabin, "15-minute doctor visits take a toll on patient-physician relationships," PBS News Hour, April 21, 2014, https://www.pbs.org/newshour/health/need-15-minutes-doctors-time.

2—Hlawulani, "New Scientific Paper Confirms 300 Million People Living with a Rare Disease Worldwide," Rare Diseases International (website), October 15, 2019, https://www.rarediseasesinternational.org/new-scientific-paper-confirms-300-million-people-living-with-a-rare-disease-worldwide/.

3—National Center for Chronic Disease Prevention and Health Promotion (NCCDPHP), "Chronic Diseases in America," Center for Disease Control, accessed June 28, 2022, https://www.cdc.gov/chronicdisease/resources/infographic/chronic-diseases.htm.

accessing providers and find their symptoms minimized or attributed to another issue (being overweight for instance), after months and even years of waiting for an appointment. Unseen and unheard. Getting insurance authorizations for required therapies and treatments is another hurdle that prevents people from accessing appropriate care; there are people employed by insurance companies who "manage patient expectations around bureaucratic hurdles"—people who are paid to tell other people why they get to be unseen.

Moreover, there is a massive resistance within the medical system against working cooperatively with practitioners of integrative and complementary modalities. Using plants to support wellness is sometimes portrayed as quaint, ineffective, hippie-era folk medicine. At the other end of the spectrum, some consider it to be risky, irresponsible, and even quackery.[4]

While the technological advances of the past century are nothing short of astounding, our ability as a society to navigate how to actually provide comprehensive care to humans has not caught up to the machines and diagnostic and surgical tools we have available. The New York Academy of Medicine, founded in 1847 to recognize highly skilled physicians and to bring credibility to a troubled profession, in an inaugural move voted that practitioners of homeopathy (which is not at all the same as herbalism) be barred from the medical field. This was almost *two decades* before Louis Pasteur developed modern germ theory.

How (and why) did the use of pharmaceuticals overtake the use of botanical remedies so quickly? In a nutshell, they are easy to standardize and dose appropriately. Aspirin was originally derived from the bark of the white willow tree. Prior to it being commercially available, a person would need to find the tree, harvest the

---

4—People who practice herbalism call it traditional medicine because it has been used effectively for thousands of years. The world of medical and pharmaceutical research is starting to catch up, and currently there are well over one hundred plant-derived compounds used in medications for anything from a headache to lymphoma.

bark, make some type of extraction, and then decide when and how much to take. That requires a lot of work and the knowledge to do it. It is much simpler to buy an effective anti-inflammatory at the store. It's not formulated so differently from the tree bark, plus it's convenient, and the side effects are manageable.

In some cases, a medication might be very strong and upset the equilibrium of a person's system in a more significant way. Antibiotics undoubtedly save lives; they are also well-known for disrupting the gastrointestinal tract because they do not discriminate between the unwanted bacterial visitors and the microorganisms that keep our digestion functioning smoothly. Naturally, it is important to address illnesses or conditions that may be life-threatening. And in modern medicine, sometimes the solution is akin to attacking a fly on the windowpane with a baseball bat. It will probably kill the fly, but the window won't be in great shape either.

One of the advantages of using the whole plant (with exceptions for those that have a degree of toxicity) is that it gives us access to all of the constituents that already work together harmoniously, rather than separating out the chemical compound that we think is doing the heavy lifting. Herbs that are known as "tonic herbs," "adaptogens," and "amphoterics" often are very effective at toning imbalances, helping the body adapt to stress, and even have the wisdom to normalize a system of the body that is expressing symptoms. I think of these more subtle actions as an embroidery needle, precise and much better for the overall health of the organism than knocking the daylights out of it. Plants used properly both remove the fly and result in a windowpane that is a little cleaner and shinier.

Moreover, facilitating and empowering the individual to implement health strategies that work for them increases and broadens wellness accessibility and autonomy. Empowering the consumer to make decisions with gentle guidance toward best

practices rather than insisting on compliance builds trust and expands the opportunity for effective intervention.

I need to emphasize that accessibility is critical and fundamental. Wellness is not an elitist sport. Nor is it a moral issue. Wellness is a sign of a body in harmonious equilibrium. Rippling outward, the state of health of the people indicates the state of health of the larger society. The phrase "getting to the root cause" comes up often, and the individual "puts roots down" into the soil of their communities. There is no healthy garden if the earth is unattended or undernourished in any area. That is because land, plants, humans, communities will compensate for their imbalances and deficiencies in any way possible.

Years ago, I attended a lecture given by Henry Niese, an artist and herbalist in the Lakota tradition, in which he described a certain plant gradually creeping closer and closer to his home. After tuning into and listening for the energetic messages of the plant spirit, he discovered that the constituents and actions as determined by scientific exploration were helpful for a health imbalance or condition he was challenged by. I, too, have found that the plants that "approach" me are springing up for a reason. Just this morning, on my daily walk, I had a thought: *I haven't seen many Cleavers[5] this year.* A moment later I turned my head to the left and spotted a healthy patch by the creek.

Nature intelligence has sophisticated communication capabilities that go beyond what can be seen and heard. We do not exist apart from nature, despite all of our efforts to protect our vulnerable bodies. Tapping into that massive potential unleashes the body's ability to readjust itself to equilibrium and harmony. This can co-exist with deepening our understanding of the known scientific information about the effects of the plants as we continue to have more revelations about matter at the microcosmic level. There are over 120 medications derived from plants, and

---

5—Galium aparine, a wonderful lymphatic that proliferates in April and May, which, not-so-coincidentally is considered a good time in TCM to focus on releasing any stagnation that has built up over the winter.

research continues to expand. We have the capability of maximizing health on all levels by acknowledging that traditional and integrative care techniques can work synergistically with the system we have created for now.

The privilege of being an herbalist is immense, as is the responsibility—to our clients, to the earth, to the plants, to our colleagues. I am using my expertise to be a passionate advocate for those who are unseen by the medical system and on the vanguard of a new wellness paradigm. One where healthcare consumer is offered an array of modalities within a cooperative and collaborative framework. One where there is a trained herbalist accessible in every medical office and a living apothecary in every medical center. One in which the medical system has the capacity to fully see every human that they care for, ensuring better wellness outcomes for all.

In case you were curious, the baby from the beginning of this story got to have a gentle and joyful birth and is now twenty-four years old fiercely pursuing her own dreams in the world.

ABOUT DAWN SCHIMKE

Dawn Schimke is an herbalist, wellness coach, and advocate for her clients. Her first life-altering experience involving herbs was when a skilled practitioner of TCM saved her high-risk pregnancy in 1997. She shared the story at a TEDx Charlottesville open mic event in 2019.

Her formal herbal education began in 2007, with her mentor, Teresa Boardwine of Green Comfort School of Herbal Medicine. Dawn initially focused on applying her training as a pastry chef to formulating in the apothecary. Gradually she developed clinical skills and a love for research. She interweaves storytelling, nature metaphors, and a keen eye for energetic patterns into her work.

Dawn provides support and coaching for people who experience complex conditions helping them have more good days so they learn to love and trust their bodies again. She also offers mini workshops to HerbCurious people who desire simple, delicious techniques to upgrade their wellness autonomy.

Diagnosed with Ehlers-Danlos syndrome in 2013, Dawn uses her knowledge and insights to help medical "zebras," neurodivergent people, and those unseen by the dominant medical paradigm.

To learn more about how you can work with Dawn, please visit her website www.leafandpetalalchemy.com.

Facebook: Leaf and Petal Alchemy
Instagram: @leafandpetalalchemy
Pinterest: Leaf & Petal Alchemy

FROM WISHES TO DREAMS

Bobbie Jo Yarbrough

As I sit in our Sacred Circle drinking my cacao, I clear my mind of expectations. My gaze follows the flames, dancing in the center of the beautiful mandala, calling in the Four Directions, the Universe, and the heart-centered connections from above and below. The beauty of being present in myself now. My body begins flowing in the music and the movement of my Shakti energy—connecting to my life force, my Divine Feminine, in ways that feel like the first time.

Settling and silent, I listen to the sacred words guiding me as I walk through my portal door to merge with my future self in the sacredness of the quantum realms. Here, my beautiful highest spiritual self and I are integrated. *I Am* her and she is me. *I Am* loved and safe. *I Am* seen and heard. All my dreams, all my desires, everything *I Am* creating and more is now. I'm filled with the truth, that each day I will expand more, desire more, and love my family and myself more. My soul shines brightly and fills me with more joy. I know that my dreams are meant to be created and lived. Living my dreams is the embodiment and integration of who I truly am. *I Am.*

———

Now I didn't always believe dreams were real. I think as small child, I would associate them with wishes and prayers. I would make wishes and say prayers every night hoping that my life would be better. I was scared to fall asleep and have literal dreams because I would always have nightmares. When I closed my six-year-old eyes every night, I would play out scary scenarios of being abandoned, unloved, and unsafe. I would be running and running, so very scared, and no one would help me. I still said my wishes and prayers and tried to give myself hope, but when I opened my eyes, everything was still the same.

I was learning at the very core of me, during my crucial developmental stages, to be silent and to be invisible. As I grew up, I immersed myself in books and music. I would lose myself in the stories and lyrics. I would stay up all night just to finish a whole book. I would constantly think about the characters and who they were while I was going about my days. I loved book series like, Carolyn Keen's original Nancy Drew young sleuth stories and Stephen King's The Dark Tower series. These adventurers and heroes helped others, led others, close friends with them, and most of all were who they wanted to be, no matter the challenges they were facing. I would think about the characters so much, it was like they were in my actual world. I longed to go on adventures and see the world, but most of all, have the freedom to be myself. Every now and then I would bravely write songs, poetry, and journal about my wishes and dreams, but it never made my life better. I never felt like I could share the creative stories and parts of me that I felt needed to be shared. Some feeling or small whisper made me believe deep down I wasn't alone in how my life was. I knew there were others who lived or felt the way I did, but in my youth and before social media, I never knew how to find or reach out to them.

I was popular in school and had some good friends, but growing up, I went to small-town schools where everyone knew

everyone. We were the foster kids and the kids who had ethnic hair and darker skin, but were "white" too, so we usually, naturally stood out. I was nice and well liked; however, inside I was awkward, ashamed, and hidden. I wished my life was like the kids I went to school with, who seemingly had parents who loved them, money to do all the fun things, and more than a few outfits for school clothes. I just knew deep down this wasn't truly how I was supposed to feel about myself. I was just riding out time till I could get out of foster care and be on my own. I knew this couldn't be my life forever. I was still just making wishes, not knowing I was actually dreaming my future life into creation.

As I was thrust into adulthood, I was naturally forced into new challenges. I was in a new part of the country, with all new people, trying to figure out who I was and where I would fit in, all at once, no time to take breaks or have introspection. At this point in my life, it was all about survival, and there was no time to dream or make wishes. All of those were put on hold while I tried to work or start college so I could set myself up for some distant future that I couldn't connect to. I lived in my car at times, sleeping in the parking lot of my work so I wouldn't waste gas or have to worry about being attacked. I became friends with some people who weren't always the best to be around so I had a sense of protection from the scariness of the streets.

At some point, actually living a better life became just as important as just surviving it. I took a job in another city. I was still just asking and dreaming, but now I had more freedom to seek out how to get the life I wanted. I loved where I was and who I was with. I finally felt like I could be understood more and breathe. My new best friend and I did everything together: we spoke about our dreams, we lived in various cities together, we struggled together, and we supported each other in every way. In retrospect, I can see one of the most powerful aspects to our friendship was our mutual support for each other. We both

believed we could achieve the futures we both wanted, no matter how long it took.

Then my life took a very unexpected turn. The events of 9/11 happened, and within two days I had signed up to serve in the US Navy. There was something that happened or changed inside me while watching the events unfold in the next few days. I was shocked, scared, and sad for those who couldn't find their family members. The call to help others feel safe was stronger than I had ever felt before. I had to do something.

So, the little girl who grew up feeling abandoned, the teenager who dreamed of being on adventures helping people, now was the young adult doing just that. My first four years in the military were spent living overseas at various duty stations, two of which were islands, one of those in the Middle East. Later while stationed in Italy, I got to visit many other countries, such as Germany, Amsterdam, Ireland, etc. I got to explore Rome, Pompeii, and beautiful off-the-coast getaways. I had fun and created friendships that are still strong today. I'm not sure if I knew then; however, now I can see how all my wishing, prayers, and dreams growing up became parts of my real life as an adult.

When a traumatic event happened to me while serving overseas, it felt like my happiness was halted. I was catapulted into the space of feeling scared, abandoned, and shamed. When I got stationed back home in the US, I was in a different mindset. Being myself wasn't safe. My coping skills were all over the place. I didn't understand at the time how my anxiety and depression were being masked every day to help me seem normal. I felt like I stopped dreaming again and was just longing to feel happy. Like being happy was something I had to find or just accept was out of my reach. Even being part of a group of friends, I never felt like I fit in or was wanted. Internally, I was always questioning everything and everyone. "Fake it till you make it" does not happiness make at all. I know—I lived it for a lonely long while.

When I reflect now, I still couldn't tell you how I came to find the path to the journey I've been on for so many years now. I could say that my friend and I went to a metaphysical mixer one evening out of curiosity and found out about a magical, esoteric, sustainable-living community in rural San Diego. Then I was introduced to an intuitive school that tapped me into all my natural spiritual gifts and self-healing. And for years to follow, there has been more intensive self-healing, learning various powerful healing modalities, and intentional living every day. That is the easy explanation. It's true, it's simple, it's to the point. This journey has been so much more than that though.

As I was taught how to tap into the magic of who I truly was, I could connect with my higher self. I was learning to trust my intuition and have the discernment to know what wasn't mine to feel. I remember when I was learning Pranayama breathing and setting a timer to meditate in silence, how uncomfortable and scared I felt. I remember when we would have Karma yoga together in silence for hours, working side by side together, how anxious I would get, thinking everyone was thinking I didn't belong there. Sometimes I would want to just run away from everyone or leave. Sometimes I wished I could do that to myself, just leave myself and live my safe, pretend life.

As I dove more and more into accessing myself so deeply and spiritually, I still didn't realize that all the fear, shame, and invisibility I had wrapped myself in for so long had actually become me. This is how I saw myself and believed others saw me too. The shifting was so uncomfortable because I was seeing my true self, I was connecting to my highest self, I was healing and rewriting my new stories; however, I wasn't believing yet who this me was. I was learning how to pause and sit in my stuff, weed out the lies, and believe in my dreams, but I wasn't in alignment with me. Literally, I was struggling with which me was going to be the real me moving forward. It is so mind-blowing to think about not

resonating with your true self so much that you are not sure of who you really are and it feels safer to stay miserable. I wanted to be in alignment with my true self more than anything now. I knew it was time for me to choose my true self. I was top priority. I was learning how to make my dreams, of truly being me, bigger than my fears.

And I dreamed big. I was dreaming bigger than ever before. I believed what was inside of me could be healed. I believed that I didn't have to hold on to old identities, beliefs, contracts, relationships, etc., that no longer felt good or resonated with me. I dreamed I could help people transform their lives in different sustainable ways. I believed in self-healing. I believed I could heal all of me. I believed I could help others do the same. I believed I could be a mom, after being told by my doctor I wouldn't be able to carry a child. I believed I could have a completely different family life than I had growing up. I was listening to Abraham-Hicks daily, and I truly believed that I could figure my life out and find true happiness. I finally believed that dreams were not just wishes. Dreams were more than just my wishes; they were my big asks to the Universe—of the life I believed I wanted. The life I knew I could have.

What I didn't clearly understand at the time was I couldn't just bypass the deeper healing that still needed to be done in order to have all the things I wanted. Being that my identity was shame and hiding for so long, and now I wanted to be my authentic self and live a fun life with my children, there was a huge disconnect I wasn't even aware of yet. I was going in cycles of standing in my power, using my voice, and still not being heard, valued, or treated with integrity. This went on for a few years and was very confusing.

I was asking for a very different soul-led life, but I was picking the same environments, friends, and situations that put me in situations forcing me to go home and yell in discord, "This is not the life I want. Universe, please help me." Even as I type this.

Universe, please help me. There is calm. A quiet among the tears. A belief. A hope. A dream. A knowing that there is better. I am better. My life can be better. I can have a soul-led life of abundance, soul family, healing, ascension, expansion, and most of all, love. I can have a heart-centered, love-led life. Breathe that in. Pause. Exhale that out.

Yes, I am still learning. I am still healing. I am still learning my value, my worth, and my voice. I am learning what and who I can let go of. I am learning how to create new beliefs every day. And I never stop creating new dreams. Every day the kiddos and I talk about what we want or where we want to explore and who we want to visit. My children are growing up in a house of trial and error as I navigate through my personal healing journey. And also, they are learning healing, they are learning not to give up, and they are learning unconditional love. They are learning to dream big, to ask the Universe for the things they want, and we celebrate and give gratitude every time we receive.

I continue to put myself in rooms, connect in ceremonies, and tap into my personal energies and flow in order to bravely be more and more of my authentic self. When I need to integrate, process, and rest, I rest. Each day I remind myself that I know my dreams are meant to be created and lived. Living my dreams is the embodiment and integration of who I am. *I Am.*

ABOUT BOBBIE JO YARBROUGH

Meet Bobbie Jo, founder of Bravely Authentic, LLC. An intuitive alchemist, master healer, spiritual teacher, artist, and coauthor of the bestseller *Faces of Mental Illness: A Journey from Stigma to Health.*

Bobbie Jo graduated from San Diego State University, school of social work, after serving in the US Navy. She is a graduate of Intuitive Insights: School of Intuition San Diego, certified Sacred Soul Alignment Advanced Practitioner, and Usui Reiki Master.

Bobbie Jo assists people to heal their heart, body, mind, and soul from the inside out. She uses a combination of powerful quantum energy healing modalities, essential subconscious reprogramming techniques, and advanced intuitive techniques to create heart-centered spaces of growth and healing for those that want to live in their joy again.

If you are ready to take a new course of action in your life or just want to start feeling better in your day-to-day, then she can help you. Bravely Authentic also regularly sponsors various PTSD trauma healing programs.

By healing ourselves, we create ripples of healing for the whole world.

How you can connect and work 1:1 with Bravely Authentic:

Linktr.ee: /bravelyauthenticliving
Instagram: @bravelyauthenticliving
Facebook Group: Bravely Authentic Conversations

Have you ever dreamed of
becoming a published author?
Do you have a story to share?
Would the world benefit
from hearing your message?

Then we want to connect with you!

The *Inspired Impact Book Series* is looking to connect with
women who desire to share their stories with the goal of
inspiring others.

We want to hear your story!

Visit www.katebutlerbooks.com to learn more
about becoming a Featured Author in the #1 International
Best-selling *Inspired Impact Book Series*.

Everyone has a story to share!
Is it your time to create your legacy?

May Your Soul be uplifted, and the words of these pages inspire
you to continue to DREAM your infinite light living the fullest
expression of your divine life.

the women who dream

REPRINTED WITH PERMISSIONS

Abby Steurer
Addy M. Kujawa, CAE, DES
Amalai
Bobbie Jo Yarbrough
Candice Shepard
Christina Macro
Cori Solomon Santone
Dawn Schimke
Ellen M. Craine
Ellie D. Shefi
Ericha Scott, PhD
Erin Bonner Hudyma
Erin McCahill
Jennifer Weaver
Keri Gavin
Laura Mount
Lauren Oberly
Linda Gonzalez
Linda Yang
Lori Anne De Iulio Casdia
Mary Gervais
Maya Comerota
Melissa Malland
Michele Gambone
Susan Meitner
Suzette Perez-Tate
Teja Valentín
Teri P. Cox, MBA
Tiffany Donovan Green
Tracey Watts Cirino
Tracy Richards

Made in the USA
Monee, IL
20 July 2022

ABOUT BOBBIE JO YARBROUGH

Meet Bobbie Jo, founder of Bravely Authentic, LLC. An intuitive alchemist, master healer, spiritual teacher, artist, and coauthor of the bestseller *Faces of Mental Illness: A Journey from Stigma to Health.*

Bobbie Jo graduated from San Diego State University, school of social work, after serving in the US Navy. She is a graduate of Intuitive Insights: School of Intuition San Diego, certified Sacred Soul Alignment Advanced Practitioner, and Usui Reiki Master.

Bobbie Jo assists people to heal their heart, body, mind, and soul from the inside out. She uses a combination of powerful quantum energy healing modalities, essential subconscious reprogramming techniques, and advanced intuitive techniques to create heart-centered spaces of growth and healing for those that want to live in their joy again.

If you are ready to take a new course of action in your life or just want to start feeling better in your day-to-day, then she can help you. Bravely Authentic also regularly sponsors various PTSD trauma healing programs.

By healing ourselves, we create ripples of healing for the whole world.

How you can connect and work 1:1 with Bravely Authentic:

Linktr.ee: /bravelyauthenticliving
Instagram: @bravelyauthenticliving
Facebook Group: Bravely Authentic Conversations

Have you ever dreamed of
becoming a published author?
Do you have a story to share?
Would the world benefit
from hearing your message?

Then we want to connect with you!

The *Inspired Impact Book Series* is looking to connect with
women who desire to share their stories with the goal of
inspiring others.

We want to hear your story!

Visit www.katebutlerbooks.com to learn more
about becoming a Featured Author in the #1 International
Best-selling *Inspired Impact Book Series.*

Everyone has a story to share!
Is it your time to create your legacy?

May Your Soul be uplifted, and the words of these pages inspire you to continue to DREAM your infinite light living the fullest expression of your divine life.

the women who dream

REPRINTED WITH PERMISSIONS

Abby Steurer
Addy M. Kujawa, CAE, DES
Amalai
Bobbie Jo Yarbrough
Candice Shepard
Christina Macro
Cori Solomon Santone
Dawn Schimke
Ellen M. Craine
Ellie D. Shefi
Ericha Scott, PhD
Erin Bonner Hudyma
Erin McCahill
Jennifer Weaver
Keri Gavin
Laura Mount
Lauren Oberly
Linda Gonzalez
Linda Yang
Lori Anne De Iulio Casdia
Mary Gervais
Maya Comerota
Melissa Malland
Michele Gambone
Susan Meitner
Suzette Perez-Tate
Teja Valentín
Teri P. Cox, MBA
Tiffany Donovan Green
Tracey Watts Cirino
Tracy Richards

Made in the USA
Monee, IL
20 July 2022

table of contents

This book is dedicated to you. We see you, we feel you, we relate to you, and we connect with you, because . . . we are you. At the core we are more alike than we are different. We are beings of light and love who deeply desire to make a positive influence in the world with our unique type of brilliance. The pages of this book promise to fill you with the wisdom, insights, and inspiration that will align you further with your soul's path. Our hope is that the vulnerability and authenticity of these stories will remind you deeply of who you are and inspire you to rise up and shine your light in the world.

It is your time. It is our time. It is time.

Enjoy the unfolding . . .

First Edition

Copyright © 2022 Kate Butler Books

www.katebutlerbooks.com

All rights reserved.

ISBN: 978-1-957124-07-0

Design by Melissa Williams Design
mwbookdesign.com

WOMEN
WHO
dream

30 STORIES TO INSPIRE
BIG BELIEFS AND BIG DREAMS

WOMEN
WHO
dream

CHAPTER ONE

Shenty Street, Bolton, Lancashire

SHE'D SEEN HIM around here only a couple of times before, a scruffy-looking man with his cap pulled low and his collar raised high. He had a furtive air, not looking directly at anyone in the street and skulking in the shadows instead of greeting folk with a cheery 'All right?' in the usual way. Round here, everyone knew everyone else – and their business – so Evie was certain this man was a stranger. And, from his manner, he was up to no good.

The question was, what did he want with her dad?

She'd now come into the kitchen to make sure her brothers, Peter and Robert, were getting on with their homework, leaving her mum and Grandma Sue folding the dried clothes ready to be ironed. Now, standing just inside, the back door partly closed

3

to conceal her, Evie watched her father and the stranger. The two men faced each other in the shadowy alleyway between the Carters' house and the next row of terraces. Evie could plainly see both men in profile, her father taller, younger and more handsome than the weaselly-looking fella. The stranger was saying something in a voice too low for her to hear and then Dad, who had been smiling, no doubt laying on the charm, muttered something in return and began to look less happy. The next moment the man, his expression aggressive, was wagging a finger in Dad's face. Evie was surprised to see her father's shoulders slump and he no longer met the other man's eye. She was half ashamed to be snooping and half afraid that here was bad news on the way and she ought to see if she could do something about it before her mum heard. This wouldn't be the first time Dad had got in a bit of a tight corner, and Mum had lost a bit of her sparkle of late.

Since Evie had left school to help her mother and Grandmother Sue with the washing business she was more aware of what everyone in the family was up to. It wasn't always bad news with Dad, but there had been some weeks when money was especially tight after he'd had a long evening at the pub, celebrating or commiserating some event with 'the lads', especially if the bookie's runner had been there collecting the stake on some nag that Dad had been told was 'a certainty' to win and make his fortune, and which had eventually cantered in well down the field.

Michael Carter was never down for long and, with his irrepressible high spirits, would shrug off his setbacks and carry on regardless, sweeping aside any difficulties as if they weren't happening. But Mum was sometimes impatient with him these days, and the older she got the more Evie could see Mum's point of view. Somehow Dad's jokes weren't as funny as they used to be, and Evie understood why her mother was beginning to look worn down and her smile had grown, like herself, thin. You couldn't live on laughs, after all.

What was that word Mary had used when Evie had once confided how annoying Dad's charm could be when you recognised how he worked it on you? *Exasperating.* Mary Sullivan, Evie's best friend, was clever. She always had her head in a book and knew a whole dictionary of good words. She even *had* a dictionary, so Evie reckoned 'exasperating' was probably exactly the right word for her father.

Evie glanced to where her brothers were labouring over their schoolwork at the kitchen table. Their heads were down in concentration so she risked opening the door a fraction wider and craned her neck through the gap. The two men were talking intently but their voices remained low. Then the stranger, with another jab of his pointed finger, turned and disappeared from view. Evie waited a minute, then made a show of opening the back door wide and treading heavily up the alleyway to greet her father where he had moved to stand in the open in front of the house. The summer's evening sun was low between the rows of back-to-back houses and for a moment a golden beam shone through the sooty air directly onto his face, showing his furrowed brow and his tired eyes with a fine trace of lines she had never noticed before. He was standing with his hands in his pockets, facing into the sun with his eyes closed, almost as if he were praying. Suddenly Evie saw that her handsome dad looked older than his years.

Michael Carter looked up at his daughter's approach and turned to her, his smile instantly back in place.

'You all right, Evie?'

'Just taking a rest before I tackle a pile of ironing. Grandma's got a bit of mending to do so I said I'd iron. She's really feeling the heat today.'

'Well, your gran's got her own insulation,' he said, winking. 'It's certainly hot work for a July evening.'

'It is that. But Gran will be taking the good stuff back early tomorrow, so we need to get on.'

'Oh, leave it, lass. Don't be beating yourself up. It'll wait for you.'

'That's what I'm afraid of, Dad. There'll be more tomorrow and I'll not have Mum or Gran doing my share. Gran's complaining about her feet, and I don't blame her. She's been on them since seven this morning.'

'She's a tough old bird, and a good 'un. Don't tell her I said so, mind.'

Evie and her father exchanged smiles.

Michael called across to Marie Sullivan, who lived in the house opposite and was sweeping dust off her doorstep. 'All right, Marie? Tell Brendan I'll see him for a drink later.'

'I'll tell him.'

He waved to old Mrs Marsh, who lived next door to the Sullivans, and who was out rubbing Brasso onto her doorknocker. Mrs Marsh was known to be house-proud. 'Evening, Dora. That's looking good. I'll find you a job at ours, if you like.'

'Give over with your cheek, Michael Carter,' she grinned.

Evie laughed along with her father. This street was home. She knew no other, and nor did she want to. But the question remained, who was that man with the creeping manner who had caused her father's smile to slip? She took a breath and decided to plunge in.

'Dad . . . who was that man?'

'What man?'

'Here, a few minutes ago. In the ginnel.'

'Here, you say?'

'Ah, come on, Dad. Talking to you. Just now.'

'Oh, *that* man . . . '

'Yes, *that* man. I don't think he lives round here. Is he a friend of yours?'

'Well, I wouldn't exactly call him a friend, love . . . '

'What then?'

'What?'

'Oh, for goodness' sake, Dad, do you have to be so *exasperating*? Who is he and what does he want, lurking round here? Is everything all right? Only you didn't look too pleased and it set me wondering.'

Michael turned the full beam of his smile on Evie, but she noticed that it didn't quite reach his eyes. 'It's a bit of business, that's all, love. Nothing for you to worry about.'

Evie fixed him with a hard stare. 'If you're sure, Dad,' she said doubtfully.

'As I say, sweetheart, nothing to bother yourself over. Or your mum.' He looked at her meaningfully until she nodded. 'Now why don't you go and look in the pantry where I think you'll mebbe find a bottle or two of cold tea cooling in a bucket on the slab. That'll help that ironing along, d'you reckon?'

Evie knew there was no point pursuing the matter of the stranger so she shrugged off her anxiety as Michael took her arm with exaggerated gallantry.

'C'mon, let's see if the boys have abandoned their homework yet. Your cold tea and ironing await, your ladyship,' he grinned.

'Too kind, your lordship,' Evie beamed, and, their noses in the air in a pantomime of the gentry, they spurned the alleyway and the back door, and let themselves in through the front, laughing.

~

'I don't know what you two have got to be so cheerful about,' Grandma Sue said, easing a swollen foot out of a worn and misshapen slipper. 'My ankles are plumped up like cushions in this weather. It's that airless I can hardly catch my breath.' She slumped down on one of the spindle-back kitchen chairs and began to massage her foot.

'Here you are, Gran, a cup of cold tea,' said Evie, emerging from the pantry and putting Gran's precious bone-china cup and saucer down on the kitchen table beside her. Sue had been given the china as a present when she left her job as a lady's maid to get married. No one else in the family would even think of borrowing it, knowing that the crockery was doubly precious to Sue because it had not only survived the war, it had outlasted Granddad Albert, too.

'Here you are, Mum . . . boys.' Evie placed mugs of the tea, which was no longer particularly cold, in front of her mother, Jeanie, and her younger brothers. Peter and Robert were frowning over their school homework, applying themselves to it with much effort and ill grace.

9

'Thanks, Sis,' Peter smiled on her. 'I'll just get this down me and then I'm off out to play football with Paddy.'

'Football, in this heat?' Sue shook her head and smiled. 'You're a tough one, an' no mistake.'

'Lazy one, more like,' said Jeanie, taking off her pinny. 'What have I said about not going out to play until you've done your homework?' She sat easing her back, then removed the turban she wore when she was working to try to prevent the steam from the copper frizzing her hair. As her mother raised her arms and pushed up her flattened curls, Evie noticed how sore her hands were. Mum liked to look nice but it was difficult in this heat, with all the steam and hard work. In winter it was even worse, though.

'It's too hot to do schoolwork. It's the play next week and no one's bothered about doing sums when there's the play to rehearse.'

'But you're not even in the play, are you, Pete? Isn't it just the little 'uns that are doing the acting?'

'I'm in the choir *and* I'm playing the whistle,' said Peter. 'You can't have a play without music.'

'That's right,' Robert had his say as always. 'Pete's got a solo.'

'Two solos,' Peter corrected. 'Anyway, it's only one more year before I'm fourteen and then I can leave school. I can read and write already – what more do I need when I'm going to be a musician?'

'A musician, is it now?' smiled Sue. 'I don't know where you get such fancy ideas.'

'Fifteen,' Michael corrected, coming out of the pantry with a second bottle of cold tea. 'You can't leave until you're fifteen.'

'But that's not fair. Evie left at fourteen. Why can't I?'

'Evie left to help Mum and Grandma Sue with the washing,' Michael reminded his elder son, not for the first time. 'The authorities turn a blind eye if you've got a family business to go into, especially when it's the best in Bolton.' He beamed at Jeanie and she rolled her eyes at his nonsense.

'And if I don't get on with that last pile of ironing I might as well have stayed at school,' Evie said, getting up and moving to the ironing board, beside which was a pile of pretty but rather worn blouses.

'I could always go and help you at the brewery until the music takes off, Dad,' Peter went on, adding innocently, 'I'm sure we need the money.'

'And you wouldn't be spending it in the pub like Dad does either,' Robert said, unwisely. 'Or betting on horses.'

Typical, thought Evie, in the brief silence that followed. When would Robert ever learn to keep quiet?

Jeanie, Sue and Michael all spoke at once.

'Shut up, Bob, and get on with your homework. I won't have you cheeking your father,' said Jeanie.

11

'I think you're asking for a clip round the ear, my lad,' said Sue.

'Ah, come on, son. A man's got a right to have some fun,' said Michael.

Robert lowered his head and began snivelling over his exercise book while Peter got up very quietly, collected his books into a neat pile and sidled over to the door.

'I'll see you later,' he muttered and left, taking his mug of tea with him.

Sue eased herself off the chair and made for the living room, where the light was better and where she kept her workbasket. 'I'll just finish that cuff on Mrs Russell's blouse and you can add it to the pile. I'm that grateful for your help this evening.'

'Oh, and I've found one with a missing button. Do you have a match for this?' Evie followed her grandmother through with a spotlessly white cotton blouse and showed her where the repair was needed.

Sue turned to her button box and Evie went back to the ironing, mussing up Robert's fair hair supportively as she passed. Robert was still sniffing over his schoolbooks, writing slowly with a blunt pencil. The distant sound of Peter's voice drifted up the alleyway from the street, Paddy Sullivan answering, and then the dull thud of a football bouncing.

'Right,' said Michael, 'I'll be off out. See you later, love.' He planted a kiss on the top of Jeanie's head and was gone. Jeanie didn't need any explanation.

She got up and took her tea into the living room to sit with her mother.

'Let's hope he comes back sober,' Sue muttered under her breath.

'He's usually better on a weekday,' Jeanie said loyally, 'and it's Thursday as well, so I reckon there isn't much left to spend anyway.'

They each lapsed into silence with a sigh.

~

Evie shared the attic bedroom with her grandma. It was hot as hell that night, as if all the heat from the street and the scullery and the kitchen had wafted up into the room and lingered there still. It was dark outside, although the moon was bright in the clear sky. Sue was lying on her back on top of her bed, her head propped up high on a pillow and with the bedclothes folded neatly on the floor at its foot. She was snoring loudly. Evie thought she looked like an island – like a vast landmass such as she'd seen in the school atlas – and Sue's swollen feet, which Evie could just see in the dark, looked enormous, being both long and very wide. Poor Gran, thought Evie, it must be a trial carrying all that weight on your bones in this weather.

It was Sue's snoring that had woken Evie and now she was wide awake and too hot to get back to sleep. The bed seemed to be gaining heat as she lay there and the rucked-up sheet was creased and scratchy. Lying awake and uncomfortable, Evie thought of the weaselly stranger she had seen earlier, how Dad had swerved her questions and obviously didn't want her to know anything about the man. He'd more or less admitted it was a secret from Mum, too, and therefore from Grandma.

I bet it's about money, Evie thought.

Her dad had a job at the brewery loading drays and doing general maintenance. She had long ago realised that it wasn't very well paid. Despite Jeanie's scrimping and all the doing without, though, Dad didn't seem to care. He just carried on going for a drink or three, and enjoying what he called 'a little flutter' on the dogs or the horses. 'You have to place the bet to have the dream of winning,' he had explained to Evie. 'A few pounds is the price of the dream.' Sometimes he did win. Mostly he didn't.

The laundry helped to support them. For someone so old – she was sixty-three and didn't care who knew it – Grandma Sue was full of go, always trying to think of ways to improve the little business. She offered mending and alterations, and had found new customers away from the immediate neighbourhood – people with a bit more to spend on the extra service.

Enterprise, Mary Sullivan had called it. 'Everyone admires your gran,' Mary had said. 'She doesn't sit around being old, she gets on with it.' Evie had to agree that Grandma Sue was amazing.

Evie looked at her now, lying on her back, snoring like billy-o, and grinned.

Getting up silently, Evie went to stand in front of the open sash window, desperate for a breath of cool fresh air. The rooftops of the houses opposite were visible but, from where she stood, there was no one in sight in the street. She lingered, breathing deeply of the hot, sooty air, leaning out and turning her head to try to catch any breeze.

Then she heard the echoing sound of approaching uneven footsteps and recognised her father coming down the street, weaving slightly, not hurrying at all, although it must be very late as he was the only person in sight. But – no, there was another man. Evie hadn't heard him, but suddenly the man was right there, outside the house. She leaned out further to see who had waylaid her father; it was the man she'd seen earlier. In the quiet of the night their voices drifted up to her, and her heart sank. Something was not right.

'I told Mr Hopkins what you said and he isn't prepared to wait that long,' growled the stranger. 'He wants his money now.'

'And I told you I don't have it,' Michael said. 'I'll pay him what I owe, I promise, but I need more time.'

'Mr Hopkins says you've had long enough. He'll be charging the usual rates from now.'

'Please, I can get it all by next month. I just need a bit longer to get sorted, that's all.'

'I'll be sorting you out if Mr Hopkins doesn't see his money soon,' snarled the man, leaning in close. Evie felt hot all over, the beginnings of panic flipping her stomach.

'Next week, then,' she heard her father pleading. 'I'll get it by the end of next week. C'mon now, I can't say fairer than that.' He tried for a friendly tone, a man-to-man kind of banter, but Mr Hopkins' man was not to be charmed from his purpose.

'Next week it is, then,' he said, 'but there'll be interest, too, don't forget. You should have paid up straight away, Carter. It's going to cost you more now. I'll be back to collect what you owe. All of it, *and* the interest. And if you don't pay – and I mean every pound of the debt – I wouldn't want to be in your shoes. You won't be able to talk your way out of it with Mr Hopkins. Let this be fair warning to you.' It was a dark warning.

The stranger seemed to melt away in the darkness, and Evie slowly sank down to the floor beside the window. She had a sense of trouble. Oh dear God, *every pound*. Dad owed Mr Hopkins pounds! And he had only until the end of next week to pay. And tomorrow was Friday already. How on earth had Dad got himself into that kind of mess? It couldn't be a bad bet on the horses. That might have wiped out his wages but wouldn't have led to such a debt, surely. Maybe this Mr Hopkins was a moneylender. Oh good grief, this was serious . . .

She sat numbly thinking about pounds of debt for a while, then got up stiffly and crept back to bed. Sue's snoring had subsided, thank heaven, and she was blissfully asleep. Evie lay down and tried to work through the situation in her head. Who else knew? No one, she guessed.

Evie wished that she didn't know, and her father's secret was so terrible that she couldn't unburden herself by sharing it with anyone, especially when her mum and grandma were so tired after working all hours doing laundry. She didn't want to worry them until she knew what was going on and how bad things were. First she'd have to confront Dad and see what he had to say, though she didn't hold out much hope of getting a straight answer. She'd already tried asking about the stranger and he'd pretended there wasn't anything wrong. No doubt he'd try to fob her off with some tale when she questioned him about what she'd overheard . . .

It didn't occur to her to leave the matter to her father to deal with alone. Now the truth was out she couldn't sweep it under the rug and forget what she knew. That was the kind of thing he did, and look where it had got him. He needed to face facts and do something about the trouble he was in. That awful man had sounded dangerous.

She tried to think of people who might be able

to help. The Sullivans were good friends. Perhaps she should go to Mary and Geraldine's father, Brendan. Dad might listen to Brendan. But it wasn't the Sullivans' problem and it would be unfair to burden them. Besides, money was probably tight there, too, as there were so many of them.

What about Billy? He was such a good man, so reliable, and she knew he'd do anything for her. But he hadn't got any money, she was sure. He was a postman but he hadn't been all that long in the job. He'd got his mother to support, too, as his dad had been killed in the war. And anyway, why should Billy give over whatever savings he might have to help her dad? But he was so wise, maybe he'd know of a way out of this mess . . .

Who did she know who could lend Dad the money he owed to this Mr Hopkins? Evie racked her brains but could think of no one. The most well-to-do person she knew was Mrs Russell, whose blouses she had been ironing that evening. But then she remembered the mended cuff Gran had worked on, the missing button and how worn the once-fine fabric now was with repeated washing. Mrs Russell was a step up from Shenty Street, but she was widowed and lived on what she had, which was not much. And anyway, Grandma would die of shame if the Carters took their problems to Mrs Russell. So would Evie herself, for that matter.

The burden of her secret and the anger she felt towards her father kept Evie awake until the early hours, when she eventually fell into a restless sleep. It was with heavy eyes and a heavier heart that she faced the next morning.

~

'You're looking peaky, love,' Jeanie remarked to Evie as they finished their breakfast of bread and scrape. 'I've got the copper heating and if you help me fill the dolly tub first, you can go with your gran to Mrs Russell's, if you like? Your dad's already gone and Pete can see to Bob so there'll be no one under my feet.'

Evie filled the dolly tub with hot water, then put in some washing soda, followed by some small items from the latest bundle. Then the sheets went in the copper with more washing soda and Evie pushed them underwater with some long wooden tongs.

'Help me load up, then.' Michael had made the trolley for them out of some orange boxes set on a frame with two axles, some pram wheels and a steering column handle. The box part was lined with an offcut of old sheeting to prevent splinters snagging the clothes. Evie laid the ironed and neatly folded bed linen inside, then placed the blouses carefully on top and covered them with a piece of fabric to keep off the dust. This had been Sue's idea, to keep the clothes clean and dry, and she'd fashioned the mac to fit snugly over the boxes like a pram cover.

19

Evie nearly blurted out her worries about her dad to Sue before they were two streets from home, but then she remembered her resolve of the previous night: not to say anything until she simply had to. There might yet be a way to deal with the mess Dad was in without spreading the worry around.

Mrs Russell lived not far from Queen's Park, and Sue and Evie cut through the back alleys, chatting about their washing schedule. But it didn't stop Evie worrying that the end of next week was the deadline for her father to pay back Mr Hopkins. She fell silent while Sue chatted on, unaware of her granddaughter's preoccupation.

'. . . We'll go to the boys' play, I reckon,' Sue was saying. 'I think we need to get tickets. I hope there's no charge for them. I'll ask Peter. It's no use asking Bob, bless him.'

Before long, they arrived at Mrs Russell's, a tall old-fashioned red-brick house that had been divided into two. Sue opened the gate and Evie wheeled the pram up along the tiled path, then round to the back door. A rose bush was in full bloom in the small front garden and she noticed its delicate scent was like the perfume Mrs Russell wore.

Mrs Russell's 'girl', Annie, opened the door, beaming at Sue and Evie.

'Come in and I'll go and tell the missus that you're here.'

Sue and Evie unloaded the trolley, passing the

items between them to lie neatly on a chair in Mrs Russell's large kitchen.

Annie showed them to the sitting room, then went to make a pot of tea. Mrs Russell's sitting room was like the lady herself, all pink and white and pretty.

'Good morning, Mrs Goodwin. And, Evie, my dear, how lovely to see you. Please, sit down. Annie will bring us some tea,' Mrs Russell greeted them.

Evie liked Mrs Russell, who was always friendly and fair and didn't treat Grandma Sue as if she wasn't fit to set foot in her house, as a couple of the women who sent them their washing did.

'How did you get on with that cuff that needed your expert attention?' asked Mrs Russell.

'I'll show you. Evie, love, will you fetch that blouse so Mrs Russell can see?'

Evie did as she was asked, admiring the soft colours of the wallpaper, so different to their home on Shenty Street with its constant smell of washing soda and damp sheets draped over the maidens. How quiet this house was, too. Kind of restful . . . Evie glanced into another room opening off the corridor before she reached the kitchen. There was a large comfy-looking sofa, and a small pile of books that looked as if they'd been read a lot. A piano, far bigger than the one at the school, stood at the window end.

Mum would love to sit there and sing a few songs around that piano, Evie thought. So would I . . .

She knocked on the kitchen door and retrieved

the blouse, then Annie followed her back with a tray of tea and some plain biscuits.

Mrs Russell admired the mend, which pleased Sue, although Evie knew that it had been an easy job for her, and then the two women drank their tea and chatted while Evie sipped hers and gazed round the room, daydreaming about living in such a house. On a side table in a smart frame there was a photograph of a man in air force uniform. Evie guessed it was Mr Russell.

'Well, must be getting on,' said Sue as soon as she'd finished her tea.

Mrs Russell counted the payment for the washing into her hands and Sue put the coins in her jacket pocket and thanked her for the tea.

'Annie will bring round the next wash on Wednesday morning as usual, Mrs Goodwin,' Mrs Russell assured her.

'Thank you, Mrs Russell. I'll see you next week,' answered Sue with a smile.

Then Annie showed Sue and Evie to the back door where they'd left the trolley.

'She's so nice,' said Evie as she wheeled the empty trolley back along the footpath.

'And a good woman. Doesn't think that just 'cos she's seen a bit of money she's any better than the rest of us. But poor woman lost her husband in the war, like Granddad Albert. She's got no children either and I think she might be a bit lonely. It's family that's important, not how smart your house is. Always remember that.'

'Yes, Gran,' said Evie, though she thought it would be nice to have some pretty things at home as well as her family.

The thought of family started her worrying about Michael and Mr Hopkins' man again. The coins Mrs Russell had paid Sue for the washing and mending would go nowhere towards a debt of *pounds*.

~

By the time Evie and Sue had wheeled the trolley as far as the top end of Shenty Street, they were both hot and tired.

'Look, there's Billy,' said Sue, seeing the postman pushing some mail through the last letterbox in the road.

'Hello, Mrs Goodwin. Hello, Evie. That's lucky, seeing you now. I've just finished my round for the day. Been up since cockcrow.'

'So have we,' Evie smiled. 'Best bit of the day, first thing.'

'I'll take the trolley home and you can join us in a minute, Evie,' suggested Sue, fully aware that her granddaughter and Billy had a special fondness for each other.

Evie had never been so glad to have a few moments alone with Billy. All the way home the worry about her father's debt had festered and she couldn't keep it to herself any longer. Billy was so wise and, not being family, he might be able to see straight what needed to be done.

Evie perched on the low wall at the side of the end house and Billy sat next to her, putting his empty bag down at his feet.

'What's up, Evie? You look like something's fretting you.'

'Oh, Billy,' her brown eyes filled with tears, 'it's a family thing really but I don't want to worry Mum and Grandma unless I have to. Trouble is, it's too big. I don't think I can deal with it on my own.'

'Is it your dad?' Billy knew Michael Carter had a reputation for being feckless but then a lot of men round here put their beer and their bets before their families. 'What's he done that's so bad you can't even tell your mum and grandma?' He'd heard Michael had been placing some heavier bets lately, more than just the odd shilling. He hoped it hadn't got out of hand.

Evie told Billy about the creepy man sent by Mr Hopkins and what she'd heard in the night.

'Oh, Evie, Hopkins is bad news,' said Billy, lowering his voice. 'He runs a card game. I've heard all sorts about it: that it's held upstairs at the King's Head. It sounds as if your dad's been playing cards there and has run up this debt.'

24

'Cards? Are you sure? Not horses or dogs? What do you think's going to happen, Billy?'

Billy thought better of telling Evie everything he'd heard about Mr Hopkins. 'Let me think . . . Hopkins will want to get the money off your dad if he can. Maybe your dad can agree to pay it back a bit at a time.'

'But it's pounds already. That might mean it's never paid off!' Evie was indignant.

'I don't see that he's any choice if he can't pay it all. He has to take responsibility, love.'

'But I'm afraid if I tell Dad all this he'll take no notice of me. He never likes to face up to problems and I'm sure he'd rather carry on as usual at the pub and betting on the races than pay what he owes Mr Hopkins. And I don't want Mum and Grandma to be scrimping and doing without because of what Dad owes, Billy. They've been working so hard and Mum's getting all worn out, and Grandma's feet are so swollen in the heat and she's bone-tired. She should be sitting down in a comfy chair and drinking tea like that nice Mrs Russell, not working to keep Dad in beer and card games.' Evie felt hot, angry tears springing to her eyes.

Billy put his arm around her shoulders and drew her to him, wrapping her in his comforting embrace.

'Do you want me to talk to your dad?' he asked after a minute in which Evie's tears subsided as he hugged her against his jacket.

Dad might take some notice of Billy, who was

older than she, and a man, of course, but she felt the responsibility for her family should be hers.

'Shall we both talk to him?' she suggested. 'I think he'll listen to you but it was me that found all this out, and he *is* my dad, after all.'

Billy stood up and took her hand. 'I'll come round this evening after he's had his tea and we'll say our piece then, all right?'

'Thank you,' said Evie, giving Billy a hug. 'I'll see you later.'

Billy kissed the top of her head, then let her go. As he took up his bag to go back to the depot, he watched Evie walking back to her house halfway along Shenty Street. Before she disappeared down the passage she turned to wave with a little smile and Billy felt his heart lift.

He retrieved his bicycle from where he'd chained it to a lamp post, worried about Evie's future.

Mr Hopkins had a reputation as a bully and there were some nasty stories about him. Billy didn't want anything violent to happen to Michael Carter. He was Evie's dad, and Evie's happiness was very close to Billy's heart. She was a hard worker and everything she did was to help her family, even giving up school, for all she loved it, to help her grandmother with the washing business.

As he cycled back to the mail depot, Billy resolved to help Evie in whatever way he could. She was an angel and he would never let her down.

CHAPTER TWO

Evie met Harold Pyke from down the road at the back of her house as he was leaving.

'What did Mr Pyke want?' she said, going into the scullery.

'He brought us some peas from his allotment. Says they're the first of the season,' Jeanie said.

Sue was wringing out some garments from the dolly tub and putting them in a large bucket, her hands red-raw from the morning's work. She winked at Evie and looked sideways at Jeanie, who was poking stray curls back under her turban with a damp hand.

'Just an excuse to come round and admire you in your pinny, if you ask me,' laughed Sue.

'Go on with you. He was only being kind,' said Jeanie, though she looked pleased.

'It wouldn't be the first time Harold Pyke's come round offering veg,' said Sue. 'You want to be

27

careful, our Jeanie. He'll be asking for something in return before long.'

'Well, what a thing to say!'

'Don't encourage him, then, lass.'

'I can't help it if the fella's taken a shine to me,' Jeanie gave a comical but telling little grin.

'Not just that fella, either,' said Sue. 'I'm not surprised he's bringing round peas, the way you've been tossing your hair around. It's nice to have the peas and that, but be careful not to fascinate him with your smiles and tossing your curls around.'

'How can I toss my hair when I'm wearing a scarf?'

'It's what you were doing, turban or no turban. And, as I say, there are others, too. That Derek Knowles, for instance. And Patrick Finlay from round the corner. We're not doing their washing for nowt but a cabbage and a bit of flirting.'

'I'm a happily married woman and I'm certainly not labouring over a hot copper for a cabbage or a bag of peas, so don't you worry.'

'So long as you've got that straight,' said Sue. 'Now, our Evie, what's Billy's news?'

'He's coming round later, after tea.'

'He's always welcome. He knows that,' said Jeanie.

Evie wished the business of her father's debt wasn't the reason for Billy's visit, but maybe with his help it could all be resolved without upsetting Mum and Grandma. Evie was feeling better now she'd spoken to Billy.

As she carried the bucket of clean wet clothes to the mangle in the outhouse, she decided not to worry any more about her dad until she had to. There was work to be done, and plenty of it.

~

It was mid-afternoon when the boys erupted into the house. Jeanie made them each a jam sandwich – thick bread, thin jam – and they went off noisily to play in the street with Paddy and Niall Sullivan, passing the Sullivan boys' sister Mary on their way out.

'Hello, Mrs Carter,' said Mary from the back door.

'Come in, lass,' Jeanie called out. 'That frock's come up smart, hasn't it?' she added to Mary. The school summer dress was second-hand, and Sue had altered it to fit Mary a treat. School uniform was expensive and Mary didn't mind that hers wasn't new. She was well aware how fortunate she was to be allowed to continue at school and study, the only one of the seven Sullivan siblings to do so.

'Mrs Goodwin's done a stupendous job with it,' said Mary.

Stupendous – whatever next? thought Jeanie.

'Is it all right if Evie and I go for a stroll up to the park? I won't be keeping her from her work, will I?'

'I've just finished,' announced Evie, beaming at

her best friend. 'Gran says she's got mending to do and I'll help Mum with the tea, so we won't have to be long.'

Mary looked to Jeanie for confirmation.

'Best get going, then,' Jeanie smiled.

Mary produced a paper bag of bull's-eyes from her pocket as the girls went outside and Jeanie could hear them giggling as they skipped down Shenty Street as though they didn't have a care in the world.

She smoothed down her pinny and put the kettle to boil, pleased to hear Evie's laughter. Her daughter had been oddly preoccupied today. Evie worked hard, and Jeanie worried that she sometimes forgot Evie was only sixteen, barely a woman yet.

Sue and Jeanie were enjoying a few minutes' sit-down with a well-deserved cup of tea when they recognised Michael's heavy footsteps approaching.

'Got the sack, didn't I?' Michael told them, untying his work boots before hurling them through the open back door in a show of temper. 'There was a mix-up about the maintenance of some pipes and there was a bad leak this afternoon and a lot of beer was lost. Mr Denby called me in. It was like he'd made a note of every single thing I've ever missed. I reckon he's had it in for me for a long while.'

'Oh, Michael!' Jeanie's face was completely white. Deep down she knew her husband was a slacker. He sometimes went into work the worse for wear from the night before, but he was popular at the brewery with his mates and it hadn't occurred to her that he might be less popular with his boss.

Sue kept quiet but her expression was grim.

'Couldn't you go and ask him for another chance?' Jeanie suggested quietly.

Michael gave a hollow laugh. 'No hope of that. I told him he could stuff his job and I was well out of it. He never remembers when I've done summat properly, only when he wants to pick holes. I told him that straight. I've had it with smarming round Denby, at his beck and call all day.'

'But he's the *boss*, Michael.'

'Aye, well, not any longer,' muttered Michael. 'I'll be my own boss from now on. I'll answer to no one. If you women can do it then so can I. I can tout my skills around, earn some money from my own gumption.' He gave a brief smile. 'Give folk a bit of the old charm, butter 'em up, like, I'll soon have plenty of satisfied customers.'

'Like you did Mr Denby, you mean?' muttered Jeanie.

Sue passed Michael a strong cup of tea with sugar in it. 'I think Jeanie means you'll need to find paid work straight away,' she said diplomatically, trying to keep the peace. 'It can take a while to build up customers when there's only you to do it.' She was fond of her son-in-law but she thought he lived too much by his belief in his luck, and not enough by hard graft.

'Look, I'm sorry, love. It's not your fault,' he went on, taking Jeanie's hand. He lifted it to his lips and planted a kiss on her rough skin. 'Mebbe I do need to find work with someone else. I'll have a look around and see what's going. There's proper house-building now – I'm sure I'll be able for summat. I'm going to have to be,' he added quietly, sounding unusually forlorn.

Jeanie got up and hugged him to her. 'Don't worry, you'll find a new job,' she said. 'In the mean-time the washing's going well and we can take in some more for a week or two, just to tide us over.'

'I'll ask around at church,' said Sue, though they were already working to capacity. 'That's where I heard about Mrs Russell, after all.'

As the two women rallied their own spirits and tried to pull him up with them Michael felt even worse. He wondered when would be the best time to break the news of his debt from the card game, realising even as he considered it that there would never be a good time. Maybe if he held his peace something would turn up . . .

'Dad, you're home early,' said Evie, appearing with the boys at the back door. 'Here, have one of these sweets – they were giving them away at the shop 'cos the box got wet or something. Anyway, they're all right.' She passed round the sweets and then looked properly at her parents.

'What? You two are a bit gloomy. You haven't had

bad news, have you?' she asked, wondering whether her father had told her mother about the debt to Mr Hopkins. Then again, it might be something quite different that was making them look so down; perhaps they'd heard someone was ill or even dead.

'Evie, would you go and collect Bob, please – you've probably seen him playing in the street – and Peter, too?'

'Yes, Mum.'

Evie's stomach was churning by the time she'd rounded up her brothers and they all trooped into the kitchen where their parents and Grandma Sue were now sitting round the table. Whatever it was, it was very serious.

'Mum, Dad, tell us. What's happened?' asked Evie.

'I'm out of work, lass,' said Michael solemnly.

'Oh, Dad . . . ' Peter said. 'But you'll find another job.' He sounded confident.

'Of course, Pete. I shall have to.'

'Will we starve?' asked Robert, looking anxious. 'Will we have to go and live in the woods, and eat berries and boiled nettles?'

'Give over your nonsense,' said Jeanie. 'I don't know where you get such daft ideas. We've got the washing, and your dad's going to find another job, so in a week or two it'll all be back to normal.' She ruffled Bob's hair and gave him a reassuring smile.

'But it won't be,' Evie blurted out. It was as if her mouth suddenly had a mind of its own.

33

They all turned to look at her and in that moment her suspicions were confirmed: Dad hadn't told Mum and Grandma Sue a word about the debt. It was time to face up to the truth. She couldn't keep quiet a second longer, as if she didn't know, while Mum and Grandma Sue tried to make the best of things and Dad sat there taking them in, pretending it was all going to be all right.

'What do you mean, love?' asked Sue. 'There's no need to get upset. We'll manage somehow.'

'I mean, what about Mr Hopkins? How on earth are we going to pay what you owe him, just from the washing, Dad?'

Michael sat open-mouthed and there was total silence. It was broken by Sue, who sprang to her feet with surprising speed, looming over Michael, her face a picture of fury.

'And who the hell is Mr Hopkins?' she roared.

~

'Right, Mum, I'm off to see Evie,' said Billy, putting a cup of tea down beside his mother's armchair. 'Have you got everything you need? I won't be late.'

'You're a good lad, Billy. I'm right as rain, don't you fret.'

Billy wasn't looking forward to helping Michael Carter sort out his problems repaying Mr Hopkins. Being a postman, Billy tended to know more than most what happened in several neighbourhoods, though he wasn't a gossip. He'd heard of at least two men who had been beaten up when they couldn't pay Hopkins, and some who had had their possessions taken by Hopkins' men in payment of their debts. Billy had thought before now that, what with Michael's drinking and his betting, if it hadn't been for the laundry the family would probably have gone under.

Billy got as far as the corner shop on Lever Lane, at the junction with Shenty Street, when Geraldine Sullivan emerged, rummaging in her handbag and bringing out a packet of Craven 'A' cigarettes.

'Hello, Gerry. Just finishing work, are you?'

'Yes, it's been a long day. Mr Amsell does the evening papers but it's my job to sweep up and tidy the storeroom. I'll be glad to get home and take these shoes off – and these stockings. It's that hot in the shop.' She fanned herself prettily and Billy tried not to think about her taking off her stockings.

Geraldine Sullivan was a real looker, with her glossy dark hair and her big blue eyes. If Mary had more than her fair share of brains, there was no doubt that her elder sister had got the beauty. Geraldine had worked at the corner shop ever since she'd left school. Billy thought she was seventeen or eighteen now but it was hard to tell, what with her red lipstick and her hair always nicely done. She had an easy way with the customers and Billy thought Mr Amsell had realised her beauty was an asset behind the counter as well as her manner, because he knew of several men, old and young, who would choose to go to Amsell's shop just to be sold a paper by Geraldine Sullivan.

'It's the way her hand brushes mine when she counts out the change,' Patrick Finlay had joked. 'Gives a man hope.' Patrick Finlay was sixty if he was a day, and was sweet on half the women in the neighbourhood, including Evie's mum.

'I hope Ma's got something nice saved for my tea,' Geraldine was saying. She laughed and added, 'That's if Da, Stephen, Jamie, Paddy, Niall and especially Cormac haven't scoffed it all.' Cormac was her youngest brother, aged five, who of all her siblings resembled her most. Plump and cute, he looked like a dark-haired cherub.

Billy joined in her laughter. 'Aye, you want to watch out for the little 'un. I reckon he's got the appetite of a brickie.'

Geraldine offered the open packet of cigarettes but Billy shook his head.

'No, thanks. That's one vice I haven't taken up,' he smiled.

Geraldine lit her cigarette, tipped her head back with a flick of her hair and blew a plume of smoke into the air. 'Why, Billy, what vices have you taken up, then?' She looked him directly in the eye. 'Do tell. I'm interested.'

'Ah, man of mystery, me,' Billy replied.

'I like a mystery,' Geraldine said. 'That's what we need round here, a bit more excitement, don't you agree?'

'Mmm . . . ' Billy nodded, unsure quite what he was agreeing with. Still, it was pleasant strolling down to Evie's in easy and attractive company, and fortunately, before Geraldine's flirting got too much for him, they reached her house.

'Thanks for walking me home, Billy. Always nice to see you.' She gave the merest wink, produced her key from her bag and opened the front door. 'See you soon,' she promised with a glamorous red smile over her shoulder, and closed the door behind her.

Phew, that Geraldine is getting to be quite a girl, Billy reflected. Not many round here had her style. She reminded him of Elizabeth Taylor in that comedy he'd seen with Evie at the cinema – *Father of the Bride*. Evie's prettiness was more homely, with her short brown hair clipped back behind her ears, her natural complexion and her girlish figure.

Reluctantly his thoughts turned to the task ahead of him at the Carters'. Best get it over with, and he'd be pleased to help allay Evie's worries if he could. She was a darling girl and she shouldn't have to be worried about her father owing money. He crossed over the road, went up the side to the back door and was surprised to find it closed. He gave a knock and Evie came to open it. Her eyes were red and it was clear she'd been crying.

'Oh, Billy, thank goodness you're here.' She pulled him inside and closed the door. 'It's worse than I thought. Dad's lost his job and there's all this money to find to pay that Mr Hopkins and we don't know what to do now.'

'Sit yourself down, love.' Sue poured Billy a mug of tea. 'Michael's told us the worst and it's twenty-five pounds he owes.'

'It'll never be paid,' sobbed Jeanie, wiping her eyes with an already sodden handkerchief. 'How on earth will we ever get that much?'

'We need to know a bit about this Mr Hopkins,' said Sue. 'Evie says you've heard of him.'

'I have, Mrs Goodwin.' Billy glanced around to see if Peter and Robert were within earshot but there was no sign of them.

'I've sent the boys to their bedroom,' said Sue, correctly understanding him.

'It's not good news, I'm afraid. Mr Hopkins runs a card game upstairs at the King's Head. I've heard the stakes start low, but once you're drawn in they soon get a lot higher.'

'The King's Head?' gasped Jeanie. 'Michael, you told me you went to the Lord Nelson with Brendan as usual. I thought this was something to do with the horses. How many other lies have you told me?'

'I did go to the Nelson with Brendan,' said

Michael. He added in a small voice, 'But I hadn't had much luck with the horses lately so when I heard there was a card game at the King's Head I thought I'd give it a go. I didn't mean to get in deep. I thought if I went on a bit longer my luck would change and I'd be on to a winning streak.'

'Pathetic!' said Sue wrathfully. 'Go on about this Hopkins, lad.'

'Well, he tends to win at the cards and then he makes a point of collecting his debts.'

'You mean by force?' asked Michael, looking even more worried.

'By any means he can. He'll bring in bailiffs to take your furniture, and he's been known to be violent if he thinks you're withholding what you could be paying him. And I've heard that once he starts adding on the interest it's difficult to clear the debt.'

'What are we going to do?' sobbed Jeanie. 'We'll be ruined . . . '

Billy looked down at his hands, reluctant to agree that this was exactly the situation. A miserable silence settled on the five of them as they tried to think of a solution.

'When did you say the money is due?' asked Billy.

'Friday,' said Michael, nervously.

The silence resumed. Billy was beginning to see the only possible course of action but it seemed so drastic that he was unwilling to suggest it.

39

'Nothing for it but to leave,' said Sue.

Billy was glad she had been the one to voice what he was thinking.

'What, leave our house and the washing and everything, and go right away?' said Jeanie, aghast.

'It isn't our house, it's rented,' said Michael. 'And we'll be out of here anyway if we can't pay the rent.'

'So whose fault would that be?' Jeanie screamed. 'I married you for better or for worse, Michael Carter, but I never thought the worst would be this bad. You'll have us all homeless. I can't believe what you've brought us to.'

'C'mon on, love. No need to get hysterical.'

'What do you expect me to be when it looks like I'm going to lose everything I've got and it's all your fault?' She had bitten her tongue for years but now everything was pouring out. 'Where were you when Mum and I were washing and ironing half the night to make ends meet? I'll tell you where: down the Nelson, drinking your wages and putting bets on half-dead three-legged nags that should have been at the knacker's. Or was it down the King's Head, playing some card game you probably didn't understand against some crook with marked cards?'

'It was bad luck—' Michael began.

'It *was* bad luck all right,' screeched Jeanie. 'It was bad luck for me that I ever set eyes on you!'

She got up and rushed out, slamming the kitchen

door behind her. The others heard her stomping upstairs and then the bedroom door crashing shut.

Evie and Billy exchanged embarrassed glances.

'I'll go up when she's had a chance to calm down,' said Sue.

'I'll go . . . .' said Michael, rising from his chair.

'You've done enough. Sit down and stay here until we've sorted this out,' Sue barked, and Michael slumped in his chair, defeated.

Evie cleared her throat. 'What do you think, Billy? Is Grandma right? Is running away the best thing to do?'

'I'm afraid it is. If you can't pay Hopkins what you owe, he'll dog you until you do, Mr Carter. The only way to be free of him is to leave and go somewhere he doesn't know. That means right away from here, to another part of the country.'

'Leave not just our home but all our friends? But this is all we've ever known,' said Evie, looking pleadingly at Billy.

'It'll be hard, love, and I wish I could say different, but I think it's the only way. Is that what you're thinking, Mrs Goodwin?'

'I'm afraid so, Billy. We'll have to keep quiet about it, too, as we don't want Hopkins after us where we've gone. And we'll have to go soon before word gets round about Michael losing his job or Hopkins' men will be here to take what they can sooner rather than later, if they think that's all they'll be getting.'

41

Billy nodded. Evie's grandma had grasped the situation exactly.

'But where will we go?' Evie asked. 'We don't know anywhere but here. We don't even have any relatives we can go to.' She looked as if she were about to cry again and Billy passed her his clean handkerchief.

'Don't fret yourself, Evie. At least you'll all be together.'

'But I won't be together with all my friends, and if it has to be a secret I won't be able to tell them where we've gone either,' Evie sniffed. 'I won't be together with you,' she added.

'I know, love, but I won't lose sight of you, I promise. I'll know where you are and I can keep a secret. Your gran's right: it would be better to tell as few folk as possible and to go as quickly as you can before Hopkins gets to hear.'

'Then it had better be straight away,' Michael said, getting up and prowling around the kitchen worriedly. 'By Monday all the folk at the brewery will know I've been sacked.'

'Right, well, I've been thinking,' Sue declared, 'and I think we should decide where we're going this evening. We can't just set off empty-handed and with no idea where we're heading.' She took a lined writing pad and a chewed pencil of Robert's from a drawer behind her. 'Let's make a list of what we know.'

Evie looked blank. 'I don't know anything, Grandma.' Michael was shaking his head, too.

'Nonsense,' said Sue. 'Buck up, the pair of you. And you, Billy. Let's put our heads together and see what we can manage.'

'Right,' said Billy, determined to rise to Evie's grandma's expectations. 'As I say, it'll have to be somewhere far enough away that Hopkins doesn't know it. You'll have to sort of . . . disappear. North is what Hopkins knows. So that means going south.'

'Good thinking,' Sue muttered, writing it down. 'And we'll need to find somewhere to live and then some work.' She looked up and gave Michael a meaningful stare.

'We don't know about those things, but I've an idea who might be able to help,' said Evie. 'Mr Sullivan.'

'Aye, Brendan can be trusted to keep quiet and he has family all over the place,' Michael said. 'I'll go over and get him, shall I?'

'You do that,' said Sue, 'but remember not to say anything while you're there. The Sullivans are good folk but you don't want to let slip our business to the entire houseful in case it accidentally gets passed on.'

Michael collected his boots from where he'd thrown them out of the back door, put them on and went to fetch Brendan.

~

It was late that night that Evie let Billy out through the back door and the Carters went wearily to bed. To Evie it felt as if years had passed since she'd gone to Mrs Russell's that morning with Grandma Sue.

There wouldn't be another wash for Mrs Russell, though. When Annie came with the bundle on Wednesday she'd find the house empty and the family gone. Evie felt sorry to be letting down the kindly widow and the other loyal customers.

Brendan had shown himself to be a true friend that evening. He'd listened to Michael's account of how he'd been kicked out so unfairly from his job and commiserated wholeheartedly. He'd been less sympathetic about the card game and the debt to Mr Hopkins – 'I told you not to go near the King's Head, Michael. You may as well be playing cards with the devil himself as that Hopkins fella' – and then he got down to practicalities in a way that made Evie think how lucky Mary was to have such a clear-thinking and sensible father.

Not only had Brendan got a cousin with a big van, who could transport them and as many of their belongings as could fit in it, but he also had a friend who lived well over a hundred miles south. Brendan's friend Jack knew of an empty property that he thought the Carters would be able to rent, at least until they found something better. Jack had his ear to the ground and he said he'd look out for any jobs going for Michael, too.

Brendan fixed all this up from the public telephone box outside Mr Amsell's shop, waiting for
incoming calls to learn the facts and confirm the
details, and writing them all down. The arrangements for renting the empty place were hazy, to say
the least, but the Carters had the address and
Brendan's word on the reliability of his friend. In
the circumstances, even such vague progress felt
like something to be positive about.

Not long after Brendan came over, Jeanie had
been persuaded to come downstairs and she'd
brought the boys down with her to join in the discussion.

'They're in this with us. It affects all of us, and
Peter and Robert need to know what's going to
happen . . . and why,' she said, looking at Michael
with her eyes narrowed.

'You're right, lass,' said Michael. 'It's all going to
be an exciting adventure, eh, fellas?'

Robert nodded dumbly, not really understanding.
Peter, his mouth a tight line, looked away, ignoring
his father.

Brendan had brought a couple of bottles of
Guinness across with him 'to help things along',
which pleased Michael, who emptied and refilled
his own glass with remarkable speed.

By the end of the evening Sue's bold handwriting
covered several pages of the writing pad and the
plan for the Carters to move had a timetable. Fergus

45

Sullivan, Brendan's cousin, was bringing the van at dawn on Sunday morning and the family were to have everything they wanted to take packed ready and piled by the front door, to be loaded quickly and discreetly.

'I'll come over and give you a hand,' Billy said. 'It's my day off and I'm used to getting up early.'

'Thank you,' Jeanie said. 'What will we do without you?'

'Oh, Mum . . . ' Evie's heart was heavy with her grief. 'We're going to have to find out, that's for sure.'

Now, as she climbed into bed in the stuffy attic room and wished Grandma Sue a goodnight, she felt hot tears running down her face. One more day in this house, the only home she had ever known. Even now she could hardly believe it. And in about . . . she totted it up quickly . . . thirty hours she would be parted from Billy.

Please, let it not be for ever, she whispered.

CHAPTER THREE

'IT'S HERE,' SAID Peter, who had been looking out of the front window for Fergus Sullivan's van.

It was four o'clock on Sunday morning, the summer daylight pale. To the Carters, the air felt unusually clear. All the previous day they had packed their belongings, choosing carefully what was essential and what could be left behind. Even some of the furniture was to remain here because, as Sue reminded her family, the van would need to be loaded as fast and as quietly as they could do it so they could make their escape.

'Escape' – as if from a prison, Jeanie thought. As if staying here would be a punishment instead of the life she had made for herself and her family. She was finding it difficult to be civil to Michael even now, though she'd tried to encourage her children to pack up their belongings and clothes with light hearts and a sense of adventure. Evie and

Peter were old enough to pretend they were excited for Robert's sake, but as Robert was not a naturally light-hearted child anyway they soon abandoned this pretence.

Evie was in charge of extracting suitcases from under beds and she helped Robert to fold his clothes into one of them. There was so much to do in so little time, and keeping busy helped prevent her from becoming more upset. She knew Mum and Grandma Sue were furious about the move but it was no good stoking the flames of their anger with her own.

Peter had been very quiet since the decision to go had been made. He'd packed a duffel bag with his few treasured possessions, and silently helped bring items downstairs until the front room was full of boxes, cases and bagged-up bits and pieces, mainly chosen by his mother.

Sue, with Evie's help, had been busy finishing the washing. Luckily, it was the end of the week, so they weren't due to take in any new bundles. All that remained was collected by the owners, who came to the back door, so there was no need to hide the evidence of the approaching early morning flit piled high in the front room. It was an uncomfortable lie to call a cheerful 'See you next week' to loyal customers, but there was no alternative.

Now, as a large dirty white van pulled up in front

of the house, it was time to move. Evie had imagined a huge removal lorry but this was half the size and had no name painted on the side.

Fergus was let in through the front door and greeted Michael, Jeanie and Sue with a friendly handshake and a smile.

'Right, let's be having you,' he said, speaking softly so as not to disturb the quiet of the sleeping street. 'Beds first and we'll see what else we've got room for after that.'

'What! I'm hoping to take the settee and the chairs and table, at least,' said Jeanie. 'And the mangle has to go.' She was realising it was the size of the van that would dictate what went with them and what was left, not the speed of loading it.

'I'll do what I can, Mrs Carter, don't you worry,' beamed Fergus.

During the next hour it became clear to Evie that this was his answer to everything, and his smile never faded.

Brendan came over to help and the men began to load the heavy items while Sue supervised them and ticked items off her list. Evie packed up some smaller things that they'd needed the previous day, and Jeanie got weepy and wrung her hands.

As Evie was wrapping the last of the crockery in newspaper, being extra careful with Grandma Sue's precious cup and saucer, there was a tap at the back door and Billy let himself into the kitchen.

'Hello, Evie. Let me take that box through to the front,' he said quietly, coming over and giving her a hug. 'You all right?'

'Oh, Billy, thank you for coming to help. I'm that glad to see you.'

'Now don't get upset. You know why this has to be done.'

'We're going away from everything and everybody that we know and care for.' Her heart felt as if it was going to burst.

'You've still got all your family around you. That's what your grandma always says, isn't it: it's family that's important. As long you have each other, nothing else matters.'

'And *you*, Billy. *You* matter to me. I won't have you where we're going.'

'I'll be waiting for your return, never fear, Evie.'

'You mean that, Billy? You'll wait for me to come back? But what if I never do?'

'You will. Here is where you belong, Evie. You'll know where to find me when you come home to Lancashire. But even supposing you don't return here, you can be sure that I'll come and find you where you are. We won't be apart for ever.' He wrapped her in his strong arms and kissed her tenderly. 'In the meantime, we can write to each other. We'll write often. I've never been south and I should like to know what it's like,' he smiled.

'Yes . . . of course. I'll send a letter with the address

when I know we're going to be staying there and not moving on at once.'

'Then do it as soon as you can, my darling, 'cos I'll be looking for that letter every day.'

He gave her another hug and wiped a treacherous tear away from her face with his thumb.

'Now, to work. As I came past I saw all the beds are stowed, and your gran and mum are organising the men moving furniture from the front room. I'll take this box while you make sure you've got a couple of pans packed up, and the knives and forks.'

'Gone already,' said Evie with a brave smile. 'Come on, you can help Dad, Brendan and Fergus with putting the big stuff in the van and I'll help Grandma tick off what's done on her list. Remember, keep your voice down. We don't want half the road in on the act.'

As the van got ever fuller, final decisions were made about what had to be left, and the time to depart grew closer, Evie dreaded having to say goodbye to Billy. She was taking a last look round upstairs when she heard the voice of Brendan's wife, Marie.

'Just wanted to wish you luck, me darlin',' said Marie. 'You're in safe hands with Fergus. Don't forget to let us all know how you're doing. It won't be the same round here without you.'

'Thank you. We'll miss you too, Marie,' sniffed Jeanie, who was looking sadly at all the furniture left behind with no room in the van.

'Thanks for everything,' said Sue, hugging each of her neighbours, including Brendan. 'You've been right good friends to us and I won't forget that.'

'Yes,' said Michael. 'Thank you. I'm sorry to have put you to all this trouble.'

'Go on with you,' said Marie, just as Sue said, 'I should think so, too.'

'Goodbye, Mary,' Evie whispered to her friend, hugging her close. 'You're the best friend a girl could ever have – and the cleverest. I'll write, I promise.'

'Dear Evie, there'll be a hole in my life when you've gone. I shall miss you dreadfully.'

'And I'll miss you, Mary.' Evie tried to smile. 'Who's going to teach me long words now?'

'Come on, we'd better get going.' Sue gathered up her handbag, which was bursting at the seams. 'We'd better get off now before we attract unwelcome visitors,' she added meaningfully.

As Michael pulled the door to and posted the key back through the letterbox, the family moved towards the van and their neighbours went back over the road. Billy and Evie turned to one another for the last time.

'Goodbye, Billy,' said Evie, hugging him tight. 'I'll be in touch very soon, I promise.'

'Bye, my Evie,' Billy said, his voice raw with emotion. Then he bent down and kissed her mouth and their tears mingled.

'Don't forget me, will you?' she pleaded.

'I said I'll be waiting,' he reminded her as they drew apart.

'I love you,' Evie whispered, but he'd already turned away to hide his tears and she wasn't sure he'd heard.

It was a terrible squash to fit everyone in the van, although there were big extra seats that folded down behind, sideways on to the front ones. Sitting there meant finding room for your legs around the luggage, however, so it was hard to get comfortable. Peter and Evie were sharing a seat and Robert had to sit on Jeanie's knee. Fergus started the engine and all the Carters waved to their friends congregated outside the Sullivans' house to give them a silent send-off.

Evie fixed her eyes on Billy's face, but within a few seconds it was lost from her sight. The van turned the corner at the end of the road and Shenty Street was gone.

As Fergus happily negotiated the streets heading to the road that would take them south, the Carters sat nursing their regrets. Jeanie was openly sobbing and even Sue was tearful, which set off Evie, and Robert was crying, too. Michael was subdued but, wisely for once, decided to say nothing. Evie, squashed up beside Peter, took his hand in hers to comfort him, but when she looked into his face she saw not sadness but such fury that she felt a strange and terrible foreboding and withdrew her own hand in shock.

The van reached the southern outskirts of the town and the blackened industrial buildings gave way to houses with gardens and, soon, green fields. The Carters dried their eyes, made themselves as comfortable as they could and accepted the inevitable. The old life was gone and a new one, whatever it held, lay ahead of them at the end of this journey.

'I still wish I'd been able to say goodbye to Mrs Russell,' said Grandma Sue over her shoulder to Evie, who sat behind her. 'And Dora Marsh. I've known Dora . . . must be forty years. We were young brides together.'

'There are a lot of folk I'd like to have said goodbye to. Seems rude just to go, like they meant nothing to us,' Jeanie agreed. She paused for a few moments and then added: 'I wish I'd been able to say cheerio to Harold Pyke.' Then she started laughing rather shakily and soon everyone joined in, even Robert, who didn't know what was funny.

The mood lifted as they drove on and the sun rose higher on the promise of a beautiful day.

After a while Robert piped up: 'I spy with my little eye something beginning with . . . '

Sue and Evie caught each other's eye in the wing

mirror and pulled faces. It was going to be a long journey.

~

'Where are we?' said Peter, waking from a deep sleep. Sue and Evie had also nodded off, and Robert was still asleep on his mother. 'It must be the sight of those mattresses that sent me to sleep. They look so comfy compared to this seat.'

Everyone gazed out of the windows at the countryside they were passing through. In the strong summer sunshine the scene was glorious.

Evie wished she hadn't slept and missed seeing some of this: on either side of the road hedges grew tall and green, dog roses twining through them. At breaks in the hedges, through field gates, she could see cows and sometimes horses grazing. It was all so huge and so green that she couldn't quite believe her eyes.

'Countryside – there's just so much of it,' said Peter. 'I'd no idea it was so big.'

'And the air smells different – sort of nice,' said Sue, winding down the window.

They continued travelling south, amazed at how green everything was and how clean. Sometimes they passed through a town or village and Jeanie would point out a pretty house and wonder aloud if they were heading for one like that.

Eventually Sue looked at her watch and declared

it was 'dinnertime' and if Fergus would like to find a suitable place to stop they could have something to eat. Fergus turned off the road in the next market town and pulled up in a car park where there was, everyone was pleased to see, a sign for public lavatories. The little town was quiet on a Sunday lunchtime and the shops were closed when Jeanie took her children for a short walk to stretch their legs after enduring the cramped seats.

When everyone was back at the van and standing around in the sun, Sue got out a cake tin, which was filled with rather warm sandwiches, and when they'd eaten those, another in which there was cake, and Jeanie poured lemonade from a flask. Michael produced a bottle of beer with a flourish, which Fergus declined to share because he was driving. Evie noticed that her father drank it all himself then.

The sandwiches and most of the cake eaten, the Carters and Fergus climbed back into the van and set off again. There was a stop at a petrol station, where Sue paid for the van to be refuelled and bought some boiled sweets, but by mid-afternoon the novelty of the journey had worn off and everyone was bored, fidgeting and eager to arrive. They had long since passed signs for the city of Birmingham and still they headed south.

'Not too far now,' said Fergus when Robert asked for the tenth time if they were nearly there. 'We'll be there before nightfall, don't you worry.'

'Thing is, Fergus,' said Peter, reasonably, 'it isn't dark until nine o'clock, so that's quite a long time yet.'

'It could well be,' said Fergus, vaguely. 'We'll have to see how it goes . . . '

'Do you know what this place is like, Fergus? Have you ever been there before?' asked Jeanie.

'No, I haven't, Jeanie. I just said to Brendan that I'd take you in the van. I think it might be quite a small village as I've never heard of it and I had to look up the way on a map. I don't think Brendan knows much about it either. But he trusts his friend Jack Fletcher so it'll be all right, don't you worry.'

'But it is all right for us to be there?' asked Jeanie, beginning to get anxious. 'We don't know this Jack Fletcher, and Brendan's a long way away now.'

Seeing Jeanie quietly wringing her hands, Evie picked up her mother's mood and began to worry too. What if there had been a mistake and there wasn't an empty house after all? What if someone else was living there? Or maybe there'd been a mix-up and they'd been given the wrong address? Or he could have been misled by the owner of the house . . .

Peter, sensing her distress, nudged her gently with his elbow. 'C'mon, Evie, it might even be nice,' he whispered bravely.

~

57

It was late afternoon when Fergus drove past a shabby-looking farm and slowed down at a sign announcing a village.

'Here we are,' he said. 'Church Sandleton.'

Everyone sat up and peered out to try to get the gist of the place. There was an assortment of old and new houses lining the road, a pub and a couple of shops.

'Slow down, Fergus, and let's remind ourselves what it is we're looking for,' Sue said, fishing the writing pad out of her handbag. Then she had a rummage around for her reading glasses and Fergus pulled into the side of the road while she found them and put them on. 'The house we're looking for is called Pendles, so keep your eyes peeled for that name,' she said.

'Pendles . . . ' Michael murmured, looking to the right and left, while Evie, Peter and Jeanie craned forward in their seats to see the nameplates on gates as Fergus drove slowly on.

Jeanie caught sight of a cottage with a garden full of blooming roses and lavender. 'Slow down, Fergus. Is that it?' She squinted hopefully at the sign on the gatepost, then saw it said Lavender Cottage. 'No . . . ' Disappointed, she sat back.

'Wait, wait, what's that one?' said Sue, pointing over to Fergus's side of the road where a fine square house was set back with a black front door and steps up to it from a wrought-iron gate. 'P . . . It's

P-summat, I can't quite see . . . ' She couldn't keep a note of hope from her voice.

'Prospect House,' said Fergus, and everyone sighed and subsided in their seats.

'It must be on this road somewhere because the address is "High Street",' said Sue.

'Brendan told me that Jack Fletcher said it's towards the end of the village. I thought we'd find it easily,' Michael added.

The end of the high street was in sight as the buildings became more widely spaced and gave way to hedges and fields ahead of them. Evie felt a flicker of panic. What if there was no such place? Would they end up living out of Fergus's van? She dismissed the ridiculous thought immediately but her stomach was now churning nervously.

'It's just a derelict shop this side and what looks like it might be a market garden over there,' said Sue. 'We must have missed it. Let's turn round and go through again.'

'No, wait,' said Michael. 'There! Over the shop. It's called Pendle's. It must be that.'

'It can't be,' breathed Jeanie faintly. 'No one said anything about a shop. We're looking for a house.'

'It has to be that,' insisted Michael. 'Stop here, Fergus, and let's have a look.'

Fergus pulled up and Michael climbed stiffly out and went to the front of the boarded-up shop. There was a door at one side with wood planks nailed over it and a heavy padlock securing a hasp. Next to it was a large expanse of window, also covered in planks. The paintwork around the window, what was visible of the door and on the fascia, was a dull green. The deep fascia spanned the whole of the front and on it in peeling gold capital letters was painted the name 'PENDLE'S'.

There was no doubt this was the right name, Jeanie saw. She hoped it wasn't actually the right building, that there would somehow be another place called Pendles, and it would look more like, if not Prospect House then at least that cottage with the pretty garden they'd passed earlier.

'Brendan said the key would be here, is that right, Sue?' called Michael, looking up at the building, his back to them all waiting in the van.

Evie guessed her father was disappointed too and hiding his face until he was ready to put on a brave show.

'Round the side, under a brick, apparently,' confirmed Sue.

Michael went up the side of the shop, saw a ruined-looking wooden door, lifted the sneck and disappeared through it. A few moments later he reappeared holding up a key.

Oh dear, thought Evie. That means it really is the right place. And it's going to be awful, I know it is.

She could hardly bear to watch as her father fitted the key to the padlock and it opened. Everything now had a dreadful inevitability. He removed the padlock, eased open the door with its planks attached to the frame and went inside.

'Come on,' said Sue, heavily, climbing out of the van. 'I think we're home.'

~

The Carters and Fergus stood in the shop part of the building. The good news was that the electricity was on so they could at least see how awful the place was behind the boarded-up window. There was long counter parallel to the interior wall and floor-to-ceiling drawers and shelves against the far wall. They were empty and dusty, a few dead flies littering the surfaces and the front window, and mouse droppings on the floor. There was no indication what Pendle's had ever sold or how long the place had been empty, but the smell was stale as if it had been abandoned a while ago.

'God save us,' muttered Jeanie, her voice trembling. 'A shop. Not even a proper house.' Her face was white with tiredness and disappointment.

'You stay here. I'll go and look upstairs,' said Sue. She thought she'd better learn the worst and break it to Jeanie gently rather than risk her kicking off unprepared. It had been such a long day, it didn't look like they would be able to get to bed for ages yet and Sue had the unhappy idea that Jeanie's fuse might just be ready to blow. 'Come with me, Peter, Evie, and let's see what we can find.' She opened the door behind the counter and sure enough it led to a hallway with two rooms opening off and a flight of stairs to the floor above.

'Right, you two,' Sue began when the door had closed on weighted hinges behind them. 'Your mum's had enough and I don't blame her. Let's see what works, what we can get working this evening, and decide where everyone's going to sleep. Everything else can wait until tomorrow.'

'Are we really going to live here, Grandma?' asked Peter. 'Did Dad know it was a shop?'

'I don't know and I don't know, Pete, but we're here tonight and the main thing is we're all together. So far as I know no one on earth has ever heard of Church Sandleton, so we're most likely safe from that Mr Hopkins.'

As she spoke she led her grandchildren into the first of the downstairs rooms behind the shop. It was a large sitting room, empty of furniture, with a dirty wooden floor and a bare light bulb suspended from the centre of the ceiling. Evie tried the switch and the bulb glowed dimly. Through the unboarded window they could see into a small backyard, paved but with weeds peeping through between the slabs. There was a little brick building at the end, which they all guessed was a privy.

'It'll do,' said Sue stoutly, looking round the room.

'Your mum and I will know what to do with this, I reckon.'

Evie smiled, feeling less dismal, and she saw Peter was bucking up, too.

'The kitchen will be the other room,' said Sue. 'It's make or break there, I reckon,' she added, leading Evie and Peter back to the cramped hallway and into the room next to the sitting room.

'It can be put right and your mum will come round to it – if we're allowed to do as we like, that is. It's not our place, don't forget. I haven't had a chance to work it out yet, but I think we're renting it from Jack's friend, and we don't even know who he is yet . . . Oh, this is big. It must be twice the size of Shenty Street's kitchen. Needs a lot of cleaning, though,' she added, looking at a solidly built but very grubby cream-coloured electric cooker.

Evie opened a door at the back and found a pantry with a cold slab and a vent to the outside to keep the air cool. It was empty except for a cardboard box on one of the shelves. It looked like a recent addition, being free of dust, and she opened it and gasped in astonishment.

'Look, Grandma,' she said, bringing it out and putting it on the built-in dresser. 'There's a note with Dad's name on it and a loaf of bread and a packet of tea. Who can have left this?'

'One way to find out,' said Sue, unfolding the

lined sheet of paper and holding it at arm's length because she'd left her glasses in her handbag in the shop room. 'It's no good, Evie, you'll have to read it to me. Never mind it's addressed to your dad.'

Evie saw that the letter was elegantly written with a fountain pen:

> *Dear Mr Carter,*
>
> *I hope you have had a good journey. I am sorry about the state of the shop. Jack Fletcher says you are a friend of his and need a place to stay, so I hope it will do for now.*
>
> *The electricity is working. Please accept the bread and the tea.*
>
> *I look forward to meeting you shortly.*
> *Yours sincerely,*
> *Frederick Bailey*

'Well I never!' exclaimed Sue. 'Our first piece of good luck, and I'm hoping not the last. 'Course, we've never met Jack Fletcher, but let's not fret about details. Obviously Brendan has some influence with folk, even down here. Maybe things aren't as bad as we thought.'

'I'll go and show Mum,' said Evie.

'You do that, love. It might just pull her back from the brink. Peter and I will go and look upstairs and see if we can cope, eh? Whoever this Frederick Bailey is, at least he knows this place is a shambles. Mebbe

he'll be round in the morning to sort it all out.'
Though I wouldn't bet on it, she thought.

Upstairs was pretty grim, too, but there was an
electric water heater over a wash basin, and even a
working lavatory. The three bedrooms were bare of
furniture, dusty and stuffy in the heat, but there
would be room for all of them, as there had been
in Shenty Street.

'I think we're staying, at least until we sort out
summat better, don't you?' Sue asked her grandson.

'I reckon you're right, Grandma. Let's go and tell
Fergus we can start unloading the van. It's going to
be dark soon and I'm that hungry I can hear my
tummy singing.'

'Good thinking, young fella,' said Sue. 'I won't
put up with an unclean house, but just for tonight
I think I may have to break that rule.'

~

The van was unloaded far quicker than it had been
packed up that morning. Fergus and Michael took
the bedsteads and then the mattresses upstairs
between them while Jeanie and Evie carried in the
chairs and the boxes for the kitchen. The mangle
went into a corner of the kitchen.

Fergus was invited to stay the night, Peter agreeing
to double up with Robert so as to leave his bed free
for the helpful Irishman, but Fergus said he'd rather

be getting home. He didn't mind driving late at night if it meant his own bed at the end of it, and his wife, Kate, waiting for him, so Sue made him a cup of tea and gave him some of the cake left from earlier, and then the Carters waved him on his way with heartfelt thanks and love to be passed on to Brendan and the family.

The sun was setting in a red sky as the forlorn family watched the rear lights of Fergus's van disappear down the road and they waved until he was out of sight. Then they filed back into the shop through the boarded-up door and Sue, Michael and the boys went to make up the beds.

'We won't unpack more than necessary,' said Jeanie to Evie, leading her into the kitchen. 'I don't know as we're staying, despite that Frederick Bailey's letter.'

'But it will be better when we've cleaned it up and got our things where we want them, I'm sure, Mum. And at least we've got Dad away from Mr Hopkins.'

'Thank the Lord.' Jeanie looked around the big filthy kitchen and shook her head. 'You know, Evie love, I'm really trying to see this as the start of a new life, a hope that things will be good for us from now on in a different place. That's what your grandma would be saying to you.'

'And she'd be right, Mum. We've got somewhere to stay, at least for now, and Mr Bailey must be a good sort, don't you think, as he thought to write that note and leave the tea and bread?'

'Yes, love, but we don't know him, do we? We've never even met Fergus's friend Jack, who arranged this with Mr Bailey. And if we do stay here we'll have to pay rent. Your grandma and I have a bit of money saved from the washing but it won't go far. We've lost our laundry business now, and your dad'll need to find a job straight away.'

'I know, Mum, but didn't Brendan say Jack Fletcher has an ear to the ground and might come up with something? And Dad can start looking tomorrow. I know he's been a bit . . . daft with the betting, and then this card game with Mr Hopkins, but mebbe he's learned his lesson.'

'I want to think so, love, I honestly do. But somehow I can't see your dad changing, and that's what's worrying me. I've seen the road he's been going down for a while. Mebbe it's too late for him to be any different.'

Evie wanted to argue that their lives *would* get better now they had a chance to start again, all of them together in a new place, but they'd lost so much by running away – all their friends, not least – and she couldn't bring herself to lie to her mother. In her heart she knew that Mum was probably right: Dad would never change. She only hoped he wouldn't drag them down further.

She thought about Billy – how he had kissed her

farewell and told her he'd wait for her to come back. Was it only this morning? It seemed like days ago.

Quietly contemplating their new lives, she felt furious with her father. Stupid man! Stupid and selfish. His selfishness had caused his family to lose everyone they knew and cared for, everything Mum and Grandma Sue had worked for, and their little home in the town where they belonged. Now they had only each other.

For a moment she stood breathing deeply until her anger subsided.

'We've got each other and we always will have,' she said, trying for a smile. 'Together, who knows what we can manage?'

CHAPTER FOUR

As Evie woke up very early in a strange room, the light streaming through the uncurtained window, and remembered the upsets of the weekend and her parting from Billy, she was comforted to see the familiar bulk of Sue in her own sagging bed close by.

'Awake, Evie?' Sue smiled. 'New home, new life, lass. Shall we be up and at it? I'm keen to see what that shop part is like. I had a few thoughts about it in the night. Let's get your dad busy taking down the boards and we'll see better what's what.'

'Gran, you always know how to make the best of things,' Evie said, feeling less anxious. 'So much to do . . . I'll go down and make a pot of tea while you get up.'

It was impossible for Evie to feel miserable for long with Sue's remarkable energy and enthusiasm rallying her.

69

Sue and Evie were up and making toast when Peter appeared, playing a cheery ditty on his penny whistle.

'You're in a good mood,' Evie remarked to Peter, as he smiled at the music, quietly tapping his toes.

'No school,' said Peter simply.

'But you'll have to go sometime.'

'Not for ages and ages. It's the summer holidays from the end of this week. Mum and Dad won't send Bob and me to school for one week, will they, Grandma?'

'They haven't even had the chance to think about school, Pete,' Sue replied. 'I reckon you're safe now until September.'

'Yippee! Though I won't tell Bob just yet. Let him stew, like.'

'Don't be cruel,' laughed Evie. Within five minutes it was smiles all round. The music was jolly and lifted their spirits.

'You can help your dad with those boards and let some light into the front,' said Sue, as Michael and Jeanie came running in.

Peter gave his father a look that said he'd rather not help him but his words belied that. 'Of course,' he said. 'I'm good on ladders – if we have one, that is?'

'Saw one round the side yesterday when I fetched the key,' Michael told him. He took a piece of toast and went off with it to find the ladder and his tools.

All their things had been unpacked so quickly from Fergus's van the previous evening that it was difficult for everyone to remember where they'd put their belongings.

'You sound keen to get on,' said Jeanie to her mother, sounding anything but keen herself. She looked as if she hadn't slept at all and her eyes were red.

'No point in delaying,' Sue replied. 'You never know what you'll find.'

'You're right, Mum, of course,' Jeanie pulled herself up, 'though it'll have to be an awful lot better than I think it's going to be if we're to stay here. The place is rundown – and a shop, for goodness' sake!'

'I'll have no defeatist talk,' Sue answered, though she was smiling. 'We don't even know who owns it, and we've yet to meet Brendan's friend Jack Fletcher, either. Or maybe he owns it? I'm confused about that, I admit.'

'Me, too,' said Jeanie. 'I expect someone will appear to tell us – especially if they want some rent,' she added.

'Come on, get that toast down you – and you too, Peter,' Sue commanded, passing over mugs of tea. 'It could be our lucky day.'

'Give over, Mum. No need to go overboard,' said Jeanie, but she winked at Evie and Peter.

'Maybe there'll be buried treasure,' said Peter, as

he led the others through to the front, bringing the plate of toast with him. 'A secret cellar full of gold.'

'Aye, and I'm the Queen of Sheba,' said Jeanie. 'Where's Bob? Is he getting up?'

'Sort of. He said his stomach aches but I told him to stop whingeing and see if it felt better when he came down,' said Peter without a trace of sympathy. 'I think he's worried about going to a new school. I haven't told him yet we're not going,' he grinned.

'I'll go and tell him and see if he's all right. You know what he's like with his sensitive stomach.'

~

It took most of the morning for Michael and Peter to remove the boards from the window to the street and stack them out of the way, while Jeanie and Evie found some dusty curtains in the attic and tried to get the place cleaner and more comfortable, and Sue unpacked their boxes. The whole family went to view the unboarded shop from the pavement, eager to see if it looked more promising than it had the previous evening.

'At least we'll be able to see out,' said Michael. 'And it's a big room.'

'A big room for what?' snapped Jeanie, her anger with him not yet dampened down. 'And everyone else can see in now, too. What are we going to do there, sit having our tea like goldfish in a bowl?'

Robert started pulling fish faces, his mouth silently working like a guppy until Peter gently cuffed him round the ear.

'No, love, I only meant—'

A young woman with a baby in a pram and a toddler clutching her arm came along the pavement and the Carters moved aside to let her pass.

'Good morning,' the woman said, smiling. 'Nice to see the old shop opened up.'

'Morning,' said Michael. He peered into the pram, turning on the charm in front of the pretty lady. 'Now that's a bonny baby . . . We're new here and know nowt about the place. What was the shop, do you know?'

'Yes, I can hear you're not from round here,' said the woman, but kindly. 'It was a general household store. Mr Pendle sold buckets, brooms, seeds, string – you know the kind of thing. There's still a call for it but people go to the new shop in the village now. Mr Pendle was old and couldn't keep the business going when his health started to fail. That was a while ago. I'd heard that Mr Bailey was talking about finding new tenants.'

'Mr Bailey?' prompted Sue.

'Frederick Bailey. The owner.' The woman looked puzzled, evidently expecting Sue to know that.

'Oh, aye? Well, Mrs . . . ?'

'Lambert. Josie Lambert.' She held out her hand to shake Sue's.

'Mrs Lambert, we're all very pleased to meet you.' Sue introduced herself and her family. 'Would you care for a cup of tea? I'm sure we can find summat for the little 'un, too, though I'm afraid we've nowt suitable for the baby,' she added. 'It's nice to meet new folk and we know no one around here. If you have a few minutes we'd be glad to learn about the old place and this Mr Bailey.'

'Yes, I can spare a few moments. Thank you.' Mrs Lambert parked the pram and lifted the baby out, murmuring to her and smoothing her fine blonde hair. 'Come along, Archie,' she told the toddler, smiling.

'Archie – that's nice,' said Evie, taking the child's hand and leading him in, though he clutched his mother's skirt in his other little fist.

'Excuse the mess. We only got here last night,' said Jeanie.

'It's all right,' said the friendly woman, though she perched rather tentatively on the chair in the dismal kitchen. 'So how did you come to be here if you don't know Church Sandleton?'

Michael and Jeanie exchanged looks.

'A friend of a friend had heard of a job hereabouts that might suit,' said Michael vaguely. 'It's a pretty part of the country . . . good place to bring up children,' he improvised, looking at young Archie and his baby sister.

'Would that be the job at Clackett's market garden?' asked Mrs Lambert, accepting a cup of

Ribena for Archie and tea for herself. 'I heard Mr Clackett was looking for some help.'

'If the job's still going,' said Michael. Having been working all morning at the front he couldn't have failed to notice the sign for Clackett's a few yards further down on the other side of the road.

Sue gave him a meaningful look. 'So do you know Mr Bailey?' she asked Josie Lambert. 'We haven't met him yet.'

'Oh, no, I don't know him personally. He lives in Redmond but he's seen about the village sometimes. Drives a smart car and owns here and a couple of other properties.'

'Well, no doubt he'll be round before long,' said Sue, and, having extracted what information she could about the landlord, she changed the subject to the village generally while Jeanie cooed over baby Nancy and little Archie.

As soon as Josie Lambert had waved goodbye with promises to call again when Jeanie was settled, Sue turned to Michael.

'Right, you get over to that market garden, lad, and see what this job's about.'

'But I know nowt about growing vegetables,' he protested.

'Who said you'd be growing the veg? You won't know if you don't go.' She shooed him out of the door, then turned to Jeanie. 'Now, I've an idea about the front room. Come through and see what you think. You, too, Evie. It was us women that held the place together in Shenty Street and we can make a go of it here with luck and a fair wind. And as I said earlier, this could be our lucky day.'

'It's looking that way so far,' Peter said, grabbing his whistle and playing a jaunty fanfare. 'Come on, Bob. I'll wash, you dry, and Grandma can think up ways to make our fortune.'

~

Billy immediately recognised Evie's neat round handwriting on the envelope Ada Taylor had left on the kitchen table for him to find when he got in from work. He snatched it up as he called out to her that he was home, then went upstairs to read it in private.

Pendle's
High Street
Church Sandleton
Near Redmond

Thursday

Dear Billy,
  I hope you and your mother are well. I'm missing you like mad and I hope you're missing me, too.
  I can't believe so much has happened since we waved off Fergus Sullivan on Sunday evening. Dad's

got a job – the first one he tried for! It's at the market garden across the road and he's helping to pick the crops. There's a huge amount of them at the moment and Dad says it gets very hot in the glasshouses. He says it's backbreaking work, especially the strawberries, but luckily they're nearly finished. Another really good thing is that Mr Clackett, the owner, gives Dad some of the stuff he says won't sell so we're eating lots of very ripe fruit and vegetables.

The boys are on holiday from school and play outside all day. Pete is making friends with Mr Clackett's son, Martin, and Bob usually tags along with them. There are miles of fields for them to play in around here as it's proper countryside.

Where we're living is an old shop, which makes a strange house with the shop window, but Grandma has hatched a plan for her, Mum and me to open a little business. I'm so excited that we'll be working together again. We've looked around the village and there's no one advertising their dressmaking services or doing alterations and repairs so we think we may have found what Grandma calls 'an opening'. We need to get in touch with Mr Bailey, who owns the building, to see if that's all right, but so far we haven't met him.

It's nice here but it doesn't feel like home and I don't know if it ever will. It's so different from everything we know and love in Bolton. The people in the village are friendly but we're all missing you and the Sullivans and Mrs Marsh – our kind of people.

Please give my best to your mother, and write soon.
I shall look for your letter every day. Remember not
to tell anyone the address, just in case.
With lots of love,
Evie xxx

So, Evie was missing him 'like mad' – which was exactly how he felt about her. How he longed to see her pretty face, with her pointy chin and big hazel eyes. It seemed far longer than five days since he'd waved her goodbye and he'd been thinking of her constantly since then.

Billy reread the letter, then changed out of his postman's uniform and returned downstairs.

Ada had a pot of strong tea brewing and a toasted teacake waiting for him – 'to put you on till teatime, love.'

'Thanks, Mum. You'll have guessed the letter was from Evie. Guess what: seems her dad has a job already.'

'Well, bless me, who'd have thought it?'

'It's great news. Things will turn out better for them all from now.'

'I wouldn't bet on it with that Michael Carter. I reckon Jeanie Goodwin has long rued the day that she married him. She's a bonny woman and could have had her pick. What she wanted to choose him for I don't know. I'd have thought Sue might have talked her out of it, but no.'

'Sounds like he's doing all right now, anyway.'

'That's if he can keep this job, whatever it is,' Ada muttered darkly. 'He'd do well to change his ways and be a bit more reliable. What news of Sue and Jeanie?'

'Mrs Goodwin wants to start a dressmaking business. Seems they live in an old shop so there are ready-made premises for customers – I expect that gave her the idea.'

'Well, Sue was always a hard worker, and a talented seamstress, too. It's a step up from taking in washing, but if anyone can make a go of it, she can.'

'Evie is going to help her, she's good with a needle, and a fast learner. She worries about getting things just right and she'll apply herself to it. She has the same eye for a job well done as her grandma.'

'They'll be all right with Sue in charge,' said Ada confidently. She looked carefully at her son. 'Sounds like they're making a whole new life for themselves down south.'

'I think Evie's missing everyone here,' Billy replied. 'It's not the same as where she was brought up and what she knows. And I reckon we're all missing her, too,' he added boldly.

'You say that now, Billy, but she's not been gone long. Sometimes folk move on, love, and it's not a good idea to be wanting everything to be as it was. She's not here now and probably won't come back. You've got to accept that or be disappointed.'

But Billy wasn't at all ready to accept that Evie was gone for good. He'd never forget the promise he'd made to her that they wouldn't be apart for ever, though he decided not to share this thought with his mother.

He'd write a reply to Evie that evening. After they'd had their tea his mother liked to doze while listening to the Light Programme on the wireless so there'd be a chance then for him to write a long letter full of news about Evie's friends in Bolton. And to send her his love.

~

'I can't believe we've been here over a week and still haven't met this Mr Bailey,' said Jeanie as she chopped some of the twisty-shaped carrots Michael had returned with that evening. Sue, Evie and Peter were busy in the front room, cleaning it in preparation for a coat of paint.

'Well, that's good, isn't it?' said Michael as he scrubbed soil from under his fingernails at the kitchen sink. 'At least he hasn't come asking for any rent.'

'We'll have to pay him eventually,' Jeanie replied. 'And Mum is full of ideas for our little business and wants to get started. We'll need to have enough money for the rent when the time comes, and there's no one else offering a sewing service in Church

Sandleton. So far, anyway. We can't be the only ones with a sewing machine and Mum's worried someone may pip us at the post if we don't get started soon.'

'Can't she set up business without asking Bailey?' Michael sank into a chair to watch Jeanie work.

'I expect so, but it *is* his property, after all. It's only polite to tell him what we want to do, see if it's all right with him.'

'Why would he object, though? It's not like you're opening a – I don't know – a pub or summat you'd need legal permission for.'

'Or an undertaker's,' piped up Robert, at the far end of the kitchen table. 'That would be horrible and creepy. You'd have dead people in the front room and, Dad, you'd have to wear a tall black hat.'

'Good grief, Bob, I don't know where you get such ideas,' laughed Jeanie, pulling a quizzical face at Michael. 'Anyway, I've decided that if Mr Bailey's not coming to us then I'm going to him. Mum looked out her sewing machine this morning, oiled it and everything. Evie's written a neat little notice to pin up in the shop, offering alterations, curtain- and dressmaking, and mending. Once that's up we'll need to be ready for our customers.'

'I'd leave it if I were you, love,' said Michael. 'Wait and see what happens. We're living rent-free at the moment – no use courting expense and creating problems for ourselves.'

'If you think it's rent-free here then you're dafter than you look,' said Jeanie wearily. 'Come on, Michael, we've lost so much, but let's start as we mean to go on. The laundry and mending business was what kept us going many a week in Bolton. The boys will need new school uniform come September and we can't live for ever on what Mum and I saved from the washing.'

'I do my bit—'

'Picking tomatoes!'

'But we get given vegetables, too.'

'Mr Clackett's been very generous, and I'm grateful, but we can't eat nowt but vegetables.'

'By heck, Jeanie, you're a grand cook and few others could make them veggies taste as good as you do, but what I wouldn't give for a helping of hotpot.'

'Evie and I are to catch the bus to Redmond in the morning and we shall find Mr Bailey, introduce ourselves and make sure our plans are all straight and above board with him. What if there's been some mistake and he doesn't even know we're here?'

'You're right, of course . . . ' said Michael, getting up and stretching his stiff back. 'I'll just go out and take a stroll up the street while you're making that carrot thing.'

'Don't be too long, love. You're looking tired and the veg doesn't take much cooking.'

Michael grunted as he went down the hall, past Sue, Evie and Peter still scrubbing the walls, floor and ceiling of the front room. He stepped out into the street and turned towards the Red Lion, thinking he'd already left it far too long to make the acquaintance of his new local.

~

Jeanie and Evie got off the bus in the market square in Redmond. It was market day and on this sunny July morning the place was thronging with shoppers carrying baskets, women pushing prams and traders shouting their wares from the brightly coloured stalls.

'Oh, Mum, let's have a quick look,' begged Evie.

'A look won't hurt,' agreed Jeanie, 'but we won't buy anything until we've found Mr Bailey and seen about the rent and if we can go ahead with the sewing. Look, there's Mr Clackett behind that stall. And Martin's helping him.' She waved and the market gardener called out cheerily to her.

'Let's see if there's a fabric stall or a haberdasher's,' suggested Evie. 'We can report back to Grandma if anything looks good.'

'Aye, your gran has high standards,' said Jeanie, 'though we may have to make do to start with and work our way up to best quality as we earn a bit of money.'

'It sounds like you think Grandma's idea really will work out.' Evie's smile lit up her face. 'I'm so glad, Mum. The washing was hard, but it was nice when us three were all working together. It'll be like that again.'

'From oldest to youngest, we all stick together,' Jeanie agreed.

'It's going to be brilliant. I can't wait to get started.'

They soon spotted a stall heaped with bolts of cloth, but the prices were high compared to those the Carters were used to up North.

'No mill shops here either,' said Jeanie. 'Well, I suppose we couldn't expect it to be as cheap as it is straight from the factory. That lace is nice, though.'

'We'll remember to tell Grandma. Come on, let's go and see if we can find Mr Bailey.'

They had already made a plan. The public library was a grand-looking building on one side of the square and they went in and found the reference library where a sign instructed 'SILENCE'. Josie Lambert had mentioned that Frederick Bailey drove a smart car so it was highly likely he was the kind of man who also had a telephone in his house. Jeanie and Evie quickly found the local telephone directory and in less than two minutes were coming out of the library with the addresses written down of two people: 'F. Bailey' and 'F. W. Bailey'.

'We've no way of knowing so we'll just have to try one, and then the other if we have to,' said Jeanie.

'Maybe look out for a policeman – they always know where places are – but we'll ask Mr Clackett in the meantime.'

They went back over to the market and had to wait while Mr Clackett did a brisk trade in salad before he was free to give them his attention.

'Woodfall Road – don't know that, I'm afraid, Mrs Carter. Eh, Stanley,' he called across to a man selling sausages. 'Woodfall Road – ring any bells?'

Stanley scratched his head. 'Off the main road out towards Church Sandleton,' he said eventually.

'What about Midsummer Row?' asked Jeanie.

'Oh, that's just behind here,' said Mr Clackett. 'Next to that shoe shop there's a side road that goes down into a little square.'

'Thank you,' beamed Jeanie, and she and Evie set off for the nearer place.

'Oh, I suddenly feel quite nervous,' said Jeanie as they walked through into the pretty square with trees in a tiny central garden and tall thin town houses overlooking it all round.

'Perhaps he'll be really nice,' suggested Evie, though she, too, was anxious and her stomach was churning.

'Do I look all right?' asked Jeanie. 'I don't want to appear down at heel. I want Mr Bailey to think we're respectable folk who can be trusted.'

Evie stopped walking and pulled her mother round to face her. She tipped her straw hat a fraction further forward and brushed a tiny speck of dust off the lapel of her floral print jacket. It was old but Sue had made it from quality cotton spun and woven in Bolton and, with its eye-catching colours and sharp tailoring, it had stood the test of time and was a fine advertisement for Sue's dress-making skills.

'Mum, you look lovely,' Evie told her mother truthfully. 'Now let's see which one's Marlowe House.'

They walked round the square, reading the names on smart plaques beside the front doors, and soon came to the right one. Evie opened the iron gate and Jeanie led her through and up the steps to the front door.

She took a deep breath and had just put her hand out to ring the bell when the door was flung open and a furious-looking woman, wearing an overall and with her hair tied up with a scarf, erupted out of the house.

'You can keep your flipping job, you old bastard!' she yelled back through the open door. 'Don't you threaten me with the police. Years I've slaved for you, and poor thanks I've had for it. I've seen pigs keep themselves cleaner. You can stew in your own muck. I deserve better and I only took what should have been mine. I've had enough!'

She picked up an ornament from a side table beside the door and hurled it back down the hall. Evie and Jeanie heard the tinkle of shattering china and unconsciously they clutched each other as the harridan, oblivious, stomped past them, down the steps and through the gate, leaving it open in her wake.

Evie's heart was pounding as she turned to see her mother was white with shock.

'Oh, Mum, whatever can have happened? I think we ought to go. I don't like it here at all.'

'Me neither, Evie. Come on . . .'

As they began to retrace their steps a calm and educated voice called behind them, 'Please don't mind Mrs Summers. She can be a bit ill-tempered, though, truth be told, she was a very good cleaner. Pity she wasn't a more honest one.'

Jeanie quickly tried to gather herself as she turned back to see who had spoken.

He was a tall, very lean and good-looking man in his fifties, his greying dark hair in need of a cut. He was wearing a moth-eaten old cricket pull-over, and a kerchief – such as a pirate might wear in an adventure story, thought Evie – knotted round the frayed neck of his collarless shirt. Jeanie looked him up and down in astonishment and thought without a doubt that he was the most untidy – and the handsomest – man she'd ever seen.

'Mr Bailey?' she asked, suddenly feeling strangely breathless.

'I am Frederick Bailey,' the tall man replied with astonishing dignity considering what his ex-cleaner had just called him in front of strangers.

'Er . . . I'm Ginette Carter, and this is my daughter, Evelyn.'

'How do you do,' said Mr Bailey. 'How can I help you?'

Oh dear, he doesn't seem to have heard of us. Living at Pendle's is all an awful mistake. Or maybe this is the wrong person and we should be at the other Bailey's house? As this thought flashed through Evie's mind she saw her mother's puzzled face reflecting the very same thing.

'I . . . I'm wondering if you might be our new landlord,' Jeanie persevered. 'Pendle's? In Church Sandleton?'

'Yes, I suppose I must be, if that's where you're living,' Mr Bailey replied vaguely. 'Come in, please . . . '

He stood back to let Jeanie and Evie pass through the smart front door and into the hall where shards of pink and white porcelain lay strewn across the floor.

'Pity about the shepherdess,' he said. 'I'd got a buyer lined up for her, too. Still, there we are . . . '

Evie caught Jeanie's eye behind the man's back and shrugged nervously. This man wasn't like anyone she had ever met, and though the coarse, shouting woman had gone she still didn't feel at all comfortable here.

Jeanie, too, felt out of place in this strange house, with this odd man, but as she looked around the elegant little hallway Mr Bailey turned to her and smiled, and it was a smile she understood.

CHAPTER FIVE

Frederick Bailey showed Evie and Jeanie into a beautifully decorated room overlooking the square. Evie realised she was gaping at all the ornaments on every surface and quickly closed her mouth.

'So, Mrs Carter . . . Pendle's. I do hope everything is all right. I haven't been over to the old place for a long while. I've a man who sees to things like that for me.'

'Oh, yes, I haven't come to complain,' said Jeanie, sitting down in an armchair that Frederick Bailey indicated. 'But we've been there more than a week now and hadn't heard from anyone, and I was wondering . . . that is, we wondered . . . about the rent . . .'

When her mother seemed to have ground to a halt, Evie continued, 'And my grandmother is a very talented seamstress and wants to open a sewing business in the shop part. We thought we'd better make sure that was all right . . . that you'd allow it and that we can paint the place and make it more suitable.'

'You may do as you like,' Frederick Bailey said. 'I'm not a man for strict rules and regulations.'

'So we can go ahead?' asked Evie eagerly. She couldn't help her wide grin – this was exactly what she had hoped for. 'Thank you.'

Mr Bailey laughed. 'Well, I'm glad about that,' he said.

'What about the rent?' prompted Evie. She looked sideways at her mother but Jeanie seemed lost in thought and was gazing around the room with real interest. 'We mean to make a go of the sewing, and my dad has a job, too, so we can pay what's fair.'

'Ah, so there's a Mr Carter . . . I was wondering about your father,' said Mr Bailey. 'What is it he does?'

'He works at Clackett's market garden, across from Pendle's.'

'Does he indeed?' Mr Bailey paused to think. 'Well, how about ten shillings a week? How does that sound?'

'Oh, Mr Bailey, that's marvellous! Ten shillings? Are you sure that's all?' gasped Evie. Again she looked at her mother, but she was still distracted by the unusual room and gave no reaction.

Frederick Bailey waved a hand as if to dismiss the subject. 'I'll have my man, Jack, collect the payments.'

'Jack? Would that be Jack Fletcher? We haven't met him yet but it was he who arranged for us to come to Pendle's.'

'Yes, Jack Fletcher works for me. No doubt you'll meet him soon. There's nothing for you to worry about, Evelyn.'

'It's all becoming clearer now.'

Evie realised how anxious she'd become about their new home and these people none of them had met. What a relief it was to have it all sorted out. Coming here today had been exactly the right thing to do.

'Thank you, Mr Bailey,' she said. She nudged her mother, who was still occupied with her own thoughts. 'Mum . . . ?'

'Thank you, Mr Bailey. That's right good of you,' Jeanie said, smiling up at him.

'Please, call me Frederick. Now, forgive my manners, I should have offered you tea, but I'm without Mrs Summers, as you know only too well.'

'Let me help,' Jeanie said without hesitation, throwing off her distraction. She was on her feet instantly.

'That's uncommonly kind of you, Mrs Carter.'

'Jeanie, please.'

'Jeanie. Why don't we all go down?'

He led the way into the hall, pushing fragments of the broken ornament aside with his foot, then down a curving staircase at the end to a basement

91

kitchen that looked old-fashioned and equipped very much as Mrs Russell's was, to Evie's eye. She could imagine Annie being quite at home here, though Annie wouldn't have had the dirty breakfast crockery piled up in the sink. The cups Mr Bailey set out were a strange mix: a pot mug and a couple of delicate teacups of different sizes with mismatched saucers. Didn't he have a tea set to use when visitors came, Evie wondered.

'This is pretty,' she said, taking up one of the fine cups to admire it while her mother saw to the kettle.

'Yes, but almost worthless without its own saucer, I'm afraid,' said Frederick. He searched absent-mindedly for the tea caddy, which Jeanie found in an obvious cupboard next to the stove, then asked his two visitors about their plans for the sewing business while the tea was brewing in a brown Bessie pot, just like the one at home.

'My mother's idea,' said Jeanie.

'It's Grandma who's the expert,' said Evie proudly. 'She's brilliant at sewing and can do all sorts of things – make clothes and do alterations and mending, too. She made that jacket Mum's wearing.'

'Evie . . . ' tutted Jeanie.

'Very pretty,' said Frederick, looking at Jeanie, who gazed straight back at him, smiling.

'And she can make up a pair of curtains in no time.'

'She sounds very special, your grandmother,'

Frederick said, handing round the china cups and saucers and taking up the mug of tea himself. 'And are you both going to work with her?' He looked at Jeanie when he asked this but it was Evie who answered.

'Oh, yes. Grandma wouldn't have it any other way,' she prattled on. 'She's a great one for family sticking together.'

'Well, I've been thinking about that,' said Jeanie quietly but firmly. 'It's you and Grandma who have the eye and the patience for sewing. I never helped with the mending in Shenty Street. I reckon you could get on fine without me.' She ignored Evie's open mouth of astonishment. 'What I was wondering, Frederick, was if you think Mrs Summers has left for good and whether you are in need of a cleaner? Or . . . ' she looked around and then back to him with her pretty smile, ' . . . a housekeeper?'

Frederick began laughing quietly.

What on earth was funny? And what was Mum on about? Evie felt her heart thumping loudly. Starting the sewing business had been decided, hadn't it? She looked from her mother to Frederick Bailey and suddenly felt something was happening here that she didn't understand.

Jeanie was standing waiting quite calmly for him to answer her.

'A housekeeper . . . Do you know, Jeanie, I think you'd be quite perfect,' he said eventually.

'But, Mum, what about the sewing?' Evie didn't want to question her mother in front of Mr Bailey but she *had* to say something before it was too late. 'It was going to be the three of us working together, same as in Shenty Street,' she reminded her, her voice almost pleading. Where had this new idea come from? It wasn't part of the plan at all. And what would Grandma Sue have to say?

'Well, Evie, we're not in Shenty Street any more. It's different now,' Jeanie said. Though she spoke quietly her tone was very sure. She smiled at their new landlord to show there was no criticism in her words and then looked around at the pile of unwashed dishes, the newspapers strewn across the kitchen table and the loaf of bread left out drying among a pile of crumbs.

'You've grasped the situation precisely,' Frederick replied, sounding delighted. 'When were you thinking of starting?'

'Tomorrow – would that suit you? Shall I do mornings and see how we get on?'

Evie gasped. She couldn't believe what she was hearing. Even Grandma Sue didn't take the lead like that without discussing things first.

'But, Mum—' she started.

'I don't doubt we'll get on brilliantly, Jeanie,' said Frederick, extending his hand to shake hers.

~

94

'So what happened then?' asked Sue, pouring cups of tea to wash down their lunchtime sandwiches. Michael had returned to Clackett's for the afternoon, pleased with the news of the low rent and his wife's new job, and the boys had gone out to play somewhere.

Jeanie and Evie were telling Sue more about their morning in Redmond. The way her mother recounted the events once she and Evie had entered Frederick Bailey's house lacked some detail; so much so that Evie thought it was just one version of the meeting with their landlord and she might have told it in altogether another way. Nonetheless, it was a sort of truth.

'He showed us round the house so that I could see exactly how much work it's going to be. He's an art and antiques dealer – buys and sells old things like paintings and ornaments, pretty but useless – and the house is full of the stuff. It's everywhere and it all needs to be dusted. He says some of it is quite valuable and I'm to be careful.'

'Must be odd to live in a house that's full of things you mean to sell,' said Sue. 'I wonder he doesn't become fond of them and want to keep them.'

'He may, for all I know. It's nowt to do with me,' said Jeanie with a shrug. 'But I think this job will suit me better than sewing. I was never one for stitching – you know that.'

'I know no such thing,' said Sue, sharp as a

tack. 'But I reckon you've made your mind up. And at least you got the rent sorted out, so that's one good thing.' She looked at Evie. 'Come on, love, let's decide on the colour for the walls now we've got the front room all prepared. We can get on since we've got permission, even if it's only us two.'

They went through to the front, leaving Jeanie to wash up.

'We'll have to choose a nice light colour. I can't be sewing anywhere dark with my old eyes,' said Sue.

'I'd like yellow,' said Evie. 'A light shade of yellow – like primroses. Do you think that would be all right for your eyes, Grandma?'

'I reckon it would, lass. We'll see what we can find. Now tell me, you're not too sorry your mum's not to be working with us after all, are you?'

Evie knew better than to deny it but she was surprised at the surge of disappointment that swept through her once again as she said, 'I wanted it to be like it was in Shenty Street – all us women together, like you said. I couldn't believe it when Mum said to Mr Bailey that she could be his house-keeper without even asking me if I minded – or if I thought you would mind either.'

'I'm disappointed, too, love, but your mother will go her own sweet way. She always was one for getting what she wants. It was the same when she first set eyes on your dad. Nowt I could say would change her mind – not that I haven't got used to him and his ways,' she added kindly.

~

'You've another letter from Evie,' said Ada, handing it to Billy as he came in from work. 'She's a keen writer, I'll say that for her.'

'I'm glad of that,' Billy grinned.

'Well, just remember what I've said. I know you're fond of her but Evie doesn't live here any more,' Ada advised. 'It's hard to keep up a . . . a friendship in letters. She might not always be so keen to stay in touch, lad. You don't know what folk she'll meet in the south. She's Michael Carter's daughter, don't forget, and we all know how reliable *he* is.'

'Yes, Mum, but she's Sue Goodwin's granddaughter, too, and there's no one more sound than Mrs Goodwin. I'm thinking of getting a train down one weekend and meeting up. It'll be lovely to see her and nice to see where she lives.'

'Oh, aye? Well, don't go getting your hopes up, our Billy. There's girls round here, too, you know.'

'Yes, Mum, I know there are girls round here,' said Billy patiently, and took his letter upstairs to read in peace.

Dear Billy,

Thank you for your letter. I always look forward to hearing from you. Your letters are the best thing to happen and I can't wait for them to arrive.

I hope you've had a good week.

Grandma and me have been really busy getting ready for our first customers. I've put a notice up in the village store and our shop is painted now. It's a sort of cream colour. We wanted yellow but we couldn't find anything nice so we went for the nearest. Pete and Bob helped. Pete did the ceiling, bless him, but Bob just made a mess. I suppose he is only little.

Mum is enjoying being housekeeper to Mr Bailey. She's started taking more care of herself and is more cheerful – I'd got quite worried about her in Shenty Street when we were working so hard on the washing – and though I saw for myself that Mr Bailey's house is a big job she doesn't look too weary when she gets home. It seems odd that Mr Bailey pays Mum and then Mum pays Jack Fletcher, Mr Bailey's man, who comes for the rent!

We all like Jack. He's very friendly and knows all kinds of people. He found a big table for the shop, which will be useful when we're cutting out or making curtains. He even delivered it to us.

Jack and Dad sometimes go together to the Red Lion in the village. I'm glad Dad's got someone to go with and see him home in good time, although if Jack isn't around Dad goes on his own and tends to stay later.

*Mr Clackett doesn't hold with drinking, he says,
though Dad sometimes goes to the Lion at dinnertime
instead of coming here for his dinner. There aren't
card games or bookies' runners at this pub so I'm
hoping no harm will come of it.*

*I know Sundays can be difficult travelling by train
but you said you were thinking of coming down. It
would be lovely to see you, Billy. Let me know when
you can manage it, and make it soon, please!*

Lots of love,

Evie xxx

Billy read the letter twice through, laughing at the
thought of the kind of mess Robert would have
made with the paint, and happy that Evie and her
grandmother were about to open for business after
all their hard work to make the premises smart.

It wasn't good news that Michael Carter was
drinking during the day but at least it was unlikely
that he'd get into the kind of trouble he had with
Mr Hopkins.

At that moment there was a knock at the front
door. He opened it to find Geraldine Sullivan
standing there, looking lovely in a flowered summer
dress and clutching a packet of custard creams.

'Hello, Gerry,' Billy said. 'This is a nice surprise.'

'All right, Billy? Your mum was at the shop earlier
and left these on the counter by mistake. I only
noticed after she'd gone.'

'Ah, Geraldine. Nice to see you, love,' said Ada, appearing from the kitchen. 'Come in. I've just boiled the kettle.'

'Oh, thank you, Mrs Taylor, but I won't stop,' Geraldine said. 'I only came round to drop these off for you.'

'Thank you, love. Isn't that kind of her, Billy?' said his mother. She took the packet of biscuits without so much as glancing at them. 'Are you sure you won't have a cup of tea, love?'

'No, thanks, Mrs T. I'd best be getting home. Bye, now. See you around, Billy.' She beamed her glamorous smile at the Taylors, then turned and click-clacked down the street on her high heels.

Ada looked put out and Billy followed her into the kitchen to find the teapot already under the cosy and three cups and saucers on the table.

'Expecting a visitor, were you, Mum?' he asked pointedly.

Ada couldn't hide her discomfort that she'd been rumbled though she tried to make the best of it. 'I thought Geraldine might bring my biscuits round when I found I'd come home without them,' she said.

'You could have gone and got them, Mum. It's only down the street.'

'I know, but she's so friendly – and works so hard at Mr Amsell's . . . I just thought – she's a lovely girl, isn't she, Billy?'

'Geraldine Sullivan is a right bonny lass, and a nice one, no one could deny that.'

Billy sat back in a kitchen chair thinking his mother wasn't cut out for scheming. If only Evie's father were so easy to read, the Carters would have had a far smoother ride.

That got him thinking about Evie's letter. He'd write back tonight and tomorrow he'd look for a pretty card to send with the letter to congratulate Mrs Goodwin and Evie on opening for business. It wouldn't be too long before he got to see them for himself and he couldn't wait!

~

'Looks a bit bare,' said Evie, surveying the sewing room. The only relief from its plainness was a colourful card with a bunch of flowers on the front, which Billy had sent. 'If only our fabric had arrived.'

Sue had written to Marie Sullivan to ask if she'd choose some fabric in autumn shades for her from the mill shop near Shenty Street. She'd sent Marie a postal order to cover all her costs and Marie had been only too pleased to help, but the parcel still hadn't arrived. Evie was feeling anxious about that – its absence seemed a big setback on top of her mother deciding not to work with them.

Peter had made an 'OPEN' sign and hung it on the front door. They'd closed the door in the passage so that the house part was private but Evie thought they needn't have bothered about that. She hadn't imagined a stampede of customers this first morning of business, but nor had she thought she'd be sitting here twiddling her thumbs.

'What you need,' said Peter, 'are a few props.'

'Props? What on earth do you mean?' asked Sue.

'Like in a theatre. They set the stage with things to make it look like what it's supposed to be. This looks like an empty room with a big table and chairs in it to me, so what you need is to make it look like a dressmaker's. It doesn't have to be real, it just has to look as if it is.'

'Clever lad.' His grandma was impressed.

'When did you get to be so wise?' laughed Evie, nudging her brother with her elbow.

'We need fabric,' said Sue, getting the idea at once. 'It needs to look like we're already working on summat – busy, like. Right, you three, go and find anything you can think of to drape about the place. But make sure it's clean,' she added as her grandchildren disappeared into the house.

Half an hour later the room had been transformed. The bedroom curtains were folded neatly and stacked on the shelves like bolts of fabric, Jeanie's best dress was displayed on a hanger hooked over the dado rail, and a pile of used paper dress patterns in their envelopes were arranged on a corner of the table opposite Sue's sewing machine.

Leftover trimmings and spare buttons that Sue had saved over the years were displayed on Jeanie's pretty cake plate, and finally Sue's workbasket was placed prominently in the window, open and with spools of thread cascading colourfully over the edges.

'That's more like it,' said Sue, standing back to survey their handiwork.

'And you can hardly see where I spilled the paint,' said Robert, drawing everyone's attention to the stain, just as they were beginning to overlook it.

'Ideally I would place a pile of fashion magazines over that,' said Peter seriously, 'but we don't have any.'

They were interrupted by the arrival of the postman, wearing a uniform so like Billy's that Evie's heart gave a little skip. He pushed open the door and brought through a huge box wrapped in brown paper.

'Mrs Goodwin? Delivery for you.'

'Ooh, looks like Marie's parcel, right on cue. Thank you,' she said to the postman, and let the boys cut away the wrapping. 'Save that brown paper and string. You never know when they will be useful,' Sue, for whom wartime habits were still second nature, reminded them. Then they opened the cardboard box to reveal what Marie had come up with.

There was much oohing and aahing from Evie and Sue over the printed cotton remnants and end-of-rolls that Marie had found. Sue had been a bit unsure about shelling out for fabric without specific commissions, but now she knew she'd done the right thing. These pieces hadn't cost much at the mill shop but the quality was second to none.

'Pete, Bob, get those bedroom curtains back upstairs, and we'll put these pieces in their place,' instructed Sue.

She and Evie had no sooner finished folding the remnants into a pretty display when the door opened and Josie Lambert came in carrying a bag.

'Thought I'd get in early before you get busy,' she said. 'I've left Nancy and Archie with my mother. Oh, the shop looks lovely. You've got a good eye, Mrs Goodwin. Do you think you could take in this frock I wore when I was expecting Nancy? It's too good to throw away and I like the colour.'

'I can completely refashion it for you, if you'd like,' offered Sue, getting into her stride at once. 'There's yards in this front panel – what kind of dress were you thinking of . . . ?'

Evie let Sue do the talking but listened carefully to what she was saying, while Peter went to make a pot of tea, bringing through a cup for Mrs Lambert, too. All Evie's worries about starting up the sewing business were evaporating. Sue looked happier than she had for weeks and Evie saw how confident and in control she was at being her own boss again.

Then she thought about the arrangement Billy had made to come to see her on Sunday and she felt happiness bubbling up inside her. The fabrics had arrived and they were beautiful, she and Sue had their first customer, and Billy was coming to see her – it was all just about perfect.

~

Jeanie arrived home from Redmond early in the afternoon as usual. She came into the workroom to see how Sue and Evie were getting on, and was impressed with their efforts and also with the fabrics Marie had chosen for them from the mill shop.

'Not thinking of joining us after all?' asked Sue without rancour.

'I'm getting on fine at Frederick's, thank you,' said Jeanie with a big smile. 'Oh, but I can understand why that Summers woman thought it a big job. You should see his study! Luckily he was out all morning at an auction so I was able to get on in the sitting room at least.'

'He trusts you with the run of the place and his precious things, then?' Sue enquired. She'd yet to meet Frederick Bailey and Evie suspected that for some reason Sue hadn't formed a very high opinion of him so far, despite the low rent he was asking.

'And why wouldn't he?' said Jeanie. 'I'll get on and make us some sandwiches. I got a bit of cheese from Mrs Sutton on the way home so they won't be just salad today.'

'The day's getting better and better,' said Sue as Jeanie went to make their lunch.

'Mum's in a very good mood,' said Evie. 'She's a lot more cheerful altogether these days.'

'Mmm . . . ' Sue replied noncommittally, taking her tailor's shears to Josie Lambert's maternity dress.

~

Michael didn't come home to eat the sandwiches and Sue tutted that he must have gone to get some chips and a pie at the Red Lion, which cost pennies that they didn't have. The boys went off to play in the field at the back of the market garden with Martin Clackett, leaving Sue and Evie in peace to work. Evie watched and learned as her grandmother turned Josie Lambert's vast garment into a swathe of fabric, which Evie pressed and then Sue recut into a stylish new shape. Evie machined the seams as directed and the afternoon passed, Evie feeling more settled than she had in weeks.

They were interrupted by Mrs Sutton from the village store, who came to ask about having some curtains made.

'I've seen a few people reading your notice, Evie,' she said. 'It wouldn't surprise me if you weren't rushed off your feet before the summer's out.'

'We'll cope,' said Sue, winking at Evie. 'Now, are

you wanting them lined, Mrs Sutton? I would recommend it . . . '

'Two customers already,' beamed Evie when Mrs Sutton had gone.

'It's a good start,' Sue confirmed. 'What d'you reckon? Will we manage without your mum?'

'I still wish she was in here working with us but we've had a lovely day, just the two of us, and Pete was such a help putting the finishing touches to the shop.'

'And you've also got Billy coming to visit next weekend – something for you to look forward to, love.'

'He'll be at Redmond station on the first train of the morning, and he's getting a train back in the late afternoon, so we won't have very long, but he wants to see us all and the village, too.'

'He's a grand lad,' said Sue. 'We'll make sure there's more than vegetables for his dinner,' and Evie hugged her.

~

Michael was woken by someone shaking his arm. He opened his eyes slowly, blinking in the glare of the sun through the greenhouse windows. He must have dozed off for a moment in the heat . . . Distantly he could hear the sound of children playing. What time was it now . . . ?

'Michael! Michael Carter! What do you think you're doing, asleep on the job?'

Mr Clackett was leaning over him, looking furious.

'Oh, Mr Clackett, it's the heat in here . . . made me a bit sleepy, like.'

'Heat? Beer, more like. I can smell it on your breath, and your clothes smell like the inside of the Red Lion. You've been drinking, haven't you?'

'Well, it was only a couple of pints. It's thirsty work in these glasshouses—'

'Couple of pints! And how is beer better than good honest water when I'm paying you to pick tomatoes? I don't hold with drinking, Michael, and I certainly don't hold with slacking. If you're paid to do a job I expect you to do it. If you don't then I'd rather employ someone else. There's a ton of veg to be picked and you're not doing your share.'

'I'm that sorry, Mr Clackett. I must have dozed off for a minute, that's all.'

'It's two hours since you left at lunchtime. It's not fair if you take your wages but don't do the hours.'

'Two hours? Oh, surely not,' said Michael, trying to jolly his boss out of his outrage. 'Can't possibly be that long. Tell you what – why don't I stay a bit later to make up? I'll do that as a favour, seeing as there's so much to pick.'

'A favour! You'll do it to make up for sleeping away half the afternoon at my expense, never mind any favours.'

'Oh . . . that's what I meant,' said Michael sheepishly.

'And let me tell you this. I'm a fair man and I don't hold with taking and not giving in return. If I find you asleep on the job again you won't be working here any longer.'

'No, Mr Clackett. And I'm sorry. It won't happen again.'

'If it does it will be the last time,' Mr Clackett reiterated, shaking a finger at Michael. He turned and walked away, muttering, 'Favour indeed . . . ' and the sound of his heavy boots faded into the distance, leaving Michael with a dislocated feeling.

The afternoon was silent, save for the hum of bees among the tomato plants. The children's voices he had heard earlier had faded away at some point and he wasn't sure what time it was or exactly where he'd left off what he'd been doing. He pulled himself upright and stretched, feeling seedy and weary, and regretful of his pints at the pub.

Still, Mr Clackett hadn't actually sacked him. And there was no reason why anyone else should hear of this . . .

~

When Michael came in at the end of the afternoon he looked worn and weary, and he grumbled that he had a headache coming on.

109

'Hard day, love?' sympathised Jeanie as Michael sat down at the table. 'Never mind, I've a delicious vegetable stew for you.' She laughed lightly because she made the same joke every evening, but today Michael could barely raise a smile.

'I've had it up to here with vegetables,' he said.

'What d'you mean, love? You've not been there more'n a few weeks, and Mr and Mrs Clackett have been very generous towards us with the rejects. I don't know what we'd have done without all this food.'

'Aye, you're right, of course, Jeanie, but I don't know as the job suits me all that well.'

Peter was scowling into his stew and Robert began bouncing on his chair as if he wanted to say something but his mouth was zipped shut.

'What do you mean, Michael?' Jeanie looked anxious. 'It's only picking vegetables – there's nothing about it to suit or not suit. You just do it.'

'I don't know . . . might be looking for another job.'

'That's exactly what Mr Clackett said!' burst out Robert, then clapped a hand over his mouth as if to silence himself as Peter gave him an almighty kicking under the table.

'What!' shrilled Jeanie. 'Boys, Evie, take your stew into the yard, please,' instructed Jeanie, and there was a scraping of chairs and a gathering of bread, spoons and bowls as they did as they were asked.

'All right, you two,' said Evie, when they'd made themselves as comfortable as they could in the shady backyard on a rotting garden bench and an upturned flowerpot. She put her bowl of stew down on the ground. 'What have you heard? Pete?'

'We were playing out the back of Clackett's with Martin late this afternoon and we overheard Mr Clackett giving Dad a warning. It sounded like he'd spent the afternoon asleep in one of the sheds instead of doing his work. Mr Clackett said he'd sack him if he did it again.'

'Yes,' said Robert, his eyes huge with the importance of his news. 'And Mr Clackett said Dad wasn't to go to the Red Lion at dinnertime and then go back to work the worse for drink *ever again*.'

Evie raised her hands to her face in horror and tears sprung into her eyes. The thought of Dad losing this job so soon after the last one, especially now the family were working so hard at making a new life, and with everyone in the village having been so friendly, was more than she could contemplate. People might not be nearly so kind if the Carters got a reputation for being unreliable. It could even mean she and Grandma Sue would lose potential customers before they'd even got their business started. That would be so unfair. Evie pulled the boys into her arms, and as the row started indoors, they huddled together wishing they were back home on Shenty Street.

111

CHAPTER SIX

EVIE WALKED AS quickly as she could to the railway station in Redmond. Billy's train wasn't due for half an hour but already she couldn't stop smiling at the thought of seeing him. Her stomach was doing a little dance of anticipation. She'd chosen to wear a pretty cotton frock that Sue had made her and which Billy had once told her looked nice.

Redmond station had only two platforms so there was no problem for Evie finding out where Billy's train would be pulling in. In the way of all stations it felt draughty, even on this hot July day, so Evie decided to sit in the ladies' waiting room. There were a couple of other women in there but when the northbound train was announced they left, so Evie had the place to herself, which was just as well as she was finding it impossible to sit still. She got up and walked about the room, then sat down again, swinging her legs, frequently glancing at her watch all the while until she made up her mind not to, to make the time go quicker.

At last the southbound train was announced and she jumped up and hurried out. With a shrill whistle it approached, gigantic wheels turning, the familiar smell of soot thick in the air and smoke engulfing the platform. The train halted, steam hissed fiercely, and then slowly the fug cleared and Evie looked up and down, smiling widely, ready to greet Billy. Doors were opened and a few people climbed out. No sign of Billy yet. No doubt he'd be collecting his things off the luggage rack, making sure he hadn't left anything. A few doors were slammed and Evie focused on those that remained open. He'd be here any second now . . .

Then the stationmaster went down the train shutting the doors. Evie's heart started to thud and she tried not to panic as she began to walk quickly along the platform, looking in at the carriage windows. Where was Billy? What was going on? He'd said he'd be on the ten thirty train. She checked her watch again but she knew she wasn't mistaken. This was his train, but where was he?

When she got to the last carriage the guard leaned out, seeing her looking worried. 'You all right, miss?'

'I was supposed to meet a friend on this train but he doesn't seem to be here,' she said, thinking she might disgrace herself by bursting into tears of disappointment like a little child.

'Maybe your friend has missed this train. There's

another southbound in forty minutes. Why not get yourself a cup of tea and wait for that one?'

'Thank you,' said Evie, though she thought it unlikely that Billy would have missed the train if he could possibly have helped it. What was more important than their meeting up? They'd planned the whole day so carefully: going back to Pendle's café for dinner, which was going to be special and not just vegetable stew. And then afterwards a lovely walk around the village and by the pretty stream that ran through the woods bordering the fields at the back . . .

Right now though, the stationmaster loudly blew his whistle and the guard waved a flag. There was a piercing answer from the driver's whistle and with a lot of hissing and rumbling the train pulled away, leaving Evie feeling very lonely on the platform all by herself.

Now what? Better wait for the next one, and if Billy wasn't on that then she'd have to decide whether to go home or wait longer. She returned to the ladies' waiting room, subdued now, and sat despondently in the corner, prepared to wait for the forty minutes until the next train was due. So, she sat and waited and worried, constantly glancing at the big old station clock on the wall.

The distant chime of the bells of the parish church sounded at eleven o'clock, and then there was a station announcement. Evie managed to make out from the very loud yet strangely unclear voice that the southbound train had been delayed and was going to be twenty minutes late.

She sat back with a deep sigh, wondering how this morning would end. Would she ever get to meet up with Billy? She'd started off so excited and so hopeful; now she was just fed up.

Everyone had a little grumble as the late train eventually rolled in with a huff and a puff and a loud whiste. It was half-past eleven and Evie was on the platform again, looking and hoping. Again, passengers alighted and a few people boarded, the whistles were blown and the huge wheels turned, gathering speed and leaving Evie alone.

Except she wasn't alone this time. From the very last carriage Jack Fletcher had climbed down with Monty, his terrier, on a lead.

'Hello, Evie. What brings you here?' asked Jack. 'Is something wrong?'

'Hello, Jack. I'm that glad to see you. I was supposed to meet a friend off the train before this one and he still isn't here and I don't know what to do. I don't want to go home in case he turns up, but I can't stay here all day.'

'So how long have you been here?' asked Jack.

'Since well before half-past ten. We've been planning today for ages and he's not the sort to let me down.'

'Maybe he hasn't been able to help it. Perhaps he's been delayed through no fault of his own?'

116

Evie thought about this and decided that Jack was right. Billy was always so reliable that there could be no other explanation. She couldn't help the hot tears of disappointment that started to form, and she tried to sniff them away.

'Now, come on. I've got the motorbike rig parked round the back. Me and Monty can give you a lift home, if you like.'

'Oh, but you'd be going out of your way. You're nearly home.' Evie knew Jack lived on the edge of Redmond, where the countryside ended and the town started.

'It's no trouble. Can't leave you looking miserable, with a long walk home. How could I face your grandma if I left you here? Come on, we'll get you home by dinnertime.'

'Thank you,' Evie smiled. She blew her nose, straightened her shoulders and her spirits lifted slightly as she went with Jack and Monty round behind the station where a few cars and Jack's motorbike and sidecar were parked.

'Hop in, Evie,' Jack offered his hand to help her climb into the sidecar. 'Thing is, you'll have to share with Monty.' He indicated to the restless dog by his leg.

Evie looked at the long-haired Jack Russell. Monty was, she noticed now, absolutely filthy, with dirt drying in his curly coat, the comical brown patch over one eye and ear less distinctive now the little dog was mostly brown all over. She looked down at her pretty dress, then at Jack's kindly face and the cute way Monty had of looking at her with his head on one side. What does it matter about the dress? she thought. It isn't as if Billy is here to see me in it.

Giving a little shrug, she climbed into the sidecar and made herself comfortable. 'Come on, then, Monty.'

Monty sat on Evie's lap, and gave her a big lick.

Evie laughed, past caring about her dress now, as Jack started the bike and drove her home, Monty sitting up on her knee with the wind in his ears and pride on his face at a morning well spent.

~

Monty leapt out of the sidecar when Jack parked the rig in front of Pendle's. Evie climbed out after him and brushed the dirt off her dress as best she could. She'd enjoyed the journey home on the hot day, the rush of air through her hair and the different view of the countryside from so low down had been special. This must be how Monty saw life, she thought. She was trying hard to overcome her disappointment over Billy's failure to show. As Jack had said, there would be an explanation.

She'd had plenty of time to study the back view of Jack as he carefully drove the motorbike – rather slower with her as a passenger, Evie suspected, than he usually did. He was wearing an old waxed jacket, despite the heat, with many pockets. She wondered how old he was. Older than Dad, no doubt, but not as old as Grandma Sue. Maybe about the same age as Mr Bailey? But Jack had such an easy way with him that he was almost like a much older brother or an uncle. All the Carters liked him.

Jeanie was at the door.

'Oh, Evie, but what's happened? Where's Billy?'

'He didn't come, Mum,' said Evie, her voice wobbling with threatened tears again. 'I waited and waited, and then I saw Jack and he gave me a lift.'

'There'll be a good explanation, don't you worry, Evie,' smiled Jack.

'Oh, no, what a shame, Evie! You were that excited about Billy coming here today. Come here, love,' said Jeanie, giving her daughter a big hug. 'We were all keen to see Billy again and we were hoping he'd bring news of Shenty Street and all our friends, too.' She sighed heavily, also disappointed. 'Well, we're one less for dinner, Jack,' she said. 'I've cooked some brisket and you're very welcome to have some.'

'Jeanie, my dear, that would be perfect,' said Jack. 'If I can just wash my hands . . . Monty and I have been busy this morning and neither of us is fit to be seen.'

Jeanie laughed and welcomed them in, and in a few moments she could hear greetings all round, and Peter and Robert making a fuss of Monty.

'Sorry, love,' she said to Evie, and hugged her

again. 'As Jack says, there'll be a good explanation. Billy would never let you down. I wouldn't be at all surprised if there wasn't a letter from him, come Tuesday, explaining everything.'

Dear Evie,

I'm so very sorry not to have got down to see you as we'd planned. I hope you weren't waiting a long time at the station before you realised I wasn't coming. I am that disappointed that I couldn't go at the last moment and it was impossible to get word to you. I expect you were a bit upset and I was, too.

Mum was taken poorly with one of her migraines on Sunday morning, early, just as I was getting ready to leave. It struck her down very quickly and she was quite helpless so I had to help her into bed and stay to look after her. She said she thought she was going blind, and she'd been sick in the night, too, and knew that one of her heads was coming on then, but I have to admit I must have slept through that. Poor Mum, she did seem very bad and I was going to go for the doctor but she insisted I wasn't to. She was much better in the afternoon, though. I really couldn't leave her, when she felt so ill. I'm sure you understand.

I'd been looking forward more than anything to our day together and I wouldn't have let you down if I could possibly have helped it. Please apologise to your parents and Mrs Goodwin, too, who I know had planned their day around me being there.

120

*We must make another arrangement soon to make
up for this one falling through. I truly am very, very
sorry.*

Missing you lots.

Love from Billy xxx

Evie sighed. 'That was bad timing. Poor Mrs Taylor.
I do hope she soon recovered,' she said, having read
the letter through for a second time aloud while
Sue tacked a replacement zip into a skirt for Josie's
mother.

Sue's mouth was a thin line and she didn't look
particularly sympathetic. 'Oh, I expect she did,' she
said dismissively. 'As you say, love, bad timing. Now,
Evie, let me show you how to get a zip in invis-
ibly . . . '

They got down to work on the skirt and then Sue
turned up the short trousers of Robert's new school
uniform, which were completely covering his knees,
while Evie machined together some curtain widths,
stopping frequently to check that the pattern
matched exactly.

'Come here, Bob, and let's see how these look,'
called Sue. He came in dragging his feet and
hunching his shoulders. She held the short trousers
against him. 'They'll do,' she decided.

Robert looked even more miserable.

'What's the matter?' asked Evie. 'You look like
someone's done you a bad turn.'

'It's school,' said Robert glumly. 'I don't want to go. I want to stay here with you and Grandma.'

'Don't be such a baby,' Sue replied. 'Whoever heard of a boy your age stopping at home with his grandma and sister? Why, I bet little Archie Lambert won't be making such a fuss when he starts school. It's not as if you haven't been to school before, either.'

'Yes, but, Grandma, I won't know anyone,' whined Robert. 'Pete and Martin are going to school in Redmond and I'll be all by myself at the village school.'

'You'll soon make friends,' Evie assured him. 'You won't get to meet new people if you don't go, will you?'

'S'pose not . . . '

'And it is only down the road. And you'll be home by the middle of the afternoon.'

'S'pose . . . '

'No "suppose" about it. Get on with you and put the kettle on,' ordered Sue, giving him a wink to show she understood but was taking no nonsense anyway.

'Do you think he's all right?' asked Evie, once Robert had disappeared to the big kitchen.

'Just nerves, I reckon, though I've noticed he's made no friends of his own over summer. Martin Clackett is Pete's friend and they let Bob tag along with them. And Pete's been playing music with those

Thomas boys next door to Josie, but Bob doesn't go there any more. I think he was soon bored because he can't play an instrument himself.'

'Well, he's always been a bit of an odd one out,' said Evie. 'I'll make a cake or summat for after school on the first day. That'll cheer him up.'

'Good idea, love.' Sue raised her voice. 'Bob, put the cups on the tray to bring them through, please. And I think there's a packet of biscuits in the tin.'

'Biscuits, Grandma! We must be doing well,' laughed Evie, and she pedalled the sewing machine treadle furiously to race to the end of the seam.

～

Jeanie was enjoying her work at Frederick Bailey's house. She liked that it was something she was doing on her own, away from her family for once. She, Sue and Evie had worked well together at their little laundry but, though she loved her family dearly, now that Robert was no longer a child she wanted to get away from them sometimes. The thought of working on her own – working here – had come to her all of a sudden on the day she'd met Frederick Bailey. It had felt so exactly the right thing to do: something she'd chosen for herself when the new life in Church Sandleton had been forced upon her by Michael. She'd just had to be bold for once. And it had worked out fine. Maybe she'd be bold a bit more often from now on.

She laughed aloud at that thought as she opened the ornate gate and walked up the steps to Frederick's smart front door. Of course, she'd swapped one lot of domestic chores for another, but here was cleaning such as she'd never done at home!

It was nice to come to such a pretty house. Nothing here was ordinary. She felt her shoulders straighten as she produced the key Frederick had given her and let herself in. At such moments she could almost pretend that this was her own house. The hall floor was polished wood and the central light was a brass lantern with shiny glass. They were so perfectly suited to the space that Jeanie thought she would have chosen to have exactly the same, if this were her house. But what had happened to the painting that hung on the wall next to the sitting room? The wall was bare and Jeanie noted a trace of cobwebs where the frame had rested at the top.

'Frederick – hello,' she called.

'Ah, Jeanie . . . ' He came out of his study at the back, reading glasses perched on the end of his nose. 'Thought we'd have a little outing today, if you're agreeable?'

'An outing?' she smiled. 'But I'll need to tackle those cobwebs, and give the kitchen a once-over.'

'Cobwebs and kitchen be damned. There are

more important things in life than cleanliness,' he replied mildly. 'Rise above it all and see what's important in life.'

'A clean kitchen is important,' said Jeanie, pretending to be severe. 'That's what you employ me for.'

'Ah, but today, I shall take you out of the kitchen and on a trip to a place of beautiful things.' He spread his hands like a showman, looking faintly ridiculous with the baggy knees of his worn trousers and his fraying shirt, but a little bit dashing, too, with his red kerchief knotted at his throat. He looked a jolly, peculiar little man with a smile wider than his face.

'Don't talk rot, Freddie. Just tell me where we're going. I'm not sure I'm dressed for anything but cleaning.' Jeanie was learning to give as good as she got, which Frederick evidently appreciated. She wore a pretty summer coat that Sue had made for her out of a remnant, but underneath were her everyday worn slacks and a cheap sleeveless blouse. These were quite good enough for cleaning Frederick's kitchen but possibly not the right outfit for any form of outing.

'Actually,' Frederick said in his normal voice, 'there's an auction in Kingsford and I thought I'd take *Flora* along. There will be other paintings of the period and I suspect a few experts will be in to have a look.'

'Sounds exciting,' beamed Jeanie. 'So long as you don't mind the mess waiting until next time . . .'

'Excellent. You make us some coffee and I'll go and put on my glad rags.'

Jeanie left her coat and bag on the hall chair and went down to face the electric coffee percolator, which she'd learned to operate but which still made her nervous. Frederick drank mostly coffee in the mornings and Jeanie was getting a taste for it.

In a few minutes Frederick appeared in a sports jacket and flannel trousers that Jeanie had pressed for him the previous week. His shirt was clean and tidy, and he wore a natty silk tie.

'*Flora*'s already in the boot,' he said. 'Drink your coffee and let's go.'

He led Jeanie out and through a narrow ginnel at the back of the square, which opened out into garage space.

'I wondered where you kept the car,' said Jeanie. 'I did know you had a car. A friend in the village mentioned it.'

'Oh, yes? And what else did this friend say?' he asked casually.

'Nowt really. Just that you have some properties in Church Sandleton and you drive a car.' Jeanie felt defensive. She wasn't a gossip.

'Best not to believe everything you hear,' he said, looking pointedly at her. Then he beamed his handsome smile and opened the garage to reveal a little red car. Surprisingly, considering the volume of stuff in the house, aside from the car the garage was completely empty.

As he drove to the auction, Frederick explained that he'd decided to submit the painting only at the last minute and they had to be there early so it could be included in the viewing. 'I know the people there, so it'll be all right,' he said.

Kingsford was about the size of Redmond, and the auction was to take place on the premises of an auctioneer who occupied a grand building behind the town hall. Jeanie hadn't been to Kingsford before and she looked around eagerly as Frederick parked right outside the auctioneer's and took the painting, wrapped in brown paper, out of the boot. She felt a world away from Shenty Street and all she knew, and that felt exciting and scary all at once. Jeanie took a deep breath and followed him inside and went to wait in a room where there were other paintings on view and some precious objects in cases, while he saw to business. There were pretty pieces of jewellery and great piles of crockery, and some gloomy old paintings that Jeanie wouldn't even consider buying if she had a home like Marlowe House to furnish. She'd have only beautiful things, she decided. She saw a whole dinner service decorated in a way that looked very like the pattern on Sue's precious cup and saucer that she had been given by her employer when she got married. Jeanie must remember to mention that when she got home . . . Then there was a glass case of brooches, some small and neat, others big and gaudy. A tiny one was shaped like a bow, the loops and tails set with shiny white stones. Jeanie traced a finger over the glass of the case: *so pretty* . . .

'Nice,' said Frederick, suddenly beside her. 'You've got good taste.' He gave a little chuckle. 'Aren't folk strange, eh?'

Jeanie laughed. She'd never heard that she'd got *any* taste before.

'Right, I'd like to see how *Flora* does, and I might have found something interesting that will replace her, at the right price, but the sale won't start for a while so let's go and have something to eat.'

'Lovely – thank you,' said Jeanie, pleased she was wearing the summer coat. At least she hadn't got her pinny on! She wasn't worried about getting home to feed her family. Now the boys were back at school, dinner was a more casual meal.

~

Jeanie finished her lunch and sat back, feeling full.

'Thank you, Freddie,' she said. 'That was delicious. I've never had fish with grapes before. Perhaps I'll try it at home, see what Michael thinks of it.' She laughed, then stopped suddenly, feeling disloyal.

'Good. Glad you liked it,' Frederick said. 'I'll pay the bill and then we need to get to the sale, or there will be nothing left worth having!'

'What do you do at an auction?' asked Jeanie as the waitress, wearing a black dress and frilly white apron, came over with the bill on a plate.

Frederick barely glanced at the total, just put down a note and some coins, then helped Jeanie on with her coat, which she slid into without properly standing up, in order to hide her work clothes.

'Hmm? Oh, sometimes I bid but often I just look and make a note of what's selling. You need to know the market in this game. Then I'll perhaps sell a piece privately at a good price.'

'I don't understand,' Jeanie confessed.

'That doesn't matter. So long as I do,' he laughed. 'You'll soon work it out. But remember not to make any gestures that could be mistaken for a bid.'

They sat in a large and stuffy room where rows of hard chairs were set out. Frederick acknowledged a few people with nods and smiles. Most of the chairs were occupied but when the auction got under way people wandered in and out between the lots.

Jeanie tried to concentrate on everything at first but after a while she started to get bored. The room was hot and she wanted to take off her coat but was too ashamed of her work clothes to do so.

After what seemed like hours of countless dreary paintings and ugly vases, relieved only by the occasional piece of any beauty at all, her attention was grabbed by the sound of a familiar name.

' . . . portrait . . . thought to be Flora MacDonald, the heroine of Skye . . . '

'Your *Flora*!' Jeanie whispered.

'Indeed.' Frederick squeezed her hand and they settled down to listen to the bids.

At first the bidding was slow and Jeanie was disappointed. It seemed few people were interested in *Flora*, after all. But then a few started to show interest and the price rose more quickly. Soon Jeanie was jiggling in excitement in her seat like Robert did when there was a sponge pudding, and she found herself clutching Frederick's arm in excitement. He gave her hand a squeeze and smiled into her happy face as the bids came thick and fast.

When the portrait sold for £150 Frederick declared himself well satisfied and Jeanie felt as if her eyes were on stalks at the sum.

They went outside for some fresh air then.

'That's better. It's getting a bit crowded and airless,' Jeanie said. 'Oh, but that was fun! I felt as if I was holding my breath with the suspense.'

'Why don't you go and get a cup of tea? There are a couple of things I might be interested in, which are coming up shortly, and I've got to sort out the business with the portrait, too. There's a teashop over there. I'll come and find you in a little while, if that's all right?'

'Thank you,' said Jeanie, glad to stretch her legs.

When Frederick joined her it was rather longer than 'a little while' and she'd lingered over her tea for so long that the miserable-looking waitress had asked her three times if there was anything else she wanted. Jeanie, however, refused to be cowed by her surliness. *Be bold*, she told herself. That was going to be her touchstone from now on. Michael had imposed this new life on her but she was determined to make of it what she could. And if that meant sitting waiting in a teashop, then that's what she would do. She had as much right to be here as anyone else.

The doorbell tinkled and Frederick was there, dominating the room, turning every head. The waitress approached but stepped back as he strode over to Jeanie's corner table and helped her to her feet as if she were a princess.

'I'm sorry to have kept you waiting, Jeanie,' he said. 'If you're ready, shall we go home?'

'Thank you, Freddie. Oh, but the bill . . . '

'Allow me.' He left a ten-shilling note on the table and they made for the door.

'Thank you so much,' said Jeanie graciously to the ill-tempered waitress, who was now simpering at Frederick, having seen the fortune on the table.

Jeanie emerged into the street, laughing. Frederick looked down at her with a twinkle in his eye as he took her arm and led her to the car, and Jeanie knew that he understood her exactly.

131

'Did you bid for anything?' he asked.

'I did.' She felt proud.

'And were you successful, Freddie?'

'I was. You'll see all in good time.' He gave a satisfied grin.

The drive back in the golden light of late summer was a treat for Jeanie. It had been an extraordinary day and she didn't want the drive to end. She'd thought she'd be scrubbing the kitchen and dusting the books this morning, instead, she'd been on an adventure.

'I shall take you home,' said Frederick.

'Thank you. That's kind. I'm a lot later than usual. But Mum and Evie will have fed themselves earlier and Michael goes to the Red Lion if he doesn't like the sound of what's for dinner.'

As Church Sandleton came in sight, she turned to him and said, 'I've had a lovely day, thank you. It was a bit of a holiday as I haven't done a scrap of work, but I have done all sorts of interesting new things instead.'

'My pleasure,' said Frederick, driving down the main street and pulling up in front of Pendle's.

'I'll see you tomorrow,' said Jeanie, grinning. 'Better tackle that kitchen then.'

Frederick came round and opened the car door for her, then gave her his hand to help her out. 'I've had a good day, too, Jeanie,' he said. 'Thank you.' And then he bent and kissed her hand.

As she stood gaping in astonishment he got back into the car and drove away without a backward glance.

Well, I never . . . Jeanie watched him go, her hand raised in a wave he didn't acknowledge. Jeanie gave a little chuckle, and quickened her steps as she went.

Robert came to the door, having heard the car.

'You're late, Mum. Who is that? What kind of car is that? Where have you been all this time?'

'I don't know, love,' she said vaguely, not really listening, watching the red car until it was out of sight. She felt as though the day had been rather good, and that she would love to do it again.

CHAPTER SEVEN

'**Y**OU'RE LATE,' SAID Sue, echoing Robert.
Jeanie knew her mother was much too sharp
to let the wool be pulled so easily. Yet she felt she
didn't want to share the whole day with her family.
What was the point of her going to work to make
her own way if she had to account for herself every
time she came home, she muttered softly.

'Out with it,' Sue said, peeling some carrots, while
the boys did their homework at the end of the table,
just like they had in Shenty Street.

'Frederick wanted to sell a painting and he took
me with him to the auction, that's all,' she said, grinning as she remembered the excitement of the sale.

'An auction?' Peter looked up, his face full of
interest. 'Tell us what it was like, Mum.'

'Hot and smoky,' she laughed. 'But it was exciting
when the bidding started. The picture went for quite
a lot in the end – I mean, *we'd* think it quite a lot

– and Frederick was pleased. That's how he makes his living.'

She wouldn't mention the lunch at the hotel, she decided, and nobody asked whether she'd eaten earlier.

'Tell me about your day,' she asked Sue to distract her. 'Where's Evie?'

'Oh, we've had a good one,' said Sue. 'Evie's getting to be a neat hand at stitching a hem. She's upstairs writing to Billy. She's still disappointed about the other week when he didn't turn up.' She and Jeanie exchanged meaningful looks. They'd keep their views on Ada and her convenient headaches between themselves for the time being.

'So what are you working on?' Jeanie asked, laying her coat over a chair back and putting on her pinny.

'I've a fancy blouse to make out of one of those lengths from Marie's fabric parcel, and tomorrow I'm going to go and measure up some curtains at Lavender Cottage.'

'Oh, aye? That's the one I spotted the day we arrived here, isn't it? On the way into the village – looks really pretty?'

'That's right. Miss Richards, she's called. Nice woman, fifty-ish, sensible shoes and good clothes. I'll be sure to give you a full report of the house,' laughed Sue.

'I shall expect nowt less,' Jeanie replied. 'Not a lot gets past you, Mum.'

'You're right there, lass,' said Sue, and gave her daughter a sideways look. 'At dinnertime Michael said he's going to be a bit later this evening. Something about a lot of marrows . . .'

'So how was school today, Bob?' Jeanie asked.

Robert had sunk lower and lower in his chair as Peter talked about what fun he was having at school. He'd watched how quickly Peter had done his homework, too, even though it was maths. And he had noticed earlier, as he sat reading a comic in the shop window while Sue and Evie worked, that Peter had got off the school bus with a whole group of other children, some of them older than he was, and they'd all been chatting and laughing. Robert had walked home from school along Church Sandleton High Street alone, as usual.

''S all right, I s'pose,' he mumbled.

'Only all right?' questioned Jeanie. 'Why, what's wrong with it?'

'Nothing . . . .'

'Have you found someone to play with at playtime?'

'No . . . They all know each other already. They don't want to play with me,' Robert said.

'Early days yet,' said Sue. 'You've not been there long, love. Just stick with it and you'll be all right.' She gave him a hug and he emerged from her well-padded pinafore with tears in his eyes.

'There, love, don't take on. Do you want me to

speak to your teacher – what's her name again?'
Jeanie asked.

'Miss.'

'Her *name*, Bob?'

'Miss Grainger.'

Robert shook his head and Jeanie decided she'd
try to speak to Miss Grainger anyway before the
week was out.

They were disturbed by a thumping noise from the
yard behind them and everyone turned to look
through the window. Michael had come in down the
side passage and was dragging something heavy with
him.

Jeanie went to the back door. 'What the . . . ?
Good grief, Michael, what on earth are those?' She
looked in horror at the contents of a large wooden
box. 'They're not . . . ? Oh, please, tell me they're
not all marrows?'

'They are indeed,' said Michael, straightening his
back with a groan. 'Mr Clackett says it's a bumper
year for them and he's got these to spare so I thought
you'd be able to do something with them.'

'Oh, you did, did you?' Jeanie gave him a hard
stare. 'Like marrows, do you, Michael?' she asked
meaningfully.

He looked taken aback. 'Well, it is all food, Jeanie.'

'They're *marrows*, Michael. No one likes marrows,
as far as I know,' she said, shaking her head at the
stupidity of her husband.

The others all crowded round to see and the boys lifted a few out of the box to test the weight of the monstrous vegetables.

'This one's as big as Bob,' said Peter, raising one above his head like a weightlifter.

'This one's as big as Grandma,' laughed Robert in turn, his tears forgotten as he tried and failed to lift the biggest marrow in the box.

'Oh, Michael, I hope you like marrows,' said Sue, 'because you're going to be eating an awful lot of them. And it was you that made such a fuss about having to eat so many vegetables over the summer.'

'Well, you know what you can do with these marrows,' said Jeanie, a smile playing about her mouth.

She caught Peter's eye and they spoke in unison. 'Stuff 'em!'

~

After they'd eaten their evening meal – possibly the last one for a long time that wouldn't include marrow – Michael took himself off to the Red Lion, as he so often did, saying there was a chance he'd be seeing Jack Fletcher there.

'So,' said Sue, as she and Jeanie sipped cups of tea at the kitchen table, 'seems a funny sort of job, gallivanting off to auctions when you reckon to be a housekeeper?'

'It was only a little trip. I think Frederick wanted some company on the drive to Kingsford and he asked me, that's all.'

'And does he intend paying you for a day's work while you provide him with "company"?'

'Don't you make it sound like something it's not,' said Jeanie. 'I expect he'll pay me for my time. I'll be there tomorrow cleaning and getting in a bit of shopping for him, and doing all the work I usually do. Don't make more of it than it was, please.'

Sue reached out and patted Jeanie's hand. 'I do understand why you want to make a bit of a life for yourself after being a wife and a mum and a washer of other people's clothes, but you won't forget that you're still a wife and a mum, will you?'

'I won't be forgetting that ton of marrows,' Jeanie sighed wearily, looking with distaste at the box of the vegetables now taking up a lot of space in the kitchen.

'We can store some of them. If they're kept dry they'll last a long time,' Sue said.

'We'll need a saw to get through them by November,' Jeanie smiled. 'They'll become armour-plated if we leave them too long. Don't you have a recipe for marrow jam somewhere?'

'Aye, lass, I believe so.' Sue heaved herself to her feet and went to find it, leaving Jeanie feeling happier now that her mother's attention was distracted from herself.

It has been a lovely day – not like any day she'd ever had before – and if Frederick asked her to go on another such trip with him she wouldn't hesitate to say yes. Why should every day be alike, stretching ahead for ever, just the same old thing and so little fun? Why shouldn't new and exciting things happen, even to her?

Evie and Robert made a miserable pair as they skirted a field of stubble, the greying stalks scratchy against their legs above their ankle socks.

Evie had been pleased to receive the letter of explanation and apology so quickly from Billy. It really hadn't been his fault that he'd had to stay to look after his mum, and Evie would have thought very badly of him if he'd taken the train and left Mrs Taylor feeling poorly. But it was such bad luck – the one day they had arranged to meet . . .

Since then they'd exchanged a few letters but it wasn't the same as meeting up, and Evie was missing Billy so much that it felt like a weight in her stomach. The only good thing was that the sewing business had taken off even better than she and Sue had hoped. People had been friendly when they came to the little dressmaker's premises and it felt like the family was beginning to settle into village life. Only Robert was finding it hard.

Evie looked at him now as he slouched along, hands in pockets, shoulders hunched, a look on his face that would sour milk.

'What is it, Bob? Is it just school that's bothering you?' she asked.

'*Just school? Just?* School's everything – it's all that happens to me, and it's awful, Evie.'

Robert mooched along in silence for a few minutes, his eyes fixed on the dusty field. They climbed a stile into the woods, which was a favourite place they'd discovered over the summer. Now, the first leaves were beginning to show gold in the evening sun, and the pathway they liked to take felt cool and damp.

'Let's go to the stream,' suggested Evie, remembering happy times in the summer holiday when Robert had gone there fishing with Peter and Martin Clackett.

Robert grunted and let himself be led along the rough dry track to the stream. In summer the water level had been low, but with the arrival of autumn it had started to rise. They sat down on a fallen tree trunk and watched the stream flow by, alive with insects, midges dancing in the golden light.

'Look,' whispered Evie. She raised her arm slowly and pointed to a rabbit on the path down which they'd come. It was nibbling on some plant in the verge, then hopped away. It made her smile.

Robert looked up into Evie's face, smiling.

'Brilliant,' he said. 'That's something we didn't see in Shenty Street.'

'Too right, Bob.'

'Though I think I prefer there to here.'

'Do you, now? Why's that, then?'

''Cos Pete and I went to the same school, and . . . I knew what it was like there. It's different here.'

'Can't stay the same for ever, Bob. You know that. But we've still all got each other and that's not going to change.'

'Well, I don't have any friends. At home . . . Shenty Street . . . I had Paddy, Niall and Cormac Sullivan to play with.'

'You'll make new friends—'

'No I won't! The other children are horrible. They talk different and they make fun of me.'

'How?' Evie was concerned.

'By pretending to talk like I do – like *we* all do – and making fun of it.'

Evie sighed. 'I think they must be daft,' she said. 'Folk speak like us in Lancashire, and here they speak differently. Who's to say who's better? If they were in Shenty Street they'd be the odd-sounding ones, I reckon. We know that, and if they don't then I think they're a bit stupid. If they keep on at you, you've got to tell Mum or Grandma.' Robert looked happier but he mumbled something about not wanting to be a sneak, which Evie ignored.

As they lapsed into daydreaming about Shenty

Street, the Sullivans and Billy, a water vole swam up the stream right in front of them. They both saw it at once and remained completely still and silent until it disappeared.

'Time for us to go home, too, Bob,' said Evie. 'It's getting damp.' She shivered, then took his hand. 'Come on,' and she ruffled his hair as they set off home together.

~

For a while, as everyone chatted, the clock ticked and the day grew closer to evening, everyone set about their business and the house grew quiet.

~

The children and Sue had gone to bed by the time Michael staggered his way home down the main street from the Red Lion, but Jeanie was up waiting for him. She'd spent the evening looking out recipes for cooking marrow, but then her mind wandered and she'd gone over every moment of her day with Frederick from when she'd first let herself into Marlowe House and daydreamed it was her own.

'Oh, Michael! You look like you've had a busy evening . . .' He stumbled inside, beer on his breath, and Jeanie quickly locked the front door.

'I have that,' said Michael with a hiccup, taking

144

the cup of tea from her hand. 'We had a few games of darts.'

'Get up to bed and keep your voice down. The children and Mum will be asleep by now.'

'You comin' with me?' Michael asked with a leering kind of smile.

Jeanie turned her head away from the beer fumes in disgust. This was not a fitting end to such a lovely day.

'Yes, I'll be up in a minute,' she told him, and pushed him in the direction of the stairs.

'Ah, come up with me now, lass,' slurred Michael, turning back and flinging an arm heavily around her waist.

'I'll be there in a minute, love,' she said, unwinding herself from his clumsy embrace. 'You go and warm the bed.'

He grinned then gave another hiccup. 'Good idea . . . warm the bed,' he said, and clumsily made his way upstairs.

Jeanie thought she'd give it several minutes so there'd be no danger of his being conscious when she went up.

She climbed into bed ten minutes later, moving slowly, careful not to wake Michael, though there seemed little danger of that. He was flat on his back and snoring like a pig. She lay beside him, sighing, filled with disgust. At least he wasn't a violent drunk, merely a pathetic one.

145

She pulled the blankets round her ears to block out his snoring and closed her eyes, remembering her elegant lunch at the hotel, the excitement of the auction, the happy journey home in the red car, neither she nor Frederick needing to say much, and most of all, she remembered how Frederick had helped her from the car at the door, and kissed her hand. He was unlike any man she had ever met before.

And what about tomorrow? she thought. Work, of course! I am, after all, his housekeeper, and nothing got done today. Well, *no work* got done today, though a lot did happen. And I don't mean that pile of marrows . . .

She sighed, thinking of the monster vegetables, wondering whether she could just get rid of them, even though they were food. No doubt Sue would object . . .

One thing is clear, though, Jeanie decided, remembering sitting in the hot auction room, trapped in her coat by her shabby clothes beneath. I'm not going to work *wearing* my work clothes again. I'll take them in a bag – mebbe leave them there. Just in case there's to be another outing . . .

CHAPTER EIGHT

EVIE PICKED THE post off the doormat. No letter from Billy today, but there was one addressed to her, from Mary Sullivan, if she wasn't mistaken in the handwriting. She opened it immediately, eager to hear about her friends in Shenty Street.

'What news?' asked Sue, who was washing up the breakfast things before beginning work.

'Mary says Geraldine is having a big birthday party and they've invited me to be there!' Her heart lifted for a moment. 'Oh, can I go, Grandma? Could we afford the train? I could go up on Saturday and come back on the Sunday.'

Sue looked at the hope in young Evie's face, and knew she'd work night and day to make this trip happen. 'You can get all the news and give our love to everyone. Yes, of course you can go, Evie. No doubt Billy will be there so you'll have a grand time.' She looked up and beamed at Evie, giving her a wink.

147

'But I don't know if I'll be able to afford the train fare and a present for Gerry, and I'll have to arrange somewhere to stay as well . . . ' Evie was beginning to worry already.

'Don't fret yourself, love. I'll give you the train fare, and in return you can do summat for me while you're up there.'

'Of course, Grandma. Anything!'

'I think we could make use of a few lengths from the mill shop, so if you go up on the Friday you'll have time to see everyone – including Billy – and do a bit of shopping for the dressmaking as well. It can be a sort of business trip and we'll put the train fare down to expenses. How does that sound?'

'Thank you, Grandma, that sounds brilliant, if you're sure I'll get the right things.'

'Of course you will. Why wouldn't you? The Sullivans' house is bursting with folk already, but if you stay at Dora's next door you'll be able to help Marie and the girls prepare for the party. Dora's always had a soft spot for you. She'll be glad of the company, too, her being by herself so much. I'll write and ask her if you can stay there for the two nights.'

'That would be nice. Though, of course, I could stay at Billy's, if Mrs Taylor wouldn't mind.'

Sue thought for a few moments, then said carefully, 'If Ada offers to put you up that would be fine, of course, but I wouldn't ask to stay there, and I wouldn't go there unless Billy says she's suggested it herself.'

'Oh . . .'

'It would be rude to ask if the offer's not already there.'

'But you said you'd ask Mrs Marsh – isn't that the same thing?'

'No, Evie. It's quite different,' said Sue firmly. 'Now let's get the kitchen tidied up before I go to measure up for Miss Richards' curtains. And I'm wondering how your mum's got on seeing Bob's teacher this morning, though we'll have to wait till she comes home from Redmond to find that out.'

'Those mean kids – they want their heads knocking together,' said Evie.

Sue nodded her agreement, then, turning to the sink, she glanced into the corner where the box of marrows stood. 'Blessed marrows,' she muttered. 'Do you think we can give them to the Harvest Festival, Evie?'

'To our village church and several others, Grandma,' Evie said. 'Tell you what, though, I'm not lugging any of them marrows up to the North on the train!'

And they both burst out laughing.

~

Jeanie arrived at Marlowe House carrying a cloth bag with her work clothes rolled up inside. Today she wore a carefully chosen dress under the summer coat – an old favourite but not something she would be ashamed of if there was another outing.

At the thought she pulled herself up. She had a job to do and yesterday had been a one-off. Frederick had wanted company on the drive, that's all, just as she'd explained to her mother.

She let herself in the front door with her key and, as always, her heart lifted at the elegance of the place. The space where the painting of Flora MacDonald had hung was still bare, the cobweb draped exactly where it had been the previous day.

'Frederick?' Jeanie called. 'Hello?'

No answer. She knocked on his study door, then tried the handle and peeped in. No one there. This was not unusual as he often was absent 'seeing people' and left her to get on. She didn't need supervision, after all.

But today, after the unlooked-for treat of the previous day, Jeanie felt strangely disappointed to find she was alone and firmly back in her house-keeper's role.

'Idiot,' she chided herself aloud. 'What exactly did you expect?'

But that was a question she preferred not to try to answer.

She took her work clothes up to a spare bedroom,

changed into them and came down determined to catch up on her chores.

~

Sue walked down to Lavender Cottage in the autumn sunshine. The lavender in Miss Richards' garden was long over, but the roses still graced the front of the house and the scent reminded her of visits to Mrs Russell. She wondered how that gracious lady was, and wished once again that she could have confided in her before the Carters had fled from Shenty Street.

~

It wasn't Miss Richards that brought the heavy curtain fabric down the road to Pendle's that afternoon, it was Letitia Mortimer, Miss Richards' niece, which pleased Sue. Although the young woman had an unusually confident manner, she had seemed a nice sort of person, and it had occurred to Sue when Evie had said that Robert was finding it hard to make friends, that Evie herself had no new friends her own age. The customers tended to be older than Evie – women with young families. To Sue's mind, Evie was continuing to look back to Shenty Street and her friendships with the Sullivan girls and with Billy Taylor, and not really making a new life for herself here, for all she had thrown herself into the sewing business.

Letty opened the shop door.

'Hello, Mrs Goodwin. I've got the curtaining in the bicycle basket – I'll just get it.'

She went back outside and returned carrying the thick chevron-patterned fabric in both arms. 'Shall I put it here? Ooh, I love the shop! Aunt Margaret said you'd got it set up nicely.' She turned to close the door, then back to Evie, who was hand-stitching a skirt hem. 'Hello, I'm Letty Mortimer.' She extended a hand and shook Evie's shyly proffered hand firmly.

'I'm Evelyn Carter – Evie,' said Evie, standing up and putting her work aside. 'Grandma says your fabric is lovely – may I see . . . ?'

Then there was the showing and admiring of the bold fabric, and then Letty looked through the dress patterns and commented on the styles, and she and Evie exchanged views on various cuts of skirts. Then Letty had to look through Sue's collection of lace and buttons, constantly asking where they had come from and drawing out the stories behind them – 'as if she really cared to know,' as Sue said afterwards – and so the afternoon passed, punctuated by cups of tea and laughter.

Robert came home from school and Letty even drew him into the conversation, asking about his school, which he said had been 'better than usual' that day, and then going with him to admire the ridiculous box of marrows.

'We're having summat called a fête at school,' Robert announced.

'Oh, yes? What happens there?' asked Letty, giving Evie a wink.

'I don't really know . . . I think it's part of Bonfire Night but with stalls to raise money. They want to get new curtains for the front of the platform in the hall so that we can do plays and stuff.'

'Well, we all know who can make curtains,' said Letty.

Sue smiled. 'It's the first I've heard of it, but I'll go in and see Miss Grainger. I reckon me and Evie could run up summat simple for free if they brought me the fabric.'

'So what are you going to do in this fête, Bob?' Evie asked. 'Got any fund-raising ideas?'

He looked downcast. 'No . . . they all want to do the Tombola. That's the best. Some of them have done this kind of thing before and know all about it, but I don't.'

'There's time yet to think of summat,' said Sue.

'And I must be getting back or Aunt Margaret will be thinking I've gone missing,' said Letty. 'Thank you for the tea and a wonderful afternoon. It's been the most fun I've had since . . . for ages.'

'It's been nice for us, too, love,' said Sue. 'Do come again.'

'Try keeping me away,' Letty replied, beaming. 'See you soon!'

Through the front window they saw her pushing off on the bicycle and she gave a wave and big smile as she passed.

For a moment Evie, Sue and Robert sat in silence as the air sort of settled and the habitual peace of the sewing room returned.

'Blimey, that girl's a whirlwind,' laughed Sue.

'She's lovely,' said Evie. 'I do hope she comes here again.'

'Oh, she will, living in a village this small – that is, I *think* she lives at Lavender Cottage. For all her chatter, I didn't quite learn whether she lives with Miss Richards or she's only there for a bit.'

'Mebbe we'll find out next time she comes,' said Evie. 'I do hope that will be soon.'

'Yes,' agreed Sue, 'but not too soon. Do you know, I haven't got owt done this afternoon.'

'Me neither,' said Evie. 'But we've had fun, haven't we? Sometimes it's good just to have a laugh.'

'Aye, I reckon you're right, love,' Sue replied. And she thought: Mebbe that's what our Jeanie was doing yesterday, going to that auction with Frederick Bailey. Mebbe she only wanted a bit of fun. And after all that's happened, I can't say I blame her.

∼

Since Jeanie had had a word with Miss Grainger, Robert was no longer being teased by his classmates, but he still came home in the afternoons heavy with the burden of having spent every playtime alone.

Evie tried to jolly him out of his misery, while trying not to make much of his loneliness in case he became more upset. If the weather was fine she and Robert had taken to walking along their favourite route round the field and into the wood, though as autumn drew on they needed to remember coats and gloves.

Letty came to visit them again and one day Evie and Robert took her with them.

'It's a bit gloomy,' said Letty, standing by the stream, which was now deep and cold-looking. 'The way those branches creak is creepy, and, look, that one is like a skinny hand – like a witch's hand.'

'Oh, don't, Letty,' Evie said, looking sidelong at Robert to indicate what she meant. When Robert had gone to collect some acorns she said quietly, 'Poor old Bob – he's not made any friends at school yet and coming here is one of his best things to do. I don't want him to become frightened about being in these woods. It would leave him with so little if he didn't have here to enjoy.'

Letty clamped her hand over her mouth in dramatic fashion. 'Oh, I'm so sorry, Evie. Me and my big mouth! I didn't think. Poor mite. Has he thought of anything he wants to organise for his school fête yet?'

'I don't think so. We've suggested a few things but he's not keen. It has to be summat nice for him to do, not a chore.'

'I've got it!' said Letty. 'I've just had the most brilliant idea! What about Guess the Weight of the Marrow? Heaven knows, you have plenty to choose from. The prize can be the marrow itself, so you'll have one fewer to get rid of.'

'Ha-ha, that is a good idea, except do you think Bob will have any takers if the marrow is the prize? Who'd want it?'

'Well, we could have a proper prize for the nearest guess – chocolate or a cake or something – but still have Guess the Weight,' said Letty.

'*We?*'

'Yes, *we*,' insisted Letty. 'I'm determined to play a part in this fête and not leave little Bob all on his lonesome with his marrow.' The girls both snorted with laughter. 'Peter and I can provide some entertainment to attract the punters and Bob can take the money and keep a note of the guesses. What do you think?'

'It sounds grand,' said Evie. 'Thanks, Letty. Hey, Bob, you'll never guess what Letty's just thought up . . .'

~

Billy was delighted that Evie was coming home for Geraldine's party. The Sullivan parties were always crowded, loud and generous, all their guests chipping in with food and drinks. He only hoped there would be a chance to see Evie properly – to really talk to her, not just at the party, where, if past Sullivan events were anything to go by, the noise would be incredible. Everyone in Shenty Street would be invited because no one would be getting any sleep that night.

' . . . arriving in Bolton on the Friday so that I can get a few things at the mill shop for the sewing business . . . ' Evie had written.

'Mum,' began Billy, one evening, as he brought her a cup of tea and placed it next to her *Woman's Weekly* on the side table. He turned down the radio and sat on the footstool beside her. 'I've been thinking, would it be all right if Evie came to stay the weekend of Geraldine's party, please?'

'What, stay *here*, you mean?'

'Well, yes.'

'Oh, I don't think so, Billy love. That wouldn't be possible at all.' Her tone implied that was the end of the matter.

'What do you mean, Mum?'

Ada looked at him as if he were daft. 'Where would she sleep, for a start? We've only got the two bedrooms.'

'Yes, Mum, but I could sleep on the settee in the front and Evie could have my room.'

157

'Oh, no, lad. I don't think that's a good idea,' said Ada, picking up her cup and sipping her tea. She turned the radio up to indicate the conversation was over.

Billy turned it down again.

'Why not?'

'You won't want to be sleeping on that lumpy old settee, Billy. Not with your back. Why, you could be crippled by morning.'

'Don't be soft, Mum, there's nowt wrong with the settee. And it would only be for the Friday and Saturday nights. Evie will be going home on the Sunday.'

'With your back! Whatever next? I've never heard nowt like it.'

'Mum, I wish I knew what you are on about. What's wrong with the settee? And what's wrong with my back, come to that? I only ask that we be hospitable to a friend, that's all.'

'But there'll be all the extra bedding to wash, love, and you know there's only me to do that. I don't know how I'll cope with a load of extra work at my age.'

'Your age? Goodness' sake, you're only fifty-two,' Billy muttered, beginning to lose patience.

'Don't you go bringing my age into this. I don't want you telling folk how old I am,' Ada grumbled. 'A lady's age is her own concern and no one else's.'

'Who's talking about your age, Mum? You are –

that's who. I'm talking about having a friend to stay for two nights so she can go to a party, that's all. If you don't want Evie to stay here just say so. At least I'll know where things stand.'

'Right then, she's not staying, so let that be the end of it,' Ada snapped.

'Fine.' Billy got up quickly and turned the Light Programme up to near-deafening volume, then went out leaving the door open, because he knew the draught from the passage annoyed Ada.

He put on his coat and went for a stroll down to the Lord Nelson to see who was there to join him for a pint, feeling that he'd been mean and childish to his mother. But then, she'd been mean first. He knew she regarded Michael Carter as unreliable, but it was Evie coming to Geraldine's party, not Michael, and she was the sweetest girl he could imagine.

He cheered up, thinking about Evie and how he would see her very soon. She'd written that her grandma had thought she'd ask Dora Marsh to put her up, so at least she'd be staying with a friend, and nearby. Of course, that wasn't as good as having her to stay at his own home, but he'd still see her most of the weekend . . . and he could hardly wait.

～

'I can't help noticing that your study is getting in a right old state, Frederick. Would you like me to clean it this week?' asked Jeanie. She hadn't been invited to clean the study yet, nor even to set foot in it. It was chaotic and, although Frederick hadn't said so, more private than the other rooms in the house.

Frederick looked around the small room at the back of the hall as if he didn't see it every day. Cobwebs festooned the tiny crystal chandelier and the fringed rug was rucked up by the desk, its pattern almost invisible under a layer of dust and balled-up scraps of paper that had missed the waste-paper basket.

'If you're going out, I can do it while you're gone so you won't be disturbed,' suggested Jeanie.

'Jeanie, the way you disturb me has nothing to do with vacuuming the rug,' said Frederick, 'but I have lost a receipt I need to file so I think it would be a good idea if we have a tidy-up.'

'We?' asked Jeanie, but wondering more whether she'd heard the first part correctly. *He surely didn't say that?*

'Of course *we*. My dear Jeanie, you may be the best housekeeper on this earth but there's no way I'm allowing anyone loose in my study unsupervised.'

'Oh . . . I . . . '

'It's not that I don't trust you, but only I know

what things are and where they go, and, despite how it appears, there is some order here.'

'Oh, aye? I'll take your word for that,' said Jeanie.

'We can start now, if you like, as I do need to find that receipt,' suggested her employer.

'Right, we'll remove all the paper to a safe place and you can go through it while I get rid of the dust. Would that suit you?'

'Perfectly, Jeanie. You're a woman in a million. Now please go and make us some coffee and I'll get started on the paper.'

Jeanie went down the winding stairs to the basement kitchen to face the complicated coffee percolator, trying to make sense of what Frederick had said earlier about her disturbing him. In the end she decided she had misheard and she calmly brought up the coffee, stopping to admire the new painting that had taken the place of *Flora* in the hall.

Suddenly it occurred to her how different her life was now from how it had been in Shenty Street. Here she was, a housekeeper to a nice man in a posh house, drinking coffee, of all things, surrounded by beautiful items that came and went as Frederick bought and sold them, so there was always something new to admire and to wonder at. Even the smallest of these treasures would be like the very best thing she owned if it were removed to Pendle's. Who'd have thought that Jeanie Carter of Shenty Street, up to her elbows in other folks' washing, would, just a few months later, be working here – and for such a kind man?

Michael, with his charm and his twinkly-eyed smile, had turned out to be a right slacker, there was no doubt about that. Her mother had warned her but Jeanie wouldn't listen and she knew that was down to her and no one else. He'd been lazy and a drinker when she'd met him, and he hadn't changed a bit. But this time his stupidity seemed, against all odds, to have landed them all on their feet. She worried about Michael, but then she probably always would. He was bound to get into another fix before long. But the others were all doing all right.

And what about Evie? She was less anxious about everything since Letitia Mortimer had come into her life. Letty was such a nice girl. It was sad about her parents, though, killed in a car crash at the beginning of summer, and the poor child orphaned and now living with Miss Richards, her mother's sister. Letty hadn't decided what to do with her life just yet, and who could blame her after that amount of upset?

With a sigh Jeanie took the coffee through to the study where Frederick had put all the loose paper and files into three enormous random heaps.

'Now, we can take all these piles of paper into the sitting room and you can sort it out while I get to work on those filthy windows,' she said.

'Jeanie, you're an angel. I bet you can clean the entire room before I've sorted the filing, though.'

'I bet I can,' she laughed, looking at the tottering heaps of files. 'Just take that waste-paper basket with you, will you? I reckon you'll need it . . . '

They worked all morning in adjacent rooms, calling across to each other occasionally but mostly busy in silence. Jeanie was very careful with the chandelier and the little pictures. Early on, Frederick had given her a special brush to stroke the surfaces and she took it slowly, knowing she'd never be able to pay for any breakages.

Eventually, Frederick emerged from the sitting room into the hall and held up his hands, which were black with dust. 'I'll just go and wash my hands and then we'll have some lunch. How do you fancy going to get some fish and chips?'

Jeanie held up her own hands, laughing. 'Snap! And I bet my face looks the same.'

'Jeanie, your face looks lovely,' he said seriously, and as her heart started to beat with a furious excitement he stepped forward and gently kissed her mouth. Before she knew it – before she had grasped a rational thought – he had wrapped her in his arms and was kissing her fiercely, with a passion she couldn't help but return.

'I've wanted to do that since the moment I set eyes on you,' he said.

And in that moment, Jeanie's decision that would change her family's life forever was made. There was no turning back.

CHAPTER NINE

ROBERT WAS JUMPING up and down on the spot with excitement as Evie locked the front door of Pendle's and the family set off together for the school Bonfire Night celebrations and fund-raising event.

'Have you got your gloves, Bob?' asked Jeanie.

'Yes. And Dad's going to carry the marrow because it weighs—'

'Shush! We don't want to know. There may be spies about and this is secret information known only to you,' said Peter.

Robert covered his mouth with his hand briefly. 'My lips are sealed,' he announced.

'I've got you a tin for the takings,' said Evie, holding up an old sweet tin.

'And I've got the chocolate cake for best guess,' said Jeanie, picking up her basket.

'And there's some pennies for toffee apples in my pocket,' said Sue. 'So I think we're ready.'

Streetlamps lit the way down the High Street. As the Carters neared the school gates they slowed with the throng of people heading into the school grounds, which were illuminated with electric lanterns hung on wires.

'I'll go on ahead with Bob and we'll find his table,' said Michael. 'I'll be glad to put this blessed marrow down.'

'You'll need the tin,' said Evie, handing it to Robert.

'Look, there's James and Brian,' Peter said, pointing out the Thomas twins. The boys were carrying violin cases. Peter had only his penny whistle as he'd declared his guitar playing, a recent interest at school, not yet up to public performance standard. 'And Letty and Martin, too. I'll see you all later.' He went off to join his fellow band members. Letty gave the Carters a big smile and a wave and then the musicians disappeared to get themselves ready to play.

'We'll give Bob a few minutes to set up his stall – he can manage that, or at least he can with his dad's help – and then I'll go and pretend to guess the weight to start him off,' said Jeanie. 'I'll hang on to the cake – he'll only lose it or step on it or summat – and the prize-giving isn't until after the fireworks.'

'Look, there's Jack,' said Evie. She ran over to greet her friend. 'What are you doing here, Jack? Aren't there fireworks in Redmond?'

'Hello, Evie. You look snug in that hat. Yes, there are, but I'd a bit of business for Mr Bailey out this way today and Mr Clackett said he'd like some help with the bonfire, so I've been here most of the afternoon building it up with last-minute contributions. People have been generous with their old timber,' he laughed. 'Mrs Clackett made the guy and it's pretty life-like.'

'Ooh, I must go and see it before you light the bonfire,' Evie said, and Jack gallantly extended his arm to escort her to the field behind the school.

Just as they approached the band struck up 'The Irish Rover', Letty playing her guitar and singing as purely and sweetly as Evie had ever heard anyone sing. Peter played a tune between verses, the Thomas boys lent depth and heart on their fiddles, and Martin shook and tapped his tambourine and sang harmony to Letty's lovely voice.

There was plenty of applause at the end and Letty said, 'If you like what you hear, guess the weight of the marrow. It's only a penny a go.' A queue formed at Robert's table and for a minute he looked panicked, but he gathered himself and loudly instructed every punter to 'Write your name and the weight clearly, please.'

Letty smiled and waved at Evie and then counted the band in for the next number, a song Evie had never heard before about . . . a gigantic marrow! She guessed it had been written by Peter because

167

familiar names were mentioned: Mr Clackett and Michael Carter, and the chorus had a catchy tune about a marrow that 'grew and grew'.

Evie was laughing so much by the end that her sides ached, and the queue in front of Robert was enormous.

~

Jeanie had met up with Josie Lambert, who had brought her children but lost her husband in the crowd.

'Never mind,' she said, 'he'll turn up. Gives me a chance to ask you . . . ' and she started to ask about solutions to baby Nancy's teething problems, which Jeanie didn't mind at all because the baby was so cute and she loved to hold her.

Sue wandered off to see what she could make of the stalls. She didn't often go out after dark these days and she'd noticed as soon as she left the house how difficult it had become to see where she was going without proper light, and to make out who people were. She could hear Peter's band distantly, sounding very professional, and she thought that Peter's talents would take him far from them before very long.

The fund-raising stalls were either games with prizes, or food and drink. There was treacle toffee, shattered into pieces with a hammer and sold in paper cones for a penny ha'penny, and toffee apples, too. There was mulled ale on a stand run by the Red Lion – Michael was standing there with a large beaker of it – and the Tombola. Sue looked at the prizes but decided she didn't fancy winning any of them, but she did buy toffee apples for Robert and Peter.

She had just turned away when her ears pricked up at the mention of a familiar name. Two women were standing close by, obviously unaware of Sue in the dim light.

'. . . owned by Frederick Bailey, you know, him that lives in Redmond and drives a red car.'

'Oh, yes? I've heard mention of his name. Sells this and that, I gather.'

'Antiques – overpriced bric-a-brac, I expect. But his real claim to fame is the number of times he's been married.'

'Oh, the poor man. Widowed more than once? I gather he's not old.'

'Not widowed,' said the gossip. '*Divorced.*' She hissed the word with horror in her voice. 'Three times, no less.'

'No!'

'Yes! And the second and third Mrs Baileys were someone else's wives before they took up with him. Lured them away from their husbands, so I heard.'

'Who'd have thought? So he isn't still married, then?'

169

'No, I told you, divorced the lot of them. Men like him should carry a sign to warn women what they're like, dangerous. You wouldn't catch me keeping him company.'

At this Sue, whose stomach was flipping like a pancake, chanced a peek over her shoulder to glimpse the gossip: a hugely fat woman in her early seventies, with a face like an unplumped cushion. If she hadn't felt so upset Sue would have dealt the gossip a put-down. As it was, she moved away to calm herself and have a quiet think.

Could it be true? And even if it were, what had it to do with her – with Jeanie? Sue had to acknowledge now what she'd tried to ignore these past weeks: that Jeanie was obviously fond of Frederick Bailey. But was there more to it than that? Jeanie could be wayward and Sue knew that, as her only child, Jeanie had been a bit spoiled and allowed much of what she wanted. She was still very pretty, and recently Sue had been pleased to see that Jeanie was looking after herself much better than she had in Shenty Street. She'd started doing her hair in a new way and she now walked with a spring in her step that had not been there in recent months.

Sue looked across to where Michael was buying himself another beaker of mulled ale, laughing with Jack, who now had Letty beside him. Michael's face had coarsened over the years and he was less obviously charming and more obviously lazy these days.

Could it be Michael that was bringing the roses to Jeanie's cheeks? Somehow Sue doubted it.

'Mrs Goodwin? Are you all right?'

It was Miss Richards.

'I'm fine, thank you, Miss Richards. Just getting away from the crowd for a moment, that's all. Your Letty's got a lovely voice. I had no idea she was such a talented singer. I saw quite a gathering where the band was playing. It's good of her to support Robert that way.'

'She loves an audience,' said Miss Richard indulgently 'It's good that she's doing something so cheering after all her troubles.'

'Your troubles, too, love,' said Sue, giving Miss Richards' arm a squeeze. 'Come on, let's go and see this bonfire being lit.'

'Good idea – and I still haven't had a go at Guess the Weight . . .'

The bonfire was lit and was soon blazing fiercely, then the stalls were closed while the fireworks were set off so that those doing the fund-raising could enjoy them along with everyone else. There was much oohing and aahing from the crowd and applause at the end. Then the stallholders returned to do more business or announce the results of the games. The Red Lion's mulled ale was going fast, and already over-tired little ones were being taken home to bed.

Robert took a long time to go through all the

entries for Guess the Weight of the Marrow, so Jeanie helped him in the end and the winner of the chocolate cake was declared to be Mr Clackett. Jeanie privately thought he'd weighed more than a few marrows in his time so had an advantage over most people, but he had paid to have a go, so that was all that mattered.

'I think I'll just go and see who's in the Lion,' Michael told Jeanie, and shuffled off out of the school gate.

'Aren't you going to stop and help us with . . . ?'

Too late, Michael had wandered away and seemed not to hear.

Jeanie and Sue tidied up Robert's stall and made sure the tin of money was safely in Jeanie's basket while Evie and Peter said goodbye to their friends.

Jack approached Jeanie and Sue as they were wondering what to do with the marrow. 'Have you seen Michael?' he asked. 'Mr Clackett and I could do with a hand taking down the lanterns and making the fire safe before we go.'

'Oh . . . he said he was going to the Lion,' said Jeanie, embarrassed. 'I'm sure he didn't mean to abandon you.'

'I'll help,' said Peter. 'Here, Mum.' He handed Jeanie his penny whistle. 'I'll see you at home.'

'The more help we have, the quicker we'll be,' said Jack. And he and Peter went off together to tackle dismantling the lighting.

'I can't believe Michael's not here,' Jeanie fumed. 'It's blinkin' typical of him these days. In fact, it's typical of him altogether.'

'Well, he was never a grafter, love, you always knew that.'

'I did, Mum. Somehow I never used to mind.'

'And you do now?'

'Mmm . . . The rest of us – we're all doing our bit. And you and Evie are doing amazing with the sewing, and I've got my own job, too. But Michael – he's content to do as little as possible. He can hardly even manage his job properly. I haven't forgotten Mr Clackett giving him that warning. For goodness' sake, Mum, he only has to turn up and do as he's asked. It may be cold and mucky now it's autumn but it's not exactly difficult, is it?' She realised she'd raised her voice and she looked around to make sure no one else had heard. 'Sorry, Mum, but I lose all patience with him sometimes.'

'And how are you getting on with "your own job"?' asked Sue. 'Do you know, I've yet to meet Frederick Bailey? What's it like, working for him?'

'It's fine, Mum. I've told you, I do a lot of dusting and tidying up. He's very untidy and tends to lose things and leave the place in a mess, but it's clean dirt, if you know what I mean. The kitchen's the worst because he has no idea about washing stuff up and putting it away. In fact, I meant to tell you, I've said I'll cook his dinner – lunch, he calls it –

and wash up afterwards, so I shan't be home so early from now on. And he wants me to get the shopping in, too, which means the job's a bit more interesting than just keeping the place clean.'

'Oh, aye?'

'Yes, and I've organised a system for his post. He was always losing his letters and receipts and stuff, but I put it in a special tray when it arrives and he works through it.'

'You sound very organised,' said Sue. 'I gather there isn't a Mrs Bailey or he wouldn't need a house-keeper,' she ventured.

'No, he isn't married.'

'*Was* there a Mrs Bailey?' Sue persisted, trying to find a way of telling her the truth. 'I wonder a man who seems to have so much doesn't have a wife. And he's not bad-looking – Evie told me that.'

'It's none of my business, Mum,' said Jeanie care-fully. 'I've never asked him. But you're right, there certainly isn't a Mrs Bailey these days. Maybe she died or summat. I don't like to ask.'

'Oh, I'm sure Frederick wouldn't mind you asking,' Sue said. 'After all, if you knew the full picture you wouldn't put your foot in it by mistake. It isn't like you'd gossip about him or anything. But you'd know not to say the wrong thing, then.'

'I hope I wouldn't say the wrong thing anyway,' said Jeanie. 'All I know is, there's no Mrs Bailey at Marlowe House, and that's all I need to know.'

'All right, love. Just wondering, that's all,' Sue replied. 'Now let's get some cocoa on. It's getting cold and I think Peter will want some after helping with the clearing up.'

'Good idea,' said Jeanie. They were now back at Pendle's and she pushed the door open and went through, calling out to Evie.

~

'I must sing "The Marrow Song" to Billy when I see him – only six days to go!' said Evie. 'He's been that amused by the saga of the marrows in my letters.'

'Maybe you could teach it to Harold Pyke,' said Jeanie, deadpan. 'It's a good tune, though a bit "of the moment", so to speak. Or at least I hope it is,' she added, eyeing the only slightly reduced contents of the marrow box. 'What happened to the monster marrow, Pete?'

'I left it there, by the school gate. I reckon it will have gone by Monday,' said Peter. 'There's always someone stupid enough to pinch anything, even a gigantic marrow.' And he resumed playing the song, trying out different chords.

As the children were giving the chorus one more raucous round, Michael came slowly into the kitchen, his face screwed up, looking as if his head hurt. He sat down heavily at the table and groaned.

'Can't you kids just shut up?' he snarled. 'What

kind of Saturday is it that a fella can't have a bit of peace and quiet before he does a hard day's work?'

'You only work until dinnertime on Saturdays, as you well know,' Jeanie answered, cheerfully. 'And you'll have to get a move on if you're to get over the road on time.'

'Aye, all right. Don't go on,' Michael muttered. 'I think that mulled ale must have been a bit stronger than I thought.'

'Should have drunk less of it, then,' said Peter.

There was a brief silence. 'What did you say?' said Michael menacingly.

'Shush, Pete . . . ' said Sue, who was making toast. 'Just leave it, love.'

But Peter was determined to get his opinion of his father's behaviour off his chest.

'I said you should have drunk less of it,' he repeated loudly and bravely. 'Then you could have helped pack up the lighting and the stalls. It was Jack and me, and Mr Clackett, and the twins' father who did it all, and we could have done with your help, 'specially as you said you'd be there at the end.'

'Don't you judge me in that tone, my lad,' Michael said, standing up, though his aggressive stance was undermined by his swaying on his feet.

'But everyone else is, Dad. Everyone else is saying that you skived off to the pub and left other folk to do all the work.'

'Is this true?' asked Jeanie. She couldn't help herself: even if she prolonged the argument she had to know what was being said.

'I wouldn't lie to you, Mum,' said Peter. 'Jack was trying to make excuses for you, Dad, but the others weren't taken in.' Then he added, unwisely: 'Mr Clackett was muttering about "the evils of drink" and Mr Thomas said . . . well, I heard him saying to Jack that you were a no-good drunk, and he felt sorry for Mum and Grandma. And I do, too!'

Jeanie's hands shot to her face in horror, while everyone started speaking at once.

'Peter, be quiet! You've said far too much,' shouted Sue.

And Evie said, 'Oh, Pete, that's awful. To say such a thing so that you overheard!'

'Come here, you cheeky bugger, and I'll give you a good hiding,' threatened Michael, starting towards Peter, but he lost his footing and sat down, nearly missing the chair, incapable of carrying out his threat.

'Michael, I can't believe you haven't learnt your lesson, you stupid man,' shrieked Jeanie. 'After everything that happened in Shenty Street . . .'

'Why should I shut up, Grandma, when it's only the truth?' yelled Peter.

Robert sat looking from one to another and then loudly burst into tears. Soon everyone was remonstrating with everyone else and the noise was terrible.

177

Eventually it was Sue's voice that carried above all others.

'Be quiet, the lot of you! Michael, get this cup of tea down you and get over the road to Clackett's. And take your hangover with you and don't come back until you're sober and in a better mood. Peter, Robert, go to your room, please, and don't come down until I say.'

'But, Grandma—' sniffed Robert.

'I said *go*,' snapped Sue, and the boys did as they were asked, Peter taking the guitar with him. He gave his father a filthy look in passing but he didn't appear at all contrite.

Michael got up stiffly, looking more fragile than ever, gulped down the tea, and shuffled off down the passage to the front door, grumbling and moaning in equal measure. The front door slammed and there was a sudden and deep silence.

Sue, Jeanie and Evie looked at each other.

'Well, it's better we know what folk are saying. This is a small place and if I don't learn the truth from my own family I may well hear it from others in the street or the shops, which would be far worse.'

'But here was to be our new start,' Evie said, tears spilling over. 'I thought after the to-do at the brewery and that awful business with . . . ' she automatically lowered her voice, ' . . . with Mr Hopkins, that Dad had learned his lesson and we were starting over.'

'Well, folks all know each other's business here,

so anybody steps out of line, you might as well shout it from the rooftops. If Michael can't keep sober and make an effort to be neighbourly then maybe we ought to go somewhere where we can keep our heads down more, a place where everyone *isn't* minding everyone else's business.'

'You can't mean it!' gasped Jeanie. 'What, move again? But we've hardly been here—'

'And already Michael's got a reputation for drink and idleness,' interrupted Sue.

'Oh, it's not too late, is it?' pleaded Jeanie. 'You and Evie are doing so well – I'm that proud of you – and Pete's never been so happy. He'd be heart-broken if he had to leave. And I admit I didn't like the place when I first set eyes on it, but we're settled at Pendle's now, and anyway, you're making use of the shop part. And we've got friends here. Even I have got a bit of a job of my own and I can't, I just *can't*, leave Frederick's.'

Sue sank into a chair and reached across to see if there was any more tea in the pot. Evie turned away to put the kettle on again and Jeanie could tell even from the back that she was fighting away tears. They all thought about what Sue had said for a few minutes.

Then Evie said, 'You're right about folk knowing our business here, of course, Grandma, but we can't keep running away. We had to leave Shenty Street because of Dad's debt to Mr Hopkins and it was too dangerous to stay, but if we run away this time we'll be trying to run from ourselves. We'll be taking Dad with us, so we'll be taking Dad's drinking and Dad's problems too. We could keep starting over forever, but it would always end the same.'

'Wise words, lass,' said Sue. 'Yes, you're right: better to stay where we have friends. If we move because folk know us, and know what we're like, then we'll be friendless vagabonds for the rest of our lives.'

Jeanie let out a sob and mopped her eyes. 'You're both right,' she nodded. 'And after all, no one's blaming us. Everyone here knows how hard you two work. You wouldn't be so busy if folk didn't think well of you.'

Evie refilled the teapot and, discarding the cold and soggy toast, went to find the tin of digestive biscuits.

'I've an idea,' said Sue. 'I'll have a word with Mr Clackett – or you can, if you'd rather, Jeanie, love – and see if we can get him to keep Michael too busy to think about the Red Lion. Clackett's a strict man but a fair one, and I think if he were to see keeping Michael on the straight and narrow was to his advantage, then we'd all benefit. What do you say?'

Jeanie blew her nose and gave a watery smile. 'Mr Clackett's been good to us so it's worth a try, Mum. But I reckon you're the woman to do it. He terrifies the life out of me!'

'Nonsense,' said Sue with a chuckle. 'I reckon he's soft as butter underneath. It's just that we've never got underneath to see that. I'll go over this afternoon, when Michael will have finished there for the weekend. And then we'll have to swallow our pride and rise above Michael's behaviour yesterday evening. It's the Carter women that keep the show on the road, as always.'

'And Pete and me,' said Robert, coming in to hear the last bit. 'Perhaps I can stay here with you and Evie, Grandma, and help with the sewing.'

'Perhaps you can go to school on Monday with all the money you collected for Guess the Weight,' said Jeanie.

'Oh, I forgot about the money,' said Robert. 'I haven't counted it yet.' He looked around. 'Can anyone remember what I did with the tin?'

While the others were all looking for the tin, Sue sipped her tea and thought over everything that had happened in the last day or so. Despite the upset of the morning, she found her mind returning, as it had when she lay in bed the previous night, to the gossip she had overheard about Frederick Bailey at the school bonfire. So what if he was divorced, she thought fairly, wasn't it just bad luck if his marriages hadn't worked out?

But then a little voice in her head said: And whose fault was that? It took two to make a marriage work, as she knew only too well. She didn't know anyone who was divorced, though she had known plenty of unhappy marriages in Shenty Street over the years. And *three* divorces! Could that be true – could it even be possible? She couldn't forget that awful gossiping woman had said he'd 'lured' women from their husbands, then married and divorced them. And Jeanie had already as good as said she was beginning to fall out of love with Michael. Oh Lord . . .

Well, maybe it was time to meet Frederick Bailey at last, thought Sue, but she'd have to think through very carefully exactly what she would say.

In the meantime, she remembered heavily, she'd volunteered to tackle Mr Clackett about Michael that afternoon.

'No rest for the wicked,' she muttered, heaving herself to her feet, still tired from standing all yesterday evening.

'What, Grandma?' asked Evie.

'I think I'll go and press Miss Richards' study curtains,' said Sue. 'We can take them down to Lavender Cottage and hang them this afternoon before I go to see Mr Clackett.'

'I'll give you a hand, too,' said Peter, for which Sue was grateful, though she suspected that what lay behind the offer was Peter hoping to spend the afternoon with Letty rather than with his father. And she could hardly blame him for that.

CHAPTER TEN

Evie sat on the train heading north. A case of clothes, including her party dress, and a bag containing a handmade birthday present for Geraldine, a little thank you posy for Mrs Marsh for accommodating her, and a jolly red scarf she'd knitted for Billy, was on the luggage rack above her. In her handbag was Sue's shopping list for the mill shop.

'See what you can manage to carry, love,' Sue had told her. 'Start at the top and if they've got everything then stop buying when you're spent up or you think you've run out of hands!'

Jeanie had seen her off at Redmond station, on her way to work.

'Give my special love to everyone, won't you, love? And say hello to the old house for me. But don't forget to keep quiet about where we are. We don't want Hopkins' man turning up on the doorstep at Pendle's.'

183

'No, Mum. I'll be careful who I speak to, don't worry.'

The thought of anyone trying to get information about the Carters' whereabouts from her made Evie nervous, but she was comforted by the thought that she would be among friends. After all, Brendan Sullivan knew where they all were and he'd obviously not spilled the beans.

The carriage became full before the train had stopped at many stations, but Evie was in the corner next to the window and facing forward, which she felt was the best seat. The lady sitting opposite handed round a bag of peppermints and there was some chatting between the other passengers, but Evie preferred to keep herself to herself, nervous at being on her own. She glanced at her watch and counted down the time to the change at Manchester, when she would be within an hour of seeing Billy, who had promised to meet her train in Bolton. Her stomach did that customary flip of excitement at the thought of him.

Billy had managed to swap shifts with one of his friends at work and was free the whole time Evie would be there, which was even better than she had dreamed!

After her memory of all the waiting around when Billy had been meant to visit her, Evie could hardly believe it when she changed stations at Manchester without any difficulty, the train from Manchester

Victoria was almost on time and she stepped out at Trinity Street station and looked up and down the platform for him. Quite a few passengers had alighted and there were small crowds of people blocking her view. She scanned the scene to right and left but there was no one who looked like Billy.

Oh, please, let him be here . . .

Then the other people started to move away and Evie's stomach began to change from fluttering with excitement to the nervous churning that it had done that awful Sunday at Redmond station. Her eyes searched the platform again and she suddenly had a terrible sinking feeling.

Then, just as she thought she might be out of luck a second time: 'Evie! Oh, Evie!' and he was running towards her, waving.

Evie put down her case and her bag and ran to meet him. 'Billy!' She rushed into his arms and they held each other tightly for a long, long moment. 'Oh, I thought you hadn't been able to make it. Billy, I'm that glad to see you.'

'And so am I, Evie, love. Sorry I'm a bit late. I didn't mean to worry you. Mum started fretting over nowt and getting herself worked up, and I thought I'd never get to leave the house. In the end I just ran out.'

'Well, you're here now, and so am I, and that's all that matters,' Evie said, giving him another hug and kissing his cheek.

185

'Let's get your things. Would you like a cup of tea? It's been a long journey for you.'

'No, thank you. I'm all right. I had time to have a quick cup at Manchester, but I tell you what I would like, Billy, if it fits in with your plans.'

'What's that, then?'

'I'd like to get a bag of chips and we can sit and share them in Victoria Park, just like we used to.'

'Bit parky to be sitting out, isn't it?' he asked, but smiling because he, too, treasured the memory.

'Chips always taste better in the open air, and it'll give us a chance to catch up. I mean, look at you. New overcoat, is it?'

'Aye,' said Billy. 'First time on.' He brushed imaginary dust off one shoulder.

'Come into money, have you?'

And they laughed together as they left the station, Evie carrying the bag and Billy taking her case.

~

'So tell me,' said Evie, as they sat in the park and Billy unwrapped the layers of newspaper from around the steaming chips, 'what have I been missing?'

'Nowt, so far as I can see,' said Billy. 'It's me what's done the missing. I've thought about you every single day, and you look even prettier than I remember.'

Evie blushed to the tip of her toes.

'Really, Evie,' he said seriously. 'That Sunday when

186

it all went wrong – I were that upset and it was hard to explain in a letter. I . . . I thought if you didn't forgive me . . . if you took it badly that I'd let you down—'

'But, Billy, it wasn't your fault your mother was taken poorly. And it's impossible to say if our plans are changed at the last moment when neither of us is on the telephone. I was disappointed – of course I was – but when you wrote so quickly to explain I did understand.'

'You're a good lass, Evie. One in a million.'

'So how's your mum now? No more bad head-aches?'

'She's all right, thank you, Evie. She tends to get some queer ideas into her head but it's nowt I can't deal with.'

'That good, then,' said Evie, too polite to ask about the 'queer ideas'.

'Tell me more about this Pendle's where you live, Evie. And how's your friend Letty Mortimer? I'm so glad you've found folk you like down there.'

So Evie told Billy all about Letty and Miss Richards, and how Letty's parents had been killed at the beginning of summer, but that she was being really brave about it, and then she went on to describe the Bonfire Night festivities and Robert's Guess the Weight stall, and how he'd personally raised five shillings towards buying new curtains for the school platform.

Then, as they dipped into the pile of chips, Evie told Billy about the success of Peter's band on the evening, and all about 'The Marrow Song', which made them both laugh loudly, and how Peter had abandoned the huge marrow outside the school gate where by Monday morning, it had, as he'd predicted, disappeared without trace.

'So there's someone eating marrow for breakfast, dinner and tea,' giggled Evie. 'And they're welcome to it. In fact, if they want any more I reckon Mum will be pleased to hand the wretched things over.'

'I'm glad you didn't bring me one up with you,' chuckled Billy.

'I'd have brought the whole box if I could have carried them,' Evie replied, 'but I'd have needed to take a wheelbarrow on the train. Oh, but I did bring something for you . . . '

She wiped the grease off her hands with her handkerchief, then dug around in her bag of presents until she found the scarf she'd knitted for Billy, which was wrapped in reused tissue paper.

'There. Just a little thing I made in the evenings.'

Billy unwrapped the scarf and held it out. 'Evie, it's grand – fringes at the ends and everything. You are clever. Thank you, love.' He wrapped it around his neck. 'Looks smart with my new coat.'

'You look lovely, Billy,' she said, and leaned forward to kiss him.

The kiss turned into a long one, and then it was

followed by another, so that when they drew apart Evie looked a bit shy and her face was glowing.

'I've wanted to do that since the moment we parted in July,' whispered Billy.

She nodded. 'Me, too, Billy. Oh, I've missed you so much!'

They cuddled up on the park bench and Billy put his arm around Evie and held her close. After a few minutes Evie remembered she had plans, and only this afternoon to carry them out. Tomorrow she would be busy helping the Sullivans prepare for Geraldine's party.

'I could stay here for ever, Billy, but I ought to go and say hello to Mrs Marsh, and leave my things there. She's expecting me this afternoon and she's so kind to put me up. And then I've got a shopping list for the mill shop from Grandma.'

'Then we best get on.'

Billy balled up the empty chip paper, lobbed it into a nearby waste bin, then picked up Evie's case and they set off in the direction of Shenty Street and Dora Marsh's pristine house next door to the Sullivans.

They'd just got to the top of Shenty Street – which looked to Evie as if time had stood still and was exactly as she had known it all her life – when they heard a voice calling out behind them.

'Evie! Billy!'

They turned. 'Mary!' exclaimed Evie in delight,

setting down her bag and running to meet her old school friend.

'Brilliant!' said Mary, who was wearing her school uniform and holding a bulging satchel of books. 'I hoped I'd see you sooner than later. Me and Gerry were going to come round and find you at Mrs Marsh's later. This is even better, though. Come in and have some tea with Ma and me now and tell us all about everything. You, too, Billy.'

'Oh, Mary, I'm right glad to see you,' said Evie, giving her friend a hug. 'But I need to get off to the mill shop when I've said hello to Mrs Marsh. I've a shopping list from Grandma and the shop is only open until the end of the afternoon.'

'I remember Ma getting that box of fabrics, and how pleased your gran was with them,' said Mary. 'But don't they have nice things in . . . ' she turned her head furtively to check all round in an exaggerated gesture, ' . . . you-know-where?'

'Not like they do in Bolton. It's not the same quality, and the prices are higher, too. Of course, we can't get all our fabrics here but it makes sense to stock up a bit today.'

'Then we'd best get on,' said Mary, and she took Evie's arm at one side while Billy held her hand at the other.

So Evie arrived at Dora Marsh's house surrounded by friends, and it felt just like coming home.

~

190

Geraldine's birthday party was in full swing and the noise was unbelievable. The party-goers seemed to include everyone Evie had ever met in her beloved home town, and she couldn't have been happier. There was so much news to share with her family when she got home that she was anxious she'd forget half of it.

Geraldine was the centre of attention, of course, and was looking particularly lovely in a silky bias-cut dress that showed off her fabulous figure and made her look very grown-up indeed. Evie thought she remembered Sue running it up for Marie a couple of years before, but it fit Geraldine perfectly and looked as good as new.

'Scrubs up well, doesn't she?' laughed Mary, who couldn't care less about her own appearance, though she had pinned back her hair with a couple of diamanté clips she'd borrowed from her sister in honour of this being a party. 'I think she's sweet on Colin Fraser, who works with Billy at the postal depot.'

Brendan appeared with a glass of beer for Stephen and proffering a bottle of dandelion and burdock to replenish the girls' glasses.

'Now, Evie, m'darlin', how's your dad getting on these days?'

Evie politely outlined how Michael's job was going at Clackett's, making no mention of the upsets caused by his drinking, of course. Then she told

Brendan, Mary and Stephen about the misshapen vegetables that had been the Carters' staple diet for the first few weeks, and everyone was soon roaring with laughter.

Marie was handing around plates towering with sandwiches, which she and her girls and Evie had made that afternoon, and Billy came over to join Evie, putting his arm around her.

Evie and Billy soon found themselves cornered by Mr Amsell, who was getting quite emotional on the beer he'd drunk. He was loudly declaring Gerry to be the daughter he'd never had, and the greatest asset a man who ran a busy corner shop could wish to employ, when Evie looked up and her eyes met those of Billy's mother. Ada was sitting with some of the other older ladies, including Dora Marsh and Harold Pyke's wife, and she was staring straight at Evie with an expression that could have chilled a summer's day.

Evie quickly looked away. The hostility was unmistakable, yet what could possibly be the matter? When she dared to look up again, Ada was talking to Mrs Pyke and her face was quite amicable.

I surely can't have been seeing things . . .

'You all right, love?' Billy asked, feeling Evie's tension.

'Yes . . . yes . . . '

Mr Amsell was now singing Geraldine's praises to her father, which was undoubtedly a sound diplomatic move to any proud father on his beautiful daughter's birthday, and Evie and Billy went to find Colin Fraser, as Evie said she'd heard he was a sight to behold with his Brylcreemed hair and his shiny shoes. To herself she admitted that she needed a distraction from wondering about the look she'd seen on Ada Taylor's face.

'Come on, my girl,' Billy playfully punched Evie on the arm.

'My girl'? Is that how he sees me? Yes, I reckon I am Billy's girl, but I would bet on it that his mum doesn't like to think so. Again Evie wondered what could be behind that black look on Ada's face.

'. . . Evie?'

'Oh, sorry, I got distracted. It's quite hot in here, isn't it?'

'I'll get you a glass of lemonade, if you like,' said Billy.

'Thank you.'

He disappeared and left Evie with Colin Fraser.

'I was just saying, I gather you used to live around here?' asked Colin.

'Yes, that's right,' Evie replied. 'But it's grand to come back and see everyone, especially with Gerry's birthday to celebrate.'

'Aye, the Sullivans know how to hold a party,' Colin nodded. 'Where is it you live now, Evie?'

'Oh, it's . . . it's a long way away,' she said, alarm bells suddenly ringing. This man was a stranger to her. What had Mum said as she saw her off at Redmond yesterday morning? *Don't forget to keep quiet about where we are. We don't want Hopkins' man turning up on the doorstep at Pendle's.* 'Not anywhere you'd have heard of,' she added with a smile to soften the words.

She was surprised when Colin Fraser came straight back at that. 'And how would you know whether I've heard of it or not, Evie?'

Now she felt cornered and she had to think fast. 'Because it's on the south coast,' she lied. 'Such a long way away . . . near Dover,' she improvised, remembering the name of a place on the coast from a well-known song. 'It's a very long way from here,' she repeated.

'Dover? That's nice . . . good sea views,' Colin said.

So maybe he did know Dover. Oh Lord, that was bad luck. What if he asked her about it? Evie had never been anywhere near Dover in her life! She'd simply picked the first place that came to mind.

'I think I'll just . . . go and see where Billy's got to with that lemonade,' she muttered, and backed away, leaving Colin looking puzzled until Gerry sashayed up to him and whispered something in his ear. His eyes lit up and they moved to a cabinet at the side. Soon the scratchy sound of a gramophone record rose above the already high level of conversation and a few people took partners in the centre of the room, to dance as best they could in the crowded space.

'Oh, Billy, that was difficult,' Evie murmured, joining him in the kitchen. She repeated the conversation she'd just had. 'I don't want to be unfriendly, like, but I can't be too careful.'

'You're right, of course, love,' said Billy, giving her arm a squeeze. 'I've said nowt at work about where you're living now – not to anyone – and although I've known Colin a while, and I think he's a good fella, the fewer people learn where you are, the less likely . . . ' he lowered his voice, as everyone at home always did, ' . . . Mr Hopkins is to find your dad.' Then he started laughing. 'Dover, though! That's a good one.'

'Shush,' said Evie, glancing towards the door. 'I hate lying.'

Suddenly Ada was standing in the doorway, looking fierce and disgruntled. 'Hello, Evie Carter,' she greeted her, looking spiteful. 'I think it's time we went home, Billy.'

'What, now, Mum? But it's barely nine o'clock. Party's just getting started, and I think I see a cake to cut on the side, there.' He indicated an upturned tin centred over a cake board, a pile of candles and a box of matches by the side.

'But it's that noisy now, and I'm sure I've got another of my heads coming on.'

For one terrible moment Evie felt inclined to

snigger as she pictured Billy's sour-faced mother with two heads. She decided it would be wise to keep quiet and leave this to Billy.

Evie was close enough to Billy to hear him take a deep breath. 'I'm sorry to hear that, Mum, but maybe if you have a glass of water you'll soon feel better.'

'I don't think so,' she replied. 'I don't feel up to eating cake, either.'

'Well, that's a shame, Mum, because you don't often get to celebrate birthdays with your friends, and Gerry did invite us both to join her tonight.'

'Well, Gerry Sullivan is a lovely girl, there's no doubt about that,' said Ada. 'She looks beautiful in that dress, what with her figure and her pretty hair. Always one to make an effort,' she added, giving Evie a sideways glance to dismiss her girlish party dress, which was, of course, nothing like as grown-up as Geraldine's.

'So are you staying to see her cut her cake, then, Mum?' asked Billy, trying to jolly her out of her bad mood.

Ada briefly looked again in Evie's direction and seemed to make up her mind. 'No, I reckon we've both had enough company for one evening, Billy, and it's time to go home.'

'You may well have, Mum, and I'm sorry your head's aching—'

'Oh, it is, Billy. It'll be fit to split by morning if I don't go and lie down soon.'

'—but I shall be staying a while yet. *I* don't want to miss Gerry cutting her cake—'

'Oh, I can understand that, you and Gerry being so close,' said Ada, changing tack. 'But—'

'—so I've already spoken to Mr Amsell and he's said he'll walk you to the door when you're ready to go, Mum.'

For a moment Ada looked furious. 'But, Billy—'

'That way, I get to enjoy seeing Geraldine enjoying her party on her birthday,' said Billy with exaggerated tolerance, 'and you get to walk home with someone who'll make sure you get there safely, and then you can have a little lie-down. I feared something like this might happen so I left some aspirins on the kitchen side,' he added.

Mr Amsell appeared at the kitchen door with remarkably good timing.

'Mrs Taylor, dear lady, do I gather you're ready to go home?' he asked. He leaned in close as if confiding in her. 'We old folk can't stay up so late dancing and carousing as we used to, can we?'

'Dancing and carousing . . . ?' spluttered Ada.

'Let me help you find your coat, Mrs Taylor, and I'll escort you to your door.'

'I— I don't—'

'It's really no trouble,' Mr Amsell added graciously, holding out his arm to her. 'Come, my dear, the night is young for some, and we don't want to spoil

Geraldine's party, do we? We'll just thank Marie discreetly and slip away.'

He took Ada's arm and escorted her out of the kitchen, calling, 'Goodnight, Billy and Evie,' cheerfully over his shoulder.

'All right, Billy, what's going on?' Evie asked when they'd gone.

'Let's make sure they've left and then I'll tell you,' he said, helping himself to a beer out of the crate Brendan, always a generous host.

'Yes, please. Why not?' said Evie.

Billy led her through to the main room and then out into the quiet of the passage just as Mr Amsell closed the front door behind him, Ada on his arm.

'What's the matter with your mum?' demanded Evie. 'She's been looking daggers at me and I can't think why. And how did you know she'd have a headache this evening?'

'Because I'm learning she always has a headache if she thinks things aren't going her way,' Billy replied impatiently.

'I don't understand, what's not going her way?'

'*We* aren't, Evie.' He took her hand in his and gave it a squeeze of reassurance. 'She thinks we're not suited and that it's hopeless if we . . . if we have feelings for each other and we live so far apart.'

'Not suited? Of course we're suited. We've known each other for ever,' said Evie. 'And we can't be the first folk who've been apart. I know it's difficult, and I miss you all the time—'

'And I miss you – you know I do.'

'But we write and we can meet up as often as . . . Just one minute – it was one of your mum's headaches that stopped you getting that train a few months ago, wasn't it?'

'I'm afraid it was, Evie. And I know what you're thinking. Oh, I'm that sorry. I've learned a lot these last months and I can see what her game is now. If I'd realised at the time I'd have just got the train down to see you and left her there, playing the invalid.'

Evie stood quiet for a few moments, taking all this in. 'I can't pretend I'm not angry, Billy, but I reckon you couldn't have left her. I'm trying to be fair and think if it had been my mum that felt ill, what I would have done. I can't blame you for staying to make sure she was all right.'

'But it wasn't your mum, Evie. It's my mum who's being difficult and I won't have her being nasty about you.'

'Why, what's she been saying?'

Billy realised he'd led the conversation in a direction he'd really rather avoid.

'Come on, Billy. What's she got against me? I've known your mum as long as I've known you, and she's never had cause for complaint, so far as I know.'

Billy sighed. 'It's your dad,' he said quietly. 'She thinks he's unreliable.'

'We *all* think my dad's unreliable, he's the reason we had to leave Shenty Street, after all. Most of the people in that room know about him getting the sack from the brewery, and quite a few must know about . . . ' she lowered her voice, though both were speaking softly, ' . . . about the gambling debt. Why's your mum making a fuss about him now?'

'Because she thinks I'm in love with you, of course,' said Billy, in a rush.

Evie looked at him, startled.

'And are you?' she asked quietly.

'Oh, I don't know, Evie. I think so. You're the best girl ever, and the prettiest, and I've never set eyes on anyone half as good and kind as you are . . . '

'But you can't be sure,' Evie finished for him. She knew that was true because she felt exactly the same. She loved him but was it a forever kind of love? She wanted it to be, but she couldn't yet be sure. He, too, was good and kind, but maybe he missed her so much because she was far away now. Maybe if she was nearby he wouldn't have the same yearning to be with her. She had to ask herself, of course, if the same couldn't be said of herself.

'It's all right, Billy, I do understand,' she said. 'But why should your mum mind so much if we're fond of each other?'

'I reckon she's frightened that I'll go away from

here to be with you, and leave her by herself,' Billy said. 'She's trying to make out it's because your dad begrudges going to work . . . well she says he's no good and thinks you may take after him.'

'Billy!'

'Shush, love. Hear me out. I know that's not true. She just wants me to stay with her.'

'But she must want you to have a life of your own?' said Evie. 'Children do go away from their parents sometimes – often, I suppose.'

'I know, and she does, too, but she's frightened of being left alone. She can be difficult and selfish, and she doesn't have any close friends, even though she's lived here all her life. I'm all she's got and she doesn't want to share me and she doesn't want to lose me.'

'But you can't stay in her house in Fawcett Street for ever, Billy. How old is your mum – mid-fifties? Younger than Grandma Sue. She may live for twenty or more years yet.'

'I expect she'll want the girl I marry to move in with her – with us – and look after her.'

'Good heavens, Billy, it's a good thing you've warned me,' said Evie before she could stop herself.

'Oh, so it isn't the same for your dad, living with his mother-in-law?' Billy asked angrily.

'No, Billy, it isn't the same at all. There's no one like Grandma Sue. She's kept my family on its feet through thick and thin – and it's mostly been thin, let me tell you – and she'd never stand in the way of anyone's happiness.'

'I know—'

'She's not at all like your mother. Do you think Grandma Sue would pretend to be ill to get her own way? Do you think Grandma Sue would even admit she was ill if she was? She's nothing like your mother.'

'Evie, please don't speak about my mother like that,' he said dangerously.

'Like what? Like she talks about me, you mean? Feckless? Unreliable? I'm obviously not good enough for her boy, am I?'

'Evie, please . . .'

'Well, you mustn't disappoint your mother, must you, Billy? I'm only amazed you didn't go trotting off home with her as soon as she started moaning. I wouldn't want to be in your shoes tomorrow because you'll be getting it in the neck for sure.'

'Right, I reckon it is time I went,' said Billy, 'before I hear any more of your rubbish.' He turned away and disappeared into the crowded sitting room where the heat and the noise had risen to new levels.

Evie stood breathing heavily, trying to calm her anger. Where had all that come from? She was like a woman possessed. She couldn't even remember half the awful things that had come out of her mouth. *Stupid, stupid . . .*

She waited until she thought her face was composed and then she followed Billy back into the party, determined not to spoil the occasion for anyone else. She looked around but there was no sign of him. Maybe he'd gone out the back – it really was extremely hot in the sitting room. She went into the kitchen and out to the yard but there were only smokers out there.

'What's up?' said Mary, suddenly by Evie's side when she came back indoors.

'Nothing.'

'Ah, come on, Evie. You've a face like Billy's mum. What's happened?'

'I have not got a face like Ada Taylor,' hissed Evie.

'Oh . . . I understand,' said Mary. 'That woman . . . She really is the limit, with her selfishness and her headaches. Oh, and don't think we haven't all twigged by now. She's come between you, hasn't she? Don't worry about it, darling Evie. Billy'll come round. You know what lads are like – the boys are the same with their mum. Our Cormac is only six and he's the most grown-up of the lot.'

'Oh but, Mary, I said some horrible things. And they weren't even true – well, some of them were but I still shouldn't have said them.'

'Don't fret, Evie. Everyone has a little disagreement now and again. It'll blow over. Now I think Ma is going to bring a birthday cake through in a minute. I expect she's just got delayed lighting all those candles. I hope we've got the fire brigade on standby . . . .'

So Mary tried – and mainly succeeded – in jollying Evie out of her temper and the rest of the party evening passed in catching up with old friends, dancing with Stephen Sullivan – who was very like a taller, older, more Irish version of Peter, and made Evie laugh at all his tales of the scrapes he got into at work as a gardener for the local council – and keeping an eye open in case Billy reappeared.

He didn't reappear, however, and later on Marie said he'd told her he was going home to check up on his mum, which made Evie secretly cross all over again.

It was very late when Evie escorted Dora Marsh back next door and they bade each other goodnight very wearily. So sleepy was Evie that she slipped into bed in Dora's spare room with barely a thought for Billy before she was fast asleep.

CHAPTER ELEVEN

EVIE WAS READY to leave her beloved Shenty Street again. She'd already been round to the Sullivans to thank them for a lovely party and to promise to keep in touch. Mary had given her a big hug and told her quietly not to worry about Billy.

'He'll come round. It's his mother who's being awkward, not you, Evie. You wait, he'll be down to see you with a big bunch of flowers before long,' she had reassured her friend.

'... And give my best love to your grandma, Evie, sweetheart,' called Dora.

'I will, Mrs Marsh, don't you worry.' Evie turned at the top of the street to see the kindly widow still waving.

No sign of Billy, though.

Well, what did you expect? As Mary said last night, he's a mummy's boy at heart. Ada obviously won't allow him out by himself this morning to see you off.

Mary had also said the row would blow over, Evie reminded herself, and Mary was right about most things. Obviously it hadn't blown over yet, though, she reflected as she trudged off alone to the station carrying her case and the heavy bag of fabrics she'd purchased on Friday afternoon.

It was freezing cold at the station but the train was already waiting on the platform. Evie found a seat and sat down, hot with the burden of her luggage and the remnants of her temper.

'Evie? Evie Carter? It is Evie, isn't it?'

Evie looked up at the woman sitting in the seat opposite.

'Mrs Russell, what a lovely surprise!'

'My dear, how are you? Such a long time since I've seen you,' said Mrs Russell, as the train pulled out of the station.

She looked much the same as she had when Evie and Sue had last delivered her washing to her house in summer, the day the family had found out that Michael owed money to Mr Hopkins, but somehow she had an air of purpose about her, an energy that she had never shown in the pretty pink-and-white drawing room where she sat alone.

'I'm very well, thank you, Mrs Russell, and Grandma is, too.'

'I'm pleased to hear that. I've been worried about you. Of course, I sent Annie to see if she could find out what had happened to you so I know some of it, and the rest is none of my business anyway. But I gather you live somewhere else now?'

'We do. I'm here to see some friends, that's all. We had to go away, but Grandma's said often that she was sorry not to be able to say goodbye to you.' Evie lowered her voice. 'It was a bit difficult. We had to go quickly, like.'

'And how is Mrs Goodwin doing? I imagine she's making the best of things.'

'She's set up a sewing business: a bit of dressmaking, alterations and repairs and making curtains and stuff. I'm her assistant and we're doing all right.'

'I'm glad to hear it. Give her my very best wishes, won't you?' said Mrs Russell. 'I had a lot of time for your grandmother. As I say, she makes the best of things.'

'I will. Thank you, Mrs Russell.'

'In fact, I have your grandmother to thank for a new turn in my own life.'

'How can that be?'

'Well, I always admired the way Mrs Goodwin got on with things and made her own way. I know life could be difficult for her and fate hadn't dealt her many advantages of circumstances, but so far as she could, she influenced her own destiny. She didn't just let things happen – whether good or bad – she always did her best to bring them about to her advantage. I know it was she who decided to do mending and alterations as a sideline to the washing, and that's when I heard about her. She was using her talents, and making a success of it.'

'You're right, of course,' said Evie, proud that this kind and gentle lady should think so well of her grandma.

'Now, I played the piano quite a bit when I was younger – you may have seen my piano in the back room – but when Mr Russell was killed I rather gave up. Gave up in more ways than one, I'm afraid. I didn't want to play any more. Nobody to play for, I suppose. Anyway, my cousin, who lives in Manchester, told me about a choir that needed an accompanist and she said she thought I should apply. Of course, I was very out of practice and . . . scared – yes, that's the right word – really scared that I'd make a fool of myself. But then I thought of your grandmother. I asked myself, "What would Mrs Goodwin do?" and I knew she wouldn't sit there feeling sorry for herself. Instead she'd be using her talents to make her own way. So now you find me going to Manchester to accompany the choir, as I do every Sunday.'

Evie was delighted to hear this account, and even more pleased that Grandma Sue had played a part, even if she hadn't known it.

'Congratulations, Mrs Russell. That sounds such a lovely thing to happen.'

'It is, Evie. It isn't just that I've made new friends, and I've unearthed my old and nearly forgotten love of music, but I get out and see all kinds of people now instead of sitting at home and knowing only my neighbours. We do concerts all over the place – in churches, mainly – and it's made such a difference to my life.'

She beamed at Evie, and Evie felt she could hardly wait to get home to tell Grandma Sue.

The train pulled into Manchester Victoria station and Evie and Mrs Russell said their goodbyes, Mrs Russell looking elegant and surprisingly youthful as she strode away to her rehearsal.

Evie's spirits had been lifted by this encounter and she stepped out towards London Road station with a spring in her step.

The train south was late leaving and very crowded. Evie had to stand in the corridor and there was hardly room for her luggage. A group of men came to stand nearby, smoking heavily and making lewd jokes, and Evie shifted away so she wouldn't have to listen to them.

'Can't you see it's crowded? There are no seats further down. You might as well stay where you are,' barked an ill-tempered woman as Evie tried to get past.

'Sorry . . . excuse me, please,' said Evie, edging by as best she could, certain that the cross woman was deliberately standing in her way.

'You all right, love?' said a younger woman at the end of the corridor. 'Ain't much room here, but if you sit on your case you'll be more comfortable.'

'Yes, thank you.' Evie did as she suggested, though the catches and the handle made it an uncomfortable seat, but at least she took some of the weight off her feet, which were aching after all that standing up at the party yesterday.

She got to thinking about the party, and about the disagreement with Billy, and how they'd parted without making up or even saying goodbye. Mary had seemed to think it would all be all right between them, but would it? Evie acknowledged she could never warm to Ada now she knew she had stopped Billy coming down to see her that time. She wouldn't forget the disappointment of that miserable morning at Redmond station in a hurry.

The train chugged on, seeming to take forever. It surely hadn't taken this long to go the other way on Friday?

'Something to do with signals, I reckon,' said the young woman, as if reading Evie's mind.

Evie nodded. She'd told them at home which train she'd be on and someone was going to be there at Redmond to meet her. No doubt there would be an announcement at the station of how late the train was running. She hoped whoever was waiting for her wasn't worried, and cold and bored.

'Here's my station – Kingsford,' said the young woman.

Evie stood up as the train pulled in and moved aside to let people get off and on. It was only when the train was pulling out of the station that she realised her case was no longer against the wall where she'd been sitting. Frantically she looked around, but there was no sign of it.

'Lost something?' asked an elderly man who had just got on.

'My case. I was sitting on it until Kingsford and now it's gone!'

'What's it look like?' asked the man, looking around as if Evie could possibly have missed it.

'Quite small, and covered with tweedy-looking shiny paper.'

'I saw a young woman getting off at Kingsford with a case something like that,' said the man. 'Out of this door here,' he pointed.

'Oh, no . . . '

Evie sighed heavily, wondering if there was anything she could do about it. The woman would be long gone by the time the train pulled into Redmond. Thank goodness, at least she was still holding the heavy bag of fabrics.

'Speak to the guard when you get off,' suggested the man.

'Yes, I will. Thank you,' said Evie, thinking this train journey had been horrible from the moment she'd boarded in Manchester. What with the theft and the delay, added to yesterday's row with Billy, she could hardly remember whether she'd had a nice time at the weekend at all.

The train arrived at Redmond station at last and Evie got out, making doubly sure she had her remaining bags with her. What was the point of speaking to the guard – what on earth could he do about a stolen case further up the line?

The lamps were lit on the platform and fog hung in clouds, making the globes of light dull and yellow. Evie looked along to see who had come to meet her.

'Mum!'

'Evie, love!' Jeanie came rushing up to hug her. 'So late . . . you must be tired . . . thought it'd never arrive.'

'Oh, Mum . . . ' Evie burst into tears like a small child, hugging her mother.

'Evie? What on earth's the matter, love? What's happened?'

So Evie told her mother about having her case stolen at Kingsford. This was neither the time nor the place to express her woes about Billy's mother and the row – the real cause of her tears.

Evie dried her eyes as her mother patted her back and made comforting noises, then Evie became aware of someone standing beside them.

'Mr Bailey! Oh, I'm sorry,' she sniffed. 'I know I'm being silly, it's just . . . everything . . . '

'Freddie has very kindly offered to take us home in his car,' Jeanie explained.

'Oh, but I hope you haven't been waiting for ages, as well as Mum,' Evie said to him. 'I am sorry.'

'It really is no trouble at all,' said Frederick. 'We soon discovered the train was going to be late so we quite simply went back to Marlowe House and waited in the warm until just now.' He and Jeanie smiled at each other. 'We had rather a nice time, actually. We'll speak to the stationmaster about your stolen case. You never know, it might yet turn up in left luggage, though I fear that's unlikely, and you ought to give a description of the thief, in case she's already known to the police. I hope you haven't lost anything precious or irreplaceable?'

Evie had to smile at that. She didn't own anything precious or irreplaceable.

'No, nothing like that.'

'Come on, then, let's have a word with the stationmaster and then get you home,' said Frederick.

It was cramped in the back of the car, and dark and not very warm, though Frederick had put on the heater. He drove carefully through the fog, Jeanie in the passenger seat beside him. Every so often she looked back at Evie and gave her a reassuring smile so that by the time they arrived at Pendle's all danger of more tears had passed and Evie merely felt tired and reconciled to having lost her belongings and her special friendship with Billy.

Frederick helped Jeanie out, then Evie and her bag, said goodnight, kissing Jeanie's cheek, which Evie was too tired to notice, got back in the car and made sure Jeanie had the front door open before he drove away.

'What a long way he's come, just to bring us home, Mum.' Evie stood in the passage, unbuttoning her coat.

'He's very kind,' said Jeanie.

'How come Mr Bailey was at the station? Had he been on a journey, too?'

'Mmm . . . ' said Jeanie, taking a silky patterned scarf Evie couldn't remember seeing before from around her neck and absently stowing it in her coat pocket. 'Mum, Michael, boys! Evie's back,' she called.

The door of the big kitchen at the end of the passage flew open and Peter and Robert were there, firing questions at Evie and pulling her through into the warm room.

Evie gratefully took the cup of tea her father handed her and tried to answer everyone's enquiries about who she'd seen and what their news was, but she felt too tired to deal with all their excitement.

'You look ready to drop,' said Sue. 'Off you go and get in bed, love, and I'll bring you a bowl of soup if you promise not to spill it on the sheets.'

But when Sue took the soup up, Evie was already fast asleep.

~

The fabrics Evie had chosen at the mill shop attracted the attention of customers coming in with alterations and commissions for curtains or cushion covers. Once word started to get round the village that Sue Goodwin had some stylish winter dress material of top quality on her shelves, more women came in specifically to look, and she and Evie suddenly had commissions for several garments to make up in time for Christmas.

'I thought I saw your Robert yesterday morning, going through the back into the field,' said Josie one day, as she sipped tea while she and Sue looked over romper patterns for Nancy now the little girl was starting to take her first steps.

'Robert? Surely not. He'd have been in school,' said Sue.

'Oh, well, I was surprised, but I must be mistaken,' said Josie. 'Now, a bib with a pocket would be sweet, don't you think . . . ?'

As soon as Josie had gone Sue picked up on what she had said. 'He'd better not be skiving off school,' she grumbled to Evie. 'I know he's found it difficult to settle but that's no excuse.'

'Shall I see if I can find out, Grandma? Mebbe it's a misunderstanding.'

'And mebbe it isn't,' said Sue, darkly. 'But yes, please. If there's owt the matter we need to know what it is.'

When Robert came in at around the usual time

that afternoon, but looking cold and with slightly muddy shoes, Evie suspected that Josie hadn't been mistaken at all.

'Good day at school, Bob?' she asked, making him a jam sandwich while Sue continued working in the front room.

''S'pose.'

'So what did you do?'

'Nowt much.'

'How's the Nativity play coming on?'

'Dunno . . .'

She passed him the sandwich on a plate and a mug of milky tea. 'All right, Bob, the game's up. I know you weren't at school this afternoon. Why was that?'

He tucked into the sandwich hungrily, not answering.

'And I bet you didn't have anything to eat at dinnertime, did you?'

At that, he pushed the plate away and screwed his fists into his tearful eyes.

'Tell me.'

'It's horrible at school. All the others have best friends and lots of other friends, too. I've got no one.'

'Who do you sit next to these days?'

'I told you, no one. I'm by myself at the back.'

'Oh, Bob . . .'

'And I was going to be the Innkeeper in the play, Miss Grainger said, but one of the other teachers,

216

Mrs Kelsey, said she couldn't understand what I was saying and Miss Grainger was to choose someone who was "nicely spoken".'

'Well, that doesn't sound like Miss Grainger to me. She's always been fair to you.'

'But it's Mrs Kelsey who's in charge of the play and she's got a loud voice and the other teachers have to do as she says. She's right bossy.'

Evie sighed. 'Do you want Mum to go and see Miss Grainger again?'

'No! I don't want to go at all. I'm fed up of the others poking fun and making out I'm daft.'

'But I thought you'd put all this behind you?' said Evie. 'Weren't things better after the success of Guess the Weight?'

'They were for a bit, but then it got bad again.'

'Well, you have to go to school, Bob. It's the law. You can't hide in the woods all day, especially now it's winter. You looked cold when you came in and it'll get a lot colder yet. We'll ask Mum to go and speak to Miss Grainger again, or maybe this Mrs Kelsey, as she's the one who's made things difficult for you over the play.'

'She's big and she's always shouting. She doesn't listen to other folk.'

'Can't be much of a teacher, then,' said Evie. 'Sounds like a job for Grandma.'

~

Sue was briefed about Robert's troubles and she shared this with Jeanie, but not with Michael. He'd been unusually ill-tempered of late – Mr Clackett was keeping him very hard at work since Sue had had a word – and she didn't think it would help matters if he were to box Robert's ears and shout at him.

Sue went with Robert to school the next morning, leaving Evie to get on with baby Nancy's rompers on her own. When she came back she looked grim but satisfied.

'Well, that Mrs Kelsey might say she can't tell what Bob is saying but she certainly understands me,' said Sue, and left it at that.

Robert went into school and stayed until the end every day after that, though he was now miscast as part of the Heavenly Host in the Nativity play and didn't have a speaking part. Still, it was a small triumph for him of sorts, as not every child had a part, and Sue vowed to make sure his gown was the best-fitting of all the angels' costumes.

~

Evie hadn't expected to hear from Billy for a few days after their argument and her return home, but when she still had not had a letter by the middle of December, she started to think that Mary had been wrong and that Billy was no longer interested in her.

'And have you written to him?' asked Sue, as they sat side by side, cutting and stitching.

'No, Grandma.'

'Why's that, then? Do you think the argument was all his fault and nothing to do with you?'

Evie breathed out heavily and tried to recall exactly what had been said. Strangely, she could remember little of the cause now, only that Ada had been behind it.

'Well, it was his mum that stopped him getting the train that day, I told you.'

'That was mean, I admit, leaving you standing there on the station for hours, but if the woman's scared of losing him then that's why she's acting unfriendly. You see, Evie, as things stand, you can't both have Billy, can you? He can't be with you and with Ada.'

'True, Grandma. Thing is, I don't even know for sure that I want to be with Billy for ever and ever. It's too much to think of that yet, especially if his mother comes as part of the deal. Oh, I know that's selfish, Grandma, but you should have seen her face, and she was so rude. Maybe I'll know one day, and I certainly don't want *never* to see him again. That would be terrible! I want us to be as we were – special friends – and I do miss his letters. I was so excited about seeing him when I went north.'

'So if you could make it right between the two of you now, never mind about the future, what would you do?'

Evie thought for a few minutes. 'I'd write and say I want us to be friends again,' she said quietly.

'There's your answer, then,' said Sue, not looking up from her work. 'Why don't you go and do that now? *You* choose to make it happen. Don't wait for Billy to decide. Or his mother. He's a good lad is Billy. You can have the rest of the morning off so you can get the letter in the post box by Suttons' straight away. Then you can get the darts sewn in this blouse and the collar made by teatime.'

Evie kissed Sue's bent head and went to do as she suggested. She remembered what Mrs Russell had said on the train about how Grandma Sue influenced her own destiny, and she acknowledged to herself what a wise woman her grandma was.

Dear Billy,

I'm sorry we fell out at Gerry's party and I'm sorry for the things I said. I want it to be just like it was between us, and I hope you are prepared to forgive me. I promise not speak about your mother like that again. It was very rude and I know it was wrong.

It was especially wrong because we'd had such a lovely time until then and you'd swapped shifts to be with me and make it a nice weekend, and it got spoiled.

I've missed your letters and I hope this makes up for what I said and that we can be friends again.

With love,
Evie

How could such a short letter have taken half the morning to write? Evie wasn't entirely satisfied with it but it was the best she could do. She went down to Suttons' to post it in the pillar box outside, then nipped into the shop to buy some humbugs, which were Sue's favourites.

As she was coming out she saw further down the High Street her father disappearing into the Red Lion.

But Grandma had a word with Mr Clackett, who is supposed to be keeping Dad's nose to the grindstone so he doesn't have time to go to the Lion.

'Honestly, Grandma, if it's not Bob it's Dad,' she said when she got back to Pendle's, handing the sweets to Sue and explaining what she'd seen. 'He's like another child.'

'You've realised that, have you, love?' said Sue.

'Should one of us go and fetch him out? I don't know if he'd take any notice of me, and I don't want you to have to go. It's cold outside and a bit icy.'

'It might hurt his dignity to have his wife's mother come and drag him out of the pub in front of everyone,' said Sue. 'And I don't want to ask Mr Clackett to fetch him. That'll only create more trouble.'

Luckily, at that moment there was a knock on the shop door, which was always open for customers anyway, and there was Jack, Monty beside him.

'By heck, Jack, you're the very man I need,' said Sue. 'Our Michael's been seen entering the Lion and he's supposed to be too busy at Clackett's to be having a pint or two at dinnertime. You know how Mr Clackett doesn't hold with drinking, and Michael's already been given a warning.'

'Leave it to me and Monty,' said Jack. 'I can guess what you're going to say and I'll go there right away.'

'Oh, thank you, lad. I'm that grateful. I reckon you've come for the rent. When you've done with Michael, come back and I'll pay you and we'll give you a bite to eat, too. How does that sound?'

'I'll see you directly,' Jack said, and set off for the pub, Monty trotting along beside him.

'That was lucky,' said Sue.

'Yes, Grandma. But what on earth are we going to do when Jack isn't here to help us? Dad's been in a bad mood generally lately, and I'd hate there to be a scene in the Lion.'

'I'll have to have another word with Mr Clackett,' said Sue, getting up stiffly, then taking off her glasses and rubbing her eyes. 'So dark these days. I hate winter. I think we might need a stronger bulb in that there light. It's going to be a cold one this year, I can feel it in my bones.'

~

Having dispatched Michael to Clackett's, Jack and Monty returned to Pendle's and shared Sue and Evie's lunch, and then Letty came round to have a look through the fabrics with the idea of asking Sue to make a blouse for Miss Richards as a Christmas present.

Jack had been about to depart, but when Letty appeared he stayed on and made himself useful brewing tea and entertaining 'the ladies', as he called the three of them, while Sue and Evie worked and Letty asked questions about everything in her usual vivacious way. There was much laughter, and Sue was glad to see Evie looking happier than she had for a few weeks, now she'd got her apology to Billy in the post. Sue also noticed that Jack paid a lot of attention to Letty, taking an interest in everything she said and lending a sympathetic ear when Letty admitted that she still didn't know what she was going to do with herself next, but her aunt liked her company, and her presence at Lavender Cottage allowed them to grieve together for the loss of Letty's parents without having to explain or put on a brave face.

Then Peter came home from school and there was more lively conversation. Letty showed him some new chords on the guitar and he strummed while they both sang, Jack joining in on the chorus.

'It's better than the wireless,' declared Evie. 'Has anyone seen Bob? I haven't heard him come in but maybe he went straight upstairs. Odd he shouldn't have said hello, though.'

'I'll go and look,' Peter said.

'He's been finding school hard again lately, poor lamb,' Sue explained to Jack and Letty, 'though I had thought we'd turned the corner with that.'

'No sign of him upstairs,' said Peter, returning to the front room. 'I'll look out the back. Bob! Bob! Come and say hello to Letty and Jack. Bob . . . ?' He reappeared shortly after. 'He's not there either.'

'Odd,' Evie said, putting her work aside. 'Mebbe he's been kept in at school or summat. We ought to go and make sure.'

'I'll go with you,' Peter volunteered. 'It'll take us both to face down that Mrs Kelsey, from what I've heard about her. Shan't be long.'

They put on their outdoor shoes and coats and set off down the High Street for the school.

'You and Letty will want to be getting off home,' Sue said, as the workroom, which had been so full of life all afternoon, subsided into slightly anxious quiet.

'No, I'll wait and make sure Robert's all right,' said Letty.

'And I will, too. And when we've found him I'll take you back home in the rig, Letty,' said Jack.

A quarter-hour passed and Peter and Evie returned, their cheeks red from the cold that had descended on the village with the night drawing in.

'The school was completely shut and dark,' said Letty. 'We looked all round. Everyone's gone home.'

'Right,' said Jack, 'it's getting dark now so it looks like Robert went off somewhere after school instead of coming straight home. Now don't worry, Sue. If we search around the village it's quite likely we'll find him in no time. Could he have gone to play with one of his friends?'

'Oh, Jack, the poor lad hasn't got any friends! He never goes to play with anyone.'

Jack looked taken aback for a moment. 'He hasn't mentioned anyone's name?'

Sue shook her head. 'Has he said anything to you, Peter?'

'No, Grandma. I reckon we should start on this search quickly, though. It's getting frosty already. You stay here in case he wanders in, and the rest of us can go and ask if anyone's seen him. How does that sound?'

Peter and Evie set out to ask in the Suttons' shop and up and down the High Street. When they'd gone, Jack said he'd go to the market garden and ask Michael and Mr Clackett if they'd seen Robert playing in the field at the back.

'I'm sure they'll want to help us look, too,' said Letty.

'Of course Michael will. And I dare say Mr Clackett will, as well,' Jack said, holding the door of Pendle's open for her.

225

Sue went to the shop window and stood looking out, impatient for news. After a while she saw by the light of a streetlamp Evie and Peter coming back.

'Well, love?'

'Nothing. Though Mrs Lambert did say she saw Bob coming out of school this afternoon, so we definitely know he's both been and left,' said Evie.

Sue's hand leapt to cover her mouth as she stifled a sob. She sniffed back her anxious tears and visibly pulled herself together.

'You don't think . . . he could have been kidnapped by Mr Hopkins' men?' asked Peter.

'Don't be daft, Pete,' Sue snapped. 'It's Michael they're interested in, not Bob.'

'And, anyway, they don't know where any of us are,' said Evie. 'But I've just thought of somewhere else to look – down through the field and in the woods. Bob's always liked it there. Do you remember how he said he wanted to stay there for ever with the woodland creatures?'

'But why would he be there now, in the dark and cold?' asked Sue.

'I don't know, Grandma, but at least we ought to go and look. Pete, I think there's a torch in the cupboard under the stairs. We'll need that as it'll be properly dark beyond the streetlights by now.'

'Good thinking.' He went to find it and came back with two torches. 'Grandma, you stay here and put the kettle on. I reckon Bob will need a warm drink when he comes back. And tell Dad and Jack where we've gone.'

'Off you go then, you two. Take it steady; it may be slippery.'

'We will, Grandma. Try not to worry,' said Evie, giving Sue a hug before dashing off after Peter.

It was pitch-dark in the field behind the High Street. Evie and Peter were slowed by the uneven ground, but they hurried as best they could. Their breathing sounded loud and ragged in the quiet of the field.

'There!' said Peter suddenly as something shot across the track in front of them.

'Aah!' Evie cried. 'Oh, my goodness, I nearly died of fright!'

'It was only a deer,' Peter said, but his heart was hammering, too. The animal had seemed enormous, coming out of the dark so close to them.

They paused only for a few seconds to calm themselves, then moved on, over the stile at the back of the field and into the woods.

'Bob!' called Evie. Her voice sounded high and thin.

'Bob! Bob!' Peter bellowed. 'We'll have to go slower here, Evie, or we're bound to trip over something.'

They crept along, too busy concentrating on stepping over tree roots and avoiding brambles to call out. The sound of the stream grew louder and the temperature seemed to plummet as they neared the water, which was fast-flowing now, and looked black in the light of the torches.

'Bob, Bob, are you there?' called Evie. 'If you can hear us, please answer.'

No one spoke.

'I don't think he can be here,' said Peter, training the beam of his torch over the partially overgrown track in front of them. 'Bob! Bob! No, I think we're wasting our time, Sis.' He turned to retrace his steps.

'No, wait . . . ' Evie shone her torch where Peter's had just arced over the bank of the stream. It was very muddy and there were signs of shoeprints sliding down towards the water. 'Bob, are you there?' She went forward carefully, the light slightly unsteady in her shaking hand. Peter trained his torch in the same direction.

'Oh, Bob . . . ' gasped Evie.

Her younger brother was lying on his front in the stream, his face turned to one side just under the surface.

She ran forward. 'Here, Peter, take my torch. Oh, Bob, oh, you poor little fella . . . ' She lowered herself into the stream, gasping at the coldness of the water. 'Peter, for God's sake shine those torches over here.'

Peter did as she asked, though he was sobbing loudly as Evie dragged the little boy's body up from the stream, heaving it over onto the bank with Peter's help. There was a huge graze on Robert's forehead. It looked as if he'd slipped on the bank, fallen into the stream and hit his head on some stone or log beneath the water. There was no doubt, though, that he had drowned.

'Here . . . ' Evie held out her hand and Peter pulled her onto the bank where they stood and held each other tightly, weeping with all their hearts for their brother.

That was how Michael and Jack found them a few minutes later.

PART TWO

A turn in the road
January 1955–January 1956

CHAPTER TWELVE

Evie looked up briefly from the sewing machine and waved as the postman passed the shop window of Pendle's. Then she heard the letterbox clatter.

'Aren't you going to see what's come?' asked Sue, squinting over the shirt collar she was turning.

'I don't expect there'll be a letter from Billy, if that's what you mean,' said Evie heavily, continuing with her work.

'Oh, I'll go then,' said Sue, beginning to heave herself to her feet.

'No, Grandma, it's all right, I will.'

Evie came back with two envelopes, neither of which was addressed to her. She resumed treadling and the two women continued their work in silence for a while.

Since Robert's death, Pendle's had often fallen into silence, and in the dark days of late January, no one's spirits could be lifted. The women went to their work quietly because they must, and Michael spent every evening drinking away his wages or being bought rounds by men who felt sorry for him, often returning home drunk and morose, or being brought home by Jack, or the local policeman if he happened to be around.

As she worked, Sue allowed her mind to wander. She couldn't see a way out of this and she wondered if they would ever be happy again. She thought back to the autumn when the sewing business had taken off so well, when Jeanie had blossomed in her new job, and even Michael had worked hard with Mr Clackett keeping him in order; when Peter had entertained them all with his music and his excitement about the band, and little Robert had been the hero of the Bonfire Night fête with the success of his fund-raising. It felt like a lifetime ago now – almost as if all those things had happened to a different family.

The sewing business was still going well. Evie was working hard, but there was not much laughter in her these days. Often Sue would look up while they stitched and catch Evie with red eyes, silently weeping for her brother.

Billy had not been in touch since Evie's trip to Bolton for Geraldine's birthday party. Evie had written that day Robert died and then again just before Christmas, with a card and a letter breaking the awful news, but she'd heard nothing from him. Sue thought that strange; she wouldn't have had Billy down as someone to bear a grudge. His mother, on the other hand, was exactly that kind of person, and Sue had her suspicions about Ada's role in Billy's silence. But again, she had felt too worn down with her sadness to do anything about that.

Peter was hardly here these days, and Sue knew Evie missed him. They all did. He'd practically moved in with the Thomas twins, Brian and James, and taken his music with him. Mr and Mrs Thomas had welcomed him and were glad to offer him a second home and a place where, Mrs Thomas had confided to Sue, he could be away from being reminded too much of Robert and get over his brother's death in his own way.

'How are you doing with those curtains, Evie? Will they be ready for Mrs Cooke by tomorrow afternoon? She wants to hang them herself, she says, so she's collecting them.'

'Only the hems to do once I've finished this bit, Grandma. Would you like a cup of tea?'

'I'll do it, lass. I could do to rest my eyes for a minute or two,' said Sue, getting up and shuffling through to the big kitchen.

She sat down heavily at the table while the kettle boiled, and wondered what on earth she could do to get the heart back into the family. She and Evie were fairly busy most days, and glad of the commissions, although those had tailed off a little since Christmas, but somehow they worked automatically now, without the enthusiasm and drive they'd had before Robert . . .

Sue put her head in her hands, overtaken for a moment by her sadness, and shed a few quiet tears. Then she sat up, wiped her eyes and stood up to make the tea. While it brewed she thought about Jeanie and Frederick Bailey.

Never in a million years would Sue have guessed she would meet Frederick Bailey for the first time at her grandson's funeral. Mr Bailey had sat near the back of the village church but afterwards he'd made a point of coming over to express his sympathy to the whole family and remind a tearful Jeanie that she need not go back to work until she felt up to it. Jeanie hadn't stayed away long, though.

Sue had taken a great interest in this man she'd heard so much about, and a fella who'd been divorced three times, if the gossip was true, though Sue was ashamed of listening and then remembering what she had heard – but an interesting man, with flair and imagination. Mostly what she saw, though, was a man who was clearly in love with Jeanie, and with whom Jeanie was equally clearly in love. At least, it was clear to her mother. Sue was pleased to think that no one else, especially Michael, had noticed the signs that she saw all too well.

Oh dear, what to do about that? She'd pushed it

to the back of her mind, what with feeling so tired . . . and the awfulness of Christmas, and now it was dark nearly all day and her eyes weren't so good in poor daylight.

She put the cups of tea on a tray and took it through to the front room. Evie was just finishing her seams and she stopped, smiling up at her grand-mother.

'Grandma, do you know, I don't think I ever told you about seeing Mrs Russell on the train, did I? I sort of forgot, what with Billy, and having my things stolen.'

'What, you saw her when you went to Gerry's party?'

'On the way back. She was sitting opposite me and she looked really well and happy. It was lovely to see her, but the best thing was what she told me, and that it was all down to you.'

'Are you having me on, our Evie? How could I have made any difference to Mrs Russell?'

Evie related the story of how Mrs Russell had been inspired by Sue to gather her courage and rediscover her talent for playing the piano when she thought her life held so little, how she'd used her skills to make new friends and to bring something better and more interesting into her life.

Sue laughed. 'I'm right pleased for Mrs Russell. She's a lovely woman and it's a shame she lost her confidence to play the piano, but I think she might have found her way back to her music in the end anyway, without me. Though it's nice of her to say I helped.'

'No, Grandma, she really thought it was all down to you, and how you made a go of the washing and then the fine mending and alterations. She said summat like . . . ' Evie thought carefully, ' . . . "Mrs Goodwin influenced her own destiny. She didn't just let things happen to her, she always did her best to bring them about to her advantage." Summat like that, anyway. I were that proud of you, Grandma, and Mrs Russell isn't the kind of lady who would tell lies or flatter a person, is she?'

'Well, that's true enough, Evie, love. I'm glad you've remembered you saw her. That's given me summat to think about while I finish this collar.'

'Aye, me, too, Grandma,' said Evie. 'I've felt ever so down lately—'

'We all have, lass.'

'But if we don't raise ourselves up, who's going to do it for us? Oh, I know Miss Richards and Letty couldn't have been kinder – and Jack, too – and everyone in the village has done their best to help, but in the end it's down to us, isn't it? We have to decide if we're going to sit here being sad for ever or . . . ' she looked round the workroom, at the lengths of cloth on the shelves and the partially finished curtains, ' . . . or whether we're going to move this business on.'

'You're right, love. I've been trying not to think about it, but soon everyone in Church Sandleton who wants new curtains will have them, and then what will we do? The mending and alterations don't bring in much, and though we've made quite a few garments recently there doesn't seem to be a call for a lot of dressmaking in the village now Christmas is over. We need new customers.'

'And it's up to us to find them, Grandma,' said Evie. 'We can't sit here feeling sorry for ourselves.'

'And no one wants to keep company with miserable people,' said a merry voice at the door. 'Hello, Mrs Goodwin, Evie.'

'Letty!'

'Just passing. I won't stay long and disturb you.'

'Come in, love. Evie and I were giving ourselves a talking to, telling ourselves to snap out of it,' said Sue. 'You and your Aunt Margaret know better than anyone what it's like, and we admire how you've both coped with your sadness.'

'That's kind of you to say, Mrs Goodwin. I know it's helped Aunt Margaret a lot that she's had her articles to write for the newspaper. There's nothing like a deadline to keep you focused, she says.'

'If Grandma and me take on some new customers, we'll be that busy we won't have time to mope. But we need to find them first.'

'I think you should advertise,' said Letty, pulling off her hat and gloves, helping herself to a chair and putting her elbows on the table. 'I'm sure there's a market for a top dressmaker in Redmond. Why don't you put an advert in one of the local papers?'

'I suppose we could do, if it doesn't cost very much.'

'I can't think it would in the local paper or the parish newsletter. Why don't you decide which paper your clients would most likely read and then, if you want, I can ring up from the cottage and find out what the advertising rates are?'

'Oh, Letty, thank you. That would be grand,' said Evie.

'Provided we can get a few commissions outside the village we'll have enough to keep us afloat if we've not got much from Church Sandleton folk. I think in a few weeks we could be really busy,' said Sue. 'People like to have new clothes for the milder weather.'

'I'll gather a few different newspapers and magazines when I'm next in Redmond and that can start you off,' Letty offered.

'You're an angel,' said Sue. 'But I think I might take a trip into Redmond on the bus and have a look around, see what's what, like.'

Evie felt her heart lift at this news.

'I'll come with you, if you like, Grandma. Shall we go this afternoon?'

'We'll go tomorrow morning,' Sue decided. 'You've got Mrs Cooke's curtains to finish. Mustn't forget our loyal customers.'

'I'd never do that, Grandma.' Evie found herself smiling.

'So exciting,' said Letty, while Evie began on the hand-stitched hems. 'I just wish I had an idea of what I can do.'

'Well, you've already come up with some ideas to help us,' said Sue. 'And I know you're a real help to your auntie because she told me so.'

'She lets me organise her office – I mean, as if I'm her secretary,' said Letty, 'but I don't think I want to be a real secretary. Aunt Margaret is easy to work for and, anyway, I like to play in the band and that takes up a lot of time.'

'Speaking of the band, how's Peter doing?' asked Sue. 'We don't see so much of him these days. He seems to have gone to live at the Thomases. I'll have to pay Mr Thomas Peter's keep if he doesn't come home soon.'

'I think he likes it there,' said Letty carefully. 'He doesn't want to be reminded of Bob all the time, as he would be here. The Thomases have got masses of room and Peter fits in so well. I heard Mrs Thomas telling Aunt Margaret how much she likes having him around and what a nice boy he is. And he doesn't have to see his father there.'

As soon as the words were out, Letty flushed with embarrassment. 'I'm sorry, I didn't mean to be rude.' She got up and pulled on her knitted hat and gloves. 'I should be going and let you get your work done. Let me know how you get on in Redmond tomorrow, won't you?'

She waved and blew kisses, laughing, as she left.

Evie sat sewing intently for a few minutes and then she said, 'Letty was only saying what we already know, Grandma, wasn't she? Pete still hasn't forgiven Dad for us having to leave Bolton. He doesn't like Dad at all these days, and he thinks that everything that's happened to us since we got here – all the setbacks, not the good things like our work here and Mum's job – are Dad's fault because we're here because of him.'

'So what are you saying, Evie, love?' Sue got up and draped the finished shirt over the ironing board in the corner. 'That Pete blames your dad for what happened to Bob?'

'Yes, Grandma. I'm afraid he does. After all, if we were still in Shenty Street, Bob wouldn't have slipped into the stream in the woods.'

'But it was just a horrible accident, Evie. *You* know that, don't you?'

'Yes . . . yes, and I don't blame Dad for what happened, but I can kind of see what Pete means. And . . . oh, Grandma, he's so angry with Dad. He has been for a long time now and I don't see it getting any better.'

~

242

It was evening and Michael had come back from Clackett's and then gone out again to the Red Lion, as he did most days since Robert had drowned. His neighbours in the pub felt sorry for him that his younger son had died and there were always plenty of drinks bought for him. Sometimes he even bought rounds in return, though not often. His main currency was tall stories about bets won and lost in the pubs of Bolton, how he'd single-handedly saved the brewery from crisis on several occasions, and about the toughness of life up north in general. Then, as the drink took effect, he'd descend into maudlin stories of his 'little lad' and reminisce about what a wonderful son Robert had been.

Jack Fletcher came into the Red Lion that evening, and saw that Michael had had a skinful.

'All right, Michael, maybe it's time to go home to that lovely wife of yours,' suggested Jack after a few minutes.

'Oh, there's time for another one,' said Michael, putting his empty pint glass down heavily on the bar. 'Who's for another?'

There were one or two takers, but the locals generally respected Jack, both as a good man and as Frederick Bailey's man, and they weren't going to undermine his sound suggestion.

The beer was bought and drunk, more rambling stories were told, and then Jack announced that it really was time to get off home now. 'Jeanie will have your dinner on the table, Michael, and you don't want to keep Sue and Evie waiting for theirs after they've been hard at work all day.'

'Aye, Jack, lad, that's all I ever hear: Jeanie this and that, Sue and Evie this and that . . . '

'Well, they are your family, Michael, and Jeanie's a good cook. She'll have made an effort.'

'A house of women, that's what it's become. Outnumbered, I am, and by women, with their own jobs to go to. Work that they think is better than mine.'

'I'm sure that's not true, Michael,' said Jack, taking Michael's pint and putting it out of reach on the bar. Then he steered Michael towards the door and Monty followed them. 'They work hard, but they appreciate what you do, too. You know that.'

'I know no such thing,' declared Michael. 'They all look down on me, and even my own son has left home to avoid me and gone to live with Mr pompous Thomas and his snide opinions. It's them Thomases that have bad-mouthed me to Peter – it started at the Bonfire – and now he's gone to live with them.'

'I think young Peter is having a hard time getting over his brother's accident,' said Jack quietly, 'and it's his way of coping with it.'

'We're all having a hard time getting over Bob's accident,' said Michael, raising his voice. 'One son dead and the other left home to go to live with other folk, not his family. And when I get home, what do I find? Women! Women everywhere, talking about curtains and cleaning, and other women's stuff.'

'Well, I don't know about that,' said Jack, 'but from what I know of Jeanie, she'll be happy to hear about your day and what you've been doing at Clackett's. And I'm sure Sue and Evie will be, too. You've got good women, there, Michael, and I think you should treasure them.'

'Do you, Jack? Do you?' snapped Michael. 'And what do you think I've got to tell them about my day, eh? Up to my knees in mud and nearly frozen some days. Do you think Jeanie wants to hear about that?'

Jack thought it would be wise not to answer since it was obvious that nothing he could say would smooth over Michael's drunken anger.

'And there's Jeanie going off to work as some jumped-up cleaner – *housekeeper*, she calls it, if you please – and wearing her good clothes, and her hair all nice, and, from what I see, spending her money on ladylike stuff that she'd never have worn in Bolton. Fancy scarves and bits of jewellery! She's getting above herself, that one, sorting through the post for Mr bloody Bailey, and gallivanting off with him to auctions and God knows what.'

'Michael, I don't want to hear your opinion of Mr Bailey,' said Jack. 'He's your landlord and my employer. I won't hear or speak ill of him, and I suggest you don't either.'

Michael subsided, muttering, while Jack and Monty walked him to Pendle's and Jack tapped on the front door.

Sue answered. She took in the situation at once. 'Thanks for bringing him home, Jack,' she said. 'I can see a bit of help was needed and I'm grateful.'

'I'll be getting on home myself, Sue,' said Jack as Michael shuffled past her and disappeared in the direction of the kitchen. 'I think he's missing his boys,' he said quietly.

'I know.' Sue sighed heavily. 'It's hit him as hard as any of us. We've all been feeling down but we're going to try to rise above it and it's going to take all of us, pulling together, to make a life without Robert. We can't leave Michael behind, grieving and . . . well, I tell you, if he's intending to make a habit of this he's going to come home one day and find things have changed, and in a big way.'

Jack raised an eyebrow and opened his mouth to speak.

'I'll say no more, lad. I may be wrong. But please, if you're in the Lion and you see Michael pouring his wages down his throat – and other folks' wages, too, I don't doubt – then you've got my permission to give him a kick up the backside and get the others to help you bring him out.'

'I will. You have my word on that, Sue. I think I'll tip off Frank Davis, the landlord, too, if it's all the same to you? I know he wants to sell his beer but he's a good man and he wouldn't want you Carter ladies to be upset after all that's happened.'

'Thank you, Jack. That's right good of you.'

'I'll see you next week for the rent then, Sue.'

'I'll have it ready.'

And maybe I'll invite Letty over the day the rent is due, thought Sue. She and Jack are good fun together and their company will help keep our spirits up . . .

They said goodbye, and Jack and Monty strode back to the pub where Jack's motorbike rig was parked at the back. As they went, Jack thought about Michael's resentment of the Carter women making their own way in life, then he thought about what Sue had said.

'Well, Monty,' he murmured as he put on his biking gear and made sure the little dog was safely tucked down in the sidecar, 'if Michael Carter's going to make a habit of this, and if what I suspect is true, then I bet you Jeanie won't be around to cook his meals come Easter at the latest.'

～

It was a bleak dinner with Michael sitting morosely at one end of the kitchen table, staring unhappily into his hotpot and glowering at the others while they tried to pretend he wasn't casting a pall over their evening.

Jeanie had wept for many days after Robert died but she was trying to make an effort now, and Sue didn't like to see her spirits brought low by Michael's behaviour, especially as she'd returned from work that day looking happier than she had for a few weeks.

While they'd made the hotpot together Sue had shared her plans for expanding the sewing business to take in customers from Redmond, and Evie, peeling potatoes, had chipped in with her thoughts about the level of dressmaking she felt she could take on under Sue's guidance. Of course, they knew Michael had gone to the Red Lion after changing out of his muddy work clothes, and they also knew when he was later home than usual that he would probably not reappear sober.

'Eat up, love. I thought Lancashire hotpot was your favourite,' said Jeanie, trying to jolly Michael out of his mood.

Michael made no reply and the women chatted on, eventually forgetting about his mood as they exchanged gossip. Until Michael, getting to his feet, snarled, 'Can't a man sit and have his meal in peace without you lot gabbing about dresses and curtains, and fellas with "a bit of dash"?'

'But, Dad, we're only discussing our plans, that's all,' said Evie, hoping her calm voice would smooth his drunken ill temper, as it used to do in Shenty Street. Mostly there, though, he'd been a happy drunk. Now he was always fierce and snappy. 'Why don't you tell us about your day instead, then?'

'Don't talk to me as if I'm a child, Evie, or you'll feel the back of my hand,' said Michael. Nonetheless, he sat back down: 'What do you know about the mud and the rain and the cold at that market garden, and Clackett laying on the work so hard I've hardly time to catch my breath?'

'I'm sorry, Dad, I didn't mean—'

'And one of my lads dead and the other gone to live with strangers. And all I hear is you women talking about *fabrics* and *customers* and *advertisements*, and other fancy things that don't matter a bit—'

'Michael, they're my sons, too. You're not the only one with the right to feel sad. We're *all* heartbroken about what happened.'

'Are you? Are you really?' shouted Michael, getting up again and pushing his plate to one side. 'Well, you don't look very heartbroken to me – any of you.' He looked at each of them in turn, pointing with his knife.

'It's not a competition to see who can be the saddest and who can feel worse, Dad,' said Evie quietly.

'Evie, shut up. I've heard enough from you.'

'Well, you haven't heard enough from me,' said Jeanie, both fury and resolve suddenly written all over her face. 'Because I'm fed up to the back teeth with your drunkenness and your selfishness.'

'Me, selfish?'

'Yes, you, you pathetic drunk. You haven't come in sober one evening this year and it's nearly February and I've had enough. I've kept quiet till now because I hoped you'd feel better about Bob after a bit and I wanted to be understanding about how you felt, but you're getting worse, not better. This isn't about Bob dying any more, it's about you drinking too much, as you've always done . . . as you did in Shenty Street, and look where that got you!'

Michael opened his mouth to reply but Jeanie had got into her stride now.

'Be quiet! I'm speaking! Don't you think my heart is broken, and Mum and Evie's, and Peter's? But we're trying – we're really trying, Michael – to make something of our lives because *we have to*! Because if we don't, no one else is going to do it for us. Mum and Evie have made a whole new life for themselves with their own talents, with their own efforts, no one else's, not propped up by beer and self-pity, and what do you do?'

'I—'

'You sneer at them, like it isn't the money they make that's kept us all going. Like it isn't the respect they've won in this village that has made it a nice home for us against all odds, and though we knew not a soul here when we arrived.'

'I'm doing my best—'

'You've just been brought back from the pub again by Jack. Every evening this year you've been there, drinking away your wages, and going over to Clackett's every morning looking like death warmed over. How that poor man gets a day's work out of you I'll never know. It's time for you to sober up, Michael, and start behaving like a man because, I'm warning you, I'm getting very near the end of my patience. Oh, in Shenty Street we all bowed down to "the man of the house" – but all the time you cared more for your drinks and your bets than you did for us. And in the end, how did you repay our loyalty? With an enormous debt to some violent card sharp, that's how. And so we're here, where we never chose to be, and we're all trying to do our best. Except you. You don't even know what doing your best for other people is. Because you're a bone idle drunk, Michael, and I've thought so for years now.'

'How dare—'

But there was no stopping Jeanie as years of anger were now pouring out. 'I've earned the right to speak out, Michael, that's how I dare. Because once I was too busy having babies and running about after little ones to think life could be any different. I thought I'd made my choice and I had to put up with it. But now . . . now, well, I've seen you for what you are.'

Michael sat speechless for a few moments, as if he couldn't believe what he had heard, and then he got up and lurched towards the door, slamming it behind him. Jeanie, Sue and Evie heard his uneven tread up the stairs and then, inevitably, the bedroom door slam, too.

Then there was a long, long silence during which Evie and Sue looked at each other in open-mouthed astonishment and Jeanie pretended to eat her dinner until her tears flowed and she couldn't continue. She pushed her plate away and put her head in her hands, sobbing.

Sue got up to put the kettle on the hob, patting Jeanie's heaving shoulder as she passed.

Evie went to put her arms around her mother and they held each other tight and then Sue enveloped them both in her sturdy arms, kissing the tops of their bowed heads.

'It's all right, Mum. You've got us . . . you've got us . . . ' whispered Evie, stroking her mother's hair.

Jeanie cried all the harder then, shaking her head, too upset to find any more words.

CHAPTER THIRTEEN

THE NEXT MORNING Evie kept out of Michael's way. A night's sleep hadn't improved his mood and he was quite clearly in a foul temper, seething with anger and nursing a hangover as he sat sullen and glowering over his breakfast. Where had her once cheeky and cheerful father gone, Evie wondered. Having to leave Shenty Street, the loss of his son and his disappointment in the hard work required of him at Clackett's seemed to have broken him.

After he had staggered off to work Evie heard her mother moving about upstairs and went to see if she was all right and whether she wanted some toast before she went to her job at Frederick Bailey's house in Redmond.

'Mum, what are you doing?' Evie looked askance at Jeanie's suitcase on the bed and the piles of folded clothes beside it. Among them were some pretty things she only half remembered seeing before: a brightly coloured scarf that looked as if it was silk, some fine suede gloves and a little brooch shaped like a bow of ribbon with shiny white stones set into it.

'I'm packing my things, Evie. I'm leaving.'

'What? Mum! You can't leave us! Where will you go? What will we do without you?'

By now Sue had come to stand in the doorway, and she shuffled into the room and put her arms around Jeanie.

'I guessed this would happen. In fact, I *knew* it would, though I tried to pretend it wouldn't, but when I saw how you were with him . . .'

'Grandma . . . ? Mum . . . ?' Evie looked at them, completely at a loss. 'What's happening? Please tell me.' She felt as though something important had been discussed and decided behind her back and she'd missed out on what everyone else knew all about.

Jeanie pushed her mother gently away and faced her and Evie. 'You're right, Mum,' she said. 'I made up my mind a while since, but after last night I've decided not to wait any longer.'

'What? Tell me, Mum, please.'

'I'm going to live at Marlowe House . . . with Freddie.'

'With Frederick Bailey?' said Evie, thinking she must have misunderstood.

'We're in love and he's asked me to go to him. At first I said I couldn't, but now I think it would be better if I did.'

'In love with Mr Bailey? Mum, don't leave us, please! How is it better if you're not here?'

'Don't get upset, Evie. You and your grandma have got a right good little business going in the front room. Peter doesn't live here any longer and, honestly, I don't see him coming back, not with the way he feels about his father. I went to see him a few weeks ago on my way back from Redmond and he's happy with the Thomases. He's got everything there he wants.'

'He hasn't got his mother,' said Sue quietly.

'He's always got me whenever he wants me,' said Jeanie firmly. 'I just won't be living here. Same goes for you two. You know where I am and you can come to me at any time, but I won't be living here with Michael any more, and nor do I want to.'

'So you knew all along that Peter's not coming back?'

'Frederick has been paying Mr and Mrs Thomas for Peter's keep since the beginning of the year. That's what will happen for as long as Peter wants to stay there and for as long as the Thomases are happy to have him.'

'But, Mum, please don't go,' said Evie again. 'There's only Grandma and me here now with Dad. Bob's . . . gone, and then Peter left, and now you.

There are fewer and fewer of us. We were all together when we left Shenty Street, and I thought we'd manage in this new place because there *were* all of us, but now there's only Grandma and me. And Dad, of course.'

'Oh, love, I haven't been happy for a long while but I thought I could put up with it because it was how it was going to be. I thought I had no choice. But then Frederick gave me a choice. At first it was out of the question that I could ever leave you all and go to him, even though I wanted to, but then Bob died. And then when Pete went to the Thomases – that was his decision and no one made him go – I could see that the moment would soon come when I'd know it was time to leave – when my family didn't need me any more. And that moment is now.'

'But *I* need you, Mum!' Evie cried, wringing her hands. 'What about me? Please, please, don't go.'

'Shush, our Evie. Don't take on, lass.' Sue sat down on the bed, her weight toppling the neat piles of clothes beside Jeanie's case. 'Well, Jeanie, love,' she sighed, 'I can't say I approve, but nor do I approve of the way Michael's behaved. You always were one to do exactly as you wanted, and I know nothing I can say will change your mind. You were just the same with Michael, don't forget. I warned you not to be taken in by his charm, and now it seems that his charm was all he had, and he hasn't even got that any longer. You chose him then, my girl—'

256

'And now I'm choosing someone else, Mum. I made a mistake with Michael but it's not too late to change that.'

'But you've still got two lovely children with him, Jeanie. You can't just forget them and start again.'

'Who said anything about forgetting? I'll always be a mum to Evie and Peter – even if I live in Marlowe House with Frederick, and even if Evie lives here with you and Michael, and Peter lives with the Thomases.'

'But, Mum, you won't be *here*,' said Evie. 'And I really, really need you.'

'Well, you may say that, love, but you're nearly seventeen now, and getting quite grown-up, and it may not be long before you want to go away and make a life of your own – maybe with Billy Taylor back in Bolton, or maybe with someone else.'

'Not with Billy. That's all over, Mum. I doubt I'll see him again.'

'Well, sorry, love, but I'm making a life for myself.'

'I'm not sure marriage is to be thrown off so quickly, Jeanie,' said Sue. 'You vowed to take each other for better and for worse.'

'I know that, Mum. And I'm not making this decision lightly. I wish I loved Michael as I used to, but I don't. It's Frederick I love now, and I can be so much happier with him. Don't you think I'm allowed to put my mistake behind me and be happy again?'

'I want you to be happy, Jeanie, you know I do. But I just wonder if you've thought about this properly. Michael's behaved badly on so many occasions, but maybe there are better times ahead if you stick together. It's not all bad with him.'

'I've thought about nothing else,' Jeanie said desperately. 'When we came here it was to a new life that Michael had made us have. We didn't choose it. But when I went to Marlowe House to find Frederick that day, I realised that I could have a better life.'

'Mum,' said Evie, visibly pulling herself together, 'I don't want you to go but I don't want you to be unhappy either.'

Jeanie held out her hands and took both of Evie's, pulling her towards her. 'Love, you're a good girl, and I promise I'm not abandoning you. I'm leaving Michael but I can never leave you – or you either, Mum.'

Jeanie hugged her mother and her daughter, and then they drew away from each other and wiped away their tears.

'Evie, off you go down and make us all a cup of tea,' said Sue. 'Your mum and I need to get this case together.'

Evie did as she was told.

'All right, Jeanie. I can see you're set on this,' said Sue quietly as the sounds of Evie's footsteps faded down the stairs, 'but I have to tell you summat that's

258

been bothering me since I heard it at the Bonfire Night do. Frederick Bailey might be a good man, for all I know – and he's shown us nowt but kindness, what with the low rent, and not standing in my way over the sewing business – but is it true that he's been divorced three times?'

'Good heavens, Mum, where on earth did you hear that?' asked Jeanie.

'Gossip, love, and I shouldn't have listened, but I know what I overheard and I can't unknow it. So, is it true?'

'You shouldn't be gossiping about Freddie,' Jeanie said sharply.

She turned away and started to pack her clothes into the case.

'What is the truth then, lass?' Sue was growing impatient.

'It's nowt to do with you.'

'It is if you're leaving Michael to go to live with a fella what's had three wives,' snapped Sue, pulling Jeanie round to face her by her cardigan sleeve.

Jeanie shrugged her off. 'He has had three wives—'

'So it is true—'

'But the first one died, and the second one ran off with someone else – a so-called friend of his who'd got a lot of money, and Freddie did divorce her, but can you blame him? – and the third left him too.'

'Doesn't sound like Frederick Bailey is so lucky with his women, Jeanie. Do you really think this is the man you want to spend the rest of your life with? Because I'll tell you summat for nowt, my girl, you won't want to come back to Michael – even if he'll have you – after you've got used to living the kind of life Bailey seems to lead, and which you've clearly taken to. What happened to the third wife? Did he divorce her, too?'

Jeanie looked away. 'No, Mum,' she said in a small voice. 'He's married to her still. She lives somewhere else, not nearby, by herself, I think, and she's some sort of potter.'

'Good heavens, you mean she works at a pot factory?' asked Sue, distracted from the point by this information.

'No, Mum, she's an artist. She makes special pots, one at a time, I gather, and people buy them to display rather than to use.'

'Well, I never! And you say they're still married?'

'They are.'

Sue took a few moments to digest this. 'But, Jeanie, love, to go and live with a man you can't marry, and who is someone else's husband? How do you know this woman isn't going to reappear at any moment to move back in with him? What would happen to you, then? You'd be out on your ear, because I reckon she'd have every right to return if she wanted to. You'd be the one in the wrong because you'd be living in her house. With her husband!'

'It's not like that, Mum, really it's not,' said Jeanie. 'She's been gone for years. She's never coming back. Don't you think I haven't asked Freddie about her and where I stand? Honestly, Mum, there are different folk in the world than those that live in Shenty Street. It was all we knew until we left there, but it was only one way of living – for people like us.'

Sue was silent as she watched Jeanie slowly finish putting all her clothes in her case, and gathering her second pair of shoes into a paper carrier bag. Sue thought back to her life in the big house where she'd been a lady's maid until she'd met and married Albert and left to be a housewife and then a mother. She remembered the lives of the people there, the secrets and the romances, even the scandals. She'd seen all kinds of folk there – high-born and low-born – and she recognised that poor people had less choice, less licence. Then she had got used to living a smaller life in Shenty Street and almost forgot that she had ever seen anything any different. Maybe the values of the people she knew there were sounder than those of folk with more money and more choices, or maybe ordinary working folk were long-suffering and prepared to put up with unhappy marriages because there was nothing for them outside of that and nowhere to run to.

'You go, then, lass. I only hope you're choosing

the right road. I won't put up with gossip about you but nor will I lie to our friends. I just want you to be happy.'

'Thank you, Mum.' Jeanie hugged her close again.

'All I ask is that you tell Michael. Don't leave it to me to tell him. And I want you to say it to his face, not leave him a note.'

'I've told him already, Mum. I don't know if he believed me, but he knows, and when he comes home and finds me gone, he'll believe me then.'

'And you'll see the children, won't you, lass? And me? Please don't leave us completely, Jeanie,' Sue begged quietly. 'You're the heart of this family – what's left of it – and we won't survive without you if you leave us and we never see you.'

'No, Mum, I promise.'

Then Jeanie tied the pretty scarf around her neck in a dashing new way she seemed to have copied from Frederick, pinned the bow brooch to her cardigan, picked up her case, her bag of shoes, her handbag, her coat and the beautiful fine gloves. She gave a look around the shabby bedroom one last time and then walked down the stairs with her back straight and her head held high, leaving her mother, bowed under the weight of her worry, to follow behind.

～

Evie and Sue were too upset to go to Redmond as they had planned that morning, so they stayed in working on some mending. Mrs Cooke's curtains were ready and waiting for her, and, as they sewed, the two of them spent the morning in silent worry, dreading Michael's return, with his inevitable anger.

'It feels like us two alone now, Grandma,' said Evie. 'Do you really think we'll see Mum again?'

'Not only do I think we'll see her, I *know* so,' Sue replied staunchly. 'Because I shall make sure we do. I've never been to Frederick Bailey's house, but I mean to visit my daughter there from now on and you can come with me. I can't imagine a place where everything's got a price label on it, but I expect I shall soon see what it's like.'

Evie smiled. 'It's not like a shop, Grandma. There aren't the prices on the things, it's just that Mr Bailey lives among stuff that he buys and sells. Some of it is lovely.'

'How does he know what's his and what he's got to sell on?' asked Sue.

'Does it matter?' Evie said. 'I don't suppose he has to sell anything he wants to keep. Say he bought a nice tea set and he decided he really liked it – provided he didn't need the money I expect he'd just keep it and use it.' She remembered the odd cups with no saucers. It seemed that Mr Bailey hadn't yet found a tea set he liked enough to keep. She said as much to Sue.

'Mmm . . .' said Sue, wondering if Frederick Bailey had found a woman he liked enough to keep, and hoping, if Jeanie was as much in love with him as she appeared to be, that she was at last the one he wouldn't pass on. But Jeanie had said that one wife had died and the next two had left him, so maybe his being tired of her was not something to be worrying about. The thing was, though, there were always two sides to any story, and a man who'd had three wives couldn't be entirely blameless for that situation. Could he?

~

In the days after Jeanie left, Evie couldn't stop thinking about what her mother had said about choices and making her own luck. She worked at the sewing machine in silence, turning her mother's words over in her mind, and Sue darned alongside her, also silently.

By the beginning of February Evie felt she was somehow waiting for something to happen. Maybe it was the arrival of a letter from Billy, which never came, she decided. If Billy wouldn't reply to her letters then maybe she should get in touch via Mary.

Dear Mary,
I'm sorry it's taken me a while to reply to you. I was really pleased to get your letter with your kind words about our Bob, and the good wishes of all your family.

I know your mum also wrote to Grandma Sue, Mum and Dad, and they were made up by her thoughts and a funny little story she told about him. Christmas wasn't much of a celebration, as I expect you can imagine. We were pleased to get the card from you all, though.

It's not too good here, but Grandma Sue and me are doing our best and are working hard at the sewing. Mum has left us and has gone to live elsewhere, though she's nearby and we will see her soon. I think she just got fed up when Bob died and now that Peter's gone to stay with friends in the village.

Evie read through what she had written and thought it just awful. How could she spread all this misery around? Her heart wasn't in sharing her news, especially the actual truth of it. She tore the letter up and threw the pieces on the kitchen fire. *Stupid, stupid, stupid . . .*

If only Billy would get in touch. She'd been silly to spoil the weekend when she'd gone to Bolton for Geraldine's party but now it seemed that she would never hear from him again. She felt hurt that he hadn't even written to say anything about Robert, but she'd done her best with the two difficult letters she'd sent him. He'd always been so reliable and kind, but it was clear now that he didn't want to keep in touch with her. Maybe, a bit like her mother, he'd found someone else he'd rather be with, who was kind herself and didn't fly off the handle, and who was fond of his mother and didn't say mean things about her. Maybe, more to the point, he'd found someone Ada liked, someone who Ada thought was good enough for her only son . . .

The more she thought about it, the more Evie decided that this was exactly what must have happened. How could she not have worked it out before now? How undignified. He was simply no longer interested . . . when he was probably already in love with someone else and had forgotten all about her. Someone who was all pretty and glamorous and wore fine stockings with seams in them instead of ankle socks like a schoolgirl, and maybe had red lipstick and a swirly skirt like the ones pictured in her magazines. Evie picked one up, a treat at Christmas that she had thought would help lift her spirits and inspire her and Sue with new ideas. She flipped through and admired the impossibly slim models in elegant poses, their snooty faces beneath pert little hats and offset by fur-trimmed coat collars; their slender ankles and high-heeled shoes beneath yards of well-cut skirting. She sighed again. How far they seemed from real life . . . from herself, in her thick, warm trousers and well-washed jumper with the darned elbows.

'Evie, Grandma?' It was Peter calling.

'In here, Pete.'

'He's not here, is he?' Peter appeared at the kitchen door, Letty behind him.

'No, he's at Clackett's. He won't be back for a

266

while. Grandma's gone down the road to measure up for some curtains. Let me pour you both some tea and you can tell me your news. We'll take it through to the front, shall we? I've been sitting here and sort of forgot all about the shop. I don't want folk to think we're not open for business.'

'You need a bell,' said Letty. 'If you're not in the room your clients can summon you.'

'Great idea, Letty. I can't think why we haven't thought of that before. We're always having to "keep an eye" on the shop.'

'Mebbe Frederick will have one you can use,' suggested Peter.

'Perhaps. Have you been to see them?'

'Oh, yes, a couple of times after school. He's got such an interesting house and Mum does seem much happier. She's much more smiley than she was here and she sort of looks different, too.'

'In what way?' asked Evie, handing Peter and Letty their tea and leading them through to the front room, taking her magazine with her.

Peter thought about it. 'Difficult to say. She's still the same old mum, and wears mostly the same things, but there's more . . . drama, I suppose, about the way she wears them.'

'Style?' suggested Letty. 'More style?'

'Yes, that's it. Bits of jewellery and stuff, and a smart new belt on an old frock, that kind of thing. Even the way she tucks her jumper into her slacks.'

'You always had an eye for what looks right, Pete,' smiled Evie. 'Remember how you set up the front room to look like a proper dressmaker's workroom?'

'It *is* a proper workroom,' said Letty, sitting down at the table and reaching for Evie's magazine. She turned the pages as Evie asked Peter about his guitar lessons and what else he was doing at school. Then Letty joined in as they talked about the band and Peter invited Evie to go to listen to a concert they were to play in a church hall. After a while he got up to leave.

'Don't want to have to see Dad,' he said, 'so I'd best be off now. Sorry to miss Grandma but I'll catch her soon. Don't forget to tell her about the concert and maybe she'll want to go as well.'

'I'll tell her. Bye, Pete.'

The front door shut and he waved through the window and was gone.

'All right, Evie, what's the matter?' said Letty.

'Oh, you know . . . .'

'I know about Robert, of course, and your mum going. But Pete's seen her and it sounds as if she's fine.'

'Yes, it does, and I'm glad. But, oh, Letty, I still wish she hadn't gone. Dad's hardly around these days, what with Mr Clackett keeping him busy and then his going out every evening, and it feels so empty with just Grandma and me here all the time.'

'You're missing the others, that's all, Evie.' For a

moment Letty looked sad and Evie knew that of course she understood.

'But it's something else as well, Letty. I've been thinking a lot since Mum left and what I'm really fed up with is being me,' said Evie. She looked down at the shapeless and slightly itchy trousers, at the jumper felted with wear, an old and fraying shirt underneath it. 'I wish I looked more like these women.' She pointed to the magazine, which Letty had left open on the table. 'No wonder Billy's probably found someone new – who would want a girl looking like me on his arm?'

'Good heavens, Evie, where on earth has all this come from?' asked Letty. 'You're lovely.' She laughed then. 'Though I have to admit that your clothes aren't! But then mine aren't either, and I don't care.'

'Well, I haven't got much to spend on fancy clothes – and certainly not stuff like that.' She indicated the gorgeous suit in the fashion spread. 'And anyway, at the moment it's all about keeping warm.'

'You're right there,' agreed Letty. 'I have at least five layers on most days. The forecast is for snow again, too. But everyone has to have new clothes, and there's no reason why you shouldn't have something that looks a bit more like . . . Well, take that dress, for example. I expect you and Mrs Goodwin could copy that design and come up with something similar.'

'Such a lot of fabric in it, though, Letty. I'm not sure we could run to that just for me.'

'Nonsense, Evie. You'd be a walking advertisement for the business. Or how about one of those straight skirts? No excuse about too much fabric in that. When people see how well-dressed and smart you look, and how well made your clothes are, they'll want something the same. Before you know it, there'll be commissions for all sorts – no more kitchen curtains!'

'Aye, Letty, love, I can see what you mean,' said Sue, coming in to hear the last bit. 'No use me getting done up in sharp tailoring: I haven't got a sharp figure. But I reckon it's time our Evie had a few new things, summat more grown-up and suitable for a working woman, and you're right about needing to show off our skills. Who's going to believe an old woman and a scrap of a girl could make them summat nice to wear? And Evie's the one to show off our style.'

'Hello, Mrs Goodwin.' Letty got up and kissed Sue's cheek. 'I'm so glad you agree. You see, Evie, *we* agree so *you're* outnumbered. And I've just had the most terrific idea.'

'Not another one?' laughed Sue, sitting down and unzipping her boots.

'Yes, but I'll have to ask Aunt Margaret first.' Letty got up and buttoned on the layers she'd hung on the back of the chair. 'Don't worry, I'll be back tomorrow.'

'Ask Miss Richards about what?' said Evie. 'You can't leave us guessing.'

'Oh, but I can!' laughed Letty, pulling on her knitted beret. 'Don't sit there being miserable about your clothes any longer because I may have thought of the perfect solution.'

She departed laughing and blowing kisses, and the air settled as it always did behind her liveliness.

'*The perfect solution*, indeed,' smiled Sue. 'Well, we'll see, but she's a good 'un, is Letty Mortimer. Now, let's get the kettle on and then I'll make a start on these curtains while I can still read the figures I wrote down.'

'I'll copy them out larger for you, Grandma, if you like? And while the kettle boils I can tell you what Peter said when he was here earlier, about how he's doing, and about Mum.'

'I can see from your face it's good news. Not such a bad day, after all, then?'

'No, Grandma,' said Evie, following Sue through to the kitchen. 'And I've been thinking all the time about what Mum said that morning she left.'

'Oh, yes?'

'About making her own luck, and choosing what she wanted and not what she was given.'

'And what about you, Evie? You'll be seventeen in a few days, old enough to begin on your own path through life. What destiny will you choose, love?'

Evie paused to get her thoughts in order. Then she said carefully, 'I'm choosing to link my destiny to yours, Grandma. But I won't be the same little Evie any longer. If we're to make something of this sewing business – make a success of it and grow it, not just make it something we do day in and day out, for ever, without it going anywhere – we need to make some changes. We should look for new customers, as we said we would, and take on dressmaking rather than household linen and mending so that's what people get to know us for. No more boring old kitchen curtains! Our customers can bring their own fabrics, but we need to find a source nearby of nice trimmings and some lengths for smaller garments. The mill shop in Bolton is too far away and we can't keep calling on favours from old friends, nor expect them to choose the fabrics for us. It's time to make some big decisions together – you and me, Grandma – and I reckon we can make a real go of it.'

Sue smiled. 'I like the sound of all this and you're good enough at the sewing now to take on some ambitious garments.'

Ambitious. Evie thought about it. It wasn't a word she'd ever applied to herself before. But things were going to be different from now on.

'Let's get that tea made and we'll raise a cup to toast the future and big decisions,' she laughed, and Sue agreed.

CHAPTER FOURTEEN

THE NEXT MORNING Evie and Sue got up with a renewed sense of purpose and set about finishing their current sewing tasks as quickly as they could so they could start to concentrate on exciting new projects.

Michael had gone to work quietly and dutifully on time. His anger seemed to be spent, to be replaced by sadness but also a misplaced sense of hope that Jeanie would return.

'She'll not stay away for long, I reckon,' he'd said to Sue as she poured him a mug of tea, and she smiled and offered to pack him up some sandwiches for midday in case he was too busy to come back over the road to eat. He thanked her politely and accepted, leaving meekly a few minutes later.

'It's as if his spirit has been quite crushed, poor Dad,' said Evie.

'Don't worry about him, lass,' Sue replied. 'I'll

see him mend his ways before he gets much of my sympathy . . . '

Halfway through the morning Letty appeared with a big smile, and a huge pile of clothes in her bicycle basket.

'I've asked Aunt Margaret and she isn't upset if I do what I want with these,' she announced, bringing in the first armful of garments, then going back out to the bike to get the rest.

'What are they?' asked Evie, getting up to look. 'My goodness, Letty, these are lovely. Where did you get them?'

'Mum,' said Letty simply. 'Oh, it's all right, don't get all sad about it. It's my idea to get rid of them. I can face it now. It's time.'

'But they're so pretty and . . . well, I think they were quite expensive. Your mum must have looked smashing.'

'She did,' said Letty. 'But I won't ever wear these, and I don't need them to remind me of her. I've got some photographs of her in them. Aunt Margaret has kept a few things, including a nice warm coat, and I've got one as well, and a couple of dresses that I may wear when I'm performing with the band, but all these are spare and just taking up room in the cottage. As you know, I don't care much about clothes. I thought that maybe you could use them somehow . . . if you want?'

Sue was feeling the quality of the fabrics and then

she held up one of the dresses. She could see it was a bit too wide and a lot too long for Evie.

'Would you mind if we altered them, even cut them up a bit?'

'No, of course not,' said Letty. 'I would expect you to. They're yours if you want them.'

'Oh, we do, we do!' said Evie, laughing and hugging Letty. 'You are such a love.'

'Letty, lass, you're an answer to my prayers,' said Sue. 'I've been awake half the night wondering how I can get together a few smart outfits for Evie to show off our skills without spending any money.'

'I would have explained yesterday, but I had to ask Aunt Margaret first. The clothes are mine to do with as I like but I didn't want her to be upset by my giving them away.'

'Quite right, love. You're a good girl.'

'And there are more, but I couldn't get them on the bike.'

'More?'

'Oh, yes, this is only a fraction.'

'Your mother must have been as smart as the Queen,' said Evie, holding up a light red evening dress with a row of tiny pearl buttons down the front. 'Oh, Grandma, look at this!'

'Not really, but Dad used to get asked to a lot of functions and Mum needed to look nice, too.'

'It all sounds very grand,' said Sue. 'What did your father do?'

'Oh, something in the government,' said Letty vaguely. 'Not the kind of thing I understand . . . Anyway, if you can use them I'm really pleased. Now, I'll leave you to look through these clothes and I'll bring the rest along soon.'

'Thank you, lass.'

'Yes, thank you, Letty. You've made our day,' said Evie.

'Made our year, more like,' said Sue. 'And if you need anything you're keeping altered or refashioned, I'll be glad to do it for you. Same for your auntie, tell her.'

'Thanks, I will. Bye, then.'

'That is so generous,' said Evie after they'd waved Letty off, her expert hands sorting through the lovely materials. 'It seems a shame to cut them up.'

'Well, they're no use to you if we don't,' said Sue sensibly, 'because they're probably all too big for you. I think we should go through them piece by piece and see what's what.'

'Good idea. Oh, Grandma, it's like Christmas,' said Evie, feeling a lightness in her heart for the first time in a long time.

～

The snow that had fallen in Bolton back in January turned out to be nothing compared to the amount that fell over the whole country in February.

Billy was unable to go to work because the roads were blocked and, anyway, the post wasn't getting through to be sorted and delivered, so he spent his days with a working party of local men – and some women, too – clearing the roads and making sure his neighbours were all right.

They met at the Lord Nelson, and at first there was a worry that the pub would run out of beer, but the snow-clearing gang knew where their priorities lay, and the roads between the brewery where Michael Carter used to work and the pub were among the first to be cleared. There would be beer for as long as there were barrels ready to deliver to the Nelson.

Billy wasn't a big beer drinker but clearing the roads was thirsty work.

'I'll have a half of mild, if you've got it, please,' he told the landlord, stopping by one lunchtime.

'Make that two, please,' said a soft Irish voice behind him.

'Brendan, hello. I've not seen you for a bit. You all surviving?'

'Just about, Billy, but I tell you, the house seems very small when we're all there all day long.'

'I bet it does, with the lads not at work and the schools closed.'

'I thought I'd join the working party this afternoon for a bit of peace and quiet. Only our Gerry's at work, and I reckon Mr Amsell will have to close

277

the shop in a few days if he can't get any deliveries. He's running on what's left on the shelves and then that's it.'

'Mebbe there'll be a thaw before then. I hope so, or we all might run out of food. Gerry OK, is she?'

'Oh, yes, though she says it's colder in the shop storeroom than it is outside!'

It was then that Billy, whose thoughts were never far from Evie, was reminded again of the disagreement at Geraldine's birthday party.

'Has anyone heard from the Carters?' he asked casually.

'Marie and Mary are the ones for writing letters but I haven't heard that they've been in touch with Jeanie and Sue or Evie recently. Not since before Christmas. I think that bad business with Robert hit them hard. It's difficult to write when you've lost heart.'

Billy set his glass down slowly. 'What bad business? What's happened to the little 'un?'

'Oh, dear Lord, lad, have you not heard?'

Billy was filled with dread. 'No. Tell me, Brendan. What's happened?'

So Brendan told Billy all about Robert drowning, and that the Carters were in pieces over his death.

Billy listened, shocked and pale.

'She never wrote to tell me, Brendan. How could she not have written with such news?'

Brendan knew Billy was speaking of Evie, and he

also knew from Mary something of their falling out at Geraldine's party, but he hadn't realised the rift between them had never been healed. It was clear to him that Billy had thought Evie would write eventually, but that Evie had washed her hands of the poor fella. He wasn't all that surprised. Evie was still only about seventeen and the family had been gone for months now. It was no wonder that the youthful romance between Billy and Evie had died a natural death, particularly when the Carters had so much to deal with in their new lives. But it wasn't for him to voice this opinion and he didn't answer.

'I haven't heard from Evie since . . . since Gerry's party,' Billy went on. 'Poor little Bob. What an awful thing to happen.' Downcast, he finished his beer, said goodbye to Brendan and went to collect his shovel from the pub's porch.

While he cleared snow he thought long and hard about what Brendan had told him and reached the same conclusion that the kindly Irishman had: Evie no longer wanted to keep in touch with him.

That afternoon, when Billy returned to Fawcett Street in the muffled and strangely white twilight, his face was glowing with the effort of his snow clearing, but inside he felt cold.

'I'll make a pot of tea and we'll open them biscuits I've saved from Christmas,' said Ada, seeing the weariness in his face.

'Oh, Mum, I've heard the most terrible news,'

Billy told her, as he pulled off his wellies and padded into the kitchen in two pairs of thick socks, the scarf Evie had knitted for him around his neck.

He told his mother about Robert Carter's accident. 'I haven't heard a word from Evie, so I'd no idea. How could she not have written to tell me?'

Ada had her back to him, making the tea, and she didn't dare turn round in case her face gave her away as she said, 'What an awful thing. Poor lad. But those Carters don't seem to have much luck, do they?'

'Well, that's true enough, Mum.'

Ada, who was genuinely sorry about Robert, and had heard the news from Dora Marsh at Christmas, came over then, looking sad, and hugged Billy to her where he sat on a kitchen chair. 'It's a bad business, true enough. I reckon they've got friends down wherever it is they live now and no need to share the news up here.'

'But Brendan Sullivan told me,' Billy pointed out. 'The Carters have been in touch with Marie and the girls.'

Ada thought quickly before she undermined her own point. 'Well, I know Sue Goodwin has always been one to share her news. It's a generation thing, love.'

'Maybe . . . but Evie used to write, Mum, as you know. I don't understand why she wouldn't let me know about young Bob.'

'It looks like she's stopped writing, love,' said Ada, well aware that Evie had indeed stopped writing since the two letters she'd sent after she'd visited Bolton and at Christmas – and which were in Ada's sideboard – had of course gone unanswered.

Ada hadn't opened and read them – that would have been dishonest, she reckoned – but she could guess what was in the first after Geraldine's party, and when she'd heard the sad news about Robert from Dora she knew what was in the second. No need to be bothering Billy with any of that. Though, now she thought of it, it was hardly a surprise that someone should have mentioned the little lad's accident to him eventually.

'The Carters have been gone a long time, Billy, and Evie's got new friends now, I'm sure,' said Ada. 'As I've said before, she's a long way away and she's only young. She'll know all kinds of different folk down there and it's hardly surprising if she's too busy with her new life to be thinking about Bolton.'

'Yes, I reckon you're right, Mum,' Billy said. 'But still, I thought she'd have let me know about this. We all liked poor little Bob.'

'Mmm,' said Ada, who had thought Robert an awkward child, sad though the news of his death was. 'Well, I think this proves I'm right,' she said, and Billy couldn't really argue with that, having reached the same conclusion.

'Sit down and have your tea,' she went on, pouring out a cup.

'Thanks, Mum. I think I'll take it upstairs with me,' Billy replied, and wearily went to his room to think through what he had learned.

Ada spent the rest of the afternoon alone, and the conversation over the tinned soup she heated that evening – taken from the enormous hoard she'd started to store in the larder at the sight of the first flurries of snow in January – was on her side only. Billy washed up and, as Ada settled beside the wireless to listen to the weather forecast, he came through with a cup of tea for her and declared he was very tired with all that snow shifting and he thought he'd get an early night, leaving her feeling quite alone in her own company.

~

In Church Sandleton the February snow was just as heavy as it was in the north. Michael was kept busy helping Mr Clackett to clear the market garden and lending a hand to their neighbours. The schools were closed so Peter was around, but he kept away from his father, shovelling snow with Letty and Miss Richards at Lavender Cottage at the far end of the village, the rest of the time playing music with the Thomas boys.

Evie and Sue didn't mind the snow. They were

working on refashioning the treasure trove of garments Letty had given them to make smart new clothes for Evie, and altering the ones Letty and Miss Richards had chosen to keep for themselves, in return for the generous hoard of beautiful clothes.

'You look gorgeous, Evie,' enthused Letty, when Evie put on a newly finished tailored two-piece to show her friend and Miss Richards what she and Sue had made from an old outfit.

'Good fit, Sue,' said Margaret Richards, inspecting the back of the neat jacket. 'You've done wonders with that old costume.'

'What you need now, Evie,' said Letty, always full of ideas, 'is a new hairstyle. Not that you don't look pretty as you are, but maybe something a bit more grown-up . . . ?'

'I don't know if I can afford anything very different,' said Evie. 'I usually just have the ends trimmed.'

'Well, why don't you ask your mum to pay?'

'Letty!' tutted Margaret. 'That isn't for you to suggest.'

'I know, Aunt Margaret, but I saw Mrs Carter in Redmond before the snow and she had such a lovely new hairstyle. Maybe she could pay for it for your birthday – if you asked nicely, I mean,' Letty laughed. 'With the lipstick and bits Auntie and I gave you, your lovely new outfits and smart hair, you'll have all the ladies in Redmond looking at you and asking where you get your clothes.' She pushed the ever-open fashion magazine towards Evie. 'If this model had long hair and a fringe like yours, it wouldn't really go with the dress, would it?'

'Letty, you are so rude,' said Margaret, laughing.

'But she's right, Miss Richards,' Evie agreed, and Sue was nodding, too.

'I reckon Jeanie will be all for that,' she said, 'and anyway, it's time we went to see her. Soon as this wretched snow's gone we'll get the bus to Redmond.'

~

As soon as the roads were open and the buses to Redmond were running again Sue and Evie embarked on an expedition to see Jeanie. Evie wore her two-piece with one of Letty's mother's coats over it, which Evie had turned up but otherwise was perfect for covering any number of layers in the cold weather. Her shoes rather spoiled the effect but there was nothing she could do about those until she and Sue started earning again. The snow had been bad for business even if it had been good for Evie's wardrobe.

They alighted in the market square. It was market day but what few stalls there were were a sorry-looking lot in the bleak weather. The fabric stall Evie had seen with Jeanie in the summer wasn't there, which was disappointing, but then they didn't have much money to spend anyway.

'I've had an idea,' said Evie. 'You remember how Mum and me found Frederick by looking in the telephone directory? Well, I wonder if there are any fabric shops or haberdashers in Redmond. We could look them up and see.'

Sue agreed and Evie led her across the square to the imposing library. They sat at desks in the reference room and carefully wrote down two names and addresses in Redmond and one in Kingsford. Then, in a whisper, Evie asked the librarian where the local streets were and she and Sue listened carefully to the directions.

'Let's go and see Mum first, though,' Evie suggested as they came out into the cold. 'I've missed her so much.'

'Me, too, love. Now where's this Midsummer Row . . . ?'

Evie could tell that her grandmother was impressed with the neat railings and steps up to the front door of Marlowe House, though Sue didn't say anything.

Evie rang the bell, remembering how the fierce, angry woman had rushed out just as she and Jeanie arrived that first day. How much had happened since then. Now Jeanie lived here!

The smart front door opened and Jeanie's smiling face greeted them. In a moment she was holding Evie close in a big hug, and then Sue.

'Oh, Evie, love . . . Mum, I've missed you both so much. I was beginning to think with all that snow that I'd never see you again. The roads have been terrible here and I expect they were even worse in the village.' She stepped back to let them in out of the cold as she spoke.

The first thing Evie noticed was how lovely her mother looked. She did indeed have a new hairstyle, as Letty had said, but there was something else about her. Evie thought hard about this as she gazed at her mother: less worried, not too thin any longer, and her face was a healthier colour, though that might have been the subtle make-up she wore as well. Her clothes were warm and casual – a hand-knitted jumper and trousers – but she wore them with style.

'Mum, you look so pretty,' Evie gasped.

'Thank you, love,' said Jeanie, accepting the compliment with a confidence she never used to have. 'Come in and have a hot drink. Or you could stay for lunch. I've made some soup and there's plenty.'

'We won't put you to any trouble,' said Sue.

'It's no trouble. I'd like you to stay. We've got a lot to talk about.'

Evie and Sue looked at each other and smiled. 'Yes, please,' said Evie. 'There's so much to catch up on, Mum!'

Frederick came out of a room at the back of the

hall and was delighted to see the unexpected visitors.

He hung up their coats, then showed them into the sitting room, where interesting-looking things stood on every piece of furniture.

'Why don't you and your mum go and make us that hot drink, Evie,' suggested Sue, 'and Frederick can show me some of these treasures?'

Evie and Jeanie did as they were asked.

'Now then, Frederick Bailey,' said Sue in her forthright way as soon as they'd gone downstairs to the kitchen, 'I can see my lass is looking happy here, but I've heard there have been a few Mrs Baileys and I want to be sure you mean to do right by her.'

'Well, Mrs Goodwin, I certainly mean to love and to cherish your beautiful daughter,' Frederick replied, indicating an armchair for Sue and sitting down opposite her. 'But it isn't possible for me to marry her – at least not at the moment.'

'Aye, she told me you're already married,' said Sue. 'To the *third* Mrs Bailey, isn't that so?'

'It is indeed, Mrs Goodwin. Truth be told, I don't actually know where the third Mrs Bailey is. I haven't set eyes on her for years.'

'Not know where your own wife lives? I thought I'd heard it all in my time . . . '

Frederick smiled. 'I have to agree with you, Mrs Goodwin. I've rather let matters slide. But Jeanie, of course, is still married to Michael Carter, so there

287

are two reasons why we can't be married,' he added pointedly, but with another disarming smile.

'Well, I can't argue with that,' said Sue.

'I have been married three times, though my first wife died, and I am still married to the third, and . . . well, Mrs Goodwin, I'd maybe have done things differently if I'd known how they were going to turn out. But this time I'm certain I've chosen right.'

'But she's Michael's wife, Mr Bailey. She wasn't free to be chosen by you or by anyone else.' Sue couldn't help raising this although she knew it was water under the bridge and there was no way Jeanie would suddenly remember her obligations to Michael and decide to go home.

'You want her to be happy, though, don't you, Mrs Goodwin? She is happy here.'

Sue knew there was only one answer to that, and it wasn't about asking Jeanie to honour her wedding vows.

She sighed heavily. 'She's gone against her vows and left her family for you, it's up to you to make sure she never, ever regrets it. Because she won't want to go back to Michael – I can see that, and he's certainly not been the best husband. But she's left her children and if she hasn't got you she won't have anything.'

Frederick stood and took Sue's arm to help her to her feet. 'Yes, Mrs Goodwin, I mean to keep

Jeanie with me for ever. I shall do my best to make sure she never regrets coming here,' he said quietly. 'I don't know if we shall ever be free to marry, but she is as dear to me as anyone can be and I dare to hope that she feels the same.'

'Then,' said Sue, 'I think you had better call me Sue, because whatever she is and whatever she does, Jeanie will always be my daughter.'

Frederick looked into Sue's formidable face and saw strength, kindness and good sense written there.

'Thank you, Sue, and I shall be pleased to see you – and Evie and Peter – whenever you care to visit. Now I think Jeanie said something about a cup of tea, or even soup, and you and she and Evie can catch up with all your news while you have it.'

~

When Evie and Sue eventually left Marlowe House it was late afternoon and starting to get dark. There had been so much to say that the hours had flown by and Sue had lost all track of time.

Jeanie had said she'd book an appointment for Evie at her own hairdresser, and pay for her daughter's new hairstyle and also some shoes with maybe a bit of a heel. They'd make a day of it next week and have some fun together.

Jeanie was full of praise for Evie's new outfit and the plans for expanding the sewing business into more ambitious projects. 'You should go into tailoring and make a suit for Freddie, Mum,' she grinned, looking sideways at his frayed shirt collar and trouser hems.

'No, I'm not that good. I only do dress patterns,' said Sue. She could see that although Frederick was shabbier than anyone with no money, such as those that lived in Shenty Street, it was almost an act, a kind of statement of style rather than through necessity. Kind of as though he is dressing up, she thought.

The Carters talked about Peter and shed a few tears over Robert, which they couldn't help because they all missed him so much. Jeanie wrote the date of Peter's concert in a smart diary by the telephone and promised to try to go if there was no danger of Michael being there.

'I don't want any awkwardness in public,' she said, 'and there'd be no avoiding him in a church hall.'

'I don't suppose Peter wants him there either,' said Evie.

'I've just had an idea,' Jeanie said, pen still in hand. 'You could do with a telephone at Pendle's, what with taking on customers in Redmond, couldn't you?'

'Ooh, Mum, I hadn't really thought. It would be a great help, wouldn't it, Grandma, so we'd be able to arrange fittings and tell them when their clothes were ready?'

'Yes, you're right, love,' Sue agreed.

'I'll ask Jack to arrange that for you,' said Frederick.

'Oh, thank you,' beamed Evie. 'We'll be like a proper business, with a telephone and everything.'

'It *is* a proper business anyway,' said Jeanie, smiling at Sue and Evie, 'and I couldn't be more proud of you.'

~

That night, Evie lay in bed thinking about the day and how much she'd enjoyed seeing her mother. It wasn't just that she missed Jeanie, but her spirits were raised by what she had found. She remembered how she'd begged Jeanie not to leave them, but now it was obvious that it had all been for the best. Jeanie had been different . . . happy, despite still grieving for Robert. Evie couldn't remember ever seeing her mother that happy before. She was clearly very much in love with Frederick – and he with her – so that even the house felt like a happy place to be. It was almost as if the walls had been smiling.

Evie shrugged off her fanciful notion while accepting that here was a lesson for the new Evie to learn. The new Evie was now a seamstress who was about to launch a proper business with an expert needlewoman, Sue, and she had some beautiful outfits to show off their talents and style. They were even going to have a telephone installed. All they needed was to put in some hard work and everything would be fine. It was all down to them.

The only thing the new Evie wasn't sure about was whether she would ever be as much in love as her mother and Frederick Bailey were, and as Grandma Sue and Granddad Albert had been in the old tales Sue told about how they had met and married. Billy Taylor was no longer a part of her life. He'd made his choice and she had to go along with that. Maybe he had never been the one for her. Now she'd never know. But there must be someone else out there for her. How long before she found him?

CHAPTER FIFTEEN

EVIE HAD NEVER been vain. However, she couldn't help but notice with satisfaction how, since she'd started wearing the beautiful clothes she and Sue had sewn, and had her hair cut in a new style, total strangers sometimes turned to give her a second glance in the street. This morning, in Redmond, one lady, wearing a smart outfit herself, even asked where Evie had bought her suit, and Evie was able to give her one of the business cards she and Sue had had made with their names and the number of the newly installed telephone on it:

Goodwin and Carter, Dressmakers
Telephone: Church Sandleton 325

There had, of course, been no time to find the fabric and haberdashery sellers, the addresses of

which they'd noted in the library, on that first visit
to Jeanie at Marlowe House – far too much catching-
up to do – but Evie and Sue were back in Redmond
on this spring-like morning in early March especially
to seek out the shops. Disappointingly, neither of
the places was anything special, but it was useful to
know where they could buy all the basics nearby.
The vast amount of thread and buttons that Sue
had brought with her to Church Sandleton was
beginning to run low.

'We've been spoiled by the quality of the cotton
prints from the mill shop in Bolton,' said Sue, as
they came out of the second shop with only some
tacking cotton and a card of press studs.

'You're right, Grandma,' Evie replied. 'Do you
think it's worth looking out this place in Kingsford?'

'I reckon we should. Be a pity if we didn't and it
turned out to be worth the effort.'

'You're not too tired, are you, Grandma?'

'No, lass. We'll take the train as it's quicker, so
I'll have a sit-down more comfortable than on the
bus. Come on, I gather it's only the next station.'

Neither Evie nor Sue had been to Kingsford
before and they were pleasantly surprised by the
pretty little town.

'"G. Morris, Market Passage",' Evie read from the
shorthand notebook into which she'd copied the
addresses she'd found in the library. She'd taken to
carrying the notebook these days, and with so many

prices to remember it was proving to be essential this morning. 'It must be off the marketplace.'

They walked slowly around the marketplace, admiring the shops and checking the names of the side streets.

'Here we are,' said Evie, and she and Sue walked arm in arm down a narrow cobbled side street, treading carefully on the uneven surface. 'My goodness, Grandma, I wasn't expecting this,' she gasped, gazing at two long windows filled with draped fabrics to either side of a blue shop door. 'It's enormous.'

'Best get in and see what it's like,' said Sue, looking pleased.

A bell tinkled loudly as Evie opened the door and they entered. Fabrics in every colour and pattern she could imagine were stacked on shelves, and there were racks of braid, ribbon and lace, zips in a huge variety of lengths and colours, and then buttons and threads in cabinets with glass-fronted drawers – everything a dressmaker could need.

'It's like being back in the North,' laughed Sue. 'I reckon we might be able to do a bit of shopping here.'

'Good morning. How can I help you?' A middle-aged man with thinning hair and tortoiseshell glasses came out from behind one of the polished counters.

'We've just come for a look round at the moment,' said Sue. 'My granddaughter and I are professional dressmakers and we're keen to find a source of quality fabrics and trimmings.'

'Professional?' asked the man. He eyed up Evie's stylish suit. 'So I see,' he said, admiringly. 'Well, Mrs . . . ?'

'Goodwin,' said Sue, dipping into her handbag for one of the business cards.

The man took it, looked at it and turned to Evie with a smile.

'Evie Carter. How do you do?' said Evie, offering her hand. That was what Letty would say, she thought.

'George Morris,' said the man, shaking it gently, then offering his hand to Sue. 'Well, please have a look around. The prices are retail, of course, but I can offer you a trade discount as you're in the profession.'

Sue and Evie beamed at each other. *Trade discount?*

They spent the rest of the morning oohing and aahing over the fabrics and trimmings, discussing what they could do with them. The prices, though, were much higher than they were used to and they soon realised that they wouldn't be coming away with bagsful of purchases, even with the promised trade discount.

'I love this midnight blue,' whispered Evie, 'but I don't know if we ought to buy any without a specific commission. We can't afford to buy even half a yard too much at this price.'

'I was wondering about that, love,' murmured Sue. 'I reckon it might be worth the risk for a blouse and a dress. We know well enough what most patterns take. That green broadcloth is summat special. I wonder what sort of a discount Mr Morris offers to the trade.'

'We'll have to ask him,' said Evie. 'But then he'll cotton on that we've just started out and mebbe he'll take advantage.'

'Mmm . . . ' Sue frowned, thinking hard. Luckily two other customers came into the shop and George Morris, who had been packing up some brown paper parcels for the post, became busy with them while Sue and Evie thought what they could do.

'I didn't expect there'd be so much choice,' said Evie quietly. 'But we haven't got a lot to spend and "trade" probably means buying quite a bit.'

'Yes,' said Sue, 'we'll just have to do what we can. Don't forget he's already offered a discount. Where's that notebook?'

Evie pulled the shorthand notebook and her propelling pencil out of her bag. She noted down the prices of the fabrics they liked best, and also of some lace and some special beading.

'So, Mr Morris,' said Sue, when the other customers had gone, 'you've got some nice stuff here. The thing is, we're from the north, as you can probably tell, and northern folk are canny shoppers. Now, you mentioned a trade discount, did you not?'

'I did indeed, Mrs Goodwin.'

'And might I ask how much this discount would be? You see, Mr Morris, we're mainly buying from the mill shops – and as you know, Lancashire cotton is the best in the world – so not only are we used to buying quality, but we always get a good trade discount at the mill. It's the personal service, you see. They know us up there and they know how to keep us going back.'

George Morris looked taken aback at Sue's forthright words, but he quickly regained his cheerful smile.

'But if you're a regular customer of the mill shops, Mrs Goodwin – and I do agree with you about the quality of Lancashire cotton – why would you need to shop here as well? I can't compete with the mill shop prices.'

'Because you're local to us now, and if we were to shop here we'd be able to choose not only the fabrics but also all the special trimmings that are such a feature of our work, and all in one place, Mr Morris,' said Evie. 'The mill shops don't have these kinds of things, and we're having to buy them elsewhere . . . in London,' she said, inspiration suddenly striking. She indicated the racks of lace and decorative bindings. 'We'd rather buy local, if the price is right, and we'd be able to recommend that *our* regular clients come to you to choose their fabrics and trimmings for themselves, though, of course, you'd be selling to them at full retail price.'

'Yes . . . I can see that would be beneficial to both of us.'

'And we're *two* dressmakers, don't forget,' smiled Evie, 'so that's twice as many customers to send to you than if there was only one of us.'

George Morris raised his eyebrows. Never in his life had he seen a pair of women like these two. The nerve of the girl! Still, that suit was a work of art – if they had indeed made it themselves, that was.

'So mebbe we can talk about the discount . . . ?' suggested Evie with what she hoped was a winning smile.

She really has got a very pretty smile, though, thought George. Suddenly he didn't want Miss Carter and her formidable grandmother to leave.

'How does five per cent sound?' he asked, testing the water.

'What about twenty-five?'

George clutched the counter for support. He looked like he might actually faint away.

There was a long silence. Just as Evie was about to lose her nerve, George Morris cleared his throat.

'Fifteen per cent?' he offered, his voice sounding as if he were being strangled.

'Agreed,' beamed Sue, taking his hand and shaking it hard. 'Evie, write that down now and then we'll not forget,' she suggested pointedly, and Evie did as she was told.

'I'll be right glad to do business with you, Mr Morris,' said Sue. 'I wonder if we might have two and a half yards of that midnight-blue voile, and four yards of the green broadcloth, please, to be going on with? Our clients will be asking where we got those, don't you worry.'

'Certainly, Mrs Goodwin,' said George, unsure whether these two unusual women were in fact dressmakers or merely pretending to be. Mrs Goodwin looked old-fashioned and a bit shabby, but that didn't mean she wasn't a skilled seamstress, of course. The granddaughter, Miss Carter, looked amazing, and certainly someone had made that suit to fit her perfectly. It was difficult to place them as he'd never seen anyone quite like them before.

As he measured out the fabric an awful thought occurred to him. Perhaps they were con artists? A double act? No, that couldn't be right. If it were so then why would they be asking for a discount from a draper? It made no sense . . .

He cut the fabric lengths, folded them neatly, wrapped them in brown paper and tied the parcel with string. Then he totted up the total, deducted fifteen per cent – Sue leaning over the counter, her glasses on her nose, checking the sums from upside down – and announced the sum owing, writing out a receipt and putting his carbon copy on a spike by the till.

As Sue handed over what seemed like a large sum

even with the discount, Evie tried not to think how many remnants and blouse lengths she had bought for less than that at the mill shop in Bolton.

'Thank you, Mr Morris. A pleasure doing business with you,' said Sue graciously, folding the receipt into her purse and handing the parcel to Evie.

'We'll see you again soon,' smiled Evie, turning with a deliberate swish of her well-tailored skirt as she went towards the door.

George nipped out from behind his counter and rushed ahead to open the door for his customers. He still didn't know what to make of them but he knew for certain that they'd got very good taste. The fabrics they'd chosen were among the best he stocked.

Sue and Evie waited until they were back in the marketplace before they dare let their social smiles turn to mirth.

'Heck, love, if this is the new Evie you spoke of, I approve of her!' grinned Sue. 'You did well there, lass. I thought the old miser was going to go back on his word about a discount for a moment. And at his prices he ought to be offering fifty per cent!'

'Oh, Grandma, I have to laugh. I could see he was thinking he'd never seen owt like us before.'

'I don't know as we'll be shopping at "G. Morris" all that often,' Sue said, sounding regretful.

'I don't see why not, Grandma. I rather liked him, and we've secured a discount for the business. If we want to build a reputation for quality we'll have to get the good stuff from somewhere, and it's a long way to Bolton!'

'And a long way to London, too!' Sue laughed loudly. 'London, indeed!'

Evie joined in the laughter as they walked slowly back to the station.

~

Sue and Evie's raised spirits from the success of their shopping in Mr Morris's shop were lowered on their return to Pendle's. Evie went upstairs straight away to change out of the precious suit and put on her old clothes, which felt baggy and shapeless after a morning spent in the perfect-fitting jacket and skirt, though her feet were glad of her socks and plimsolls after so long in the elegant court shoes Frederick and Jeanie had bought her for her birthday.

Then it was back to letting down hems on summer school uniforms for a couple of children in the village, which reminded Evie and Sue of Robert and altering his school uniform, and this deflated them even more.

'I wish the telephone would ring, Grandma, and someone would ask for a blouse in midnight-blue voile,' said Evie, eyeing the lovely fabric on the shelf.

'So do I, love. I thought when we placed those adverts in the *Redmond Gazette* that we'd be turning folk away. Almost every last penny went on that ad.'

'Maybe Mum will mention us to someone. Frederick seems to know a lot of people – that is, he gets around and Mum goes with him to so many places now – and she did say she'd put a word in for us if the chance came.'

But two weeks went by and the telephone didn't ring once. Sue and Evie swallowed their disappointment and carried on with their mundane tasks. At least they still had those, though it didn't look to them as if they would be revisiting Mr Morris any time soon. Funds were getting low and every day they were more glad of the mundane work while their dreams were put on hold. They started making cutbacks at home and this further dampened their spirits. It was back to meals made of Mr Clackett's leftover vegetables, which drove Michael out to the pub in the evenings, where the locals would buy him a pint or two.

~

By the beginning of April the days were lengthening so fast that Sue declared she thought her eyesight was improving. She'd spent the dark winter peering under a table lamp as she stitched, and on a couple of occasions she'd had to ask Evie to finish something for her.

'It's sometimes difficult to get a sharp focus,' she said, 'but I reckon I'll improve with these longer days.'

Evie wasn't so sure, she worried terribly about her grandmother, but she knew better than to say anything. Evie was thinking she needed to take over some of her grandmother's work as her fingers always got stiff and swollen in the cold. She had pressed the fabric and laid it flat on the big work table when the door opened with a crash and her father stomped in with a furious look on his face.

'What's the matter, Dad?' checked Evie kindly, just as Sue said, 'Out! Get them mucky boots out of here at once, Michael Carter.'

Michael strode out without a word, almost slamming the door to the big kitchen in Evie's face as she followed him, all concern, and Sue heaved herself to her feet with a sigh and went to see what the matter was now.

When Sue saw Michael hurling his boots through the back door she had a horrible feeling she knew exactly what he was going to say.

'Go on, tell us, lad.'

'I've left Clackett's,' Michael announced, slumping down on a chair.

'Left?' she said wearily, going to put the kettle on.

'Yes, left. Clackett gave me my notice so I told

him I'd not be working it and I'd rather leave straight away.'

'But why, Dad? What's happened? I thought you were getting on all right there these days.'

'Well, you thought wrong,' he shouted. 'Seems Clackett were only keeping me on until that Martin of his were old enough to go to work there. Martin's leaving school this summer and so there'll be no job for me.'

'Oh, Dad, I am sorry,' said Evie. She went to give him a hug, which he shrugged off.

'You could have worked your notice, Michael. At least you'd have been paid until summer.'

'I'll get summat else, don't you worry,' said Michael, though he didn't sound as if he believed it.

'You could always go and tell Mr Clackett that you've changed your mind,' ventured Evie.

'I'll not set foot on that bugger's land again. He wants blood, sweat and tears for his bit of money and I've done with the mud and the cold. I don't care if I never see another cabbage.'

Sue made a pot of tea, her brain whirring with options that Michael might consider. Because there was one thing she was sure of: he wasn't going to sit here in the kitchen doing nothing while she and Evie sat stitching all day.

'Now that the days are getting warmer, it might be better there?'

'Perhaps you could ask around the village, Michael—' began Sue.

'Just shut up and let me drink my tea in peace for a minute,' Michael said wearily. 'It's all right, I'll be out of your hair before long. I won't be in the way of your precious sewing.'

Sue chose not to answer and the two women slipped away back to their work, which they took up in silence, the only sound the grind of Evie's shears through the fabric.

'Shall I go and ask Mr Clackett to give Dad his job back until Martin joins him in the summer?' asked Evie.

Sue smiled a sad smile. 'No, love, don't waste your breath. Do you think he'd go if you did?'

Quiet work resumed. Evie felt sick with worry, where was their next meal coming from if they didn't have Clackett's leftovers?

Suddenly the door opened and there were Jack and Monty.

'Hello. What's up? You two look a bit gloomy,' said Jack.

'Our Michael's lost his job at Clackett's.'

'I'm sorry to hear that,' said Jack, frowning. 'It wasn't more trouble about him being at the Red Lion, was it?'

Sue explained about Mr Clackett wanting his son to come into the business full time when he left school in the summer.

' . . . So Michael's taken umbrage and left now,' she concluded.

'Where is he? Shall I go and see him?' Jack wasn't keen but he felt he should offer support.

'I wouldn't, lad. He's in the back, but with you being Frederick's man and all, I don't want you getting caught up in something you can do nowt about. I've noticed you've not been round here of an evening, and I don't suppose you came by today to see Michael, did you?'

'I had expected him to be over the road.' Jack was keeping his voice down now. 'I came by with a little something for you that Jeanie found in a junk shop. She and Frederick thought it'd be useful so I've brought it round in the van.'

'Well, bring it in, lad,' Sue said, looking at Evie in excitement.

Jack disappeared while Monty came over to be petted by Evie. Jack reappeared a couple of minutes later with . . .

'Good grief, Jack. It's a dressmaker's dummy.'

'It certainly is,' said Jack, carrying the figure in and placing it on its castors in front of the window. 'What do you think? Jeanie was a bit anxious you wouldn't want it when she'd bought it, but Frederick said in that case you are to send it back with me and he can sell it on.'

'Oh, no, it's perfect!' Evie gasped. 'Exactly what we need. Thank you for bringing it, and please

thank Mum and Frederick for thinking of us, won't
you?' She felt sad that her mum hadn't come around
but was pleased she'd thought of them.

'Of course, Evie.'

'Thank you, Jack,' Sue joined in. 'I've never had
one of these before. I never thought I would have
either,' she smiled.

With a cheery wave, Jack was gone, his loyal dog
following at his heels.

Evie went over to inspect the dummy. A medium
size, it was covered in a fawn-coloured calico.

'I've got an idea,' Evie said, and disappeared
upstairs, returning shortly with the tailored suit. 'If
we dress the dummy it can show off the clothes
we've made – when it's not being used, that is.'

Sue watched as Evie did just that, her young
fingers working quickly and confidently.

'Looks lovely. If only we had some folk in to see it.'

'Grandma, it's only a matter of time, I know it.
In the meantime I'm going to get this blouse made
and then the dummy can wear that, too!'

'We'll have to visit your mother to thank her.'

'Will you tell her about Dad?' asked Evie.

'I suppose we'd better, love,' she replied sadly.

～

It was Easter at the end of the week, and time hadn't
improved Michael's temper. Evie guessed the news

would be all around the village now, and her dad said he'd been asking around, but he always seemed to end up in the pub.

~

Michael had just been to a farm a couple of miles outside the village where he'd heard they needed a cow man, but when he told Evie and Sue about the muck and the smell, even he had to join in their laughter at the thought of him working with a herd of cows.

'Smell was terrible,' he said.

'Well, of course it was, Dad,' said Evie. 'We may live in the country now but we're townies. I don't think farm work is for you, but I suppose you needed to go to find that out. I heard Miss Richards wants some help digging her garden – maybe you could help her?'

'Oh, that Miss Richards is a good sort,' said Michael, 'but I'm not sure I want to do any more digging.'

'You don't have much choice,' Sue said, firmly, turning Michael back out through the door. 'Don't throw away her kindness.'

That night, as she lay in bed, Evie worried greatly. Now her brothers had been gone so long, Sue had moved into what had been the boys' room so Evie had a bedroom to herself. She could hear Sue's distant snoring and she got up and went to the window, which looked onto the backyard. The sky was black and cloudless, and she shivered. Evie couldn't help thinking of that cold dark evening when she and Peter had gone to find Robert, and tears filled her eyes. She would never get over it, but was starting to learn to deal with it. But she missed her brothers and her mum so much. And all the folk on Shenty Street. Billy especially. With that thought, Evie climbed back into bed and cried herself to sleep.

The sun had barely risen when Evie made her way downstairs, hoping to get a head start on work. But Sue was already up and a little unsteady on her feet as she stepped around the kitchen making some breakfast.

'Just tired eyes, love, that's all,' she assured Evie. 'I'll be better after a good night's sleep.'

But Evie was not so sure. She'd noticed that Sue was still stitching by the light of the lamp, even during the sunnier days, and she'd had to ask Evie about colour-matching some thread several times. Evie had been too worried about the lack of work to think much about it, but now she vowed to keep a more careful watch on her beloved grandmother.

As they worked on their stitching, Evie kept a watchful eye on Sue. When Michael came in at the end of the afternoon, he declared he'd had a good day at Lavender Cottage. He looked happier than he had for months.

'Margaret only wants me to help her do the boring bits, she says,' he smiled, 'so there's a bit of digging, pots to wash and the paths to sweep. She does all the clever stuff herself, but she did show me how to do some pruning. She says I made a decent job of it.'

Evie was delighted to hear her father so cheerful. She couldn't remember him expressing any interest in his work since they'd left Bolton – and possibly long before that.

'I'm so glad, Dad,' she said. 'She and Letty are such good friends to us. We're lucky to have them.'

'We are, that,' he agreed. 'Now what's for tea? I'll peel some spuds, if you like, and you can make a start on it.' Evie had never known her dad to help, but she'd been so busy with her sewing . . .

'Oh, no, I forgot all about tea, Dad! I don't know if we've got anything much. Now that you don't get the vegetables given, we've sort of run out. I'm not used to buying them.'

She was fearful for a moment that Michael's good mood might evaporate, especially when he fell silent.

Then he said, 'Well, it's lucky I've got some pennies from Margaret. Here, Evie, you nip over to Suttons' before they close and choose summat for tonight.' And he gave her some coins.

Evie flew out without even her coat on to catch the general store, which was open every day, bank holidays included, arriving breathless.

She looked at the goods on the shelves and in the fridge and chose a minced beef pie and some carrots and potatoes.

Mrs Sutton put them in a paper carrier for her, enquiring, as she always did, about Sue.

'She all right, your grandma?'

'Yes, thank you, Mrs Sutton. Her eyes get tired with all the stitching but then she's getting old and I think mebbe she needs new glasses.'

'It's just, well, the last time she was in here she was finding it hard to see what she wanted on the shelves, though it was right in front of her and as plain as could be to me.'

'Oh? She never said.'

'I helped her out and she said she hadn't spotted it, but then she went out right past Mrs Lambert without a word. Oh, don't worry, Mrs Lambert said she thought Mrs Goodwin was preoccupied and hadn't noticed her. She's a nice woman and not one to take offence.'

'No, of course not . . . ' Josie had been polite enough not to mention it, but Evie was puzzled and not a little worried. 'Thank you for telling me, Mrs Sutton.'

She went home with her pie and vegetables, full of new worries.

After they'd eaten and washed up, Michael went to the Red Lion with some of the money Miss Richards had paid him and Evie made a pot of tea.

'You all right, Grandma?' she asked, sitting down beside Sue at the kitchen table.

'Never better, lass. Why?'

'Well, I've noticed you seem to be having trouble with your eyes. You've always got the lamp on, even during the day, and you've asked me a couple of times about matching a colour, and I think you're finding it hard to see what's right in front of you.'

Sue was silent for a few moments. Then: 'You're right, love. It is getting difficult to see to sew, but mebbe I just need new glasses.'

'Are your eyes hurting at all, Grandma?'

'No, lass.'

'No headaches – you would tell me, wouldn't you?'

'My head's fine, Evie.'

'Shall we go and see if we can get you some new glasses?'

'I'm sure I'm all right, love. I'll think about it.'

~

The following day Evie took a few coins out of the tin Sue kept to cover small expenses and went over to Suttons'. As she approached, she could see a couple of women gossiping outside the shop. Hearing the name 'Carter', she stood quite still behind the pillar box to listen.

' . . . heard their mother ran away and now lives with her fancy man in Redmond: only Frederick

313

Bailey, if you please, he that owns their place and those two houses further down.'

Evie didn't want to listen but she couldn't help it.

'What, him that's had all those wives! I don't believe it. I thought I hadn't seen her around but I'd no idea she'd done a runner. Always thought she was flighty. Far too pretty for her own good.'

'Disgraceful, if you ask me. One child dead, one living with other people, and that scruffy-looking urchin now dolling herself up and going off on the bus to Redmond. What's she doing there dressed like that, I'd like to know. It's plain to me that the mother hasn't kept her on the straight and narrow. Like mother, like daughter I should say.'

Evie was torn between running away and giving the gossips the tongue-lashing she felt they deserved. But then she remembered she was now the new Evie. Grown-up and with the courage to face the gossips down with dignity, not run away crying like a child.

She swallowed down her anger while taking note of what these two middle-aged women looked like. She knew neither of their names, but she vowed to find them out. Then she drew herself up to her full height to give herself courage. She stepped forward and they turned to see her. If she hadn't been so cross she'd have laughed at the looks on their faces.

'I think you'll find,' Evie said, 'that people who know us – people who aren't gossiping in the street like fishwives – are very pleased for my grandmother and me to be running a successful dressmaker's, and if you think wearing a nice outfit is somehow immoral, I expect you'll be making saints, the pair of you.' Leaving the gossips open-mouthed and silent in astonishment, she went into the shop.

'Hello, Evie, dear,' said Mrs Sutton. 'What can I get you?'

Evie asked for her few essentials and Mrs Sutton helped her.

'Who are those women I saw just now in front of the shop?' asked Evie casually.

'Oh, Mrs Bradshaw and Mrs Pinnock, I think you mean,' offered Mrs Sutton.

She decided not to tell Sue what she'd heard in case it upset her, but when she got back to Pendle's Sue could sense Evie buzzing with energy at the encounter.

'You all right, love?' Sue asked. 'Only you look like you're bursting with summat to say.'

'No, Gran, I'm fine,' said Evie. 'But I overheard one woman in the street saying I looked flighty, like my mum.'

'Oh love, don't you listen to them.'

'You don't think everyone is saying that, do you? I couldn't bear it if folk or you thought badly of Mum and me when we've done nowt wrong.'

'Don't you worry, Evie. No one who matters thinks badly of you at all.'

But whatever her grandmother said, Evie felt sick that everyone was thinking bad of her family. She felt that no good would come of this.

CHAPTER SIXTEEN

'I'VE GOT A job!' Michael beamed. 'I start tomorrow. It's a small place just outside Redmond, bit of a walk from the bus, though.'

'What do you have to do?' asked Evie. 'Is it difficult?'

'No, lass, I'm only sweeping up and fetching and carrying at a shoe factory, as far as I know. There's no skill involved.'

'Mebbe you'll work your way up to do the shoe-making.'

'I doubt it, our Evie. It looks to be quite a skilled job. Lots of stitching, but bigger machines than your grandma's.' He laughed loudly. 'Still, it's indoors, which has got to be better than Clackett's.'

'You won't forget to let Margaret Richards know that you've got a job now and won't be going there to help her in the garden, will you, Michael?'

'Well, Sue, I was thinking, mebbe when the

317

weather's fine, at weekends, I could go down and see what she wants doing, if that suits her.'

Evie and Sue looked at each other in astonishment. This was a turnaround!

'Good idea, Dad,' said Evie, when she'd managed to compose her face.

~

Suddenly it was just Evie and Sue alone all day at Pendle's and the atmosphere lifted slightly. They worked hard, hardly stopping to eat at lunchtime, and the workroom was abuzz with the sound of the treadle machine and the grind of scissors through fabric. Working on a client's clothes by herself, Evie sensed for the first time in her life that things had turned a corner and she felt the flutterings of happiness.

On the Thursday they took the bus to Redmond to look at the market, and to go to the doctor, as Sue's eyes were getting worse. They shuffled into the consulting room, Sue looking as if she was going to her execution and leaving her coat with Evie, who sat nervously waiting.

Time passed slowly and Evie started to worry: did it usually take this long? Eventually the door opened and a white-faced Sue emerged.

'What is it, Grandma? Tell me,' whispered Evie, her heart hammering.

'It's a *degeneration* thing, love –' Sue pronounced the word carefully '– something to do with my age, and the rest is just bad luck. It's only in one eye, though, and if I have new glasses then I'll be able to see through the other one better than at present.'

'Oh, Grandma! Oh, I'm sorry. Will it get worse? Will you . . . you won't go blind, will you?' The very idea filled her with horror.

'No, love, but it might get worse.'

Tears sprang to Evie's eyes. Just when their lives were beginning to improve at last, too! It was so unfair! Better go and tell Jeanie the bad news while they were here.

~

'Er, we wondered if we could beg a cup of tea, Mum, please? Grandma's been to the doctor's and it's not good news.'

Jeanie was at once all concern, and led Sue down the winding stairs to the kitchen.

'There's nothing to be done.' Evie explained the sad situation. 'Grandma's only sixty-four and we've got such plans for the dressmaking. It's starting to take off, and bring some money in. If Grandma can't see to sew then I shall have to do all the work myself. I don't know if I'll be able to manage that. I'm worried about Grandma and I'm worried that it might all be too much for me . . . ' She sniffed and mopped her eyes with her hankie.

~

Ada Taylor had a bit of a summer cold. She claimed she hadn't really felt well since the snow in February and now, towards the end of June, she was petulant, moany and demanding.

Billy had done his best to tend to her, and had even gone to the surgery to ask the doctor to come round. The doctor had done so, then declared Mrs Taylor had only a mild summer cold and a severe dose of self-pity, and he told Billy not to waste his time bothering him again unless she took a turn for the worse.

Billy, too, was feeling the effects of his mother's illness – not in his own health, but in the demands she made of him. For the last week she'd taken to staying in bed for much of the day, saying she was too ill to get up and do the housework. At first Billy tried to take on the chores himself when he got home from work, but then Ada fretted he might not have cleaned the kitchen well enough, or that the shopping he'd bought entirely at Mr Amsell's on the way home from work was more expensive than taking a trip to the bigger shops in the nearest high street. There was no pleasing her.

Billy had to leave her by herself all day to go to

work, which meant making her a sandwich before he left and leaving it under a plate, in case she really did feel too ill to make her own. At least there seemed to be nothing wrong with her appetite. The food was always gone by the time Billy arrived home, the plates left for him to wash.

'Are you sure you're not well enough to get up, Mum?' he asked eventually. 'If you can manage the afternoons you could do a bit of light housework then, something to occupy you, like, and it'd be to your own high standards.'

'Billy, you wouldn't ask it of me if you felt like I do,' Ada moaned, coughing into her hankie.

'Would you like me to ask someone to visit you, Mum?' he suggested. He racked his brains. He thought of Marie Sullivan, but decided she had enough to do with her large family. Dora Marsh? But Mrs Marsh, though she had a heart of gold, was of the old school, like Sue Goodwin, and she'd probably tell Ada to buck up and get on with it. Geraldine Sullivan? Gerry was a cheerful sort, and he knew his mother liked her. He would understand, though, if she declined to visit. How he wished Evie was here; she'd look in, he was sure.

Gerry reluctantly agreed, however, when he popped in to ask her as he passed the corner shop. 'I'll not be able to stop long, though, Billy,' she said, primping the back of her new hairstyle. The queues for morning papers at Mr Amsell's were even longer than before since Gerry Sullivan had changed her style.

'Oh, Geraldine, love, is that you?' called Ada in a shaky voice when she heard the key in the front door at lunchtime. Billy had given Gerry a spare key when she'd agreed to visit.

'It is, Mrs Taylor.' There was the sound of light footsteps on the stairs and Gerry put her head round Ada's bedroom door. 'Oh, you poor thing. Is it a bad cold you've got? Here, I've brought you some sweets from the shop.' She handed Ada a box of fruit gums. 'By, it's hot in here, Mrs Taylor. Shall I open the window?'

Before Ada could object the window was opened and fresher air entered the musty room.

'How are you feeling today, Mrs Taylor?'

'Not so good, Geraldine, love. I don't know if I shall make it to Christmas at this rate.'

'I'm sorry to hear that,' said Gerry.

Billy had briefed her about his mother's mood. 'I don't know what she's after, Gerry. Sometimes she just wants some attention, so if you can bear to go and see her, at least she'll have a fresh face to look at. Mebbe she'll snap out of it when she thinks she's stayed in bed long enough.'

'Would you like me to make you a cup of tea, Mrs Taylor? Billy says he's left you a sandwich.'

'Oh . . . Geraldine, that would be so kind. I haven't

anyone to make tea for me, what with Billy out all day on his rounds. He's a good lad, though.'

He's a saint to put up with you. 'He is indeed,' agreed Geraldine, sweetly.

Ada was encouraged by this reply. 'Do you see much of Billy, Geraldine, love?'

'Oh, yes, Billy and I are great friends,' she beamed. 'We've known each other for years and . . . well, you grow closer over time – you know what I mean?' she added artlessly.

Ada perked up for a moment, forgetting she wouldn't make it to Christmas.

'If you make me that tea, love, we can have a little chat,' she suggested. 'Have a cup yourself,' she added.

'Thank you, Mrs T. I'll just go down and do it.'

A few seconds later Gerry called up, 'The tea caddy's empty, Mrs Taylor. Have you another packet?'

'I keep it in the sideboard in the front room,' called back Ada, her voice surprisingly strong.

Gerry went to find it and was astonished when she saw the size of the hoard of tea. Saints above, the woman must be mad! It looked like she'd withstand a siege. How many were there? Out of sheer naughtiness she quickly pulled the packets of tea out to count them. If nothing else it would make a good tale to confide to her mother. Twenty-five!

And what was this? She reached in and extracted two envelopes that had been right at the back of the cupboard behind all the tea. Both of them were addressed to Billy and neither had been opened. Strange . . . She looked at them carefully. There was something familiar about the hand-writing . . . Mary had had letters in the same round schoolgirl hand. Suddenly Geraldine knew. There was no doubt these letters were from Evie Carter, and no doubt either that Billy's mother had taken them and hidden them from him. After all, why would Billy himself have not opened them, and why would he hide them in the sideboard, which was definitely his mother's territory?

For a moment Geraldine debated with herself whether to put the letters back where she'd found them and forget all about them. They were, after all, nothing to do with her. But she knew that Billy had been out of sorts since his split from Evie, and Brendan had said that the poor lad hadn't even known about what happened to Robert. A quick glance at the dates of the postmarks confirmed these letters had arrived last winter and Geraldine would have put money on it that they contained the vital news.

She quickly put all the packets of tea back in the sideboard, arranging them as they were but with a gap at the front to show she had taken one out. Then, as she went back into the kitchen, she slipped the letters into her handbag, which she'd left in the hall. It wasn't stealing, she told herself. It was Ada who was the thief. These were Billy's letters and she would be simply delivering them into his hands at last.

Her conscience clear, Geraldine made the tea, found the sandwich on the kitchen table and took Ada's lunch upstairs for her. Out of sheer devilment she'd put three spoons of sugar in the tea.

'Here you are, Mrs Taylor. It really is hot in here.' Fanning herself, she went to open the window even wider. 'Nothing like fresh air to bring colour to your cheeks.' She smiled kindly at Ada.

'I don't know about that—'

'So how long have you felt bad, Mrs Taylor?'

'Ooh, weeks at least. I've not been right since the snow.'

'And have you seen the doctor?' Geraldine had been told all about the doctor's visit but she was feeling spiteful since she'd found Billy's letters.

'Hmm. He was no use.'

'Oh dear, whatever did he say?'

Ada looked abashed. 'He said it's only a summer cold and we weren't to waste his time again,' she muttered.

'Oh dear, how cruel! And there's you suffering. Maybe you should get a second opinion, Mrs Taylor. Perhaps you should go up to the hospital and demand to see one of the doctors there, what with you doubtful about making it to Christmas. Still, that's six months yet,' she added cheerfully.

Ada was at a loss how to take this suggestion so she decided to move the conversation on from her health.

'So you and Billy have grown closer, you say?' she asked.

'Mmm. He's a grand lad.'

'And you're a lovely lass. You know, Geraldine, I always dreamed of having a daughter-in-law like you, someone right pretty and knows how to dress herself well. Any man would be proud to have you on his arm.'

'Well, thank you, Mrs Taylor.'

'And I reckon, with all them brothers of yours, that you know how to do things properly around the house. I'm sure you'd fit in well here, love. I'd leave you a free hand at the chores and I've never been one for eating fancy food – just plain cooking – so there'd not be owt complicated for you to learn.'

'Now, I best be getting back to the shop.' Geraldine got up, cutting Ada off. 'I'll let myself out and give Billy the key when I see him.' *And his letters, you miserable old woman.* 'I'm sure you'll be feeling better soon.'

She went downstairs, leaving the window in Ada's room wide open, rinsed out her cup and the teapot, and called a cheerful goodbye up the stairs.

Out in the street she vowed to deliver the letters to Billy at the soonest opportunity. It might be awkward to explain how she'd come by them but she could work round that. It was Ada's conscience that should be worried, not her own.

~

'It's so beautiful here,' breathed Evie, walking slowly along the track around the fields at the back of Clackett's market garden.

'Bliss,' smiled Letty, stopping to raise her face to the sun.

'It's good of Grandma to give me a bit of time off. Two women arrived with babies in prams, wanting little frocks made for them, so as Grandma likes to do the baby clothes I was pleased to leave her to it. The workroom was beginning to feel a bit crowded. The babies were good as gold but the mothers always fuss something terrible.'

They sank down onto some soft grass and Evie idly started a daisy chain.

'I didn't really notice how peaceful and nice it was last summer, what with us only just arriving here and everything to sort out,' Evie went on. 'Pete and Bob liked the other side of the road, the path that leads to the woods. I don't think I shall ever go there again, though.'

'I don't blame you, Evie. I'd feel the same.'

Letty looked down shyly. 'I think I may be a bit in love with Jack. He's just the kindest man I've ever met.'

'He is kind. I don't know where we'd be without Jack's help this last year. But I've seen the way he is with you, and how you seem . . . I don't know . . . to understand each other without owt being said.'

'Yes, it's true!' gasped Letty. 'That's exactly how I feel. It's such a special thing.'

Evie was delighted. 'And does Jack feel the same?'

'I think so. He's taken to coming round to Lavender Cottage more often, and Aunt Margaret was asking me only the other day if we had any special feelings for each other.'

'And she wouldn't mind if you fell completely in love with Jack, and he with you, would she?'

'Good heavens, no. Even though he's more her age than mine, and has all sorts of odd and part-time jobs running together, I don't think she'd care in the least if I was happy.'

'She is lovely, your aunt, and Jack's lovely, too.'

'And so am I, and so are you!' Letty giggled. 'We're the loveliest people in the entire world.'

'What are you two giggling about?' asked Peter, coming up the path unseen.

'Ah, here's lovely Peter,' said Evie, and she and Letty roared with laughter.

'Idiots,' he muttered affectionately.

'Just girls' talk. You wouldn't understand, Pete,' said Evie.

'I came with a message from Grandma,' said Peter, sinking down on the grass next to them. 'You know,

I blame Dad for everything – us having to leave Shenty Street and all our friends, and then about . . . about Bob, and then Mum going, and then losing his job, and making it so that poor Grandma and you had to work every hour to make enough money, Evie, but now I can see that Mum leaving was the best thing for her. We all want her to be happy, don't we? I went round yesterday after school and Mum and Frederick are so very happy. It's strange, but I can feel it the moment I go in the house.'

'I've felt that, too,' said Evie. 'Of course I miss her, but you're not here any more and I'm working so hard with Grandma that I feel now we can let Mum go and be glad for her. That's something else I thought would be awful but turned out right. Mum deserves to have a nice life after looking after all of us and everything she put up with in Shenty Street.'

'Dad, you mean?'

'Well, yes. But he's doing all right with his job at the shoe factory – that is, he goes to it every day and stays there until it's time to come home, and I expect he does some work in between. He's bought himself a bicycle to save the bus fare to Redmond and then the walk to the factory. He doesn't say much about the job, but at least he doesn't moan like he did about Mr Clackett.'

Letty chipped in. 'He's being a huge help to Aunt Margaret. She was saying only last weekend how pleased she is to have your father to help her keep it tidy.'

'Well, that's good,' said Peter. 'Mebbe he's found a job he can manage not to mess up. Anyway, this message from Grandma: could you pop round to see Mr Harris, please? He hasn't got something you ordered but he's got something else instead. I expect it will make sense when you speak to him.'

'It doesn't sound very urgent,' said Evie.

'It is if you want to catch him this afternoon. It's getting on for five o'clock.'

'Oh, no, I've lost all track of time. I'd better hurry. Bye, Letty. Bye, Pete. See you soon.' She rushed away down the track.

'There she goes, all in a flutter, expecting the worst,' laughed Peter. 'Will she ever learn?'

'Oh, don't be so unkind, Pete. It's worrying about getting things right that makes her such a good seamstress. If she didn't care about the details she'd be hopeless.'

'You're right, of course, and I didn't mean to criticise. I only wish . . . I don't know.'

'What?'

'I just want Evie to be happy. She holds the weight of our family on her shoulders.'

'Well, who knows what's round the corner?'

'True. Even Billy let her down. I know she was disappointed when Billy didn't reply to her letters, especially when she told him about Bob. Whatever

330

their differences, the way Billy treated her then was bad. But she's over it – and over him – now, I think.'

'She never mentions him, that's for certain.'

'So it would be nice if she were to find someone who suited her so well that she'd never have to worry again.'

'Why, Peter Carter, you old romantic! I'd never guess you're only a schoolboy. Perhaps Evie *has* found someone who suits her,' suggested Letty with a naughty glint in her eye.

'Who are you thinking of?'

'This Mr Harris, of course. Oh, but imagine if she were to marry him. She'd have all the fabrics in his vast shop to choose from and she'd never have to negotiate a discount again!'

Peter couldn't help laughing at the idea. 'Let's hope Evie's luck is about to change,' he said.

CHAPTER SEVENTEEN

BILLY SAT ON his bed and read the two letters
Evie had sent him way back at the end of last
year. Geraldine Sullivan had said they'd fallen out
of the sideboard when she was fetching a packet
of tea for his mum, and she thought Billy had maybe
put them down and forgotten about them and Ada
had tidied them away by mistake. Well, full marks
for invention to Gerry, and she was sticking to her
story even if it didn't hold much water.

The first letter was a simple and heartfelt apology
for Evie's part in the argument at Geraldine's party.
When he'd read the letter, Billy thought back to
that evening when he'd last seen Evie and the stupid
argument that had divided them. He tried to
remember who had said what but, in the way of
most arguments, the subtlety of both sides' words
had become lost in time. He did remember their
differences had turned on something Evie said

about not wanting to live with his mother, and now he wholeheartedly agreed. How could he have thought anyone would want to live with such a woman? He didn't! Oh, he'd always known she was selfish, but this . . .

Then he read the other letter and was surprised to find tears in his eyes at the account of Robert's death. The page was smudged in places and Billy thought that Evie had also shed tears as she wrote it. It was such a brave letter, and included in the envelope was a pretty Christmas card with glitter and a robin on the front, wishing both Billy and his mother a merry Christmas. At the sight of that Billy could contain his misery no longer and he gave himself up to weeping for that lovely girl and her dead little brother.

Eventually he pulled himself together. What must she have thought of him when he hadn't written back?

There was a tap at the door and Ada, who seemed to have rallied since Gerry's visit, called, 'Billy, love, your tea will be ready in ten minutes.'

Billy considered not answering her, but he didn't want her to know anything about his having the letters yet. He'd decide how to play this in his own time.

'Thank you, Mum,' he called back with little enthusiasm for the prospect of having her company over his evening meal.

C'mon, Billy, think! What's should we do about this?

Was there anything to do about it? All kinds of things could have happened in six months. Maybe the Carters weren't even living in Church Sandleton any longer. Perhaps when Robert died they couldn't face it there and had moved on. After all, there had been nothing to take them to the village in the first place except a need to escape Shenty Street, and it was just somewhere that a cousin of Brendan Sullivan's knew about.

Even if they were still there, Evie's circumstances could have changed dramatically. She was six months older – seventeen, now – and she might well have a new boyfriend. A boyfriend who lived nearby and was able to see her all the time. A boyfriend who didn't argue with her and who hadn't got a spiteful mother.

Dear God, how had he even imagined Evie would *ever* want to come to live with his mother? The idea was ridiculous! Her arguing, far from being the thoughtless response of a young girl, now appeared nothing more than common sense. It was he who had been stupid, not Evie.

But then maybe Evie hadn't got a boyfriend at all – maybe she'd got a husband! The thought, though unlikely in so short a time, was terrible, but Billy couldn't help niggling at it like a bad tooth. Soon his imagination was running riot. If Evie was married – very happily married – and lived in her own house, not at Pendle's, then if he wrote to her, Jeanie would be quite justified in withholding the letter from her. What newlywed would want a letter from an old boyfriend forwarded to her blissful new life?

All through that awkward evening meal Billy's mind churned with various imaginings, some bizarre and others credible, until he no longer knew what was plausible, or what to do about it.

He went back up to his room as soon as he could escape Ada, and then to bed, but he couldn't sleep with his thoughts in turmoil.

The next morning he got up even earlier than usual for work and went off while Ada was still asleep, leaving her a note to say he was going out that evening and she was not to cook him any tea or wait up.

After work he went down to the Lord Nelson for a pie and a pint, and the hope of catching Brendan Sullivan. Billy's friends at the postal depot were good fun but he drew the line at confiding this whole sorry story to any of them for their advice.

'All right, Billy, lad?' asked Brendan, coming in and seeing him looking miserable and nursing his pint by himself.

'Ah, Brendan.' Billy brightened. It was Brendan who had masterminded the Carters' flit from Shenty Street, and a good job he'd made of it. Plus, he was the father of two daughters around Evie's age, and possibly he even had sisters of his own. Brendan was the best man to help him sort out this mess, no question.

'What are you having? This one's on me, Brendan, and if you've got the time, I could really do with some advice,' said Billy.

Brendan agreed. He sat down with Billy and listened to the tale of woe, from the argument at the party last November to the letters Billy had been handed only yesterday by Brendan's own daughter.

'Gerry meant it for the best when she gave me the letters,' Billy finished. 'I might have found them myself one day and, as it is, they're six months old, but at least they've not been hidden from me for years. I'm only hoping it may not be too late to do summat about being reunited with Evie.'

Brendan had to smile at Gerry's part in the tale. She was a bold girl who didn't put up with any nonsense, and Ada Taylor was a bigger fool than she'd yet shown herself to be if she thought she'd have had an easy time of it had Gerry and Billy married. As it was, Gerry was seriously involved with Colin Fraser, who suited her in every way.

'Well, lad, I'm fairly certain that young Evie Carter isn't married, at least,' Brendan said. 'Sure, Marie and Mary would not have let that golden nugget of news escape circulation. I also know that most of the family still live in Church Sandleton, or they did when my womenfolk last heard from them,

337

which I think must have been Easter. Just a card and a brief letter with good wishes. It's hard to keep in touch at such a long distance as the time goes by, but I know Sue Goodwin, bless her, would have tried to let us know if they'd moved away or something big had happened in the meantime . . . as she did when that poor lad of theirs died, and when Jeanie left home.'

Billy looked surprised. 'Evie's mum's gone?'

'Aye, lad, some while ago. Don't know the details.'

Oh no, it looked as if things were going from bad to worse for the Carters. First, that awful business with Robert, and then Jeanie leaving. What must the others be feeling? Billy knew how important her family were to Evie and he started to imagine her all alone and grieving for her brother and her mother, which – he really must stop this and behave like a rational man – was absurd.

'So I don't know quite how things are with them at the minute, Billy, but circumstances have definitely changed since Evie wrote to you at Christmas.'

'What do you think I should do, Brendan? I don't want to blunder in where I'm not wanted, but how do I even know . . . ?'

Brendan ordered another couple of pints and he and Billy sat thinking on a course of action.

'There's only one thing for it, so far as I can see, young fella,' said Brendan eventually. 'You'll have to go down there, find Evie and speak to her. If you write, you can't be sure she'll get the letter, and even if she does she may not reply straight away, and in the meantime you'd be left wondering. I can see already that you can hardly live with yourself, not knowing.'

Billy acknowledged this, thinking he also had to live with his mother while he sorted this out, however long it took. At present, this was not a happy prospect.

'You're right, Brendan. I'm owed some holiday from work so I'll take time off and sort this out. Mum wants to go to Blackpool, but she can go on her own, for all I care.'

'That's the spirit, Billy, though I don't mean about your ma.'

'I'll arrange it as soon as possible – next week, even. You're right: if I explain to Evie, to her face, then I shall know once and for all.'

'Well, I hope it works out for you, Billy, I really do. Evie Carter's a grand girl and we were all sorry when you two fell out.'

'Thank you, Brendan, and thank you for your advice.'

Billy and Brendan chatted on, finishing their pints, then Billy took a stroll the long way home in the light June evening. When he let himself into the terraced house in Fawcett Street he could hear the sound of the radio coming from the sitting room, so he called, 'Goodnight, Mum,' as he passed and left Ada to her own company.

The next morning Billy went to work early again, eager to arrange a couple of days off as soon as he could. His holiday was agreed for the beginning of the following week, and he decided to withhold this information from Ada for the time being.

By the time he got home that evening Ada had worked out that something had happened to put Billy out of sorts, but she was at a loss to know what.

'What's up, love?' she asked, pouring him a cup of tea.

'Nowt, Mum.'

'Oh, but I think there is, Billy. Is it summat I can help with?'

'No, Mum. I told you, it's nowt. Thank you for the tea.' He took the cup of tea upstairs with him and spent the time before eating feeling both resentful and a bit triumphant at having secretly arranged his days off.

It was a hot evening and Ada had prepared a salad of tinned sardines, which further fuelled Billy's keenness to get away, however briefly. Ada wasn't making much of an effort domestically these days. Billy thought she'd got used to lying in bed and out of the habit of cooking. The unappetising meal passed mostly in silence, and then Billy washed up and went up to his room.

On the Saturday evening Geraldine Sullivan came calling after tea.

'There are a whole lot of us going to the pictures this evening, Billy. Would you like to come?'

Billy was delighted to accept – he didn't mind what the film was – and he quickly gathered his wallet and jacket, wished his mother a goodnight and left her alone with her wireless.

'Don't wait up,' Billy called, pulling the door to behind him.

There! Let her spend her time in her own company. Folk who stole other folk's letters didn't deserve any consideration, he thought.

It wasn't until Sunday evening, over another dismal meal, that Billy decided to tell Ada that he was getting a train south next morning to go to see Evie. He was about to come straight out with the information when Ada started talking about her hopes for a holiday.

'I've been thinking, Billy, you've been looking a bit tired of late, and not quite yourself,' she began. 'What you need is a holiday away from here.'

'I certainly do,' agreed Billy.

'Where shall we go, love? Do you fancy Blackpool again this year? Or we could go to Southport, which I always think is a bit smarter, like.'

'I fancy neither,' said Billy.

'Oh . . . ' Ada was put out. 'But we always go to the seaside. I thought you liked Blackpool.'

'I shan't be going anywhere with you, Mum. You go anywhere you fancy, but you can leave me out

341

of your holiday plans because I've made plans of my own.'

'What? Billy! You might have said. I've been looking forward to my holiday.'

'Well, as I say, Mum, you can go on your own. Don't let me stop you.'

'But, Billy, where . . . ? What . . . ? Oh, I can't believe you've made plans and not even told me.'

'And why can't you believe it, Mum? It's the truth. After all, you took Evie Carter's letters and didn't tell me, and that's the truth, too.'

Ada looked flabbergasted. For a moment she sat there with her mouth opening and closing and no sound coming out at all.

Billy was grimly satisfied. If, for even a moment, he had thought his mother could possibly be innocent of the theft of the letters, her reaction was proof of her guilt. He sat waiting to see what she would say.

'I . . . I never—'

'Oh, but you did, Mum, didn't you?'

Silence.

'How else did they get into the sideboard? Hopped in there by themselves, did they?'

Ada was backed into a corner. 'Well, I was only protecting you, Billy, love. That girl showed her true colours at Geraldine's party and I didn't want you to be hurt by her any more. Those Carters are unreliable folk and Evie's plainly as bad as her father.'

'It's not your place to steal my letters and make decisions about my life,' snapped Billy, his voice rising.

'It's my place when I can see you coming to harm, Billy.' Ada's voice was getting louder, too. 'It's a mother's role to keep her child from being hurt.'

'I'm a grown man and I can make my own mind up. I don't need you poking your nose in where it's not wanted and keeping me from the girl I love.'

'Love? I didn't see much return of love when that little madam went off back down south and didn't write for weeks, leaving you miserable. I decided then that if she could treat you like that it was better you didn't know her.'

'You decided? What right had you to decide? Don't you reckon I'm old enough to make up my own mind? You'd already taken against her before then. I haven't forgotten you wouldn't even welcome her as a guest in our home, and I'm downright ashamed of that. So you couldn't let us make up our differences – you had to stick your spoke in. You say you didn't want me to be hurt – well, how hurt do you think I feel to learn that Evie's little brother died, and she wrote to tell me and I didn't even know? How hurt do you think I am to discover that Evie wrote to make up our quarrel and I didn't know that either?'

'I only meant it for the best, Billy, love.'

'You meant to keep Evie and me apart because, you say, you don't like her father.'

'But can't you see it's over between you now? She's miles away and she's got her own life to lead down south now. She's never coming back here. You'll be hurt some more if you try to take up with her again. And leopards don't change their spots, son: she'll always be Michael Carter's daughter. She's hurt you once *and* she's shown herself to have a nasty temper—'

'Now you really are talking rubbish. The real reason you don't want me to be with Evie is because you're afraid I'll leave and go south and you'll be left here on your own. That's the truth, isn't it?'

'No, I've told you—'

'And I'm now telling you. You were never so against Evie when she lived in Shenty Street, but when you thought there was any chance I might one day go to be with her and not be here all the time, looking after you when you take to your bed for days, taking on the chores when I come home from work, listening to your moaning—'

For a moment Ada looked stricken but she had gone too far to retreat.

'I was ill, Billy. It's time for you to move on, find a new girl, someone who suits you better.'

'Someone who suits *you*, you mean. You just don't understand, do you? This is the girl I hoped one day to marry. I've booked a couple of days off work.

I'm taking the train tomorrow morning. I only hope I'm not too late. And if I am, it's all your fault, Mum, and I don't know how I'll ever forgive you.'

'Billy, don't speak to me like that,' lamented Ada. 'I can't bear it.'

'Well, Mum, you might just have to "bear it". Because you've brought it on yourself.'

With huge dignity Billy got up, scraped the remains of his lunch into the kitchen bin and went upstairs to pack a few things into his duffel bag.

~

The next morning Billy was still seething with anger, which fuelled his energy to be gone. He gathered the remainder of his belongings for the journey in his bag and put on his jacket.

There was no sound from Ada's room. Should he knock and say he was going now? He didn't fancy renewing the argument this morning, or listening to Ada's self-pity that she would be left alone. He wouldn't be gone long, anyway. That was a comfort: one way or another, this would be sorted out very soon.

He left the pot of tea he'd made under the tea cosy for her. Then he called up the stairs, 'Bye then, Mum. See you soon.'

When there was no reply he guessed she was

sulking and he wasn't going to waste time dealing with that.

He closed the front door carefully on the silent house and set off to find Evie.

~

The bell tinkled merrily at G. Morris as Evie entered the shop.

'Morning, Evie. My word, you look a picture in that striped cotton,' beamed George, coming round from behind the counter to greet her with a handshake, holding on to her hand a little longer than necessary.

Over the past weeks Evie had become a regular at the smart draper's shop and she and George were now very friendly. Evie sent her clients here if they wanted to choose their own fabrics, and she came here to choose them herself if the client preferred.

'Thank you, George. It's come out well, hasn't it? Stripes are always fun to work with.'

'Show me the back, then,' George asked, and Evie did a twirl to show off how she'd worked the stripes on the back of the bodice. 'Very nice indeed. So how are you, dear? And how is Mrs Goodwin?'

'We're both well, thank you, George. It's better for Grandma's eyes in the summer when the light is brighter.'

They exchanged more pleasantries and, as there

were no other customers in the shop, George brought out a tray of tea from the back room, and a plate of biscuits. Then they began the business of the day, Evie perched on a stool while George unfurled bolts of fabric and cards of trimmings to show her what was new while she drank her tea. Other customers came and went but although George served them all with his full attention and courtesy, no one else was privileged to the special treatment he offered Evie.

Evie chose some pretty prints for a summer two-piece and a blouse commissioned by Mrs Smedley, a client who was fast becoming a favourite: easy to fit, choosy but not fussy, and, best of all, she paid top price on delivery. This meant that Evie and Sue had money in hand to buy more fabrics, and so the small business ran smoothly. They made payment on delivery the rule now, having learned a lesson about that early on.

There had been an awkward business with Mrs Smythe, who had said she'd settle the invoice at the end of the week 'as is the usual way', and had shown Evie to the door of her house without paying. Evie had had a sinking feeling about this and she knew Sue would have demanded the money there and then, but maybe this was the way better-off folk did things. A fortnight later Mrs Smythe had still not paid and Evie had had to telephone to remind her.

'Oh, I didn't realise you were so in need of money,

dear,' said Jean Smythe, implying nastily that they were on their uppers, which, of course, they were.

'And I didn't realise it would be a problem for you to pay,' replied Evie, who'd rehearsed what she might say. 'You can always pay in instalments, if that would make it easier for you.'

There was a sharp intake of breath. 'That will not be necessary,' Mrs Smythe said haughtily.

'Then I shall expect the cheque in tomorrow's post,' said Evie. 'The address is on the invoice, or would you like me to remind you of it?'

'No thank you. I have it here.'

'Good. Then you have everything you need and I shall expect the cheque tomorrow,' finished Evie, and put down the phone. Her heart was thumping. What an awful woman Jean Smythe had turned out to be.

'She won't order anything more, I reckon,' she said to Sue, who had heard Evie's side of the conversation.

'Do you know what, love? I don't care,' Sue had replied. 'There's a name for those what take and don't pay and it's not a nice one.'

'Oh, I expect she'd have paid eventually.'

'We don't need clients like that, love. No use working and not being paid.'

The cheque had duly arrived the next morning.

'Now, Evie,' said George, parcelling up the fabrics in brown paper, 'I was wondering if . . . if you weren't too busy . . . and I can quite understand you might be . . . if, well . . . '

'Yes, George?' asked Evie. What on earth could he be trying to say?

'Well, that is . . . I was wondering if you'd care to go out to tea with me on Sunday? There's a little place that serves tea in the park, but the main draw is that there's a bandstand on Sunday afternoons in summer.'

'Oh, George, what a lovely idea.' Evie was delighted. 'Thank you for asking me. I'd be really pleased to go with you. I haven't had a day off for ages.'

George looked relieved. 'I'm so glad. I'll meet you at the station if you telephone me which train you'll be on. The music usually starts about three o'clock, but people come and go all the time.'

'I think we should try to get there at the start,' said Evie.

'I agree.'

She paid for the fabrics, put them carefully in her basket and, with a merry wave and a big smile, went to the door.

'I'll look forward to Sunday. It'll be a proper treat.'

'Goodbye, Evie, dear.'

George quickly went to open the door for her, then stood on the doorstep watching her walk over the cobbles and into the marketplace. Evie Carter really had got the prettiest smile . . .

~

Evie hadn't seen her mother in weeks so she decided to drop in. As always when she approached Frederick's tall pretty house down the tiny Midsummer Row, she remembered the first time she had come here with her mother, and how that awful woman had stomped shouting down the steps. How much had happened since then! On this glorious June morning, the square was peaceful and the garden in the middle blossomed with flowering shrubs.

Evie rang the bell and Jeanie opened the door, looking beautiful but a bit flushed.

'Hello, love, how lovely to see you. You scrub up well,' she said, indicating the striped dress as Evie went inside.

'A Goodwin and Carter special, Mum,' laughed Evie. 'I've just had Mr Morris admiring it, too.'

'I reckon that draper's soft on you, love.'

'Nonsense, Mum. He must be three times my age. He likes to see a nice bit of sewing, that's all,' laughed Evie.

'Ha, it's all right, I'm teasing. Now come downstairs and I'll make you some lunch.'

It seemed her mother was more comfortable down in the kitchen than the posh parlour, Evie pondered. She wondered how happy her mother really was.

'Thank you, Mum, I'd like summat to eat, though we're that busy now, I'd better not stay too long. Any news?'

'I do have some, but it'll wait until you're sitting down.'

~

All the way from Bolton to Manchester, and then again from Manchester to Redmond, Billy thought about what he would say to Evie. The quarrel between them was as nothing compared to Ada's thieving of his letters, and Evie had done her very best to make amends anyway. Billy acknowledged that it was he who had done badly: not writing to Evie last year to make up the quarrel but expecting her to make the first move – which, of course, she had – and then not writing when he heard about Robert's death last February. But by then he thought Evie had washed her hands of him, he reminded himself. The whole situation was a muddle. But now he meant to make it right.

Billy's train pulled into Redmond station in the early afternoon. He knew he had to get a bus from here to the village of Church Sandleton and that the bus ran from the market square, which would likely be in the middle of town.

The market square was easily found, and the bus stop for the south-travelling buses displayed a rather complicated timetable in very small print. Eventually Billy decided he had half an hour before the bus was due and standing there waiting wouldn't make it come any quicker. Better to get something to eat. He looked around and spotted a café that served plain food, and he went in and sat down near the window.

As he sat drinking his tea, he idly watched the people of Redmond passing by. They looked pretty much like Bolton folk, but no one here was shuffling down the street in carpet slippers and a pinny. He noticed a man, very tall and lean, with hair that fell into his eyes and a fine scarf knotted round his throat. He was very good-looking, kind of like a film star, for all his jacket was so crumpled. And the young woman on his arm was his equal in looks, with her pretty hair, cut short, and a stylish striped frock that showed off her slim figure, and sandals with heels.

Billy peered through the window, his eyes drawn to the glamour of the couple. Then he looked again, craning forward, slowly lowering his knife and fork to his plate, though his eyes did not leave the figure of the woman.

Good grief, that looked a bit like Evie – he turned to press his face closer to the window – looked like Evie, but yet not quite like Evie. Like Evie would look if she was the kind of girl who wore fashionable dresses and had fashionable hair, and was all sort of grown-up. Billy, his lunch forgotten, sat staring at the couple across the square. They walked past the bank, chatting, the woman holding the man's arm. His face was turned away from Billy, looking down into the woman's face, and he partly hid her from Billy's view. Then they stopped to speak to a country-looking man with a Jack Russell terrier by his side and the three stood talking. The woman bent down to pet the dog and Billy got a good view of her face at last. Oh, but she looked so very much like Evie. Could there be another with that heart-shaped face? Though this woman wore lipstick. Evie had never worn lipstick.

Billy felt confused now. Nothing he had imagined on the journey down had prepared him for this situation. He stood up, shrugged on his jacket and left what he hoped was the right money on the table as he picked up his bag and went out. He was just in time to see the couple going down a side street off the market square and he ran across the square after them, dodging traffic. 'Midsummer Row', read the sign, and it was a narrow passage. The man and woman were at the end of it now and Billy ran lightly after them. When he emerged into an attractive little square he caught sight of them going up the steps of an elegant terraced house, where the man opened the door and they both disappeared inside. 'Marlowe House' said the sign beside the door.

Now what? Billy loitered in the square, watching the house and trying to work out what he should do.

He could knock at the door of Marlowe House and ask for Evie Carter. Then if the woman turned out to be Evie he'd be able to speak to her. If she wasn't Evie he could always say he'd got the wrong house.

Oh, but that would be so clumsy. If it was Evie, and she was married to the good-looking man, she wouldn't want to see good old Billy from Bolton, the boyfriend she'd fallen out with months ago and had probably forgotten about by now. What if she invited him in that smart house and introduced her to the man – to her husband? She certainly looked very happy, and her life must have changed, what with the frock and the hairdo. And coming out of a bank! Billy would be willing to bet the Evie he had known had never been in a bank in her life. It was all so unsettling.

But Brendan had said that Evie wasn't married. It looked as though the Sullivans hadn't heard the news. Brendan said they hadn't had a letter from Sue Goodwin since Easter so all this had obviously happened since then.

As he stood there dithering and unable to decide what on earth to do, a woman with grey hair came into the square and walked up to the gate of the house across from Marlowe House. She gave Billy a long look, evidently wondering what business he had here. Billy saw a way forward and went to speak to her.

'Excuse me,' he asked, 'I'm looking for Evie Carter, though that might not be her name now. She's an old friend. I think she lives round here but I'm not sure.'

'Carter . . . Carter . . . ' The woman looked round the houses of her neighbours, thinking. 'Oh, yes, I think that's the name of the young woman at Marlowe House,' she said. She pointed across. 'You were right outside it.'

'Yes, she is a young woman,' said Billy.

'Then that's certainly her,' smiled the neighbour. 'The rest of us are all older.' She laughed lightly to show she didn't care if he thought her old.

'Thank you,' said Billy, and turned away.

Flippin' heck, Evie was living with a man old enough to be her father, and in some splendour, by the look of it. He cast his eyes over Marlowe House a last time then went slowly back down Midsummer Row, his mind once more in turmoil. Never in a million years had he imagined this situation.

He emerged back into the market square and wondered what to do now. Pointless to call on Evie, who looked so happy in her smart new life.

Face it, Billy, you've lost her. You're a part of her past now, nothing more . . .

He sat down on a bench outside the bank from which Evie had emerged only a quarter-hour earlier and thought through his options. He quickly concluded there was none. He'd just have to get the train back to Bolton and go home to his mum. What a dreary thought that was, especially after their argument. To top it all, Ada had been right and Evie, miles from Bolton, in this little southern town in the countryside, was never coming back north. She'd moved on and left him well and truly behind.

As he walked back to the station Billy was lost in miserable thought. He stepped into the road and jumped back as a red car sped by dangerously close.

No need to get yourself killed, Billy.

He continued on his way, hoping the north-bound train would not be too long.

~

Evie, sitting beside Frederick in the car, wasn't paying any attention to pedestrians, but looked up as she felt Frederick swerve.

'Oh, what was that?'

'Just some fool not looking where he's going,' said Frederick. 'Don't worry, no harm done.'

Evie glanced in the wing mirror to catch sight of the 'fool'. How strange, the slouching figure with the duffel bag receding into the distance behind them looked a lot like Billy Taylor.

Evie shrugged, settled lower in her seat and gave

herself up to planning what to do with the money in her new bank account.

~

So much for having a couple of days off, Billy thought bitterly, slowing his pace as he approached Fawcett Street. It was late evening and the sky, at the height of summer, was beginning to darken. It had been a very long day and he was not looking forward to facing his mother.

All the way home on the train the image of Evie – a new kind of Evie – had haunted his mind: the way she held onto the arm of the dashing-looking husband she gazed up at so affectionately.

Face it, Billy, she's well out of your league now, even if she wasn't married.

Might as well go back to work tomorrow, holiday or not. No point stopping at home with Mum, and I'm not bloody well taking her to Blackpool either.

He reached the house and opened the door. There were two letters addressed to his mother on the mat. She must have overlooked them. The house smelled stuffy and Billy wondered if Ada, who seemed to be allergic to fresh air, had sat in with the windows closed all day despite the warm weather.

'Mum?' he said.

Silence, but then – he glanced at his watch – she'd

probably gone to bed. It was well past the time she normally listened to the wireless.

He hung his jacket on the peg in the hall and went through to the kitchen. Strange, the teapot was still on the table under the tea cosy exactly as he'd left it many hours ago. It looked as if his mother had never got up.

'Mum!' Suddenly Billy was racing up the stairs. 'Mum! Mum, are you all right?' He barged into her room without knocking, groping for the light switch.

Ada lay sprawled untidily on her back in her bed, her eyes partially closed and her mouth slightly open on one side.

Even without touching her, Billy knew the truth. She was stone-cold dead.

CHAPTER EIGHTEEN

By September the gardens of Church Sandleton were laden with full-blown flowers with little green apples growing on the trees. Evie stopped to admire the quiet high street before she crossed the road from the bus stop and carried her heavy load of purchases back to Pendle's. The fresh prettiness of the countryside was something that she loved – even now, more than a year after coming here – and she would never take it for granted. Maybe she'd make a country girl yet. Certainly she no longer thought about going back to Bolton, going back to Shenty Street. What was there to go back for? Here was home now.

'How did you get on?' asked Sue, looking up from her work as Evie hefted her bags through the door. 'You've got quite a haul there.'

'I know, Grandma, but wait till you see it. George had got in both the green and the blue I ordered, and some lovely prints in a woollen mix. They're quite expensive so I got only two, for those autumn dresses we've taken on. George says he'll probably not sell the others too quickly yet so I've got till the end of the month to make up my mind about them, but I'd like your view on the ones I've bought first. And I found a couple of beautiful remnants in his box at the back, which we thought would make some sweet little matinee jackets. I hope you like them. George says I can always take them back if you don't. He doesn't usually allow returns of remnants, but as it's us . . .'

'"George says . . . George says . . ." Honestly, you should hear yourself, lass. It's your opinion I want, Evie, not George Morris's.'

'Sorry, Grandma, I didn't mean to go on.'

'George is in business, same as we are, love. He's out to make a profit and he'll do so even when he gives us a discount. It's nice that he's got what you ordered, and there's no doubt that he's selling lovely stuff, but he certainly knows how to sell it to you.'

'Oh, I'm not sure that's quite fair, Grandma.' Evie was stung by the implication that she was a soft touch for the draper's sales patter. 'I do think you'll like the remnants. And the other pieces.'

Evie felt that her bubble had been burst with Sue's strictly no-nonsense attitude this afternoon. And she'd had such a good morning in Kingsford, enjoying the special treatment George meted out to his favourite customer. She admitted to herself that she liked to be seen in her well-cut suit, courtesy of Letty's mother's legacy, perching on a stool in front of one of the counters while George ran about the place bringing bolts of fabric to her to view, whereas other customers had to go to find their own unless they asked for something specific. And the tea and biscuits were welcome, too.

'See you on Sunday?' asked George as he'd opened the shop door for Evie. 'I thought we could go for a picnic, as well.'

'I shan't want to miss it, then,' Evie had said. 'Usual train.'

'I'll be there.'

Now Evie busied herself opening the numerous brown-paper-wrapped parcels and spreading the fabrics over the big work table for Sue to examine. Sue felt the woollen prints for quality and, bending close to see properly, examined the patterns.

'And how much did you say you paid for these?'

Evie produced the receipt and pointed out each item on it.

'And that's with the discount?'

'No, Grandma, George took that off the total at the end – see, here? So we've got the remnants at a discount, too. He doesn't usually do that as they're reduced to clear already.'

'I bet he doesn't,' said Sue, deadpan.

361

After a silent minute Evie dared to ask, 'So what do you think, Grandma?'

Sue drew a long breath. 'I reckon you've done all right, lass, but I think you need to be careful. It's lovely stuff, but I don't want George Morris persuading you to buy what's not suitable. We're only dressmakers, not fancy designers.'

'I know that. So you're saying I'm being too ambitious?' asked Evie, feeling slapped down.

'No, but I reckon you might be if you carry on down this road. Always keep in mind what folk want and what they're prepared to pay. If you aim too high you'll be up there by yourself with no one to pay for it.'

'I suppose you're right,' Evie said in a small voice.

'You know I am,' said Sue. 'All I'm saying, love, is don't carried away with what George Morris has got in his fancy shop, that's all. We started at the mill shop and on the market, and we did all right there. There's nowt wrong with giving folk what they want, Evie, and you'll soon find it's a hard life *telling* them what they want and then trying to make them have it.'

Evie bit back her reply. There was no point in arguing with her grandmother.

At that moment the door opened and a young woman with two identical toddlers holding on to her hands struggled her way in. Evie rushed over to help.

'Hello, I'm Mrs Armitage. I telephoned earlier about pageboy outfits for the boys,' the woman said.

Sue introduced herself and Evie, and showed Mrs Armitage to a chair. There was a box of toys in the corner, which Josie had suggested would help keep small children quiet while discussions took place, and Evie showed the boys the building bricks and Dinky Toys while Sue found out what Mrs Armitage had in mind.

'Oh, but this is lovely,' said the young mother, noticing the fabrics Evie had just bought. 'This print with the tiny sailboats is exactly right for the little sailor jackets.'

Evie slipped out to make a cup of tea for their customer, and to hide her smile. She just *knew* those remnants would be useful, and they'd been snapped up before she'd finished unwrapping the parcel. Well, Sue was a canny woman – no doubt about that – but she didn't know everything.

~

'I'm glad I put my coat on,' said Evie, wrapping her summer coat around her. 'It's getting a bit nippy to be sitting out in a deck chair.'

'I expect that's what the organisers thought now they've brought the season to an end,' said George. 'It's been fun, though. I've really enjoyed having you to share it with this summer.'

'Me, too. I shall miss these lovely afternoons,' said Evie.

'Will you?' George asked, looking intently at her.

Evie frowned in puzzlement. 'Mmm, I said as much. Shall we take a last walk around the pond now the band's finished?'

'Good idea. Though I hope it's not the last walk.' George got up and helped Evie out of her deck chair.

'Well, it will be for this year,' Evie replied.

'We could find something else to do instead,' George suggested.

'I suppose we could: summat indoors, though,' Evie added with a shiver at the cold wind.

'Have a think, my dear, and I will, too,' he said.

'Oh, I hope so,' said Evie. 'It's been so lovely having Sundays off – you've been so kind.'

George beamed. 'It's been a pleasure, Evie.'

He really was a very thoughtful man, thought Evie. She guessed he was probably lonely since his wife had died several years ago. He lived in a flat over the shop, which Evie imagined was very clean and tidy. George Morris was definitely a different sort of man from her father, with his flinging his boots around, and rinsing his hands in the kitchen sink when you were trying to wash vegetables. She couldn't imagine George ever raising his voice and getting into an argument, or drinking too much. He seemed to inhabit a different planet from

Michael, with his drinking and that unforgettable business with Mr Hopkins, and, Evie realised, that planet would be quite an appealing place to live. Peaceful.

Evie said she'd better go to get the train home and George walked with her to the station while they discussed the concert. He waited with her for the train and saw her safely onto it.

'I shall miss our Sundays,' smiled Evie. 'It's been fun.'

'It has. I shall miss you, too, Evie.'

'Oh, I'm not going anywhere,' she said. 'I shall be in the shop in the next week or two.'

'I shall look forward to that,' George said seriously. 'You certainly brighten a morning behind the counter.' He took her hand through the carriage window and held on to it. 'In fact, I'd go so far as to say you brighten my life.'

Evie was taken aback. She didn't think she was a part of George's life – not really. The Sundays out were just nice outings before it was back to the sewing on Mondays, so far as she was concerned.

Before she could think of anything else to reply the train exuded a cloud of steam, the whistle sounded and the wheels started to turn. 'Bye, then, George.'

But his reply was lost under the increasingly loud chug of the departing train.

Evie sat back in her seat and tried to think what

George could have meant. She knew he had a romantic nature because of his taste for the more sentimental tunes in the band's Sunday repertoire, whereas she liked the jollier melodies she could tap her foot to.

I'd go so far as to say you brighten my life . . .

Perhaps he was merely being nice at the end of a lovely afternoon. Then suddenly a big and disturbing thought rushed into her head: George Morris was in love with her.

No, that was ridiculous. He was ten years older than her mother! No, she must be mistaken. Better get that idea straight out of her mind before she said something foolish.

To banish the thought, she began thinking about the parcel her mother had sent that morning, with a bank book for the account that she'd opened for her and a note apologising for not seeing her. Evie had bought a second sewing machine for the workroom so that she and Sue could both work on their seams without delay or the bother of changing threads. There had once been a very frustrating day when both of them had left the wrong colour thread in the bobbin and each had sewn a whole seam, red on one side and blue on the other. Now Sue sat at the treadle machine near the window, the better to catch the daylight, but with her lamp by her side, too, while Evie had set up her new electric machine on one end of the big table. There had been no more mix-ups.

Jeanie had suggested that she didn't mention the money to her father, and Evie had agreed. Michael took little interest in the sewing business since he'd started work at the shoe factory, and Evie let him assume whatever he wanted about the new sewing machine.

Sue had been a bit snappy of late and Evie guessed that her eyes were worrying her more now that the daylight was fading with the onset of autumn. Sue didn't complain but Evie noticed she was working more slowly and she herself worried about it, not just on Sue's account but because the dressmaking business was so busy that she knew she couldn't manage all the work on her own if Sue couldn't go on. This thought surfaced sometimes in the small hours of the night, but Evie had confided in no one. To speak it aloud made her worry more, but the burden of not telling her mother and brother was hard. Her grandmother was so precious to her, and she realised just how scared she was.

~

Michael wheeled his bicycle down the side passage at Pendle's and parked it in the backyard. He really must get some lights for the bike now the evenings were growing darker. It wouldn't be long before he was cycling home in complete darkness.

To Michael, sweeping the floors and keeping the premises tidy, every day was exactly the same. The men and the couple of women who made the shoes in the factory hardly acknowledged his presence as they sewed and hammered, glued and polished. Though everyone was pleasant enough, Michael had made no friendships among the employees. He felt that no one even noticed him, that he was just a part of the background of the place, rather taken for granted.

He opened the back door and let himself into Pendle's. The kitchen was empty. He'd seen the light on in the big front room as he'd passed, and Evie and Sue bending over their sewing machines, the table and chairs strewn with the cut-out shapes of garments. He switched on the kitchen light and reached for the kettle, which was empty and cold. There were a couple of used cups on the side, one of them Sue's special cup with its matching saucer, but there was no sign of any preparation of food.

He changed his shoes and went to see what time tea would be ready. He was hungry and he had hoped one of them would have started on some cooking by now.

'Oh, hello, Dad,' said Evie, hardly looking up. 'I hadn't realised it's that time already.'

'Hello, love. Are you both nearly finished?'

'Well, I just want to get these darts in before I stop, Dad,' said Evie.

'And I've got this collar to do,' said Sue. 'If I stop in the middle it won't look so smooth as if I carry on.'

Michael hovered by the door.

'Make yourself a cup of tea, why don't you?' said Evie. 'We'll eat when I've finished this.'

'If you're putting the kettle on I could do with a brew,' said Sue. 'We've been that busy this afternoon . . . '

Michael went off wearily to do as he was asked. He had to admire Sue and Evie's commitment to their work, but he felt a bit put out that they seemed to have less commitment to him as head of the household, and his need to be fed after a hard day's work.

He brought the tea through.

'Thank you, lad. Just put it on the side there,' said Sue, her eyes inches away from her seam.

'Thanks, Dad. We really have been very busy today,' said Evie.

'So have I,' Michael replied, defensively.

'Good . . . good.' Evie did not look up.

Half an hour later Michael came back to see if they had nearly finished for the day. His stomach was rumbling by now.

'Almost done, Dad,' Evie said. 'If you peel a few spuds I'll come and see to our tea in a minute. You could put the oven on . . . '

Another half-hour went by before Evie came through to the kitchen. The oven was on and the peeled potatoes sat in a pan of cold water.

Evie could have been knocked over with a feather. 'I'll get these spuds on the boil.'

'I thought you'd be finished long since,' Michael said. 'I have been at work all day, too, you know, love.'

'Yes, Dad, and I'm sorry to keep you waiting, but Grandma and me are rushed off our feet this week. Maybe if we're still hard at it tomorrow you could begin cooking?'

Michael looked sulky. 'Is this what it's going to be like now – I come home and have to make everyone's tea?'

'Well, I do usually, Dad. I know you've been at work, too, but I've only just finished now. It's been a long day.'

'A working man shouldn't have to make his own tea when there's women in the house.'

'Why ever not?' said Sue, coming through, rubbing her eyes. 'Why does your work mean you can't help around the place? We're all tired at the end of a long day. Those that get to the kitchen first can start on the cooking. That's only fair.'

'Well, I've never heard of that,' said Michael. 'Jeanie always got the tea ready.'

Evie thought that maybe that was why Mum, who had always worked, had found somewhere she preferred to live and had upped and left, but fortunately she stopped short of pointing that out.

'Well, while Evie and me are so busy, let's see if you can help us out, lad,' said Sue. 'And then, when you're extra busy at the factory, we'll do the same for you. It can work both ways, can't it?'

Michael could not argue with that point, especially as Evie now had on her pinny and was spreading sausages out in a roasting tin.

After they'd eaten he took himself off to the Red Lion, feeling unappreciated and sidelined. It seemed to him that, if he hadn't come home, Evie and Sue would have carried on working until bedtime and gone without cooked food. Far from being head of the household, Michael feared he was becoming the one whose place was juggling pans on the stove, wearing a pinny. Work at the factory was very much like housework as it involved a lot of sweeping and tidying up, and now he wondered if he'd find himself being the cook in his own home. As he opened the door of the Red Lion and greeted his neighbours he felt far more at home than he had done all evening at Pendle's.

~

The telephone rang and Evie hurried to answer, her order book open and ready. But it was only George.

'What did he want?' asked Sue, after he'd rung off.

'He's invited me to tea at his flat above the shop on Sunday.'

'Oh? Any particular reason?'

'He didn't say. Perhaps he wants someone to chat with. It must be lonely on a Sunday now that the band isn't playing any more.'

'I suppose . . . Did he say who else he's invited?'

'No, and I never thought to ask. Why?'

'Just wondering.'

The phone went again and Sue heard half of another conversation, also clearly not about ordering new clothes.

'What was that about?' she asked, when Evie, grinning hugely, came back in.

'Well, I've arranged for a bit of maintenance work on the front this afternoon. There will be a couple of men with ladders. Do you think you'll be disturbed by them? You could always go and see Miss Richards if you think they may be in your light.'

'Maintenance? When was this decided?'

'It's a surprise, so don't ask.'

~

'Come and look now, Grandma,' Evie said when the painters started to pack up.

Sue got up stiffly and shuffled out of the front door to look.

'Good heavens!'

372

There, above the shop, where before it had said 'Pendle's', there was a newly painted sign: smart dark blue with curly gold lettering: *Goodwin and Carter, Dressmakers.*

'All right for you, missus?' asked the painter.

Evie studied Sue's face. She looked amazed but also very pleased.

'Oh, Evie, love, our own names over the shop. And so smart, too.'

Evie thanked the painters and waved them off in their van.

'Do you really like it, Grandma?' she said when they'd gone.

Sue couldn't stop gazing at the sign. 'Of course I do, love. It's . . . it's like we're a real business.'

'Well, even though there's only the two of us we stuck with it and we've made a success of it. And now we're officially Goodwin and Carter, for all to see.'

'It's grand, lass. I'm that proud of it. And I'm that proud of you, too.'

'Thank you, Grandma.'

～

'So it's come to this, has it?' said Michael grumpily, coming into the workroom from the back of the house, where he'd left his bicycle.

'Don't you like our sign, Dad?' Evie asked. 'We

373

think it looks nice. There's no need to have "Pendle's" above the front. Mr Pendle left here years ago, according to Josie.'

'Goodwin and Carter,' said Michael heavily. 'Well, it's nowt to do with me, is it? Why don't you two just take over the whole place with your sewing machines and your bits of stuff lying about the place? I'm surprised you've left me a bed to sleep in, the way things are going.'

'Oh, Dad, don't be daft. You know we never take our work out of here,' said Evie, disappointed. 'We've always kept to our own space.'

'It doesn't feel like it to me,' argued Michael. 'It seems to me that this whole place is nowt but a dressmaker's these days, and there's no room or time for anything else – or anybody else – at all. I feel like I'm *living* at a dressmaker's, not a home of my own.'

'I'm sorry, Dad, I don't want you to feel like that. It's true the sewing takes up the whole of the big room, but it's how we earn our living – Grandma and me – and it needs a bit of space.'

'And what if I need a bit of space?'

'Well, there's the big kitchen. We've all always sat in there of an evening,' said Evie.

'All . . . ' said Michael sadly. 'Once there were all of us Carters. Now it's only me, facing a tide of sewing stuff piling up around me—'

'No, Dad—'

'My wife has gone off with a fancy man, my little lad is dead, and my other lad can't stand the sight of me and has gone to live with folk who aren't even his relations. And now you two have claimed the place entirely as your own and announced it with a ruddy great sign outside with your names all over it. Seems to me I'm a spare part here, a leftover. Not needed and not wanted.'

'Now you know that's not true, Michael,' Sue said. 'The old sign made no sense any longer. What would you have up outside?'

Michael looked stricken. 'I'd have nowt,' he said eventually. 'I'd live in a proper house, like we had in Shenty Street, not a rented shop.'

'Well, those days are gone,' replied Sue, looking hard at him.

Evie wanted to argue with that but she knew better than to speak out against Michael when he was feeling sorry for himself.

'Yes, we know, Dad. We all miss Shenty Street. But this is our home now.'

'It's not just you who lives here, Evie, you'd do well to remember that.'

'I think,' interrupted Sue loudly, 'that I might finish up here for the evening and go and see about summat to eat.'

'I'll do it, Grandma,' said Evie, getting up from the big table. 'Come on, Dad, cheer up. It's one of Mrs Sutton's pies for tea . . . '

She and Sue exchanged glances as Evie followed Michael out to the kitchen. She'd been so pleased with the new sign and now it felt like it was a kind of showing off. Maybe she should have considered her father's feelings, but lately he was so easily cast into an ill temper that there was no pleasing him. Well, it was too late to do anything about the sign.

No point, perhaps, but that didn't stop her worrying as she lit the oven and wearily looked out some vegetables to go with the pie.

She tried to remember a time when the whole family had been all together, and happy, and she had to cast her thoughts further and further back to the beginning of that last summer in Shenty Street, before Michael had fallen into debt with Mr Hopkins.

I've tried so hard – all of us wanting the same thing, being a happy family – and at every turn it's slipped away. No sooner do I get one bit right than another part goes wrong. If only I could make everything all right for all of us, for ever . . .

376

CHAPTER NINETEEN

'I've had a letter from Marie Sullivan,' said Sue, coming into the workroom with the letter in her hand. 'It's good to hear from her. It's a while since we've been in touch. My fault, I suppose. I'm finding it hard work to be much of a letter writer these days.'

'Are they all well, Grandma?' Evie asked, watching her grandmother carefully. She was having one of her bad days, her eyes were bad and she was shaky on her feet.

'They are. Geraldine's engaged to be married.'

Evie's heart stopped beating for a moment. Not to her Billy?

'Oh, I'm so pleased. Who's the lucky man?'

'Colin Fraser. Marie says he's a lovely lad, very good-looking . . . '

Evie felt her cheeks pinken in relief. Life on Shenty Street and Billy seemed a lifetime ago now, and she still felt so fond of him.

'What about Mary?'

'Still at school, being clever. Marie says she doesn't know where she gets it from. And she says summat else, too. She asks if it's true that you're married.'

'What? Where on earth did she get that idea?'

'I dunno, love. She doesn't say. Just asks if it's true.'

'Strange. Maybe she's muddled me up with someone else.'

Sue shrugged. 'I reckon she must have. Oh, and she says Ada Taylor's dead.'

'Ada . . . ? Billy's mum? Good grief, she wasn't especially old.'

'Not like me, you mean,' said Sue drily. 'A stroke, Marie says. Found dead in bed by Billy.'

'Oh, poor Billy. That must have been a shock.'

'Aye, poor lad, as you say.'

Sue went back to her sewing, leaning close to her lamp, and Evie resumed making her seams.

After a while Evie said, 'I do feel sorry for Billy.'

'I'm the same, love.'

They continued with their work and then the door to the workroom slowly opened and Letty came dancing in.

'Guess what,' she demanded, planting a kiss on each of their heads. 'The very best news.'

'Best tell us before you explode, then,' said Sue.

'Jack and I – we're getting married!'

Evie clasped her hands together with joy. 'You're

right, Letty, it *is* the very best news.' She stood to give her friend a big hug. 'Oh, I'm so happy for you.'

'And then we can discuss the wedding dress while we drink our tea.'

'You want us to make it?'

'Who else? I want something pretty that I can wear later, made by my very favourite dressmakers.'

'I think, then,' said Evie, 'I'd better take you to the shops.'

~

Michael was getting used to cooking when he got home in the evenings, but that didn't mean he had to like it. Since Letty Mortimer had asked Evie and Sue to make her wedding dress, the sewing took up more time and seemed, somehow, to take up more space, too, although the materials were never allowed to spread from the workroom into the rest of the house. And every time he came home from work, there was that fancy sign proclaiming the place was a dressmaker's, shouting to the world that it wasn't his home. It didn't feel like his home now, with no wife, no sons. He wasn't needed.

After a week of cooking for everyone, Michael decided that he'd had enough.

'I'm home now, Evie, so you can stop messing about and cook our tea,' he announced, standing in the doorway of the workroom.

Sue was immediately furious. 'Evie's not going anywhere. It's our money that mostly pays the bills, Michael Carter. If we've work to do we'll stick at it until it's done. There may be days to come when there is none. It's no different from the laundry we had in Shenty Street, just drier.'

'But you never carried on of an evening with the laundry and expected me to make the tea,' objected Michael.

'I think you've got a short memory, lad,' retorted Sue. 'I remember darning and mending and altering clothes well into the evening, and Evie doing the ironing then, too. It was Jeanie who stopped to cook for everyone.'

'Well, Jeanie's gone,' he said bitterly, 'so one of you will have to do it instead. We've still got to eat. What could be more important than womenfolk providing for their men?' Michael asked crossly.

'We *are*, Dad! That's exactly what all this work is about, providing for all of us.' Evie felt what she was explaining was so obvious that Michael was wilfully not understanding.

'Well, I don't know what was wrong with the stuff you used to do – repairs and curtains and that,' he said sullenly.

'Is that really what you want us to do, Dad? Repairing other folks' old clothes so that you can get your food on time? We can do better than that – and we *are* doing. And if you don't like it, well . . .'

380

'Right then . . . ' said Michael. 'I'm off to get summat to eat at the Lion. You two can do as you like,' and he stomped off to the Red Lion, slamming the front door behind him.

Evie put down her sewing and took a deep breath.

'It wouldn't be like your dad to make much of an effort for very long,' sighed Sue. 'Pop a couple of potatoes in the oven, love, and we'll carry on for a bit until they're ready.'

'He could have done that for us instead of making a fuss,' said Evie, getting up resentfully, but her concentration was shattered now and she didn't want to go on.

'Will you thread this needle for me, love?' said Sue. 'I'm finding it hard to see the fine stuff now the evenings are drawing in.'

'How are your eyes, Grandma?' It wasn't like Sue to mention her difficulties.

'Not so good, love. This right eye is getting worse, I know it. It's a good thing it's only bad in the one eye or I think I'd have had to give up by now.'

'Oh, Grandma. What would I do if you couldn't do your sewing? What would *you* do?'

'Well, Evie, love, I know the answer to the second question and so do you. I'd make your father's tea.'

Evie smiled a tiny smile and squeezed Sue's hand.

'As to the first, we'd manage. I wouldn't be completely useless. We'd have to organise ourselves differently, that's all. I'd do all the cutting out and you'd do the sewing. Don't worry, love. It's not come to that yet, though I think we should be prepared.' Sue had obviously been thinking this through.

'And I think we ought to finish for today,' said Evie. The argument with her dad had left her feeling upset and now the discussion about Sue's eyes was adding to her worries.

~

Michael ate a pie and washed it down with a few pints of beer. At first some people he knew were at the bar and he forgot his anger with Evie and Sue as he chatted with them, but after a while they drifted off, leaving him with his bitter thoughts. He looked out for Jack, but Jack was seldom in the pub these days. Michael took himself into a corner with the *Redmond Gazette*.

That was a mistake. On the first inside spread was a round-up of recent events in the town. There, looking beautiful and wearing a very fitted dress, was Jeanie! His wife, pictured in the newspaper, smiling into the camera, holding a glass of what looked like wine. And next to her, of course, was that bastard Bailey she'd gone off with. The contrast between this Jeanie and the wife he'd recalled only an hour or two ago – the woman who took in washing and cooked his tea – was overwhelming.

'Mr and Mrs Frederick Bailey' read the caption. Michael could hardly believe his eyes. That woman was not Mrs Frederick Bailey and she never would be. 'Mrs Frederick Bailey' indeed! The nerve of the man. Or maybe that was what Jeanie was calling herself these days, trying to pass herself off as a respectable married woman instead of a hussy who'd upped and left her husband and children and taken up with the fella whose cleaner she was. She was behaving as if he'd never existed! Well, it was time Jeanie Carter remembered who she was and where she came from.

Michael scraped back his chair, knocking the table and slopping beer over it. He tucked the offending newspaper into his jacket pocket as fuel to his anger and lurched out into the autumn night.

'Mrs Frederick Bailey indeed . . . ' Muttering, Michael wove his way down the road back to Pendle's. Except it wasn't Pendle's any more, it was Goodwin and Carter, Dressmakers. He'd done nothing to deserve this, nothing at all. Well, he was going to put a stop to Jeanie Carter gallivanting about Redmond, making out she was summat she wasn't.

He opened the side gate and sent it crashing into the wall, then lumbered down the side passage to collect his bicycle from the backyard.

The kitchen was lit up and Michael could see Evie and Sue sitting at the table, eating, but he grabbed his bike without acknowledging them and, with just one failed attempt, wheeled it down the side of the building and out to the street.

Evie rushed out of the front door as he emerged.

'Dad, what on earth are you doing? Where are you going?'

'I'm off to get your mother,' he slurred. 'I've had enough.'

'What are you talking about? You can't bring Mum home on a bicycle. Come inside, Dad, and tell us what's wrong.'

'Perishing women, that's what's wrong,' he hissed. 'You're all as bad. Your mother—'

'What? Dad, please, come in and tell us.'

Sue came up behind Evie. 'Come inside and sober up. You can't go anywhere like that,' she called over Evie's shoulder.

Michael ignored her and pushed off on his bicycle, starting to wobble his way past the front of the shop.

Evie stepped out to grab him and ran after him but in two turns of the wheel he was away and she was left behind.

'Dad! Dad! Come back, please,' she called, but he didn't even look back.

'Where's he going?' asked Sue. 'Not far in that state, I should think.'

'He says he's going to get Mum,' Evie answered. 'He's so angry.'

'What's that there?' said Sue. She pointed to a

newspaper lying on the pavement by the side gate. Evie picked it up. 'You look, love. I can't see nowt in the dark.'

'It's the local paper.'

They went into the kitchen and spread the newspaper on the table. Sue put on her reading glasses and in no time they both saw the photograph of Jeanie and Frederick, and read the caption.

'Oh Lord, and Dad said he's going to Redmond to get her,' gasped Evie.

'He'll never get there in that state,' said Sue. She spoke confidently but they looked at each other worriedly.

'I think I'd better telephone Mum and Frederick and warn them about Dad,' said Evie. 'He's so mad that I'm really worried. I don't want Mum being upset.'

'Good idea, love, just in case.'

They went into the workroom and Evie dialled the number.

'Redmond 786,' said Jeanie. ' . . . Oh, hello, love. You sound a bit bothered – are you all right?'

'No, Mum. Dad's been in the pub all evening and now he's drunk and he says he's coming to get you. He saw a photo of you in the *Gazette*, calling you "Mrs Frederick Bailey" and we think that's what's got him in such a fury. He's set off on his bike, but he's very wobbly. Grandma and I think mebbe he won't make it and he'll see sense and have to turn back, but then I'm worried that he might reach you, and he'll do something awful. He's ever so angry, Mum.'

'Oh, no . . . oh dear. I've never said that was my name. Freddie's not here now. He's gone to Jack's.'

'I reckon you should call him and ask him to come back, Mum. I don't want you to have to cope with Dad on your own.'

'Yes, love. I'll do that. If your dad does get here, Freddie will deal with him and send him home. Thank you for warning me. You're a good girl. Don't worry, Evie.'

She rang off and Evie told Sue what Jeanie had said. Then she made a pot of tea and they sat and waited anxiously to see what would happen next.

~

Michael was hot with anger as he pedalled out of Church Sandleton and onto the Redmond road. Once he was out of the village there were no street-lamps to light the way, but the moon was bright in a clear sky and he could find his way with his eyes shut.

The countryside was fairly flat and the road a good one so he made fast progress despite some-times weaving across to the right. One time a car approached from behind and passed him, the driver slowing down and pulling out to allow Michael his wobbly progress. Then a car came towards him and hooted. Michael hadn't realised he was so close to the other side and he moved back to the left.

'Bloody women . . .' he muttered. 'Mrs Frederick Bailey . . . Thinks she's too good for the likes of me these days . . .' He ranted on, pedalling faster, furiously, carelessly. He was approaching Redmond now – he could see streetlights in the distance.

Another car approached behind, headlights illuminating the empty road ahead. Michael tried to steer to the side but he seemed suddenly to be a long way from the verge. He wobbled on, thinking the car would pull out but it moved ever closer. Then suddenly it was right behind. Then next instant it had clipped the back wheel of Michael's unlit bike and sent him somersaulting off the road and into the ditch beyond the verge as it sped away.

The ditch was deep and Michael landed heavily on his back, the bicycle coming to rest in a tangle of spinning wheels on top of him. The last thing he heard was the sound of the car's engine fading into the distance. Lying in the ditch, he looked up and saw the huge white and grey moon above. It looked very distant and very cold. The road was now completely silent. Then the image of the moon faded from his sight and he felt darkness closing in around him.

~

After a fitful night's sleep, Evie awoke and took a few moments to remember that Michael had set off for Redmond and she hadn't heard him return. She went to see if he was in bed, but the blankets were pulled over and it looked as if the bed hadn't been slept in. She went downstairs to see if there was any sign of him there, but the kitchen was exactly as she'd left it the night before.

Oh Lord, what to do now?

She put the kettle to boil while she tried to have a sensible think, then took a cup of tea up to Sue.

'Grandma? Here, I've brought you some tea. There's no sign of Dad. I think summat might have happened to him. Should I call the police?'

'You sure he's not gone to work?'

Evie explained. 'I'm worried he's had an accident, Grandma.'

'Mmm, it doesn't sound good, love. Yes, better call the police. Do you want me to do it?'

'No, Grandma. I will while you get up.'

'Think carefully what we know, love, 'cos they're bound to ask you about the time he left and what he was wearing and that.'

Evie went back down to telephone and recited all the facts as carefully as she could. By then she was tearful and fearing the worst, though the policeman she spoke to was sympathetic and reassuring. He took the address and telephone number and promised to be in touch as soon as he could.

It was mid-morning, and neither Evie nor Sue had got much work done, when a black police car drew up outside. The women looked at each other and Evie felt her heart sink as two policemen got out of the car. Evie sprang up and ran to the door.

'It's bad news, isn't it?' she gasped. 'I knew it! I should have tried harder to stop him setting off on his bike like that.'

'Miss Carter?' asked the older policeman. They both removed their hats as they came into the workroom. 'And you are Mrs . . . ?'

'Goodwin,' said Sue. 'I'm Evelyn's grandma and Michael Carter's mother-in-law. Tell us, Sergeant, what's the news?'

'We think we've found Michael Carter, but I'm afraid I'm going to have to ask you to come with us to the hospital. It's bad news.'

Sue guessed what was coming but she had to be sure. 'He's dead?'

'I'm sorry. I'm afraid so. But we need to be certain it is him.'

'No!' wailed Evie. 'Not Dad as well! Oh, I can't bear it, I just can't bear it . . . ' and she sank to the floor, sobbing loudly, tears streaming down her face, and wouldn't be comforted.

Eventually, Sue asked the younger policeman if he'd mind going to Lavender Cottage at the other end of the High Street to fetch their friends so that she could leave Evie and go with the police to the cottage hospital in Redmond.

It wasn't until Margaret and Letty arrived, full of compassion and common sense, that Sue was able to set off on her grim task. As she looped her handbag over her arm and stepped through the front door, she turned the 'OPEN' sign to 'CLOSED'.

Goodwin and Carter would remain closed for many days.

CHAPTER TWENTY

'I THINK, EVIE,' said Sue, 'that it's high time you got back on your feet. I don't want to sound hard, my girl, but I reckon you might find doing a bit of work will take your mind off your sorrows.'

'I don't know, Grandma . . . It's all such a big effort, and I feel so exhausted. Bob's dead and Mum's gone, and Pete's not here any longer either, and now Dad's dead, too. There's only us left, Grandma. I don't think I can ever be happy again. What if summat were to happen to you? I'd be all by myself and I don't know how I could manage.'

'Nonsense. There's nowt going to happen to me. It's a bad do about your dad, and it were worse about little Bob, but you can't let your life be all about. We all lose people we love, you know that, but we have to go on without them. Look how you pulled us up after Bob died. You did it then and you can do it now. Come on, love, up you get and come and get summat done. I need you in that workroom.'

Evie sighed heavily. 'But it all seems so pointless. What does it matter what the stupid buttons are like when everyone I love is dead or gone?'

'Now listen, Evie,' said Sue sternly, sitting down on the edge of Evie's bed, where Evie had spent much of the time since Michael's funeral, a week previously, 'it's them clothes what pays our bills. *Our* bills, Evie. Yours and mine. You can't give up and leave me to do it all – my eyes are failing and I need you.' Sue was finding it increasingly hard to focus properly on the finer sewing. 'We haven't got your dad's wages now so we're relying entirely on ourselves. Don't let me down.'

Tears sprang to Evie's eyes, as they did so frequently these days. 'Please, Grandma, just let me be. Give me a bit longer to get over Dad.'

'No.' Sue stood up and wagged a strict finger at Evie, her face fierce behind her glasses. 'If you stay here nursing your sorrows any longer you'll find it's become a habit and you'll never get up. I want you washed and downstairs in ten minutes.'

'No, Grandma, please . . . ' Evie wailed.

'And if you're not then I shall come back up here and drag you out, do you hear?'

Evie sank down in her bed and threw the covers back over her head.

'Ten minutes,' said Sue, and went down to put

the kettle to boil. Every situation could be eased with a cup of tea.

Soon Sue could hear Evie moving about. Eventually she clumped downstairs, looking red-eyed and thin.

'That's better,' said Sue with an encouraging smile. 'Here, there's a cup of tea for you.'

'Thanks, Grandma.'

'You know, Peter's been going to school all this time and trying to carry on as usual. He's not given in to grieving.'

'Pete didn't even like Dad.'

'I think,' said Sue carefully, 'you'll find that's not entirely true. He's been busier than ever with the band, too, and they've all sorts of concerts lined up. It's his way of coping, and if you ask me it's a good 'un.'

'S'pose . . . '

'Now go and get started and we'll see what we can manage this morning. I shall be glad to have someone else in the sewing room. It's been a bit lonely there all by myself.'

Evie knew Sue was trying to jolly her along. When news had got out of Michael's accident there had been a stream of visitors bringing their condolences, leaving posies of late flowers, dropping by with cards, some with cakes they'd baked. Michael himself had not had many friends in the village but Sue Goodwin and her granddaughter were popular. Even Mr Clackett had come over with a box of vegetables and a few kind words about Michael, which had made Sue laugh hollowly after he'd gone.

Evie and Sue worked all morning. Already she had assumed her lifetime habit of watching the pennies, reining in on any extras. Most evenings it was vegetable soup and bread with no butter for their tea. Biscuits, and sugar in the tea, were things of the past.

Gradually, over the following weeks, Evie pulled herself out of her sadness and – Sue was right – the work helped a lot. Yet she felt she was marking time, waiting for something to happen. She hadn't the inclination to see a way forward and make a move herself. As so often since meeting Mrs Russell on the train to Manchester, she remembered how that kindly lady had made positive decisions that led her to a new and better life.

But what am I even deciding about? Where do I go from here? Do I even want to go on with hardly any of my family around me?

'You know, Grandma,' she said one afternoon, while she was stitching some beading to Letty's wedding dress and Sue was leaning as best she could over the table, cutting out pattern pieces, 'I once thought that if we could get the sewing business up and running I'd never want for anything again. I saw no further than that. I thought that would be it – all I could possibly need in life.'

'Did you, love?' Sue stopped and stretched her

back, regarding Evie seriously. 'I don't think that life is quite like that.'

'Yes, you're right.'

'We always need more work, though.' Sue thought of the bare kitchen cupboard and how grateful she'd felt to Mr Clackett for the box of vegetables, which had lasted a good few days.

'Of course, but we're here, people know that, and we can put an advertisement in the *Gazette* or summat if we need new clients. But I can't see what happens next.'

'Well, that's what it's like in this kind of business, love. The work gets finished and then we have to look for summat else to take its place. You know that. We have to keep going because otherwise we'd run out of money – and soon, too.'

Just then the phone rang and Evie went to answer it.

'Evie, my dear. I haven't wanted to bother you too much lately, what with all you've had on your mind, but I wonder if you'd like to come round to tea again?'

'George, that's a kind offer but I'm not sure I'm very good company at the moment.'

'You don't have to put up a front among friends, you know. I'd love it if you felt you could visit.'

Evie thought quickly. A few minutes ago she'd been thinking that she was waiting for something to happen with her life – well, nothing ever would if she never left the workroom.

'Thank you, George. I'll be in Kingsford on Sunday at the usual time, shall I?'

~

After the first outing to see George, Evie felt better. She enjoyed putting on a pretty dress and her lipstick, making an effort after languishing in bed in her pyjamas for so many days, consumed with misery, then keeping a low profile in the workroom. Her weekly visits to see George were resumed, although sometimes on the train home afterwards her thoughts would turn to Michael, her heart would fill with grief and she'd cry quietly, feeling suddenly lonely and bereft. But as the weeks went by and Christmas approached, these moments of intense sadness became fewer.

She and Sue had found a few more jobs, and the work was a huge relief. It had been famine and feast since Michael's death – not enough money coming in, or now two of them working flat out – and since Sue had acknowledged the limits of her sight for fine sewing Evie was working very hard for long hours at her sewing machine. But the mood in the workroom had lifted, and Evie looked forward to her Sundays off, visiting George. Sue insisted that she stopped working for one day a week, and she herself either had a nap or went to visit Margaret while Evie was in Kingsford.

Often on the way home Evie would go to see her mother before catching the bus to Church Sandleton.

'What's happened to your car, Frederick?' Evie asked the first week, when he offered to drive her. She was opening the passenger door and noticed some scratches and a dent on the front wing.

'What? Let me have a look . . . ' He peered at the slight damage in the dim light of the winter dusk. 'Must have caught it on the side of the garage or something. I hadn't realised. I'll take it to be repaired. There's a good man in Kingsford who can fix it for me . . . '

He didn't seem very worried, but then if he hadn't even noticed there was no point in getting worked up about it now, Evie thought. Frederick was like that about so many things: he had great confidence in everything working out to suit him with the minimum amount of fuss and effort.

The next time she saw the car it was all smooth and smart again, so the man in Kingsford was obviously very good at his job.

Evie observed Jeanie carefully when she went to visit, looking to see how her mother was taking her father's death. Jeanie had wept a bit at the funeral, but had been very dignified, and, Evie thought, quite a lot less upset than she'd been about Robert. Sometimes now Evie caught Jeanie with a faraway look on her face, and maybe she didn't laugh quite so readily, but she certainly wasn't heartbroken. No, Jeanie had moved on in her life and Michael had been part of the past she'd left behind. What she hadn't left behind, despite Evie's fears that she was losing all her family, were her surviving children and her mother, with whom she was in touch most days.

~

What Evie hadn't expected when she went to tea with George that Sunday, was that he'd ask her to marry him. She could feel her heart beating fast and her stomach was fluttering like a bird. There was no doubt in her mind that George Morris was quite a catch, with his kindness and his generosity, but he wasn't like Billy.

Where did that thought come from? That was her old life.

George was waiting patiently.

'I'm very fond of you, George,' Evie began, and saw his smile slip. 'You're the nicest, kindest man I've ever met and we always have such fun together . . . '

'But . . . ?'

'I know you'd be a wonderful husband and that you would look after me, as you say, but I'm not sure I'm ready to marry anyone yet. I'm only seventeen and, well, there's quite a gap between our ages.'

'But I'm not ancient, Evie. I'm good for many years yet,' George said.

'I'm sure you are. That's not what I meant. What I should have said is that, I'm sorry, I'm not in love with you and so I don't think it would be right to marry you.'

'But do you think you could ever fall in love with me, Evie? Can you give me any hope at all?'

He looked so sad that Evie reached out and clasped his hand. Immediately he put his other hand over hers and held it tenderly.

'It would be wrong to string you along, George, but if we continue to be friends then maybe I will come to love you. I'd really like it if we could still meet up as we do, which are the times I enjoy best of all. I can't make any promises about love because that wouldn't be honest, but I can promise that I'll always be your friend.'

'And you will tell me if you change your mind – if you find that, after all, you do love me, won't you, Evie?'

'Oh, George, of course I will. If I fall in love with you, you will be the very first person to know.'

~

That night, when Evie got into bed, thoughts about George's marriage proposal ran endlessly through her head. Had she said the right thing? She thought of the neat flat above the draper's shop, which was big enough to accommodate Sue if she wanted to live there, too. Then she thought of the shop with the finest selection of materials and trimmings she'd ever seen, its polished mahogany cabinets and counters, its smell of pristine new fabric. Finally she thought of George, widowed for several years now, probably a bit lonely, always kind, sober, fun and thoughtful. What did it matter that he was ten years older than her own mother, if they loved each other? Tears sprang to her eyes as she remembered the flowers George had sent when Michael died and how he'd telephoned to see if she was all right while she'd been lying miserable and selfish in her bed, leaving all the work to Sue.

If only I could love him, George would be quite perfect.

He'd said he'd give her time, but how long would that be? Typically, he hadn't asked her for a deadline. He was prepared to wait for as long as she needed to make up her mind.

I want to be in love with him – I do – but I can't make it happen. I can't hurry it or direct it, and it would be so wrong to pretend. What if, then, I met someone else and really fell in love, and wouldn't feel alone any more?

CHAPTER TWENTY-ONE

BACK IN FAWCETT Street, since Ada's death Billy had been miserable. It had been a terrible shock finding her lying in bed like that, especially as she'd been dead for many hours, all alone. And he'd just gone and left her without even looking in. What kind of son did that make him? It was true that Ada had been a bit of one for playing ill and faking to bed, but that was no excuse for not checking whether she was all right.

Billy missed his mother. He missed her gossiping and grumbling, and he missed the sound of the wireless of an evening but hadn't the heart to put it on for himself. Now the house was silent. He even missed her bad cooking. One of the worst things about his life without Ada was returning home to an empty house and having to get his own lonely tea after work, with no one to sit and eat it with. At first he'd taken to going to the pub, just for the cooked food and a bit of company, but he couldn't afford to go every evening, and, anyway, he felt he didn't deserve the company. Not after the way he'd treated his mother. It served him right that he was by himself now. After a week or so he stopped going to the pub.

At first Billy had not told the truth of that awful day to his friends. He was so ashamed of the way he had treated his mother, he'd never forgive himself. They had rallied round to try to cheer him up, but he couldn't set aside the feeling that he had let Ada down in her final hours, that the last thing he'd ever said to her had been in anger. Now he was being punished for it and he felt he shouldn't be looking for a good time with his friends. After several failed attempts to raise Billy's spirits, Colin from the postal depot, Geraldine and her older brothers gave up and left him to stew in his own misery.

One day on his delivery round, Billy saw a poster up outside Mr Amsell's shop, advertising an evening of music at a church hall in Manchester the Saturday before Christmas. He thought nothing of it, but then the fellas in the depot had organised a few festive events he'd turned down and he got to thinking he'd rather go somewhere where no one knew who he was – where no one knew what an awful son he'd been, letting down his mother in her last hours. At least he wouldn't have to speak to anyone in Manchester, as there was no one there he knew. And it had to be better than sitting alone at home, where he spent so much time he felt he was in danger of becoming downright peculiar.

The day of the concert, Billy took an early train and had a look around the city. There were rows of metal and canvas chairs and the place smelled dusty and looked a bit shabby with use. He took a seat not too near the front.

'And now for a song that may be new to Manchester,' said the girl singer, who had a very assured manner, 'but we think it will soon be sung wherever marrows are grown. It was written by Peter Carter here, on guitar, and it's called "The Marrow Song".'

As the musicians burst into a lively tune Billy stretched his neck to see the composer, his attention caught by the familiar name.

Good grief, I don't believe it. It can't be . . . Yes, it's Peter Carter from Shenty Street. Evie's little brother!

Peter was older, of course, much taller and halfway to being a man, but there was no doubt it was the same person. Billy hardly listened to the song as he tried to think what on earth he would do now. He couldn't go back home as if he hadn't seen Peter. Even if Billy had never been in love with Evie, Peter was a good lad and, although he wouldn't know, it would be ridiculous not to try to say hello, at least. And maybe there'd be some news of Evie. Despite the fact she was now married to that dashing fella, Billy would like to know how she was.

The song ended and the applause was enthusiastic. He filed out of the row of seats and headed for the front of the room. The band would be somewhere behind the stage, he reckoned. Everyone was moving that way and he heard talk of refreshments. Good, that would make it easier.

Straight away he saw Peter, talking and laughing with the twins who played violins.

'Peter! Peter Carter!'

Peter looked round, surprised. Then his face brightened. 'Billy! What a surprise. I never expected to see anyone from Bolton here.'

'It's good to see you,' said Billy, shaking his hand and slapping Peter on the back. 'I've enjoyed the concert so far. Will you be playing again?'

'We will. We're appearing last. I hope you'll stay for that. Let me introduce you to the band . . .'

Billy met each of them and shook their hands, impatient to ask Peter about Evie.

' . . . and our leader, Letitia Mortimer,' Peter finished. 'Letty, this is Billy Taylor.'

'Letty Mortimer?' asked Billy, seeing an opening. 'I know your name. You're a friend of Evie's.'

'Evie's very *best* friend,' smiled the young woman. 'And I think I've heard your name, too.' She looked

404

more serious. 'Are you the Billy Taylor with whom Evie had a falling-out at someone's birthday party last year?'

Billy didn't like the way the conversation was going now. 'That's true, I'm afraid, though I tried to make it up to her by coming down to see her.'

Letty drew Billy to one side and Peter joined them in a private huddle.

'All we know is that you didn't reply to her letters, even when she told you Bob was dead, and she never heard from you again,' said Peter, but patiently. He evidently suspected there was far more to this than a silence on Billy's part. After all, Billy would hardly be being so friendly now if he'd never forgiven Evie for her side of the quarrel.

'Oh, Peter, I did get two letters from Evie, but my mother . . . she put them aside and they got over-looked somehow . . . ' Billy still could not bring himself to blame his mother in front of these people.

'So what happened?' asked Letty. 'When you eventually found the letters, I mean.'

'It was months after Evie wrote them. I went down to see her, to tell her to her face that I was sorry about the quarrel as I know from the letters that she was sorry, too.'

'I didn't know you'd been down,' said Peter.

'Evie didn't tell me that,' said Letty.

'She didn't know. I never got to speak to her.'

'So what happened?' asked Letty, taking a cup of

tea off a passing trolley and putting it into Billy's hands.

'I stopped in Redmond to catch a bus to Church Sandleton and I happened to see her in the street there. She looked lovely – right got up – and I hardly believed it was her at first. She was coming out of a bank with an older man and they looked very close.'

'George Morris, I should think?' Letty asked Peter. 'He's a draper. He owns a shop where Evie goes to buy fabrics for the business,' said Letty. 'He's been a good friend to her, especially since her father was killed.'

'Michael, dead?' Billy's mouth was agape. 'Oh . . . oh, Peter, I'm sorry.'

Peter looked away for a moment. Then he said, 'Evie took it badly, but Grandma's got her working hard, everyone's been kind to Evie and Grandma Sue, haven't they, Letty?'

'They're very popular in the village and people always rally round their friends.' Letty said this with slight emphasis and Billy felt that in her opinion he had been found wanting as a friend. Well, that was right enough.

Just then someone rang a handbell to signal the interval was over and the audience began to troop back to their seats while the musicians gathered together and looked out their music for the second half.

'In the village?' asked Billy, confused. 'But doesn't Evie live in Redmond, in some grand house in a little square?'

'Come and find us afterwards . . . ' said Peter as Martin Clackett called him and Letty over to where he and the twins were busy preparing for their turn.

Billy sat impatiently waiting for it to end, although he could tell why The Mortimers, as the band was called, were the main draw and the last to reappear as the highlight of the evening. All he could think about was getting back to Peter and Letty and finding out about Evie – and who this George Morris was to her. It was the first time that he'd felt hope since finding his mother dead in her bed.

When the applause died away and the lights were switched back on, Billy rushed out and back to the room behind the stage.

'Billy,' said Peter, who'd been looking out for him.

Billy was bursting with questions. 'So is Evie married? Where does she live? I saw her going into a right smart-looking house in a little square in Redmond, and a neighbour said she lived there.'

'It's our mother who lives in a house like that – in Midsummer Row.'

'Yes, that's the name. But I saw Evie going there with the older man, sort of dashing and untidy, but like it didn't matter, and very good-looking.'

'Ah, Frederick Bailey,' said Peter. 'Our mother

lives with Freddie. It's his house. He's kind of like our stepfather, I suppose.'

Billy let out a long breath. Everything he'd thought about Evie and the man he'd seen her with had been of his own imagining. What an idiot he was.

'But what about Evie? You say she's still in the village? And who is this George Morris, besides a shopkeeper?'

Letty interrupted. 'Look, Billy, we have to go now to get the bus back down south.'

'Yes . . . yes, of course. But what shall I do? Do you think Evie will want me to be in touch with her again?' Suddenly he felt like a child on his first day at school, completely at a loss. These people knew all about Evie and he knew nothing any more.

'It's up to you what you do, and I can't speak for Evie. But there's one thing I do know, she's had a hard time but she's pulled herself up with the help of Mrs Goodwin and their friends, and none of us wants to see her heartbroken after all she's been through,' said Letty.

'Now hold on a minute—' began Billy.

'I only want to see Evie happy,' said Letty, 'so, please, think very carefully whether what you do is going to be the best thing for her.'

Billy was silenced for a moment by the young woman's fierceness. 'Will you tell her that we've met and I asked after her?' said Billy.

'No, I won't,' said Letty, picking up her guitar case. 'She doesn't need to know if you don't do anything about it, does she?'

She turned away and went over to join her aunt.

'Bye, Billy,' said Peter.

'Thanks, Pete . . . and mebbe I'll see you soon.'

Peter grinned and gave a wave as he went to join the others, leaving Billy with a lot to think about on the train journey back to Bolton.

~

She doesn't need to know if you don't do anything about it

The words went round and round in Billy's head. Billy's life had been brought to a standstill by Ada's death, and he had become used to the same humdrum routine of going to work and coming home to spend his evenings alone.

In his head, he planned what he would say to Evie when he saw her. Of course, he'd also planned his previous visit but the result had been completely unexpected. He knew Evie and Sue lived in the village and that Evie wasn't married and that light-ened his heart.

But then he thought about Letty's words of warning.

I only want to see Evie happy, so, please, think very carefully whether what you do is going to be the best thing for her.

Perhaps Evie had forgotten all about him. Would going to see her upset her at a time when she was recovering from the death of her father? It would be unforgivable to go stirring up feelings that may well be buried and causing her more distress.

Oh Lord, what to do?

Christmas came and went, and then the New Year. The more he tried to think what to do, the less clear it all became and the further he was from making his mind up.

Then one day on his postal delivery round he met Brendan Sullivan in the street.

'All right, Billy, lad?'

'All right, Brendan? I'm not so bad . . . you know.'

'Well, you look dreadful, if you don't mind me saying. What's the matter?'

So Billy told Brendan everything.

'What are you waiting for?' gasped Brendan. 'It was not acting quickly enough and writing to apologise for that argument at Gerry's party that got you into this mess in the first place! C'mon, Billy, if this was our Stephen I was talking to I'd give him a boot up the backside and throw him onto the train south myself.'

'I just thought—'

'Whatever you thought, you thought wrong. It may work out or it may not, but it's as certain as the love of God is there'll be nothing between you

410

and Evie if you don't go. Is that what you're choosing?'

At that, Billy pulled himself up, shouldering his mail sack with a straight back where before he had seemed bent under its weight.

'How could I be so stupid? Thank you . . . thank you . . . ' He turned to collect his bike from where it was propped and cycled down the street, waving to Brendan, determined to finish his round and then get the first train south.

~

Evie sat back in her chair and stretched. It was a dark January morning, and cold in the house, but two cardigans helped keep out the chill. They chatted on happily while Evie resumed her stitching and Sue rested her eyes.

'You know, Grandma, despite the dreary January days and Dad being gone only a few months I do feel better about . . . everything, really. I reckon this will be a good year for us.'

'Yes, love. Now you're over the worst of your grief for your dad you've been a lot more cheerful. That wouldn't have anything to do with George, by any chance, would it?'

Evie had told Sue all about George's proposal of marriage and how she'd replied to him. It was testament to George's generosity of spirit that he and

Evie had become even better friends since his proposal but that he had not referred to marriage again. Sue had observed their growing closer and she thought George was a canny man who was playing a long game.

'Ah, Grandma, I shall have to see if I fall in love with him. But you know I don't want to marry anyone yet awhile. I won't be eighteen until next month and there's so much to do here. I'm not leaving you.'

There was a knock at the workroom door.

'Come in, it's open,' called Sue, as Evie, nearest but sitting with her back to it, was half-buried under yards of skirt, unable to get up quickly.

The door opened slowly and there stood Billy Taylor.

'Good grief!' Sue gasped. 'Where the heck did you spring from, lad?'

Evie turned and her mouth fell open. There was a long, long moment of silence. Then: 'Billy? Can it really be you?' she breathed.

'Evie . . . oh, lass, I'm that glad to see you.'

Sue heaved herself to her feet and went out to put the kettle on. One way or another there would be a need for tea, that was certain. And, in the meantime, a need for privacy.

'Sit down, Billy,' said Evie, gathering herself and putting her work aside. She indicated a chair and he sat and looked around the workroom.

'I found you easy enough – that smart sign with your name on it. You're doing well for yourself, Evie,' he smiled.

Evie didn't reply. She was looking at this man who had once meant a great deal to her. What did she feel about him now? She searched her heart and her mind and discovered only confusion.

'Why are you here, Billy?' she asked politely.

Billy looked at the girl he'd last seen close to well over a year ago. She was a girl no longer. She was a beautiful young woman, taller, slim but in a womanly way and, despite the layers of cardigans, he felt clumsy and out of place all of a sudden.

'I came to see you, of course, Evie,' he stuttered.

She was looking at him with an unreadable expression on her face. After a few moments she said, 'And why have you come to see me, Billy?'

Oh Lord, she wasn't making this easy for him.

What did you expect – that she'd rush into your arms declaring undying love, you idiot?

'To say I'm sorry . . . for that stupid argument we had . . . for all the daft things I said.'

Evie turned and gazed out of the big shop window, a faraway look in her eyes. Then she sighed and turned back to him. Her face still unreadable.

'It's all right, Billy. I forgave you a long time ago. I wrote to say that I was sorry and asked you to forgive me. It doesn't matter any more.'

Billy felt tears in his eyes. This was going all wrong.

Any moment now she'd get up and thank him for coming as she showed him to the door.

'It matters to me,' he said, dashing the tears away. 'Oh, Evie, I've been a right fool! I was too proud to write and apologise straight off, and when I knew you'd written—'

'So you do know I wrote?' she asked quietly, frowning.

'I didn't get your letters for months.' He took a deep breath. 'My mum stole them and hid them and, when I found out, we argued and I came down to see you to try to put it all right. I knew I should have said I was sorry straight away.' He shrugged helplessly. 'I saw you in Redmond, looking right pretty, and with a man I thought was your husband, and I went back home without speaking to you . . . without saying all the things I needed to say.'

Evie looked away again, eyes narrowed as if she was thinking very carefully. The silence stretched out until he could hardly bear it.

'And have you said all you need to say now, Billy?' she asked him.

'No! Never mind what happened. Never mind about my mum and your dad and all the things that took place to set us apart from each other and to keep us there. I'm sorry that we argued, and I'm more sorry than I can say that I let it go on and on and was too daft to do owt about it.'

414

'It's all right, Billy. I told you, it doesn't matter.'

'But it does, Evie. Because I love you. I love you more than I can say and I can't bear to think that I hurt you and you thought I wasn't sorry. I've wasted so much time when I could have been with you, loving you as I do.'

'Oh, Billy, a long time has passed since we fell out.'

'Yes, but my love for you hasn't changed, Evie. I should have listened to my heart and not given up until I'd told you, and I should have done it months ago.'

Evie put her hands over her face and Billy thought she was crying, but when she eventually looked up she was dry-eyed though she looked troubled.

'Billy, I don't think we can just take up where we left off.'

'Why not, Evie? If I love you—'

'Because my life is different now. This isn't Shenty Street and I'm never going back to Shenty Street. I know what we said that day we put all our stuff in Fergus Sullivan's van – for a long time I thought of little else. But I have made a life here, and Grandma Sue and me have worked hard to set up this place and make it a success. I'm not going to give it up. Not because it's what Grandma and me do but because *I don't want to!*'

Billy let this sink in for a minute or two.

'I'm not asking you to give up owt, Evie,' he said

quietly. 'I can see what a success you are here.' He looked around at the shelves of fabrics, the dressmaker's dummy, the two sewing machines, the pile of fashion magazines, and the fitting room screened off in the corner. 'It's marvellous what you've done. Why would you want to give it up? All I'm asking is that you let me back into your life and allow me to love you and be proud of you.'

'Yes, Billy, we can be friends again, if that's what you mean,' Evie said. 'But I think you want more than that.'

'I did hope that you could love me in return,' Billy ventured. 'Or maybe learn to love me again, as I think you did once.'

'Oh, Billy, I don't know,' said Evie, getting up and walking over to the window, biting her nails. 'It's different now.'

'Is there someone else?' Billy thought of the name Letty had mentioned, George Morris.

'There is someone who wants to marry me, yes.'

'And do you want to marry him?'

Evie sat down again, sighing. 'Not now. Not yet. But he's a good man, very kind, and he's one of my dearest friends. I've told him I'm too young to be married and I don't know if I want to marry him. He understands that and is prepared to wait. But we are close friends.'

'And what about me, Evie?'

Evie smiled a crooked smile. 'A close friend, Billy?'

'Oh, Evie, if that's what you want. If that's the best I can hope for.'

'It is just now, Billy. We've got a lot of ground to make up before things can be the same between us as they were, if they ever can, and I reckon you know that.'

Billy nodded.

Evie reached out, took his hand and gave it a squeeze. 'But I shall be glad to have you back in my life, Billy, even if you are miles away.'

'Thank you,' he murmured.

Sue made a lot of noise outside the inner door and came in with a tea tray, looking carefully at the pair to see how things were.

'Tea,' she announced needlessly. 'Where have you got to get back to tonight, Billy?'

'Home, I suppose,' said Billy. 'Though now Mum's gone I've no one to worry about but myself.'

'Yes, we heard about Ada. We're sorry for your loss, aren't we, Evie?'

Evie nodded and they drank their tea while Sue asked about old friends in Bolton.

'Right, best be off then,' said Billy eventually.

'I'll see you out,' Evie offered, getting up.

'It's nice to see you, lad. Goodbye,' said Sue, taking up the tea things and going back to the kitchen.

'Goodbye, Mrs Goodwin,' he called after her, then turned to Evie. 'Goodbye, Evie.'

'I hope it's not really goodbye, Billy,' she said. 'I

think we'd better say farewell, and I'll see you soon.'
She smiled. 'We can't make up all that lost time if
we don't see each other again, can we?'

Billy's heart lifted and he smiled for the first time
since he'd arrived. 'No, Evie, you're right. I reckon
I might give up the postal delivery and have a look
around, try my hand at summat else, maybe elsewhere.'

'Don't rush it, Billy,' said Evie. 'Close friends,
remember? Please, you need to give me time.'

'Evie, love,' said Billy, 'you've given me hope and
I know that's more than I deserve.' He kissed her
cheek as she stood aside to let him through the
front door. 'You can have as long as you need.'

EPILOGUE

June 1956

'OH, EVIE, LOVE, you look beautiful,' said Sue, as she helped Evie arrange her hair, in which she had a pretty white band with flowers on it.

'Thank you, Grandma. Is Mum here yet?'

'She's gone to the church. I think she wants a moment with your dad and Bob.'

'Of course she does. I know she takes a posy to the grave whenever she's in the village.'

'Well, we'll have no sadness today, lass. Let's get you to church.'

'Good grief, you brush up well, Sis,' said Peter as Evie came into the workroom. 'I hardly recognise you.'

'Which was exactly what I was going to say to you,' laughed Evie.

Peter grinned and pretended to adjust his tie. 'Ready, Grandma?'

419

'I am, love. Let's go.'

When it was the moment to leave, Evie held her bouquet of white roses tightly, thinking about all of those who wouldn't be at her wedding, sending up a prayer to her dad and wishing that he could walk her up the aisle.

~

Bells rang out as the newly married couple emerged from the church and their family and friends showered them with rose petals.

'Oh, doesn't Evie look amazing? I can hardly believe she made that dress herself, even though I lived through every decision about it and every fitting,' said Letty to Margaret.

Billy looked down at Evie's glowing face, feeling so happy, aware that he'd nearly lost her, lost everything.

Evie leaned in and kissed him on the lips. 'You are *perfect*.'

'And so, my darling Evie, are you.' Billy smiled shyly.

'But I'm the luckiest, because I've got you.'